AN INSTITUTIONAL AND NORMATIVE ANALYSIS OF THE WORLD TRADE ORGANIZATION

LEGAL ASPECTS OF
INTERNATIONAL ORGANIZATION

VOLUME 46

The titles published in this series are listed at the end of this volume.

An Institutional and Normative Analysis of the World Trade Organization

by

MARY E. FOOTER

MARTINUS NIJHOFF PUBLISHERS
LEIDEN / BOSTON

A C.I.P. record for this book is available from the Library of Congress.

Printed on acid-free paper.

Layout and camera-ready copy:
Anne-Marie Krens – Oegstgeest – The Netherlands

ISBN 90-04-14961-9

Koninklijke Brill NV incorporates the imprints Brill Academic Publishers, Martinus Nijhoff Publishers and VSP.

http://www.brill.nl

Printed and bound in The Netherlands

TABLE OF CONTENTS

Acknowledgements ix

List of Abbreviations xi

Table of Cases xvii

Introduction 1

1 Background and problem 1
2 Framework for analysis and structure 6
3 Methodology and sources 8

Chapter I – Organisational and institutional aspects 11

1 Introduction 11
2 Antecedents: from ITO to WTO 12
3 Organisational and institutional bases 18
3.1 Objectives and functions 22
3.2 WTO bodies and their powers 35
a) Ministerial Conference 42
b) General Council 48
c) Specialised Councils 53
d) 'Horizontal' committees, working parties and working groups 62
e) Miscellaneous bodies: committees, working parties and working groups 64
f) Secretariat and Director General 68
3.3 Membership issues 71
4 Conclusions 74

Chapter II – The dynamics of a regime 79

1 Introduction 79
2 Regime theory and international legal scholarship 80
3 The WTO as a regime 88
3.1 The practice of regime analysis 90
3.2 Regime theory and the WTO 93
3.3 Application of regime theory: some observations 106
3.4 Prospects for institutional and normative developments 115
4 Conclusions 124

Chapter III – Decision-making 129

1 Introduction 129
2 Decision-making rules 132
2.1 Right of initiative and proposals 133
2.2 Consensus 135
a) Consensus as a primary rule 137
b) Mandated consensus 142
c) Consensus *in lieu* of voting 148
2.3 Voting 149
a) Simple majority 151
b) Qualified majority 152
c) Unanimity 156
3 Practice of decision-making 157
3.1 Equality of voting power *versus* parity of interest 157
3.2 Informal practices 163
a) Caucuses and alliance building 165
b) Small group and 'green room' meetings 167
c) Chairpersons, facilitators and 'friends' 170
4 Internal and external transparency issues 173
5 Form, legal bases and validity of decisions 176
6 Conclusions 178

Chapter IV – Principal rule-making 181

1 Introduction 181
2 Principal rule-making: primary treaty rules 184
2.1 The normative framework and primary treaty rules 186
2.2 The development of primary treaty rules through the treaty-making process 193
3 Principal rule making and the application of secondary treaty rules 203
3.1 Amendment 204
a) Amendment law of the WTO 206
b) Practice of WTO amendment 211
c) Protocols supplementing Schedules 221
d) Modification, rectification and certification of Schedules 233
e) Rectification in the event of error 239
3.2 Accession 241
3.3 Waivers 252
a) General waiver power 254
b) 'Mini' waivers 259
3.4 Authoritative interpretation 264
4 Conclusions 267

Chapter V – Subsidiary rule-making 271

1 Introduction 271
2 WTO bodies and subsidiary rule-making 279
2.1 Delegated rule-making 282
2.2 Subsidiary rule-making and the internal legal order 291
a) Rules establishing subsidiary bodies 292
b) Rules of procedure of WTO bodies 295
c) Operational rules: budget, finance and administration 302
d) Staff rules and regulations 304
e) Rules giving effect to assigned functions in the *WTO Agreement* 308
2.3 Adjudicative rule-making 310
a) Procedural rules, including evidence and proof 312
b) Substantive rules, mostly standard of review 315
3 Rule referencing 320
4 Conclusions 324

Conclusions 327

1 Institutional developments 328
2 Normative developments 335

Bibliography 339

Index 359

ACKNOWLEDGEMENTS

This book has been a long time in the making and arises from some of my earliest teaching in the field of public international trade law. Together with those students that I was privileged to teach on the University of London LL.M. course, International Economic Law, between 1987 and 1995, I began to unravel the mysteries of the GATT and to track developments in the Uruguay Round of Multilateral Trade Negotiations, which would eventually lead to the birth of the WTO as a new international economic organisation. In this respect I owe a particular debt of gratitude to Terry Daintith, an outstanding scholar and communicator, who first introduced me to some of the theoretical underpinnings of international economic law and who taught me to teach. I am also grateful to my former colleagues at the International Law Development Organization, Rome, Italy who helped broaden my horizons by affording me the opportunity to teach the law of international economic development within the framework of their technical legal assistance programmes both in Rome and in the developing world.

I wish to single out and acknowledge the following colleagues who have supported me along the way with helpful comments and insights that have contributed to this study. In particular I thank my thesis supervisor Ellen Hey and the members of my doctoral committee at the Erasmus University Rotterdam, who read and commented on the manuscript – Pieter Jan Kuijper, Jaap de Zwaan, Peter Van den Bossche, Joe François and Rogier Van den Bergh – and Maarten van der Vlugt for so ably coping with the correction of the footnote references. My thanks also go to those members of the ILA International Trade Law Committee who have been supportive of my work over thc ycars, especially Wolfgang Benedek, Jacques Bourgeois, Marco Bronckers, Thomas Cottier, Werner Meng, Ernst-Ulrich Petersmann and Friedl Weiss.

Other colleagues from the WTO, academia and the practitioner community, who have been instrumental in developing my thinking about institutional and normative developments at the WTO include José Alvarez, Arthur Appleton, Lorand Bartels, Niels Blokker, Kiki Brölmann, Michael Byers, Steve Charnovitz,

Christine Chinkin, Judy Czako, Bill Davey, Claus-Dieter Ehlermann, Julio Faundez, Ignacio García Bercero, Otto Genee, Viejo Heiskanen, Rob Howse, John Jackson, Markus Krajewski, Nikos Lavranos, Patrick Low, Vaughan Lowe, Gabrielle Marceau, Jim Mathis, Adrian Otten, Joost Pauwelyn, Denise Prevost, Elisabetta Righini, Jan Wouters and Werner Zdouc. I am also grateful to the members of the Beneleux study-group Recht van Internationale Betrekkingen (RIEB) or Law of International Economic Relations, for the lively and stimulating discussions that we enjoy at our meetings in Amsterdam and Brussels.

Completion of the research and writing for this book would not have been possible without the input of members of the *Ius Commune* research school and the ongoing project on Effective Global Economic Governance, taking the WTO as a case study, which has received initial financial support from the Netherlands Scientific Research Organisation. During 2004 I also received financial support from the Universiteit van Amsterdam through the funds for the promotion of women in higher education and research, which enabled me to complete the manuscript.

Finally, my thanks go to family and friends, in particular my two sons, Rudo and Ben Wormgoor, for their love and support, especially in the London and Rome days, and to my partner, Jack van der Wees, whose love and forbearance have been instrumental in completing the project. This book is dedicated to my father, Cyril Footer, and to the memory of my mother, Elisabeth Footer, née Raban.

LIST OF ABBREVIATIONS

AB	Appellate Body
AcDI	*Annuaire canadien de Droit International*
ACP	African, Caribbean and Pacific Group (Lomé or Cotonou Convention)
ADB	Asian Development Bank
ADP	Anti-dumping practices
AfDB	African Development Bank
AGP	Agreement on Government Procurement
AIDI	*Annuaire de l'Institut de droit international*
AJIL	*American Journal of International Law*
ATC	Agreement on Textiles and Clothing
AYIL	*Australian Yearbook of International Law*
BFA	Budget Finance and Administration
BISD	*Basic Instruments and Selected Documents*
BOP	balance of payments
Brooklyn JInt'lL	*Brooklyn Journal of International Law*
BYIL	*British Yearbook of International Law*
CalWestInt'lLJ	*California Western International Law Journal*
CBD	Convention on Biological Diversity
CEB	Chief Executives' Board for Coordination (UN)
COMTD	Committee on Trade and Development
CRTA	Committee on Regional Trade Arrangements
CTE	Committee on Trade and Environment
CTFS	Committee on Trade in Financial Services
CTG	Council for Trade in Goods
CTS	Council for Trade in Services
CVD	Countervailing duty (subsidies)
CYIL	Canadian Yearbook of International Law
DDA	Doha Development Agenda

DSB	Dispute Settlement Body
DSU	Understanding on Rules and Procedures Governing the Settlement of Disputes (or Dispute Settlement Understanding)
EBRD	European Bank for Reconstruction and Development
EC	European Communities
ECJ	European Court of Justice
ECOSOC	Economic and Social Council (United Nations)
EGD	Equitable geographical distribution
ESMs	Emergency Safeguard Measures
EJIL	European Journal of International Law
EPIL	*Encyclopaedia of Public International Law*
ETS	Council of Europe Treaty Series
EU	European Union (officially European Communities in the WTO)
FAO	Food and Agriculture Organization
FOGS	Functioning of the GATT System
GATS	General Agreement on Trade in Services
GATT	General Agreement on Tariffs and Trade
GC	General Council
GaJInt'l&CompL	*Georgia Journal of International and Comparative Law*
GSP	Generalized System of Preferences
GYIL	German Yearbook of International Law
HLCM	High Level Committee on Management (UN)
HODs	Heads of Delegation
HRQ	*Human Rights Quarterly*
HS	Harmonized Commodity Description and Coding System
ICAO	International Civil Aviation Organization
ICITO	Interim Commission for the International Trade Organization
ICJ	International Court of Justice
ICLQ	International & Comparative Law Quarterly
IDB	Inter-American Development Bank
IDHL	*International Digest of Health Legislation*
ILA	International Law Association
ILC	International Law Commission
ILM	*International Legal Materials*
ILO	International Labour Organization

ILOAT	Administrative Tribunal of the International Labour Organization
IMF	International Monetary Fund
IOLR	*International Organizations Law Review*
IPPC	International Plant Protection Convention, 1951
ITC	International Trade Centre
IntTLR	*International Trade Law and Regulation*
ITO	International Trade Organization
ITU	International Telegraphic Union
JAB	Joint Appeals Board (WTO)
JIEL	*Journal of International Economic Law*
JWT	*Journal of World Trade*
LIEI	*Legal Issues of Economic Integration*
LJIL	*Leiden Journal of International Law*
LNTS	*League of Nations Treaty Series*
LPICT	*Law and Practice of International Courts and Tribunals*
MaxPlanckUNYB	*Max Planck Yearbook of United Nations Law*
MEA	multilateral environmental agreement
MFA	Multifibre Arrangement (replaced by ATC)
MJIL	*Michigan Journal of International Law*
MFN	most favoured nation
MRA	Mutual Recognition Agreement
MTN	Multilateral trade negotiations
NAFTA	North American Free Trade Agreement
NILR	*Netherlands International Law Review*
NJIL	*Nordic Journal of International Law*
NorTIR	*Nordisk Tidsskrift for international Ret*
NorthwJInt'lLBus	*Northwestern Journal of International Law and Business Studies*
NYIL	*Netherlands Yearbook of International Law*
OECD	Organization for Economic Cooperation and Development
OIE	International Office of Epizootics
OMOV	One member one vote
OPCW	Organization for the Prohibition of Chemical Weapons
ÖZöR	*Österreichische Zeitschrift für öffentliches Recht*
PCIJ	Permanent Court of International Justice
PCWTO	Preparatory Committee for the World Trade Organization

PPA	Protocol of Provisional Application
Recueil des Cours	*Recueil des Cours de l'Académie de Droit International*
RGDIP	*Revue Générale de Droit International Public*
RIAA	*Reports of International Arbitral Awards*
RDI	*Rivista di Diritto Internazionale*
SCM Agreement	Agreement on Subsidies and Countervailing Measures
S&D, SDT	Special and differential treatment (for developing countries)
SPS Agreement	Agreement on Sanitary and Phytosanitary Measures
TBT Agreement	Agreement on Technical Barriers to Trade
TMB	Textiles Monitoring Body
TNC	Trade Negotiations Committee
TPRB	Trade Policy Review Body
TPRM	Trade Policy Review Mechanism
TRIMs	Agreement on Trade-Related Investment Measures
TRIPS	Agreement on Trade-Related Aspects of Intellectual Property Rights
UN	United Nations
UNAT	United Nations Administrative Tribunal
UNCLOS	United Nations Conference on the Law of the Sea, 1982
UNCTAD	United Nations Conference on Trade and Development
UNDP	United Nations Development Programme
UNESCO	United Nations Educational, Scientific and Cultural Organization
UNGAOR	United Nations General Assembly Official Records
UNRIAA	United Nations Reports of International Arbitral Awards
UNTS	United Nations Treaty Series
UNYB	*United Nations Yearbook*
UPaJInt'lEconL	*University of Pennsylvania Journal of International Economic Law*
UPU	Universal Postal Union
VCDR	Vienna Convention on Diplomatic Relations, 1961
VCLT	Vienna Convention on the Law of Treaties, 1969
VCLTIO	Vienna Convention on the Law of Treaties between States and International Organizations or between International Organizations, 1986
VandJTransnatL	*Vanderbilt Journal of Transnational Law*
WHO	World Health Organization
WIPO	World Intellectual Property Organization

WMO	World Meteorological Organization
WPDR	Working Party on Domestic Regulation (Services)
WPGR	Working Party on GATS Rules (Services)
WPPS	Working Party on Professional Services
WTF	World Trade Forum (see WTI)
WTI	World Trade Institute
WTO	World Trade Organization
WTO-OMC	World Trade Organization-Organisation Mondiale du Commerce / Organizacíon Mundial del Comercio
WTR	*World Trade Review*
Yearbook ILC	*Yearbook of the International Law Commission*
YIEL	*Yearbook of International Environmental Law*
ZaöRV	*Zeitschrift für ausländisches öfffentliches Recht und Völkerrecht*
ZLW	*Zeitschrift für Luft- und Weltraumrecht*

TABLE OF CASES

International Court of Justice

Application for Review of Judgement No. 158 of the United Nations Administrative Tribunal (Fasla) (*Advisory Opinion*) [1973] ICJ Rep 166 [*Fasla Advisory Opinion*]

Case Concerning Military and Paramilitary Activities in and against Nicaragua (Nicaragua v. *United States of America)* [1986] ICJ Rep 14 [*Military and Paramilitary Activities in and against Nicaragua*]

Case Concerning the Temple of Preah Vihear, (*Cambodia* v *Thailand*) [1962] ICJ Rep 1962 6 [*Temple of Preah Vihear*]

Case Concerning US Diplomatic and Consular Staff in Tehran Case (United States v. *Iran*) [1980] ICJ Rep 3 [*Diplomatic and Consular Staff Case*]

Certain Expenses of the United Nations (Article 17, paragraph2 of the Charter) (*Advisory Opinion*) [1962] ICJ Rep 151 [*Certain Expenses*]

Effects of Awards of Compensation Made by the United Nations Administrative Tribunal, (Advisory Opinion) [1954] ICJ Rep 47 [*Effects of Awards*]

Fisheries Jurisdiction Case (United Kingdom of Great Britain and Northern Ireland v. *Iceland)* [1974] ICJ Rep 9 [*Fisheries Jurisdiction*]

Legality of the Threat or Use of Nuclear Weapons (*Advisory Opinion*) [1996] ICJ Rep 226 [*WHO Advisory Opinion*]

North Sea Continental Shelf Cases [1969] *(Federal Republic of Germany* v. *Denmark and Federal Republic of Germany* v. *The Netherlands)* [1969] ICJ Rep. 3 [*North Sea Continental Shelf Cases*]

Reparation for Injuries Suffered in the Service of the United Nations (*Advisory Opinion*) [1949] ICJ Rep 174 [*Reparation for Injuries*]

International Arbitration

Trail Smelter Arbitration (*United States* v. *Canada*) (1938) 3 RIAA 1905

GATT Panel Reports

US – Manufacturing Clause, GATT Panel Report, *United States – Manufacturing Clause (Copyright)*, adopted 15/16 May 1984, *BISD* 31S/74

WTO Panel Reports

Australia – Automotive, Panel Report, *Australia – Subsidies Provided to Producers and Exporters of Automotive* Leather, WT/DS126/R, adopted 11 February 2000

Brazil – Aircraft – Second Article 21.5 Panel Report, *Brazil – Export Financing Programme for Aircraft – Second Recourse by Canada to Article 21.5 of the DSU,* WT/DS46/RW/2, adopted 23 August 2001

Canada – Aircraft (Article 21.5), Panel Report, *Canada – Measures Affecting the Export of Civilian Aircraft – Recourse by Brazil to Article 21.5 of the DSU*, WT/DS70/RW, adopted 4 August 2000

Canada –Aircraft Credits and Guarantees, Panel Report, *Canada – Export Credits and Loan Guarantees for Regional Aircraft*, WT/DS222/R, adopted, 19 February 2002

Dominican Republic – Import and Sale of Cigarettes, Panel Report, *Dominican Republic – Measures Affecting the Importation and Internal Sale of Cigarettes*, WT/DS302/R, adopted on 19 May 2005, as modified by the Appellate Body Report, WT/DS302/AB/R

EC – Export Subsidies on Sugar, Panel Report, *European Communities – Export Subsidies on Sugar*, WT/DS265/R, WT/DS266/R and WT/DS283/R, adopted 19 May 2005 as modified by the Appellate Body Report, WT/DS265/AB/R

EC – Trademarks and Geographical Indication, Panel Report, *European Communities – Protection of Trademarks and Geographical Indications for Agricultural Products and Foodstuffs*, WT/DS174/R and WT/DS290/R, adopted 19 May 2005

Indonesia – Autos, Panel Report, *Indonesia – Certain Measures Affecting the Automobile Industry*, WT/DS54/R, WT/DS55/R, WT/DS59/R, WT/DS64/R, adopted 23 July 1998

Korea – Commercial Vessels, Panel Report, *Korea – Measures Affecting Trade in Commercial Vessels*, WT/DS273/R, adopted 11 April 2005

Korea – Procurement, Panel Report, *Korea – Measures Affecting Government Procurement*, WT/DS163/R, adopted 19 June 2000

Mexico – Telecoms, Panel Report, *Mexico – Measures Affecting Telecommunications Services*, WT/DS204/R, adopted 1 June 2004

Turkey – Textiles, Panel Report, *Turkey – Restrictions on Imports of Textiles and Clothing Products*, WT/DS34/R, adopted 19 November 1999 as modified by the Appellate Body Report, WT/DS34/AB/R

US – FSC, Panel Report, *United States – Tax Treatment for 'Foreign Sales Corporations'*, WT/DS108/R, adopted 20 March 2000 as modified by the Appellate Body Report, WT/DS108/AB/R

US – Gambling, Panel Report, *US – Measures Affecting the Cross-Border Supply of Gambling and Betting Services*, DS/285/R, adopted 20 April 2005 as modified by the Appellate Body Report, WT/DS/285/AB/R

US – Lead and Bismuth II, Panel Report, *United States – Imposition of Countervailing Duties on Certain Hot-Rolled Lead and Bismuth Carbon Steel Products Originating in the United Kingdom*, WT/DS138/R and Corr. 2, adopted 7 June 2000 as upheld by the Appellate Body Report, WT/DS138/AB/R

WTO Appellate Body Reports

Argentina – Textiles and Apparel, Appellate Body Report, *Argentina – Measures Affecting Imports of Footwear, Textiles, Apparel and Other Items*, WT/DS56/AB/R and Corr. 1, adopted 22 April 1998

Australia – Salmon, Appellate Body Report, *Australia – Measures Affecting Importation of Salmon*, WT/DS18/AB/R, adopted 20 August 1999

Brazil – Aircraft, Appellate Body Report, *Brazil – Export Financing Programme for Aircraft*, WT/DS46/AB/R, adopted 20 August 1999

Brazil – Aircraft (Article 21.5 – Canada), Appellate Body Report, *Brazil – Export Financing Programme for Aircraft, Recourse by Canada to Article 21.5 of the DSU*, WT/DS46/AB/RW, adopted 4 August 2000

Brazil – Desiccated Coconut, Appellate Body Report, *Brazil – Measures Affecting Desiccated Coconut*, WT/DS22/AB/R, adopted 20 March 1997

Canada – Aircraft, Appellate Body Report, *Canada – Measures Affecting Importation of Civilian Aircraft*, WT/DS70/AB/R, adopted 20 August 1999

Canada – Dairy, Appellate Body Report, *Canada – Measures Affecting the Importation of Milk and the Exportation of Dairy Products*, WT/DS103/AB/R, WT/DS113/AB/R, Corr. 1, adopted 27 October 1999

Canada – Dairy (Article 2.5 – New Zealand and US II), Appellate Body Report, *Canada – Measures Affecting the Importation of Milk and the Exportation of Dairy Products – Second Recourse to Article 21.5 of the DSU by New Zealand and the United States*), WT/DS103/AB/RW2, WT/DS113/AB/RW2, adopted 17 January 2003

EC – Asbestos, Appellate Body Report, *European Communities – Measures Affecting Asbestos and Asbestos Containing Products*, WT/DS135/AB/R, adopted 5 April 2001

EC – Bananas III, Appellate Body Report, *European Communities – Regime for the Importation, Sale and Distribution of Bananas*, WT/DS27/AB/R, adopted 25 September 1997

EC – Computer Equipment, Appellate Body Report, *European Communities – Customs Classification of Certain Computer Equipment*, WT/DS62/AB/R, WT/DS67/AB/R, WT/DS68/AB/R, adopted 22 June 1998

EC – Hormones, Appellate Body Report, *EC – Measures Concerning Meat and Meat Products*, WT/DS26/AB/R, WT/DS/48/AB/R, adopted 13 February 1998

EC – Sardines, Appellate Body Report, *EC – Trade Description of Sardines*, WT/DS231/AB/R, adopted 23 October 2002

EC– Tariff Preferences, Appellate Body Report, *European Communities – Conditions for the Granting of Tariff Preferences to Developing Countries*, WT/DS246/AB/R, adopted 20 April 2004

India – Patents (US), Appellate Body Report, *India – Patent Protection for Pharmaceutical and Agricultural Chemical Products*, WT/DS50/AB/R, adopted 16 January 1998

India – Quantitative Restrictions, Appellate Body Report, *India – Quantitative Restrictions on Imports of Agricultural, Textile and Industrial Products,* WT/DS90/AB/R, adopted 22 September 1999

Japan – Alcoholic Beverages II, Appellate Body Report, *Japan – Taxes on Alcoholic Beverages*, WT/DS8/AB/R, WTDS10/AB/R, WT/DS11/AB/R, adopted 1 November 1996

Japan – Apples, Appellate Body Report, *Japan – Measures Affecting the Importation of Apples*, WT/DS245/AB/R, adopted 10 December 2003

Korea – Various Measures on Beef, Appellate Body Report, *Korea – Measures Affecting Imports of Fresh, Chilled and Frozen Beef*, WT/DS161/AB/R, WT/DS169/AB/R, adopted 10 January 2001

Mexico – Corn Syrup (Article 21.5 – US), Appellate Body Report, *Mexico – Anti-Dumping Investigation of High Fructose Corn Syrup (HFCS) from the United States – Recourse to Article 21.5 of the DSU by the United States*, WT/DS132/AB/RW, adopted 21 November 2001

Turkey – Textiles Appellate Body Report, *Turkey – Restrictions on Imports of Textile and Clothing Products*, WT/DS34/AB/R, adopted 19 November 1999

US – 1916 Act, Appellate Body Report, *United States – Anti-Dumping Act of 1916*, WT/DS136/AB/R, WT/DS162/AB/R, adopted 26 September 2000

US – Cotton Yarn, Appellate Body Report, *United States – Transitional Safeguard Measure on Combed Cotton Yarn from Pakistan*, WT/DS192/AB/R, adopted 5 November 2001

US – Certain EC Products, Appellate Body Report, *United States – Import Measures on Certain Products from the European Communities*, WT/DS165/AB/R, adopted 10 January 2001

US – FSC, Appellate Body Report, *United States – Tax Treatment for 'Foreign Sales Corporations'*, WT/DS108/AB/R, adopted 20 March 2000

US – FSC (Article 21.5 – EC), Appellate Body Report, *United States – Tax Treatment for 'Foreign Sales Corporations', Recourse to Article 21.5 of the DSU by the European Communities*, WT/DS108/AB/RW, adopted 29 January 2002

US – Gambling, Appellate Body Report, *US – Measures Affecting the Cross-Border Supply of Gambling and Betting Services*, DS/285/AB/R, adopted 20 April 2005

US – Gasoline, Appellate Body Report, *United States – Standards for Reformulated and Conventional Gasoline*, WT/DS2/AB/R, adopted 20 May 1996

US – Hot-Rolled Steel, Appellate Body Report, *United States – Anti-Dumping Measures on Certain Hot-Rolled Steel Products from Japan*, WT/DS184/AB/R, adopted 23 August 2001

US – Lead and Bismuth II, Appellate Body Report, *United States – Imposition of Countervailing Duties on Certain Hot-Rolled Lead and Bismuth Carbon Steel Products Originating in the United Kingdom*, WT/DS138/AB/R, adopted 7 June 2000

US – Line Pipe, Appellate Body Report, *United States – Definitive Safeguard Measures on Imports of Circular Welded Carbon Quality Line Pipe from Korea*, WT/DS202/AB/R, adopted 8 March 2002

US – Offset Act (Byrd Amendment), Appellate Body Report, *United States – Continued Dumping and Subsidy Offset Act of 2000*, WT/DS217/AB/R, WT/DS234/AB/R, adopted 27 January 2003

US – Shrimp, Appellate Body Report, *United States – Import Prohibition of Certain Shrimp and Shrimp Products*, WT/DS58/AB/R, adopted 6 November 1998

US – Wool Shirts and Blouses, Appellate Body Report, *United States – Measures Affecting Imports of Woven Wool Shirts and Blouses from India*, WT/DS33/AB/R, adopted 23 May 1997

European Court of Justice

Meroni and others v. *High Authority*, Case 9/56 [1957/8] *ECR* 133

Administrative Tribunal of the International Labour Organization

ILO Administrative Tribunal (ILOAT) Judgement No. 2232 of 16 July 2003 in the *Bustani* case

INTRODUCTION

1 Background and problem

The WTO has just celebrated its tenth anniversary in 2005 in an interesting fashion. At home in Geneva the publication of a specially-commissioned report by the Director-General reflects on the future of the organisation and considers the institutional challenges that the WTO faces in the new millennium.[1] Abroad the show has taken to the road in regional conferences across the globe in order to commemorate ten years of the dispute settlement system, which has often been referred to as 'the jewel in the crown'[2] of the WTO. To the casual observer, it may come as a surprise to discover that this particular organisation is better known for its complaints procedure than its role as the key international institution for the governance of world trade.

The role of binding dispute settlement in the enforcement of the elaborate body of rules in the world trading system is a significant contribution to the success of the WTO. Without it the promise of free trade would be endangered and the system would most likely revert to a GATT-like atmosphere of inter-governmental activity where free-riding was common-place, safeguard measures had free reign and unilateral reprisals were often implicitly sanctioned. Nevertheless, at a time when global economic governance has come under increasing

1 *The Future of the WTO — Addressing institutional challenges in the new millennium*, Report of Consultative Board to the Director-General Supachai Panitchpakdi (Geneva: World Trade Organization, 2004) [hereinafter *The Sutherland Report*]. See in particular the remarks by the Director-General in the Foreword to the Report, at 2-3.

2 No one can be certain as to the provenance of the term 'jewel in the crown', which is used in order to describe the WTO dispute settlement system. However, it seems that a former WTO Director-General Mike Moore was keen on reciting it. *See* further Debra Steger, *Peace through Trade: Building the World Trade Organization* (London: Cameron May, 2004) 17.

scrutiny with calls for major reforms of both the IMF and the World Bank[3] one might have expected the WTO as the newest global economic organisation, with its near-universal membership, its rule-making vocation and strong enforcement mechanism[4] to be at the forefront of the discourse on institutional reform. This is hardly the case.

The WTO dispute settlement system may have attracted a considerable amount of interest from governments, practitioners and commentators alike but the same cannot be said about its governance structure and functioning as an international organisation nor about its rule-making capacity. Instead, in the wake of each of the two failed Meetings of the Ministerial Conference held in Seattle in 1999 and Cancún in 2003 there were initial calls for a review of the WTO's institutional deficiencies and suggestions for possible reform[5] but all too quickly the membership reverted to the more pressing mandate of completing the Doha Development Round on time.

The reasons for this may lie in the WTO's inauspicious institutional beginnings, which originated in one of the negotiating groups of the Uruguay Round and went by the uninspiring name of 'Functioning of the GATT System'[6] or FOGS.[7] Or they may lie in the fact that the WTO has emerged almost seamlessly out of the former GATT, which was a semi-institutionalised treaty regime for the reciprocal reduction of tariffs and the management of global trade. And yet the WTO has a far more complex institutional and governance structure and its normative scope is significantly broader than was the case under the former GATT.

3 *Strengthening the International Financial System and the Multilateral Development Banks*, Report of G-7 Finance Ministers and Central Bank Governors, 7 July 2001, Rome, Italy, available at: http://www.g8.utoronto.ca/finance/, 1-13, especially at 2-3 and 7-9.

4 Claus-Dieter Ehlermann and Lothar Ehring, 'Decision-making in the World Trade Organization: Is the Consensus Practice of the World Trade Organization Adequate for Making, Revising and Implementing Rules on International Trade?' (2005) 8 *JIEL* 51-75 at 52.

5 Robert M. MacLean, 'The Lessons of Seattle and the Need for WTO Institutional Reform: Opinion' (2000) 6 *IntTLR*, 1-5, at 2. Simon Evenett, 'Systemic Research Questions Raised by the Failure of the WTO Ministerial Meeting in Cancún' (2004) vol. 31 *LIEI* 1-6.

6 *See* for details of the mandate and activities of the Negotiating Group on the Functioning of the GATT System or FOGS, Xu Yu-Chong and Patrick Weller, *The Governance of World Trade: International Civil Servants and the GATT/WTO* (Cheltenham, UK: Edward Elgar, 2004) 235-248.

7 Even so the birth of the WTO has been heralded by at least one commentator as: '[P]erhaps the most dramatic result of the Uruguay Round negotiation', *see* John H. Jackson, *The World Trade Organization: Constitution and Jurisprudence* (London: Pinter/Royal Institute of International Affairs, 1998) 36.

A brief glance at the institutional structure of the WTO reveals that its founding instrument is a model of brevity and simplicity. A mere sixteen provisions contained in the *WTO Agreement*[8] form the constitution for an international organisation, which for the first time in history places the multilateral trading system on a firm legal and institutional footing.[9] As formulated, the *WTO Agreement* performs several functions. It creates an international organisation,[10] sets out its scope and functions,[11] regulates such matters as terms of membership and withdrawal,[12] defines its institutional bodies and establishes procedures for decision making by those bodies.[13]

At the same time, the *WTO Agreement* has been regarded both as a 'constitutional contract' between the Members[14] and the product of a regime-creating exercise.[15] It reaffirms the pre-existing trade regime of the GATT, as embodied in the GATT 1994,[16] and takes up the GATT-acquis[17] besides adding an institutional structure to govern the results of a deliberate normative exercise. Taken together the *WTO Agreement*, the annexed Multilateral Trade Agreements and

8 Marrakesh Agreement Establishing the World Trade Organization (opened for signature 15 April 1994, in force 1 January 1995) 1867 UNTS 3, 33 ILM 1125 (1994) [hereinafter WTO Agreement], reprinted in *The Results of the Uruguay Round of Multilateral Trade Negotiations: The Legal Texts* (Geneva: World Trade Organization, 1999) [hereinafter *The Legal Texts*] 5-18.

9 Asif H. Qureshi, *The World Trade Organisation: Implementing International Trade Norms* (Manchester: Manchester University Press, 1996) 3.

10 Article I, WTO Agreement, *The Legal Texts*, above n. 8, 4.

11 Article III WTO Agreement, *The Legal Texts*, *ibid*, 5.

12 Articles XI and XV WTO Agreement respectively, *The Legal Texts*, *ibid*, 19 and 20.

13 Article IX WTO Agreement, *The Legal Texts*, *ibid*, 16.

14 The term 'constitutional contract' is what several GATT contracting parties understood the WTO Agreement to be, *see* Xu and Weller, above n. 6, 67-68. *See* for use of the term in international environmental law, Catherine Redgwell, 'Multilateral Environmental Treaty-Making' in Vera Gowland-Debbas, *Multilateral Treaty Making: The Current Status of Challenges and Reforms Needed in the International Legislative Process* (ed.) (The Hague: Martinus Nijhoff 2000) 81-107 with reference at 91, in fn. 9 to Oran R. Young, *International Governance: Protecting the Environment in a Stateless Society* (Ithaca NY: Cornell University Press, 1994) at 27.

15 See Redgwell, *ibid*, at 91-92.

16 The General Agreement on Tariffs and Trade 1994 [hereinafter GATT 1994] contained in Annex 1A to the WTO Agreement, consists of the GATT 1947, twelve separate agreements on trade in goods (sectoral and additional rules/disciplines), six understandings aimed at clarifying certain GATT provisions and the GATT Schedules of tariff bindings; see GATT 1994, *The Legal Texts*, above n. 8, 17-32.

17 The GATT-*acquis* is taken up in Article XVI:1 WTO Agreement, *The Legal Texts*, *ibid*, 17.

the Tariff Schedules and Schedules of Specific Commitments are the legal instruments which make up the results of the Uruguay Round.[18] They constitute a comprehensive body of trade rules, which was negotiated and is applied among all Members as a 'single undertaking'.[19]

The establishment of the WTO also marks the revision of the normative template for the conduct of international trade whereby WTO law currently comprises a matrix of principal treaty rules and subsidiary rules. Yet at the same time, many of the rights and obligations form a legal continuum with the previous GATT legal regime. In other instances, for example in the case of several of the former Tokyo Round agreements, the legal continuum takes on a different dimension because key disciplines, for example on subsidies and antidumping, have been elaborated upon and made part of the overall package of trade rules which are applicable to *all* WTO Members, rather than just a select few. The *WTO Agreement* and the annexed Multilateral Trade Agreements, provide a general legal and institutional framework within which further normative developments can occur.

While the WTO was widely considered to herald the dawn of a new phase in international economic relations[20] it has inherited the institutional practices of a post-war liberal economic policymaking body.[21] Many of the institutional problems that beset the GATT are still relevant in the WTO context. This is particularly true for such crucial matters as the institutionalised decision-making process which is out of step with the current requirements of the rule-making agenda.[22]

18 *Final Act Embodying the Results of the Uruguay Round of Multilateral Trade Negotiations*, done at Marrakesh, 15 April 1994, 1867 UNTS 3, 33 ILM 1111 (1994).

19 In the context of the Uruguay Round MTN, the term 'single undertaking' means that each WTO Member is expected to take on *all* WTO obligations in contrast to the individual Codes of the Tokyo Round MTN 1973-1979, which bound only States that became signatories to them. The term single undertaking has been criticised by John Jackson who refers to it as one of the seven 'mantras', or catch phrases, frequently invoked by diplomats, government officials and academics when referring to the internal constitution of the WTO without reflecting on its implications. John H. Jackson, 'The WTO "Constitution" and Proposed Reforms: Seven "Mantras" Revisited' (2001) 4 *JIEL* 67-78 at 72.

20 See Joel Trachtman, 'The International Economic Law Revolution' (1996) 17:1 *UPaJInt'lEconL*, 33-61 and other contributors to the inaugural edition of that journal.

21 Nicholas Bayne, 'International economic organizations – More policy making, less autonomy' in Bob Reinalda and Bertjan Verbeek, *Autonomous Policy Making by International Organizations* (London: Routledge, 1998) 195-210 at 197; also MacLean, above n. 5, 1-5 and Marco Bronckers, 'More Power to the WTO' (2001) 4 *JIEL* 41-65, at 55.

22 MacLean, *ibid*, 2.

However, calls for reform of the decision-making process have concentrated on aspects of internal and external transparency rather than on reform of the governance structure and improvement of the organisation's capacity for rule-making.[23] On the internal plane, the focus has been on reform of governance issues such as transparency and accountability of the organisation. On the external plane, the focus has been on institutional reform linked to issues of legitimacy.[24] Important as those aspects of governance are, they mask the deeper problems that arise from the institutional malaise that has set in at the WTO and is present in the ongoing Doha Development Round MTN.

The Sutherland Report on the future of the WTO reflects on the institutional challenges facing the WTO but does not go far enough in addressing institutional and normative deficiencies. Its recommendations touch upon the role and function of the Director-General and the Secretariat, the possibilities of establishing a senior-level consultative body but without any powers, and recommendations concerning improvements to the consensus decision-making process and dispute settlement. No consideration has yet been given to ways of improving institutional decision-making such that it would assist the rule-making process and, as a possible result thereof, provide a more adequate legislative response to the adjudicative process, i.e. rule-making as opposed to rule-application.[25]

Institutional matters that have not been addressed so far include, the proper functioning of the WTO as an international organisation, the separation of the executive, legislative and adjudicative powers of the organisation and respect for the principle of institutional balance, the creation of bodies of limited composition to act as sounding boards and to offer expert advice to the membership on legal and institutional improvements, a more active role for the Director-General and

23 *The Sutherland Report*, above n. 1, which devotes surprisingly little attention to the topic.

24 The issue of legitimacy of the WTO has been addressed by the following commentators: J.H.H. Weiler, 'The Rule of Lawyers and the Ethos of Diplomats: Reflections on the Internal and External Legitimacy of WTO Dispute Settlement' (2001) 35 *JWT* 191-207; Robert E. Hudec, 'Concepts of Fairness in International Trade Law' in *Essays on the Nature of International Trade Law* (London: Cameron May, 1999) 227-280. and Robert L. Howse, 'Adjudicative Legitimacy and Treaty Interpretation in International Trade Law: The Early Years of WTO Jurisprudence' in Joseph H.H. Weiler, *The EU, the WTO and the NAFTA: Towards a Common Law of International Trade* (Oxford: Oxford University Press, 2000) 35-69 at 42-51.

25 Thomas Cottier, 'WTO Dispute Settlement and Multilateral Trade Negotiations: Is There a Need for Inter-Round Negotiations?', paper prepared for the World Trade Forum 2002, *Dispute Settlement and Decision Making in the Multilateral Trading System: Current Operation and Options for Reform.*

Secretariat in proposing legislative and procedural reforms and better procedures for the preparation and formulation of WTO rules both during and outside of a negotiating round, with the assignment of this task to an expert body that is answerable to the membership. Each of these proposals raises a separate set of questions with respect to the current status of institutional and normative developments in the WTO that have so far not been the object of serious examination.

The purpose of this study is to contribute to the debate on WTO reform, with an institutional and normative analysis of the World Trade Organization.

Within the context of this study, institutional developments are understood to mean all those types of arrangements, of both a formal and informal character, that are related to the WTO as an institution and say something about its functioning. Normative developments, in the context in which they are used here, are understood to mean all those activities connected with the creation, maintenance and application of principles, rules and standards, which are shaped by the behaviour of individual or groups of States, as well as non-State actors, in their relationship with the WTO.

2 Framework for analysis and structure

A framework for analysis of the institutional and normative character of the WTO can be derived from locating the organisation in a broader theory of international institutional law, by applying regime theory in order to better understand the dynamics at work in the practice of the organisation, by examining the decision-making process which underpins and informs its institutional and normative acts and by analysing the formal rules and the established practice of the Members with respect to principal and subsidiary rule-making in the WTO.

Institutional developments in the WTO are explored through the lens of international institutional law in locating the organisation and its objectives, in determining the basis for the conferral and exercise of powers in relation to its executive, legislative and adjudicative functions, and in establishing whether the WTO fulfils the role of an international organisation, with a will of its own, separate from that of its constituent Members. The WTO is also read as an international regime in order to go beyond its formal legal and constitutional bases and to observe the Members' practice in the context of the former semi-institutionalised GATT treaty regime with which it retains strong links. A basic proposition of this study with respect to institutional developments is that the WTO is incapable of fulfilling a proper institutional role and becoming a pillar for global economic governance as long as its individual Members continue to shape the organisation to their own ends through a variety of informal arrangements and established practices.

Normative developments in the WTO are reviewed from the perspective of the creation, maintenance and revision of legally binding and non-binding or 'soft' law norms, in the sense of principles, rules and standards, as laid down in primary treaty rules, which set out the rights and obligations of the Members and some subsidiary rule-making activity by WTO bodies. Thus, various norms that are shaped by international law, such as treaties, as well as the presence of 'soft' law instruments in the form of declarations, decisions, standards of international and regional bodies, guidelines and recommendations, form the objects of the analysis with respect to normative developments. A second basic proposition of this study with respect to normative developments is that the rigidity of the WTO's amending provisions coupled with its institutional decision-making processes result in an ineffective exercise of the organisation's rule-making capacity.

In the light of these two propositions, this study seeks to demonstrate the importance of examining the institutional and normative bases of the organisation in order to better understand the organisation and to make informed recommendations about WTO reform. The structure of this book is as follows. Chapter I examines the makings of the WTO in fulfilling the role of an international organisation with an analysis of its organisational and institutional bases. After a brief historical account of the WTO's antecedents from the still-born ITO-project to the GATT, attention is directed to studying the WTO's objectives and functions, the WTO bodies and their powers, and finishes with a brief review of some membership and accession issues.

In Chapter II the WTO is read as a regime in order to test the proposition that the WTO is actually better understood as an international regime, which continues the tradition of the former semi-institutionalised GATT treaty regime alongside, and even within, the overall organisational and institutional framework of the *WTO Agreement*. The chapter begins by tracing the development of regime theory and its relationship to international legal scholarship before recalling the practice of regime analysis in the context of the former GATT trade barriers regime and the international regime for the protection of human rights. Regime theory is then applied to the WTO in order to find out what it can tell us about institutional developments in the WTO that international institutional law does not and to note some of the consequences of this exercise.

Chapter III is devoted to an analysis of the decision-making process in the WTO, which focuses on the formal and informal practices that exist in the WTO alongside the general rules on decision-making which are set out in the *WTO Agreement* and which inform and underpin the institutional and normative acts of the organisation and its institutional bodies. Beginning with a summary of the formal WTO rules on decision-making, including the right of initiative and the means of adopting decisions by consensus and/or majority voting, the discussion turns to review two specific aspects of the practice of WTO decision-making, before considering issues of internal and external transparency and the form, legal bases and validity of WTO decisions. One aspect of WTO decision-making in practice is equality of voting power *versus* parity of interest and the other relates to the myriad of informal practices in the organisation that involve varying constellations of Members and individuals, in plenary and small group, in formal and in informal meetings.

The major part of chapter IV is dedicated to examining the WTO's, or more accurately the Members', capacity to develop primary treaty rules, by means of the negotiating process, and by means of secondary treaty rules that revise or interpret primary treaty rules through the WTO's amendment law and practice, protocols supplementing Schedules, modifications to Schedules following (re-) negotiation of tariff concessions or services' commitments, the norms and procedures surrounding the accession process, which are not formally regulated in the *WTO Agreement*, exercise of the waiver power and the role of authoritative interpretation.

Chapter V complements this analysis of the normative capacity of the organisation with an examination of the extent to which WTO bodies engage in subsidiary rule-making activity in the form of delegated rule-making based on express and implied powers, subsidiary rule-making that forms part of the WTO's legal order or internal law relating to the establishment of subsidiary bodies, rules of procedures and rules relating to the organisation's operational capacity, the contribution of adjudicative rule-making to the formation of subsidiary rules and the topic of 'rule referencing'.

The final part of this book takes up a set of conclusions, which draws upon the findings and conclusions reached in the preceding chapters with respect to institutional and normative developments in the WTO, and offers some prospects for the future conduct of the organisation and its rule-making function.

3 Methodology and sources

The methodology used in this study is primarily observational in nature, and is based on a careful study of primary GATT/WTO documents in the public domain that have been published in the GATT and WTO Series of *Basic Instruments and Selected Documents* or *BISD*, de-restricted documents that are available on-line through the WTO Documentation Dissemination Facility or DDF and from the

Stanford University Library – Documentation Gateway in respect of previously unpublished GATT documents.

It is supplemented by empirical research into Members' practice in the organisation with respect to institutional and normative developments in the WTO. The material was gathered by means of a series of interviews with delegates of permanent missions to the WTO in Geneva, some former trade diplomats, Secretariat staff (including members of the WTO Legal Affairs Division, the Appellate Body Secretariat, the Rules Division, the Council and Trade Negotiations Committee (TNC) Division and some of the Appellate Body judges), officials of the European Commission, Directorate General for Trade, Brussels, practitioners who advise client governments on negotiations and dispute settlement and civil society representatives.

Additional research for this book included facilitated access as an observer at meetings of the General Council and the Anti-dumping Committee as well as the opportunity to address the Committee on Trade and Development in informal session on 'The Legal Aspects of the Doha Work Programme with a Special Focus on Special and Differential Treatment', the latter of which was made possible through a seminar organised by Aitic – the Agency for international trade information and cooperation, Geneva.

The empirical research was critical in testing two basic but contradictory assumptions that were made at the outset of this study. One was that the formal treaty-making process, which establishes the rights and obligations of the Members, is the only means by which normative developments take place in the WTO. The other was that the WTO's institutional bodies are not merely involved in the implementation of primary treaty obligations through a proces of monitoring and surveillance but are actively engaged in subsidiary rule-making in the organisation.

Secondary sources have been used as the basis for preliminary research and in order to understand some of the primary source documentation and results of interviews that have been conducted for the purpose of this research. The secondary sources include the works of publicists in the fields of public international law, international economic law and GATT/WTO law, political scientists and international relations theorists and some international civil society participants, which are held in the collections of the Library of the Erasmus University Rotterdam, the Law Library (in particular the collection of International Law materials) available in the library of the Universiteit van Amsterdam, the Peace Palace Library, The Hague, and the Library of the World Trade Organization, Geneva.

I

ORGANISATIONAL AND INSTITUTIONAL ASPECTS

1 Introduction

Over the past half century the international community has witnessed the rapid 'rise of international organisations'[1] and with it a move from co-existence among States to more intensive forms of cooperation between them. International organisations have been noted for their proliferation[2] and their pervasiveness,[3] including their propensity to usurp competences that have traditionally been reserved to States.[4] At the same time our understanding of what constitutes an international organisation has changed with the appearance of a growing number of autonomous organisations,[5] or more accurately autonomous institutional arrangements.[6] Essentially, these are bodies created within the framework of a treaty ('treaty-based organisations' or 'treaty organisations'), which are designed to establish substantive and procedural norms and regulate the conduct of States

1 The term 'rise of international organisations' is borrowed from Jan Klabbers, *An Introduction to International Institutional Law* (Cambridge: Cambridge University Press, 2002), 16-41.

2 Niels M. Blokker and Henry G. Schermers (eds.) *Proliferation of International Organizations: Legal Issues* (The Hague: Kluwer Publishing, 2001).

3 C.F. Amerasinghe, *Principles of the institutional law of international organizations* (Cambridge: Cambridge University Press, 1995) 1-6.

4 Jan Klabbers records this trend in a somewhat ambiguous piece on 'The changing image of international organizations', in Jean-Marc Coicaud and Veijo Heiskanen (eds.), *The legitimacy of international organizations* (Tokyo: United Nations University Press, 2001) 221-225, at 222-223.

5 Philippe Sands and Pierre Klein, *Bowett's Law of International Institutions* (London: Sweet & Maxwell, 2001) 16-17 and 115-148.

6 Robin R. Churchill and Geir Ulfstein, 'Autonomous Institutional Arrangements in Multilateral Environmental Agreements: A Little-Noticed Phenomenon in International Law' (2000) 94 *AJIL* 623-659.

in specialised areas such as trade, the environment, disarmament and human rights but are not necessarily part of the UN legal system.[7]

It is against this background that the organisational and institutional aspects of the WTO are examined in this chapter. The WTO presents a particularly complex institutional structure that has evolved out of a set of multilateral treaty instruments and is *de iure* an international organisation. At the same time it typifies what Oscar Schachter has described as the merger of 'a general multilateral law-making treaty into a regime'[8] (the GATT) and the *de facto* continuance of that regime despite its formal status as an international organisation (the WTO).[9] International institutional law may provide a useful scholarly source of ideas and insights into the organisational and institutional workings of the WTO but work by international relations scholars on regime theory may also be relevant in explaining the processes by which institutional structures develop and suggest ways in which norms are developed, maintained and undergo change – an issue which is taken up in the next chapter.

This chapter proceeds as follows. Section 2 provides a brief, mostly historical account of the WTO's antecedents, including the institutional failings of the ITO project and the role of the former GATT (1948-1995) in fulfilling the institutional vacuum that eventually led to the formation of the WTO. Section 3 reviews the organisational and institutional bases of the WTO, including its objectives and functions, WTO bodies and their powers and some membership and accession issues. Section 4 contains a set of conclusions, based on the findings in respect of this chapter and describes their relationship to the overall proposition concerning institutional developments that was set out in the introduction to this book.

2 Antecedents: from ITO to WTO

The WTO's organisational and institutional antecedents date back to the development of the post-war international political economy through US and UK govern-

7 Sands and Klein, above n. 5, 115.

8 Oscar Schachter, *International Law in Theory and Practice* (The Hague: Martinus Nijhoff, 1991) 76. *See* also C. Wilfred Jenks, *The proper law of international organisations* (London: Stevens/Dobbs Ferry, New York: Oceana, 1962), Paul C. Szasz and Edith Brown Weiss, *Selected essays on understanding international institutions and the legislative process* (Ardsley, NY: Transnational Publishers, 2001).

9 C.W. Jenks, 'Some structural dilemmas of world organization' (1973) 3 *GaJInt'l&CompL* 1-17.

ment efforts,[10] following the long inter-war depression and the general economic malaise, caused by 'beggar thy neighbour'[11] policies. In 1944 delegates from ministries of finance met at a specially convened conference, held at Bretton Woods in the United States[12] in order to draft the founding charters for the International Monetary Fund or IMF and the International Bank for Reconstruction and Development or IBRD or World Bank. In late 1945 US and UK negotiators called for a detailed charter or code of conduct relating to governmental restraints on international trade[13] and the establishment of an International Trade Organization or ITO, which would administer the aforementioned code of conduct, provide a forum for dispute settlement and conduct other trade-related functions such as the collection of statistical data and the preparation of guidelines for customs valuation.[14]

10 A US/UK understanding on international economic relations had already been reached in the so-called Atlantic Charter of 14 August 1941, 55 Stat. 1600 E.A.S. No. 236. *See* Richard N. Gardner, *Sterling-Dollar Diplomacy in Current Perspective* (New York: Columbia University Press, 1980) 50. At the time it was widely believed that prospects for peace and prosperity were linked to the establishment of multilateral (if possible universalist) organisations that 'could serve both as a forum for negotiations and as a guardian of the rules', *see* Andreas Lowenfeld, *International Economic Law* (Oxford: Oxford University Press, 2002) 22.

11 'Beggar thy neighbour policies' can be defined as 'trade or economic measures, such as export subsidies, import quotas and tariffs, taken with the intention of improving domestic economic conditions, e.g. raising employment, which have the effect of being a cost to other countries'; *see* Walter Goode, *Dictionary of Trade Policy Terms* (4th edn Cambridge: Cambridge University Press, 2003) 41; also Clair Wilcox *A Charter for World Trade* (New York: The Macmillan Co., 1949) 3-52.

12 *Proceedings and Documents of the United Nations Monetary and Financial Conference, Bretton Woods, New Hampshire, July 1-22, 1944, Vol. 1* (Washington, DC: US Government Printing Office, 1948) 941; *see* John H. Jackson, *The World Trading System: Law and Policy of International Economic Relations* (Cambridge, MA: The MIT Press, 1997) [hereinafter *The World Trading System*], 36, citing his earlier work, John. H. Jackson, *World Trade and the Law of GATT* (Charlottesville, VA.: The Michie Company (The Bobbs-Merill Company, Inc.), 1969) § 2.2., 40.

13 'Proposals for Expansion of World Trade and Employment to be considered by an International Conference on Trade and Employment', which were part of a more inclusive document, published by the US government and entitled *Proposals for the Expansion of World Trade and Employment*, US Dept. of State *Commercial Policy* Series 79, Publ. 2411 (Washington, D.C, 1945). *See* Lowenfeld above n. 10, 23 and Gardner, above n. 10, 146.

14 In that same year, the US Congress granted President Truman authority to negotiate and conclude an agreement for the reciprocal reduction of tariffs whereupon the US invited fifteen countries to join it in holding a round of trade and tariff negotiations. *See* US Dept. of State Press Release, 13 December 1945, (1945) 13 *Dept. State Bull.* 970 cited in Lowenfeld, above n. 10, 24.

Following a proposal for an International Conference on Trade and Employment, the first meeting of the United Nations Economic and Social Council or ECOSOC[15] was held in Paris in February 1946, at which a resolution was adopted[16] appointing a Preparatory Committee to draft a convention for international trade. Then in September 1946 the US Government published a 'Suggested Charter' with seven chapters, Chapter IV of which dealt with commercial policy. Eventually Chapter IV formed the basis for discussion at various sessions of the Preparatory Committee,[17] culminating in the completion of a text that became the basis for a Plenary Conference on Trade and Development[18] that was convened in Havana in November 1947.[19] The proposed ITO included an institutional chapter that was devoted to the structure of the organisation and regulated such

15 It was intended that the UN General Assembly and the Economic and Social Council (ECOSOC) would set policies and co-ordinate the activities of a group of narrowly defined 'functional agencies'. Each would operate within its sphere of competence, thereby clearly introducing the notion of 'functionalism' into the field of international institutions. *See* Stephen Zamora, 'Economic Relations and Development' in Christopher C. Joyner (ed.), *The United Nations and International Law* (Cambridge: American Society of International Law/Cambridge University Press, 1997) 232-286, at 233-238 and Peter H.F. Bekker, *The Legal Position of Intergovernmental Organizations: A Functional Necessity Analysis of Their Legal Status and Immunities* (Dordrecht: Martinus Nijhoff Publishers, 1994).

16 1 UN ECOSOC Res 13 (1946) UN Doc E22. As Lowenfeld points out the ECOSOC, although a principal organ of the United Nations (Articles 7:1 and 61-72 UN), played no real role in international economic relations despite having had a significant effect on the 'social' aspects of its mandate, particularly in the international protection of human rights; Lowenfeld, above n. 10, 24.

17 Report of the First Session of the Preparatory Committee of the United Nations Conference on Trade and Employment (London, 1946) UN Doc E/PCT/33. Chapters were drafted on commercial policy, restrictive business practices, commodity agreements and economic development. However, no agreement was reached on voting, other organisational provisions or on the matter of state trading and the technical articles on trade (corresponding to Articles III to X GATT) remained incomplete.

18 Report of the Second Session of the Preparatory Committee of the United Nations Conference on Trade and Employment (Geneva, 1947) UN Doc E/PCT/186. The 1947 Geneva sessions were 'an elaborate conference in three major parts', devoted to the charter for an ITO, the negotiation of a multilateral agreement for the reciprocal reduction of tariffs and the drafting of 'general clauses' of obligations relating to the tariff obligations. *See* Jackson, *The World Trading System*, above n. 12, 37.

19 The Final Act and Related Documents of the United National Conference on Trade and Employment (Havana, Cuba 21 November 1947 to 24 March 1948) [hereinafter *Final Act of the Havana Conference*], included the draft charter for the International Trade Organisation (1948), UN Doc E/Conf.2/78; ICITO/1/4 (April 1948) [draft ITO Charter] and the establishment of an Interim Committee for the International Trade Organisation

matters as membership, functions of the ITO and the establishment of institutional bodies, namely a plenary Conference of all ITO Members, an Executive Board, Commissions, Director-General and Staff. Notably, it included explicit coverage of the powers and duties of the Conference and Executive Board as well as decision-making by means of voting.

At the same time negotiations aimed at wide-ranging tariff cuts[20] were being undertaken by 23 countries[21] and were completed in Geneva by the autumn of 1947. The General Agreement on Tariffs and Trade, or GATT, together with its annexed tariff schedules, was opened for signature on 30 October 1947[22] and henceforth applied on a 'provisional' basis.[23] Bereft of institutional provisions

(ICITO), *ibid,* 69. *See* further Jackson, *World Trade and the Law of GATT*, above n. 12, §2.2., 45-46 and §2.5, 49-50.

20 It also included 'general clauses' of obligations, drawn from the ITO Charter provisions in Chapter IV on commercial policy, which were designed to protect the tariff reductions.

21 The initial 1947 Geneva 'Round' of tariff negotiations had far-reaching consequences due to: (i) 'the pace and volume of the negotiations', which set a precedent for all subsequent Rounds; (ii) the 'concessions', i.e. the negotiated tariff reductions and bindings, which were generalised to all other participants on the basis of MFN; and (iii) the fact that 'the concessions were recorded in a single document'. Not only was the GATT comprised of the schedules of tariff bindings but also it contained a code of conduct designed to provisionally safeguard the undertakings given and 'to commit the participants to a common (if incomplete) standard of behaviour with respect to international trade'; *see* Lowenfeld, above n. 10, 25.

22 Final Act Adopted at the Conclusion of the Second Session of the Preparatory Committee of the United Nations Conference on Trade and Development 55 UNTS 188, containing the General Agreement on Tariffs and Trade and the Protocol of Provisional Application (adopted 30 October 1947, *in force* 1 January 1948) [hereinafter *GATT Final Act*] 55 UNTS 194; *see* Jackson, *The World Trading System*, above n. 12, 37.

23 The legal device used was a so-called 'Protocol of Provisional Application' or PPA whereby eight of the 23 original contracting parties agreed to apply the GATT 'provisionally on and after 1 January 1948' whilst the remaining original parties would do so as soon as possible thereafter. This allowed most countries that otherwise required legislative authority for the whole package to seek executive or administrative approval in order to give immediate effect to Part I (MFN and tariff bindings) and Part III (territorial application, institutional and final provisions) of the GATT. Part II (Articles III to XXIII containing the substantive GATT obligations relating to national treatment, customs procedures, quantitative restrictions, subsidies, anti-dumping and the dispute settlement provisions) was to be implemented 'to the fullest extent not inconsistent with existing legislation'.
A contracting party was also entitled to 'grandfather' any domestic legislative provisions that were inconsistent with Part II obligations of the GATT thereby allowing governments to avoid having to seek immediate legislative approval for GATT but instead allowing

and subordinated to the ITO Charter, it was intended that when the ITO entered into force, the GATT would be extinguished.[24]

However, deep divisions existed among the participating countries as to the future of the international economic order and after much debate and acrimony the Final Act of the Havana Conference, embodying the ITO Charter, was signed on 24 March 1948, on behalf of 53 States.[25] It became apparent that the proposed ITO Charter would not be endorsed by the US and UK parliamentary constituencies[26] and this led to the demise of the ITO project. The GATT 1947 filled the institutional vacuum left by the failed ITO and eventually emerged as the permanent institutional basis for the multilateral trading system.[27]

The GATT continued to grow in terms of the number of contracting parties and in terms of the practices under the treaty that comprised all forms of explicit and implicit legal actions. In the broader analysis of legal actions, offered by Deirdre Curtin and Ige Dekker for the EU,[28] actions that contribute to such institutional practices, encompass any form of cooperation, including negotiation between participants (GATT contracting parties), adherence to general principles (such as MFN under Article I:1 GATT), the establishment of decision-making organs (this took the form of collective action by the contracting parties under Article XXV GATT) and provisions relating to the performance of GATT treaty obligations ('consultation' and 'nullification and impairment' under Articles XXII and XXIII GATT).

for the PPA to be approved by executive or administrative order. Given that the ITO Charter was ready for submission to legislatures, it was anticipated that in due course the GATT would also be submitted for 'definitive' application, pursuant to Article XXVI GATT 1947. *See* for details, *GATT Final Act* (1947), above n. 22, and Jackson, *The World Trading System*, above n. 12, 40-41.

24 Provision was made for this in a so-called 'disconnection clause', viz. Article XXIX GATT 1947, at paragraphs 1 and 2. Additionally, under the terms of paragraph 3 of Article XXIX GATT 1947 the contracting parties had already agreed that if by 30 September 1949 the Havana Charter had not entered into force then they would meet before 31 December 1949 in order to agree on whether the GATT should be 'amended, supplemented or maintained'; *see* Jackson, *World Trade and the Law of GATT*, above n. 12, § 2.4, 48-49.

25 *Final Act of the Havana Conference* and draft ITO Charter, above n. 19.

26 *See* Gardner, above n. 10, 369-380 for a detailed historical account of the issues that the US administration and the UK government of the day faced before their respective legislatures.

27 Sands and Klein, above n. 5, 116.

28 Deirdre Curtin and Ige F. Dekker, 'The EU as a "Layered" International Organization: Institutional Unity in Disguise' in Paul Craig and Gráinne de Burca (eds.), *The Evolution of EU Law* (Oxford: Oxford University Press, 1999) 83-136, at 91-92.

Despite attempts in the mid 1950's[29] and the early 1960's[30] to create some form of institutional mechanism for international trade, the GATT continued to operate for almost half a century as a semi-institutionalised multilateral treaty regime on a provisional basis. The GATT was considered to be a *de facto* international organisation although it lacked any formal institutional provisions and, where they existed, they were essentially founded upon the decision-making powers of the GATT contracting parties under Article XXV GATT (Joint Action by the Contracting Parties)[31] with no substantial treaty changes being made that could have led to institutional developments.[32] Thus, at the end of the Uruguay Round

29 The Ninth Session of the GATT Contracting Parties, held from 28 October 1954 through 18 March 1955 (the 'Review Session') was charged with examining and restructuring the GATT, in accordance with Article XXIX:4 GATT 1947 but proposals for institutional reform only reflected changes previously made to the ITO Charter at Havana. At the same time a new charter for a more simplified trade organisation was drafted, which would henceforth be responsible for administering the General Agreement, and would be called the 'Organization for Trade Co-operation', or OTC, but this also failed. *See* the Agreement on the Organization for Trade Co-operation done at Geneva, 3 October 1955, GATT Doc. PROT/5, as part of the *Final Act Adopted at the Conclusion of the Ninth Session of the Contracting Parties to the GATT.*

30 A group of experts called for the creation of a new UN agency with universal membership and substantial powers in the sphere of international trade in order to implement recommendations of a proposed United Nations Conference on Trade and Development (UNCTAD) which was eventually established pursuant to UNGA Res 1785 (XVII) (8 December 1962) and UNCTAD Final Act (1964) UN Doc E/Conf. 46/141, vols. 6-8. It became an official organ of the UN General Assembly by means of UNGA Res 1995 (XIX) (30 December 1964). The GATT would have become the agency's Committee on Tariffs. *See* Bernard M. Hoekman and Michel M. Kostecki, *The Political Economy of the World Trading System* (2nd edn Oxford: Oxford University Press, 2001) 50, citing Michel M. Kostecki, *East-West Trade and the GATT System* (London: Macmillan Press for the Trade Policy Research Centre, 1979).

31 Article XXV:1 GATT bears the heading: 'Joint action by the contracting parties', whereby the CONTRACTING PARTIES are explicitly authorised to meet '... with a view to facilitating the operation and furthering the objectives of this Agreement'; *see* Article XXV:1 GATT 1947 (now *GATT 1994*), in *The Results of the Uruguay Round of Multilateral Trade Negotiations: The Legal Texts* (Geneva: World Trade Organization, 1999) [hereinafter *The Legal Texts*] 460-461.

32 One small institutional development came about with the introduction of Part IV in 1965, Protocol Amending the GATT to Introduce a Part IV on Trade and Development, (adopted 8 February 1965, *in force* 27 June 1966) GATT Doc. PROT/2/62, L/2314, GATT *BISD* 13S/2. The CONTRACTING PARTIES established a standing GATT Committee on Trade and Development on 26 November 1964 pursuant to the mandate on joint action contained in Article XXXVIII:2(*f*) GATT, *see Analytical Index: Guide to GATT Law and Practice* (6th edn Geneva: GATT Secretariat, 1994) 992.

(and prior to the establishment of the WTO at the Marrakesh Ministerial Meeting held in 1994) the GATT 1947 bore all the hallmarks of an autonomous institutional arrangement within a treaty framework, of the type that Robin Churchill and Geir Ulfstein have noted in their analysis of institutional arrangements under a wide range of multilateral environmental agreements.[33] The following section analyses the organisational and institutional bases of the WTO that came into force on 1 January 1995, thereby seeking to end the institutional indeterminacy that surrounded the GATT.

3 Organisational and institutional bases

The WTO's organisational and institutional bases are founded upon a multilateral treaty, the *Marrakesh Agreement Establishing the World Trade Organisation* (*WTO Agreement*),[34] thereby fulfilling one of the elements for its qualification as an international organisation[35] and distinguishing it from other types of organisations such as international corporations and non-governmental organisations, or NGO's.[36] The Preamble to the *WTO Agreement*[37] records the intention of States 'to develop an integrated, more viable and durable multilateral trading system …'[38] This is reinforced by one of the key provisions in Article II:1 *WTO Agreement*, which states that the WTO 'shall provide the common institutional framework for the conduct of trade relations among its Members in matters related

33 Churchill and Ulfstein, above n. 6, *in extenso*.

34 *The Legal Texts*, above n. 31, 6-18. *See* also the WTO's own Agreement Series which contains a publication entitled *Agreement Establishing the WTO* (Geneva: World Trade Organization, 1999). It provides a description of the legal text of its constituent instrument and is intended to be 'an authoritative aide for understanding the agreements[s]' but is not to be taken as a legal interpretation of the agreement.

35 H. G. Schermers and N. M. Blokker, *International Institutional Law: Unity within diversity* (4th edn rev Boston, Leiden: Martinus Nijhoff Publishers, 2003). They provide a definition of an international organisation that comprises the following three elements: (i) constituted by an international agreement (treaty); (ii) a new legal person with a will of its own; and (iii) established under international law, *ibid* at §§32-45, 26-37.

36 Schermers and Blokker, *ibid*, §48, 39-40.

37 *The Legal Texts*, above n. 31, 6-18. *See* also the WTO's own Agreement Series which contains a publication entitled *Agreement Establishing the WTO* (Geneva: World Trade Organization, 1999). It provides a description of the legal text of its constituent instrument and is intended to be 'an authoritative aide for understanding the agreements[s]' but is not to be taken as a legal interpretation of the agreement.

38 Preamble (fourth recital), *WTO Agreement*, *The Legal Texts*, above n. 31, 6.

to the agreements and associated legal instruments...'[39] The WTO's constituent instrument or treaty bears witness to the creation of an international organisation that encompasses 'a complex of conventional and institutional provisions', as noted by the International Court of Justice when describing the World Health Organisation in its Advisory Opinion on *Legality of the Threat or Use of Nuclear Weapons* (*WHO Advisory Opinion*).[40]

Two further elements distinguish an international organisation from other sorts of organisations. One is that it should be a new legal entity having a will of its own and the other is that it be established under international law.[41] It is usually assumed that when a new international organisation like the WTO comes into existence it is *ipso facto* a new legal entity, on the basis of which it is the bearer of rights and obligations and has the capacity to act on the international plane, i.e. it has legal personality in international law. To what extent does the WTO fulfil these two elements?

39 Article I and Article II:1 *WTO Agreement, ibid,* 6-7. A number of association agreements concluded by the European Community with third states, on the basis of Article 310 EC, provide for similar common institutional frameworks. The usual reference is to 'joint institutions' where provision is made in such international agreements for bodies that take legally binding decisions; *see* for example Part Two of the African, Caribbean and Pacific (ACP)-EU Partnership Agreement (signed 23 June 2000) which replaced the fourth Lomé Convention, Decision 1/2000 of the ACP-EC Council of Ministers, 27 July 2000, [2000] OJ L 195/46 and the text of which can be found at [2000] OJ L 31/171. See Berend Martenczuk, 'Decisions of Bodies established by International Agreements and the Community Legal Order' in Vincent Kronenberger (ed.), *The European Union and the International Legal Order: Discord or Harmony?* (The Hague: T.M.C. Asser Press, 2001) 141-163 at 144.

40 The International Court of Justice has offered a definition of what is understood by a constituent treaty, noting the particular interpretative problems to which such a treaty can give rise owing to its dual conventional and institutional character:

'... the constituent instruments of international organizations are also treaties of a particular type; their object is to create new subjects of law endowed with a certain autonomy, to which the parties entrust the task of realizing common goals. Such treaties can raise specific problems of interpretation owing, *inter alia*, to their character which is conventional and at the same time institutional; the very nature of the organization created, the objectives which have been assigned to it by its founders, the imperatives associated with the effective performance of its functions, as well as its own practice, are all elements which may deserve special attention when the time comes to interpret these constituent treaties.'

Legality of the Threat or Use of Nuclear Weapons (*Advisory Opinion*) [1996] ICJ Rep 226 [hereinafter *WHO Advisory Opinion*] para. 19.

41 Schermers and Blokker, above n. 35, §§44-44A, 34-36 and §45, 36-37.

Article VIII:1 *WTO Agreement* states unequivocally that: '[T]he WTO shall have legal personality, and shall be accorded by each of its Members such legal capacity as may be necessary for the exercise of its functions'.[42] The wording of this provision comes close to one of the conclusions formulated by the International Court of Justice in its Advisory Opinion on *Reparation for Injuries*[43] in respect of the UN. In that case the Court was of the view that the UN possessed international legal personality because the Member States 'by entrusting certain functions to it, with the attendant duties and responsibilities, have clothed it with the competence required to enable those functions to be effectively discharged'.[44] Whereas in the case of the UN there was some doubt as to whether the organisation possessed legal personality, this is not disputed in the case of the WTO. What matters are the functions it can exercise as a result of having legal personality and the extent to which the WTO is an organisation with a will of its own, independent of that of its Members.[45] As we shall come on to discover when discussing the structure of WTO bodies, the powers of those bodies and the way the Members perceive them to function, together with the extent to which the organisation can be said to have a will of its own, is not easy to determine.[46]

A final aspect of the *Reparation for Injuries* opinion, which is relevant in the WTO context, is the conclusion that the Court reached in recognising the international legal personality of UN vis-à-vis its members, not on any objective basis, or irrespective of the will of the members but precisely because this must have been what they intended.[47] The Court reasoned that the capacity of the UN to undertake acts, which are legally binding on the international plane, is limited to the extent necessary for it to be able to exercise its respective functions. Additionally, whereas an international organisation will have a number of powers expressly conferred upon it by means of its constituent treaty or charter, it 'must

42 Article XIII:1, *WTO Agreement* on 'Status of the WTO', *The Legal Texts*, above n. 31, 10.

43 *Reparation for Injuries Suffered in the Service of the United Nations* (*Advisory Opinion*) [1949] ICJ Rep 174 [hereinafter *Reparation for Injuries*].

44 *Reparation for Injuries*, *ibid*, 179. *See* Schermers and Blokker, above n. 35, §1566, 989-990. One commentator has remarked that the Court effectively equated the possession of rights by an international organisation in relation to its Member States with international personality; *see* Philippe Gautier, 'The Reparation for Injuries Case Revisited: The Personality of the European Union' (2000) 4 *Max Planck UNYB* 338.

45 Schermers and Blokker, above n. 35, §44A, 35-36.

46 *See* below, section 3.1 relating to the functioning of the WTO as a 'forum organisation' and section 3.2 on the plenary nature of WTO bodies and the perception of the Members that this is a 'member-driven organisation'.

47 *Reparation for Injuries*, above n. 43, pp. 178-179.

be deemed to have those powers which, though not expressly provided in the Charter, are conferred upon it by necessary implication as being essential to the performance of its duties', i.e. it may also have implied powers.[48] Indeed, certain powers may be implied whenever they are 'essential' for the fulfilment of the objectives and purposes of the organisation.[49]

By analogy the capacity of the WTO to undertake certain acts on the external plane may be limited to those that are necessary for the exercise of its functions as described in Article III *WTO Agreement*. However, this is without prejudice to such implied powers that the WTO as an international organisation, or one of its constituent bodies, may have, which are not expressly provided for in the *WTO Agreement* or its Annexed agreements and associated legal instruments but are necessary for it in order that it may fulfil its objectives and purposes. Reference will be made to the exercise of implied powers, as an articulation of the WTO's legal personality, when analysing its functions and the competences of its various bodies to act.

One final element that needs to be considered in determining the existence of the WTO as an international organisation is whether it is constituted under international law. It could be argued that implicit in the wording: 'The WTO shall be accorded by each of its Members such privileges and immunities as are necessary for the exercise of its functions' (Article VIII:2 *WTO Agreement*),[50] lies a recognition by States of the existence of the WTO under international law. Although not specifically elaborated upon in the *WTO Agreement*, as a matter of international institutional law, the privileges and immunities of the WTO are held to exist for most international organisations in five main areas: absolute

48 *Reparation for Injuries*, *ibid*, p. 180 and p. 182. *See* also *Certain Expenses of the United Nations (Article 17, paragraph2 of the Charter)* (*Advisory Opinion*) [1962] ICJ Rep 151 [hereinafter *Certain Expenses*] 177, dealing with the UN Security Council and General Assembly's competence to establish peacekeeping operations otherwise not provided for in the UN Charter, and the *WHO Advisory Opinion*, above n. 40, para. 25, dealing with the exercise of implied powers, not otherwise expressly provided for in the organisation's constituent instrument.

49 *Reparation for Injuries*, *ibid*, p. 168. Elihu Lauterpacht has suggested that 'essential' does not mean that the implied power is 'indispensably required' and that the ICJ in another advisory opinion on *Certain Expenses* was somewhat liberal in its interpretation of the word. *See* E. Lauterpacht, 'The Development of the Law of International Organizations by the Decisions of International Tribunals' (1976) 52 *Receuil des Cours* 377, at 430-432.

50 The text of paragraph 2 of Article VIII of the *WTO Agreement* mirrors that of Article 105 UN Charter and other international organisations, with privileges and immunities flowing directly from the source of obligation which in this case is the treaty basis of the WTO.

immunity from the adjudicative jurisdiction of States; immunity from measures of execution; inviolability of the premises, property and archives of the organisation; enjoyment of various currency and fiscal privileges; and freedom of official communication.[51]

Similarly, it could be argued that provided an international agreement like the *WTO Agreement* does not specifically state that the organisation is *not* established under international law then a presumption is raised that it is.[52] Since there is nothing in the *WTO Agreement* to the contrary, it can be concluded that the WTO is established under international law and *ipso facto* is therefore governed by international law.

3.1 Objectives and functions

The reasons for establishing the WTO are specified in the Preamble to the *WTO Agreement*[53] and are not without legal relevance, as is evident from a number

51 *See* Dapo Akande, 'International Organizations' in Malcolm Evans (ed.) *International Law* (Oxford: Oxford University Press, 2003) 269-297, at 288-290.
There is a further set of privileges and immunities pertaining to 'the officials of the WTO and the representatives of the Members' (or delegates) who 'shall similarly be accorded by each of its Members such privileges and immunities as are necessary for the independent exercise of their functions in connection with the WTO' (Article VIII:3 WTO). In other words, they enjoy limited functional immunity. *See* further Chanaka Wickmerasinghe, 'Immunities enjoyed by Officials of States and International Organizations', in Evans, *International Law*, *ibid*, 387-413, at 404-406.
Finally, Article VIII:4 *WTO Agreement* makes clear that such privileges and immunities 'to be accorded by a Member to the WTO, its officials, and the representatives shall be similar to' those set out in the *Convention on the Privileges and Immunities of the United Nations* (adopted by the UN General Assembly on 13 February 1946, *entry into force*, 17 September 1946) 1 UNTS 15 (corr. 90 UNTS 327). The WTO Members formally approved the relationship between the organisation and the government of the host State, Switzerland, by means of a *Decision by the General Council* concerning the *Headquarters Agreement*, being the *Agreement between the WTO and the Swiss Confederation* (WT/GC/1 and Add.1) and the *Infrastructure Contract*, WT/GC/2 adopted on 31 May 1995, WT/L/69 (1 June 1995); *see* also Minutes of the Meeting of the General Council, 31 May 1995, WT/GC/M/4 (1 June 1995), para. 5. Although not specifically stated in the General Council's decision, this was done pursuant to Article VIII:5 *WTO Agreement*. *See* further *WTO Analytical Index: Guide to WTO Law and Practice* (Geneva: WTO Secretariat/Bernan, 2003), [hereinafter *WTO Analytical Index*] 78.

52 Schermers and Blokker, above n. 35, §45, 36-37.

53 Preamble to the *WTO Agreement*, *The Legal Texts*, above n. 31, 2.

of rulings of the WTO Appellate Body[54] which has emphasized its importance with respect to the scope of the new organisation,[55] its status as successor to GATT 1947[56] and as an aid to interpretation in construing certain substantive provisions in the various multilateral trade agreements.[57] The ultimate objectives of the WTO are three-fold: 'raising standards of living, ensuring full employment and a large and steadily growing volume of real income and effective demand, and expanding the production of and trade in goods and services' and point in the direction of a light institutional structure for the fledgling organisation in order to preserve the status quo of the former GATT that gave pre-eminence to a minimum of constraints to the negotiating process.[58] In seeking to achieve these objectives, the WTO should take into account the preservation of the environment and the needs of countries at differing levels of development.[59]

The means for achieving these objectives are reminiscent of those set out in the Preamble to the GATT 1947 on which they are based, thereby reinforcing the WTO as the institutional successor to the former GATT treaty regime. The instruments that are to be employed in achieving the WTO objectives can be summarised as the continued agreement among Members on 'substantial reduction of tariffs and other barriers to trade' and 'the elimination of discriminatory treatment in international trade relations'. While both of these objectives endorse the

54 *See* the *WTO Analytical Index*, above n. 51, 34-38.

55 *See US – Gasoline*, Appellate Body Report, *United States – Standards for Reformulated and Conventional Gasoline*, WT/DS2/AB/R, adopted 20 May 1996, p. 31 and *US – Shrimp*, Appellate Body Report, *United States – Import Prohibition of Certain Shrimp and Shrimp Products*, WT/DS58/AB/R, adopted 6 November 1998, paras. 129-131 (both with respect to the environment and sustainable development); *India – Quantitative Restrictions*, Appellate Body Report, *India – Quantitative Restrictions on Imports of Agricultural, Textile and Industrial Products*, WT/DS90/AB/R, adopted 22 September 1999, para. 7.2. (developing country needs).

56 *Brazil – Desiccated Coconut*, Appellate Body Report, *Brazil – Measures Affecting Desiccated Coconut*, WT/DS22/AB/R, adopted 20 March 1997, p. 17 (WTO as successor to GATT) and *US – Shrimp*, *ibid*, paras. 152, 153 and 155 (preamble to GATT 1947 as template for WTO preamble).

57 *US – Shrimp*, *ibid*, paras. 130, 153 and 155 (Article XX(g) GATT) and *Turkey – Textiles* Appellate Body Report, *Turkey – Restrictions on Imports of Textile and Clothing Products*, WT/DS34/AB/R, adopted 19 November 1999, paras. 9.161-9.163 (discussion on Article XXIV GATT) and *Brazil – Aircraft (Article 21.5 – Canada)*, Appellate Body Report, *Brazil – Export Financing Programme for Aircraft, Recourse by Canada to Article 21.5 of the DSU*, WT/DS46/AB/RW, adopted 4 August 2000, paras. 6.47, fn. 49 (WTO's concern with interests of developing countries).

58 *See* Andrew L. Stoler , 'The Current State of the WTO', paper for a *Workshop on the EU, the US and the WTO,* Stanford University, 28 February – 1 March 2003.

59 Preamble to the *WTO Agreement* (first recital), *The Legal Texts*, above n. 31, 6.

practice of the contracting parties with respect to substantive and procedural norms under the former GATT treaty regime, thereby ensuring a certain continuity of principle and practice in the WTO, there is no reference in the overall objectives to institutional continuity and that is because there simply was none – at least in the formal sense of the word.

Instead, the institutional rationale for the organisation is set out for the first time in Article II *WTO Agreement* where it is stated that the WTO 'shall provide the common institutional framework for the conduct of trade relations among its Members in matters related to the agreements and associated legal instruments included in the Annexes to this Agreement',[60] i.e. Annexes 1,[61] 2[62] and 3[63] (the 'Multilateral Trade Agreements'), which are 'an integral part' of the *WTO Agreement* and bind all Members.[64] These Annexes are important in three respects. First, they define the substantive rights and obligations of WTO Members. Second, each Annex and/or Agreement has its own institutional body or organ,

60 Article II:1 *WTO Agreement, ibid*, 6-7. The wording is reminiscent of Article 3 (ex Article C) of the Treaty on European Union, as amended by the Treaties of Amsterdam and Nice (*in force* 1 February 2003) [hereinafter TEU], which states that the Union 'shall be served by a single institutional framework' even though no institutional bodies (or organs) are explicitly mentioned in the Treaty. *See* Curtin and Dekker, above n. 28, 98.

61 Annex 1A contains the *Multilateral Agreements on Trade in Goods*, including the GATT 1994 (i.e. GATT 1947 as amended and complemented with various understandings mostly related to the interpretation of key GATT provisions). Some of these have their origin in previous MTNs, notably the Tokyo Round MTN (1973-1979); Geneva (1979) Protocol to the General Agreement on Tariffs and Trade, L/4875, and Protocol Supplementary to the Geneva (1979) Protocol, L/4812, BISD 26S/3 and 7 and Annexes (1978-1979). They include the current *Agreement on Technical Barriers to Trade*; *Agreement on Implementation of Article VI of the General Agreements on Tariff and Trade* ('*Anti-dumping Agreement*'); *Agreement on Implementation of Article VII of the General Agreements on Tariff and Trade* ('*Customs Valuation Agreement*'); *Agreement on Import Licensing Procedures* and *Agreement on Subsidies and Countervailing Measures.* Others were negotiated during the Uruguay Round MTN (1986-1994). They include the *Agreement on Agriculture; Agreement on the Application of Sanitary and Phytosanitary Measures*; *Agreement on Textiles and Clothing; Agreement on Trade-Related Investment Measures*, *Agreement on Preshipment Inspection*, *Agreement on Rules of Origin* and the *Agreement on Safeguards.*
Annex 1B is the *General Agreement on Trade in Services (GATS)* and Annex 1C is the *Agreement on Trade-Related Aspects of Intellectual Property Rights (TRIPs)*, both of which were negotiated during the Uruguay Round MTN.

62 Annex 2 is the *Understanding on Rules and Procedures Governing the Settlement of Disputes (DSU)*, which is the common dispute settlement mechanism of the WTO.

63 Annex 3 is the *Trade Policy Review Mechanism (TPRM)*, which is a new instrument for the surveillance of individual Member trade policies.

64 Article II:2 *WTO Agreement, The Legal Texts*, above n. 31, 7.

i.e. a Council and/or a committee (or a number of committees), operating under that particular Annex and/or Agreement, which forms part of the overall institutional structure of the WTO. Thus, a reading of the Annexes and/or Agreements leads to an institutional reading of the organisation. Third, the WTO provides the legal framework for the conduct of trade under the agreements and associated legal instruments, which are taken up in Annex 4[65] to the *WTO Agreement* (the so-called 'Plurilateral Trade Agreements') and which are part of the *WTO Agreement* for those Members that have accepted them and on whom they are binding.[66]

The approach taken in the *WTO Agreement* of describing the organisation's mandate in terms of its functions follows the approach taken by the drafters of the abortive ITO in the late 1940's.[67] The WTO has five functions that are explicitly laid down in Article III *WTO Agreement.*

The first function is set out in paragraph 1 of Article III, where it is stated that the WTO 'shall facilitate the implementation, administration and operation and further the objectives of this Agreement and of the Multilateral Trade Agreements…'[68] Implicit in the wording of this provision lies the institutional structure of the organisation since each of the agreements contains provisions designating an institutional body (usually a Council or Committee in which all Members participate) that is tasked with exercising certain functions on behalf of the organisation within the discrete subject matter area of the relevant agreement on the basis of an attribution of powers.[69] Indeed, such is the preoccupation of the various Councils and Committees with the implementation, administration and

65 Article II:3 *WTO Agreement, ibid.* Annex 4 currently has just two Plurilateral Trade Agreements (the *Agreement on Trade in Civil Aircraft* (*Civil Aircraft Agreement*) and the *Agreement on Government Procurement* (*GPA*), which are legal instruments dating from the Tokyo Round MTN. During the Uruguay Round, the negotiators tried unsuccessfully to negotiate new Agreement but at the end of the Round the 1979 *Aircraft Agreement* was simply annexed, unchanged to the *WTO Agreement*. In the case of the *GPA*, negotiations began during the Uruguay Round in order to revise it (adopted 15 April 1994, *in force* 1 January 1996, for those WTO Members that are party to it) 1915 UNTS 103.

66 It is specifically stated in Article II:3 that the Plurilateral Trade Agreements 'do not create either obligations or rights for Members that have not accepted them'.

67 For further details concerning the origins of functionalism in post-war international organisations, *see* Zamora, above n. 15.

68 Article III:1 *WTO Agreement*, *The Legal Texts*, above n. 31, 7.

69 *See* for example, Peter Van den Bossche, *The Law and Policy of the World Trade Organization* (Cambridge: Cambridge University Press, 2005) 89, where he describes the function of the *WTO Committee on Sanitary and Phytosanitary Measures* or *SPS* on the basis of Article 12 of the Agreement on Sanitary and Phytosanitary Measures

operation of the many annexed agreements that it may be possible to speak of an 'executive power' that overshadows the exercise of other powers such as legislative powers.[70] Some commentators have applied the traditional separation of powers doctrine to the WTO, which usually applies in respect of the functions of a State (and sometimes an international organisation), and have found it wanting.[71] However, it may be more appropriate to apply the doctrine of institutional balance rather than the separation of powers doctrine in assessing the proper functioning of WTO bodies, as will be discussed hereunder.

A second function of the WTO is to 'provide the forum for negotiations among its Members concerning their multilateral trade relations in matters dealt with under the agreements in the Annexes to this Agreement'.[72] The wording 'among its Members' is somewhat anomalous and stands in contrast to the other paragraphs in Article III describing the WTO's functions. It reflects the practice of Members, as former GATT contracting parties, in regarding the WTO as an area for interaction between them rather than as an institution where individual States perform collective tasks. In this respect the WTO continues to portray the characteristics of a 'forum organisation', in the sense that Robert Cox and Harold Jacobson used the term to describe organisations, which provides a framework or forum 'for member states to carry on many different activities ranging from the exchange of views to the negotiation of binding legal instruments'.[73]

In exercising this function as a forum for negotiations, the WTO runs counter to the idea that international organisations are 'multi-layered' in character, embodying within their structures the competing images of the international organisation as 'a forum of states' and as 'an independent international actor'.[74] Instead, the WTO represents a single dense layer of state activity where Members operate as

and of the WTO Committee on Safeguards on the basis of Article 13 of the *Agreement on Safeguards*.

70 *See* below at chapters IV and V.

71 This reading of the WTO's functions is attributable to Armin von Bogdandy in 'Law and Politics in the WTO – Strategies to Cope with a Deficient Relationship' (2001) 5 *Max Planck Yearbook of United Nations Law* 614. However, he is critical of the WTO because in his view 'adjudication' is the only element in the traditional separation of powers doctrine that is not part of the WTO's political realm – both the executive and legislative functions of the organisation are firmly rooted in the political domain.

72 Second full sentence, Article III:2 *WTO Agreement*, *The Legal Texts,* above n. 31, 7.

73 Robert W. Cox and Harold K. Jacobsen (eds.) *The Anatomy of Influence – Decision Making in International Organization* (New Haven: Yale University Press, 1973) 5-6.

74 Catherine Brölmann, 'A Flat Earth? International Organizations in the System of International Law'(2001) 70 *Nordic Journal of International Law* 319-340.

if taking part in a forum of States and where there is little place for the development of the organisation as a separate organisational entity.

A further point to note about this second function is that the negotiating mandate, which the Members have given themselves, is broader than under the WTO's predecessor, the GATT. The function is not restricted to dealing with tariff reductions and the scheduling of service commitments but 'may also provide a forum for further negotiations among its Members concerning their multilateral trade relations, and a framework for the implementation of such negotiations, as may be decided by the Ministerial Conference'.[75] The wording in the second full sentence of Article III:2 *WTO Agreement* hints at the intention of governments to create a permanent forum for negotiations not only on matters already covered in WTO Agreements and in some instances to build upon the results of prior negotiations, for example in the case of trade in services,[76] but also to provide a basis for negotiating on matters not currently dealt with in the WTO. This is reinforced by the practice of the organisation in the Ministerial Declaration adopted at the first Ministerial Conference held in Singapore in 1996, where Members agreed, without prejudice to future negotiations, to establish 'a working group to examine the relationship between trade and investment' and 'a working group to study issues raised by Members to examine the relationship relating to the interaction between trade and competition policy'.[77]

Potentially paragraph 2 of Article III *WTO Agreement* is the basis for the exercise of legislative power emanating from, and responding to, the needs of the Members themselves. However, it is at the discretion of the Members to decide

75 Second full sentence of Article III:2 *WTO Agreement*, *The Legal Texts*, above n. 31, 7.

76 The results of certain built-in negotiations in trade in services have thus far led to certain 'supplemental protocols' to the *General Agreement on Trade in Services* or *GATS*. *See* the *Second Protocol to the General Agreement on Trade in Services*, S/L/11 (24 July 1995) and the *Fifth Protocol to the General Agreement on Trade in Services*, S/L/45 (3 December 1997), both of which are the results of extended negotiations on financial services, while further negotiations on basic telecoms have led to the *Fourth Protocol to the General Agreement on Trade in Services*, S/L/20 (30 April 1996) and similarly the *Third Protocol to the General Agreement on Trade in Services*, S/L/12 (24 July 1995) has dealt with issues relating to Natural Persons. *See* further below, chapter IV, section 3.1(c).

77 WTO Ministerial Conference, Singapore, 9-13 December 1996, *Ministerial Declaration*, WT/MIN(96)/DEC, 18 December 1996, [hereinafter *Singapore Ministerial Declaration*], para. 20. Members also decided to establish 'a working group to conduct a study on transparency in government procurement practices' and instructed the General Council 'to undertake exploratory and analytical work … on the simplification of trade procedures in order to assess the scope for WTO rules in this area', i.e. trade facilitation; *see* further *Singapore Ministerial Declaration*, *ibid*, para. 21.

upon its actual exercise, i.e. the right of initiative in rule-making lies solely within their domain. Here again the practice of the organisation, or more properly its Members, as stated in the Doha Ministerial Declaration[78] indicates that they continue to view the WTO 'as the unique forum for global trade rule-making and liberalization'. Armin Von Bogdandy is critical of the 'peculiar relationship between politics and law in the WTO', resulting from the way in which the executive and legislative powers[79] are defined, such that they do not institutionalise any autonomous political process. This institutional failure combined with a certain subservience of the organisation to the will of its Members, i.e. the idea that it merely exists to serve the Members in what has come to be known as a 'member-driven' organisation,[80] casts doubt on whether the organisation has a will of its own and functions separately from its Members.

It is further supported by the Members' own view that the WTO is a *sui generis* organisation in character,[81] which when coupled with its own identity as a member-driven organisation sets it apart from other international organisations and may over time contribute to the WTO's sense of self-imposed isolation.[82] The WTO stands in stark contrast to an international economic organisation like the IMF, which owing to the greater operational autonomy of the Executive Board can be considered as 'institution-driven'.[83]

Even so, given the implicit reference in the WTO Agreement to the exercise of a legislative function three issues arise in connection therewith. First, which institutional bodies may exercise this rule-making competence on behalf of the

78 WTO Ministerial Conference, Fourth Session, Doha, 9-14 November 2001, *Ministerial Declaration*, WT/MIN(01)/DEC/1, 20 November 2001 [hereinafter *Doha Ministerial Declaration*], para. 4. *See* also Van den Bossche, above n. 69, 91.

79 Von Bogdandy, above n. 71, 617; he refers to such 'powers' as 'functions'.

80 This comment is reinforced by the WTO's own web-site where it is stated that: 'In fact: it's governments who dictate to the WTO.' The concept of a 'member-driven' organisation is examined by the Consultative Board in *The Future of the WTO – Addressing institutional challenges in the new millennium*, Report of the Director-General's Consultative Board (Geneva: World Trade Organization, 2004) [hereinafter *The Sutherland Report*], 76-77, paras. 359-364, which is of the view that the WTO needs a convincing and persistent voice. However, the *Report* does not consider the issue on its own merits which would mean questioning the status of the WTO as an international organisation with a will of its own, independent of that of its Members.

81 This notion of *sui generis* character stems from the WTO's establishment in 1995 when it was decided by the contracting parties to the GATT that the new organisation should be neither a specialised UN agency nor form part of the UN system.

82 *See* Joost Pauwelyn, 'The Sutherland Report: A Missed Opportunity for Genuine Debate on Trade, Globalization and Reforming the WTO' (2005) 8 *JIEL* 329-346 at 334.

83 Von Bogdandy, above n. 71, 617.

Members? Second, is that competence granted on the basis of an attribution or delegation of powers? Third, is the competence specifically granted or is it derived, i.e. does it involve an express or an implied power? A preliminary answer to these three questions, which are fundamental to any analysis of the normative scope of the WTO, is dealt with below in section 3.2 when considering various WTO bodies and their powers. Fourth, to what problems might the fusion of executive and legislative powers give rise when it comes to rule-making and how, if at all, can they be overcome? The answer to this last question is taken up in the final conclusions to this book following completion of a normative analysis of the WTO, which is the subject of chapters IV and V.

A third function of the WTO is the administration of the *Understanding on Rules and Procedures Governing the Settlement of Disputes*.[84] This adjudicative power forms part of the *trias politica* of 'constitutional' powers that are usually ascribed to a State or in this instance an international organisation.[85] As von Bogdandy remarks, it is the only function which the WTO exercises autonomously, i.e. the WTO is not limited to providing a forum or facilitating an activity. Instead the WTO is charged with 'administering' the *Dispute Settlement Understanding* or *DSU*, with the actual function being discharged through the two reporting bodies (the panels and the Appellate Body) thereby ensuring some degree of independence and compulsory (quasi) judicial adjudication.[86]

However, von Bogdandy goes too far in describing the WTO's exercise of adjudicative power as 'autonomous' and the separation of powers doctrine is hardly applicable in this case. The practice of the Dispute Settlement Body or DSB – a WTO political organ in which *all* Members have representation – in administering the rules and procedures governing complaints raised by Members in the dispute settlement system,[87] i.e. the exercise of an executive function, as an emanation of the General Council, is not as autonomous as it might appear.

84 Article III:3 *WTO Agreement*, *The Legal Texts*, above n. 31, 7.

85 Lorand Bartels, 'The Separation of Powers in the WTO: How to Avoid Judicial Activism' (2004) 53 *ICLQ* 861-895 at 861-862.

86 Von Bogdandy, above n. 71, 615-616, where he cites three bases of evidence to support his claim that the WTO's adjudicative function is the only truly autonomous one. This is because (1) it 'does not rely on the consent of the respondent member' (Article 6.1 DSU), (2) 'the nomination of the panelists is a function of the Secretariat and the Director-General' (Articles 8.6 and 8.7 DSU) and (3) 'political blockage of the dispute settlement procedures is prevented' (Articles 16.4 and 17.14 DSU).

87 Article 2:1 *DSU*, *The Legal Texts*, above n. 31, 405. Von Bogdandy himself acknowledges that 'formally the adjudication function remains a competence of a political organ' but at the same time discounts it because of the principle of 'reverse consensus' in Articles 16.4 and 17.14 of the DSU, which has the practical effect of leading to the

Besides, an adjudicative system that allows the Members to retain ultimate political control over its functioning,[88] to be held responsible for adopting panel[89] and Appellate Body reports,[90] for maintaining surveillance over the implementation of rulings and recommendations[91] and for authorizing retaliatory measures in the case of non-compliance,[92] while the *ad hoc* panels and the Appellate Body exercise a (quasi-)judicial function, is not consistent with the separation of powers doctrine.

At the same time, if the WTO's exercise of its powers in fulfilling its various functions is examined through the lens of the principle of institutional balance rather than the separation of powers doctrine, it becomes clear that the potential for institutional conflict and infringement of the principle of institutional balance abound, given the inevitable tensions that arise from a hybrid system for the investigation of complaints, arising out of the review of Members' conduct and potential violations of their obligations. This is because the exercise of decision-making powers in fulfilment of rule-making (legislative) and (quasi-)judicial competences involving review processes by the Councils and Committees, which are political bodies, and by the *ad hoc* panels and the Appellate Body, which are (quasi-)judicial bodies, together with the DSB as a political body, by means of the dispute settlement system, may threaten the fragile principle of institutional balance between them as has already been demonstrated in practice.

For example the Balance-of-Payments Committee or BOP Committee, as a standing WTO body, has continued to keep under review India's prolonged use and justification of quantitative restrictions for balance-of-payments difficulties on the basis of Article XVIII:12 *GATT 1994*. However, this did not prevent the United States from invoking the dispute settlement system against India when it felt that the measures proposed by the BOP Committee for India's compliance were unsatisfactory.[93] Similarly, the report issued by the Committee on Regional Trade Arrangements or CRTA, a subsidiary body of the General Council, concerning the question whether the regional trade agreement between Turkey and the European Union was in fact a 'customs union' and met the criteria set out in

automatic adoption of panel and Appellate Body reports; *see* von Bogdandy, above n. 71, 616.

88 Article 2:1 *DSU*, first full sentence, *The Legal Texts,* above n. 31, 405.

89 Article 16:4 *DSU*, *The Legal Texts*, *ibid*, 417.

90 Article 17:14 *DSU*, *The Legal Texts, ibid*, 419.

91 Article 21 *DSU*, *The Legal Texts, ibid*, 420-421.

92 Article 22 *DSU*, *The Legal Texts, ibid*, 422-425.

93 *India – Quantitative Restrictions*, Appellate Body Reports, above n. 55. *See* Asif H. Qureshi, 'Challenging Quantitative Restrictions for Balance-of-Payments Purposes under the WTO', (2000) 6 *IntTLR* 28-31.

paragraphs 8(a) and 5(a) of Article XXIV *GATT 1994*, did not prevent India from challenging Turkey afresh in the dispute settlement system even though the Appellate Body noted that arguably 'panels do not have the jurisdiction to assess the overall compatibility of a customs union with the requirements of Article XXIV'.[94]

In particular, the first of these two examples is noteworthy because India, as respondent, in the claim brought by the United States, argued that a review by a panel of its justification for balance-of-payments restrictions would violate the principle of institutional balance which requires that panels, in determining the scope of their competence, should take into account the competence conferred on other bodies in the WTO to take binding decisions on related matters.[95] In India's view, this was essential in order to ensure a proper institutional balance between the judicial and political organs of the WTO with respect to balance-of-payments restrictions and in light of the powers attributed to the BOP Committee and the General Council under Article XVIII:12 *GATT 1994* and was inconsistent with Article 3:2 *DSU*. The Appellate Body ruled otherwise, taking the approach that the BOP Committee and panels exercise different functions and that the complaints procedures under these two WTO bodies 'differ in nature, scope, timing and type of outcome'.[96]

A fourth function of the WTO is the administration of the Trade Policy Review Mechanism (TPRM)[97] which was begun during the Uruguay Round MTN[98] with the Montreal Mid-Term Review Process in 1988[99] but institutionalised upon

94 *Turkey – Textiles*, Appellate Body Report, above n. 57, para. 60, where the Appellate Body in an *obiter dictum* recalled its almost contemporaneous decision in *India – Quantitative Restrictions* with respect to the application of the principle of institutional balance.

95 *India – Quantitative Restrictions*, above n. 55, Appellate Body Report, paras. 80 and 98.

96 *India – Quantitative Restrictions*, *ibid*, Appellate Body Report, paras. 99-106. *See* further Frieder Roessler, 'The institutional balance between judicial and political organs of the WTO' in Marco C.E.J. Bronckers and Reinhard Quick (eds.), *New directions in international economic law: essays in honor of John H. Jackson*, (The Hague: Kluwer International, 2000) 325-346 and Bartels, above n. 85, 877-882.

97 Article III:4 *WTO Agreement*, *The Legal Texts*, above n. 31, 7.

98 The Uruguay Round MTN was launched at the Ministerial Meeting held in Punta del Este, Uruguay; *see Declaration of Punta del Este*, Ministerial Meeting (Uruguay Round Declaration), GATT *BISD* 33S/19 (1987).

99 General Agreement on Tariffs and Trade: Decisions Adopted at the Mid-Term Review of the Uruguay Round held at Montreal, 28 ILM 1023 (1989). *See* further Asif Qureshi, 'The Trade Policy Review Mechanism', in *The World Trade Organization: Implementing International Trade Norms* (Manchester: Manchester University Press, 1996) 108-125.

completion of the Round. The notification and surveillance function of the TPRM involves 'the regular *collective* appreciation and evaluation of the full range of Members' trade policies and practices and their impact on the functioning of the multilateral trading system'[100] thereby enhancing the transparency of the organisation and contributing to its stability and predictability.[101]

A fifth function of the WTO is to cooperate, as appropriate, 'with the International Monetary Fund and with the International Bank for Reconstruction and Development and its affiliated agencies' with a view 'to achieving greater coherence in global economic policy-making'.[102] The so-called 'principle of coherence' in economic policy-making is supported by a Ministerial Declaration, taken at the end of the Uruguay Round,[103] on the basis of which the WTO General Council took a decision to conclude agreements between the IMF and the World Bank and the WTO.[104] The respective agreements provide for consultations and the exchange of information between the WTO, through its Secretariat, and the staff of the IMF and the World Bank, besides granting observer status to each organisation in certain of the other's meetings.[105]

100 Van den Bossche, above n. 69, 95.

101 Others have viewed Article III:4 *WTO Agreement* 'as a new strategy of implementation which embraces elements of execution and adjudication'; *see* von Bogdandy, above n. 71, 614.

102 Article III:5 *WTO Agreement*, *The Legal Texts,* above n. 31, 7.

103 *Declaration on the Contribution of the World Trade Organization to Achieving Greater Coherence in Global Economic Policymaking*, *Final Act Embodying the Results of the Uruguay Round of Multilateral Trade Negotiations, The Legal Texts ibid*, 442-443. The principle of coherence, as set out in this *Ministerial Declaration*, has subsequently been endorsed by the Appellate Body in *Argentina – Textiles and Apparel*, Appellate Body Report, *Argentina – Measures Affecting Imports of Footwear, Textiles, Apparel and Other Items*, WT/DS56/AB/R and Corr. 1, adopted 22 April 1998, para. 70.

104 *Agreement between the International Monetary Fund and the World Trade Organization*, in Annex I and *Agreement between the International Bank for Reconstruction and Development and the World Trade Organization* in Annex II to WT/GC/W/43 (4 November 1996), entered into by the WTO, pursuant to a General Council Decision to conclude 'Agreements between the WTO and the IMF and the World Bank', WT/L/94 (18 November 1996).

105 *See* Van den Bossche, above n. 69, 98. It should be noted that pursuant to Article V:1 *WTO Agreement* the WTO General Council 'shall make appropriate arrangements for effective cooperation with other intergovernmental organizations that have responsibilities related to those of the WTO'. It has subsequently entered into various forms of cooperation with the World Intellectual Property Organization (WIPO) and UNDP while the WTO is continuing a cooperative venture begun under the former GATT, with the UNCTAD and the International Trade Center (ITC), Geneva, to assist developing and transition economy countries with establishing effective trade promotion programmes

A sixth function, which the WTO is said to fulfil, is that of technical assistance to developing country and LDC Members[106] although there is no explicit reference to it in Article III *WTO Agreement*. Peter Van den Bossche is of the view that such a function is implicit in that of facilitating the implementation, administration and operation, and in furthering the objectives, of the WTO.[107] It could also be argued that the Members intended the WTO to exercise this function because it was 'essential'[108] to achieving the WTO's objective of taking into account the needs of countries at differing levels of development,[109] i.e. it is exercised on the basis of an implied power.

The practice of the organisation attests to this when at the Fourth Ministerial Conference held at Doha in November 2001 recognition was given to the function of technical assistance, in the form of technical cooperation and capacity building, as 'core elements of the development dimension of the multilateral trading system' in the *Doha Ministerial Declaration*.[110] The means of achieving this technical assistance function were taken up in the Doha work programme, which forms part of the aforementioned *Doha Ministerial Declaration*[111] and has led to an enormous expansion in training and capacity building activities, which have been undertaken under the heading of technical assistance, and in an increasing number of individual financial donations by individual Members in fulfilment of these activities.

for their imports/exports.

The WTO has also entered into a large number of Memoranda of Understanding with a range of intergovernmental and non-governmental organisations, mostly in the field of technical cooperation.

Likewise, the WTO has a mandate to cooperate with non-governmental organisations, or NGO's, pursuant to Article V:2 *WTO Agreement*, which has been achieved through various means, including NGO attendance on the periphery of Ministerial Conferences (NGO's and other non-state actors are not allowed to take part in the actual plenary sessions of the Ministerial Conference), NGO symposia on specific trade-related topics, regular briefings on the work of WTO committees and working groups and notification of NGO documents, position papers and newsletters on the WTO web-site. A set of *Guidelines for arrangements on relations with Non-Governmental Organizations*, was adopted by the General Council on 18 July 1996, WT/L/162 (23 July 1996).

106 Van den Bossche, above n. 69, 100-103.

107 *Ibid*, at 100.

108 *See* above n. 49 and accompanying remarks in the main text to this footnote which relate to the doctrine of implied powers that was discussed in the introduction to this section.

109 *WTO Agreement*, Preamble (first recital), *The Legal Texts,* above n. 31, 6.

110 *Doha Ministerial Declaration,* above n. 78, para. 38

111 *Doha Ministerial Declaration*, *ibid*, para. 41.

However, the use of a Ministerial Declaration, as a basis for ascribing a further function to the organisation is questionable not least because Ministerial Declarations are generally considered to be statements of a political nature, as reflected in their hortatory language,[112] and therefore not capable of imposing binding obligations on Members.[113] Were the legal basis of this sixth function to be subject to challenge before a court or tribunal then it would be incumbent upon the WTO, or more likely its Members, to demonstrate that it is based upon an implied power.[114] Moreover, within the WTO's own adjudicative process from an evidential point of view there is nothing to prevent a Member from relying on a Ministerial Declaration as persuasive authority before a WTO panel[115] or the Appellate Body in much the same way as the Preamble to the *WTO Agreement*.[116] In practice, at least one Ministerial Declaration has been invoked in WTO dispute settlement proceedings to date, although with a view to construction, as an aid to interpretation, rather than as persuasive authority.[117]

112 *US – Lead and Bismuth II,* Appellate Body Report, *United States – Imposition of Countervailing Duties on Certain Hot-Rolled Lead and Bismuth Carbon Steel Products Originating in the United Kingdom*, WT/DS138/AB/R, adopted 7 June 2000, para. 49.

113 *Argentina – Textiles and Apparel*¸ Appellate Body Report, above n. 103, para. 72.

114 *See* the decision of the ICJ with respect to the implied powers doctrine in its advisory decisions on *Certain Expenses* and the *WHO Advisory Opinion*, above n. 48 and 40 respectively. On the possible legal effects of *ultra vires* acts of international organisations or *détournement de pouvoir*, *see* E. Lauterpacht, 'The Legal Effect of Illegal Acts of International Organisations', in *Cambridge Essays in International Law: Essays in honour of Lord McNair* (London: Stevens & Sons/ Dobbs Ferry, New York: Oceana Publications, Inc., 1965) 88-121.

115 *See Turkey – Textiles*, Panel Report, *Turkey – Restrictions on Imports of Textiles and Clothing Products* WT/DS34/R, adopted 19 November 1999, as modified by the Appellate Body Report, above n. 57, paras. 9.98-9.100 with respect to the Singapore Ministerial Declaration as evidence of the Members' general view of the desirability of concluding Article XXIV GATT 1994 (regional trade agreements) as a means of increasing freedom of trade.

116 *US – Shrimp*, Appellate Body Report, above n. 55, paras. 130, 153 and 155, for a statement by the Appellate Body on the relationship of the WTO's objectives to sustainable development.

117 *See US – Lead and Bismuth II*, Panel Report, *United States – Imposition of Countervailing Duties on Certain Hot-Rolled Lead and Bismuth Carbon Steel Products Originating in the United Kingdom*, WT/DS138/R and Corr. 2, adopted 7 June 2000, as upheld by the Appellate Body Report, above n. 112, para. 6.17 for a discussion of the differences between a Ministerial Declaration and a Ministerial Decision. Both parties to the dispute (US and the EC) called on the panel to determine the 'meaning' that should be ascribed to the term: 'need for consistent resolution of disputes arising from anti-dumping and countervailing measures', which is taken up in the *Declaration on Dispute Settlement Pursuant to the Agreement on the Implementation of Article VI of the General*

The expansion of the WTO's functions in this way raises a more significant institutional problem if the organisation were to overreach itself in the fulfilment of this function to the extent that it might become something of a development agency, which is something that is strongly resisted by the majority of the membership.[118] It also makes additional demands upon the organisation in terms of its coordination role with other institutions and agencies in the field of development in the international community because it calls for greater policy coherence not only in terms of global economic policy-making – a function which we have just noted that the WTO exercises with the IMF and the World Bank on the basis of Article III:5 *WTO Agreement* – but also in terms of development policy.[119]

3.2 WTO bodies and their powers

The WTO has a hierarchical, almost pyramid-like structure (see fig. 1 below), at the apex of which stands the Ministerial Conference. At a second level there is the General Council, which also functions as the Dispute Settlement Body or DSB (charged with the overall administration of the dispute settlement system)[120] and as the Trade Policy Review Body or TPRB. A third level consists of the specialised Councils on Trade in Goods, Trade in Services and Trade-Related

Agreement on Tariffs and Trade 1994 or Part V of the Agreement on Subsidies and Countervailing Measures, *The Legal Texts,* above n. 31, 453. The Panel was of the view that a Ministerial Decision imposes an obligation on Members; presumably, although not explicitly stated by the Panel, a Ministerial Declaration does not.

118 Faizel Ismail, 'A Development Perspective on the WTO July 2004 General Council Decision'(2005) 8 *JIEL* 377-404 at 402.

119 There is also a possible danger of the WTO's scope and mandate creeping into the functions of other institutions and agencies, especially the World Bank and UNDP. This is not an entirely unthinkable scenario, given a similar development in the past with respect to the IMF. This particular institution has been accused of 'mission creep' in fulfilling its functions with respect to international cooperation and crisis management through various extended loan facilities and the establishment of economic development goals that potentially encroach on the functions of the World Bank and other agencies; see *Report of the International Financial Institutions Advisory Commission,* under the chairmanship of Allan H. Meltzer, to the Joint Economic Committee of the US (2000) [hereinafter the *Meltzer Report*].

120 On the basis of Article 2:1 DSU, *The Legal* Texts, above n. 31, 405, the DSB's administrative functions extend to 'the authority to establish panels, adopt panel and Appellate Body reports, maintain surveillance of implementation of rulings and recommendations, and authorize suspension of concessions and other obligations under the covered agreements.'

Intellectual Property Rights (or TRIPs Council) and also a number of 'horizontal' committees, consisting of standing or permanent committees, working parties on accession, various working groups, and the committees established under the two plurilateral agreements. All of these bodies report to the General Council. Finally, there is a fourth layer of committees, working parties and the former Textiles Monitoring Body or TMB, established under the separate Multilateral Trade Agreements, which report to the specialised Councils.

Altogether, the WTO comprises some seventy bodies, of which a total of thirty-four are standing bodies, whereas the remaining thirty-six or so bodies are *ad hoc* and include such bodies as the Trade Negotiations Committee or TNC (and its two negotiating groups on 'Market Access' and 'Rules') together with twenty-six working parties on accession and five plurilateral bodies.[121] With a few exceptions *all* of the aforementioned bodies, including working parties on accession, are bodies of the whole, in which there is absolute equality of voting power among the Members but where decisions are usually taken on the basis of consensus, conform the rules on decision-making in Article IX:1 *WTO Agreement.*[122]

Where a WTO body at a lower level of the organisation is unable to reach a consensus decision then Rule 33[123] of its Rules of Procedure[124] allows it to be moved (or 'kicked up') to a higher body.[125] This so-called 'kick-up' provision is common to all WTO bodies since it is replicated in each of their individual Rules of Procedure. In practice, the kick-up rule may give rise to some peculiar situations when combined with express and implied powers mixed with

121 Statement by former WTO Deputy Director General, Miguel Rodriguez Mendoza to the General Council on 13 February 2002, WT/GC/M/73.

122 Article IX:1 *WTO Agreement, The Legal Texts,* above n. 31, 11.

123 The actual wording of Rule 33 will differ in the individual Committees, depending upon which body they report to. In the case of the specialised Councils, all of which report to the General Council, the wording of Rule 33 is as follows: 'Where a decision cannot be arrived at by consensus, the matter shall be referred to the General Council for decision.' In the case of the committees, the wording is changed slightly to reflect the difference in reporting such that 'General Council' is replaced by the name of relevant specialised Council(s).

124 *Rules of Procedure for Sessions of the Ministerial Conference and Meetings of the General Council*, WT/L/161 (25 July 1996) [hereinafter *Ministerial Conference and General Council Rules of Procedure, W/T/161*] together with the Rules of Procedure as adopted by the other WTO councils and committees, are reproduced in *OMC/WTO Rules of Procedure for Meetings of WTO Bodies* (Geneva: WTO Secretariat, 1997).

125 Pieter Jan Kuijper, 'Some institutional issues presently before the WTO', in Daniel L.M. Kennedy and James D. Southwick, *The Political Economy of International Trade Law: Essays in Honour of Robert E. Hudec* (Cambridge: Cambridge University Press, 2002) 81-110 at 85 and 86.

the conferral of powers by attribution or delegation, reference to which will be made in passing when reviewing the different WTO bodies and their powers.

There are a few exceptions to WTO bodies of the whole and they can be placed in one of three categories, dependent upon whether their composition is drawn from the WTO membership or from outside 'experts'. First, there are a few bodies of limited composition, which are drawn from the membership. An example is the TMB, which existed until 1 January 2005 and was charged with supervising the Agreement on Textiles and Clothing or ATC until its full and final integration into the *GATT 1994*.[126] The TMB was a standing body of limited composition, consisting of a Chairman and ten Members that must be 'balanced and broadly representative of the Members'. TMB members were appointed on a rotational basis 'by Members designated by the Council for Trade in Goods to serve on the TMB'.[127]

Second, there are a few bodies of limited composition that are drawn from part of the membership and that are only open to those Members that are parties to the underlying agreements. The reference here is to WTO bodies that are established on the basis of one of the remaining plurilateral agreements in Annex 4 to the *WTO Agreement*, i.e. the *Agreement on Government Procurement* (with 28 Members)[128] or the *Agreement on Trade in Civil Aircraft* (with 30 Mem-

126 The Textiles Monitory Body or TMB was established as a standing body pursuant to Article 8 of the Agreement on Textiles and Clothing (ATC), *The Legal Texts,* above n. 31, 99-101. It was the primary means for integrating the textiles and clothing sector into the GATT 1994 over a period of 10 years, beginning on 1 January 1995. Pursuant to Article 8:1 ATC, the mandate of the TMB was to supervise the implementation of the ATC, to examine measures taken under the ATC and their conformity with it and to take any actions specifically required by the Agreement. The TMB held its 117th and final meeting on 9 December 2004, T/TMB/R/116 (8 February 2005) since when the ATC is no longer in effect, as of 1 January 2005. Instead, the trade in textiles and clothing products are now governed by the general rules and disciplines embodied in the GATT 1994.
The TMB's supervisory tasks extended to providing a forum for bilateral consultations in respect of any matter that affected the operation of the ATC, as a possible prelude to dispute settlement, thereby effectively substituting for consultations under Article 4 DSU, *The Legal Texts*, *ibid*, 407-409. There was one subtle difference, namely the fact that the TMB could make recommendations or observations to the Members concerned pursuant to Article 8, sections 5 and 6 ATC, *The Legal Texts*, *ibid*, 100.

127 During its existence the TMB reported to the Council for Trade in Goods or CTG, charged with reviewing the implementation issues, on the basis of Article 8:11 ATC, *The Legal Texts*, *ibid*, 101.

128 Article XXI:1 *GPA*, above n. 63, which provides for a 'Committee on Government Procurement composed of representatives from each of the Parties', which elects 'its own Chairman and Vice-Chairman'.

bers),[129] or on the basis of an Agreement that was reached at one of the Meetings of the Ministerial Conference. An example of the latter is the *Agreement on the Expansion of Trade in Information Technology Products* (with 44 Members), which was established pursuant to the First Session of the Ministerial Conference, held at Singapore in 1996[130] although the Committee was not established until a few months later in early 1997,[131] due to the initial difficulties in getting sufficient participation from the membership to take the Agreement forward.

Third, there are bodies of limited composition that are made up of experts from outside the organisation, chosen by the Members. Examples of such bodies include the quasi-judicial *ad hoc* WTO dispute settlement panels, consisting of three (or exceptionally five) members,[132] and the WTO Appellate Body, which is a standing judicial body composed of seven persons (known confusingly as 'Members' rather than judges), only three of whom serve on any one appeal.[133] Both bodies report directly with their findings to the Members in plenary sessions of the DSB. Another example is the Permanent Group of Experts or PGE under the *Agreement on Agreement on Subsidies and Countervailing Measures* or *SCM*,[134] consisting of five highly qualified independent specialists in the field of subsidies and trade relations, who may at the request of the SCM give 'an advisory opinion on the existence and nature of a subsidy'.[135]

These exceptions notwithstanding the fact is that the WTO is an organisation that is effectively 'managed' or 'run' by its plenary bodies and where no executive functions are attributed or delegated to a body of limited composition, such as an executive committee or consultative board. It is a situation that may not be

129 Article 8:1 *Civil Aircraft Agreement*, above n. 65, which states that a Committee on Trade in Civil Aircraft shall be established 'composed of representatives of all Signatories' and that the Committee 'shall elect its own Chairman'.

130 *Ministerial Declaration in Trade in Information Technology Products*, 13 December 1996 (WT/MIN(96)/16) [hereinafter *Trade in Information Technology Declaration*].

131 The Committee of Participants on the Expansion of Trade in Information Technology Products was established in accordance with the *Decision on Implementation of the Ministerial Declaration on Trade in Information Technology Products*, 26 March 1997, G/L/160 (2 April 1997), para. 3.

132 Pursuant to Article 8 DSU, *The Legal Texts,* above n. 31, 411-412, panels are selected for each new dispute.

133 Each Appellate Body Member serves a term of four years, renewable once on a rotational basis; *see* Article 17, paragraphs 1 and 2, DSU, *The Legal Texts*, *ibid*, 417-418.

134 Article 24.2 of the *Agreement on Subsidies and Countervailing Measures* (SCM), *The Legal Texts*, *ibid*, 296.

135 On the basis of Article 24.3 SCM, *The Legal Texts*, *ibid*, 296.

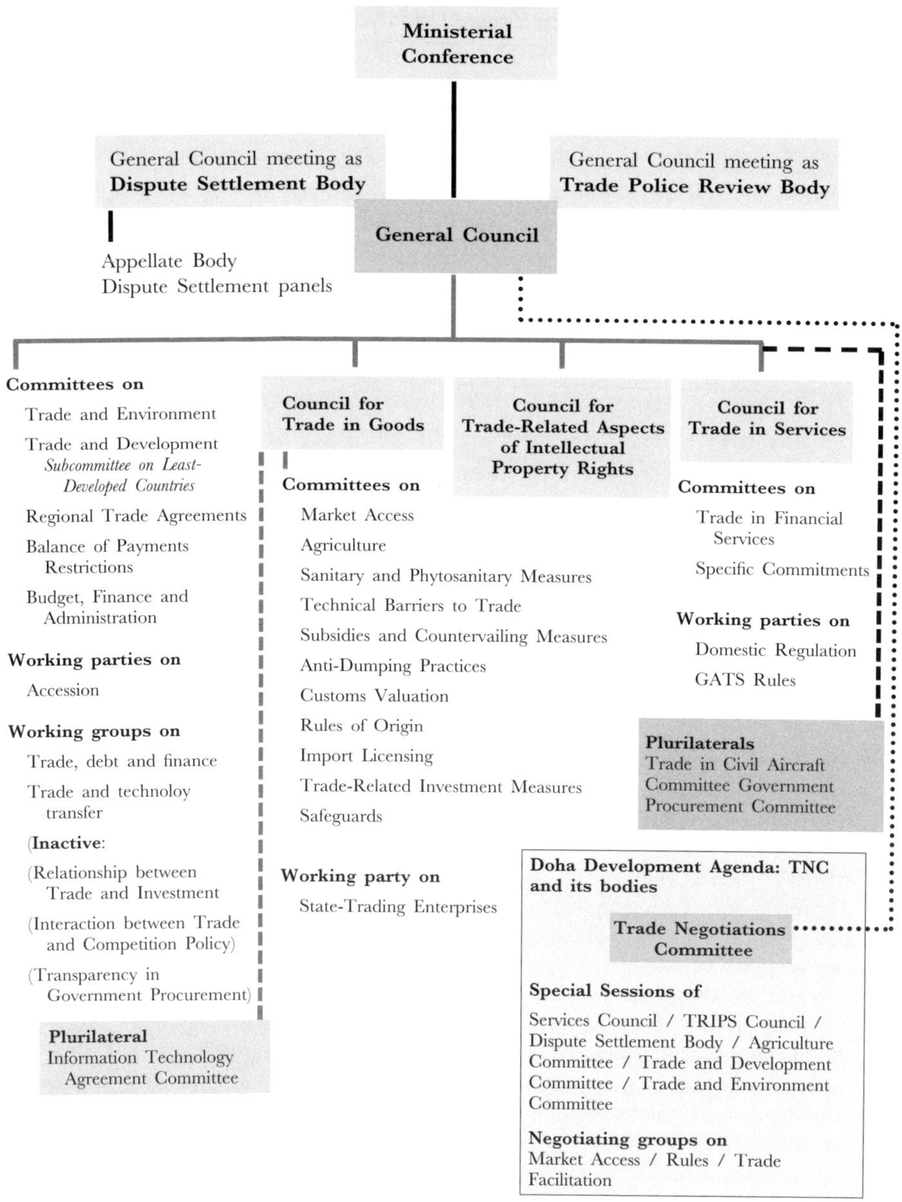

Fig. 1. WTO Structure (Source: World Trade Organization, Geneva, 2001-2005)

unique but is somewhat unusual in the field of international institutional law.[136] The fact is that in many major international organisations rules on majority voting have been relaxed over the past half century in favour of consensus decision-making[137] but without prejudice to the retention of the original institutional structure of those organisations which invariably include a mixture of plenary and non-plenary bodies. It is also common for most international organisations to have a separate executive body, comprising a core group of members that facilitate the process of decision making in the organisation and provide some guidance in policy-making, as is the case in the IMF and the World Bank.

The idea of a member-driven organisation[138] has come in for some harsh criticism not least because of the sheer impossibility of managing an organisation of this size and calibre. As Jeffrey Schott has pointed out, the WTO 'cannot be run by a committee of the whole. Mass management does not lend itself to operational efficiency or serious policy discussion'.[139] The lack of a separate executive body means that the Members, by exercising various functions of the organisation through the Councils and committees, *are* the executive.[140] More recently the Consultative Board, established by Director-General Supachai Panitchpakdi, has reported on institutional challenges that the WTO faces in the new millennium and recommended that a consultative body be established with limited participation

136 It contrasts for example with the United Nations and its various specialized agencies where there exists a mixture of plenary and non-plenary bodies, which may include regular standing committees that are numerically defined and apply a system of rotation for seats on those committees combined with selection based on any number of criteria, including equal geographical distribution or EGD, level of contribution, or subscriptions, to the relevant organization, and so on. *See* for a brief overview Klabbers, above n. 1, 169-196.

137 Mary E. Footer, 'The Role of Consensus in GATT/WTO Decision-making' (1996/97) 17 *NorthwJInt'lLBus* 653-680, which traces the development of consensus decision-making in preference to voting in the UN and the GATT/WTO.

138 *See* WTO's own web-site, www.wto.org/wto/about/organsn1.htm, at 'The organisation – Whose WTO is it anyway?' The characterisation of the WTO as a 'member-driven organisation' has given rise to considerable comment; *see* John J. Jackson, 'The WTO "Constitution" and Proposed Reforms: Seven "Mantras" Revisited' (2001) 4 *JIEL* 72. *See The Sutherland Report*, above n. 80, 76, para. 359, where the role of the Secretariat as a Member-driven organisation is criticised. *See* also Xu Yi-chong and Patrick Weller, *The Governance of World Trade: International Civil Servants and the GATT/WTO* (Cheltenham, UK: Edward Elgar, 2004) 264-267, who record this point in greater detail.

139 Jeffrey J. Schott of the Washington-based Institute for International Economics, as quoted on the WTO's own web-site, www.wto.org/wto/about/organsn1.htm.

140 Schott also believes that an executive board, composed of a certain number of WTO Members, drawn predominantly from industrialised countries will be necessary in order for the WTO to operate more efficiently.

(and composed of a maximum of 30 senior level officials, drawn from the membership and filled on a rotational basis), chaired and convened by the Director-General and meeting on a quarterly or half-yearly basis.[141] However, no executive or negotiating powers[142] are foreseen for the proposed consultative board and thus it would most likely function in the manner of the Consultative Group of Eighteen or CG18, which was an informal steering group that existed in the former GATT,[143] rather than along the lines of the IMF or World Bank executive boards.[144]

The institutional structure of the various WTO bodies and the division of powers between them reflects a more general observation in international institutional law that the underlying relationship between many international organisations and their members is often problematic, even schizophrenic.[145] A certain tension arises between States, as primary subjects of international law, and as members of an international organisation, which may lead to States seeking to control the capacity of the international organisation to act on the international plane, at times demonstrating how (legal) acts of the organisation may become indistinguishable from the acts of individual participating members. Jan Klabbers has suggested that '[T]his constant oscillation between the organization and its members has given rise to a rather volatile set of legal rules and principles' governing international organisations.[146]

Implicit in this statement is the reference to the internal law of an international organisation, which according to Article 1(j) of the 1986 Vienna Convention on the Law of Treaties between States and International Organisations or between

141 *The Sutherland Report*, above n. 80, 70-71, paras. 323-326, with recommendations at para. 327.

142 *The Sutherland Report*, *ibid*, para. 324.

143 The Consultative Group of Eighteen was established by Decision of the Council of 11 July 1975, GATT Doc. L/4204, *BISD* 22S/15, later confirmed by means of a further Decision of the CONTRACTING PARTIES, 22 November 1979, being the 'Mandate of the Consultative Group of Eighteen', GATT Doc. L/4869, *BISD* 26S/289-290; *see* further *Note by the GATT Secretariat*, 9 June 1987, GATT Doc. MTN.GNG/NG14/W/5. *See* Xu and Weller, above n. 138, 231-233.

144 *See* further chapter II, section 3.4.

145 Klabbers, above n. 4, 227.

146 *Ibid*. *See* also Committee on the Accountability of International Organisations 'Final Report' in International Law Association *Report of the Seventy-First Conference (Berlin 2004)* (International Law Association London 2004) New Delhi Conference (2002), Section One: Applicable Law: *The relations between an IO and its Member States*, 188-189, which refers to a number of possible sources of applicable law governing the relations between an international organisation and its members.

International Organisations[147] consists of 'constituent instruments, decisions and resolutions adopted in accordance with them, and established practice of the organisation', which have been characterised by the ILC in its work on the law of international responsibility between States and International Organisations or between International Organisations as the internal law of international organisations.[148] In the case of the WTO the situation is volatile precisely because the organisation *is* the Members and does not always properly exist as an autonomous legal person. The efficacy of its internal law can only be measured against the practice of the Members and this will be borne in mind when discussing the competences of the organisation, exercised by various WTO bodies in this chapter, and also when reviewing subsidiary rule-making by WTO bodies relating to the internal rules of the organisation in chapter V.[149]

With this limitation in mind, we turn briefly to a consideration of the main WTO bodies and analysis of their powers, including such matters as the basis of those powers, i.e. the provenance of their competence to act,[150] the nature of those powers, i.e. whether such powers are expressly conferred by means of treaty or are implied, and whether their conferral is by means of attribution or delegation.

a) Ministerial Conference:

The Ministerial Conference is the main plenary body in the WTO (see fig. 1 above) and meets at least once every two years. *Rules of Procedure* governing its meetings and that of the General Council[151] were adopted upon establishment

147 United Nations Conference on the Law of Treaties between States and International Organisations or between International Organisations (adopted 18 February – 21 March 1986, *not yet in force*) A/CONF.129/16.

148 *See* Report of the International Law Commission (ILC) 'Report of the International Law Commission on the Work of its 55th Session (5 May – 6 June and 7 July – 8 August 2003), UN Doc. A/58/10, 37 (fn. 33) and 48 (para (10)).

149 *See* below chapter V, section 2.2.

150 As Bekker has stated, '[T]he notion of *competence* lies at the heart of an organization's legal status. Competence describes what a given international organization, being a subject of law endowed with the potential capacity to act, is specifically empowered to do'; *see* Bekker, above n. 15, 75.

151 *Rules of Procedure for Sessions of the Ministerial Conference and the General Council*, WT/L/28 (7 February 1995), adopted at the Meeting of the General Council, held on 31 January 1995, WT/GC/M/1 (28 February 1995), at 5, para. 4.I.(a), as amended by the General Council on 3 April 1995 with regard to Chapter V – Officers, and on 18 July 1996 with regard to Annex 3. The extant version is *Rules of Procedure for Sessions of the Ministerial Conference and General Council,* WT/L/161, above n. 124.

of the organisation and form part of the internal law of the organisati importance of the Ministerial Conference in the overall WTO institutiona flows from the fact that it is the only forum where the Members meet at Ministerial level[153] and it is the highest decision making authority, as explicitly stated in the *WTO Agreement*. Its primary task is to 'carry out the functions of the WTO and take actions necessary to this effect' on the basis of Article IV *WTO Agreement*.[154] On the decision-making powers of this body, the *WTO Agreement* is explicit:

> ...the Ministerial Conference shall have the authority to take decisions on all matters under any of the Multilateral Trade Agreements, if so requested by a Member, in accordance with the specific requirements for decision-making in this Agreement and in the relevant Multilateral Trade Agreements.[155]

The broad decision-making powers of the Ministerial Conference have led to the adoption of decisions by Members, in the form of Ministerial Declarations, at three of the five Ministerial Conferences that have so far taken place (decision's were taken at Singapore 1996,[156] Geneva 1998[157] and Doha 2001[158]).

There has been some question as to whether on the basis of very broad, general powers the Ministerial Conference is in a position to take decisions that are legally binding on WTO Members.[159] This is because, as Pieter Jan Kuijper remarks,[160] in most international organisations such broad decision-making powers of a plenary organ do not normally produce binding decisions. In practice, it has the effect

152 Schermers and Blokker, above n. 35, §§1196-1200, 752-754, especially at §1205, 757-758.
153 The GATT Contracting Parties occasionally met at Ministerial level but formally there was no equivalent to the WTO Ministerial Conference. One consequence of this former practice under the GATT was that the trading regime lacked continuity in political leadership.
154 Article IV:1 *WTO Agreement*, *The Legal Texts,* above n. 31, 8.
155 Article IV:1 *WTO Agreement,* third full sentence, *The Legal Texts*, *ibid*, 8.
156 WTO Ministerial Conference, Singapore, 9-13 December 1996; *see* also *Singapore Ministerial Declaration*, above n. 77.
157 *Ministerial Declaration*, adopted on 20 May 1998, at the Second Session of the Ministerial Conference, Geneva, 18 and 20 May 1998, WT/MIN(98)/DEC (25 May 1998) [hereinafter *Geneva Ministerial Declaration*].
158 *Doha Ministerial Declaration,* above n. 78.
159 This issue was raised above with respect to the potential addition of a sixth function to the WTO's mandate by means of the *Doha Ministerial Declaration*; *see* above n. 110 and accompanying text.
160 Kuijper, above n. 125, 82.

that when taking decisions in such bodies Members may be unsure as to whether they are ascribing to a political or legal commitment.[161] A further confusion has arisen for Members with respect to the character of decisions taken at sessions of the Ministerial Conference, due to their format, language and drafting – an issue which is taken up briefly in chapter III.[162]

While the desirability of the Ministerial Conference's exercise of broad, general powers is open to question, it may be explained on historical grounds. Under the former GATT, the mandate granted to the CONTRACTING PARTIES on the basis of Article XXV[163] was very broad indeed. The number and range of actions that the contracting parties were authorized to take collectively 'permeat[ed] the administration and effectuation of the General Agreement on Tariffs and Trade'[164] and while individual delegations were free to seek limitations on this

161 In the case of the Ministerial Conference this issue arose in 2003 with respect to the mandate which the Members had given themselves at the First Ministerial Conference, held in Singapore in 1996, to establish working groups on *inter alia* (i) the relationship between trade and investment, (ii) the interaction between trade and competition policy and (iii) the conduct of a study on transparency in government procurement *Singapore Ministerial Declaration*, above n. 77, with particular reference to paras. 20 and 21. According to its wording the first two working groups were established 'on the understanding that the work undertaken shall not prejudge whether negotiations will be initiated in the future' (para. 20) but without any time-frame being set for completion of that work.
At the Fourth Session of the Ministerial Conference (Doha 2001), it was decided that negotiations on a multilateral framework for trade and investment and trade and competition policy, as well as negotiations on a multilateral agreement on transparency in government procurement, and more generally modalities for negotiations on trade facilitation, would only 'take place after the Fifth Session of the Ministerial Conference on the basis of a decision to be taken, by *explicit consensus*, at that Session on modalities of negotiations' (emphasis added), *Doha Ministerial Declaration*, above n. 78, paras. 20, 23, 26 and 27.
Following the failure of the Fifth Session of the Ministerial Conference, held at Cancún in 2003, to arrive at any decision, the Members were left wondering what (legal) consequences, if any, this could have for the working groups, in particular the working groups on the relationship between trade and investment and interaction between trade and competition policy. Had their mandate, as set out at Singapore and elaborated upon at Doha, effectively come to an end and, if so, should they be wound up?

162 *See* chapter III, section 5.

163 *See* Jackson, *World Trade and the Law of GATT*, above n. 12, §5.4., 126-128 for 'Powers of the CONRACTING PARTIES Acting Jointly', and Appendix to §5.4, at 128-132; wherever the term 'contracting parties' appears in capitals in the text of the GATT 1947, it shall mean that the General Agreement grants 'authority' for 'joint action' by the contracting parties, i.e. for them to take a collective decision.

164 Jackson, *ibid*, §5.4., 126.

very broad mandate, they rarely did.[165] It is therefore hardly surprising that the Members, acting through the Ministerial Conference, have not taken any action to (re-)allocate powers, previously granted to the CONTRACTING PARTIES acting jointly under the GATT (Article XXV:1),[166] to various WTO bodies as they are exhorted to do in paragraph 2(b) of *GATT 1994*.[167] A simple explanation for this failure to act by the Ministerial Conference might be that Ministers are reluctant to relinquish the broad powers they previously enjoyed under the GATT in favour of a number of autonomous institutional bodies that function within a larger and more structured institutional setting in which a greater number of diplomats and bureaucrats representing Member governments exercise those powers through a range of WTO bodies.

Since the establishment of the WTO in 1995, the Ministerial Conference has met on five occasions, beginning with its first meeting at Singapore in 1996.[168] At some of those Ministerial Conferences the Members have established new committees or working groups, with mandates that are dedicated to specialist trade functions or involve a work programme of new issues that have linkages with trade.[169]

165 Jackson cites one or two examples in section §5.4, including an opinion from the German Government concerning the legal scope of Article XXV GATT, Doc. L/1301 at 7 (1960), *ibid*, 128.

166 Some examples of a (re-)allocation of powers include: the authority to formulate rules together with the IMF concerning currency conversion rates in the matter of customs valuation (Articles VII:4(c) GATT); authority to initiate discussion concerning persistent and widespread import restrictions that indicate the existence of a general disequilibrium (Article XII:5 GATT) and authority to specify an exchange agreement for non-IMF Members (Article XV:6 GATT). *See* further Jackson's Appendix to §5.4., in which he lists all the provisions in the GATT 1947 that specifically grant authority to the CONTRACTING PARTIES to act jointly, *ibid*, 128-130.

167 The wording of Article 2(b), last full sentence explicitly states: 'The other functions that the provisions of GATT 1994 assign to the CONTRACTING PARTIES acting jointly shall be allocated by the Ministerial Conference.' Article 2(b) is taken up as the Preamble to the GATT 1994, *The Legal Texts,* above n. 31, 21.

168 Ministerial Conference, Singapore, 9-13 December 1996, WT/MIN(96)/DEC (18 December 1996).

169 For details of the three working groups that were established on the Relationship between Trade and Investment, on the Interaction between Trade and Competition Policy and in order to study Transparency in Government Procurement, *see Singapore Ministerial Declaration*, above n. 77 and especially n. 161. The Committee of Participants on the Expansion of Trade in Information Technology Products was also set up in order to give effect to a decision taken at the Singapore Ministerial Conference of 1996, *see* the *Ministerial Declaration in Trade in Information Technology Products*, above n. 130, and the subsequent decision establishing the Committee, above n. 131.

Drawing on the precedent set in the Uruguay Round MTN and previously under the GATT,[170] the Members established a special second level body, the so-called the Trade Negotiations Committee or TNC, at the Doha Ministerial Conference in November 2001 for the duration of the Doha Round MTN.[171] Once the negotiations are over and the Round has been finalised the TNC will cease to exist as has been the practice in previous GATT/WTO negotiations rounds. The TNC is an emanation of the General Council, to which it reports and is charged with overseeing the work of the special negotiating groups, on trade in services, market access, rules, trade and environment, TRIPs, dispute settlement, agriculture and trade and development, all of which report directly to the TNC on the results of the special negotiating sessions.

Alongside broad decision-making powers, the Ministerial Conference is allocated a number of specific powers that are explicitly set out in various treaty provisions in the *WTO Agreement*. The specific powers of the Ministerial Conference include (a) the power to 'appoint the Director General' and to 'adopt regulations setting out the powers, duties, conditions of service and terms of office of the Director-General' (Article VI:2 *WTO Agreement*), (b) the power to adopt regulations governing the duties and conditions of service of the Secretariat (Article VI:3 *WTO Agreement*), (c) 'the exclusive authority to adopt authoritative interpretations' of WTO Agreements (Article IX:2 *WTO Agreement*),[172] (d) the power (in exceptional circumstances) to waive (or set aside) an obligation imposed on a Member (Article IX:3 *WTO Agreement*), (e) the power to adopt amendments to WTO Agreements (Article X *WTO Agreement*) and (f) the authority to approve accessions to the WTO (Article XII *WTO Agreement*).

Thus far during the first ten years of the WTO (1995-2005), of the six aforementioned powers, three of them have never been exercised by the Ministerial Conference. In the case of (a) the appointment of the Director General, it will be recalled that all five Director Generals have been appointed by the General

170 Jackson, *World Trade and the Law of GATT*, above n. 12, §7.3, 157.

171 *See* the *Doha Ministerial Declaration,* above n. 78, para. 46; *see* further Van den Bossche, above n. 69, 92 and 130-131.

172 It should be noted that this 'explicit authority' to provide an authoritative interpretation of *WTO Agreements* is also granted to the General Council on the basis of the same provision. Authoritative interpretation of any *WTO Agreement* should be understood in the light of Article 31 of the Vienna Convention on the Law of Treaties (adopted 23 May 1969 *in force* 27 January 1980) 8 *ILM* (1969) 689 [hereinafter VCLT) and Article 21 of the Vienna Convention on the Law of Treaties between States and International Organizations or between International Organizations (adopted 21 March 1986, *not yet in force*) 25 *ILM* (1986) 543 [hereinafter VCLTIO]. *See* further, chapter IV, section 3.4.

Council[173] and not by the Ministerial Conference. Similarly, at (c) and (e) no authoritative interpretations[174] of or amendments,[175] to the *WTO Agreement* or the annexed Multilateral Trade Agreements have ever been adopted by the Ministerial Conference. As for the remaining powers, the Ministerial Conference has only partially exercised the power at (b) in respect of the adoption of regulations concerning the duties and conditions of staff of the Secretariat pursuant to Article VI:3 *WTO Agreement* when it took a decision at Marrakesh relating to the necessary organisational and financial consequences that would flow from the establishment of the WTO including staffing of the secretariat.[176] As for the exercise of the waiver power[177] at (d) and the authority to approve accessions[178] at (f), these two powers have invariably been shared between the Ministerial Conference and the General Council. This is because the Ministerial Conference only meets at regular two-yearly intervals and thus the majority of waiver decisions are taken by the General Council in the intervening period on the basis of Article IV:2 *WTO Agreement* together with Article IX:3 and 4 *WTO Agreement*.

173 Peter Sutherland, former Director-General to the GATT 1947, served as the first Director-General pursuant to Article XVI:2 *WTO Agreement*, for three months immediately following the entry into force of the WTO from January 1995 to 30 April 1995. At its meeting of 24 March 1995, the General Council appointed Renato Ruggiero as Director-General, WT/GC/M/2 (20 April 1995) at 1; a function he filled from 1 May 1995 to 30 April 1999. This was followed by the appointment of Mike Moore, to serve as Director-General from 1 September 1999 to 31 August 2002 and Supachai Panitchpakdi from 1 September 2002 to 31 August 2005, at the meeting of the General Council on 22 July 1999, WT/GC/M/46 (22 July 1999), in particular, at 18; *see* further *Appointment of the next Director-General*, Decision of the General Council, 22 July 1999, WT/L/308 (2 August 1999) in which the General Council resolved, 'in order to improve and strengthen the current rules and procedures [for the appointment of the Director-General], a comprehensive set of rules and procedures for such appointments shall be elaborated and adopted by the end of September 2000.' Finally at the end of 2002, the General Council adopted *Procedures for the Appointment of Directors-General*, at its meeting of 10 December 2002, WT/L/509 (20 January 2003). Pascal Lamy was confirmed as the fifth Director-General, for a period of four years from 1 September 2005, at the meeting of the General Council held on 26 May 2005, WT/GC/M/95 (21 June 2005). *See* further concerning the appointment of the Director-General, *WTO Analytical Index*, above n. 51, 72-73

174 *See* chapter IV, section 3.4.

175 *See* chapter IV, sections 3.1(a) and (b).

176 *See* chapter V, section 2.2(d).

177 *See* chapter V, section 3.3(a).

178 *See* chapter IV, section 3.2.

The Ministerial Conference has exercised its specific decision-making powers, on the basis of Article IV and/or Article IX of the *WTO Agreement*, with respect to three matters, all of which relate to the Fourth Session of the Ministerial Conference, held in Doha in 2001. These are the Ministerial Decision on Implementation-related Issues and Concerns,[179] the Ministerial waiver on the 'European Communities – the ACP-EC Partnership Agreement'[180] and related thereto the second waiver decision on 'European Communities – Transitional Regime for the EC Autonomous Tariff Quotas on Imports of Bananas'.[181]

b) General Council

The General Council meets at a second level and consists of all WTO Members, represented by government or diplomatic representatives (usually at ambassadorial level) rather than ministers (see fig. 1 above). On the basis of Article IV:2 *WTO Agreement*, it is primarily responsible for the continuing day-to-day management of the organisation in between the two-yearly sessions of the Ministerial Conference and involves the exercise of the full powers (general and special powers) of the latter body.[182] In essence, the General Council provides the vehicle for the membership's exercise of an executive function, since it is specifically charged

179 *Implementation-related Issues and Concerns*, Decision of 14 November 2001, adopted at the Fourth Session of the Ministerial Conference, Doha, 9-14 November 2001, WT/MIN(01)/17, (20 November 2001) [hereinafter *Implementation-related Decision*].

180 *European Communities – the ACP-EC Partnership Agreement*, Decision of 14 November 2001, adopted at the Fourth Session of the Ministerial Conference, Doha, 9-14 November 2001, WT/MIN(01)/15, (14 November 2001).

181 *European Communities – Transitional Regime for the EC Autonomous Tariff Quotas on Imports of Bananas*, Decision of 14 November 2001, adopted at the Fourth Session of the Ministerial Conference, Doha, 9-14 November 2001, WT/MIN(01)/16, (14 November 2001).

182 When the Ministerial Conference is in session (Singapore, 1996), Geneva (1998), Seattle (1999), Doha (2001) and Cancún (2003), it may cover a range of issues that include an exercise of its specific powers, although it does so pursuant to prior General Council action. For example in the matter of the grant of a general waiver at Doha (2001) in respect of a new partnership agreement (Cotonou Agreement) between the African, Caribbean and Pacific (ACP) countries and the European Communities, Decision of 14 November 2001 on the European Communities – ACP-EC Partnership Agreement, Minister, taken at the Fourth Session of the Ministerial Conference, held at Doha, 9-14 November 2001, WT/MIN(01)/15, 14 November 2001 or decisions on accession, or in respect of accessions to the WTO, for example the Accession of the People's Republic of China, Decision of 10 November 2001, WT/L/432, 23 November 2001.

with 'the implementation, administration and operation' of the WTO and the annexed Agreements, or the oversight of that function.

Institutionally speaking, the General Council exercises its 'executive' powers on three different planes by means of: general decision-making powers (these powers revert to the Ministerial Conference when it is in session); specific powers attributed to it on the basis of the founding Treaty, the *WTO Agreement*; and a further general power that is one of surveillance, since the General Council has overall supervision over lower WTO bodies, like the specialist Councils and Committees, which report to it within the hierarchical structure of the organisation. Under its general decision-making powers, the General Council conducts the functions of the Ministerial Conference between the two-yearly sessions, meeting 'as appropriate'[183] but on a regular basis;[184] in practice this is usually five or six times a year.

Additionally, and somewhat confusingly, the General Council has been attributed the explicit power to 'convene as appropriate to discharge the responsibilities' of the Dispute Settlement Body (DSB),[185] which is part of the WTO's quasi-judicial dispute settlement system, and of the Trade Policy Review Body (TPRB),[186] the role of which is surveillance of Members' trade policies.[187]

183 Article IV:2 *WTO Agreement*, *The Legal Text*, above n. 31, 8.

184 Van den Bossche, above n. 69, 124.

185 The General Council exercises this power on the basis of Article IV:3 *WTO Agreement* in conjunction with Article 2.1 *DSU* in Annex 2 to the *WTO Agreement*, *The Legal Texts*, above n. 31, 8 and 404-433, at 405 respectively. Article 2.1 *DSU* states that the DSB shall administer the rules and procedures of the DSU, and accordingly it has been assigned a number of specific powers such as the power to establish panels (Article 6 *DSU*), to adopt panel and Appellate Body reports (Article 16 *DSU*), to maintain surveillance of implementation of rulings and recommendations (Article 21 *DSU*) and to authorise the suspension of concessions (Article 22 *DSU*). *See* von Bogdandy, with respect to the competence exercised by the DSB as a political organ in the WTO dispute settlement process and his view on the proper exercise of the organisation's adjudicative function, above n. 71, 616.

186 The General Council exercises this power on the basis of Article IV:4 *WTO Agreement* and the *TPRM* in Annex 3 to the *WTO Agreement*, *The Legal Texts*, above n. 31, 434-437.

187 The Trade Policy Review Body or TPRB is established pursuant to section C of the *TPRM*, *The Legal Texts*, *ibid*, 434, with the explicit power 'to carry out trade policy reviews [of Members]'; the procedures for review are also set out in this same section of the *TPRM*. In essence it amounts to a peer review system, utilised by all WTO Members in reviewing one another's trade policies and performance in adhering to rules, disciplines and commitments under the Multilateral Trade Agreements (and where applicable the Plurilateral Agreements on Government Procurement and Civil Aircraft); *see* section A of the *TPRM*, *ibid*.

These two emanations[188] of the General Council are separate WTO bodies, in their own right. They appoint their own chairmen, as distinct from the chairman of the General Council, and have their own rules of procedure.[189] As Kuijper points out, it seems that both the DSB and the TPRB only exercise the specific powers granted to them under the relevant agreements, i.e. they function on the basis of express or 'enumerated powers' contained in the *WTO Agreement* and the relevant Annexes containing the instruments on which they are founded.

Even so, there have been other instances, for example in 1996 when the DSB took a decision to establish *Rules of Conduct* for panel members and for members of the WTO Secretariat who assist the panels in their work,[190] which can only be described as the exercise by the DSB of an implied power.[191] Again in October 2000 the DSB was acting on the basis of an implied power when it decided to modify by one month the 'reasonable period of time' for compliance with its recommendations by the United States in the *Foreign Sales Corporations (US–FSC)*[192] dispute because the US Congress needed more time to amend the FSC provisions in US tax law.[193] While the DSB is expressly authorized on the basis of Article 21:3 *DSU*, at the request of a Member, to grant a reasonable time-period for compliance, including recourse to binding arbitration concerning

188 Van den Bossche refers to them as the *alter ego* of the General Council; *see* above n. 69, 126.

189 *Rules of Procedure for Meetings of the Dispute Settlement* Body, WT/DSB/9 (16 January 1997) and *Rules of Procedure for Meetings of the Trade Policy Review Body*, approved by the TPRB at its meeting of 6 June 1995, WT/TPR/6 (10 August 1995), both of which follow the *Rules of Procedure for Meetings of the General Council*, almost *mutatis mutandi.*

190 *Rules of Conduct for the Understanding on Rules and Procedures Governing the Settlement of Dispute*, adopted by gavel without an actual decision at the meeting of the Dispute Settlement Body on 3 December 1996 (WT/DSB/M/27, item 1); the document embodying the rules can be found at the WT/DSB/RC/1 (11 December 1996) [hereinafter *Rules of Conduct for the DSU*]. *See* chapter V, section 2.2(b).

191 *See* further Kuijper, above n. 125, 87.

192 *US – FSC*, Appellate Body Report, *United States – Tax Treatment for 'Foreign Sales Corporations'*, WT/DS108/AB/R, adopted 20 March 2000. Subsequently the matter went to a compliance panel, on the basis of Article 21:5 *DSU*, and was appealed again; *see* further *US – FSC (Article 21.5 – EC)*, Appellate Body Report, *United States – Tax Treatment for 'Foreign Sales Corporations'*, *Recourse to Article 21.5 of the DSU by the European Communities*, WT/DS108/AB/RW, adopted 29 January 2002.

193 *See* request by the United States, WT/DS108/11 (2 October 2000) and Statement of the United States representative, made at the Meeting of the Dispute Settlement Body, 12 October 2000, WT/DSB/M/90 (30 October 2000), at 1, para. 1.2., and ensuing discussion (European Communities and Japan) followed by the adoption of the decision at paras. 1.3-1.7.

the 'reasonable period of time' under section (c),[194] the power to modify this period, by means of a simple extension rests on an implied power.[195]

It should also be noted that there exists an in-built institutional conflict in the dispute settlement system, which arises from the DSB's exercise of its powers. WTO Members effectively 'control' the organisation's adjudicative system through their powers of administration of the system and adoption of recommendations and rulings of the panels and Appellate Body.[196] Additionally, and by way of contrast with some other international courts and tribunals in the international community, the extent to which the Appellate Body acts autonomously or enjoys 'inherent powers' may from time be subject to restraint by the Members acting through one of the WTO's political organs such as the DSB or the General Council; ironically the *ad hoc* panels have to date enjoyed more freedom in this respect.[197] The scope of this work does not allow for an extensive discussion of these two adjudicative bodies and the exercise of actual or potential 'inherent powers'[198] except to say that the practice of the organisation does not completely support the notion of inherent powers of (quasi-)judicial bodies as one might expect to find in respect of the panels or the Appellate Body.[199]

194 Members can agree to binding arbitration under Article 21:3(c) *DSU* , *The Legal Texts,* above n. 31, at 421, whereby a sole arbitrator will determine the 'reasonable period of time' for the implementation of panel or Appellate Body recommendations

195 See also subsidiary rule-making in the sense of rules of procedure of WTO bodies, discussed in chapter V, section 2.2(b) below.

196 The exercise of general powers with respect to the administration of the rules and procedures in the DSU are set out in Article III:3 *WTO Agreement* and Article 2 DSU (Annex II), *The Legal Texts,* above n. 31, 7 and 405 respectively. More specifically the DSB adopts recommendations and rulings of WTO Panels and/or the Appellate Body on the specific powers, enumerated on the basis of Articles 16:4 and 17:14 *DSU*, *The Legal Texts*, *ibid.*, 417 and 419 respectively. *See* further Bartels, above n. 85, 861.

197 See below, chapter V, section. 2.2(b).

198 Bartels, above n. 85, 862, who gives some examples of the lack of authority of the dispute settlement bodies but is not explicit as to why this is so. *See* Steve Charnovitz, 'Judicial Independence in the World Trade Organization' in Laurence Boisson de Chazournes, Cesare Romano and Ruth Mackenzie, *International Organizations and International Dispute Settlement* (Ardsley, New York: Transnational Publishers, Inc., 2002), chapter 11, 212-240. Also Friedl Weiss, 'Inherent Powers of National and International Courts' in Federico Ortino and Ernst-Ulrich Petersmann (eds.) *The WTO Dispute Settlement System 1995-2003* (The Hague: Kluwer Law International, 2004) 177-190, for an extended discussion, with particular reference to the 'inherent powers' of the Appellate Body compared and contrasted with other national and international courts and tribunals.

199 *See* further chapter V, section 2.2(b).

An example of that practice is the special (additional) procedure that the Appellate Body established, pursuant to its *Working Procedures for Appellate Review*,[200] in order to manage the submission of *amicus curiae* (or friends of the court) briefs in the case of *European Communities – Measures Affecting Asbestos and Asbestos Containing Products (EC-Asbestos)*.[201] This additional procedure was subsequently circulated to Members and posted on the WTO website.[202] Within a week an extraordinary meeting of the WTO General Council was called at which the membership expressed its dissatisfaction with the Appellate Body's handling of such briefs, and which was described by one representative as a decision that 'went far beyond the Appellate Body's mandate and powers'.[203]

While the Appellate Body is empowered under Article 17.9 *DSU* to draw up its own working procedures,[204] it must do so '*in consultation* with the Chairman of the DSB and the Director-General, and [be] communicated to the Members *for their information*' (emphasis added).[205] The extraordinary action by the WTO

200 WTO Appellate Body, *Working Procedures for Appellate Review*, WT/AB/WP/3 (28 February 1997) [hereinafter *Working Procedures*]. Rule 16(1)of those *Working Procedures* allows the Appellate Body to deal with a 'procedural question [that] arises that is not covered by these Rules' by adopting 'an appropriate procedure for the purposes of that appeal only, provided that it is not inconsistent with the *DSU*, the other covered agreements and these Rules.' *See* further, Bartels, above n. 85, 861.

201 *EC – Asbestos*, Appellate Body Report, *European Communities – Measures Affecting Asbestos and Asbestos Containing Products*, WT/DS135/AB/R, adopted 5 April 2001.

202 *Additional Procedure Adopted under Rule 16(1) of the Working Procedures for Appellate Review ('Additional Procedure'*, WT/DS135/9 (8 November 2000)). The *Additional Procedure* was communicated to the parties and third parties in *EC – Asbestos* on 7 November 2000. The following day, the Chairman of the Appellate Body, Florentino Feliciano, informed the Chairman of the DSB in writing of the *Additional Procedure* adopted and the procedure was circulated to WTO Members.

203 *Minutes of the Meeting of the General Council*, 22 November 2000, WT/GC/M/60 (23 January 2001), para. 12.

204 The Appellate Body has revised its rules of procedure on five occasions since the establishment of the WTO in January 1995, most recently on 7 October 2004. The current *Working Procedures for Appellate Review* (4 January 2005), is a consolidated, revised version, and reflects amendments to Rules 1, 18(5), 20, 21, 23, 27 and Annex I, as well as the addition of a new Rule 23*bis* and a new Annex III, as discussed in documents WT/AB/WP/W/8 and WT/AB/WP/W/9. The new rule of procedures will be applied to appeals initiated after 1 January 2005.

205 *See* the second full sentence of Article 17:9 DSU, *The Legal Texts,* above n. 31, 418. *See* also Decision of the DSB, *Additional Procedures for Consultation between the Chairperson of the DSB and WTO Members in Relation to the Working Procedures for Appellate Review* of 19 December 2002, WT/DSB/31 (20 December 2002).

membership with respect to the special procedure for *amicus curiae* briefs might look like an attempt by the Members to curtail the implied or inherent powers of the Appellate Body in determining its own (additional) working procedures and placing limits on this body's competence but the better view is that this may have been an isolated action on the part of the General Council and one which went too far in seeking to undermine the authority of this judicial organ.

The General Council has also been assigned a number of specific powers, i.e. it 'shall carry out the functions assigned to it by this Agreement',[206] as explicitly set out in the treaty. They include: making 'appropriate arrangements' for cooperation with other intergovernmental organizations and non-governmental organizations in matters related to those of the WTO (Article V *WTO Agreement*) and adopting 'the financial regulations and the annual budget' (Article VII *WTO Agreement*). The General Council is responsible for establishing its own rules of procedure.[207] It also approves the rules of procedures for certain 'horizontal' Committees, which are standing committees, such as the Committee on Trade and Development, the Committee on Balance-of-Payments Restrictions and the Committee on Budget, Finance and Administration all of which report to the General Council.

Finally, the General Council exercises a general, surveillance power on the basis of paragraph 5 of Article IV *WTO Agreement*, according to which the Council for Trade in Goods, the Council for Trade in Services and the TRIPs Council 'shall operate under the guidance of the General Council'.[208] Kuijper has pointed out that actual instances of such guidance have been few in number and mostly related to implementation issues,[209] particularly with respect to implementation under the *Agreement on Trade-Related Investment Measures* or *TRIMs*.[210]

c) Specialised councils

The three specialised Councils for Trade in Goods or CTG, Trade in Services or CTS and the TRIPs Council operate at a third level, directly below the General Council, and its other emanations in the form of the DSB and the TPRB (see fig. 1

206 Article IV:4 , second full sentence, *The Legal Texts,* above n. 31, 8.
207 *Ministerial Conference and General Council Rules*, above n. 124.
208 Article IV:5 *WTO Agreement*, first full sentence, *The Legal Texts,* above n. 31, 8.
209 Kuijper, above n. 125, 83.
210 *See* Chapter IV, section 3.3(b) for further details.

above). Just like most other WTO bodies, all Members are represented[211] in each of the specialised Councils although in practice some developing country Members are unable to attend all meetings.[212] It is also intended that the three specialised Councils assist the Ministerial Conference and General Council in carrying out their functions but in practice there are limits to the exercise of such powers.[213]

For example, in the matter of authoritative interpretation of any of the multilateral trade agreements the powers of the specialised Councils are purely recommendatory and limited to the particular Council, which is responsible for oversight of the Agreement that may be the object of an authoritative interpretation. The actual power to adopt an authoritative interpretation, on the basis of Article IX:2 *WTO Agreement*, is reserved exclusively to the Ministerial Conference or the General Council. Similarly, the specialised Councils may play a role in the adoption of waivers and in the amendment procedure, both of which are the preserve of the Ministerial Conference (or the General Council acting between sessions

211 *See* Von Bogdandy, above n. 71, 630, noting the practice whereby all Councils and Committees, which are sub-organs of the Ministerial Conference and the General Council, are composed of representatives of the members, also deals at some length with the relationship between these political bodies and the adjudicative process, in a constitutional sense. Kuijper, on the other hand, while not discounting issues of constitutionality, nevertheless gives a broader institutional reading to the situation, given the quasi-political, quasi-legal competence of the Council for Trade in Goods or CTG and some of its subsidiary bodies; *see* above n. 125, 99-106.

212 Regular formal and informal meetings of these specialised Councils are held throughout the year, often with a dozen or more of such meetings being held for each of them. Representations at such meetings can be difficult for all Members but especially for developing country and LDC Members, without government representation in Geneva, or where the matter at issues is of a very technical nature and may require specialist input from government officials, flown into Geneva from capitals; for example with respect to issues laid before the TRIPs Council.

213 It should be noted that the Ministerial Conference and the General Council can only exercise their power to adopt an authoritative interpretation of one of the Multilateral Trade Agreements in Annex 1 'on the basis of a recommendation by the Council overseeing the functioning of that Agreement' (Article IX:2 *WTO Agreement*, second full sentence). In the matter of treaty amendments, the specialised councils enjoy a right of initiative in submitting proposals to the Ministerial conference 'to amend the provisions of the corresponding Multilateral Trade Agreements in Annex 1 the functioning of which they oversee' (Article X:1 *WTO Agreement*, second full sentence). *See* also Van den Bossche, above n. 69, 128, who is critical of the general and special powers entrusted to the specialised councils.

of the Ministerial Conference).[214] Alongside a general power of oversight[215] the three Councils enjoy specialist powers, which are attributed to them on the basis of the functions assigned to them under the individual agreements although in the case of the CTG they are limited in number due to the lack of an overarching agreement for the trade in goods agreements.[216]

On the basis of Article IV:5 *WTO Agreement* the CTG is charged with the general power of overseeing the functioning of the Multilateral Trade Agreements in Annex 1A, almost all of which in turn have their own committees and are subsidiary bodies of the CTG. The eleven Annex 1A committees all report to the CTG but in the exercise of the competences, which have been attributed or delegated to them, either on the basis of express or delegated powers, they differ considerably from one another (see below, section (e)). The CTG also enjoys a general power under Article IV:6 *WTO Agreement*, whereby it may establish additional subsidiary bodies (committees, working parties and working groups), which it has done on a limited number of occasions. Examples include: the establishment by the CTG of the Working Group on State Trading Enterprises,[217] pursuant to paragraph 5 of the *Understanding on the Interpretation of Article XVII of the GATT 1994*,[218] in order to review notifications and counter-notifications on state trading enterprises by WTO Members; the Working Group on Notification Obligations and Procedures, established pursuant to Part III of the *Marrakesh*

214 The specialised councils play a similar role with respect to decisions by the Ministerial Conference or General Council concerning a request for a waiver (Article IX:3(b) *WTO Agreement*) and in respect of amendments (Article X:1 *WTO Agreement*), both of which require that the request for a waiver or amendment be initially submitted to the relevant Council under the multilateral trade agreements; *see* also Van den Bossche, above n. 69, 128.

215 Kuijper has queried 'whether the "overseeing" function [of the specialised Councils] contains any decision-making powers independent from the functions specifically assigned to the subordinate Councils in their respective agreements'; *see* Kuijper, above n. 125, 84.

216 Instead, as Kuijper points out, the Council for Trade in Goods, or CTG, has taken on the role of the previous CONTRACTING PARTIES in the matter of trade in goods under the GATT 1994; *see* Kuijper, above n. 125, 99; *see* chapter II for the significance of this when discussing the application of regime theory to the WTO.

217 Meeting of the Council for Trade in Goods, 20 February 1995, G/C/M/1 (27 March 1995), para. 5(A), *WTO Analytical Index*, above n. 51, 53-54.

218 *Understanding on the Interpretation of Article XVII of the GATT 1994*, *The Legal Texts*, above n. 31, 25-26.

Ministerial Decision on Notification Procedures;[219] and some ten working parties on various regional trade arrangements.[220]

However, there have been occasions where the CTG has not exercised this general power, attributed to it on the basis of treaty, but has allowed the decision to be taken by a higher body, in this case the General Council, thereby effectively giving *de facto* recognition to the kick-up rule. An example of this is the establishment of the Committee on Market Access by means of a decision of the General Council,[221] on the basis of Article IV:7 *WTO Agreement*.[222] There is no appar-

219 *Marrakesh Ministerial Decision on Notification Procedures*, *The Legal Texts,* above n. 31, 444-445. The Ministerial Decision was later endorsed by General Council (rather than the CTG) in its *Decision on Notification Procedures*, adopted at the first Meeting of the General Council, 31 January 1995, above n. 151, para. 9. The Council for Trade in Goods drew the Members' attention to this latter Decision in its first meeting, where it formally established the 'Working Group on Notification Obligations and Procedures'; *see* Meeting of the Council for Trade in Goods, 20 February 1995, above n. 217, section 6, *WTO Analytical Index,* above n. 51, 55.

220 The ten working parties were established in relation to: (1) *Enlargement of the European Union: Accession of Austria, Finland and Sweden to the European Communities*, Minutes of the Meeting of the Council for Trade in Goods, 20 February 1995, *ibid,* section 7; (2) *Interim Agreement between the Republic of Bulgaria and the European Communities, ibid*, section 8; (3) *Interim Agreement between Romania and the European Communities, ibid*, section 8; (4) *Free Trade Agreement between Latvia and the European Communities*, Minutes of the Meeting of the Council for Trade in Goods, 26 September 1995, G/C/M/6 (23 October 1995), section 4; (5)) *Free Trade Agreement between Estonia and the European Communities, ibid*, section 5; (6)) *Free Trade Agreement between Lithuania and the European Communities, ibid*, section 6; (7)) *Free Trade Agreement between the Republic of Hungary and Republic of Slovenia, ibid*, section 8; (8) *EFTA-Slovenia Free Trade Agreement*, Minutes of the Meeting of the Council for Trade in Goods, 1 December 1995, G/C/M/7 (26 January 1996), section 6; (9) *Agreement between the European Community, on the one part and the Government of Denmark and the Home Government of the Faroe Islands on the other part, ibid*, section 7; (10) *Agreement between the Government of Denmark and the Home Government of the Faroe Islands, of the one part, and the Government of Iceland, of the other part, on free trade between the Faroe Islands and Iceland*, Minutes of the Meeting of the Council for Trade in Goods, 29 January 1996 and 14 February 1996, G/C/M/8 (18 March 1996), section 3, *WTO Analytical Index, ibid*, 56.

221 *WTO Committee on Market Access, Decision of the General Council on 31 January 1995*, WT/L/47 (17 February 1995), adopted at the first Meeting of the General Council on 31 January 1995, above n. 134, para. 7(2). Decision WT/L/47 contains the Terms of Reference for the Committee on Market Access.

222 *WTO Agreement*, *The Legal Texts,* above n. 31, 9.

ent explanation as to why this particular body[223] should have been established by the General Council rather than the CTG. It was the very first meeting of the General Council and it was largely devoted to what the Chairperson called 'housekeeping issues'.

The CTS oversees the functioning of the *General Agreement on Trade in Services* or *GATS*, on the basis of Article IV:5 *WTO Agreement* and Article XXIV:1 *GATS*, the latter of which states: 'The Council for Trade in Services shall carry out such functions as may be assigned to it to facilitate the operation of this Agreement and further its objectives.' The language of Article XXIV:1 *GATS* is ambiguous since it begs the questions as to who may attribute functions to the CTS and on what basis. Kuijper points out that from an institutional standpoint such an attribution of power to the CTS can only be done on the basis of treaty or by the General Council. In the case of the former, attribution of powers on the basis of treaty always yields specific powers while in the case of the latter, the General Council has so far taken no steps to assign specific powers to the CTS.[224]

The inclusion of the wording 'to facilitate the operation ... and ... further its objectives' would seem to indicate that the CTS may exercise an implied power where it is 'essential' to the operation or the achievement[225] of one of the objectives of the Agreement.[226] In practice, the general power of oversight, which the CTS exercises under the *GATS* covers information gathering,[227] including receipt of notifications from Member.[228] It does not extend to pro-active monitor-

223 The *Rules of Procedure of the Committee on Market Access* were adopted at its first meeting, which was held on 25 April 1995, G/MA/M/1 (31 May 1995), 3, para. 1.

224 Kuijper, above n. 125, 88.

225 The wording is reminiscent of that contained in the *Reparation for Injuries* case, above n. 43, p. 168 in respect of the implied powers of the UN, about which *see* also above n. 49.

226 Progressive liberalisation is one of the key objectives of the *GATS*, 'as a means of promoting the economic growth of all trading partners and the development of developing countries' (Preamble to the GATS, second recital), *The Legal Texts,* above n. 31, 327.

227 The CTS undertakes to be informed by the Members of 'any new, or any changes to existing, laws, regulations or administrative guidelines which significantly affect trade in services covered by ... [their] specific commitments' or 'any measure taken by a Member, which it consider affects the operation of [the GATS]' in Article III:3 and 5 *GATS*, *The Legal Texts,* above n. 31, 329.

228 Notification or provision of information by Members to the CTS of: so-called 'Labour Market Integration Agreements', Article V *bis GATS*, *The Legal Texts*, *ibid.*, 332-333; mutual recognition agreements, Article VII:4 *GATS*, *ibid.*, 335; inconsistent, i.e. unlawful, competitive practices by another Member, or grant of monopoly rights, Article VIII:3 and 4 *GATS*, *ibid.*, 335-336; modification or withdrawal of a specific services commit-

ing in the form of regular reviews of Member's implementation or to amendments of primary treaty text in order to bring Members WTO obligations into line with their (pre-)existing obligations in other multilateral agreements.

The CTS also exercises a general power attributed to it under the treaty to establish subsidiary bodies, such as committees or working parties, that flows from Article IV:6 *WTO Agreement* in conjunction with Article XXIV:1 *GATS*.[229] Since the WTO entered into force in 1995 the CTS has established the following subsidiary bodies: the Committee on Trade in Financial Services or Financial Services Committee;[230] the Committee on Specific Commitments or CSC;[231] the Working Party on Professional Services or WPPS[232] (in 1999 it was transformed into

ment by a Member, as a safeguard, Article X:2 *GATS, ibid.*, 336 and measures taken by a Member under the security exception involving its compliance with the protection of essential security interests or pursuant to a UN obligation for the maintenance of peace and security at Article XIV:2 *bis GATS, ibid.*, 341.

229 'The Council may establish such subsidiary bodies as it considers appropriate for the effective discharge of its functions', second full sentence of Article XXIV:1 *GATS, The Legal Texts,* above n. 31, 347.

230 The power of the CTS to establish the Financial Services Committee was explicitly granted in one of the Ministerial Decisions taken at the end of the Uruguay Round; *see Marrakesh Decision on Institutional Arrangements for the General Agreement on Trade in Services, The Legal Texts,* above n. 31, 456, para. 3. The mandate of the Financial Services Committee is the same as for any subsidiary body that the CTS may establish in respect of particular services' sector, as set out in paragraph 2 of that *Decision* and is confined to the responsibilities listed therein that fall to be dealt with under individual sectoral annexes. The Ministerial Decision was later endorsed by the Council for Trade in Services in its *Decision on Institutional Arrangements for the General Agreement on Trade in Services*, 1 March 1995, S/L/1 (4 April 1995).
The six areas of responsibility named in the decision as applied to the financial services sector include such responsibilities as keeping the GATS *Financial Services Annex* under continuous review and surveillance, formulating proposals or recommendations for consideration by the Council (including proposals for amendments to the aforementioned *Annex*), providing a forum for technical discussions, providing technical assistance to developing countries and cooperating with other subsidiary bodies under the auspices of the CTS and/or international organisations active in the financial sector.

231 The Committee on Specific Commitments, or CSC, was established by the CTS in 1995; *see Decision Establishing the Committee on Specific Commitments*, adopted by the Council for Trade in Services on 22 November 1995, S/L/16 (24 November 1995).

232 The Working Party on Professional Services or WPPS, was established pursuant to the Uruguay Round *Ministerial Decision on Professional Services,* and the *Decision on Professional Services*, adopted by the Council for Trade in Services, 1 March 1995, S/L/3 (4 April 1995).

the Working Party on Domestic Regulation or WPDR);[233] and the Working Party on GATS Rules or WPGR.[234] The role of these particular subsidiary bodies in the formation of WTO rules is discussed in chapter V, as part of the normative analysis of the WTO and its law-making competence.

Some specific powers are attributed to the CTS and, where they exist, their potential to influence the overall rights and obligations of the Members may be significant, as for example, with the power of the CTS[235] to establish procedures for the rectification and modification of schedules of specific commitments.[236] Another example is the power of the CTS to develop 'through appropriate bodies [that] it may establish ... any necessary disciplines', i.e. additional rules on the basis of Article VI:4 *GATS*.[237]

Additionally, on a strict reading of Article XXVI *GATS*[238] it might appear that the CTS enjoys some sort of external relations power but as Kuijper points out this is an anomaly.[239] The power to enter into consultations and cooperation

233 The Working Party on Domestic Regulation or WPDR, is the successor to the WPPS, and was established by *Decision on Domestic Regulation* adopted by the Council for Trade in Services on 26 April 1999, S/L/70 (28 April 1999).

234 The Working Party on GATS Rules or WPGR, was established at the second meeting of the Council for Trade in Services in order to carry out the negotiating mandates contained in the GATS on emergency safeguard measures, government procurement in services and subsidies, *see* Council for Trade in Services, Report of the Meeting held on 30 March 1995, Note by the Secretariat, S/C/M/2 (28 April 1995), paras. 23-25.

235 This general power is set out in Article XXI:5 *GATS, The Legal Texts,* above n. 31, 345-346. The Council for Trade in Services has adopted *Procedures for the Implementation of Article XXI of the General Agreement on Trade in Services (GATS) (Modification of Schedules)* on 19 July 1999, S/L/80 (29 October 1999), followed by *Decision on Procedures for the Certification of Rectifications or Improvements to Schedules of Specific Commitments* on 14 April 2000, S/L/83 (18 April 2000) and *Procedures for the Certification of Rectifications or Improvements to Schedules of Specific Commitments* of even date, S/L/84 (18 April 2000) as well as *Procedures for the Certification of Terminations, Reductions and Rectifications of Article II (MFN) Exemptions* on 5 June 2002, S/L/105 and S/L/106 (11 June 2002).

236 Kuijper, above n. 125, 91-92, points out that the practice of modifying schedules of services' commitments closely follows that of modifying tariff schedules under the GATT, i.e. it is a well-established practice that falls under 'the customary practices followed by the CONTRACTING PARTIES to the GATT 1947', by which the WTO shall be guided, pursuant to Article XVI:1 *WTO Agreement.*

237 Article VI:4 *GATS, The Legal Texts*, above n. 31, 333.

238 Article XXVI *GATS* states: 'The General Council shall make appropriate arrangements for consultation and cooperation with the United Nations and its specialised agencies as well as with other intergovernmental organisations concerned with services.'; *see The Legal Texts*, *ibid*, 348.

239 Kuijper, above n. 125, 89.

with the UN and its specialised agencies as well as other intergovernmental organisations in the field of services is a power that is reserved to the General Council, exercisable on the basis of Article V *WTO Agreement*.[240] Arguably, the General Council could delegate this power to the CTS since it is generally understood in the law of international institutions that a delegation of powers can take place 'whenever an organ of an international organization which possesses an expressed or implied power under its constituent instrument conveys the exercise of this power to some other entity'.[241]

In accordance with Article IV:5 *WTO Agreement* and various provisions in Part VII of the *TRIPs Agreement*, the *TRIPs* Council oversees the functioning of that Agreement. The general power of oversight attributed to the TRIPs Council is extensive and includes: establishing and operating a programme of review of all Members' domestic laws and regulations in the field of intellectual property protection over a five-year period;[242] monitoring the operation of the *TRIPs Agreement* and Members' compliance with substantive TRIPs obligations[243] as well as carrying out 'such other responsibilities as assigned to it by the Members';[244] maintaining under review the further negotiation by Members of pro-

240 Moreover, the scope of Article V *WTO Agreement* is broader since the General Council is also empowered to 'make appropriate arrangements for consultations and cooperation with *non-governmental organizations* concerned with matters related to those of the WTO (paragraph 2 of Article V *WTO Agreement*).

241 *See* Danesh Sarooshi, *The United Nations and the Development of Collective Security* (Oxford: Oxford University Press, 1999) 4-5, when discussing the general legal framework for delegation of powers in the UN system, noting also that: first, a specific delegation of powers is distinguishable from a general delegation of powers; second, delegation of powers is not the same as delegation of functions, authority for which can be found in the ECJ case *Meroni and others* v. *High Authority*, Case 9/56 [1957/8] *ECR* 133; third, delegation of powers is further distinguishable from delegation of authority to carry out a specific objective, authority for which can be found in *Application for Review of Judgement No. 158 of the United Nations Administrative Tribunal (Fasla)* (*Advisory Opinion*), [1973] ICJ Rep 166 at 174; and fourth, immediate delegation is not the same as contingent delegation; Sarooshi, *ibid.,* 10-15.

242 The monitoring process and role of the TRIPs Council in operating it is set out *in extenso* in Article 63 *TRIPs*. Paragraph 2 of that same article also includes oversight by the TRIPs Council of notifications made pursuant to an extra-WTO treaty, namely notifications of protected emblems, hallmarks and the registered trademarks of States and international organisations on the basis of Article 6ter of the Paris Convention (1967).

243 Article 68 *TRIPs*, *The Legal Texts,* above n. 31, 400.

244 Second full sentence of Article 68 *TRIPs*, *ibid.* The different approach taken by the drafters of the TRIPs Agreement compared to that of the GATS is evident. Kuijper has indicated an institutional inconsistency, where reference is made in this sentence to 'the Members' instead of 'the General Council'. This possible drafting error could imply

tection of geographical indications on the basis of Article 24 *TRIPs*; and carrying out a review at two-yearly intervals of TRIPs implementation by developing country Members upon expiry of the transitional period in Article 65:2 *TRIPs*,[245] i.e. after 1 January 2001, which in some cases might lead to amendments to the *TRIPs Agreement* by means of the amending clause of Article X:6 *WTO Agreement*.[246] Thus, in both the matter of monitoring Members' obligations on the basis of Article 71:1 *TRIPs* and in the matter of treaty amendment on the basis of Article 71:2 *TRIPs*, the TRIPs Council enjoys broader powers than the CTS.

The TRIPs Council has also been assigned some limited specific powers. First, it may extend the ten-year transition period granted to LDC Members for the implementation of the *TRIPs Agreement,* on the basis of Article 66:1 *TRIPs*, provided that the request for such extensions are 'duly motivated'[247] although, as Kuijper points out, this could be construed as the grant of a mini-waiver,[248] a power that is normally reserved to the Ministerial Conference on the basis of Article IX *WTO Agreement*. Second, the TRIPs Council has been expressly assigned the power to examine the scope and modalities of continuing the WTO practice of non-application of the so-called non violation and situation complaints clause under Article 64 *TRIPs*, and of '[submitting] its recommendations to the Ministerial Conference for approval'.[249]

that 'the Members, somehow outside the treaty, extra-constitutionally ... could charge the TRIPs Council with new responsibilities' or act as an invitation for the Members to conclude a simplified treaty, or 'traité en forme simplifiée' between them, outside the WTO framework. However, as Kuijper himself states, this is an error , derived in part from excessive reliance on the retention in some of the Uruguay Round agreements, such as TRIPs, of language found in the Tokyo Round Codes; *see in extenso* Kuijper, above n. 125, 96 and 100-101.

245 The *TRIPs* Council began fulfilling this oversight function in 2000, following the end of the transitional period for some developing countries. *See* Annual Report (2000) of the Council for *TRIPs*, IP/C/22 (6 December 2000).

246 *See* Article 71:2 *TRIPs*¸ *The Legal Texts,* above n. 31, 402.

247 Second full sentence of Article 66:1 *TRIPs*, *The Legal Texts*, *ibid*, 399.

248 Kuijper, above n. 125, 97; see for further details below chapter IV, section 3.3(b).

249 This process was due to be completed by the end of 1999, in accordance with paragraphs 2 and 3 of Article 64 *TRIPs*, *The Legal Texts,* above n. 31, 398. In fact, the TRIPs Council failed to reach a decision on the matter and the WTO Ministerial Conference addressed the issue at Doha in 2001. In its *Implementation-related Decision*, the Ministerial Conference directed the TRIPs Council to continue its examination and make recommendations to the Fifth Session of the Ministerial Conference and called on Members to observe a standstill with respect to the invocation of the non-violation clause, above n. 179, para. 11.1.

d) 'Horizontal' committees, working parties and working groups

A number of committees, working parties and working groups, in which all WTO Members participate, also operate at this third level (see fig. 1 above). They can best be described as 'horizontal' in the overall institutional structure of the WTO, in the sense that they report directly to the General Council and not to one of the three specialised Councils. They represent a mixture of permanent or 'standing committees' and *ad hoc* committees.

The WTO has the following standing committees: the Committee on Trade and Development, the Committee on Balance-of-Payments Restrictions and the Committee on Budget, Finance and Administration, all three of which existed under the former GATT.[250] Their basis in the WTO is founded upon Article IV:7 *WTO Agreement* which states that they shall be established by the Ministerial Conference. However, in practice, it was the General Council that took the Decision to establish these three standing committees at is first meeting,[251] on the basis of a general delegated power in Article IV:2 *WTO Agreement* whereby the General Council conducts the functions of the Ministerial Conference in the intervals between its meetings. These three standing committees are charged with 'carry[ing] out the functions assigned to them by this Agreement and by the Multilateral Trade Agreements, and any additional functions assigned to them by the General Council',[252] i.e. they enjoy a mixture of attributed and (potential) delegated powers.

The General Council has similarly established a further two standing committees on exactly the same basis (acting for the Ministerial Conference in its stead, and on the basis of Article IV, paragraphs 2 and 7 *WTO Agreement*). One of these is the Committee on Trade and Environment or CTE[253] and the other is the Committee on Regional Trade Arrangements or CRTA in which *all* Members

250 Article IV:7 *WTO Agreement, The Legal Texts,* above n. 31, 9.

251 First Meeting of the General Council on 31 January 1995, above n. 151, para. 7.A(1).

252 Article IV:7, first full sentence, *WTO Agreement, The Legal Texts,* above n. 31, 9. Exceptionally, the Committee on Trade and Development has been assigned the specific function of periodically reviewing the special provisions on special and differential treatment in the Multilateral Trade agreements and reporting to the General Council; *see* second full sentence of Article IV:7 *WTO Agreement*, *ibid.*

253 The Committee on Trade and Environment (CTE), was also established at the first meeting of the General Council, held on 31 January 1995, *ibid*, pursuant to the *Ministerial Decision on Trade and Environment* adopted by Ministers at the Meeting of the Trade Negotiations Committee in Marrakesh on 14 April 1994 (the *Marrakesh Ministerial Decision on Trade and Environment*), *The Legal Texts,* above n. 31, 469-471.

participate.[254] Likewise, all working parties on the accession of new Members, of which thirty-three have been established since the WTO entered into force,[255] are plenary in composition and fall under the direct and exclusive competence of the General Council, to which they report. They are *ad hoc* in nature since, upon the successful completion of negotiations and the entry into force of the relevant Protocols of Accession, these working parties cease to exist.

There are also a number of *ad hoc* working groups, open to participation by *all* Members, which have been established at meetings of the Ministerial Conference, or subsequently, in order to examine particular linkage issues between trade and other areas of economic activity, such as trade and investment, trade and competition or dealing with procurement principles and reporting directly to the General Council. In all cases, the competences of these horizontal working groups are expressly set out in the decisions of the Meetings of the Ministerial Conferences at which they were established, which prescribe their terms of reference and may ultimately decide upon their termination or winding up. They include the Working Groups on the Relationship between Trade and Investment, the Interaction between Trade and Competition Policy and Transparency in Government Procurement, all three of which were established at the first Meeting of the Ministerial Conference, held in Singapore in 1996,[256] the Working Groups on Trade, Debt and Finance and Trade and Transfer of Technology, both of which were established at the Fourth Meeting of the Ministerial Conference, held in Doha in 2001[257] and the Negotiating Group on Trade Facilitation, which was set up in October 2004, a full year after the Fifth Meeting of the Ministerial Conference, held in Cancún in 2003.[258]

254 The Committee on Regional Trade Arrangements or CRTA was established by a Decision of the General Council of 6 February 1996, at its meeting of even date, WT/GC/M/10 (6 March 1996), para. 11.

255 In addition there are a further twelve working parties on accession dating back to the previous GATT period, which were carried over into the WTO; *see* the decision granting these countries the status of 'observer', taken at the first Meeting of the General Council on 31 January 1995, above n. 151, para. 2; *see WTO Analytical Index,* above n. 51, 56.

256 *See* the *Singapore Ministerial Declaration*, above n. 77 paras. 20 and 21 and also the text above n. 133.

257 *See* the *Doha Ministerial Declaration*, above n. 78, paras. 36 and 37 respectively.

258 The Negotiating Group on Trade Facilitation, was established by the Trade Negotiations Committee on 12 October 2004, following the *Doha Work Programme*, Decision of the General Council of 31 July 2004, adopted at the Meeting of the General Council, 27 and 31 July 2004, WT/GC/W/535 (31 July 2004), [hereinafter *Doha Work Programme Decision*], Annex D, Modalities for Negotiations on Trade Facilitation.

e) Miscellaneous bodies: committees, working parties and working groups

There are numerous WTO committees and working parties, which operate at a level below those of the three specialised Councils and report to those Councils, i.e. they form a fourth institutional layer in the organisation (see fig. 1 above). The majority of them are established on the basis of a treaty provision in one of the multilateral trade agreements, from which they derive their competence to act. In some instances the committee or working group's mandate is clearly stated in the relevant agreement, decision or declaration that gives rise to its establishment. In other instances, the committee or working group's mandate may be elaborated upon either at the first meeting of that body or at the meeting of the WTO body, which was responsible for its establishment and to which it reports. Irrespective of their denomination all of these bodies are open to participation by *all* Members although the extent to which some may be able to participate may be hampered by lack of resources in human and financial terms. This is particularly true for some developing country Members that either do not maintain any diplomatic presence in Geneva or are unable to send experts from capitals to attend the increasing number of technical meetings that WTO bodies hold, for example meetings of the TRIPs Council or the Committee on Sanitary and Phytosanitary Measures, where extensive knowledge and expertise of the subject matter may be required but is not present among some of the Geneva-based delegations.

Equally, the scope and exercise of competences in these different committees differ widely across the organisation. For example, the eleven committees operating on the basis of the multilateral trade agreements in Annex 1A and the Market Access Committee are variously responsible for the oversight of 'rules-based' measures,[259] the implementation of integration[260] and/or harmonisation meas-

259 The Annex 1A committees, which derive their functions and their competence to act directly from specific GATT 1994 articles, include the following:
Article VI GATT 1994: the Committee on Anti-dumping Practices and its mandate is set out in Article 16:1 of the *Anti-dumping Agreement*, *The Legal Texts,* above n. 31, 191;
Article VII GATT 1994: the Committee on Customs Valuation and its mandate is set out in Article 18:1 of the *Agreement on Implementation of Article VII of the General Agreement on Tariffs and Trade 1994* or *Customs Valuation Agreement*, *The Legal Texts*, *ibid*, 207;
Article XVI GATT 1994: the Committee on Subsidies and Countervailing Measures and its mandate and provision for the establishment of a Permanent Group of Experts or PGE, can be found at Article 24:1 and 3 of the *Agreement on Subsidies and Countervailing Duties* or *SCM Agreement, The Legal Texts*, *ibid*, 296; and
Article XIX GATT 1994: the Committee on Safeguards and its very specific mandate,

ures[261] and for monitoring implementation and/or transitional matters.[262]

Under some of the Multilateral Trade Agreements in Annex 1A, the committees have been granted the express power to establish subsidiary bodies. An example is the Working Party on Subsidy Notifications, established pursuant to Article 24.2 SCM,[263] with the mandate '[T]o review the contents and form of the questionnaire as contained in BISD 9S/193-194 and to undertake such other tasks as the Committee may decide', which includes advising the SCM Committee on the existence and nature of a subsidy. Another is the establishment by the SCM

whereby its relationship to the CTG is clearly established, is set out in Article 13 of the *Agreement on Safeguards*, *The Legal Texts*, *ibid*, 323-324.

260 The Committee on Agriculture was established pursuant to Article 17 of the *Agreement on Agriculture*, *The Legal Texts*, *ibid*, 53, without any details as to its mandate, or whether it has the power to establish subsidiary bodies (evidently it does not). As Kuijper points out this oversight on the part of the drafters of the Agreement meant that it was necessary to adopt a separate decision wherein the powers and functions of the Committee were set out in greater detail. *See WTO Committee on Agriculture*, Decision by the General Council of 31 January 1995, WT/L/43 (17 February 1995) and *Organization of Work and Working Procedures of the Committee on Agriculture* adopted by the Committee at its Meeting on 28 March 1995 G/AG/1 (30 March 1995), which basically comprises the general power of oversight over the implementation of the *Agreement on Agriculture*; *see* Kuijper, above n. 125, 99-100.
The Textiles Monitoring Board was established pursuant to Article 8 of the *Agreement on Textiles and Clothing* or *ATC*, *The Legal Texts*, *ibid*, 99-101. It is considered to be a standing body (Article 8:3 ATC) that reports to the CTG.

261 The Committee on Sanitary and Phytosanitary Measures or SPS Committee was established pursuant to Article 12:1 of the *Agreement on Sanitary and Phytosanitary Measures* or *SPS Agreement*, *The Legal Texts*, *ibid*, 76.
The Committee on Technical Barriers to Trade or TBT Committee was established pursuant to Article 13.1 of the *Agreement on Technical Barriers to Trade* or *TBT Agreement*, *The Legal Texts*, *ibid*, 154.
The Committee on Rules of Origin or RoO Committee and a Technical Committee on Rules of Origin or Technical RoO Committee were both established pursuant to Article 4, paragraphs 1 and 2 of the *Agreement on Rules of Origin*, *The Legal Texts*, *ibid*, 246, with the Technical Committee being established under the auspices of an external body, the Customs Co-operation Council or CCC, to which it reports, on the basis of Annex 1 to the Agreement.
The Committee on Import Licensing was established pursuant to Article 4 of the *Agreement on Import Licensing Procedures*, *The Legal Texts*, *ibid*, 261.

262 The Committee on Trade-Related Investment Measures was established on the basis of Article 7 of the *Agreement on Trade-Related Investment Measures* or *TRIMs Agreement*, *The Legal Texts*, *ibid*, 166.

263 The Working Party on Subsidy Notifications was established a special meeting of the Committee on Subsidies and Countervailing Duties or SCM Committee of 22 February 1995.

Committee of a body of limited composition, the Permanent Group of Experts or PGE, on the basis of Article 24.3 SCM,[264] in order to assist a panel in dispute settlement proceedings with a determination as to whether a measure in question is a 'prohibited subsidy'[265] or to give 'an advisory opinion on the existence and nature of a subsidy', if the SCM Committee seeks such an opinion of it.[266] However, in practice the PGE has never functioned.

Some of these fourth level bodies exercise broad general powers to grant 'specified time-limited exceptions', i.e. to developing country Members that are facing 'special problems, including institutional and infrastructural problems' in preparing and applying technical regulations, standards and conformity assessment procedures (the TBT Committee)[267] or to determine whether the request for the extension for a special transitional period should be granted (the SCM Committee),[268] both of which are forms of 'mini-waivers'.[269] In these situations, the exercise of broad general powers by a fourth level body may be a means of 'depoliticising' certain matters by institutionalising them and according a certain procedure to their enactment rather than raising the matter in a third or level body, such as the Council for Trade in Goods or the General Council. This fact notwithstanding where a WTO body at a lower level of the organisation is unable to reach a consensus decision concerning such matters then the kick up rule will apply, ensuring that the decision-making is moved to a higher body.[270]

Other committees like the SPS Committee and the Rules of Origin Committee, but more particularly such subsidiary bodies as the Working Party on Domestic Regulation or WPDR or the Working Party on GATS Rules or WPGR, may exercise specific powers with respect to the formation of rules or disciplines that are called for on the basis of a built-in agenda contained in a treaty provision (for

264 The Permanent Group of Experts or PGE [to the SCM Committee] is also one of the few bodies of limited composition that draws on experts outside the membership to fill its ranks.

265 This is a prohibited subsidy in the sense of Article 4.5 *SCM*, *The Legal Texts,* above n. 31, 267.

266 The wording of Article 24.3 *SCM*, *The Legal Texts*, *ibid*, 296, makes clear that the PGE, does not do this on its own initiative but the Committee must 'seek' an advisory opinion of it.

267 The TBT Committee exercises this specific power under Article 12.8 of the *TBT Agreement*, *The Legal Texts*, *ibid,* 154.

268 The SCM Committee can do so with respect to the extension of special transitional periods for the maintenance of export subsidies, Article 27.4 SCM, *The Legal Texts*, *ibid*, 299-300.

269 *See* below, chapter IV, section 3.3(b).

270 *See* above, section 3.2 for details.

example development by the WPDR of further disciplines with respect to domestic regulation, pursuant to Article VI:6 *GATS*)[271] or because it is necessary for them to exercise that function in order to further the objectives of the Agreement (for example the development by the SPS Committee of a standard of equivalence, pursuant to Article 4:2 *SPS*).[272]

Additionally, there are some informal and *ad hoc* committees and working groups that function alongside the main Committees with respect to specific matters. One example is the Informal Group on Anti-Circumvention, presided over by the Chairman of the Committee on Anti-dumping Practices, which was constituted pursuant to a series of decisions that Members took in regular meetings of the Committee during the latter part of 1995 and 1996.[273] Another is the *Ad hoc* Working Group on Implementation, which was established at a regular meeting of the Anti-Dumping Practices Committee on 21 October 1996 in order to refer certain topics to it for consideration.[274] While both of these two bodies are in theory open to *all* Members, in practice it is the most active WTO Members in the field of anti-dumping, and which have specific anti-dumping legislation in place in their domestic jurisdictions, that are participating in meetings of those bodies. Neither of them was established pursuant to the express power attributed to the Committee, on the basis of Article 16:2 of the *Agreement on Implementation of Article VI of the General Agreement on Tariffs and Trade 1994* or *Anti-dumping Agreement*.[275] Instead, the Members delegated such responsibility to the Com-

271 *See* chapter V, section 2.1 for a discussion of delegated rule-making by the Working Party on Domestic Regulation or WPDR on the basis of express powers contained in Article VI:4 *GATS*, and that of its predecessor, the WPPS with respect to the development of a set of *Accountancy Disciplines*.

272 *See* chapter V, section 2.1 for a similar discussion of delegated rule-making by the Committee on Sanitary and Phytosanitary Measures or SPS Committee on the basis of implied powers.

273 The Informal Group on Anti-Circumvention came into being following discussion in the Committee on Anti-Dumping Practice, at its meeting of 30 October 1995, G/ADP/M/4 (21 February 1996) and more specifically its meeting of 29 April 1996, G/ADP/M/7 (2 October 1996). The Committee authorised the Chairman of the Committee to engage in informal consultations among Members with a view to reporting back to the Committee on how the Committee was going to respond to the *Ministerial Decision on Anti-Circumvention*, *The Legal Texts,* above n. 31, 453.

274 *Note from the Secretariat, Committee on Anti-Dumping Practices*, G/ADP/W/401 (29 October 1996) and Summary Report of the Meeting of the *Ad Hoc Working Group on Implementation of the Committee on Anti-dumping Practices*, 22 October 1996, G/ADP/AHG/ADP/R/1 (10 April 1997).

275 Article 16:2 of the *Anti-dumping Agreement*, *The Legal Texts,* above n. 31, 191, which specifically sets out a treaty base for such subsidiary bodies.

mittee in relation 'to the operation of the Agreement or the furtherance of its objectives',[276] i.e. on the basis of an implied power.

WTO practice also attests to the establishment of a number of informal institutional bodies in recent years or the reactivation of some that existed in the previous GATT *era* on the basis of practice under the GATT treaty.[277] Further consideration of such informal institutional practices, some of which have been developed over the years in order to thrash out difficult issues and build consensus among the Members, is taken up in the next chapter when analysing the WTO as a regime, and is deemed necessary in order to gain a more realistic picture of the overall institutional landscape of the organisation than would otherwise arise from a purely institutional law perspective.

f) Secretariat and Director General

Aside from the fact that the WTO, unlike the IMF or the World Bank, does not have a separate executive body or organ, for example an Executive Board, about which there has been much discussion,[278] the Secretariat and the Director-General are absent from the institutional structure of the organisation (see fig. 1 above). While the legal basis for the Secretariat and the Director-General are regulated for the first time in the history of GATT/WTO on the basis of Article VI *WTO Agreement* their powers and duties are not further circumscribed.[279]

Not unlike some permanent secretariats that assist the parties to multilateral environmental agreements or MEAs,[280] the WTO Secretariat and the Director-

276 Article 16:1 of the *Anti-dumping Agreement, The Legal Texts, ibid.*

277 It will be recalled that Article XVI:1 *WTO Agreement* forms the basis for the WTO to be 'guided by the decisions, procedures and *customary practices* followed by the CONTRACTING PARTIES to GATT 1947'; *see* above n. 236.

278 A preliminary overview of the ongoing discussion can be found in Van den Bossche, above n. 69, 131-132, who notes that WTO Members have consistently rejected a number of proposals to create an executive body within the institutional structure in order to facilitate WTO decision-making, citing as an example the reaction of the Members at the Meeting of the General Council held on 17 and 19 July 2000, WT/GC/M/57 (14 September 2000), paras. 132-170.

279 In the case of the Director-General, the *WTO Agreement* is slightly more explicit in stating that the Ministerial Conference 'shall appoint the Director-General and adopt regulations setting out the powers, duties, conditions of service and terms of office'; *see* Article VI:2 *WTO Agreement, The Legal Texts,* above n. 31, 9.

280 Churchill and Ulfstein, above n. 6, 627-628. However, it should be borne in mind that MEA Secretariats are of a very different kind to the WTO Secretariat. They exist primarily to provide services to the Conference of the Parties or COPs and various subsidiary bodies under the individual multilateral environmental agreements or MEA's.

General are considered as merely fulfilling a supportive role for the Members,[281] which is supposed to be of a strictly professional and technical nature.[282] Similarly, like those permanent secretariats to MEAs, neither the Director-General nor the staff of the Secretariat exercises any independent decision-making powers, including any formal right of initiative,[283] although they do from time to time act informally in launching initiatives and tabling proposals for the membership to consider, as well as advising Members on trade matters.[284] Were either the Director-General or the Secretariat to pursue a more pro-active and direct role in the affairs of the organisation, the Members would no doubt issue a reprimand.

This is essentially what happened in 2002 when fifteen developing country Members, headed by India, issued a joint communiqué[285] concerning the role of the Director General and the WTO Secretariat at sessions of the Ministerial Conference. The Members in question were of the view that the Director General and the Secretariat 'should assume a neutral/impartial and objective role', which meant that they should not 'express views explicitly or otherwise on the specific issues being discussed'. The action of this group of Members is reminiscent of the former GATT contracting parties where the Director General and the Secretariat were expected to play an equally insignificant role[286] whereas other inter-

281 Wolfgang Benedek, 'Die Konstitutionalisierung der Welthandelsordnung: Kompetenzen und Rechtsordnung der WTO' in *Entschädigung nach bewaffneten Konflikten. Die Konstitutionalisierung der Welthandelsordnung* (Heidelberg: C.F. Müller Verlag, 2003), 283-330 at 289. *See* also *The Sutherland Report*, above n. 80, 73, para. 338.

282 Van den Bossche, above n. 69, 137-138.

283 *See The Sutherland Report*, above n. 80, 73, para. 338, where it is recorded that the Secretariat's role is 'not of initiative or even of institutional defence of the WTO system', which basically comprises seeing it as the 'guardian of the treaties that comprise WTO law', 77 at para. 363.

284 For more details of the informal role of the Director-General in informal consultations among Members (sometimes together with the Chair of the General Council or one of the specialised Councils) in steering the discussions that take place, see chapter II, section 3.3.

285 *See Preparatory Process in Geneva and Negotiating Procedure at the Ministerial Conferences – Communication from Cuba, Dominican Republic, Egypt, Tanzania, Uganda and Zimbabwe*, WT/GC/W/471 (24 April 2002), 3, cited in Van den Bossche, above n. 69, 138.

286 Jackson, *World Trade and the Law of GATT*, above n. 12, §§6.1. -6.3, 145-150, on the lack of a legal basis for the GATT Secretariat and the 'trifurcated' position of the Director General.

national organisations allocate a more important role to their secretariats[287] and especially, their Director-Generals.[288]

In view of such public demarches, it is unlikely that the membership will change its view of the Director General and the Secretariat in order to attribute a more prominent role to either of them, as recommended by *The Sutherland Report*,[289] which should begin with the adoption by the Ministerial Conference of regulations setting out the powers, duties, conditions and terms of office of the Director-General.[290] The *Report* also suggests that specific provision be made for the Director-General to chair the General Council meetings and to establish the duties of the Director-General with respect to management of the Secretariat.[291] This action would not only clarify the position of the Director-General, as head of the organisation, internally vis-à-vis the Members and externally vis-à-vis the international community but would institutionalise the role of the WTO Director General in keeping with the institutional character of the WTO and bring it into line with other international organisations in the international community.

A strengthened Secretariat[292] could provide a greater level of management[293] and expertise to Members in running the WTO,[294] the mandate of

287 Schermers and Blokker note that the position of secretariats is particularly strong in large, technical organisations where members of the organisation place greater reliance on the expert knowledge of staff members, above n. 35, §§439-468, 318-332.
An example in the field of international economic relations is the World Bank where the staff plays a key role in the gathering and processing of economic data, the negotiation of loan agreements and is instrumental in implementing development programmes. *See* Ibrahim F.I. Shihata, *The World Bank in a changing world: selected essays* (The Hague: Nijhoff, 1991) 171.

288 *See* for example the practice of the UN with respect to the Secretary General, who enjoys extensive powers, including under Article 99 UN, the right 'to bring to the attention of the Security Council any matter which in his opinion may threaten the maintenance of peace and security', Schermers and Blokker, *ibid*, §461, 328. In the IMF and the World Bank the Director-General is president of the Board of Governors, on the basis of Article XII:4 of the Fund Agreement and Article V:5 of the Articles of Incorporation of the International Bank for Reconstruction and Development or IBRD or World Bank, and plays a more vital role in both organisations.

289 *The Sutherland Report*, above n. 80, 73-76, paras. 342-356.

290 *The Sutherland Report*, *ibid*, 73-74, paras. 342-347.

291 *The Sutherland Report*, *ibid*, 74, at para. 345.

292 *See* Xu and Weller, above n. 138, 274-277.

293 The idea of a strengthened role for the Secretariat was pursued at an earlier stage with a consultancy report, commissioned by former WTO Director-General, Mike Moore; the results can be found in Terry Slater, *Strategic Organizational Review: Structure and Staffing Resources of the World Trade Organization Secretariat*, (Geneva: World

which still encompasses lengthy preparations for the bi-annual Ministerial Conference, provides the forum for a broad range of monitoring and surveillance activities of an increasingly more technical nature and has broadened its mandate to provide training-related technical assistance or TRTA and capacity building exercises for developing (and acceding developing) country Members. However, there remains much ambivalence among the membership as to the proper role of the Secretariat, and the suggestions contained in *The Sutherland Report* for a reappraisal of the role are unlikely to change the view of the membership on the matter.[295]

3.3 Membership issues

In this concluding part we turn to briefly consider some membership issues. At first sight the WTO would appear to be a 'universalist' organisation,[296] i.e. it is open to all States, but this is not the case. As Donald McRae points out an application by a State for membership of a universalist organisation like the UN is a mere formality even though certain criteria for membership must be fulfilled whereas in the WTO membership (at least for those States that were not original Members) membership must be negotiated.[297]

There are two forms of WTO membership, either original membership or accession. On the basis of Article XI:1 *WTO Agreement* original membership was only open to those States that were contracting parties to the GATT 1947 *and* the European Communities, at the date of entry into force of the WTO (January 1995) and had accepted the *WTO Agreement* and the multilateral trade agreements, including the Schedules of Concessions and Commitments annexed to the *GATT 1994* (Tariff Schedules)[298] and the Schedules of Specific Commitments annexed to the *GATS* (Schedules of Services' Commitments).

Trade Organization, 2001), *see* further Xu and Weller, *ibid*, 251-279 on 'The World Trade Organization: The Secretariat and its Influence'.

294 *The Sutherland Report*, above n. 80, 77-78, paras. 365-366.

295 *See The Sutherland Report*, *ibid*, 76-78, paras. 359-366.

296 The term universalist organisation has been used by Georg Schwarzenberger to denote an organisation that 'aims at universality but falls short of attaining this object'; *see* Georg Schwarzenberger, *A Manual of International Law* (5th edn London: Stevens & Sons Ltd., 1967) 239.

297 D.M. McRae, 'The Contribution of International Trade Law to the Development of International Law' (1996) 261 *Receuil des Cours* 99-237 at 179.

298 On the basis of *EC – Computer Equipment*, Appellate Body Report, *European Communities – Customs Classification of Certain Computer Equipment*, WT/DS62/AB/R,

The WTO is one of the few international organisations that can count another international organisation – the European Communities[299] – among its original Members since traditionally international organisations have been created by and between States. The EC is explicitly designated in the *WTO Agreement*[300] as a Member but there is no general clause in the WTO's charter that opens the way for other international organisations to become WTO Members in the future, which is an indication of the *lex specialis* character of the EC's participation in the WTO.[301]

A further requirement for original membership was that all GATT contracting parties, and other States wishing to accede to the WTO, should accept the *WTO Agreement* and all other obligations, without reservation on the basis of Article XVI:5 *WTO Agreement*.[302] The possibility for former contracting parties to the

WT/DS67/AB/R, WT/DS68/AB/R, adopted 22 June 1998, para. 84, the Schedules are an integral part of the legal instruments that constitute the rights and obligations of the Members in the WTO.

299 This is specifically provided for in Article XIV:1 *WTO Agreement* in the case of the European Communities but not the European Union because at the time of the conclusion of the *WTO Agreement* in 1994 the latter did not have any competence to conclude international agreements; *see* Van den Bossche, above n. 69, 105.
The European Community is a member of the Food and Agriculture Organization or FAO, the European Bank for Reconstruction and Development or EBRD and a number of fisheries organisations; for details *see* Piet Eeckhout, *The External Relations of the European Union* (Oxford: Oxford University Press, 2004) 200-205.

300 Article XI:1 *WTO Agreement*, *The Legal Texts,* above n. 31, 14, where the 'original membership' clause speaks of '[T]he contracting parties to GATT 1947 as of the date of entry into force of this Agreement, and the *European Communities* ...' [emphasis added].

301 There is a further aspect to EC membership since it is also a customs union in the sense of Article XXIV GATT 1947, thereby forming a major exception to MFN, provided certain criteria are fulfilled. The GATT 1947 traditionally provided for customs territories to accede to the GATT on the basis of a territorial clause (Article XXVI:5 (c). It was previously used for example in the case of the accession by Hong Kong China and by Macau, China. More recently, the separate Customs Territory of Taiwan, Penghu, Kinmen and Matsu (Chinese Taipei) has been admitted as a WTO Member at the Doha Ministerial Meeting in November 2001, on the basis of Article XII *WTO Agreement, The Legal Texts*, *ibid*, 15, which nominally carries this idea forward into the WTO; *see* below n. 304 for further details.

302 On the basis of paragraph 2 of Article XI *WTO Agreement*, *The Legal Texts*, *ibid*, least developed countries that became original Members of the WTO are subject to the same conditions of membership as all other Members except that they 'will only be required to undertake commitments and concessions to the extent consistent with their individual development, financial or trade needs or their administrative and institutional capabilities'.

GATT and other States to become original WTO Members only existed for the brief period of two years following the entry into force of the WTO.[303] A total of 131 States are considered to be original Members.[304]

All other States (and customs territories)[305] can only acquire membership by means of accession on the basis of Article XII *WTO Agreement*, which remains indefinitely open to them. That same provision does not say what the conditions for membership are other than to announce that they will be 'on terms to be agreed between it and the WTO'.[306] In practice, the process of accession means that acceding countries must negotiate on a bilateral basis with existing Members in seeking to reach agreement on commitments involving market access (reduction of tariffs and scheduled services' commitments). In fact, this process largely remains a reciprocal undertaking between the acceding State or customs territory and the Members with which it has major trading interests. The acceding State or customs territory must also be in a position to assume all of the necessary WTO obligations, upon its entry into the WTO, which may require it to produce evidence that it is in the process of enacting (or reforming) its domestic laws and regulations and provide a reasonable assurances that it can meet its WTO obligations.

As McRae points out, 'admission to membership in the WTO resembles admission to the membership in the European Union' due to the way in which the existing Members set the conditions for entry and the fact that there is no inherent right to participate in the organisation.[307] Whereas the process of ac-

303 This is specifically provided for in Article XIV:1 *WTO Agreement, The Legal Texts,* above n. 31, 17, which should be read in conjunction with the Ministerial Decision that was adopted pursuant to paragraph 3 of the *Final Act of the Uruguay Round*, i.e. *Decision on Acceptance of and Accession to the Agreement Establishing the World Trade Organisation*, *The Legal Texts,* above n. 31, 466-468.

304 At its first Meeting on 31 January 1995, the General Council agreed that where requests for WTO accession under Article XII *WTO Agreement* had been made by States and separate customs territories for which a GATT 1947 working party on accession already existed, those existing working parties should continue their work as WTO working parties on accession, with standard terms of reference and their respective current chairpersons, Minutes of the Meeting of the General Council, above n. 151, para. 4.I(g). At that meeting, on the basis of its request of 27 January 1995 WT/L/21 (31 January 1995), Belarus was granted the same status, *ibid*; *see WTO Analytical Index,* above n. 51, 93.

305 The territorial scope of Article XII:1 *WTO Agreement* extends to a 'separate customs territory possessing full autonomy in the conduct of its external commercial relations …' on the basis of which Chinese Taipei is a Member, *see* above n. 300.

306 See for more details of the norms governing the accession process, chapter IV, section 3.2.

307 McRae, above n. 297, 177-178.

cession for new Member States to the EU is conducted according to Article 49 TEU[308] and a series of political decisions adopted by the European Council and the European Parliament[309] the case of the WTO is rather different.

Since the entry into force of the WTO the practice of the membership in admitting new Members demonstrates an ever increasing number of terms and conditions that in some cases have proven to be onerous and have led to the assumption of different sets of basic rights and obligations between a number of acceding States and existing Members. This has potential consequences for the organisation because it extends the scope and application of some basic WTO rules and adds new obligations in respect of some acceding Members.[310] Final decisions on the accession of new Members are normally taken by the Ministerial Conference (or the General Council in the interim), on the basis of Article XII:2 *WTO Agreement*, i.e. by voting,[311] or more usually on the basis of consensus.[312]

4 Conclusions

While the WTO has been established as a fully-fledged international organisation its governance structure is the product of the autonomous institutional arrangement that existed under the former GATT trade regime between 1947 and 1994. During that period the General Agreement functioned as a semi-institutionalised multi-

308 In accordance with Article 49 TEU of the Treaty on European Union or EU (Nice – consolidated version): 'The conditions of admission [to the European Union] and the adjustments to the Treaties on which the Union is founded … shall be the subject of an agreement between the Member States and the applicant State.'

309 Currently the process of EU membership via the accession process is governed by a mixture of primary and secondary law together with the adoption of a series of political decisions by the European Council, the European Parliament and the European Commission on the basis of Article 49 TEU, in accordance with the Conclusions of the European Council, adopted at Copenhagen on 13 December 2002, the so-called 'Copenhagen criteria', which contain more specific EU requirements on accession and cover a range of political, economic and legal criteria.

310 *See* further, chapter IV, section 3.2.

311 Since the establishment of the WTO only one accession of a new Member – Ecuador has been decided by means of a vote. *Accession of Ecuador*, Decision of the General Council, adopted on 16 August 1995, WT/ACC/ECU/5 (22 August 1995).

312 *See* decision of the General Council on *Decision-making procedures under Article IX and XII of the WTO Agreement*, adopted at its meeting of 15 November 1995, item 3, WT/GC/M/8 (13 December 1995), section V, pp. 7-8; the relevant decision was issued as WT/L/93 (24 November 1995); for more details on consensus *in lieu* of voting, see below in chapter III, section 2.2(c).

lateral treaty regime, parts of which were applied on a provisional basis, and under the auspices of which several new stand-alone treaties were added at the end of the Tokyo Round.

The WTO's complex institutional structure has evolved out of the *ad hoc* and pragmatic approach to institutions under the General Agreement and has ended the institutional indeterminacy that surrounded the GATT trade regime, following the still-born ITO. Henceforth the multilateral trading system rests on a common institutional framework for the organisation, which is laid down in the *WTO Agreement*. An institutional analysis of the WTO in terms of its structure, functions and powers, as set out in the *WTO Agreement*, brings us to the following conclusions.

The WTO is characterised by its hierarchical institutional structure which operates at four different levels through more than 70 different bodies. It is distinguishable by the fact that formally-speaking every institutional body is open to *all* Members on *all* matters of common interest to them in their trade relations, i.e. the WTO is an organisation with a strong collective action element. Its institutional structure is reinforced by the notion that the WTO itself perpetuates of being a *sui generis* organisation and member-drive. This latter notion in particular begs the question as to the status of the WTO as an international organisation with a will of its own, independent of that of its Members

Despite the collective action element and the concept of a member-driven organisation, in practice, meetings of the second and third level bodies, i.e. General Council and specialised Councils, are generally well represented by the membership, while meetings of other fourth level bodies are more often attended by those Members most interested in a particular trade matter and, not insignificantly, by those with adequately staffed permanent representation in Geneva.

Decision-making is also a process of collective action, which proceeds by means of absolute equality of voting power, and *all* decisions are taken in accordance with the principle of consensus. The Director-General and the Secretariat only fulfil a supportive role for the Members and have no right of initiative; they are not even considered to form part of the organisation's institutional structure. *The Sutherland Report* contains recommendations aimed at enhancing the role of both the Director-General and the Secretariat, beginning with the adoption by the Ministerial Conference of regulations setting out the powers, duties, conditions and terms of office of the Director-General.

Further provision for the Director-General to chair the General Council meetings and for the establishment of that person's duties with respect to management of the Secretariat, are solid recommendations and would help clarify the role of the Director-General internally vis-à-vis the Members and externally vis-à-vis the international community. The process would also institutionalise the role of the

WTO Director General in keeping with the institutional character of the WTO and that of other international organisations.

The scope of the organisation is expressly laid down in the *WTO Agreement* in terms of its mandate, which is divided into five main functions but arguably the organisation has expanded the scope of its constituent treaty when Member governments conferred a sixth function on the organisation, in adopting the Doha Ministerial Declaration in November 2001. Henceforth, the WTO also fulfils the function of providing technical assistance and capacity building to developing country Members and this could prove problematic if the WTO were to overreach itself in its fulfilment of this function such that it might become a development agency.

The exercise of executive, legislative and (quasi) adjudicative functions by different institutional bodies in the overall hierarchy takes place overwhelmingly within the political sphere. The majority of the institutional bodies are mostly concerned with the functioning of the organisation, which involves implementing, administering, operating and furthering the objectives of the organisation, although some of them also have specific oversight functions involving monitoring and surveillance of Members' compliance with their WTO obligations.

In the absence of a separate executive body, most of those activities concerned with the functioning of the WTO come close to an executive one which is more along the lines of collective management by the Members. The exercise of the executive function in plenary is unusual in international institutional law and raises serious challenges for the Members in terms of the management and implementation of the Multilateral Trade Agreements and with respect to leadership of the organisation. The WTO characterises itself as a member-driven organisation but the reality is that it is prone to member-domination, due to its institutional structure and the exercise of its executive function by a politically-driven collective membership.

Unlike some other international economic organisations such as the World Bank and the IMF, the WTO does not have an executive body of limited membership, which is functionally separate from a plenary body that could retain a 'legislative' oversight function and provide for a genuine separation of powers in the organisation. *The Sutherland Report* recommends the creation of an executive body, in the form of a 'senior level consultative body' along the lines of the Consultative Group of Eighteen (CG18) in the GATT, but without any executive or negotiating powers and it is difficult to see how this could bring any changes in the current situation with respect to the WTO's executive function.

The WTO exercises a limited legislative function, which emanates from and is circumscribed by its function as a forum for further multilateral trade negotiations, the results of which may be implemented within the framework of the

WTO, as decided by the Ministerial Conference (or the General Council), which means that any rule-making activity is Member-generated and exclusively politically-driven. The consequence of this is that the WTO fails to properly institutionalise the rule-making process and instead allows the Membership to retain absolute control over the legislative function, from proposals for rule-making to their negotiation and their enactment, thereby providing it with the possibility to shape the normative process to its own ends. The lack of separation of powers has the potential for the executive function to encroach upon the legislative function, or vice-versa, as will be noted in chapters II and IV when discussing some of the informal means which Members have resorted to in order to amend primary treaty rules in the interests of greater operational freedom surrounding the budget estimate.

The adjudicative function is exercised by a mixture of (quasi-)judicial bodies (*ad hoc* panels and Appellate Body) and a political body (Dispute Settlement Body), which is a somewhat unusual occurrence in the law of international institutions and is not completely autonomous, despite appearances to the contrary. The dispute settlement system operates only with respect to Members (*ratione personae*) and concerns only matters arising under one of the 'covered agreements', i.e. the rights and obligations of the Members that flow from the *WTO Agreement* and its annexes (*ratione materiae*) with no provision for third parties, including individuals or international organisations.

The adjudicative function proper, i.e. clarification and interpretation of WTO rules, falls to the *ad hoc* panels and the Appellate Body, neither of which enjoys the inherent power to determine its own competence and authority vis-à-vis the membership and to establish its own jurisdiction as necessary for the proper exercise of its judicial function, such as is normally found with respect to an arbitral or judicial body in international law. Where a system for the investigation of complaints exists under some Multilateral Trade Agreements this can lead to review by both a political body (Council or committee) and a (quasi-)judicial body (panel or Appellate Body), which has on occasion called into question the application of the principle of institutional balance.

The various bodies within the institutional framework exercise the functions of the organisation on the basis of a mixture of general and specific powers, which are either expressly laid down in the *WTO Agreement* and its annexed Multilateral Trade Agreements or are implied because it is necessary for the WTO to exercise a particular function in order to further the objectives of those agreements. The conferral of powers in the WTO is by means of attribution or delegation.

From the foregoing, we can conclude that the WTO is a specialist international organisation with a governance structure, which continues to display many of the characteristics of its predecessor the GATT and prides itself on being member-driven. As currently structured, it does not fit the classical mould of an international organisation but is more of a forum organisation, i.e. a meeting place for discussion among the Members in order to coordinate policies or exchange views, with institutional characteristics.

The overall conclusion in international institutional terms is that the WTO does not fulfil the requirement of an international organisation that has a will of its own, separate and distinct from that of its individual Members and is able to function separately from its Members. Moreover, the manner in which the WTO operates suggests that individual Members, even when acting collectively, retain considerable power and can continue to shape the organisation and its institutional developments to their own ends.

II

THE DYNAMICS OF A REGIME

1 Introduction

Contemporary international society is the most institutionalised in history and yet the rise of international institutionalism has not necessarily been accompanied by any far-reaching analysis of this phenomenon. In particular, the rise in international organisations has focused our attention on the peculiar blend of institutionalism and normativity that lies at the heart of so many of their activities. The establishment of the WTO as an international organisation, the founding instrument of which forms a constitution for the governance of world trade, raises a number of institutional and constitutional issues that are not readily explainable by reference to international institutional law.

Whereas in the previous chapter international institutional law was applied in analysing the extent to which the WTO fulfils the role of an international organisation, in this chapter regime theory is applied to explore the proposition that the WTO is better understood in terms of an international regime, which continues the tradition of the former semi-institutionalised GATT treaty regime alongside, and even within, the overall organisational and institutional framework of the *WTO Agreement*[1] and its Annexes. The WTO will be read in the light of international relations theory pertaining to international regimes, or so-called 'regime theory', in order to better understand some of its institutional and normative dynamics.

Such a reading allows us to go beyond the constitutional and legal bases set out in the *WTO Agreement* and its associated legal instruments and to study the institutional and normative bases of the organisation from the broader perspect-

1 *Marrakesh Agreement Establishing the World Trade Organisation* (adopted 15 April 1994, *in force* 1 January 1995) 1867 *UNTS* 3 [hereinafter *WTO Agreement*] in *The Results of the Uruguay Round of Multilateral Trade Negotiations: The Legal Texts* (Geneva: World Trade Organization, 1999) [hereinafter *The Legal Texts*] 6-18.

ive of Members' practice. One of the underlying notions that will be examined is whether the Members view the organisation as an area for interaction between themselves rather than as an independent actor, with separate legal personality, with a will of its own and capable of acting on its own accord.[2] Put differently, do Members see the WTO as just a forum organisation[3] for the governance of world trade rather than a formal international economic organisation?

This chapter proceeds in the following manner. In section 2, we explore the nature of regime theory and its relationship to legal scholarship. This is followed in section 3 with a reading of the WTO as a regime, beginning with an examination of the practice of regime analysis with respect to the former GATT trade barriers regime and the international regime for the protection of human rights. Regime theory is then applied to the WTO and in doing so three specific questions are addressed. First, what does regime theory tell us about the development of the WTO that international institutional law does not? Second, what are some of the consequences of reading the WTO as a regime rather than as an international organisation? Third, do those consequences say anything about prospective institutional and normative developments at the WTO? In section 4 a number of conclusions are drawn from the preceding analysis that results from reading the WTO as a regime.

2 Regime theory and international legal scholarship

The term 'regime' and the development of regime theory became the subject of intense discussion by political scientists, and in particular international relations theorists, during the early eighties, following a conference on co-operation held in Los Angeles in 1980 where the concept was conceived.[4] Serious thinking about the concept of regime came about as a result of a series of four analytical shifts in identifying and describing the phenomenon of international governance in the

2 Catherine Brölmann, 'A Flat Earth? International Organizations in the System of International Law' (2001) 70 *Nordic Journal of International Law* 320-322.

3 Robert Cox and Harold Jacobson in their introduction to the collection of essays, which they edited, use the specific term 'forum organization' to denote organisations that provided a framework or forum 'for member states to carry on many different activities ranging from the exchange of views to the negotiation of binding legal instruments.' *See* Robert W. Cox and Harold K. Jacobson (eds.) *The Anatomy of Influence – Decision Making in International Organization* (New Haven: Yale University Press, 1973) 5-6.

4 *See* for a discussion of this development and a critique of it, Richard M.A. Crawford, *Regime Theory in the Post-Cold War World* (Aldershot: Dartmouth Publishing Co. Ltd, 1996) 81-86 at 82.

study of international organisation, which began in the 1970's but which took on greater significance in the 1980's.[5]

The first analytical shift was the abandonment of the formal institutional approach that linked international organisations to international governance in order to identify the precise role of international organisations *in* international governance. The formal institutional approach maintained that international governance was whatever international organisations *did* and that *what organisations did* could be deduced from such formal attributes as their constitutive charters, voting procedures, committee structures and so on. An example in the field of international economic relations is the Bretton Woods group of institutions (the IMF and World Bank), the operations of which were examined by scholars of institutionalism in order to measure how closely they approximated to the constitutional mandates of their respective institutions.[6] By placing international organisations at the heart of international governance arrangements and adopting an integrationist approach, it was hoped that a systematic concept of international governance would emerge.[7]

A second analytical shift related to decision-making processes in international organisations. The individual study of formal institutional arrangements and objectives gave way to more generalised examinations of such things as patterns of influence, which were perceived as shaping organisational outcomes. The sources of influence that were most often studied included 'the power and prestige of individual states, the formation and functioning of the group system, organizational leadership positions, and bureaucratic politics.'[8] Organisational outcomes included such things as the adoption of specific resolutions or the development of programmes by certain international organisations, the appearance of broader voting alignments in organisations like the UN General Assembly and the general orientation of specific international institutions, which could be explained on the basis of States' behaviour[9] in those particular institutional arrangements.

A third analytical shift was the turn towards identifying the actual and potential roles of normative and institutional developments in the process of international

5 *See* for an overview, Friedrich Kratochwil and John Gerard Ruggie, 'International organization: a state of the art on an art of the state' (1986) 40 *International Organization* 753-775 at 755-763.

6 Klaus Knorr, 'The Bretton Woods Institutions in Transition' (1948) 2 *International Organization*, 19-38.

7 Kratochwil and Ruggie, above n. 5, 759.

8 Kratochwil and Ruggie, *ibid*, 756.

9 The key study on the behaviour of states in relation to international organisations can be found in a collection of essays published by Cox and Jacobson, above n. 3.

governance. For example, the potential role of institutions like the UN (and in particular the General Assembly) in restructuring North-South economic relations became a major preoccupation of many international scholars from the mid-1970's onwards. In the field of international economic relations this was reflected by extensive analysis of UN General Assembly resolutions[10] concerning the *Declaration on the Establishment of a New International Economic Order*[11] and a *Charter of Economic Rights and Duties of States*.[12] Similarly, there emerged some scholarly analysis of developments in the field of international environmental protection[13] pursuant to the Stockholm Conference on the Human Environment in 1972 and the adoption of a programme of action for the management of sustainable development.[14]

The fourth analytical shift, which emerged in the 1980's, is the move away from identifying international organisations as a separate field of study and instead considering them as part of the institutional arrangements inherent in international regimes. Indeed the study of the phenomenon of international regimes became all-encompassing.[15] One definition of regime, which enjoyed wide support from regime theorists,[16] and is thought to articulate a consensus definition on the

10 G.W. Haight, 'The New International Economic Order and the Charter of Rights and Duties of States', (1975) 9 *The International Lawyer* 591-604; Mark E Ellis, 'The New International Economic Order and General Assembly resolutions: the debate over General Assembly resolutions revisited' (1985) 15 *CalWestInt'lLJ* 647-670; Pieter Verloren van Themaat, *The Changing Structure of International Economic Law: a contribution of legal history, of comparative law and of general legal theory to the debate on a new international economic order* (The Hague: T.M.C. Asser Institute/Nijhoff, 1981); Kamal Hossain, *Legal Aspects of the New International Economic Order* (London: Pinter, 1980) and E. McWhinney, ' The international law-making process and the new international economic order' (1976) 14 *CYIL* 57-72.

11 Declaration on the Establishment of a New International Economic Order, UNGA Res 3201 (1974) (S-VI) (1 May 1974) UN Doc A/9559.

12 Charter of Economic Rights and Duties of States, UNGA Res 3281 (1974) (XXIX) (12 December 1974).

13 David A. Kay and Eugene B. Skolnikoff (eds.) 'special issue on international institutions and the environmental crisis' (1972) 26 *International Organization*, 169-478.

14 Declaration of the United Nations Conference on the Human Environment (Stockholm) UN U.N. Doc. A/CONF.48/14/Rev.1 (1973), reprinted in 11 ILM (1972) 1416, (the Stockholm Declaration).

15 Kratochwil and Ruggie, above n. 5, 759.

16 The definition was accepted by the contributors to a conference of international relations scholars, held in Los Angeles in October 1980, which included not only international relations theorists like Stephen Krasner but also John Ruggie, Jock Finlayson, Mark Zacher and Charles Lipson. The papers from that conference, which contain the most extensive analytical exploration of the concept of 'regime', were subsequently published

matter,[17] is that offered by Stephen Krasner in 1980:

> 'A regime is composed of sets of explicit or implicit principles, norms, rules, and decision-making procedures around which actors' expectations converge in a given area of international relations and which may help to co-ordinate their behaviour.'[18]

In other words, for international relations theorists (and more particularly regime theorists) this 'standard' definition considered regimes to be normative and regulatory frameworks encompassing governance arrangements that were developed by States and other relevant international actors, such as international organisations, in order to co-ordinate their expectations and organise aspects of international behaviour.

Despite fairly widespread acceptance by international relations scholars of this definition, it has also come in for a fair amount of criticism because it is employed to accommodate a variety of understandings about regimes. Thus, it has been argued that the terms such as 'principles, norms, rules, and decision-making procedures', while conceptually distinct have been 'conflated, for the sake of expediency, into the umbrella concept or definition of regime' and that Krasner's definition, both in its origin and in its application is more of a general proposition than an actual definition.[19] Others have considered the definition of regime employed by Krasner to be 'woolly', or vague and 'value-loaded' because it distorts reality, by implying an exaggerated measure of predictability and order.

in a special issue of (1982) 36 *International Organization*. *See* for the actual definition of regime, Stephen D. Krasner, 'Structural Causes and Regime Consequences: Regimes and Intervening Variables', *ibid*, 185-205 at 185.
The contributions to the conference and the special 1982 issue of *International Organization* were later taken up and published as Stephen D. Krasner (ed.) *International Regimes* (Ithaca: Cornell University Press, 1983). *See* Oran B. Young, 'International Regimes: Problems of Concept Formation', *ibid*, 332 *et seq*., especially at 333-339 for an elaboration of the terms used in Krasner's definition.

17 Thomas Gehring, *Integrating integration theory: neofunctionalism and international regimes*, EUI Working Papers no. 95/39 (San Domenico: European University Institute, 1995) 16-17.

18 *See* Krasner's extended definition in Krasner, *International Regimes,* above n. 16, at 185 and the further discussion in Jock A. Finlayson and Mark W. Zacher, 'The GATT and the regulation of trade barriers: regime dynamics and functions', in Krasner, *International Regimes*, *ibid*, 273-314 at 274.

19 Crawford, above n. 4, 81-86, especially at 81, for some useful theoretical thinking on regime debates among scholars of international relations. He underscores the definitional problems which Krasner generates with this commonly accepted definition, which can lead to conceptual, empirical and epistemological tensions.

Moreover, the definition takes for granted that regimes are necessarily 'good' and everyone wants more of them.[20]

When defining regimes international relations theorists apply basic terminology differently to the way in which international lawyers apply it. In international relations theory 'principles' are those prevailing beliefs, which underlie the policy choices of States in various issue areas, 'norms' are standards of behaviour that can be defined in terms of rights and obligations, 'rules' are specific prescriptions and proscriptions regarding behaviour and 'decision-making procedures' are the prevailing practices for making and implementing collective choices.[21] This approach contrasts with that of legal scholarship where 'principles' and 'rules' are usually understood as legal principles and legal rules, which together with standards, form part of a broader set of norms.[22]

However, it should be noted that the international political economist, Robert Keohane, in reiterating his earlier definition of regimes, attempted to be more precise when he stated that regimes are 'institutions with explicit rules, agreed upon by governments, which pertain to particular sets of issues in international relations'.[23] Andrew Hurrell points out that Keohane's definition, with its emphasis on 'explicit, and connected sets of rules brings regime theory and international law much closer together'.[24]

20 Susan Strange, '*Cave! hic dragones:* a critique of regime analysis' in Krasner, above, n. 16, 337-354, challenges the validity and usefulness of the concept of regime, noting in particular that the definition advanced by Krasner is simply stressing old things in new ways. In her view, Krasner's definition neither circumscribes the regimes debate nor advances it.

21 Robert Keohane and Joseph Nye had previously defined regimes as 'governing arrangements that affect relationships of interdependence' and, more precisely, as 'networks of rules, norms, and procedures that regularize behavior and control its effects' in a particular issue-area; *see* Robert O. Keohane and Joseph S. Nye, *Power and Interdependence: World Politics in Transition* (Boston: Little, Brown, 1977) 19. *See* also Ernst. B. Haas, 'Why Collaborate? Issue-Linkage and International Regimes' (1980) 32 *World Politics* 357-405 at 358.

22 *See* chapter IV, section 2.1.

23 Robert O. Keohane, 'Neoliberal Institutionalism: A Perspective on World Politics' in Robert O. Keohane, *International Institutions and State Power: Essays in International Relations Theory* (Boulder, Colo: Westview Press, 1989) 1-20.

24 *See* for a discussion of the relationship between regime theory and international law, Andrew Hurrell, 'International Society and the Study of Regimes: A Reflective Approach', in Volker Rittberger (ed.) *Regime Theory and International Relations* (Oxford: Clarendon Press, 1993) 49-72, at 54-57.

It is precisely in this latter sense that international legal scholarship has traditionally considered regimes,[25] and more particularly 'international regimes', as norms and decision-making procedures accepted by international actors (predominantly States) in the regulation of a particular activity or set of issues. For example, in the 1938 *Trail Smelter Arbitration* between the US and Canada a central matter was that of establishing a regime, or system of principles, rules and procedures for regulating the discharge of noxious fumes by the offending smelter and one that would prevent future injury.[26] The concept of (international) regime has also been used in the matter of ascribing a special legal status to certain physical manifestations that are linked to territory (and jurisdiction over that territory), such as river systems,[27] or navigational 'straits',[28] to certain situations beyond the sovereignty of any one State irrespective of a physical or territorial link,[29] such as the Antarctic regime[30] or the regime governing outer space,[31] in the matter of certain codifying treaties[32] and the creation of particular inter-

25 Winfried Lang, 'Regimes and Organizations in the Labyrinth of International Institutions' in Konrad Ginther, Gerhard Hafner, Winfried Lang, Hanspeter Neuhold, Sucharipa Behrmann a.o. *Völkerrecht zwischen normativem Anspruch und politischer Realität*, Feschrift für Karl Zemanek zum 65. Geburtstag (Berlin: Duncker & Humblot, 1994) 275-289, at 275-276.

26 *Trail Smelter Arbitration* (*United States* v. *Canada*) (1938) 3 RIAA 1905, also reported in (1939) 33 *AJIL* 185-212.

27 Josef L. Kunz, 'The Danube Regime and the Belgrade Conference', (1949) 43 *AJIL* 104-113.

28 John Norton Moore, 'The Regime of Straits and the Third United Nations Conference on the Law of the Sea' (1980) 74 *AJIL* 77-121.

29 Lang, above n. 25, at 276-277.

30 The Antarctic Treaty (adopted 1 December 1959, *in force* 23 June 1961) 402 *UNTS* 71 and Protocol on Environmental Protection to the Antarctic Treaty (adopted 4 October 1991, *in force* 14 January 1998) (1991) 30 *ILM* 1461; Gillian D. Triggs *The Antarctic Treaty regime: law, environment and resources* (Cambridge: Cambridge University Press, 1989) and S.K.N. Blay 'New trends in the protection of the Antarctic environment: the 1991 Madrid Protocol' (1992) 86 *AJIL* 377-399.

31 Treaty on Principles Governing the Activities of States in the Exploration and Use of Outer Space, including the Moon and other Celestial Bodies (adopted 27 January 1967, *in force* 10 October 1967) 610 *UNTS* 205.

32 Examples of such codifying treaty regimes include the Vienna Convention on the Law of Treaties (adopted 23 May 1969, *in force* 27 January 1980) 1155 *UNTS* 331, (1969) 8 *ILM* 689. In some of its preparatory work on codifying the rules of treaty law, the International Law Commission or ILC considered including an article on 'Treaties providing for an objective regime', which is usually taken to mean that the treaty establishes a situation which every other State, even those not parties to the treaty, are bound to respect and abide by (an example being the Panama Canal zone) *see* Third

national entities.[33]

More significantly the term international regime has been applied to international regulatory systems with a functional link, which are premised on the underlying treaty (or system of treaties) and which seek to achieve a certain object and purpose. Examples of international regimes include the regimes for the international protection of human rights,[34] international arms control[35] and international protection of the environment[36] as well as the GATT/WTO multilateral trading system. Oscar Schachter even considered the GATT to be a prime example

report on the law of treaties, by Sir Humphrey Waldock, Special Rapporteur, UN Doc.A/CN.4/167 and Add.1-3, Yearbook ILC 1964-II at 26-27 and 32-33.
Another is the Vienna Convention on Diplomatic Relations (adopted 18 April 1961, *in force* 24 April 1964) 500 *UNTS* 95 [hereinafter VCDR]. In the *Case Concerning US Diplomatic and Consular Staff in Tehran Case (United States* v. *Iran*) [1980] ICJ Rep 3 at 40 the International Court of Justice described the rules of diplomatic law in the *VCDR* as constituting 'a self-contained regime' (para. 85).
The rules on state responsibility, developed by the ILC, may in the fullness of time come to be recognised as the extant regime governing this area of international law, or certain aspects thereof; *see Articles on Responsibility of States for Internationally Wrongful Acts*, annexed to UNGA Res. 56/83 (12 December 2001) UN Doc A/RES/56/83.

33 The creation of particular international entities, such as the cities of Krakow, Danzig or Trieste, is well documented. *See* further with respect to such regimes, Eckhart Klein, 'International Régimes' in Rudolf Bernhardt (ed.) *Encyclopedia of Public International Law (EPIL)* vol. 2 (edn rev Amsterdam: North-Holland, 1995) 1354-1359 who puts forward certain criteria for the existence of an international regime, including (i) a treaty between States (or States and international organisations), regulating the status of the area; (ii) a general interest underlying the regime; and (iii) the intention of the parties to serve the general interest by creating a regime which endows the area with a general status *erga omnes*, *ibid*.

34 Jack Donnelly, 'International human rights: a regime analysis' (1986) 40 *International Organization* 599-642.

35 Harald Müller, 'The Internationalization of Principles, Norms and Rules by Governments: The Case of Security Regimes', in Rittberger (ed.), *Regime Theory and International Relations*, above n. 24, 361-388.

36 In the field of international environmental law it is commonplace to speak of an international waste regime, which recognises separate treaty regimes for each of the following: land-based sources of marine pollution, dumping at sea and the transport of hazardous wastes for transboundary disposal. Patricia Birnie and Alan Boyle view such environmental regimes as the emergence of 'institutions of multilateral governance' because they 'rely principally on treaties, protocols and soft law to provide a regulatory system capable of dynamic evolution'. Such regulatory systems have a normative function and provide an alternative to the previous development of relevant rules through third party dispute settlement. *See* further Patricia Birnie and Alan Boyle, *International Law & the Environment* (2nd edn, Oxford: Oxford University Press, 2002) at 180.

of a general multilateral law-making treaty that had *merged* into and become an international regime. The collaborative treaty mechanism of the GATT was operationally sustained through decisions of the contracting parties, which gave the regime an institutional character and ensured its continuing regulatory function.[37]

International relations theorists have traditionally looked to regime theory to explain the connection between the emergence of institutions and the distribution of power. In applying regime theory, they seek an explanation to a common perception that States only pursue policies out of self-interest and do not co-operate with one another unless there is some reciprocal benefit to be gained by doing so. Thus, those international relations scholars, who are termed 'regime theorists', believe that the reason why States obey principles, norms and rules and why they implement the decision-making procedures embodied in a regime is because of the functional benefits that a particular regime appears to deliver.[38]

Regime theory may contribute to our understanding of why an institution like the WTO has developed in the way it has and what functional benefits Members may derive from its normative and procedural bases. It may also help us to gain a better insight into what principles, rules and standards induce Members to cooperate and why certain decision-making practices that were developed at the time of the GATT continue in the WTO, which is something that the theoretical aspects of international institutional law, with its positivist emphasis on systems of norms and rules and their validity rather than the underlying conditions for those norms and rules, cannot do. As Jack Donnelly points out 'the real norms and procedures of a regime arise from the practice of its participants, which rarely is unrelated to but often is not exactly what is specified in the legal texts.[39]

Thus, while the broader notion of regime finds its origins in work undertaken by regime theorists, it can also be of relevance to international legal scholarship in understanding complex governance structures like the WTO, which combine a mixture of legal and non-legal norms, in the sense of principles, rules and standards, and a variety of formal and informal decision-making procedures and practices that are of a hard law or of a 'soft' law[40] variety.

37 Oscar Schachter, *International Law in Theory and Practice* (The Hague: Martinus Nijhoff, 1991) 76.
38 Hurrell, above n. 24, 56.
39 Donnelly, above n. 34, 605.
40 The term 'soft law' is usually employed to characterise a variety of non-legal norms and informal decision-making procedures. It is used to describe decisions in the form of institutional resolutions and declarations issued at ministerial conferences, codes of conduct, joint communiqués, and so on, which are not intended to be legally binding upon those parties ascribing to them. For an overview of the concept of soft law together

Winfried Lang[41] provides a further six reasons why regime theory may have some importance for international law. The reasons he gives can be summarised as follows: (i) treaties alone provide an insufficient basis for the comprehensive regulation of complex (and often very technical) subject matter; (ii) the notion of regime suggests that organisations should be able to evolve beyond their legal basis in order to adapt their constituent instruments to changing circumstances; (iii) the idea of regime may help us understand the emergence of different levels of normativity in international law, including hard law and soft law; (iv) regimes may highlight latent conflicts of interest; (v) regimes may allow ambitious States to accept meagre initial results that can be offset by the in-built perspective of implicit evolution; and (vi) they may allow the combination of treaties of different origins into one regulatory scheme.

3 The WTO as a regime

By reading the WTO as a regime it is possible to move beyond the formality of the legal texts of the *WTO Agreement* and its Annexes and to focus on the practice of the Members, including their application of the GATT *acquis* norm contained in Article XVI:1.[42] This should help us to gain a better understanding of how the WTO operates institutionally, thereby expanding our perspective on the organisation's proper vocation and allowing us to question the belief that the WTO could become a key pillar of global governance.[43]

Regime theory may reveal and help explain certain incoherencies and inconsistencies between substantive, procedural and institutional WTO norms. Additionally, there are at least two observable shifts in the conceptual underpinnings of the multilateral trading system which have come about as a result of the transformation

with the variety of instruments, the actors that employ them and the various degrees of compliance; *see* Christine Chinkin, 'Normative Developments in the International Legal System' in Dinah Shelton (ed.), *Commitment and Compliance, the Role of Non-Binding Norms in the International Legal System* (Oxford: Oxford University Press, 2000) 21-42, especially at 39-41. For a critique of the concept of soft law and the move towards relative normativity in international law, *see* Prosper Weil, 'Towards relative normativity in international law?' (1983) 77 *AJIL* 413-442.

41 Lang, above n. 25, at 277.

42 It will be recalled that Article XVI:1 *WTO Agreement* specifically states that 'the WTO shall be guided by the decisions, procedures and customary practices followed by the CONTRACTING PARTIES to the GATT 1947 and the bodies established in the framework of the GATT 1947'.

43 Marco Bronckers, 'More Power to the WTO', (2001) 4 *JIEL* 41-65 at 41 and 44-45.

of the GATT into the WTO, about which regime theory may have something to say.

One is the subtle change in regulatory philosophy underlying the multilateral trading system. There is a perceivable shift from a process of negative integration under the GATT, where the major concern of the contracting parties was the progressive reduction of tariffs and the complimentary goal of non-discriminatory international trade, to that of positive integration in the WTO where Members must also undertake to legislate and enforce measures aimed at positive prescription in fields such as technical standards, health and safety standards, intellectual property rights and trade-related investment measures (minimum standards for investment), often with the goal of harmonising those standards.[44]

The other is the change in institutional design of the WTO in comparison to the former GATT. The WTO is institutionally embedded[45] (or 'nested') in a broader network of norms and institutions which means that compliance with basic WTO norms, in the form of principles or rules, may occur because those norms find their provenance in another, horizontal legal order, such as those elaborated by standards organisations like the FAO Codex Alimentarius or the International Standards Organization or ISO.[46] Similarly, the intellectual property rights regimes, established by the Berne and Paris Conventions, which are referenced in the *Agreement on Trade-Related Aspects of Intellectual Property Rights* or *TRIPs,* act as frames of reference for compliance with and enforcement of those particular norms. By analysing the WTO as a regime, it may allow us to position the organisation within the broader parameters of a more complex institutional theory.[47]

44 Veijo Heiskanen, 'The Regulatory Philosophy of International Trade Law' (2004) 38 *JWT* 1-36 and Dirk De Bièvre, 'Judicialisation and Positive Integration in the WTO', paper prepared for 5th Pan-European International Relations Conference organised by the Standing Group on International Relations (SGIR) of the European Consortium for Political Research (ECPR), Netherlands Congress Centre, Den Haag, 9-11 September 2004.

45 The term 'embedded' was developed by Kratochwil and Ruggie, above n. 5. Also: José E. Alvarez, 'The WTO as Linkage Machine' (2002) 96 *AJIL* 146-158 at 152, who refers to the 'norm diffusion or laundering functions' of organisational treaty regimes like the WTO, relying on Michael N. Barnett and Martha Finnemore, 'The Politics, Power and Pathologies of International Organizations' (1999) 53 *International Organization* 699-732 at 699.

46 This issue is taken up, when discussing the phenomenon of 'rule referencing' in chapter V, section 3.

47 *See* the introductory section of the essay by Müller in 'The Internationalization of Principles, Norms, and Rules by Governments: The Case of Security Regimes', above n. 35, at 363.

3.1 The practice of regime analysis

The WTO has emerged from the former GATT regulatory framework, which was studied by regime theorists Jock Finlayson and Mark Zacher in 1982 and considered by them to be 'virtually coterminous' with the term 'global (or quasiglobal) trade barriers regime'.[48] In their study, they designated the following as substantive norms of the GATT regime: the principle of non-discrimination which is applied through the norm of unconditional MFN; the principle of market access or trade liberalisation norm; the principle of reciprocity which is manifested through the reciprocal trade concessions norm; the right to waive an obligation, i.e. the exceptional clause, or safeguard norm; and the principle of special and differential treatment or development norm.

Finlayson and Zacher also listed procedural norms and mechanisms, which they principally located around types of decision-making activities in the GATT. The first type of procedural norm was what they termed the 'major interests norm', which is a procedure that was followed by certain contracting parties known to be both 'principal suppliers' and key decision-makers involved in trade negotiations, monitoring, rule interpretation and dispute settlement (the US, the EEC and Japan within the GATT context). The second procedural norm was a collective decision-making procedure, in the form of joint action of the CONTRACTING PARTIES to the GATT (Article XXV:1 GATT), which they designated as the 'multilateralism norm'. Finlayson and Zacher then combined their analysis of substantive and procedural GATT norms with their analysis of decision-making activities in order to ascertain inconsistencies and to highlight conflicts in the GATT, or as they termed it the 'trade barriers regime', and to define the GATT as regulatory regime. Our analysis proceeds by way of reference to Finlayson and Zacher's early work on the identification of substantive and procedural norms in the GATT trade barriers regime but only to the extent that their analysis is useful and assists us in understanding the WTO as a regime.

The overall approach advanced in this chapter also borrows from Jack Donnelly's typology of norms and the types of decision-making activities, which he used in his analysis of the creation, evolution and current status of the inter-

48 Finlayson and Zacher, above n. 18 at 273-314. Other international relations scholars like James Fawcett considered the GATT to be 'a model of law as process' and 'an amalgam of specific obligations, codes of conduct and commercial policy considerations, working through consensus and organized persuasion'; *see* James Fawcett, *Law and Power in International Relations* (London: Faber and Faber, 1982) 90.

national human rights regime in the mid-1980's,[49] because they may have something to say about our reading of the WTO as a regime. There are certain similarities between the multilateral trade regime and the international human rights regime. Both regimes are characterised by a set of treaty-based norms which embrace a complex system of principles, rules and standards and are managed through (semi-)institutionalised treaty bodies. Both regimes also reflect the difficulties that arise with respect to the interface between international standard-setting and the strictures of domestic policy-making, that may strongly influence the decision-making activities of individual governments when performing collective tasks in international *fora* such as attendance at meetings pertaining to the creation, maintenance or amendment of substantive and procedural norms and institutions.

Even so, the norms underlying these two regimes are clearly different in character. On the one hand, substantive human rights norms, including basic principles and standards, are embodied in a range of international, regional and single-issue human rights regimes whereas each individual human rights norm (right, principle or standard) in its own way makes a universal and absolute (deontological) claim on global and national policies and/or resources.[50] On the other hand, substantive trade norms, in the form of principles, rules and standards, are embodied in international, regional and bilateral regimes (in some instances comprising a complex of norms and regulations through a number of treaty instruments) but individually (or collectively) those rights, principles or standards only make relative claims on global and national policies and/or resources.

Similarly, when it comes to procedural norms, there is strong public support for human rights but, with the exception of some regional systems (for example the European Convention on Human Rights[51] or ECHR), the enforcement of those rights in the international system displays serious weaknesses. Conversely, public support for international trade, in the form of the MFN and market access, may seem limited but the WTO has an effective dispute settlement mechanism with strong enforcement measures, which is assisted by the availability of (quasi-)

49 Donnelly provides an analysis of the creation, extension and ongoing status of international human rights regimes, including regional and single issue human rights regimes; *see* above n. 34 *in extenso*.

50 *See* Frank J. Garcia, 'The Universal Declaration at 50 and the Challenge of the Global Markets: Trading Away the Human Rights Principle', (1999) 25 *BrooklynJInt'l Law* 51-97.

51 The European Convention for the Protection of Human Rights and Fundamental Freedoms (adopted 4 November 1950, *in force* 3 September 1953) *ETS* 5, as amended, which amendments and additions have subsequently been replaced by Protocol No. 11 (adopted 11 May 1994, *in force* 1 November 1998) *ETS* 155.

judicial and administrative procedures in national courts and tribunals of WTO Members.

There is also a difference in reading the WTO as a regime as opposed to reading the system for the international protection of human rights as a regime. Donnelly undertook his analysis in order to assess the strengths and weaknesses of the international human rights regime and specifically sought to identify incoherencies arising from inconsistencies between individual norms or from gaps in the overall structure of norms. He typified regime norms as principles, rules and standards, which descend along a vertical axis beginning with the authoritative international norm at the top, moving downwards through international standards (with self-selecting national exemptions), non-binding international standards (and guidelines) and ending with national standards.[52]

Donnelly combined his analysis of basic human rights norms with decision-making activities, in much the same way as Finlayson and Zacher did for the GATT trade barriers regime a few years earlier, although he distinguished between four principle types of decision-making activities, ranged along the horizontal axis. The four forms of international decision-making activities that he identified relate to norm creation, norm enforcement, norm implementation and norm promotion. Within these horizontal decision-making activities he distinguished at least six types of applicable decision-making procedures: (i) authoritative international decision-making, including generally effective enforcement powers, i.e. institutionalised, binding decision-making; (ii) international monitoring, including the formal review of state practice; (iii) international policy co-ordination; (iv) international information exchange; (v) international promotion or assistance; and (vi) national decision-making.

The levels at which the various decision-making activities of norm promotion, norm implementation and norm enforcement take place in the WTO regime are similar to those that apply in the international human rights regime, with authoritative treaty obligations at the top of the vertical axis, descending through international standards (with self-selecting national exemptions), non-binding international standards (and guidelines) and ending at the bottom with national standards. In the next section we analyse some of the substantive and procedural norms as well as decision-making procedures noting, where relevant, their provenance in the GATT and their continuation in the current WTO as part of the practice of the Members.

52 Donnelly, above n. 34, 603-605.

3.2 Regime theory and the WTO

The first and most prominent level of norm in the WTO, which is the product of norm creation, is the set of authoritative treaty obligations, i.e. the primary treaty rules[53] that arise from the legal agreements, which were agreed to by the GATT contracting parties participating in the Uruguay Round as a single undertaking. They include the Final Act Embodying the Results of the Uruguay Round of Multilateral Trade Negotiations, the *WTO Agreement* and the Annexed Multilateral Trade Agreements, the tariff schedules[54] and the schedules of services' commitments,[55] the two sets of GATT Ministerial Decisions (but not the Ministerial Declarations)[56] relating to the fulfilment of WTO obligations, which were adopted by the Trade Negotiations Committee on 15 December 1993 and by the Trade Negotiations Committee in Marrakesh on 14 April 1994,[57] as well as any additional Protocols,[58] adopted by the Members subsequent to the entry into force of the *WTO Agreement*.[59]

53 In chapter IV, authoritative treaty obligations, in the sense of binding international standards as more generally accepted by States in Donnelly's analysis, above n. 34, 603, are analysed from a positivist point of view as primary treaty rules and the application of secondary treaty rules that affect those primary treaty rules.

54 It was determined by the Appellate Body in *EC – Computer Equipment,* Appellate Body Report, *European Communities – Customs Classification of Certain Computer Equipment*, WT/DS62/AB/R, WT/DS67/AB/R, WT/DS68/AB/R, adopted 22 June 1998, that although 'each Schedule represents tariff commitments made by *one* Member, they represent a common agreement among *all* Members' (para. 109).

55 The Appellate Body has confirmed this interpretation with respect to Schedules of services' commitments, in *US – Gambling*, Appellate Body Report, *US – Measures Affecting the Cross-Border Supply of Gambling and Betting Services*, DS/285/AB/R, adopted 20 April 2005, para. 159.

56 Ministerial Declarations are generally not considered to be legally binding on Members; *see* further chapter I, section 3.1, esp. fn. 117 and the cases cited therein.

57 Ministerial Decisions are considered to be legally binding on Members. In this respect the Decisions adopted by Ministers in the Trade Negotiations Committee on 15 December 1993, at the close of the Uruguay Round, together with the Decisions adopted by Ministers at the Meeting of the Trade Negotiations Committee in Marrakesh on 14 April 1994 relating to the establishment of the World Trade Organization and its legal consequences, form part of the legal results of the Uruguay Round.

58 *See* further chapter IV, section 3.1(c) for a discussion of Protocols supplementing Schedules.

59 According to Article XIV:2 *WTO Agreement, The Legal Texts*, above n. 1, 16, Members accepting the *WTO Agreement* after its entry into force, i.e. acceding Members, are similarly bound by all the results of the Uruguay Round, as negotiated and bound in

The authoritative treaty norm was central to the GATT as a multilateral treaty. Even so, the General Agreement was only amended twice,[60] due to the onerous treaty amending clauses in Article XXX GATT.[61] The first amendment was adopted by Protocol, following the 1954-1955 Review Session, and included *inter alia* such amendments as the inclusion of a new section B to Article XVIII GATT, which henceforth allowed developing countries to use quantitative restrictions for balance-of-payments purposes, and the addition of paragraph 4 of Article XVI, which brought some discipline into the matter of export subsidies.[62] The second amendment was the addition by means of Protocol of Part IV on 'Trade and Development' to the GATT, which was made ten years later in a special session of the GATT, held in 1964-1965.[63] A third development was not an amendment to the GATT 1947 but an expansion of the authoritative treaty norm at the end of the Tokyo Round MTN (1972-1979) by means of a separate set of legal instruments, or 'side codes' (the so-called 'Tokyo Round Codes'), to which GATT contracting parties could choose to become a party.[64]

accordance with their individual Protocols of Accession, the latter of which are attached to the Final Act; *see* further chapter IV, section 3.2.

60 John. H. Jackson, *World Trade and the Law of GATT* (Charlottesville, VA: The Michie Company (The Bobbs-Merill Company, Inc.), 1969) 68-69 as part of a broader discussion surrounding the difficulty of amending the GATT 1947.

61 Article XXX GATT 1947, *The Legal Texts*, above n. 1, at 466. It was originally intended that this burdensome procedure also be applied to the disconnection clauses, taken up in Article XXIX GATT 1947, which regulated the relationship of the GATT and its contracting parties to the Havana Charter, once the latter entered into force; *see The Legal Texts*, *ibid*, at 465-466.

62 *Protocol Amending the Preamble and Parts II and III of the GATT* (adopted 3 October 1955, *in force* 10 July 1957) GATT Doc. PROT/6, *BISD* 3S/79 (1955), 278 *UNTS* 168 [hereinafter *1955 Amending Protocol*].

63 *Protocol Amending the GATT to Introduce a Part IV on Trade and Development* (adopted 8 February 1965, *in force* 27 June 1966,) GATT Doc. PROT/2/62, L/2314, GATT *BISD* 13S/2, 572 *UNTS* 320 [hereinafter *1964 Amending Protocol*]. The *1964 Amending Protocol* was a key amendment permitting modification of the most fundamental treaty obligation in the General Agreement (the grant of MFN) by stating that developed contracting parties do not expect reciprocity in the reductions or removal of tariffs and other non-tariff barriers from developing countries, which in turn meant that the latter did not have to reciprocate or at least not fully. Henceforth developing countries were not expected to apply concessions which were 'inconsistent with their individual development, financial and trade needs, taking into consideration past trade developments'; *see* paragraph 8 of Article XXXVI GATT 1947 and the *Ad* note, *Ad Article XXXVI,* paragraph 5, *The Legal Texts*, above n. 1, at 469 and 492 respectively.

64 The following agreements were opened for acceptance by the contracting parties to the GATT and by the EEC: *Agreement on Implementation of Article VI of the General*

The authoritative treaty norm continues to be applied in the WTO. At the end of the Uruguay Round the GATT contracting parties (and future WTO Members) adhered to the concept of a 'single undertaking', meaning that *all* the Members would be bound by the *WTO Agreement* and the annexed Multilateral Agreements. At the same time, there was still a need to take account of the remaining Tokyo Round Codes, which had not been included in the renegotiation process, namely the *Agreement on Trade in Civil Aircraft*, the *Agreement on Government Procurement*, the *International Dairy Agreement* and the *International Bovine Meat Agreement*. The decision was taken to include these four agreements in Annex 4 to the *WTO Agreement* as so-called plurilateral agreements, indicating that they were outside the single undertaking and Members could choose whether to become parties to them.

Although a decision was eventually taken during the Uruguay Round to re-negotiate the *Agreement on Government Procurement* or *AGP*, negotiations were undertaken and concluded separately from the other Uruguay Round negotiations.[65] The *International Dairy Agreement* and the *International Bovine Meat Agreement* did not undergo any re-negotiation but were eventually wound up in 1997 through lack of support, owing to their perceived lack of usefulness in the post-Uruguay Round trading environment.[66] The significance of the *Agreement*

Agreement on Tariffs and Trade, *BISD* 26S/171, 1186 *UNTS* 2; *Agreement on Interpretation and Application of Articles VI, XVI and XXIII of the General Agreement on Tariffs and Trade*, *BISD* 26S/56, 1186 *UNTS* 204; *Agreement on Import Licensing*, *BISD* 26S/154, 1186 *UNTS* 372; *Agreement on Trade in Civil Aircraft*, *BISD* 26S/162, 1186 *UNTS* 170; *Agreement on Technical Barriers to Trade*, *BISD* 26S/8, 1186 *UNTS* 276 (all *in force* 1 January 1980); *Agreement on Implementation of Article VII of the General Agreement on Tariffs and Trade*, *BISD* 26S/116, 1235 *UNTS* 126 and *Agreement on Government Procurement*, *BISD* 26S/33, 1235 *UNTS* 258 (both *in force* 1 January 1981) and the following agreements, which were opened for acceptance by UN members, or one of the UN specialised agencies, and by the EEC: the *Arrangement Regarding Bovine Meat*, *BISD* 26S/84, 1186 *UNTS* 344 and *International Dairy Arrangement*, *BISD* 26S/91, 1186 *UNTS* 54. *See* John H. Jackson, *The World Trading System: Law and Policy of International Economic Relations* (Cambridge, MA, and London: The MIT Press, 1997) [hereinafter Jackson, *World Trading System*] 43 and 75-78.

65 The decision to re-negotiate the *Agreement on Government Procurement* or *GPA* was taken during the course of the Uruguay Round but the negotiations did not form part of the single package. Instead the revised GPA, which still only has 28 parties, is a designated plurilateral agreement under Annex 4 of the *WTO Agreement* (adopted 15 April 1994, *in force* 1 January 1996) 1915 *UNTS* 103.

66 The *Arrangement Regarding Bovine Meat*, *BISD* 26S/84, 1186 *UNTS* 344 and *Termination of the International Bovine Meat Agreement*, Decision pursuant to Article VI:3, IMA/8 (30 September 1997) respectively the *International Dairy Arrangement*, *BISD* 26S/91, 1186 *UNTS* 54 and *Termination of the International Dairy Agreement*, Decision

on Trade in Civil Aircraft and the *AGP* lies in the fact that these two remaining plurilateral agreements have been considered as potential models for the future development of other 'elective' agreements on matters such as trade and investment, trade and competition policy and the matter of trade facilitation.

The process for the adoption of further authoritative treaty norms is by one of two means. Either this takes place on the basis of the adoption of new primary treaty rules, which are the results of further negotiations between participating Members at the end of an MTN, or by means of supplemental protocols to existing agreements. Or else primary treaty rules are amended on the basis of secondary treaty rules and/or the established practice of the organisation, the latter of which can take the form of subsidiary rule-making. Such secondary treaty rules may also include the grant of a general waiver or an authoritative interpretation, in both cases agreed to by the membership on the basis of a collective action decision.

So far, there have been no formal amendments of the *WTO Agreement* or any of the annexed Multilateral Trade Agreements even though a treaty amendment to Article 31 of the *TRIPs Agreement* has been proposed, which if adopted, will replace the current exception granted by Ministerial Decision on the basis of a general waiver.[67] Similarly the current process for review (and revision) of the *Understanding on Rules and Procedures Governing the Settlement of Disputes* or *DSU*, on the basis of a Ministerial Decision taken at Marrakesh in 1994[68] and formally outside the negotiations launched at the Fourth Meeting of the Ministerial Conference, held at Doha in 2001,[69] may lead to further amendments of the *DSU* but have so far proved inconclusive.[70]

However, a decision was adopted by the General Council in 2003, upon a recommendation of the Committee on Budget, Finance and Administration or BFA Committee, to request the Director-General to present to the BFA Committee two estimated budgets covering a biennial period, with effect from the estimates for

pursuant to Article VIII:3, IDA/8 (30 September 1997). Both treaty instruments had a termination date of 31 December 1997.

67 For further details *see* further chapter IV, section 3.3(a).

68 *Decision on the Application and Review of the Understanding on Rules and Procedures Governing the Settlement of Disputes*, *The Legal Texts*, above n. 1, 465.

69 *See Ministerial Declaration*, adopted at the Ministerial Conference, Fourth Session Doha, 9-14 November 2001, WT/MIN(01)/DEC/1 (20 November 2001) [hereinafter *Doha Ministerial Declaration*], and the 'Work Programme' that forms part of the *Doha Ministerial Declaration*.

70 See chapter IV, section 3.1(b).

2004 and 2005, instead of annually, as required by Article VII:1 *WTO Agreement*.[71] This 'creative' interpretation of that particular constitutional provision could be read as a *de facto* amendment. More important for the purposes of our analysis, it demonstrates the Members' continuing practice in adopting *ad hoc* procedural measures in order to deal with particular institutional situations as they arise.

The second type of norm creation is the development of standards at the international level that allows States to adopt or maintain certain national exceptions (usually on policy grounds). In the GATT regime this process was made operational for the contracting parties through the safeguard norm, which was identified by Finlayson and Zacher. It was (and still is under the WTO) the conditional right of a Member to take safeguard measures (and some variants, including safeguard measures for balance-of-payments or BOP purposes) and various corrective measures, or trade remedies, such as antidumping, and countervail in the event of 'unfair trade'. The safeguard norm could also be applied horizontally, i.e. it could be invoked as a defence by a GATT contracting party, and currently by a WTO Member, in order to provide a general exception from key obligations like the application of MFN or national treatment, or the prohibition on quantitative restrictions, usually in order to protect specific values that are enshrined in national policies.[72]

The third type of norm creation is the category of international standards, guidelines and recommendations, which are not legally binding but are nonetheless widely commended to Members, for the purposes of harmonising measures or bringing domestic measures into conformity with WTO obligations. As a result of the entry into force of the WTO the role of non-binding international (or even regional or national) standards such as those which are applied to food safety, animal and plant health, technical regulations, conformity assessment procedures, professional qualifications and intellectual property standards, have assumed an importance which did not exist under the former GATT, where such matters remained almost wholly within the domain of individual States.

71 *See* Minutes of the Meeting of the General Council of 25, 26 and 30 August 2003, WT/GC/M/82 (13 November 2003), p. 2, para. 3.

72 Considerable practice by both the GATT contracting parties and WTO Members has built up over the years with respect to the application of this norm; *see* for example the overview of the GATT/WTO case law with respect to the general exception provision of Article XX GATT, prepared by the WTO Secretariat for the Members of the WTO Committee on Trade and Environment, *GATT/WTO Dispute Settlement Practice Relating to Article XX, Paragraphs (b), (d) and (g) of GATT: Note from the Secretariat – Revision*, WTO Doc WT/CTE/W/103 (8 March 2002).

The reason for this development is the paradigm shift in the underlying philosophy of the multilateral trading system from negative integration to positive prescription that we noted earlier. In the context of the WTO, certain Multilateral Trade Agreements encourage Members to harmonise existing domestic measures, by bringing them into conformity with international standards, such as the *Agreement on the Application of Sanitary and Phytosanitary Measures* or *SPS Agreement*[73] in the case of the Codex Alimentarius[74] standards on food safety, or recommend the encourage the adoption of higher levels of protection, based on international norms, such as the *TRIPs Agreement*[75] with respect to copyright and patent protection on the basis of the Berne[76] and Paris[77] Conventions. A further point to note is that these international standards are exogenous to the multilateral trade regime but are incorporated into the WTO by means of a reference in the respective Multilateral Trade Agreements – a process known as 'rule referencing'.[78] At the same time, they are forging a new regulatory regime that aims at greater harmonisation and mutual recognition of Members regulatory systems in a way that did not occur under the GATT trade regime where greater deference was given to States to pursue their own substantially divergent regulatory policies.[79]

The fourth type of norm creation in the WTO is the national standard (or deference to the national standard), as evidenced by national regulations or policy measures where there is an absence of international principles, rules or standards. This is relevant because either the matter in question is not dealt with substantively in the WTO (e.g. investment guidelines, competition rules, or consumer protection standards) or the reach of international norms has been reserved exclusively to other international (or regional) regulatory bodies (e.g. standards of airworthiness

73 *Agreement on the Application of Sanitary and Phytosanitary Measures*, *The Legal Texts*, above n. 1, 69-84.

74 The *Codex Alimentarius Commission* was created in 1963 by FAO and WHO to develop food standards, guidelines and related texts such as codes of practice under the Joint FAO/WHO Food Standards Programme; *see* further http://www.codexalimentarius.net/.

75 *Agreement on Trade-Related Aspects of Intellectual Property Rights*, *The Legal Texts*, above n. 1, 365-403.

76 Berne Convention for the Protection of Literary and Artistic Works (adopted 9 September 1886, *in force* 5 December 1887) as revised through the Paris Act of 24 July 1971 and amended on 28 September 1979 (*in force* 29 January 1970) 888 *UNTS* 67.

77 Paris Convention for the Protection of Industrial Property (adopted 20 March 1883, *in force* 6 July 1884) as revised through the *Stockholm Act* (adopted 14 July 1967, *in force* 26 April 1970) 828 *UNTS* 305.

78 See chapter V, section 3 for a more detailed description of the process of rule referencing.

79 Heiskanen, above n. 44, 13.

that are regulated by ICAO)[80] or else national authorities have been allowed to maintain domestic standards (prudential regulation in the case of central banks). Despite the change in the underlying philosophy of the multilateral trading system, there are still areas of national policy and decisions of national regulatory authorities that the WTO has not yet intruded upon.

However, the degree of deference that the GATT regime showed to national standards when compared with the WTO can be explained on other grounds, which although now largely of historical note, continue to play a significant role in some Members' trade relations.[81] The reasons for this are the following. Unlike the WTO, Part II of the GATT 1947 contained substantive obligations such as the national treatment standard, customs procedures, the prohibition on quotas and rules on subsidies and antidumping, which under the former GATT were to be applied 'to the fullest extent not inconsistent with existing legislation', conform the Protocol of Provisional Application or PPA.[82]

This device effectively grandfathered any domestic legislative provision, which existed at the time a State became a party to the GATT and which was inconsistent with Part II obligations. In practice, many GATT contracting parties continued to justify various forms of national legislation and domestic regulatory practices that were essentially GATT-inconsistent and thereby thwarted the objective of the trade liberalisation norm.[83] The situation has now been 'cured' in the WTO

80 International Civil Aviation Organization or ICAO, created pursuant to the Convention on International Civil Aviation (adopted 7 December 1944, *in force* 4 April 1947), 15 *UNTS* 295. The *Annex on Air Transport Services* to the GATS, *The Legal Texts*, above n. 1, 353-354 contains a specific savings clause, excluding the reach of bilateral and multilateral agreements in the field of air transportation sector from coverage, including any related standards, at least for the time being.

81 *See US – 1916 Act*, Appellate Body Report, *United States – Anti-Dumping Act of 1916*, WT/DS136/AB/R and WT/DS162/AB/R, adopted 26 September 2000.

82 It was decided to sign and authenticate the GATT 1947 and bring parts of it into force on a provisional basis. *See* Final Act Adopted at the Conclusion of the Second Session of the Preparatory Committee of the United Nations Conference on Trade and Development (30 October 1947) 55 *UNTS* 188, containing the General Agreement on Tariffs and Trade and the Protocol of Provisional Application (1947) 55 *UNTS* 194. The effect of the Protocol of Provisional Application was to fully implement Part I (containing the most-favoured nation (MFN) clause and tariff obligations) and Part III (mostly procedural and treaty provisions). Part II (Articles III to XXIII – containing the substantive obligations relating to national treatment, customs procedures, quantitative restrictions, subsidies, anti-dumping and the dispute settlement provisions) was to be implemented "to the fullest extent not inconsistent with existing legislation".

83 *See* Jackson, *World Trading System*, above n. 64, concerning the effect of the Protocol of Provisional Application or PPA on the negotiating process in the Tokyo Round of

by the introduction of paragraph 4 of Article XVI *WTO Agreement*[84] which 'imposes an affirmative obligation on each Member to bring its legislation into conformity'[85] with its WTO obligations.

Following Donnelly's framework for analysis, there are a number of decision-making 'activities' in the WTO that can be distinguished as further norm creation, enforcement norms, implementation norms and promotional norms. Underlying these decision-making activities there are five of the six types of decision-making 'procedures' in the WTO, which Donnelly identified for his human rights regime.[86]

First, there is the development of new norms in the form of additional treaty obligations as well as other substantive and procedural rules, which are binding upon the Members, coupled with enforcement of those norms. Since the *WTO Agreement* entered into force in 1995, the Membership has dealt with a number of so-called 'built-in agenda' items, i.e. matters left unregulated at the end of the Uruguay Round, due to lack of time or lack of political will but for which specific provision has been made in the legally binding instruments that make up the Uruguay Round Agreements.[87] When it comes to enforcing international norms, the WTO dispute settlement system represents one of the strongest exercises of such powers in the international community as a result of changes made to the process of enforcement, at the end of the Uruguay Round,[88] which provides for the automatic adoption by the Members in the Dispute Settlement Body or DSB

Multilateral Trade Negotiations (MTN) (1973-1979) and on the settlement of trade disputes, for example the GATT panel on the *US – Manufacturing Clause*, GATT Panel Report, *United States – Manufacturing Clause (Copyright)*, GATT *Basic Instruments and Selected Documents*, adopted 15/16 May 1984 *(BISD)* 31S/74 (1985).

84 Article XVI:4 *WTO Agreement* requires that: '[E]ach Member shall ensure the conformity of its laws, regulations and administrative procedures with its obligations as provided in the annexed Agreements'.

85 *US – 1916 Act*, above n. 81, para. 78.

86 Donnelly, above n. 34, 604.

87 Examples include the 'built-in' agenda items under various provisions of the *General Agreement on Trade in Services* or *GATS* for completing the GATS framework with specific disciplines on subsidies (Article XV:1 *GATS*), emergency safeguard measures or ESMs (Article X:1 *GATS*), government procurement (Article XIII:2 *GATS*) and domestic regulation (Article VI:4 *GATS*), the so-called 'rules-making' part of further negotiations on the liberalisation of trade in services.

88 Enforcement has been a characteristic of the strengthened dispute settlement system under the WTO, in particular the monitoring and surveillance of compliance by Members with decisions of the Dispute Settlement Body or DSB and the authorisation of counter-measures for non-compliance, pursuant to Articles 21 and 22 of the Understanding on *Rules and Procedures Governing the Settlement of Disputes* or *DSU, The Legal Texts*,

of panel and Appellate Body reports, combined with the task of monitoring Members' compliance and with the imposition of sanctions for non-compliance by a Member.

Second, the implementation norm has taken on a new importance in the heavily rules-dominated system of the WTO through the improved monitoring and surveillance of Members' conduct. The process of monitoring and surveillance has been institutionalised in the WTO and has come to resemble more fully the decision-making activity common to norm implementation conducted at inter-State level in other regimes but substantially different from human rights regimes. WTO monitoring and surveillance consists primarily of 'peer review', which only involves the Members *inter se* and does not seek to protect community or common interests nor the rights of third parties.[89] The only possible exceptions to the foregoing are in the dispute settlement process when a Member raises a 'systemic concern',[90] i.e. a concern that is shared by all Members in the system as a whole, or when a Member has a substantial interest in a matter and intervenes as a third party.[91]

Examples of international monitoring at the WTO include: the collective exercise by Members of their powers of surveillance over individual Members' compliance with recommendations or rulings of the DSB in accordance with the *Understanding on the Rules and Procedures Governing Disputes* or *Dispute Settlement Understanding* or *DSU*; the institutionalised 'peer review' monitoring of Members' trade policies and regulatory practices in accordance with regular, scheduled reviews by the Trade Policy Review Body or TPRB under the *Trade*

above n. 1, 420-425. *See* Joost Pauwelyn, 'Enforcement and Countermeasures in the WTO: rules are rules: towards a more collective approach' (2000) 94 *AJIL* 335-347.

89 This is in contrast to human rights regimes that provide for a peer review system at inter-state level concerning the protection of human rights of individuals and groups, occasionally with the possibility of individual review, provided that a system for the right of individual complaints has been established.

90 Systemic issues have from time to time arisen and been considered in the dispute settlement process; see for example *US – Certain EC Products*, Appellate Body Report, *United States – Import Measures on Certain Products from the European Communities*, WT/DS165/AB/R/, adopted 10 January 2001, para. 91, concerning the 'systemic issue of the relationship between Articles 21.5 and 22 of the DSU' relating to the sequencing of surveillance and the imposition of sanctions (suspension of concessions) for non-compliance with a recommendation or ruling of a panel or the Appellate Body.

91 Paragraph 10 of Article 2 DSU, *The Legal Texts*, above n. 1, 413, states that '[A]ny Member having a substantial interest in a matter before a panel and having notified its interest to the DSB … shall have an opportunity to be heard by the panel and to make submissions to the panel.'

Policy Review Mechanism or *TPRM* (Annex 3),[92] the primary purpose of which is to ascertain Members' adherence to the rules, disciplines and commitments made under the Multilateral Trade Agreements in the interests of transparency,[93] and the monitoring by the TRIPs Council of Members' compliance in bringing their national intellectual property laws and other regulations into line with their obligations under the *TRIPs Agreement*.[94]

Third, and also relevant to the implementation norm, is the increased scope for international policy co-ordination at the WTO, some of which lead to some delegated rule-making in the form of subsidiary rule-making by WTO bodies.[95] This includes such procedures as the review of Members' domestic practices, an example being the *Agreement on Implementation for Article VII of the GATT 1994* or *Customs Valuation Agreement*, a feature of which is the elaboration of a system of rules for customs valuation of goods by national customs authorities which is fair, uniform and neutral and which is intended to be generally applicable, irrespective of the source of supply of those goods.[96] However, in some cases international policy co-ordination may also consist of more extended forms of implementation as is the case with the *SPS Agreement*, where Members are under an obligation to ensure that sub-central government bodies, i.e. local governmental bodies, as well as non-governmental bodies and regional bodies, do not adopt WTO-inconsistent policy measures at the national level.[97]

At the inter-agency level the international policy coordination has taken on new dimensions. Greater macro-economic policy coherence was a key area for the Negotiating Group on the Future of the GATT System or FOGS during the

92 Xu Yi-chong and Patrick Weller, *The Governance of World Trade: International Civil Servants and the GATT/WTO* (Cheltenham: Edward Elgar, 2004) 268-269.

93 *See* the objectives in section A of the *Trade Policy Review Mechanism*, Annex 3 to the *WTO Agreement*, *The Legal Texts*, above n. 1, 434. A trade policy review consists of two elements. One is a policy statement prepared by the government of the Member under review. The other is a detailed report written independently by the WTO Secretariat. The two reports are then considered in a meeting of the Trade Policy Review Board or TPRB, whereupon they are published, together with the proceedings of the TPRB's meeting.

94 Article 68, *Agreement on Trade Related Intellectual Property Rights*, or *TRIPs Agreement*, *The Legal Texts*, *ibid.*, 400.

95 See chapter V, section 2.1.

96 This last consideration, which is found in the fifth recital of the preambular text to the *Agreement on Implementation for Article VII of the GATT 1994* or *Customs Valuation Agreement*, would seem to suggest that such rules could even bind states, which are not WTO Members, *The Legal Texts*, above n. 1, 198.

97 Article 13 *SPS*, *The Legal Texts*, *ibid*, 77.

Uruguay Round MTN.[98] The so-called 'principle of coherence' in economic policy-making between the WTO, the IMF and the World Bank is one of the five functions of the organisation, explicitly laid down in the *WTO Agreement*,[99] which is supported by a Ministerial Declaration adopted at the end of the Uruguay Round.[100] In practice, this international policy coordination exercise has not progressed very far; other than one special session of the General Council each year in order to debate the issue of coherence, there has been no substantial increase in coherence decision-making.[101]

Fourth, the international exchange of information, involving various notification procedures, has become a positive obligation, which is taken up in several primary treaty texts and which primarily gives effect to the promotional norm of transparency but may be linked to the implementation norm. Transparency is recognised as one of the fundamental norms of the multilateral trading system in providing clarity for Members and predictability for economic actors. In the WTO it is promoted between Members and additionally within a Member's territory.[102] Further examples of the transparency norm in primary treaty provisions include: annual notifications by Members of subsidies in accordance with Article 25 of the *Agreement on Subsides and Countervailing Measures* or *SCM Agreement*;[103] and the establishment of enquiry points by Members with respect to information about technical regulations, standards and conformity assessment procedures, in accordance with Article 10 of the *Agreement on Technical Barriers to Trade* or *TBT Agreement*[104] or with respect to 'all relevant measures [i.e. all domestic regulatory barriers],[105] that pertain to or affect the operation' of the *General*

98 For the mandate of the Negotiating Group on the Future of the GATT System or FOGS, *See* Xu and Weller, above n. 92, 235 and 242-243.

99 Article III:5 *WTO Agreement, The Legal Texts*, above n. 1, 7.

100 *Declaration on the Contribution of the World Trade Organization to Achieving Greater Coherence in Global Economic Policymaking, Final Act Embodying the Results of the Uruguay Round of Multilateral Trade Negotiations, The Legal Texts ibid*, 442-443.

101 Xu and Weller, above n. 92, 270.

102 Robert Wolfe, 'Regulatory transparency, developing countries and the WTO' (2003) 2 *WTR* 157-182, at 159.

103 Article 25, *Agreement on Subsidies and Countervailing Measures* or *SCM Agreement, The Legal Texts*, above n. 1, 297.

104 Article 10, *Agreement on Technical Barriers to Trade* or *TBT Agreement, The Legal Texts, ibid*, 149-151.

105 This would include but not be limited to such domestic regulatory measures as qualification requirements and procedures, technical standards and licensing requirements and so on. *See* Article VI:4 *GATS, The Legal Texts, ibid.*, 333-334.

Agreement on Trade in Services or *GATS*, in accordance with Article III thereof.[106]

Additionally, some international promotion or assistance activities, which are adopted in pursuit of the promotional norm, have come to play a more prominent role in the WTO and have been institutionalised in the WTO, most noticeably in the partial application of what Finlayson and Zacher call the development norm, i.e. the grant of special and differential treatment to developing country and LDC Members. In many of the Multilateral Trade Agreements the overriding emphasis is on providing a limited number of flexibilities for developing country and LDC Members to accept binding obligations and/or to allow them to enjoy preferential access to markets, in some instances coupled with the provision of technical assistance. Further institutionalisation of the development norm with respect to special and differential treatment is being pursued in the Doha Development Round, as part of the work programme on special and differential treatment.[107]

Essentially this comes down to the application of Part IV *GATT 1994* (and the GATT Decision on the Enabling Clause),[108] coupled with flexibility on services' liberalisation on the basis of Article XIX *GATS*. Additionally, developing country and LDC Members have been granted protection for temporary periods in order to encourage the development of new industries (Article XVIII: section C *GATT 1994*) and to allow them to take restrictive measures when balance of payments difficulties arise (Article XVIII section B *GATT 1994* reinforced with the BOP Understanding of *GATT 1994*). At times special and differential treatment has been coupled with arbitrarily determined transitional periods for the implementation of WTO obligations while on other occasions, developing country and LDC Members are exempted from certain specified obligations (*SCM*) or their WTO commitments are 'modulated' (*AoA*). In some instances the special and differential norm reflects the simple generation of a large number of ancillary support efforts to developing country and LDC Members, some of which are

106 Article III *GATS, The Legal Texts*, above n. 1, 329-330, articulates the transparency norm as a positive obligation for Members, with respect to the promptness, openness and availability of information concerning 'all relevant measures of general application which pertain to or affect the operation of this Agreement', i.e. the *GATS* (paragraph 1 of Article III *GATS*).

107 *Doha Ministerial Declaration*, above n. 69, para. 44 which refers to the work programme set out in the *Decision on Implementation-Related Issues and Concerns* Decision of 14 November 2001, adopted at the Fourth Session of the Ministerial Conference, Doha, 9-14 November 2001, WT/MIN(01)/17, (20 November 2001), para. 12.

108 Differential and More Favourable Treatment, Reciprocity and Fuller Participation of Developing Countries, Decision of the CONTRACTING PARTIES, 28 November 1979, L/4903 (1979) *BISD* 268/203-205 [the *Enabling Clause*].

completely ineffective, or else they are articulated as broad technical assistance provisions, which are mostly to be conducted on a best efforts basis. They are therefore largely aspirational in character and can be designated as programmatic norms.[109]

Since the Fourth Meeting of the Ministerial Conference, held in Doha in 2001, it is possible to include in the category of promotional or assistance decision-making activities, those activities that relate to technical assistance and capacity building.[110] For the first time in the history of the WTO, the *Doha Ministerial Declaration*[111] explicitly recognises that trade-related technical assistance and capacity building are 'core elements of the development dimension of the multilateral system' and it goes on to endorses a 'New Strategy for WTO Technical Co-operation for Capacity Building, Growth and Integration'. As we noted in the previous chapter,[112] this event is not without significance since arguably in institutional terms it expands the functions of the WTO beyond its present scope and raises serious issues for the organisation in terms of coordination with other international institutions and agencies in order to ensure greater policy coherence on matters of development policy.

The strengths and weaknesses of the WTO when read as a regime in terms of its effectiveness are, for our purposes, less important than the practical realities of its acceptance by the Members and its overall coherence. Normative incoherencies can arise in international regimes through inconsistencies between individual norms or as a result of significant gaps, or loopholes, which may lead

109 For a matrix of the special and differential norms in the Uruguay Round agreements, *see Implementation of Special and Differential Treatment Provisions in WTO Agreements and Decisions, A Review of Mandatory Special and Differential* Addendum, WT/COMTD/W/77/ Rev.1/Add.2, 21 December 2001; *Implementation of Special and Differential Treatment Provisions in WTO Agreements and Decisions, Mandatory and Non-Mandatory Special and Differential Treatment Provisions*, Note by the Secretariat, Corrigendum, WT/COMTD/W/77/Rev.1/Add.1/Corr.1, 4 February 2002; *Non-Mandatory Special and Differential Treatment Provisions in WTO Agreements and Decisions*, Note by the Secretariat, Addendum, WT/COMTD/W/77/ Rev.1/Add.3, 4 February 2002; and *Information on the Utilisation of Special and Differential Treatment Provisions*, Note by the Secretariat, Addendum, WT/COMTD/W/77/ Rev.1/Add.4, 7 February 2002. Some, but not all, of the special and differential norms listed in these provisions are merely aspirational, and require substantial efforts by State for their realisation, hence the term 'programmatic norms'; see further chapter IV, section 2.1.

110 Xu and Weller, above n. 92, 269-270.

111 *Doha Ministerial Declaration*, above n. 69, which makes a call 'to place the needs and interests of developing countries at the heart of the Work Programme', set out in the *Doha Ministerial Declaration*, at paras. 2 and 38.

112 See chapter I, section 3.1.

to one norm cancelling another out, while procedural incoherencies can arise either from inconsistent or incomplete decision-making activities or from their articulation through decision-making procedures. Due to the more complex institutional setting in which the WTO is situated, the issue of institutional incoherence may arise as a result of the mixture of attributed and delegated, explicit and implicit powers distributed over a vast range of institutional bodies, as was observed in chapter I. Thus, regime theory can expose aspects of the WTO that institutional legal theory does not touch upon. In the next section, we seek to discover what can be learnt from reading the WTO as a regime.

3.3 Application of regime theory: some observations

The WTO in terms of a regime is characterised by its overriding normative character, in strong contrast to its predecessor the GATT. The rights and obligations of the Members are clearly set out in the Results of the Uruguay Round, which acts as code of conduct for the liberalisation of world trade[113] among them. The typology of substantive norms that were operative in the GATT trade barriers regime and regulated global trade for nearly half a century are still identifiable in the WTO and in some cases have been reinforced. Examples include the non-discrimination norm in the form of national treatment, complaints about which have substantially increased in WTO dispute settlement proceedings,[114] the trade liberalisation or market access norm, which is more prominent as a result of the completion of the Uruguay Round MTN,[115] and the norm of reciprocity in trade concessions. The norm of reciprocity has also taken a new direction, since some Members have viewed it as forming the basis for the mutual recognition of other Members' regulatory measures on the basis of equivalency.[116]

113 The IMF is another international economic organisation, which lays down a similar code of conduct for its Members in the Fund Agreement, *see* Andreas Lowenfeld, *International Economic Law* (Oxford: Oxford University Press, 2002), 507.

114 For application by the Appellate Body of the national treatment norm in various complaints brought by Members, primarily involving Article III GATT 1994, but also Article XVII GATS and Article 3.1 TRIPs, *see WTO Appellate Body Repertory of Reports and Awards, 1995-2004* (Cambridge: Cambridge University Press, 2005) [hereinafter *WTO Appellate Body Repertory*], 221-242

115 *See* Peter Van den Bossche, *The Law and Policy of the World Trade Organization* (Cambridge: Cambridge University Press, 2005) 41-42.

116 *EC – Trademarks and Geographical Indications*, Panel Report, *European Communities – Protection of Trademarks and Geographical Indications for Agricultural Products and*

Similarly the safeguard norm has been strengthened by the introduction of specific rules to discipline the use of exceptions to WTO obligations. This applies in the matter of the grant of a general waiver, which is now subject to specific terms and conditions set out in paragraphs 3 and 4 of Article IX *WTO Agreement*, as well as to specific waivers for emergency safeguards on goods, conform Article XIX *GATT 1994* and the *Agreement on Safeguards*,[117] or safeguards for BOP purposes (Article XIV *GATT 1994*).[118] Other norms such as the development norm have not faired so well. Attempts are still ongoing to provide a more normative content to the special and differential treatment norm, which was adopted by the GATT contracting parties, and to make it more operational in the WTO context.[119] A further substantive norm that has been added to the WTO is that of transparency which is evident throughout the Multilateral Trade Agreements.[120]

In procedural terms, the process of 'collective decision-making' (or 'multilateralism' norm), and the 'major interests' norm were of key importance in the GATT since both reflected the prevailing belief of many countries at the time 'that those with the most obvious stake in a given issue or negotiation should exercise paramount influence in related decision-making'.[121] On the one hand, the norm of multilateralism encouraged governments to participate in rule-making conferences through a collective decision-making process (usually by consensus) and to allow multilateral surveillance by other contracting parties over their trade policies. It also symbolised the regime members' acceptance of the proposition

Foodstuffs, WT/DS174/R and WT/DS290/R, adopted 19 May 2005, finding that EC Regulation on geographical indications or GI's violates its WTO obligations because foreign nationals do not have guaranteed access to the EC's system for the protection of their GI's since access to the EC market is contingent upon the government of other Members adopting a system of GI protection that is *equivalent* to the EC's, and offering *reciprocal* protection to EC GI's, paras. 7.102 and 7.103.

117 *Agreement on Safeguards*, *The Legal Texts*, above n. 1, 315-324.

118 *See* also the transitional safeguard measure on textiles and clothing (Article 6 *ATC*), which has now expired, and the special safeguard measures during the tariffication process in agriculture (Article 5 *AoA*).

119 While the current round of MTN, which was launched at the Fourth Meeting of the Ministerial Conference, held at Doha, 9-14 November 2001, has been named the 'Doha Development Round', progress on further gains with respect to trade and development are proving limited. For example, despite the specific mandate, contained in paragraph 44 of the *Doha Ministerial Declaration*, above n. 69, in which Ministers called for a review of special and differential treatment provisions in order to strengthen them and make them 'more precise, effective and operational', the work of the Committee on Trade and Development and the General Council in doing this remains inconclusive.

120 *See* Van den Bossche, above n. 115, 41-42.

121 Finlayson and Zacher, in Krasner, *International Regimes*, above n. 16, 297-298 and 302.

that each had a legitimate interest in the other's trade policies and conduct thereof. On the other hand, the major interests' norm upheld the contrasting belief that participation by GATT contracting parties in decision-making activities should be restricted to those countries that were most affected or exercised the most influence over the outcome of the issue being decided upon. The tension between these two norms still persists and has even been strengthened as a result of the way in which these procedural norms have further developed in the WTO.

The multilateralism norm was articulated by the CONTRACTING PARTIES, acting jointly under Article XXV:1 GATT,[122] whereby they took decisions under the treaty regime which gave effect to the General Agreement and facilitated its operation and eventually led to the development of some form of *de facto* organisational capacity.[123] Procedurally, the multilateralism norm was simple, straightforward and at the outset, when there were few participants, fairly easy to operate. Once it was realised that the ITO would not materialise, attention turned to finding ways of making the GATT operate more efficiently and a list was drawn up of some ten or twelve functions and responsibilities of the CONTRACTING PARTIES, acting jointly under Article XXV:1 GATT.[124] This procedural norm was never formalised during the lifetime of the GATT. Instead, and in keeping with early GATT practice, the CONTRACTING PARTIES simply approved the

122 According to Article XXV:1 GATT, *The Legal Texts*, above n. 1, at 460 whenever the designation 'CONTRACTING PARTIES' appears in the General Agreement, it means the GATT Contracting Parties 'acting jointly'. Such joint action by the CONTRACTING PARTIES is primarily aimed at the power of the Contracting Parties to interpret the General Agreement by way of (i) decision making, (ii) the adoption of reports of panels and working parties, (iii) chairman's rulings, (iv) action by the GATT Council, or (v) exceptionally, a legal opinion from the GATT Director General, or his representative. *See Analytical Index: Guide to GATT Law and Practice* (6th edn Geneva: GATT Secretariat, 1994) [hereinafter *GATT Analytical Index*] 812. *See* Jackson, *World Trade and the Law of GATT* above n. 60, §5.4., 126-132, where he also lists all the actions that can be taken under what was essentially a broad mandate for action by GATT Contracting Parties.

123 Gerard Curzon, *Multilateral Commercial Diplomacy: The General Agreement on Tariffs and Trade and its Impact on National Commercial Policy and Techniques* (London: Michael Joseph, 1965) 70-107 and Jackson, *World Trading System*, above n. 64, 62-63.

124 Thereupon, a recommendation was made for a standing committee for intersessional business although ultimately governments did not adopt it (GATT Doc. CP.5/SR.25 at 6 (1950)), reported in Jackson, *World Trade and the Law of GATT*, above n. 60, §7.1, 154.

establishment of an *ad hoc* structure to manage the periods between sessions of the contracting parties, although this later took on more permanence.[125]

The situation is very different in the WTO where the procedural norm of multilateralism has been retained and formalised in the *WTO Agreement*. The multilateralism norm underlies every type of decision-making activity undertaken by the Members since potentially every WTO body is a body of the whole.[126] The procedural norm of multilateralism has actually been reinforced and made more coherent through its institutionalisation in the WTO, beginning with the Members' continued adherence to regular meetings of Ministers in its highest decision-making body, the Ministerial Conference.

On the basis of paragraph 1 of Article IV *WTO Agreement*, this policy-making body must meet at least once on a biennial basis not unlike some other major international organisations such as WIPO, the FAO, UNESCO and the ICAO or some of the Conference of the Parties or COPs that are common to multilateral environmental agreements or MEAs.[127] The COPs meet at regular intervals as part of a treaty-management arrangement but also fulfil an important law-making function, which operates through a process of collective decision-making based on consensus.[128] As part of the process of reinforcing the political involvement of Member governments in the WTO, it has been proposed that meetings of the Ministerial Conference be held on an annual basis and be more like annual meet-

125 The 'Ad Hoc Committee for Agenda and Intersessional Business' was established, based on a recommendation in the Second Report adopted by the CONTRACTING PARTIES on 24 October 1951, GATT, CP.6/41 *BISD* Vol. IIS/205-209, at 206 (1952) for the period between the Sixth and Seventh Sessions of the Contracting Parties. Following a revision of the intersessional rules, the Committee became permanent and was known as the 'Intersessional Committee' which, as its names suggests, met between the ordinary sessions of the Contracting Parties; *see* Organizational and Functional Questions, Report adopted by the CONTRACTING PARTIES on 28 February, 5 and 7 March 1955, (L/237), *BISD* 3S/9, 231-252, at 245-247 (1955).

126 *See* chapter I, section 3.2.

127 *See* H. G. Schermers and N. M. Blokker, *International Institutional Law: Unity within diversity* (4th edn rev Boston, Leiden: Martinus Nijhoff Publishers, 2003), §309, 240-241; Robin R. Churchill and Geir Ulfstein, 'Autonomous Institutional Arrangements in Multilateral Environmental Agreements: A Little-Noticed Phenomenon in International Law' (2000) 94 *AJIL* 623-659 at 656. Churchill and Ulfstein draw an analogy between the organisational features under Article XXV GATT 1947 and the Conferences of the Parties or COPs under a range of multilateral environmental agreements or MEA's.

128 Jutta Brunnée, 'COPing with Consent: Law-Making Under Multilateral Environmental Agreements' (2002) 15 *Leiden Journal of International Law* 1-52.

ings of the World Bank/IMF or OECD Ministerial gatherings as a sign of renewed commitment to multilateralism in the multilateral trading system.[129]

By contrast the major interests' norm has also changed in the WTO regime but its further development has been informal in character. The major interests' norm was articulated in the GATT-*era* largely by means of a decision-making process which is known as the 'club model'. In political science terms[130] the club model is a means by which international institutions facilitate co-operation although potentially at the expense of shallow integration. Robert Keohane and Joseph Nye describe the model as allowing a discrete group of States, which are members of the relevant international institution, to work together through established rules and practices and, basing themselves on specific information as to the extent to which governments follow such rules and practices, to focus on 'issue-areas' in terms of clusters of issues.[131]

The club model of decision-making, in the international relations sense, has been particularly prevalent in facilitating multilateral co-operation in single issue regimes in the fields of economic affairs (IMF, GATT) and defence (NATO). It conveniently demarcates the boundaries of subject-matter competence for government officials negotiating agreements within issue-areas and allows members of the club to develop rule to govern those arrangements, supplemented by less obligatory or informal practices.[132] Indeed the latter might include practices,

129 *The Future of the WTO: Addressing institutional challenges in the new millennium*, Report by the Consultative Board to the Director-General Supachai Panitchpakdi (Geneva: World Trade Organization, 2004) [hereinafter *The Sutherland Report*], 69-70, paras. 316-319 with a specific recommendation at para. 320 that Ministerial Conferences of the WTO be held on an annual basis.

130 In economic terms the club model is defined as 'a voluntary group deriving mutual benefit from sharing one or more of the following: production costs, members' characteristics … or a good characterized by excludable benefits'. *See* Richard Cornes and Todd Saddler, *The Theory of Externalities, Public Goods and Club Goods* (2nd edn Cambridge: Cambridge University Press, 1996) at 33-34. Applied to the GATT the overall reduction of tariffs on a MFN basis has been seen as something from which the contracting parties (now WTO Members) can derive exactly such mutual benefit.

131 Robert O. Keohane and Joseph S. Nye Jr., 'The Club Model of Multilateral Co-operation and Problems of Democratic Legitimacy' in Roger B. Porter et al. (eds.) *Efficiency, Equity, and Legitimacy: The Multilateral Trading System at the Millennium* (Washington, D.C.: Brookings Institution Press, 2001) 264-294 at 265.

132 This particular manifestation of traditional international regimes has sometimes been referred to as 'decomposable hierarchies'. They are 'hierarchic' in the sense that particular states become members (one could even speak of hierarchic governments) and 'decomposable' in the sense that membership of those particular hierarchies, and related issues, set them apart from the rest of the regime and allow them to operate without

processes and techniques of a 'soft' law type that are espoused in order to deliberately avoid creating binding obligations.[133]

During the GATT-*era* the major interests' norm was prevalent in the forms of decision-making that were initially undertaken by a relatively small group of States, mostly wealthy industrialised nations, which were able to dictate the pace of developments in respect of decision making and rule making.[134] The club model was a manifestation of the major interests norm that was both informal and highly effective. It proved very convenient for trade diplomats in keeping outsiders at bay because government bureaucracies and officials from other organisations in other issue-areas could be excluded from the informal trade negotiations.

The club model also allowed national political constituencies to be presented with a series of *faits accomplis* with respect to the results of trade negotiations, which made it easier for some governments to manage domestic trade and economic policies.[135] This latter aspect has not been lost on WTO Members. As Kal Raustiala points out,[136] it allows them to deal with difficult policy decisions at the national level by claiming that their State's membership of the WTO effectively ties their hands. He goes on to point out that continued use of the club model actually helps certain governments to enhance their sovereignty at the cost of shallow co-operation.

This may be so but the major interests' norm has undergone further changes in the WTO regime that have arisen from the practice of the Members and, in contrast to the multilateralism norm, are informal in character. The club model has survived even though it has come under challenge. At the same time the club model appears to be less effective in dealing with the complexity of normative and procedural issues that arise from the WTO's burgeoning agenda. The increasing number of 'linkage' issues, such as trade and environment, trade and intellectual property protection, trade and health and safety, or specialised issues such as agricultural or textile trade[137] call for the intervention of policy makers and

close links to other parts of the regime, *ibid.*, at 266; *see* also Herbert A. Simon, *The Science of the Artificial* (3rd edn Cambridge, MA.: MIT Press, 1996) 197-207.

133 *See* above, n. 40 for the use of soft law in order to avoid creating binding obligations.

134 *See* also Charles Lipson, 'The transformation of trade: the sources and effects of regime change' in Krasner, above n. 16, 233-271.

135 Keohane and Nye, above n. 131, 266.

136 Kal Raustiala, 'Rethinking the Sovereignty Debate in International Economic Law' (2003) 6 *JIEL* 841-878.

137 The absence of agricultural trade from the GATT for more than forty years can be partly explained in terms of the success of the club of industrialised states, which sought on protectionist grounds, to remove agriculture as a legitimate target for liberalisation during

officials from government departments other than trade and nowadays affect a broader range of WTO Members than just the industrialised countries.[138]

Yet the club model, as a manifestation of the major interests' norm, continues to attract new supporters in the WTO regime,[139] including countries drawn from the ranks of its critics. A good example is the constant oscillation of groups of developing country Members in the WTO that have not hesitated to embrace the 'club-pattern' on a range of issues that they feel strongly about. The reasons for this are not hard to discern. On the one hand, they remain suspicious of the industrialised country leadership in the WTO, which continues to represent the traditional major interests' norm that was predominant in the GATT. They are also resentful of the club's 'rules', which they had no hand in making but by which they are expected to abide.

This resentment has been compounded in the eyes of many developing and LDC Members by the introduction of a slate of further 'new issues' by a core of developed country Members, involving trade and investment standards, competition rules, labour standards and transparency in government procurement at

the 1950's. The US was the first to successfully negotiate an open-ended waiver for itself under Article XXV:5 GATT, whereby it was exempted from its obligations under the General Agreement, relating to various aspects of its domestic agricultural programme under the Agricultural Adjustment Act (of 1933). Decision of 5 March 1955, *BISD* 3S/32, at 35 (1955); *see GATT Analytical Index*, above n. 122, at 823 and footnote 80 therein. This 'agricultural waiver' led to a virtual exclusion of agricultural trade from the multilateral trading system for close to 40 years.

The development by the European Economic Community (EEC) of its Common Agricultural Policy from the early 1960's onwards marked a similar forum shift for a group of dominant European agricultural exporters from the GATT to the EEC. *See* William A. Dymond and Michael M. Hart, 'Post-Modern Trade Policy: Reflections on the Challenges to Multilateral Trade Negotiations after Seattle' (2000) 34 *JWT* 21-38 at 28. *See* also Rordern Wilkinson, 'The WTO in Crisis: Exploring the Dimensions of Institutional Inertia' (2001) 33(3) *JWT* 397-419 at 405. He makes the same argument with respect to the trade in textiles and clothing, which escaped GATT regulation and instead was made the subject of a series of special arrangements between importing and exporting countries, culminating in the Multi-Fibre Arrangement, or MFA.

138 Even today in such areas as agriculture, trade and intellectual property, technical standards, product health and safety standards arising from the use of sanitary and phytosanitary measures and some service areas, permanent missions to the WTO in Geneva are not necessarily staffed with experts. Instead governments bring in specialists from capitals for key meetings of the TRIPs Council and such Committees as those on Agriculture, Technical Barriers to Trade, Sanitary and Phytosanitary Measures, Financial Services, etc.

139 Keohane and Nye, above n. 131, 269 *ff*.

the First Ministerial Meeting, held in Singapore in 1996.[140] On the other hand, many of these same developing country Members have come to realise that their interests are best served by the club model and are acting accordingly in order to advance their point of view in the WTO.[141] As Keohane and Nye have observed 'developing countries do not want to destroy the club; they want to join it and to have more power within it.'[142]

A tangible sign of this was the vociferous protest by developing countries against use of the small group or 'green room' meeting format,[143] which is used for informal consultations of a select group of WTO Members, particularly at Meetings of the Ministerial Conference, or on the fringes of those Meetings.[144] Not surprisingly the process has often led to controversial outcomes where countries with strong interests on particular trade issues have been excluded, as was the case in Seattle, where the situation exploded for two reasons.

First, during the run-up to the Third Meeting of the Ministerial Conference in Seattle a large number of developing country Members had tabled over half of all the proposals on the draft agenda for the launch of a new MTN. Second, at Seattle itself use of the small group meeting succeeded in excluding many of those developing country Members from building the necessary consensus needed to arrive at a generally acceptable mandate for carrying on negotiations.[145]

As a result of the debacle at the Seattle Ministerial Conference in 1999, for which the aforementioned process was partly to blame, there emerged a new set of separate interest groups and alliances between developing country and/or LDC Members, such as the African Group, led by Kenya or the Group of LDC Mem-

140 All but the introduction of labour standards were placed on the WTO agenda, pursuant to the *Singapore Ministerial Declaration*, adopted at the Ministerial Conference, First Session, Singapore, 9-13 December 1996, WT/MIN(96)/DEC (18 December 1996), paras. 20 and 21.

141 Many delegates, i.e. representatives of Members, see themselves as part of a club and still speak of the WTO in these terms; *see* LeRoy Trotman, 'The WTO: the institutional contradictions' in Mike Moore (ed.) *Doha and Beyond: The Future of the Multilateral Trading System* (Cambridge: Cambridge University Press, 2004), 19-25.

142 Keohane and Nye, above n. 131, 270.

143 The term 'green room' is derived from the use of a conference room, adjacent to the Director General's offices, in the former GATT Secretariat (now WTO Secretariat) building at the Centre William Rappard in Geneva which was painted in this colour, *see* Bernard M. Hoekman and Michel M. Kostecki, *The Political Economy of the World Trading System* (2nd edn Oxford: Oxford University Press, 2001) 60-61.

144 *See* chapter III, section 3.2(b) for a discussion of the use of such informal practices in WTO decision-making.

145 Robert M. MacLean, 'The Lessons of Seattle and the Need for WTO Institutional Reform', Opinion (2000) 6 *IntLR* 1-5 at 1.

bers, which exemplify the continuance of the club model in the WTO. Third, such practices as the small group or green room meeting can lead to a group of Members not being kept properly informed and consulted on proposed deals, as was the case at the failed Fifth Ministerial Meeting, held at Cancún in 2003.[146] Following the failed Cancún Ministerial Conference in 2003, there emerged a Group of 21 (later 20) developing countries led by Brazil, China and India[147] which voiced their anger at being forced to agree to talks on new-issue linkages[148] such as trade and investment in return for a standstill on the removal of agricultural export subsidies by developed country Members.

What is clear is that through the formation of separate blocks or group of country interests under the WTO regime, these developing countries can effectively challenge the major interests' norm and at the same time sustain it. Keohane and Nye believe that while the club model may be continued, it may face new challenges primarily in terms of the sheer numbers of countries involved in the process and the business of effectively organising them.

One of the consequences of the informality of the club model is that this process is subject to new permutations. It continues to attract a proliferation of non-state actors, such as NGO's, producer alliances, consumer organisations, labour unions, firms, business associations and a whole range of civil society organisations, which are not part of the membership but are capable of exerting pressure on individual Members with respect to a whole host of linkage issues. Yet the involvement of many of these groups, alongside old-style trading club

146 *Summary Record of the Ninth Meeting* of the Ministerial Conference, Fifth Session, held at Cancún, 10-14 September 2003, WT/ MIN(03)/SR/9 (closure of the Session of the Ministerial Conference) and adoption of the *Ministerial Statement* of the Ministerial Conference, Fifth Session, held at Cancún, 10-14 September 2003, WT/MIN(03)/20. The requiem for yet another failed Ministerial Meeting is currently being held; *see* 'The WTO under Fire: Why did the world trade talks in Mexico fall apart? And who is to blame?' *The Economist*, 18 September 2003 and Claudia Decker and Stormy Mildner, 'Wo ware der Wille in Cancún: der Fehlschlag der WTO-Ministerkonferenz' (2003) 58 *Internationale Politik* 57-60.

147 The full list of 21 developing countries is as follows: Argentina, Bolivia, Brazil, Chile, China, Colombia, Costa Rica, Cuba, Ecuador, Egypt, Guatemala, India, Indonesia, Mexico, Nigeria, Pakistan, Paraguay, Peru, Philippines, Thailand and Venezuela.

148 *See* for a brief survey of how this process of 'issue linkage' has come about in the GATT/WTO context, through successive GATT MTN rounds, by means of a process of iterated discourse (i.e. repetition), cross-issue (or linkage) bargaining and embedding (or 'nesting') of policy issues within a broader framework of trade, for which, *see* Alvarez, above n. 45. His contribution served as a prologue to a discussion on the reach and scope of the WTO, entitled 'Symposium: The Boundaries of the WTO', published in (2002) 96 *AJIL* 1-158.

members, in a variety of transnational linkages has the potential of undermining the process, possibly through new shifts in the form of transnational-transgovernmental coalitions with trade government officials, pitted against other transnational-transgovernmental networks with different goals and objectives.[149]

Such transnational linkages further have the potential to harness the increasing assertiveness of WTO developing country Members in actions that can lead to far-reaching consequences for the WTO both as a regime and as an international organisation. New organisational forms, which operate both within and outside the membership, add to the complexity of the WTO and may potentially influence both institutional and normative developments.

3.4 Prospects for institutional and normative developments

Based on our reading of the WTO as a regime we may enquire as to what institutional and normative developments might be expected to evolve in the multilateral trading system, based on its transformation from a trade barriers regime to a more complex institutional and regulatory regime? In institutional terms, the WTO regime has been built upon the meagre institutional basis of the former GATT which was effectively only a multilateral treaty with a number of semi-institutionalised arrangements not unlike those that currently exist under various MEAs. Even so, there is a difference between the two. In the case of MEAs the institutions came about by design[150] whereas in the case of the GATT they came about largely in an *ad hoc* fashion.[151]

The decision to create an institutional framework for the results of the Uruguay Round MTN, and the pragmatic fashion in which it was done, sustains the notion that WTO Members simply endorsed the merger of 'a general multilateral law-making treaty into a regime'.[152] One consequence of this development is that while it may provide some continuity between the GATT and WTO, and afford stability and predictability to users of the multilateral trading system, it allows

149 Keohane and Nye, above n. 131, 271.

150 For a description of the commonalties of autonomous institutional arrangements in MEAs, Churchill and Ulfstein, above n. 127, 625-631.

151 Jackson notes that a number of GATT sub-bodies came into being 'without the existence of authorizing provisions ... in the basic treaty', which he considered to be one of the 'interesting structural developments in GATT'. In his view it could even 'be cited as an important precedent in international law for the development of the institutions necessary to carry out a multilateral treaty that makes no provisions for those institutions'; *see* Jackson, *World Trade and the Law of GATT*, above n. 60, § 7.1 at 153.

152 Oscar Schachter, above n. 37, 76.

Members to further entrench their positions in a previously established regime, thereby enhancing their sovereignty at the expense of co-operation.[153] It is worth briefly recalling the reasons for this transition between regimes because they highlight the pragmatism of the GATT contracting parties and help to explain why the WTO members have continued such institutional practices.

The original GATT 1947 treaty text was bereft of institutional provisions since, as noted previously,[154] preparations were under way for the creation of an ITO. Therefore, a simple resolution was adopted to establish an Interim Commission for the International Trade Organization or ICITO.[155] It was charged with preparing the administrative basis for the entry into force of the ITO and was also expected to provide secretarial services for the GATT treaty.[156] At the same time, the ICITO made arrangements with the UN Secretary General regarding its personnel and the benefits, privileges and immunities provided in the Convention on Privileges and Immunities of Specialized Agencies,[157] which were extended to ICITO staff. After the failure of the ITO, GATT Secretariat employees continued to be hired under contracts concluded with the ICITO and their status

153 Raustiala, above n. 136, 860. Similarly, in the context of the European Union, it has been argued that the European Commission has reinforced rather than undermined the authority of national governments; *see* Andrew Moravscik, 'Why the European Union Strengthens the State: Domestic Politics and International Co-operation', Center for European Studies, Harvard University, Working Paper Series #52 (1994); and Susan Strange, 'Why do international organizations never die?' in Bob Reinalda and Bertjan Verbeek (eds.) *Autonomous Policy Making by International Organizations* (London: Routledge, 1998), 213-220, at 218.

154 *See* chapter I, section 2.

155 Final Act of the Havana Conference, above n. 18, UN Doc ICITO/1/4 (1948) at 69. The ICITO later became known as the GATT Secretariat and following entry into force of the *WTO Agreement*, the Secretariat of the GATT 1947 became the WTO Secretariat, Article XVI:2 *WTO Agreement*, *The Legal Texts*, above n. 1, at 17.

156 The First Session of the CONTRACTING PARTIES of the GATT, met in Havana and arrangements were made for secretarial services related to the GATT to be dealt with by the ICITO. Jackson points out that it was simply assumed that the Secretariat of the future ITO would perform the necessary staff functions for operating the General Agreement; *see* Jackson, *World Trade and the Law of GATT*, above n. 60, § 6.1, at 145 and also London Report, First Session of the Preparatory Committee, 1946 at 5 and UN Doc EPCT/C.6/42 at 65 (1947). This was endorsed by the fact that the CONTRACTING PARTIES adopted Rules of Procedure, Rule 15 of which clearly stated that '[T]he usual duties of a Secretariat shall … be performed by the Executive Secretary of the Interim Commission on a Reimbursable Basis', GATT/1/SR.1, 3, 4 (1948) and ICITO docs., especially UN Doc ICITO/EC.2/1-21 (1948).

157 Convention on Privileges and Immunities of the Specialized Agencies (adopted 21 November 1947, *in force* 10 February 1949) 33 *UNTS* 261.

remained unchanged until well after the entry into force of the WTO.[158] Neither the legal position of the Secretariat, nor that of the GATT's chief administrative officer,[159] was ever formally regulated under the GATT trade regime, even though, as Jackson points out,[160] the CONTRACTING PARTIES could have taken a decision to do so pursuant to their general powers under Article XXV:1 GATT.[161]

If this had happened then it would have clarified the legal relationship of the Secretariat to the General Agreement and given the Secretariat 'GATT status'. The permanent GATT Secretariat would then have had more in common with the type of permanent secretariats that have been created under a variety of multi-

158 For a detailed analysis of the ambiguous legal relationship of the ICITO Secretariat to the GATT and the peculiarities of the system of privileges and immunities that were applied to Secretariat officials and representatives (delegates) from contracting parties attending GATT meetings, and granted by the headquarters host country, Switzerland, *see* Jackson, *World Trade and the Law of GATT*, above n. 60, §5.7 at 139-141. *See* also chapter V, section 2.2(d).

159 It was merely provided in Rule 15 of the *Rules of Procedure of the GATT* that the 'Executive Secretary of the Interim Commission' would perform the duties of a Secretariat; *see* UN Doc ICITO/4, at 70 (1948). Sir Eric Wyndam-White was selected by the Havana Conference to head this interim institution and ICITO staff began conducting the functions of a Secretariat for the GATT while making all necessary preparations for the ITO itself, UN Doc ICITO/1/36 (1948).
A pragmatic solution to the problem of the chief administrative officer's institutional status was found by providing for a mere textual amendment in the original GATT provisions, whereby a change in reference was made from the 'Secretary-General of the United Nations' to the 'Executive Secretary to the Contracting Parties', as part of the 1955 Amending Protocol, above n. 62, and in particular Articles XVIII, paragraph 12(e), XXIII, paragraph 2, and XXVI, paragraphs 4, 5(a) and 5(b) GATT 1947, *The Legal Texts*, above n. 1, at 451, 457 and 461. By means of a further decision, taken at the Twenty-second Session of the CONTRACTING PARTIES to the GATT, the title of the chief administrative officer was changed from 'Executive-Secretary' to 'Director General'; *see* Decision of the CONTRACTING PARTIES of 23 March 1965, GATT *BISD* 13S/19 (1965).

160 Jackson in *World Trade and the Law of GATT*, above n. 60, § 6.1, at 146-147, reflected on some of the obstacles to achieving this goal, which included the need to revise the status of privileges and immunities, the problem of staff participation in the UN pension fund, the issue of property with respect to equipment and property at GATT headquarters in Geneva and the indebtedness of the ICITO to the Swiss Government.

161 According to Article XXV:1 GATT, *The Legal Texts*, above note 1, at 460-461 whenever the designation 'CONTRACTING PARTIES' appears in the General Agreement, it means the GATT Contracting Parties 'acting jointly'.

lateral environmental agreements (MEAs) since 1992.[162] This institutional inhibition about granting legal status and specific powers to the Secretariat and its chief administrative officer, i.e. the Director General of the GATT, has persisted to this day. As we noted in chapter I, the *WTO Agreement* does not set out their competences nor define their responsibilities to the organisation other than to state that they are 'exclusively international in character' (Article VI:4 *WTO Agreement*). This fact notwithstanding, a complex set of subsidiary rules and procedures, adopted by the Members in the General Council, combined with informal practices, have been developed within the organisation to regulate the position of the WTO Director-General and the Secretariat.[163]

The inhibitions about developing institutions under the GATT regime extended into other areas too. At the Fifteenth Session of the Contracting Parties of the GATT, a special committee was set up to review the organisational structure of the CONTRACTING PARTIES and to make proposals for its reform. It eventually led in 1960 to the establishment of one of the first formal institutional bodies in the GATT regime – a Council of Representatives, composed of all GATT Contracting Parties that were willing to accept the responsibilities of membership therein.[164] This treaty body eventually became known as the GATT Council and continued in existence until the entry into force of the WTO on 1 January 1995.[165]

162 The different modalities for creating permanent secretariats under MEAs are discussed by Churchill and Ulfstein, above n. 127, at 627-628. *See* also for a more recent development related to the issues involved in creating a permanent secretariat under the older, but still extant, treaty regime of Antarctica, Karen Scott, 'Institutional Developments within the Antarctic Treaty System' (April 2003) 52 *ICLQ* 473-487 at 478-481.

163 *See* chapter V, section 2.2(d).

164 Decision of 4 June 1960, *Establishing the Council of Representatives*, GATT Docs. SR.16/11, at 160; W.16/15 corrigendum 1,2 (1960), reproduced under 'Procedures', sub-heading 'Other Procedures', in *BISD* 9S/7-9, at 8 (1961). *See* Jackson, *World Trade and the Law of GATT*, above n. 60, §7.2, at 154-155. The creation of a Council of Representatives in 1960 was enough for one publicist to state that the GATT was effectively an international organisation. *See* Wolfgang Benedek, *Die Rechtsordnung des GATT aus völkerrechtlicher Sicht* (Berlin: Springer-Verlag, 1990) 248-280.

165 Initially its mandate was to: consider urgent matters between the sessions of the CONTRACTING PARTIES and to make recommendations; supervise the work of committees, working parties and other subsidiary bodies of the CONTRACTING PARTIES operating intersessionally; prepare for sessions of the CONTRACTING PARTIES; and exercise 'such additional functions' … as might be '*expressly delegated* [*sic*] to it by the CONTRACTING PARTIES'. Since the latter included any action on behalf of the CONTRACTING PARTIES (other than under Article XXV:5 GATT – the waiver power) and action 'under decisions and other formal actions taken by the CONTRACTING PARTIES', the way was open for the GATT Council to also consider requests from contracting parties for consultations under Article XXII GATT and for dealing with

The GATT Council enjoyed fairly broad general powers and detailed specific powers,[166] which appear to be more extensive than the powers of its successor the General Council under the *WTO Agreement* but that is mainly because there are a number of subordinate bodies, including three specialist Councils, which report to the WTO General Council.

Other institutional bodies were created on an *ad hoc* basis as the need arose and usually in order to meet certain contingencies. Thus, various committees existed at different times and for different reasons, e.g. the Agriculture Committee,[167] the Committee on Industrial Products[168] and the Cotton Textiles Committee in order to administer the Cotton Textiles Arrangement.[169] Later, after the Tokyo Round MTN, a separate committee in respect of each of the Tokyo Round Agreements was established, composed only of representative of parties to those individual, plurilateral Agreements.[170] Even so some standing bodies were established, the two most important of which were the Balance-of-Payments Committee or BOP Committee and the Committee on Trade and Development, both in response to an ongoing *ad hoc* situation.

The Balance-Payments-Committee under the GATT regime was a typical response to the *ad hoc* practice of the contracting parties whereby contingencies were dealt with as they arose. Meanwhile, the imposition of trade measures for balance of payments purposes was in itself a prime example of what Finlayson and Zacher call the safeguard norm. What is interesting is the way in which decision-making with respect to the sanctioning of the imposition of safeguard

matters involving a nullification or impairment of a benefit accruing to a contracting party under Article XXIII GATT, i.e. for dealing with complaints and their resolution. *See* Decision of 4 June 1960, *Establishing the Council of Representatives*, *BISD* 9S/8 (1961).

166 Jackson, *World Trading System*, above n. 64, 63-64.

167 Originally called Committee II: Agricultural Protection, established by Decision of the CONTRACTING PARTIES of 17 November 1958, *BISD* 7S/27 (1959), it was concerned mostly with agricultural protection and was later superseded in 1967 by another Agriculture Committee in order to examine problems in the agricultural sphere.

168 A Committee on Industrial Products was also established by a Decision of the Council of Representatives in December 1967, pursuant to the conclusions adopted by the CONTRACTING PARTIES on 24 November 1967, *BISD* 15S/67-74 at 69 and 74 in order to explore ways of achieving further liberalisation of international trade.

169 Long Term Agreement Regarding International Trade in Cotton Textiles (adopted 1 October 1962, *in force* 1 October 1962 – 30 September 1967) 471 *UNTS* 296 (1962) and Protocol Extending the Agreement Regarding International Trade in Cotton Textiles, GATT Doc. L/2892 (adopted 1 May 1967, *in force* 1 October 1967 – 30 September 1970).

170 Jackson, *World Trading System*, above n. 64, 76.

measures became increasingly formalised under the GATT and finalised institutionalised under the WTO.

As far back as the Third Session of the Contracting Parties in 1949, it was recognised that some decision-making procedure, involving *ad hoc* consultation, would be needed to deal with (quantitative) restrictions to safeguard balance-of-payments.[171] At the Thirteenth Session of the Contracting Parties in 1958, the CONTRACTING PARTIES established a Committee on Balance-of-Payments and provided both terms of reference and procedures for its continued existence as a standing committee.[172] In the WTO the position of the BOP Committee has been institutionalised and finds its legal basis in Article IV:7 of the *WTO Agreement* in addition to which a special *Understanding on the Balance-of-Payments* provisions was added to the Uruguay Round Agreements,[173] which represents a consensus among Members about the application of such measures, including the need for ongoing consultations and notification.

Developments by the Committee on Trade and Development under the GATT also reveal a deliberate attempt on the part of the contracting parties to formalise an *ad hoc* practice relating to special and differential treatment of developing countries, or what Finlayson and Zacher called the development norm. As a response to the process of decolonisation that began in the late 1950's and an upsurge of new GATT contracting parties, there was a growing realisation that changes were needed in order to advance the interests of developing countries[174]

171 Article XII:4 GATT 1994, *The Legal Texts*, above n. 1, 502. *See* further Jackson, *World Trade and the Law of GATT*, above n. 60, §7.3, at 158.

172 The Committee on Balance-of-Payments Restrictions was established pursuant to paras. 11-16 of a Report adopted by the CONTRACTING PARTIES, on 22 November 1958, GATT Doc. L/931, *BISD* 7S/94-95 (1959).

173 *Understanding on the Balance of Payments Provision of the General Agreement on Tariffs and Trade*, *The Legal Texts*, above n. 1, 27-30.

174 In particular the 1958 Haberler Report, which highlighted the problems that developing countries faced from agricultural protection in industrialised countries, the lack of stability in commodity prices and the effect of regional trading blocs on developing countries, was very influential in the matter. *See GATT: Trends in International Trade: A Report by a Panel of Experts* (Geneva: GATT Secretariat, 1958) (*The Haberler Report*).

At the Thirteenth Session of the GATT a 'Programme of Action Towards Expansion of International Trade' was adopted, *BISD* 7S/27 (1959), leading to the establishment of a GATT Committee III (Trade of Developing Countries) which produced four reports; *see BISD* 8S/132, 135 (1960), GATT *BISD* 9S/120, 144 (1961). Eventually in 1963 a 'Committee on the Legal and Institutional Framework of GATT in Relation to Less-Developed Countries' was founded at the Twenty-first Session of the GATT in order 'to enable the Contracting Parties to discharge their responsibilities in connexion with and this eventually led to the adoption of a new part IV to the General Agreement.[175]

Significant though is the fact that Part IV contained a direction to the Contracting Parties to 'establish such institutional arrangements as may be necessary to further the objectives set forth in Article XXXVI and to give effect to the provisions of this Part'.[176] In anticipation of the entry into force of Part IV, the CONTRACTING PARTIES established the Committee on Trade and Development on 26 November 1964 and assigned to it the tasks contemplated, and set out, in Part IV of the GATT.[177] It remains the only formal treaty-based designation of an institutional body under the entire GATT regime.[178] Just like the Committee on Balance-of-Payments Restrictions, the Committee on Trade and Development has been given a new institutional basis, pursuant to Article IV:7 *WTO Agreement* but it is essentially a continuation of the former GATT Committee on Trade and Development.

The inhibitions, which the GATT regime harboured about developing formal treaty bodies was structural and may have arisen due to the reluctance of States to yield sovereignty, as John Jackson has suggested.[179] Despite the achievements of the Uruguay Round and the institutionalisation of the WTO regime, the practice of the Members once again reveals how reluctant they are to entertain further institutional developments or to engage in the reform of existing ones. A good example of this are the stalled negotiations on reform of the *Dispute Settlement Understanding* and some of the proposals made thus far where Members have demonstrated the desire to reassert political control over the judicial process and to favour less rather than more institutionalisation.[180]

the work of expanding the trade of less-developed countries', with a separate 'Committee on the Legal and Institutional Framework of the GATT in Relation to Less-developed Countries', which drafted a new Part IV to the General Agreement on 'Trade and Development'; *see* Conclusions and Resolutions adopted by Ministers on 21 May 1964, GATT, *BISD* 12S/45-46 (1964).

175 *1964 Amending Protocol*, above n. 63 and a 'Declaration on *De Facto* Implementation' (of Part IV), was opened for signature by those countries wishing to implement Part IV, GATT Final Act 2nd Sp. Sess. 25, *BISD* 13S/10 (1965).

176 Article XXXVIII:2*(f)* GATT, *The Legal Texts*, above n. 1, at 537.

177 *Establishment of the Committee on Trade and Development*, Decision of the CONTRACTING PARTIES, 26 November 1964, *BISD* 13S/75-76 (1965).

178 Jackson, *World Trade and the Law of GATT*, above n. 60, §7.3, at 160.

179 Jackson, *ibid.*, §7.1 at 153.

180 In total 42 proposals for clarification and amendment of the DSU have been taken up in draft legal texts prepared by the Chairman of the Special Session of the DSB,

Finally, there are some *ad hoc* consultative processes that developed under the auspices of the GATT regime, two of which merit our attention because they have either been continued, or are being reconsidered in the WTO context. The first of these is the informal consultative process, which evolved from meetings of 'Heads of Delegation' or HODs[181] of the Contracting Parties to the GATT and never underwent any formal recognition by the CONTRACTING PARTIES. The HODs were largely self-selecting, they sometimes met in private and they represented a special high level body whose actions were then approved by the CONTRACTING PARTIES.[182] The tradition of HODs has been retained in the WTO regime where on a strictly informal, *ad hoc* basis just as it did under the GATT[183] and details of which in relation to decision-making are taken up in the next chapter.[184]

Another consultative process, which was established under the GATT regime but which became institutionalised over time was the creation in July 1975 of an informal steering group, the 'Consultative Group of Eighteen' (CG18).[185] It was established upon the recommendation of the Committee of Twenty Finance Ministers, following the breakdown of the Bretton Woods system. Its membership contained a balance of representatives from Contracting Parties, based on a com-

Ambassador Péter Balas, on his own responsibility in April 2003 and known as the 'Chairman's Text', which was effectively reported to the Special Session of the Dispute Settlement Body in *Report of the Chairman to the Trade Negotiations Committee*, TN/DS/9, 6 June 2003 [*Chairman's Report*]. A revised version of the Chairman's Text, issued on 28 May (Job(03)/91/Rev.1), is appended to the *Chairman's Report*, which has so far failed to yield a single concrete decision with respect to any aspect of the reform agenda.

181 Heads of Delegation or HODs are those government representatives, usually representing their governments at ambassadorial level in the permanent missions to the UN and other international organisations that are based in Geneva.

182 Jackson, *World Trade and the Law of GATT*, above n. 60, §7.3, at 158.

183 In the GATT *era*, it was generally understood that the Heads of Delegations met in 'private, constituting a special high level body whose actions [were] then ratified by the CONTRACTING PARTIES', Jackson, *World Trade and the Law of GATT, ibid.*

184 *See* chapter III, section 3.2 (b).

185 The Consultative Group of Eighteen was established by Decision of the Council of 11 July 1975, GATT Doc. L/4204, *BISD* 22S/15, later confirmed by means of a further Decision of the CONTRACTING PARTIES, 22 November 1979, being the 'Mandate of the Consultative Group of Eighteen', GATT Doc. L/4869, *BISD* 26S/289-290; *see* further *Note by the GATT Secretariat*, 9 June 1987, GATT Doc. MTN.GNG/NG14/W/5.

bination of economic weight and regional representation, with provision for other countries to attend as alternates and observers, or by invitation.[186]

The CG18 was not established in order to challenge the authority of the GATT Council but instead, it provided a forum for senior policy officials to meet and discuss policy issues and to seek to improve the co-ordination of (macro) economic policies. The CG18 usually met and discussed papers prepared by the GATT Secretariat on global economic issues, such as balance-of-payments, related financial matters and the nature and scope of co-operation with the IMF. Upon the conclusion of its meetings, a comprehensive report was submitted to the GATT Council. In 1979, the GATT Council agreed to make the CG18 permanent but it only continued in existence for a further eleven years before being suspended in 1990.[187]

Under the WTO there have been calls for the (re-)establishment of a policy forum, or an executive body, in the form of an executive committee[188] or a 'WTO consultative board',[189] as a means of fostering structural institutional reform in the new organisation. While the Members have thus far failed to respond directly to such a call, in the meantime Director General Dr. Supachai Panitchpakdi has established a Consultative Board, chaired by former GATT Director-General, Peter Sutherland in order to examine the future of the WTO in terms of the institutional challenges that it faces in the new millennium. The Consultative Board has recommended that a senior level consultative body be established, convened by the Director-General, which would meet 2-4 times a year and provide 'political

186 Sylvia Ostry, 'World Trade Organization: Institutional Design for Better Governance' in Robert B. Porter, Pierre Sauvé, Arvind Subramanian and Americo Beviglia Zampetti (eds.) *Efficiency, Equity, and Legitimacy: The Multilateral Trading System at the Millennium* (Washington, D.C.: Brookings Institution Press, 2001) 361-380 at 368; Friedl Weiss, 'WTO decision-making: is it reformable?' in Daniel M. Kennedy and James D. Southwick (eds.) *The Political Economy of International Trade Law: Essays in Honor of Robert E. Hudec*' (Cambridge: Cambridge University Press, 2002) 68-80 at 74.

187 Richard Blackhurst and David Hartridge, 'Improving the Capacity of WTO Institutions to Fulfil their Mandate' in Ernst-Ulrich Petersmann (ed.) *Preparing the Doha Development Round: Challenges to the Legitimacy and Efficiency of the World Trading System*, Conference Report (Badia Fiesole: Robert Schumann Centre for Advanced Studies, EUI, 2004) 233-248 reproduced in (2004) 7 *JIEL* 705-716 at 708-716.

188 Minutes of the meeting of the General Council of 17-19 July 2000, WT/GC/M/57 (14 September 2000), at paras. 132-170. *See* also Jackson, *World Trading System*, above n. 64, 64-65; Ostry, above n. 186, at 369.

189 Richard Blackhurst, 'Reforming WTO decision-making: Lessons from Singapore and Seattle' in Klaus Günter Deutsch and Bernhard Speyer (eds.) *The World Trade Organization Millennium Round: Freer Trade in the Twenty-first Century* (London: Routledge, 2001) 295. Also Blackhurst and Hartridge, above n. 187, 708-716.

guidance to negotiators', i.e. it would be policy-orientated body, along similar lines to the CG18 of the GATT.[190]

4 Conclusions

A reading of the WTO as a regime has allowed us to go beyond the institutional framework set out in the *WTO Agreement* and to take greater account of the underlying dynamics at work in the practice of the organisation. As a consequence we are able to trace the evolution of certain institutional and normative developments in the transformation of the GATT trade regime into the WTO, in particular with respect to a number of informal, unregulated practices, to note what changes have taken place and why, to gain a better insight into the behaviour of the Members with respect to the development and application of substantial and procedural trade norms, and to observe some of the normative and procedural inconsistencies and incoherencies that have arisen in the practice. Finally, regime theory has enabled us to form some opinion about prospective institutional and normative developments in the WTO.

On the basis of this analysis, we can conclude that the WTO is a dynamic and evolving institution, which operates in a more complex regime of norms, decision-making activities and procedures than did its predecessor, the GATT. Its dynamic institutional character derives from the fact that while it remains the principal forum for the negotiation of trade concessions, as laid down in the *WTO Agreement*, the results of the Uruguay Round have led to an expansion of the responsibilities of WTO with respect to their implementation, enforcement and promotion on a normative and institutional level. There have been four notable shifts in this process.

First, the multilateral treaty bodies, which came into existence in an *ad hoc* fashion under the GATT, have been institutionalised in the WTO and take their place alongside and within the hierarchy of new institutional bodies created by the Multilateral Trade Agreements. All of those institutional bodies continue to give effect to the norm of multilateralism, as identified by Finlayson and Zacher with respect to the GATT trade regime, for the following two reasons. One is because almost all those bodies are plenary in character, i.e. *all* Members may be represented. The other reason is the collective decision-making process involving *all* Members in regular bi-annual sessions of the Ministerial Conference

190 *The Sutherland Report*, above n. 129, 70-71, paras. 323-326, with recommendation at para. 327.

or more usually in regular meetings of the remaining WTO bodies, i.e. the Councils and Committees, which is further reinforced by the adoption of decisions on the basis of consensus.

Second, the Ministerial Conference remains the primary forum for rule-making, with a minimum of rule-making activity in the regular sessions of the WTO Councils and Committees. However, there is greater emphasis on monitoring and surveillance of prevailing norms in the rules-based regime of the WTO, where 'peer review' system has been institutionalised in a number of Councils and Committees, for example in the TRIPs Council, through the DSB monitoring of Members' compliance with recommendations and rulings, and by means of the regular scheduled review of Members' trade policies by the TPRB.

Third, the WTO is more actively involved in international policy coordination through its institutional bodies with regular reviews of Members' domestic policies and practices on a range of non-trade barriers and the use of disciplines to counter unfair trade practices involving subsidies, dumping and safeguards, the latter traditionally having been considered as essential elements in the safeguards norm. This has led to the development of elaborate notification processes in order to achieve better international policy coordination and at the same time forms part of the exchange of information between Members, which is designed to enhance transparency and to provide predictability and certainty for trading partners in the multilateral trading system. In this respect, the WTO has evolved from being a treaty management regime, as was the GATT, and has become more of a policy management organisation, with enhanced interaction between the organisation and Member governments.

Fourth, as a result of the increasing number of participating, and to some extent influential, developing countries in the WTO, as compared to the GATT, combined with the thrust of the Doha Development Round agenda, there has been renewed emphasis on granting special and differential treatment to developing country Members as part of the development norm. The process of institutionalisation of this norm began in the GATT with the establishment of a Committee on Trade and Development under Part IV and the adoption of the Enabling Clause Decision at the end of the Tokyo Round but has been given greater prominence with its inclusion in a number of provisions in the Multilateral Trade Agreements and the introduction of technical assistance and capacity building efforts in the WTO.

The prospects for further institutional and normative developments must be read in the light of current WTO practice, which leads to two further conclusions. One is that the practice of the Members reveals their continued adherence to a variety of informal decision-making processes and practices, most noticeably through the club-model and other consultative processes, which continue to give weight to the major interests' norm and this may influence normative developments where the adoption of a decision has normative effect – an issue which is taken up at various points in chapters IV and V. Another conclusion is that Members continue to resort to *ad hoc* measures in order to regulate a particular situation, including the establishment of institutional bodies and procedures for the exercise of their functions as the need arises. This *ad hoc* approach can even extend to informal treaty amendments. The prospects for institutional developments in the WTO cannot be fully appreciated without taking these informal procedures and practices into account and noting the Members' preference for their continued use.

The WTO derives its dynamic normative character from rights and obligations set out in the legal instruments that comprise the results of the Uruguay Round, in particular the scope and breadth of its substantive and procedural norms not all of which were present in the GATT trade regime. However, it also owes much to the formal and informal practices, which the Members have employed in shaping the WTO to their own ends. A number of conclusions follow concerning the normative structure of the WTO based on the changes that have come about as result of its transformation from the GATT trade barriers regime to an institutionalised trade regime.

First, the underlying philosophy of the multilateral trading system has undergone a paradigm shift from one of negative integration in the GATT to positive prescription in the WTO. This shift is characterised by certain Multilateral Trade Agreements, which encourage Members to harmonise existing domestic measures, by bringing them into conformity with international standards as called for under the *SPS, TBT* and *TRIPs Agreements.*

Second, the number of normative decision-making activities has increased in two respects. One is that the Members' task of developing new authoritative treaty rules did not end with the results of the Uruguay Round but has been extended on the basis of built-in-agenda items, as we shall see in chapter IV. The other is that there is an increased amount of rule-making taking place in the WTO in the form of regulatory harmonisation which seeks to strike a balance between the global harmonisation of a range of norms, in the form of principles, rules and standards and the exercise of authority by domestic regulators. This particular normative development is institutionally embedded in a broader network of norms and institutions, which arises from such Multilateral Trade Agreements as the *SPS, TBT* and *TRIPs Agreements,* that incorporate 'by reference' rules and standards found in other treaty instruments and institutional bodies – a process which is taken up in chapter V.

Third, the Members view of normative development still focuses on principal rule-making involving their rights and obligations, which must, in their view, take place in regular negotiating rounds, where reciprocal bargaining concessions can be traded for progress on rule-making. However, this is changing with the introduction of a regulatory process that requires ongoing attention by the Members to the adoption and enforcement of harmonising and mutual recognition measures in order to ensure consistency with their WTO obligations.

The shift in underlying regulatory philosophy of the multilateral trading system from negative integration under the GATT to positive prescription under the WTO suggests the emergence of a new regulatory norm alongside the age old norm of non-discrimination. This poses significant challenges for the WTO in terms of normative developments that have thus far not been addressed in any substantive form by the membership, as will be become evident from the normative analysis in chapters IV and V.

III

DECISION-MAKING

1 Introduction

Decision-making is undoubtedly the most important activity in any international institution since it is the process by which the individual wills of Members are coordinated in a given body of an organisation and become the will of the organisation.[1] In its broadest context it can be understood as any formulation used to conclude debates in an international institution, irrespective of whether the decision is an institutional one or has, or is intended to have, normative effect. This is because there are a whole range of decisions that are taken by institutional bodies in an international organisation, which are informal and more operational in character and are necessary for the orderly functioning of the organisation. However, in the context of this book, the focus in this chapter is on analysing the process of decision-making, which informs and underpins the institutional and normative acts of the WTO.

The following analysis of WTO decision-making is set again the background of frequently heard complaints that the process is ineffective, lacks transparency and legitimacy. Already at the First Meeting of the Ministerial Conference held in Singapore in 1996,[2] there was widespread protest from some Members about the unfair manner of WTO decision-making but arguably it was the Third Meeting of the Ministerial Conference held in Seattle in 1999 that brought matters to a

1 Henry G. Schermers and Niels M. Blokker, *International Institutional Law: Unity within diversity*, (4th edn rev Boston, Leiden: Martinus Nijhoff Publishers, 2003), §703-§704, 491, citing E. Ustor, 'Decision-making in the Council for Mutual Economic Assistance' (1971) 134 *Receuil des Cours* 163-295 at 174.

2 Richard Blackhurst, 'Reforming WTO decision-making: Lessons from Singapore and Seattle' in Klaus Günter Deutsch and Bernhard Speyer (eds.) *The World Trade Organization Millennium Round: Freer Trade in the Twenty-first Century* (London: Routledge, 2001) 295.

head.[3] The WTO was challenged both internally and externally for the manner in which the Members took decisions that were 'undemocratic, non-transparent and accountable to none'[4] and led to questions as to whether the system was 'reformable'.[5] This critique forms part of the discussion on the reform of global institutions, which is being pursued within the broader framework of international (economic) governance[6] and has partially been taken up in the Report by the Consultative Board to the Director General on *The Future of the WTO (The Sutherland Report)*.[7] While it is not the intention to engage fully in the wider debate on international economic governance, since it would take us beyond the scope of this chapter, the protests that have taken place both within and outside the organisation raise questions as to the precise nature of WTO decision-making in practice.

This chapter therefore analyses, by means of a combination of international institutional law and regime theory, the formal and informal practices in decision-making that exist in the WTO, in addition to the general rules on decision-making

3 *See* Jeffrey J. Schott, 'The WTO after Seattle' in Jeffrey J. Schott (ed.) *The WTO after Seattle* (Washington DC: Institute for International Economics, 2000) 3-41; Ignacio Garcia Bercero, 'Functioning of the WTO System: Elements for Possible Institutional Reform'(2000) 6 *IntLR* 103-115.

4 Peter Van den Bossche, *The Law and Policy of the World Trade Organization* (Cambridge: Cambridge University Press, 2005) 141.

5 Robert M. MacLean, 'The Lessons of Seattle and the Need for WTO Institutional Reform' (2000) 6 *IntTLR* 1-5; Garcia Bercero, above n. 3, 104-105; Friedl Weiss, 'WTO decision-making: is it reformable?' in Daniel M. Kennedy and James D. Southwick (eds.) *The Political Economy of International Trade Law: Essays in Honor of Robert E. Hudec*' (Cambridge: Cambridge University Press, 2003) 75-77, relying on Jeffrey J. Schott and Jayashree Watal, *Decision-making in the WTO*, International Economics Policy Brief No. 00-2, Institute for International Economics, Washington, DC, March, 2000 available at http://www.iie.com/publications/pb/pb-002.htm, and Blackhurst, above n. 2, 299 *et seq.*

6 The arguments can be traced to parallel discussions on globalisation, democratic institutions and the legitimacy of international organisations. *See* for example the contributions by Susan Marks 'Democracy and international governance' and G.C.A. Junne, 'International Organizations in a period of globalization: New (problems of) Legitimacy', in Jean-Marc Coicaud and Veijo Heiskanen (eds.), *The legitimacy of international organizations* (Tokyo: The United Nations University Press, 2001) 47-68 and 189-220 respectively.

7 *The Future of the WTO: Addressing institutional challenges in the new millennium*, Report by the Consultative Board to the Director-General Supachai Panitchpakdi (Geneva: World Trade Organization, 2004) [hereinafter *The Sutherland Report*], chapter VII under the heading: 'A results-orientated institution – decision-making and variable geometry' 61-68, paras. 269-311.

as set out in the *WTO Agreement* and other legal instruments. Where possible links are made to relevant decision-making activities and informal decision-making procedures, which existed in the GATT trade regime[8] and which have been continued in the WTO, and notes those instances where such practices have been institutionalised. For the purposes of this chapter III, the term 'decision-making' is understood broadly to encompass the process of arriving at a decision in a WTO institutional body. Chapters IV and V illustrate the point that eventually the normative process is the one by which decisions are formalised, even if they are initially taken elsewhere.

The term 'decision' is also used in the sense in which it is applied in regime theory to include all forms of legally binding and non-binding decisions and even non-decisions (for example the decision *not* to take a decision on a particular matter), provided that such decisions embody the coordination of the wills of the individual Members.[9] This departs from the more common usage of the term in positive law, and in the sense in which it is used in chapters IV and V, whereby decisions of international organisations are defined as 'all the various legal formulations used in concluding debates within international organizations'.[10]

The rest of this chapter proceeds as follows. Section 2 provides a brief summary of the existing WTO rules on decision-making, including such matters as the right of initiative and the formal means of adopting decisions by consensus and/or majority voting. In Section 3 we turn our attention towards two aspects of the practice of WTO decision-making. The first aspect is equality of voting power *versus* parity of interest, i.e. the fact that formally-speaking each Member has one vote but in practice, and in line with our findings in chapter II, the WTO continues to subscribe to the major interests norm which also informs the decision-making process. The second aspect is the myriad of informal, but institutionalised, practices that exist in WTO decision-making, and some of which we briefly noted in chapter II. An example of such informal practices are consultative procedures, which involve either the entire membership, by means of caucuses, alliances and various coalitions, or select groups of members, as is the case with the small room or 'green room' meetings. A further practice that comes under scrutiny is the role of the chairpersons, facilitators and 'friends' in building consensus, as part of the informal decision-making process.

In section 4 we consider issues of internal and external transparency in decision-making, which are at the heart of the debate of governance at the WTO,

8 John H. Jackson, *World Trade and the Law of GATT* (Charlottesville, VA: The Michie Company (The Bobbs-Merill Company, Inc.), 1969) § 7.1, 153.

9 See chapter I, section 3.

10 Schermers and Blokker, above n. 1, §707, 492-493.

in particular the accountability of the organisation. Section 5 briefly examines the form, legal bases and validity of WTO decisions. The subject matter of both sections 4 and 5 addresses the broader issue of the effectiveness of WTO decision-making and its relationship to principal and subsidiary rule-making, which is taken up in the next two chapters of this book. It also raises questions as to the appropriateness of the current decision-making process, the potential for its reform and the likely effect such reform might have on the future of the organisation. In the final section to this chapter, some preliminary conclusions with respect to the decision-making process are presented and discussed in light of their potential impact on normative developments in the WTO.

2 Decision-making rules

WTO rules on decision-making can be found in the organisation's constituent document, i.e. the *WTO Agreement*, primarily in Article IX (entitled *Decision-Making)*[11] and elsewhere in that Agreement as well as the annexed agreements and the various subsidiary rules such as the *Rules of Procedure for Meetings of WTO Bodies*,[12] which provide supplementary conventions applicable to the conduct of meetings of various WTO bodies and sometimes encompass more specific rules on decision-making,[13] the *Procedures for the Appointment of Directors General*,[14] the *Procedures for the Appointment of Officers to WTO Bodies*[15] and even some practices carried over from the GATT such as the *Procedures for*

11 *Marrakesh Agreement Establishing the World Trade Organisation* [hereinafter *WTO Agreement* or *WTO Agreement*] in *The Results of the Uruguay Round of Multilateral Trade Negotiations: The Legal Texts* (Geneva: World Trade Organization, 1999) [hereinafter *The Legal Texts*] 6-18.

12 *Rules of Procedure for Meetings of WTO Bodies*, (Geneva: WTO-OMC, July 1997) [hereinafter *Rules of Procedure for Meetings of WTO Bodies*].

13 For example, the organisation of ballots, the manner in which a vote will be taken at a meeting of one of the WTO bodies, i.e. by roll call or the raising of hands, the means by which consensus will be determined and the action to be undertaken when a decision cannot be arrived at (by consensus).

14 *Procedures for the Appointment of Directors-General*, adopted by the General Council on 10 December 2002, WT/L/509 (20 January 2003).

15 *Procedures for the Appointment of Officers to WTO Bodies*, adopted by the General Council on 11 December 2002, WT/L/510 (21 January 2003).

Negotiations under Article XXVIII.[16] Before describing the rules on decision-making that are taken up in the *WTO Agreement*, we turn to consider how the right of initiative with respect to WTO decisions and the issue of proposals are dealt with in the organisation.

2.1 Right of initiative and proposals

A pre-requisite for any decision-making in international institution is that there should be some form of initiative.[17] This is necessary in order to stimulate discussion and to build 'consensus' or agreement on an issue, prior to the engagement of the formal decision-making process. In the case of the WTO, the right of initiative formally (and exclusively) rests either with individual Members or with the membership as a collectivity, depending upon the subject matter. This can be inferred from language in the *WTO Agreement* where it is stated that: The Ministerial Conference [the General Council in the intervening period] shall have the authority to take decisions on all matters under any of the Multilateral Trade Agreements, *if so requested by a Member* ...[18] An example of this is the right of an individual Member, on the basis of Article X:8 *WTO Agreement*, to 'initiate a proposal to amend the provisions' in either Annex 2 (the *DSU*) or Annex 3 (the *TPRM)* by 'submitting such a proposal to the Ministerial Conference'.

In addition, there are a number of specific instances in the *WTO Agreement* (coupled with provisions in the annexed Multilateral Trade Agreements) where the right of initiative resides with a particular WTO body, i.e. the membership acting collectively. An example of a 'collective initiative' is when the Council for Trade in Goods, on the basis of Article 9 *TRIMs*, following a review of the operation of the *TRIMs Agreement* within five years of its entry into force, 'propose[s] to the Ministerial Conference amendments to its text'.

It should be recalled that there is no provisions in the *WTO Agreement* or any of the Multilateral Trade Agreements, on the basis of which either the Director-

16 *Procedures for Negotiations under Article XXVIII*, adopted by the GATT Council, 10 November 1980 (C/113 and Corr.1), GATT *Basic Instruments and Selected Documents* [hereinafter *BISD*] 27S/26, which form part of the GATT *acquis* under Article XVI:1 *WTO Agreement*.

17 On the right of initiative in the decision-making machinery of international organisations, *see* generally Schermers and Blokker, above n. 1, §710, 494.

18 Article IV:1 *WTO Agreement*, *The Legal Texts*, above n. 11, 8.

General[19] or the Secretariat[20] may explicitly exercise the right of initiative. However, the Director-General and the Secretariat are nowhere denied the possibility of making proposals and in fact this practice exists on an informal basis.[21]

Neither is the possibility excluded that other inter-governmental bodies, non-governmental organisations (NGO's) and various interest groups may bring substantial pressure to bear on Members in order to persuade them to exercise their right of initiative in WTO bodies or to make proposals over matters that may come to form the basis of a WTO decision. While this pressure can only ever be indirectly applied to the actual process of WTO decision-making the increasing outreach of the organisation through a variety of external policy initiatives in the fields of information exchange, technical assistance, capacity building, and so on, increase the number and scope of occasions for the involvement of

19 Contrast this situation with the UN where the Secretary-General may propose items for the agendas of the primary UN bodies, e.g. General Assembly, Rule 13(g); Security Council, Provisional Rule 6, ECOSOC Rule 10; Trusteeship Council, Rule 9, and also for secondary bodies on the basis of the *Rules of Procedure of the Functional Commissions of the ECOSOC* (E/5975), Rule 5. The foregoing is notwithstanding the power of the initiative that the UN Secretary-General enjoys on the basis of Article 99 UN whereby he may 'bring to the attention of the Security Council any matter which in his opinion may threaten the maintenance of international peace and security'. The latter was strengthened by the *Declaration on Fact-finding by the UN in the Field of Maintenance of International Peace and Security*, UNGA Res. 47/59 of 9 December 1991 (17 January 1992). *See* Bruno Simma (ed.) *The Charter of the United Nations: A Commentary* (2[nd]edn Oxford: Oxford University Press, 2002) Vol. II, 1196.

20 Some of the UN specialised agencies recognise a more or less limited right of initiative for their secretariats with respect to certain matters. One example is Article VI:3(a) UNESCO together with Rule 10 of the Rules of Procedures of the General Conference of the Constitution of the United Nations Educational, Scientific and Cultural Organization 1945, as amended, concerning the right of the Director-General (and implicitly that of the Secretariat) to formulate proposals for action by the UNESCO Conference and Executive Board. Another more explicit example is the IMF where some decisions can only be taken upon the initiative of the Secretariat; *see* Joseph Gold, *Voting and Decisions of the International Monetary Fund: an essay on the law and practice of the Fund* (Washington, DC; International Monetary Fund, 1972) 95-97, cited in Schermers and Blokker, above n. 1, §461, 328. *See* also Constantin P. Economides, *Le pouvoir des décisions de organisations internationales européenes* (Leiden: Sythoff, 1964) 70-71.

21 Dencho Georgiev, 'The Decision-making Process in the World Trade Organization', in Kim van der Borght (ed.), with Eric Remache and Jarred Wiener (ass. eds.) *Essays on the Future of the WTO: Finding a New Balance* (London: Cameron & May, 2003) 39. *See* also, Xu Yi-chong and Patrick Weller *The Governance of World Trade: International Civil Servants and the GATT/WTO* (Cheltenham: Edward Elgar, 2004) 264, noting that the influence is usually indirect.

outside influences on the policy making and potentially the rule-making activities of the organisation.

Turning to the decision-making process proper, the two principal means of adopting decisions in the WTO are by consensus and by voting, each of which is discussed in light of the procedural rule, the substance of the decision (and relevant WTO body), with reference to relevant rule in the *WTO* Agreement, as set out in the accompanying table 'Rules on decision-making under the WTO Agreement' (see fig. 2 below).

2.2 Consensus

Under the GATT trade regime the formal rules on decision-making were very basic. Each contracting party had one vote[22] and, except as otherwise provided for decisions were taken by simple majority[23] although in practice the GATT contracting parties usually adopted decisions by consensus.[24] As we shall presently come on to note, that practice has been endorsed by the WTO and reinforced in practice.

22 Article XXV:3 GATT 1994, *The Legal Texts*, above n. 11, 525. *See* Jackson, *World Trade and the Law of GATT*, above n. 8, § 5.2, 122.

23 Article XXV:4 GATT 1994, *The Legal Texts, ibid.*, the two exceptions to the simple majority rule were as follows: one was a general waiver decision, pursuant to Article XXV:5 GATT, which called for a super qualified majority (2/3 majority of the votes cast and such majority had to comprise more than half of the contracting parties) and the other was a decision on the accession of new contracting parties, pursuant to Article XXXIII GATT, which required a 2/3 majority decision of the CONTRACTING PARTIES. Simple majority decisions were endorsed in Rule 28 of the Rules of Procedure, adopted in 1964, which provides that 'Except as otherwise specified in the General Agreement on Tariffs and Trade, decisions shall be taken by a majority of the representatives present and voting', GATT *BISD* 12S/10-16 (1964), containing the most recent consolidated text. *See* also *GATT, Analytical Index: Guide to GATT Law and Practice* (6th edn Geneva: GATT Secretariat, 1994) [hereinafter *GATT Analytical Index*] at 1009 and 1012; also Jackson, *World Trade and the Law of GATT*, above n. 8, § 5.2, 123.

24 Georgiev, above n. 21, 27-29; Friedl Weiss, 'From Havana to Marrakesh: Treaty Making for Trade' in Jan Klabbers and René Lefeber (eds.) *Essays on the Law of Treaties: A Collection of Essays in Honour of Bert Vierdag* (The Hague: Martinus Nijhoff Publishers, 1998) 155-170 at 167.

Fig 2. Rules on decision-making in the WTO Agreement, © M.E. Footer, 2005

Means for adoption of decision	*Procedural rule*	*Substance of decision (relevant WTO body)*	*Provision in WTO Agreement*
Consensus	Continuation of practice of consensus as primary rule	All decisions (Ministerial Conference and General Council, other Councils and Committees)	Article IX:1
Consensus	Mandated consensus	Decisions of the Dispute Settlement Body	Note 3 to Article IX:1 and Article 2.4 *DSU*
		Waiver of obligations subject to transition period (Ministerial Conference)	Note 4 to Article IX:3
		Amendment of Annex 2: *DSU* (Ministerial Conference)	Article X:8
		Addition of a Plurilateral Trade Agreement (Ministerial Conference)	Article X:9
Consensus	Consensus in lieu of voting	Waiver of obligations (Ministerial Conference and General Council)	WT/L/93* in lieu of Article IX:3
		Approval of terms of accession to the WTO (Ministerial Conference and General Council)	WT/L/93*in lieu of Article XII:2
Simple majority	Majority of votes cast	All decisions, except as provided for in *WTO Agreement*/Annexes (Ministerial Conference and General Council)	Article IX: 1
Qualified majority	2/3 majority of Members	Entry into force of amendments	Article X:3, 4 and 5 (part only in relation to *GATS*)
Qualified majority	3/4 majority of Members	Amendments effective for *all* Members	Article X: 3 and 5
		Adoption of interpretations of *WTO Agreement* and other multilateral trade agreements (Ministerial Conference and General Council)	Article IX:2
Super qualified majority	2/3 majority comprising more than 1/2 Members	Financial regulations and budget estimates (General Council)	Article VII:3
Unanimity	Unanimity	Entry into force of certain amendments	Article X:2

* *Decision-making Procedures under Articles IX and XII of the WTO Agreement*, statement by the Chairman, as agreed by the General Council on 15 November 1995, WT/L/93 (24 November 1995).

a) Consensus as a primary rule

The customary practice of consensus decision-making has been continued in the WTO to the extent that it is now understood to be the main means of reaching a decision and can be considered as forming part of the GATT *acquis*, details of which are to be found below. This is reflected in the relevant overview of decision-making under the *WTO Agreement* (see fig. 2 above) where it appears at the top of the chart. The language of paragraph 1 of Article IX *WTO Agreement* specifically endorses the primacy of the consensus principle:

> The WTO shall continue the practice of decision-making by consensus followed under the GATT 1947. Except as otherwise provided, where a decision cannot be arrived at by consensus, the matter at issue shall be decided by voting.[25]

The language of Article IX:1 *WTO Agreement* makes it clear that unless a particular provision calls for a decision by voting, consensus will be used. In other circumstances where a decision cannot be reached by using the primary rule of consensus, then the resort will be made to voting as a fall-back, i.e. voting has a residual character.

Use of consensus decision-making is reinforced by one of the final provisions of the *WTO Agreement* (paragraph 1 of Article XVI *WTO Agreement*), under the heading 'Miscellaneous Provisions', which gives weight to the continuation of a practice that evolved under the GATT. The GATT *acquis*, as it is known, implies that 'the WTO shall be guided by the decisions, procedures and customary practices followed by the CONTRACTING PARTIES to GATT 1947 and the bodies established in the framework of GATT 1947'.[26]

The wording of Article IX:1 *WTO Agreement* is explicit on two points. First, it formally recognises the practice of consensus decision-making[27] at the same

25 Fn. 1 to Article IX:1 *WTO Agreement*, *The Legal Texts,* above n. 11, 11.

26 Article XVI:1 *WTO Agreement*, *ibid*, 17. In *Japan – Alcoholic Beverages II*, Appellate Body Report, *Japan – Taxes on Alcoholic Beverages*, WT/DS8/AB/R, WTDS10/AB/R and WT/DS11/AB/R. adopted 1 November 1996, p. 15 the Appellate Body stressed the importance of this provision in bringing ' ... the legal history and experience under the GATT 1947 into the new realm of the WTO in a way that ensures continuity and consistency in a smooth transition from the GATT 1947 system' and stating that '[A]dopted panel reports are an important part of the GATT *acquis*.'

27 This is not to deny that there has not previously been some formal recognition of the practice of consensus decision-making in the GATT era. *See* for example, the Annex to the 1979 *Understanding Regarding Notification, Consultation, Dispute Settlement and Surveillance*, GATT *BISD* 26S/217 (1980), paragraph 6 (i), which states:

time the practice is institutionalised.[28] Second, the language in the *WTO Agreement* effectively endorses consensus as the primary rule for decision-making in all WTO bodies (Ministerial Conference, General Council, specialised Councils, Committees, sub-committees and working parties) with simple majority voting as the residual rule when consensus cannot be reached. A footnote to the text of Article IX:1 *WTO Agreement* explains the meaning of consensus thus:

> The body concerned shall be deemed to have decided by consensus on a matter submitted for its consideration, if no Member, present at the meeting when the decision is taken, formally objects to the proposed decision.[29]

Used in this sense, consensus refers both to the type of decision-making process[30] and the form which that consensus takes, i.e. it is a process of 'non-objection',[31] which is sometimes known as 'passive consensus'. WTO Members understand passive consensus to mean that unless they object to the adoption of a decision, they agree to it, i.e. silence denotes assent.[32] While it has its origins in GATT

'The report of the Working Party represents the views of all its members and therefore records of different views is necessary. Since the tendency is to strive for consensus, there is generally some measure of negotiation and compromise in the formulation of the Working Party's report.'

28 The formalisation of consensus decision-making is mirrored in the field of international environmental law within the *fora* of international conferences, and more recently, within the Conferences of the Parties or COP's to multilateral environmental agreements or MEA's. *See* Robin R. Churchill and Geir Ulfstein, 'Autonomous Institutional Arrangements in Multilateral Environmental Agreements: A Little-Noticed Phenomenon in International Law', (2000) 94 *AJIL* 623-659. However, neither these processes in the field of international environmental law nor the previous practice under the GATT 'institutionalises' the process of consensus decision-making in the way Article IX:1 *WTO Agreement* does.

29 *See* footnote 1 to Article IX:1 *WTO Agreement*, *The Legal Texts*, above n. 8, 11.

30 Krzysztof Skubiszweski, 'The Elaboration of General Multilateral Conventions and of Non-Contractual Instruments having a Normative Function or Objective, Resolutions of the General Assembly of the United Nations: Provisional Report'(1965) 61 *AIDI* 154-158

31 Karl Zemanek, 'Majority Rule and Consensus Technique in Law-Making Diplomacy' in R.St. J. MacDonald and D.M. Johnston (eds.), *The Structure and Process of International Law* (Dordrecht: Martinus Nijhoff, 1993) 857-887 at 863 and also 872.

32 Shefali Sharma, 'The Decision-making Process and the Single Undertaking', Institute for Agriculture and Trade Policy, paper for Panel on 'Investment in the WTO? Myth and Realities' WTO Symposium, 17 June 2003 at www.nadir.org/nadir/initiative/agp/free/wto/news/0623process_cancun.htm, 3

practice,[33] this form of consensus has much in common with the 'non-objection' procedure, as it has developed in the UN system.[34]

However, consensus can also refer to the type of decision-making process that involves negotiation and conciliation in order to arrive at a compromise position,[35] which is known as 'active consensus'. Used in this sense, consensus is the process that precedes 'formal' consensus decision-making or even initiates it.[36] It can even have a 'fonctionnement doublé' because when combined with words such as 'procedure', 'process' or 'technique' consensus denotes *both* the specific form of decision making and the process of negotiation and compromise in order to reach agreement.

What distinguishes active consensus decision-making from non-objection or passive consensus decision-making is that it allows for the elimination of controversial points by means of negotiation or mediation thereby facilitating wider participation and support for specific action, including law-making,[37] which may

33 *See* the Chairman of the GATT Council, at the Council Meeting held in March 1981 when dealing with a working party report on *EEC-Refunds on Exports of Sugar*. '[I]n his view, consensus was understood in GATT to mean that no delegation maintained its objections to a text or attempted to prevent its adoption.' Discussion of L/5113, Director General's report to the Council on Article XVI:1 discussions on 'EEC-Refunds on Exports of Sugar', adopted on March 10, 1981, GATT *BISD*, 28S/80.

34 The technique of decision-making by 'non-objection', or passive consensus, was purportedly first used at the notorious 19th Session of the UN General Assembly in 1964, during which no votes were taken in order to avoid applying Article 19 UN to the Soviet Union, France and some other States (i.e. where a UN Member is in arrears it is precluded from voting). *See* J. Charpentier, 'La procédure de non-objection (À propos d'une crise constitutionnelle de l'ONU)' (1966) 70 *RGDIP* 862-877; C. Wilfred Jenks, 'Unanimity, the Veto, Weighted Voting, Special and Simple Majorities and Consensus as Modes of Decision in International Organisations' in R.Y. Jennings (ed.) *Cambridge Essays in International Law: Essays in honour of Lord McNair* (London: Stevens & Sons/Dobbs Ferry, New York: Oceana Publications, Inc., 1965) 48-63 at 62.

35 In this broader (deliberative) sense consensus is: '[A] kind of agreement, often loosely formulated, which concludes the deliberations, usually conducted in an organ [of an international organisation] or by a conference'; *see* Skubiszweski, above n. 30, 155.

36 Consensus has also been used in order for an institutional body to be able to commence its work. For example, in 1959 the only way for the UN Committee on the Peaceful Uses of Outer Space, GAOR 1472 (XIV), to be able to function was for the Committee members to continue negotiating draft texts for the peaceful use of outer space until none of them objected to the recording of the results as an agreement. *See* Zemanek, above n. 31, at 862-863, citing Manfred Lachs, *The Law of Outer Space: an experience in contemporary law-making* (Leiden: Sijthoff, 1972) 27-41.

37 Gennady M. Danilenko, *Lawmaking in the International Community* (Dordrecht: Nijhoff, 1993) 277-286.

affect all Members[38] and may substitute for unanimity.[39] In other words, it contributes 'to a genuine consultation and bargaining process' among Members because they are able to express 'their support, opposition and doubts regarding various aspects of the process and [thus] consensus emerges from the discussion'.[40] Where negotiating positions are taken up in international *fora* like the WTO consensus is used as a technique in order to avoid formal voting, which might otherwise divide or alienate certain groups of states, and to move the consensus process forward.[41]

Active consensus lies at the heart of much WTO decision-making and like passive consensus has its origins in the GATT practice.[42] The two forms of consensus complement one another. Since the ultimate aim of consensus is to try and reach agreement on something, the importance of negotiations, as a means of resolving underlying conflicts and moving the process forward, is inherent to the technique and its success.[43] Active consensus allows participants to be able to identify with the result as a whole even where dissent may be registered on

38 Jenks, above n. 34 at 59, where he discusses the use of consensus in the light of the practice of another trade body, the United Nations Conference on Trade and Development (UNCTAD), which was established pursuant to UNGA Res. 1785 (XVII) (8 December 1962) and UNCTAD Final Act (1964) UN Doc E/Conf. 46/141, vols. 6-8. It became an official organ of the UN General Assembly by means of UNGA Res 1995 (XIX) (30 December 1964).

39 Stephen Zamora, 'Voting in International Economic Organizations' (1980) 74 *AJIL* 566-608, at 573-574. Alain Pellet, citing Luigi Condorelli, refers to consensus as a 'kind of bastard unanimity'; *see* Alain Pellet, 'The Normative Dilemma: Will and Consent in International Law-making' (1992) 12 *AYIL* 22-53 at 47.

40 Amrita Narlikar, *WTO Decision-making and Developing Countries*, Working Paper, no. 11, Trade-Related Agenda, Development and Equity' (T.R.A.D.E.) (Geneva: South Centre, November 2001) 7, who discusses the concepts of 'active' and 'passive' consensus in these terms.

41 Van Meerhaeghe, M.A.G. *International Economic Institutions*, (5th edn rev Dordrecht: Kluwer Academic Publishers, 1987) 49; *see* also Barry Buzan, 'Negotiating by Consensus: Developments in Technique at the United Nations Conference on the Law of the Sea' (1981) 75 *AJIL* 325, who distinguishes between *active consensus*, which is used to move the consensus process forward, and *passive consensus*, which he characterises as the 'mere substitution of consensus for voting as a way of making decisions'. His formulation approximates to our observation of consensus as a means of negotiation and compromise as opposed to consensus merely as a means of adopting a decision.

42 Mary E. Footer, 'The Role of Consensus in GATT/WTO Decision-making' (1997) 17 *NorthwJInt'lLBus* 653-680 at 659, 665 and 680.

43 Zemanek, above n. 31, 876.

details.[44] The eventual adoption of a decision by consensus, in the sense of passive consensus, means that Members do not jeopardise any previously agreed positions that they may have reached between themselves and masks any differences that may have existed between them.

A specific type of active consensus that has appeared on the WTO agenda is the notion of 'explicit' consensus, which is a concept that the Members apply to specific subject matter on which no consensus has yet been reached as to whether future negotiations will take place. Its usage dates back to the First Meeting of the Ministerial Conference, held in Singapore in 1996 when, despite opposition from many developing countries, four separate issues – trade and investment, trade and competition, transparency in government procurement and trade facilitation (known collectively as the 'Singapore Issues') – were added to the agenda with one *proviso*. The Singapore text states: 'It is clearly understood that future negotiations, if any, regarding multilateral disciplines in these areas, will take place only after an *explicit consensus* decision is taken among WTO Members regarding such negotiations.'[45]

The language was re-iterated in the text of the Doha Ministerial Declaration, which was issued at the end of the Fourth Meeting of the Ministerial Conference, held in Doha in 2001.[46] WTO delegates understood this to mean that unless there was (prior) approval to negotiate, it was not possible to speak of explicit consensus on the matter[47] and this proved to be the case with respect to the four Singapore Issues, prior to the Fifth Meeting of the Ministerial Conference, held in Cancún in 2003. The insistence of the European Communities' delegation on commencing negotiations for a plurilateral agreement relating to trade and investment, despite the lack of an explicit consensus from the membership to do so, is largely blamed

44 Consensus is '...compatible with objections and reservations, provided, however, that they do not affect major points of the decision to be taken', Antonio Cassese, 'Consensus and Some of its Pitfalls' (1975) 58 *RDI* 754-761, at 754.

45 WTO Ministerial Conference, First Session, Singapore, 9-13 December 1996, *Ministerial Declaration*, WT/MIN(96)/DEC, 18 December 1996 [hereinafter *Singapore Ministerial Declaration*], para. 20, last sentence.

46 WTO Ministerial Conference, Fourth Session, Doha, 9-14 November 2001, *Ministerial Declaration*, WT/MIN(01)/DEC/1, 20 November 2001 [hereinafter *Doha Ministerial Declaration*], para. 20 (relationship between trade and investment), para. 23 (interaction between trade and competition policy), para. 26 (transparency in government procurement) and para. 27 (trade facilitation).

47 Sharma, above n. 32, 3.

for the failure of the Cancún Ministerial Conference.[48] Subsequently in July 2004 Members have reached explicit consensus to start negotiations on one of the other Singapore Issues – trade facilitation[49] – and have accordingly established a Negotiating Group on Trade Facilitation.[50]

b) Mandated consensus

Consensus is called for in a number of *WTO Agreement* provisions, either stand-alone provisions or provisions that must be read in conjunction with the wording of another provision, contained in an annexed agreement. For example, a footnote 3 to Article IX:1 *WTO Agreement*[51] requires that a decision taken by the General Council, when convened as the Dispute Settlement Body or DSB, must be taken in accordance with Article 2:4 *DSU* (see fig. 2 above).[52] The latter provision states that where the *DSU* rules and procedures call for the DSB to take a decision, it shall do so by consensus.[53]

However, WTO practice on decision-making in the field of dispute settlement differs markedly from the practice under the GATT treaty regime. During the GATT era there was an unwritten rule whereby a respondent contracting party

48 Faizel Ismail, 'A Development Perspective on the WTO July 2004 General Council Decision' (2005) 8 *JIEL* 377-404 at 396-398, who also highlights the concern expressed by developing countries about the development impact of new rules on trade and investment and the problem of scheduling a decision on this and other Singapore Issues before agriculture and non-agricultural market access (NAMA) had been dealt with.

49 *Doha Work Programme*, Decision of the General Council of 31 July 2004, adopted at the Meeting of the General Council, 27 and 31 July 2004, WT/GC/W/535 (31 July 2004), [hereinafter *Doha Work Programme Decision*], at para. 1.g. where it is specifically stated that the Members are acting through the General Council and the Council for Trade in Goods, in accordance with paragraph 27 of the *Doha Ministerial Declaration*, and that the General Council has decided by 'explicit consensus to commence negotiations on the basis of the modalities set out in Annex D'; *see Doha Work Programme Decision*, at 3 and Annex D.

50 Ismail, above n. 48, 396-397; the Negotiating Group on Trade Facilitation was formally established at the Meeting of the Trade Negotiations Committee held on 12 October 2004, TN/C/M/14 (2 November 2004) para. 1 at 1.

51 In accordance with footnote 3 to Article IX:1 *WTO Agreement*, *The Legal Texts*, above n. 8, 11.

52 Article 2:4 *DSU*, *The Legal Texts*, *ibid,* 405

53 In clarifying what is meant by consensus, fn. 1 to Article 2:4 *DSU* repeats, almost verbatim, the wording in fn. 1 to Article IX:1 *WTO Agreement*: 'The DSB shall be deemed to have decided by consensus on a matter submitted for its consideration, if no Member present at the meeting of the DSB when the decision is taken, formally objects to the proposed decision.' *See The Legal Texts*, above n. 8, 405.

had the right during any phase of the dispute settlement process, including the request for a panel or the adoption of an adverse ruling, to block a decision that the GATT Council might adopt by consensus.[54] This process of decision-making by consensus has been formalised in the institutional setting of the WTO and currently operates at two levels in the *DSU*.

First, in the matter of panel establishment, where a claimant has notified the DSB that it has requested consultations and these have failed to lead to a satisfactory resolution of the issue within 30 days (Article 4.3 *DSU*), it can bring the matter before the DSB. The DSB must then establish a panel at the second time of asking, i.e. at the latest in the second meeting at which it is tabled on the DSB agenda, unless it 'decides by consensus not to establish a panel' (Article 6:1 *DSU*). This is the ordinary process of consensus decision-making at work, i.e. the process of non-objection.

Second, unless a party to the dispute (complainant, defendant, or both) formally notifies the DSB of its intention to appeal the Panel's report, the DSB moves in its regular meetings to adopt panel reports within 60 days after their circulation to all WTO Members. Where no appeal is lodged then the DSB will adopt the panel report at its next scheduled meeting unless 'the DSB decides by consensus *not* to adopt the report' (Article 16:4 *DSU*). Likewise, an Appellate Body report will be adopted by the DSB and unconditionally accepted by the parties to the dispute, i.e. no further recourse to appeal is available, 'unless the DSB decides by consensus *not* to adopt' it within 30 days from its circulation to the membership, on the basis of Article 17:14 *DSU*.

This is the process of 'reverse' consensus decision-making,[55] which introduces a novel but very effective change into the dispute settlement machinery and which, as Dencho Georgiev has pointed out,[56] virtually ensures automatic approval of panel and Appellate Body reports since the 'winning' party is unlikely to agree that a report in its favour be rejected. It also marks a radical departure from former GATT practice whereby the 'losing' party could effectively block the adoption of a panel report.

54 The continued use of consensus for the adoption of panel reports was specifically endorsed during the Uruguay Round with the adoption in 1988 of the so-called Montreal Mid-Term Review Agreement on *Improvements to the GATT Dispute Settlement Rules and Procedures* wherein GATT contracting parties agreed that: '[T]he practice of adopting panel reports by consensus shall be continued, without prejudice to the GATT provisions on decision-making.'; *see* Rule G.3, GATT *BISD* 36S/61.

55 *See* Georgiev, above n. 21, 31. Sometimes the means of consensus decision-making is referred to in tautological fashion as 'negative' consensus.

56 Georgiev, *ibid.*

In all other instances of decision-making by the DSB the general rule expounded in Article 2.4 *DSU*, i.e. ordinary consensus – most commonly in the form of passive consensus – applies to *all* types of decisions that it may adopt. This includes such matters as the extension of time frames for a panel or the Appellate Body to be able to provide its report for adoption by the DSB (Article 20 *DSU*), issues of implementation of adopted recommendations (of panels) and rulings (of the Appellate Body) (Article 21 *DSU*) and authorization of suspension of concessions or other obligations (Article 22 *DSU*).

On the basis of Article 2.4 *DSU* consensus decision-making even extends to the adoption of the DSB agenda. While the ramifications of this might not appear immediately obvious it has been demonstrated in practice that Members are quite capable of challenging the rule on consensus decision-making when it comes to the implementation of DSB recommendations and rulings and the matter of sequencing.[57] The issue is as follows. Since the *DSU* does not spell out clear procedures for dealing with a disagreement between parties as to whether a DSB ruling has been implemented or not, controversy has arisen as to whether the authorisation to retaliate can be given before the DSB has reached a determination as to whether compliance has taken place, the so-called 'sequencing problem' of Article 21.5 and 22 *DSU*.[58]

As long as negotiations on the clarification of the *DSU* remain stalled, a practice has developed among some Members of concluding bilateral agreements, which interpret the way in which those provisions will be applied to a particular dispute, such that a compliance panel, headed by an arbitrator pursuant to Article 22.6 *DSU*,[59] can make a finding on non-compliance before a party can seek DSB authorisation to retaliate for failure to comply. At least three such bilaterals[60]

57 Sylvia A. Rhodes, 'The Article 21.5/22 Problem: Clarification Through Bilateral Agreements?'(2000) 3 *JIEL* 553-558, at 555-558.

58 Article 21.5 *DSU* and Article 22 *DSU*, *The Legal Texts*, above n. 8, 421-425.

59 Article 22.6 *DSU*, *The Legal Texts*, *ibid*, 422.

60 *See WTO Analytical Index: Guide to WTO Law and Practice* (Geneva: WTO Secretariat/ Bernan, 2003), [hereinafter *WTO Analytical Index*] 1399-14001, where reference is made to three bilateral agreements between (i) the Governments of Malaysia and the United States with respect to implementation of the DSB recommendations and rulings in *US – Shrimp*, Appellate Body Report, *United States – Import Prohibition of Certain Shrimp and Shrimp Products*, WT/DS58/AB/R, adopted 6 November 1998 (notification to the DSB in WT/DS58/16); (ii) Australia and the United States where the two Members agreed to refrain from appealing panel findings in the forthcoming report on *Australia – Automotive,* Panel Report, *Australia – Subsidies Provided to Producers and Exporters of Automotive* Leather, WT/DS126/R, adopted 11 February 2000, under Article 21.5 *DSU*; and (iii) in the cases of *Brazil – Aircraft*, Appellate Body Report, *Brazil – Export*

include agreement to limit procedural objections to the establishment of a compliance panel and the possibility that the DSB will order retaliation in the case of a finding of non-compliance, which might otherwise be blocked through the ordinary consensus process.

A further example of mandated consensus is in footnote 4 to Article IX:3 *WTO Agreement* (see fig. 2).[61] This provision excludes the operation of the normal decision-making rule, whereby a three-fourths majority vote of the Ministerial Conference is required for the grant of a waiver to an obligation imposed on a Member, provided that the waiver in question concerns an obligation that is 'subject to a transition period or a period for staged implementation that the requesting Member has not performed by the end of the relevant period'. In the case of what can best be termed 'a transitional waiver', the decision granting the waiver shall be taken 'only by consensus.'

Arguably, the waiver decisions in respect of each of the EC-ACP Partnership Agreement,[62] the EC-transitional banana tariff quota regime[63] and the decision relating to the implementation by developing country Members of the *Agreement on Trade-Related Investment Measures* or *TRIMs* and other WTO obligations (the so-called *Implementation Decision*)[64] were adopted at the Doha Ministerial Conference by means of consensus because they all concerned matters that were

Financing Programme for Aircraft, WT/DS46/AB/R, adopted 20 August 1999, and *Canada – Aircraft*, Appellate Body Report, *Canada – Measures Affecting Importation of Civilian Aircraft*, WT/DS70/AB/R, adopted 20 August 1999, where the two governments reached identical agreements on the conduct of the proceedings (notification to the DSB in WT/DS46/13 and WT/DS70/9).

61 *See* footnote 4 to Article IX:3 *WTO Agreement*, *The Legal Texts*, above n. 8, 11-12.

62 *European Communities – The ACP-EC Partnership Agreement*, Decision of the Ministerial Conference, adopted on 14 November 2001, at the Fourth Session of the Ministerial Conference, Doha, 9-14 November 2001, WT/MIN(01)/15 (14 November 2001); the first recital of the Ministerial Decision refers only to paragraphs 1 and 3 of the Article IX *WTO Agreement*.

63 *European Communities – Transitional Regime for the EC Autonomous Tariff Quotas on Imports of Bananas*, adopted on 14 November 2001, at the Fourth Session of the Ministerial Conference, Doha, 9-14 November 2001, WT/MIN(01)/16 (14 November 2001); the first recital of the Ministerial Decision refers to paragraphs 3 and 4 of Article IX *WTO Agreement*.

64 *Implementation-related Issues and Concerns*, Decision of the Ministerial Conference, adopted on 14 November 2001, at the Fourth Session of the Ministerial Conference, Doha, 9-14 November 2001, WT/MIN(01)/17 (20 November 2001). This Ministerial Decision unlike the two waiver decision refers to the general decision-making powers of the Ministerial Conference and the specific decision-making powers of the General Council and the Council for Trade in Goods in paragraphs 1 and 4 of Article IV *WTO Agreement* respectively as well as to the decision-making process in Article IX WTO

'transitional' in character, possibly on the basis of footnote 4 to Article IX:3 *WTO Agreement*.[65] However, the lack of specificity in the drafting of the recitals to those transitional waiver decisions, coupled with what we know about the pragmatic nature of WTO decision-making would probably indicate that the Members' preference for consensus decision-making over voting stems from the practical advantage it affords. The use of a qualified majority vote for a waiver or an accession requires that the decision be taken according to the *number* of WTO Members present and voting at the meeting, whereas the use of consensus requires that a decision be taken on the basis of those present at the meeting without regard to the exact number of Members actually participating in the decision-making.

Consensus is also required when amending Annex 2 to the *WTO Agreement*, i.e. the *DSU* itself (see fig. 2 above). As we saw in section 2.1 any Member may initiate a proposal to amend the provisions in the *DSU* by means of a proposal to the Ministerial Conference. It is intended that the actual decision on amendment of the *DSU* will be taken by consensus and that amendments 'shall take effect for all Members upon *approval* by the Ministerial Conference' on the basis of Article X:8 *WTO Agreement*.[66] The provision is unique in that it is the only treaty amending provision in the *WTO Agreement* that calls for a consensus decision whereas all other decisions on amendments must be adopted by qualified majority or unanimity (see section 2.3).

Moreover, *DSU* amendments unlike amendments to other WTO treaty provisions are not submitted to the Members for acceptance and subsequent ratification but 'take effect for all Members upon approval by the Ministerial Conference'.[67] Ironically, this latter aspect, which effectively means that ratification (usually by national parliaments) is not a prerequisite for the entry into force of *DSU* amendments for Members, coupled with the observation by Peter Van den Bossche that

Agreement. *See* below, chapter IV, section 3.3(b) concerning further law-making aspects of this type of decision, as a type of mini-waiver.

65 Footnote 4 to Article IX:3 *WTO Agreement* states: 'A decision to grant a waiver in respect of any obligation subject to a transition period or a period for staged implementation that the requesting Member has not performed by the end of the relevant period shall be taken only by consensus.'

66 Second full sentence of Article X:8 *WTO Agreement*, *The Legal Texts*, above n. 8, 14.

67 *Ibid.* Noteworthy is the fact that Article 64:3 *TRIPs*, *The Legal Texts*, *ibid*, 398, provides for recommendations concerning the lifting or extension of the moratorium on non-violation complaints or their removal altogether from the *TRIPs Agreement* to be taken 'only by consensus' and for those 'approved recommendations' to become 'effective for all Members without further formal acceptance process'.

'[D]ecision-making by consensus gives all Members *veto power*'[68] may go some way to explaining the difficulties that the WTO membership is having with the current *DSU* review,[69] which commenced in 1999 and is still incomplete six years later.[70]

A final example of mandated consensus in the *WTO Agreement* concerns paragraph 9 of Article X *WTO Agreement* (see fig. 2) where the Ministerial Conference, at the request of Members parties to a trade agreement, decides to add an agreement to the list of Plurilateral Trade Agreements in Annex 4. Conversely, where Members are parties to an existing Plurilateral Trade Agreement and they wish to see it terminated, i.e. deleted from Annex 4, then the Ministerial Conference may also decide the matter by consensus, as has happened in practice with two former Tokyo Round Agreements – the *International Dairy Agreement* and the *International Bovine Meat Agreement* – that were continued for a short while after the establishment of the WTO in 1995 before being terminated by the consent of the participating Members.[71]

68 Van den Bossche, above n. 4, 142. The actual 'veto' aspect of consensus decision-making is implicit. It can also be a source of unfairness, as noted by Chayes and Chayes in respect of the former GATT Council practice where a losing party could block the adoption by consensus of a panel report. *See* Abram Chayes and Antonia Handler Chayes, *The New Sovereignty: Compliance with International Agreements* (Cambridge, Mass.: Harvard University Press, 1995) 131.

69 The *DSU* review process was launched in 1999 on the basis of a Ministerial Decision, taken at the end of the Uruguay Round, the *Decision on the Application and Review of the Understanding on Rules and Procedures Governing the Settlement of Disputes*, which in the third recital called for a 'full review' within four years of the entry into force of the WTO, *The Legal Texts*, above n. 8, 465.

70 *See* Report by the Chairman of the Special Session of the Dispute Settlement Body, Ambassador David Spencer, to the Trade Negotiations Committee, TN/DS/10 (21 June 2004), discussed at the Special Session of the Dispute Settlement Body, held on 28 May 2004, TN/DWS/M/19 (17 June 2004) and further comments in chapter IV, section 3.1(b).

71 The *International Bovine Meat Agreement* and the *International Dairy Agreement*, were two Tokyo Round Agreements that continued to exist on the eve of the establishment of the WTO in 1995 but were eventually wound up in 1997, viz. *Termination of the International Bovine Meat Agreement*, Decision pursuant to Article VI:3, IMA/8 (30 September 1997) and *Termination of the International Dairy Agreement*, Decision pursuant to Article VIII:3, IDA/8 (30 September 1997), effective 31 December 1997. Since both of these Agreements were stand-alone treaties the parties in question then proceeded to withdraw by means of formal notification in accordance with Article 67 of the Vienna Convention on the Law of Treaties (adopted 23 May 1969 *in force* 27 January 1980) 8 *ILM* (1969) 689 [hereinafter VCLT].

c) Consensus *in lieu* of voting

There has been further recognition of the preference for consensus decision-making over voting, when WTO Members early on in the life of the new organisation resolved that future decisions on waivers (pursuant to Article IX:3 *WTO Agreement*) and accessions (pursuant to Article XII:2 *WTO Agreement*) could be adopted by consensus instead of being put to a formal vote, as required by Articles IX and XII *WTO Agreement* (see fig. 2). In both instances the normal procedure is for the adoption of decisions on waivers to be carried by a qualified majority of three-fourths of the Members, unless it concerns a waiver related to a transitional period in which case consensus may be used,[72] and for decisions on accessions to be carried by a two-thirds majority of the Members.[73] The statement by the Chairman of the WTO General Council records the Member's agreement in November 1995 on 'Decision-making Procedures under Articles IX and XII of the WTO Agreement',[74] as follows:

> On occasions when the General Council deals with matters related to requests for waivers or accessions to the WTO under Articles IX and XII of the WTO Agreement respectively, the General Council will seek a decision in accordance with Article IX:1. Except as otherwise provided, where a decision cannot be arrived at by consensus, the matter at issue shall be decided by voting under the relevant provisions of Articles IX of XII.

Even so, the use of consensus for decisions on waivers and accession does not preclude a WTO Member from requesting a vote at the time a decision is taken although should such a Member have 'a particular problem with a proposed decision regarding a request for a waiver or an accession to the WTO' then it must ensure its presence at the meeting in which the matter is considered.[75] This residual rule on voting in WT/L/93 mirrors the general one in respect of consensus decision-making which is taken up in the second full sentence of Article IX:1 *WTO Agreement* and is known as the 'qualified consensus' approach.[76] It is

72 Article IX:3(a) *WTO Agreement* and fn. 4 therein, *The Legal Texts*, above n. 8, 11-12.

73 Article XII:2 *WTO Agreement*, *The Legal Texts*, *ibid*, 15.

74 The General Council adopted the decision on *Decision-making procedures under Article IX and XII of the WTO Agreement* at its meeting of 15 November 1995, item 3, WT/GC/M/8 (13 December 1995), section V, pp. 7-8; the relevant decision was issued in the 'L' or Legal Series, as a Statement by the Chairman, WT/L/93 (24 November 1995).

75 *Ibid*., second and third recital of the *Decision*.

76 Paul Szasz, 'Improving the International Legislative Process' (1979) 9 *GaJInt'l&CompL* 519-533 at 529.

commonly found in the rules of procedure of some international conference processes, including those on the law of the sea and environmental resources.[77] It can also be found in some contemporary multilateral treaty bodies,[78] in the constitutions of some other international organisations[79] and, more generally, in the practice of other international economic organisations.[80]

2.3 Voting

In accordance with the wording of Article IX:1 *WTO Agreement*: '[E]xcept as otherwise provided, where a decision cannot be arrived at by consensus, the matter shall be decided by voting.' Implicit in this statement is the notion that consensus is the preferred means for adopting a decision while voting is residual[81] and gives

77 *See* Robbie Sabel, *Procedure at International Conferences: A study of the rules of procedure of conferences and assemblies of international inter-governmental organizations* (Cambridge: Cambridge University Press, 1997) 311, citing the examples of the Rules of Procedure of the Third Law of the Sea Conference, UN Doc A/CONF.62/30/Rev.3 and the Rules of Procedure of the UN Conference on Straddling Fish Stocks and Highly Migratory Fish Stocks (1993) UN Doc A/CONF.164/6, Rule 33. However, he notes that in both instances the words 'general agreement' are used rather than the word 'consensus'.

78 *See* the Rule 40.1 of the Rules of Procedure for Meetings of the Conference of the Parties to the Convention on Biological Diversity (adopted 5 June 1992, *in force* 29 December 1993) (1992) 31 *ILM* 818, which are available at: http://www.biodiv.org/doc/handbook/cbd-hb-03-en.pdf; see also Schermers and Blokker, above n. 1, §779A, 528-529 for discussion of this rule in practice..

79 *See* for example the rules for decision-making of the Conference of the States Parties of the Organization for the Prohibition of Chemical Weapons or OPCW, which can be found in Article VIII.18 of the Convention on the Prohibition of the Development, Production, Stockpiling and Use of Chemical Weapons and on their Destruction (adopted 13 January 1993, *in force* 29 April 1997), (1993) 31 *ILM* 800, cited in Schermers and Blokker, *ibid*, §779, 528.

80 The IMF is a good example of an international economic law organisation that prescribes voting but operates more usually on the basis of consensus; see below at notes 108 and accompanying remarks in main body of text, and also in this respect, Gold, above n. 20, at 195.

81 The GATT 1947 contained few provisions related to formal voting. One such rule concerned the performance of multilateral treaty obligations. A condition of the decision to grant a waiver by the CONTRACTING PARTIES '[I]n exceptional circumstances', including any other conditions that the CONTRACTING PARTIES might wish to attach, was that it be approved by a super qualified majority vote comprising a two-thirds majority of the votes cast, with such majority comprising more than half of the contracting parties. Another was in the matter of accessions to the General Agreement

formal recognition to the continuance of GATT practice where voting was seldom carried out.[82] Paradoxically, the preference for consensus has continued in the WTO despite the fact that the actual number of matters which call for a formal vote have increased in absolute terms. Indeed, this survey would not be complete without briefly naming those instances where formal voting rules exist and ascertaining what type of majority[83] is required in order for a decision to be adopted (and whether a particular quorum is needed in the meeting where the decision is taken) and on what matters majority voting is called for.

We begin with paragraph 1 of Article IX *WTO Agreement*, which establishes the basic principle of equality of voting rights for WTO Members, by stating that where voting takes place in meetings of the Ministerial Conference and the General Council, each Member has one vote.[84] There is no weighted voting[85] as is the case of the IMF and the World Bank although in practice both of these institutions rely heavily on consensus (see section 3.1. below). Were weighted voting ever to be applied in the WTO then it might depend upon the Member's size, financial

(Article XXXIII GATT 1947). Decisions on accessions of new contracting parties had to be taken by a two-thirds majority (Article XXXIII GATT 1947).

82 Weiss, above n. 24, 167-168, where he draws on earlier published work, Friedl Weiss, 'The WTO Dispute Settlement System and the Economic Order of WTO Member States', in Pitou van Dijck and Gerrit Faber (eds.) *Challenges to the New World Trade Organization* (The Hague: Kluwer Law International, 1996) 77-91 at 82 *et seq.*; Jackson, *World Trade and the Law of GATT*, above n. 8, §5.2, 123; and Olivier Long, *Law and its Limitations in the GATT Multilateral Trade System* (London: Graham & Trotman/ Martinus Nijhoff, 1987) 54-55.

83 The trend towards majority rule began in the latter part of the 19th and early part of the 20th century with administrative and technical unions, such as the International Telegraphic Union or ITU and the Universal Postal Union or UPU, *see* Zamora, above n. 39, 574-575 but the battle for majority rule was largely fought out in the League of Nations at the beginning of the last century; *see* Zemanek, above n. 31, 859.

84 The fourth full sentence of Article IX:1 *WTO Agreement* indicates that where the European Communities exercise their right to vote, the number of votes is always equal to the number of their member States. The rule is set out in a footnote to Article IX:1 *WTO Agreement* as follows: 'The number of votes of the European Communities and their member States shall in no case exceed the number of the member States of the European Communities.' *See* the *Legal Texts*, above n. 8, 11.

85 The concept of weighted voting was unknown in the GATT treaty regime. Each contracting party and associated government was required to pay contributions to the GATT budget, based on its share in the volume of foreign trade of the Contracting Parties but those contributions were never linked to an apportionment of votes in the GATT Council, i.e. the plenary session, or general assembly, of the Contracting Parties, nor were they weighted to voting on intersessional committee business (the intersessional committee was the forerunner to the GATT Council).

contribution and/or share of world trade.[86] We return to this issue in section 3 of this chapter, in considering the practice of WTO decision-making and the spurious relationship between equality of voting power and parity of interest.

The table in fig. 2 above provides a systematic overview of the different types of WTO decisions that call for voting, the precise sort of majority decision, as set out in the procedural rule, the substance of the decision and the relevant WTO body for its adoption, as well as the corresponding provision in the *WTO Agreement*.

a) Simple majority

Should voting take place in any WTO body then the general rule is for a simple majority to suffice in order for the vote to carry, just as it did in the former GATT;[87] the rules for the ascertainment of a quorum are set out in the *Rules of Procedure for Meetings of the Ministerial Conference and the General Council (Rules of Procedure for Meetings of WTO Bodies).*[88] Simple majority is understood to mean that, of those Members entitled to vote half plus one are actually recorded as voting (see fig. 2). This is clear from the wording of the last sentence in paragraph 1 of Article IX *WTO Agreement,* which states that '[D]ecisions of the Ministerial Conference and the General Council shall be taken by a majority of the votes cast' unless otherwise provided in the *WTO Agreement* or one of its annexed agreements. It is further endorsed by the quorum requirement in the *Rules of Procedures for Meetings of WTO Bodies*[89] and other secondary procedural rules that endorse the simple majority principle in determining whether a meeting is quorate.[90]

86 Georgiev, above n. 21, 29. *See* Thomas Cottier and Satoko Takenoshita, 'The Balance of Power in WTO Decision-Making: Towards Weighted Voting in Legislative Response' (2003) 59 *Aussenwirtschaft* 171-214.

87 *See* above n. 23 and references therein to the *GATT Analytical Index*, at 1009 and 1012.

88 Rule 16 of the *Rules of Procedures for Meetings of the Ministerial Conference and the General Council*, WT/L/161, in *Rules of Procedure for Meetings of WTO Bodies*, above n. 12, at 3 make it clear that 'a simple majority of the Members shall constitute a quorum'.

89 See for this simple quorum requirement the *Rules of Procedures for Meetings of the Ministerial Conference ..., ibid.*

90 Rule 29 of the *Rules of Procedures for Meetings of the Ministerial Conference ..., ibid,* 5.

b) Qualified majority

Qualified majority voting[91] is called for on WTO decisions involving treaty amendments (other than *DSU* amendments), membership, authoritative interpretations, financial issues and decisions granting a general waiver of obligations. A qualified majority of two-thirds of the Members is required for entry into force of certain amendment decisions (Article X *WTO Agreement*) and for the approval of the terms of accession of new Members (Article XII:2 *WTO Agreement*), which is not surprising since both types of decision substantively affect the basic rights and obligations of Members.

In the case of treaty amendments (other than *DSU* amendments), aside from the potential changes that this might bring in the rights and obligations of Members vis-à-vis one another, there is the additional requirement that Members transform such amendments into domestic law in accordance with their national laws and regulations, which in the case of most Members calls for the amendment to be laid before parliament as part of the ratification process.[92] In the case of accessions, the decision of the Members approving the Protocol of accession of an acceding country records the outcome of a process of bilateral negotiations involving the exchange of reciprocal tariff concessions and services' commitments. The acceding country does not become a Member of the WTO until its Protocol of accession has been accepted by its national authorities (usually by means of ratification), whereupon it will enter into force 30 days later. This is the date upon which membership of the organisation commences and all of the benefits of the commitments previously agreed by the new Member, as part of the bilateral negotiating process, will be extended to the rest of the membership on the basis of MFN.[93]

91 Qualified majority voting can take two forms. Either a 'simple qualified majority' of half or three quarters of those Members entitled to vote are actually recorded as voting, or a 'super qualified majority' where not only must a majority of half or three-quarters of those Members entitled to vote actually be recorded as voting but also the *forum* in which the vote is taken must be 'quorate' according to the voting rules of the *forum*, i.e. half or three-quarters of those Members 'entitled' to vote are actually present and voting at the meeting where the decision is adopted.

92 A WTO Member remains at all times under the obligation to '… ensure the conformity of its laws, regulations and administrative procedures with its obligations as provided in the annexed Agreements' pursuant to Article XVI:4 *WTO Agreement*, *The Legal Texts*, above n. 8, 17.

93 This will differ in the case of services' commitments, pursuant to Article II *GATS*, which allows for MFN exemptions; *see* Article II:2 *GATS* and the Annex on Article II Exemptions, *The Legal Texts*, above n. 8, 329 and 352 respectively.

The normal procedures for the adoption of decisions relating to treaty amendments and for those amendments to become binding on Members are spread throughout Article X *WTO Agreement* and can be divided into substantive and non-substantive amendments, which carry different voting majorities depending on whether they *alter the rights and obligations of the Members*. The WTO follows the basic amending rules contained in Article XXX GATT 1947[94] but the provisions taken up in Article X *WTO Agreement* are far more extensive than under the former GATT. However, as we shall note in chapter IV, the practice of amending the WTO is no easier than that of amending the GATT.

A two-thirds majority[95] is normally required in the case of the following substantive treaty amendments. First, an amendment to the *WTO Agreement* or one of the Multilateral Trade Agreements listed in Annex 1A – Trade in Goods (other than the MFN obligation) or Annex 1C-*TRIPs* (other than the adjustment to higher intellectual property standards in line with other multilateral agreement to which all Members subscribe), which is *of a nature that would alter the rights and obligations of the Members*, on the basis of paragraph 3 of Article X *WTO Agreement.* Second, in the case of an amendment to certain *GATS* provisions found in Parts I and II (other than the MFN obligation of Article II:1 *GATS*) and Part III of *GATS*. All of the foregoing types of substantive amendment take effect for *all* Members 'upon acceptance [i.e. by expressing 'consent to be bound'] by two thirds of the Members' and thereafter for each Member upon acceptance by it,

94 The basic rule under Article XXX GATT 1947, *The Legal Texts*, above n. 8, 531, was that unanimity was required for certain amendments to Part I (containing the MFN obligation and the schedules of tariff bindings) and provisions related to the Havana Charter in Article XXIX GATT 1947. In practice, the increasing difficulty which GATT contracting parties experienced with amending the General Agreement led to the development of 'side codes' during the Tokyo Round and other special arrangements in order to avoid amendments. *See* further John H. Jackson, *The World Trade Organization: Constitution and Jurisprudence* (London: The Royal Institute for International Affairs/Pinter, 1998) 44.

95 The growth of quasi-legislative international treaty instruments, often doubling as the constitutional basis of an international organisation, together with the increasing number of states becoming Members of a range of international organisations made it almost impossible to achieve unanimity for amending purposes. Consequently the amending clauses of many constitutions of international organisations and their related instruments, as in the case of the former GATT and current WTO, were normally adopted by a majority of two-thirds of the votes cast at a conference or similar plenary session of the Members, called especially for that purpose. *See* in detail, Egon Schwelb, 'The Amending Procedure of Constitutions of International Organizations' (1954) 31 *BYIL* 49-95, with particular reference to the amending provisions of the ILO and UNESCO and Article 108 and 109 UN.

on the basis of paragraphs 3 and 4 of Article X *WTO Agreement*. It should be noted that for *all* Members, the acceptance or consent to be bound process, must be followed by ratification of the amending instrument, by whatever means is prescribed in their national laws and regulations.

A two-thirds majority is also required in the case of the following non-substantive treaty amendments. First, where a decision of the Ministerial Conference to submit a treaty amendment to the Members for acceptance, i.e. consent to be bound, cannot be reached by consensus within a period of 90 days (or longer if the Ministerial Conference so determines) then, in accordance with a qualified majority procedural rule, Members *shall* decide by a two-thirds majority (Article X:1 *WTO Agreement*). Second, in the case of (a) non-substantive amendments to the *WTO Agreement* or one of the agreements listed in Annex 1A or Annex 1C (minus the aforementioned exceptions), which would *not* alter the rights and obligations of the Members, or (b) an amendment to Parts IV, V and VI of *GATS*, such treaty amendments take effect for *all* Members 'upon acceptance by two-thirds of the Members' on the basis of paragraphs 4 and 5 of Article X *WTO Agreement*, which effectively means that the minority can be bound by the majority of Members expressing their consent to be bound.

Finally, a two-thirds majority is required in respect of decisions taken by the Ministerial Conference approving the terms of accession of new Members (Article IX:2 *WTO Agreement*). Actual WTO practice reveals that the Members have only ever voted once and this was with respect to the accession of Ecuador in 1995.[96] Subsequently, all accession protocols containing the agreement on the terms of accession of new Members have been adopted by a decision, which refers to the statement of the Chairman of the General Council back in 1995, who noted that Members normally adopt decisions on accessions and waivers by consensus, by

96 *Accession of Ecuador*, Decision of the General Council, adopted on 16 August 1995, WT/ACC/ECU/5 (22 August 1995). The Decision states that the accession of the Republic of Ecuador is in accordance with Article XII *WTO Agreement*, with footnote 1 recording the fact that Decision was 'adopted by the General Council by a two-thirds majority'. *See* also WT/ACC/ECU/6, which takes note of the General Council decision and informs Members that the Protocol of Accession (annexed as *Protocol for the Accession of the Republic of Ecuador to the Agreement Establishing the World Trade Organization*) is open for acceptance in the Office of the Director of the Accessions Division, Room 2079. In fact a postal ballot was necessary for Ecuador's accession because the meeting of the General Council at which a vote should have been taken was inquorate – it would have needed two-thirds of the Members present and voting at the meeting to satisfy the rule in Article XII:2 *WTO Agreement* in conjunction with Article X:3 *WTO Agreement*; *see* Lorand Bartels 'The Separation of Powers in the WTO: How to Avoid Judicial Activism' (2004) 53 *ICLQ* 861-895 at 864-865.

what may be termed the 'WT/L/93 process' that foresees the practice of consensus decision-making *in lieu* of voting (see section 2.2 (c) above).

A three-fourths majority is required in the following instances. First, and with reference to what can also be termed substantive treaty amendments under paragraphs 3 and 5 of Article X *WTO Agreement*, the Ministerial Conference can decide by a majority of three-fourths of the Members that any amendment under the amending provisions in those paragraphs are *of such a nature* that any Member, which has not accepted such amendment within a period specified by the Ministerial Conference, shall be free to withdraw from the WTO or alternatively to remain a Member but only with the consent of the Ministerial Conference; a provision that has thus far not been used.

Second, a qualified majority of three-fourths of the Members is required for the adoption of a decision by either the Ministerial Conference or the General Council, pursuant to Article IX:2 *WTO Agreement*, which contains an authoritative interpretation of a provision in the *WTO Agreement* or in one of the Multilateral Trade Agreements.[97] This interpretative power is not only 'exclusive' to the Ministerial Conference and the General Council but also binds the Members, at least on the internal plane. The importance of an authoritative interpretation is underscored by the additional wording in this provision that emphasizes that this power should not be used in a manner which would undermine the amending power of the Article X *WTO Agreement*.[98] This provision can be read effectively as a prohibition on *détournement de pouvoir* by the organisation's highest body or the Members acting collectively.

Finally, the *WTO Agreement* calls for a super-qualified majority in the adoption of financial regulations[99] and the annual budget (see fig. 2 above). The second paragraph of Article VII *WTO Agreement* specifically states that '[T]he General Council shall adopt the financial regulations and the annual budget estimate by a two-thirds majority comprising more than half of the Members of the WTO'. However, once again the established practice of the organisation demonstrates that Members normally do not vote on such matters but adopt all such decisions

97 If it concerns the authoritative interpretation of a provision in one of the Multilateral Trade Agreements in Annex 1 – Trade in Goods, Trade in Services of TRIPs, then the Ministerial Conference or the General Council shall exercise on this power on the basis of a recommendation from the WTO body overseeing the functioning of the relevant Agreement; *see* second full sentence of paragraph 2 of Article IX *WTO Agreement*, *The Legal Texts*, above n. 8, 11.

98 Final sentence of paragraph 2 of Article IX *WTO Agreement*, *ibid.*

99 *Financial Regulations of the World Trade Organization*, Committee on Budget, Finance and Administration, WT/L/156 (5 August 1996), as revised WT/L/156/Rev.1 (21 November 2003).

by consensus, including changes to the requirement that the Director-General present an bi-annual budget estimate to the Committee on Finance, Budget and Administration or BFA Committee instead of an annual one.[100]

c) Unanimity

When it comes to the application of the rule on unanimity, the WTO largely follows the rules laid down in the GATT. In the case of the General Agreement, Article XXX GATT 1947 called for the unanimous decision of the Contracting Parties in changing Part I of the GATT, i.e. the MFN obligation under Article I as well as the tariff bindings under Article II (and the related tariff schedules), Article XXIX GATT 1947, regulating the relationship of the General Agreement to the Havana Charter, which subsequently became a dead letter, and Article XXX itself.[101] In the case of the WTO, unanimity is reserved for decisions relating to certain amendments to Article IX *WTO Agreement*, which is the decision-making provision in the organisation's constituent charter, and any proposal to amend the MFN obligation in respectively Articles I and II of *GATT 1994*, Article II:1 of the *GATS* or Article 4 of the *TRIPs Agreement*. This is specifically laid down in paragraph 2 of Article X *WTO Agreement*, in which it is stated that any such amendments shall only take effect 'upon acceptance by *all* Members', i.e. the entire membership must give its consent to be bound by such amendments (see above fig. 2).

100 *See* Minutes of the Meeting of the General Council held on 25, 26 and 30 August 2003, WT/GC/M/82 (13 November 2003), para. 2 at 1-2, adopting the proposal of the BFA Committee, WT/BFA/W/105/Rev.1; for further details of the implications for treaty amendment of this decision by consensus by a WTO institutional body, *see* chapter IV, section 3.1(b).

101 The GATT 1947 provisions relating to unanimity had more to do with the still prevalent belief in the post-war period that a multilateral convention expressed the common will of States parties to it and therefore required their common will to amend it and owed much to the way in which international trade was previously organized along bilateral lines. *See* Jackson, *World Trade and the Law of GATT*, above n. 8, § 3.6, at 73 and Zamora, above n. 39, 579.
Thus in 1947 it was decided that: '[T]he General Agreement is a trade agreement and the rule in ordinary trade agreements is that they "can only be modified with the unanimous consent of the parties taking part in them", *Report of the Second Session of the Preparatory Committee of the United Nations Conference on Trade and Employment: Tariff Committee* (Geneva, April-October, 1947), UN Doc EPCT/TAC/PV/15, p. 6 *et seq.*, reported in *GATT Analytical Index*, above n. 23, 931. It would appear that the WTO Members have been reluctant to abandon this notion.

3 Practice of decision-making

While the *WTO Agreement* and its related annexes provide the formal legal and constitutional bases for the adoption of decisions by the Members, the reality of WTO decision-making is somewhat different. In the following two sections, we turn our attention to the practice of decision-making, beginning first with an assessment as to how and why the formal rule on equality of voting power does not offer the same guarantees as the use of consensus, which is essentially because consensus decision-making better reflects Members' interests, in particular the major interests' norm that underpins the GATT/WTO regime.[102] We then turn our attention to the various informal practices that have evolved in the WTO, some of which have their origins in the GATT multilateral trading system, and all of which bear the hallmarks of the continuance of the former GATT trade regime.

3.1 Equality of voting power *versus* parity of interest

While the principle of one-member one-vote, as set out in Article XI:1 *WTO Agreement*,[103] appears to place all WTO Members on an equal footing and suggests a degree of egalitarianism in decision-making,[104] it masks the actual practice of WTO decision-making which favours powerful majorities or parity of interest. The fact is that the Members never vote on anything. Instead, WTO practice follows that of the GATT where consensus is used to try and accommodate as many countries as possible but importantly gives 'weight to the views of countries that have power in the trading system'. John Jackson has even suggested,[105] in light of GATT practice, that consensus may allow for the symbolic preservation of economic power in the absence of weighted voting such as is common to both the IMF[106] and the World Bank.[107] This statement calls for

102 See chapter II, sections 3.1 and 3.3.

103 In many other international institutions, especially those in the UN system, the principle of one member one vote or OMOV is often combined with equitable geographic distribution or EGD representation, which dates back to a 1965 decision of the UN General Assembly where it was used in order to elect six Vice-Presidents to help manage the expanding UN.

104 Narlikar, above n. 40, 1-2 and 6

105 Jackson, *World Trade and the Law of GATT*, above n. 8, § 5.2, 123.

106 The IMF allocates votes, or quotas, subject to a five-yearly general review by the Board of Governors (Article III, Section 2(a) Fund Agreement), based on a mathematical formula with several variables in order to determine relative economic strength. This ensures that weighted voting power in the respective organisations reflects the relative

clarification since both the Board of Governors and the Executive Directors of the IMF and the World Bank frequently resort to the use of consensus instead of voting when taking decisions.

In the case of the IMF the use of consensus by its Board of Governors[108] may mitigate the effects of weighted voting.[109] This is because the IMF Executive Directors know that they have sufficient votes to carry an issue if it were put to a vote and therefore they may support, by means of consensus, a position adopted at a meeting of the Board of Governors. In that case the absence of a formal vote simply reinforces the underlying balance of economic power, which is implicit in weighted voting organisations. In practice the Executive Directors usually avoid voting wherever possible, instead preferring to take decisions by consensus for the same reasons as in the WTO and that is because the process of consensus decision-making depends upon and better reflects the underlying power relationships of the Fund Members.[110]

In the case of the World Bank the practice of taking decisions by consensus rather than by a vote in meetings of the Board of Governors and the Executive Directors is a well-established practice that goes back to the very inception of the World Bank and reflects a preference for informality. The usual means of adopting a decision in both World Bank bodies is for the chairman to 'ascertain the sense of the meeting'.[111]

So how does the practice of decision-making differ, if at all, in the case of the GATT/WTO multilateral trading system where weighted voting has never

economic strength of the individual IMF Members (Article XIII, Section 5 Fund Agreement).

107 The World Bank also recognises a system of weighted voting; Article V, Section 3 Articles of Agreement of International Bank for Reconstruction and Development. Other regional development banks have followed suit, *viz.*, the Inter-American Development Bank (IDB), the Asian Development Bank (ADB) and the African Development Bank (AfDB). *See* Zamora, above n. 39, 576-578 and Zemanek, above n. 31, 859-860.

108 Rule C-10 of the *Rules and Regulations of the Board of Governors of the IMF* states that: '[T]he chairman shall ordinarily ascertain the sense of the meeting in lieu of a formal vote'. Rule C-10 adopted September 25, 1946, amended September 18, 1969 and April 1, 1978 in *By-Laws, Rules and Regulations*, (43rd issue Washington, D.C: International Monetary Fund, 1986) 23.

109 Van Meerhaeghe, above n. 41, 49.

110 J.E.S. Fawcett, 'The Place of Law in an International Organisation', (1960) *BYIL*, 321-342 at 328 and 331, cited in Charles H. Alexandrowicz, *The Law-Making Functions of the Specialised Agencies of the United Nations* (Sydney: Angus & Robertson in association with the Australian Institute of International Affairs, 1973) 136-137.

111 *See* Andrés Rigo Sureda, 'Informality and Effectiveness in the Operation of the International Bank for Reconstruction and Development', (2003) 6 *JIEL* 572-576.

existed? Very little it would seem. In the former GATT, even when there were relatively few contracting parties[112] and most were industrialised countries with relatively homogenous trading interests, the practice soon emerged among the contracting parties of not voting but instead of allowing the chairman of the meeting, at which a decision was adopted, to determine that a consensus had been reached.[113] The preference for consensus decision-making has clearly been continued in the WTO and institutionalised. Arguably, the GATT/WTO system has not needed weighted voting when consensus appears to have worked effectively. This may be explained on the following grounds which trace the evolution of consensus decision-making from the GATT to the WTO.

First, the practice of consensus decision-making in the GATT was (and still is in the WTO) informal in nature[114] and stemmed from a practice commonly found in international relations of an issue having been negotiated to consensus outside the meeting in which the formal decision was taken.[115] This separate 'consensus-building' went on, as it does today, in corridors and lobbies outside the main meeting where only delegates participate but where it is possible for various interested parties, networks and alliances, such as corporations, producers' alliances, consumers and NGO's, to influence the proceedings. In this way, practical recognition was afforded to issues of power in deliberations and to vital trading interests among GATT contracting parties – a situation which remains unchanged in the WTO.

Second, the informality of consensus decision making under the General Agreement meant that all GATT contracting parties, even those that were considered to be *de facto* contracting parties, could 'participate without regard for

112 Only 23 countries were original signatories to the GATT 1947 although a further 13 States acceded to the GATT by means of the 1949 Annecy and 1951 Torquay Protocols. By the time of the Dillon Round in 1962 the total of GATT contracting parties numbered 43.

113 An example of an early GATT meeting, where the Chairman took the sense of the meeting, is in a 1953 Report of the Working Party on 'Arrangements for Japanese Participation'. It was noted that 'the CONTRACTING PARTIES do not usually proceed to a formal vote in reaching decisions; generally, the Chairman takes the sense of the meeting...' G/55/Rev.1, adopted on 23 October 1953, *BISD* 2S/117, at 118, para. 4, *GATT Analytical Index*, above n. 23, 1014.

114 In GATT, the practice of using consensus remained unwritten until 1982 when it gained some formal recognition in paragraph (x) of the Ministerial Decision: '[T]he CONTRACTING PARTIES reaffirmed that consensus will continue to be the traditional method of resolving disputes...' Thirty-eighth session at Ministerial level, *Ministerial Declaration* adopted on 29 November 1982, Doc. L/5424, *BISD*, 29S/13 (1983)

115 Jackson, *World Trade and the Law of GATT*, above n. 8, § 5.2, 123.

their formal lack of vote'.[116] The situation is not dissimilar in the WTO although *de facto* Members do not exist but perhaps have been replaced by the group of 30 or so countries seeking accession, which while they have no 'voting' rights as non-Members, may attend all meetings, take part in all discussions and be present when a decision is adopted by consensus.

Third, consensus decision-making then, as now, was open to the making of a large number of explanatory statements by the presiding officer (GATT) or by the Chair (WTO) who announced that consensus had been reached. The role of Chair in the overall decision-making process can be pivotal, especially if the Chairperson manages to steer the agenda – an issue to which we return when discussing the increase in informal decision-making practices (see section 3.2). Moreover, building on a practice that was established under the GATT trade regime, it has become an increasingly common practice in various WTO bodies for Chairman's statements[117] and Chairman's notes to be issued at the time a decision is adopted, which reflects the views of certain Members or a group of Members.

Fourth, consensus decision-making held out the possibility that no numerical superiority of any group of states could dominate the process, as might be the case through the one-member one-vote or OMOV and equitable geographical distribution or EGD systems of voting but at the same time gave procedural significance to variations in economic power and status among GATT contracting parties, and this still applies in the case of WTO Members. Put differently, it articulates best the major interests' norm that we noted in the previous chapter.

Fifth, consensus decision-making is often held out to be a good means for conducting negotiations among states in treaty regimes like the GATT/WTO where law-making decisions are the intended outcome because it maintains 'an egalitarian procedure which in practice may assure that multilateral negotiations reflect the real geopolitical power of the participating nations'.[118]

Despite the popularity of consensus decision-making over voting for all of the above reasons, what we observe today is that many Members, most of them former GATT contracting parties, consider the process of consensus decision-making to be flawed. It can lead to the adoption of decisions taking the lowest common denominator into account or the decision *not* to adopt a decision which

116 Jackson, *ibid* and also § 4.4, 95.

117 For the influence of Chairman's Statements on the treaty amendment process, see chapter IV, section 3.1(b).

118 Jonathan Charney, 'United States Interest in a Convention on the Law of the Sea: The Case for Continued Efforts' (1978) 11 *VandJTransnatL* 43.

may even result in paralysis on occasions.[119] Due to the fact that consensus is a non-objection process and any Member can veto a decision, its continued use in the WTO means that at times it resembles the process of unanimity. Not surprisingly, various suggestions have been made for reform, including the introduction of a weighted voting system.

One such proposal is that of Thomas Cottier and Satoko Takenoshita, who have examined the feasibility of weighted voting at the WTO in order to promote more efficient decision-making for inter-round legislative responses and authentic interpretations of existing treaty provisions.[120] Using economic theory and relying on an intricate method of calculation, combined with a number of variables and formulae, they have produced a template for what they believe to be appropriate weighted voting for groups of Members.

A similar approach is that of the 'critical mass' where Members agree to refrain from blocking consensus where a critical mass of them support a proposed change. The critical mass would be assessed on the basis of an overwhelming majority of Members in the forum adopting the decision and/or taking into account their overall trade weight, such as 90% of total share of world trade, or a combination of both factors.[121] A variation on this is a recommendation contained in *The Sutherland Report*[122] that a Member considering blocking a measure, which otherwise has the very broad consent of the membership, can only do so if it declares this in writing, with reasons included, and its action pertains to a vital national interest.

However, this runs counter to the major interests' norm that underlies consensus decision-making in GATT/WTO practice. While the critical mass approach has proven to be a good process of decision-making for negotiations on tariff reductions and the scheduling of services' commitments, initially involving only a few Members but with the results ultimately benefiting the entire membership on the basis of MFN,[123] it is considered to be inapplicable for general rule-

119 Georgiev, above n. 21, 33.

120 Cottier and Takenoshita, above n. 86,

121 John H. Jackson, 'The WTO "Constitution" and Proposed Reforms: Seven "Mantras" Revisited' (2001) 4 *JIEL* 74-74.

122 *The Sutherland Report*, above n. 7, 64, paras. 287 and 289.

123 The process has been endorsed in the WTO, for participating Members, by means of the scheduling of improved or additional concessions or commitments, following further sectoral negotiations on the liberalisation of telecommunications, financial services and labour mobility, *see* chapter IV, section 3.1(c), and the scheduling of the elimination of all customs duties and other charges on information technology products in accordance with the plurilateral *Agreement on the Expansion of Trade in Information Technology*

making, as experience with the GATT Tokyo Round Codes[124] and other attempts at rule-making in the WTO testify.[125]

Besides, the issue of reform of the decision-making process is not quite so straightforward in practice. Members generally perceive consensus to offer more legitimacy than majority voting, if only because the decisions are adopted collectively.[126] Paradoxically, the process of consensus decision-making also allows individual Members to prevent the adoption of decisions by means of collective action in various WTO bodies if those decisions might be unfavourable to their interests.[127] In other words, consensus can operate as a veto, thereby giving Members a sense of controlling the process on an individual basis while acting collectively.

Complex mathematical formulae on which weighted voting is worked out or the critical mass approach fail to take into account such subtleties and the GATT *acquis* on consensus decision-making. The issue is of particular significance when applied to decisions related to the modification of existing rules or the development of new ones, as we shall see in chapter IV, and which may affect the outcome of law-making processes. There is no doubt that the process of consensus decision-making calls for reform but the introduction of weighted voting, even allowing for certain flexibilities, or the use of a critical mass approach, is unlikely to win the day and is no guarantee that more successful decision-making will come about as a result of it. Even in other international economic organisations like the IMF and World Bank where it is supposedly used, formal rules on weighted voting have given way to the practice of consensus decision-making. Why is this so? This is because consensus decision-making for all its flaws sustains the delicate balance between equality of voting power and parity of (economic) interest among the Members. It is therefore unlikely to yield easily to proposals for a radical

Products or *Information Technology Agreement*, pursuant to the Singapore Ministerial Declaration of 1996, for which *see* chapter I, section 3.2.

124 Georgiev, above n. 21, 34-36.

125 An example where a rule-making forum has failed to achieve any critical mass among the Members is the TRIPs Council in its attempts to evaluate the scope and modalities for non-violation complaints in disputes under the *TRIPs Agreement,* pursuant to Article 64 *TRIPs* and paragraphs 1(b) and 1(c) of Article XXIII *GATT 1994;* whereas the United States and Switzerland are broadly in favour of non-violation complaints a critical mass of the Members favour its abolition of an extension of the moratorium on bringing such complaints in the dispute settlement system, on the basis of Article 64:2 *TRIPs*.

126 Van den Bossche, above n. 4, 148.

127 Georgiev, above n. 21, 33.

overhaul in the form of weighted voting or indeed any other form of representation that might restrict Member participation.[128]

3.2 Informal practices

In this section, we turn our attention to the myriad of informal practices, which exist in WTO decision-making and which continue to exert a considerable influence over the process.[129] These are the practices or usages by which Members discuss debate and negotiate issues in order to arrive at consensus, prior to the formal adoption of a decision; they are distinct from the means by which a decision is adopted, i.e. by consensus.[130]

The practice of informal consultations operates at every level of decision-making in the organisation[131] and this is even recognised on the WTO website where it is stated:

> Informal consultations in various forms play a vital role in allowing consensus to be reached, but they never appear in organization charts… They are necessary for making formal decisions in the councils and committees.[132]

Some informal consultations potentially involve the entire membership of the WTO, for example the meetings of the Heads of Delegations or HODs of Members (and Observers) to the WTO.[133] Informal HODs meetings take place all the time, whenever there is an issue that Members wish to consult on, outside of an official meeting of a WTO body or a negotiating body. These meetings are open to the

128 *See* the comments made by the former Bulgarian Ambassador to the WTO, Dencho Georgiev, *ibid*, 40, with respect to proposals for abandonment of the 'green room' or small group process, in favour of a consultative body, based on various criteria for representation.

129 Sharma, above n. 32, 3.4.

130 Richard Blackhurst and David Hartridge, 'Improving the Capacity of WTO Institutions to Fulfil their Mandate' in Ernst-Ulrich Petersmann (ed.) *Preparing the Doha Development Round: Challenges to the Legitimacy and Efficiency of the World Trading System*, Conference Report (Badia Fiesole: Robert Schumann Centre for Advanced Studies, EUI, 2004) 233-248 reproduced in (2004) 7 *JIEL* 707-716, at 708.

131 For a discussion of the place of these consultative processes in the former GATT trade regime and their continuance in the WTO, see chapter II, section 3.3.

132 *See* under the heading: 'Whose WTO is it anyway?' under the sub-heading: 'HODs' and other bods: the need for informality' at http://www.wto.org/english/thewto_e/whatis_e/tif_e/org1_e.htm.

133 Sharma, above n. 32, 1.

entire membership but usually involve senior officials and/or diplomats, assigned to their government's Permanent Mission to Geneva or coming from capitals, particularly if the meeting has been called to discuss an issue that requires specialist knowledge or expertise. It is quite common for the Director-General (and sometimes the Chair of the General Council or one of the other Councils or Committees) to be party to these informal consultations and to help steer the discussions.

Informal meetings of the HODs are usually open-ended, i.e. participants take part on the understanding that the process may lead to consensus-building but that it is not the intention to adopt decisions, since this is the prerogative of Members in the formal meetings of WTO bodies. A good example is the informal HOD meeting held on 13 September 2003, during the Cancún Ministerial Meeting.[134] At that meeting the four co-sponsors of the cotton initiative drew attention to the proposal, which had been made by Benin, Burkina Faso, Chad and Mali on 'Poverty Reduction: Sectoral Initiative in Favour of Cotton' (the 'Sectoral Cotton Initiative'). This Sectoral Cotton Initiative called for specific measures to be taken concerning trade in cotton, including the complete elimination of export subsidies over a period of three years, and the elimination of production-related domestic support over a period of four years, as of 1 January 2005.

The actual decision concerning the Sectoral Cotton Initiative, while being dealt with at various meeting of the General Council throughout the remainder of 2003 and part of 2004 was formally adopted as part of the Doha Work Programme Decision of 31 July 2004.[135] The decision included the establishment of a new subcommittee on cotton, reporting to the Special Session of the Committee on Agriculture, which in turn is charged with reviewing progress on negotiations on cotton subsidies as part of the broader issue of agricultural subsidies.

Smaller group meetings are also a commonly used device to reach consensus. We turn first to consider the use of caucuses and alliances in the process of deliberation, before reviewing the so-called small group or 'green room' meetings process and the role of chairpersons and facilitators in building consensus.

134 *Statement by Benin on Behalf of the Four Co-Sponsors of the Sectoral Initiative in Favour of Cotton*, to the General Council of 21 October 2003, WT/GC/74 (10 November 2003); for details of the function of 'Heads of Delegations' or HODs meetings of the Contracting Parties to the GATT, John Jackson, *World Trade and the Law of GATT*, above n. 8, §7.3, 157-158.

135 *See Doha Work Programme Decision*, above n. 49, para. 1.b and relevant sections in Annex A thereto.

a) Caucuses and alliance building

It has been commonplace both in the GATT and the WTO for countries to form groups and alliances in order to speak with one voice on a particular issue of concern to a number of contracting parties or Members. The actual process of consensus-building may focus around a single spokesperson or a common negotiating team. From its inception the GATT witnessed a number of geographical groupings, some of which represented regional economic integration initiatives whereas others were simply groups or alliances of neighbouring countries with historically close economic and trade ties. Examples of the former include the most far-reaching type of closer economic integration – the European Communities, which began as a customs union (European Economic Community or EEC) with a single external tariff and its own tariff schedule but has since become an original Member of the WTO[136] – to looser, less formal types of economic integration such as the Association of South East Asian Nations or ASEAN.[137] Examples of the latter include the Nordic group of countries, which regularly operated as an alliance under the GATT trade regime but has now largely disappeared in the WTO as a result of Denmark, Finland and Sweden's membership of the European Union. Another well-known alliance, which is neither a geographical nor a neigh-

136 Legally speaking it is the European Communities and not the European Union that is a Member of the WTO pursuant to Article XI *WTO Agreement*, see chapter I, section 3.4 with respect to membership issues. The trade policy of the 25 Members of the European Union, which for WTO purposes make up the European Communities, is coordinated in Brussels and Geneva. It is the European Commission that takes the lead in most day-to-day WTO matters, negotiating on behalf of and speaking for the European Communities on all matters within the scope of the European Communities' competence under Article 133 of the Treaty of Rome (the European Commission does so under the guidance of the Article 133 Committee). At WTO meetings it is usual for the 25 Members to sit together with the spokesperson for the Commission thereby reinforcing the notion of a regional economic grouping speaking with one voice.

137 The ASEAN consists of the following WTO Members Brunei Darussalam, Cambodia, Indonesia, Malaysia, Myanmar, Philippines, Thailand and Singapore. Two other members – Laos and Viet Nam – are in the process of joining the WTO. It is usual for the ASEAN countries to speak with a single voice, with the role of spokesman rotating among its Members.

In principle MERCOSUR, which is the Southern Common Market consisting of Argentina, Brazil, Paraguay and Uruguay, with Bolivia and Chile as associate members, also acts as an alliance in WTO trade matters but in practice it does not always speak with a single voice at Geneva-based meetings.

bour alliance, is the Cairns Group of countries,[138] which was established just prior to the Uruguay Round in 1986 and can best be characterised as a functional or sectoral alliance since its all its Members have a specific interest in the full liberalisation of agricultural trade. The Cairns Group has been extremely active since its foundation, including during the current agricultural negotiations in the Doha Development Round.

To this we can add a new wave of groups and alliances that have come into being in the WTO and are focused around specific initiatives, which reflect common interests, and may be tied into proposals for rules and disciplines in new areas such as investment competition, geographical indications in the field of *TRIPs,* amendment of the *DSU* or the non-trade aspects of agricultural trade reform. The coalitions that result from such groups and alliances are 'variable, changing and sometimes even not very clearly delineated'.[139] They should be distinguished from other groups, similarly without a formal status in the WTO that are formed around specific criteria such as regional, political or functional issues.[140] Examples of the latter include the African Group, the Group of Least-Developed Members or LDC Group, the African, Caribbean and Pacific Group or ACP Group, the Group of Latin American and Caribbean Members and, most recently since the Fifth Meeting of the Ministerial Conference, held in Cancún in 2003, the Group of 20. Jeffrey Schott goes so far as to note that deliberations among Members have become the 'subject of intense coalitional politics that were unknown in the GATT era when the United States and the European Community were the hegemonic powers' and have led to the need for alliance building by issue, by region or by groups of developing countries.[141]

These groups or alliances of Members perceive such consensus building practices as useful (and no doubt of crucial importance) in increasing their bargaining power in negotiations with larger, more powerful economic trading partners or in getting specific items onto the agenda in the first place but equally for their success in preparing and adoption decisions in the ordinary course of WTO business.[142] Just as groups and alliances of WTO Members can be formed to

138 Named after the Australian city where the first meeting of the group was held, the Cairns Group currently consists of Argentina, Australia, Brazil, Canada, Chile, Colombia, Fiji, Indonesia, Malaysia, New Zealand, Paraguay, Philippines, South Africa, Thailand and Uruguay.

139 *See* Georgiev, above n. 21, 38.

140 Georgiev, *ibid.*

141 Jeffrey J. Schott, 'The WTO after Cancún', paper prepared for the Conference on Sustainable Development in the WTO: Trade, Investment and Environment after Cancún', RIIA, 23 February 2004, 2.

142 Georgiev, above n. 21, 38.

adopt common positions in attempt to arrive at a consensus, they can also be formed in order to create compromise or to break a deadlock.

While it is difficult to gauge the overall impact of groups and alliances on WTO policy-making and rule-making because their composition undergoes frequent change and their existence may be ephemeral, there is evidence to support the view that they are becoming increasingly influential, as has recently happened with respect to the Sectoral Cotton Initiative in July 2004 and throughout 2003 with respect to various proposal made by the African Group and the LDC Group in the ongoing *DSU* reform process.[143]

b) Small group and 'green room' meetings

One of the problems with the use of consensus in formal meetings of WTO bodies is that Members often fail to adopt a decision and in some cases, consensus acts as a veto (see above, section 2.2.). This is where small group meetings may be used to bring the diverse views of some 148 Members together and to reach consensus ahead of the adoption of a formal decision by a WTO body, particularly the higher level councils, including the General Council. Small group or green room[144] meetings belong to this genre.

The informal practice of green room meetings during GATT years formed part of a consultative process by which self-selected developed countries and a representative from a set of developing countries – some twenty to twenty-five or so delegations at any one time – met and discussed proposals or negotiating agendas, with the active participation of and input from the Director General.[145] Richard Blackhurst describes the 'inner circle/green room' process in the GATT (and now the WTO) in order to stimulate discussion and consultation among small

143 *See* for example *Negotiations on the Dispute Settlement Understanding*, Proposal by the African Group, TN/DS/W/15 (25 September 2002) and *Negotiations on Improvements and Clarifications of the Dispute Settlement Understanding* – Communication from Mexico to the Dispute Settlement Body, Special Session, LDC Group, Special Session, TS/DS/W/17 (9 October 2002).

144 For the origin of the term 'green room', *see* chapter II, fn. 143. This is a reference to a conference room, adjacent to the Director General's offices, in the former GATT Secretariat (now WTO Secretariat) building at the Centre William Rappard in Geneva. Georgiev also draws attention to the fact that the term 'greenroom' on the English stage was a 'back-stage' room that was usually reserved for actors to receive visitors and has led some Members to characterise green room meetings as 'back-stage encounters'; *see* Georgiev, above n. 21, fn. 39 at 40.

145 Weiss, above n. 5, 76.

groups of participants, as the 'concentric circles model'.[146] He notes that it usually comprises '[A]n issue specific inner circle of members varying in number ... depending on whether the topic is narrow and of interest to only a few members, or broader and of interest to a large number of members'. Whatever the issue and the number discussing it, the results of decisions taken in a green room meeting are then conveyed to the wider membership for adoption of a consensus decision,[147] based on the recommendations of the more restricted concentric circles of the Membership.

One of the hallmarks of the sheer informality of the process is that no objective basis for participation in such meetings exists although traditionally it is the most active countries, with an interest in the outcome of a particular trade matter, that take part. In the past it has been usual for a number of developed countries (including the 'Quad', composed of the US, EC, Canada and Japan) together with Australia, New Zealand, Switzerland, Norway and one or two middle to large-ranking developing countries, such as Argentina, Brazil, India, which have always played a significant role in shaping GATT policy and rule-making, to be the main participants in green room meetings.[148]

There was even a point in 1975 when a consultative body – the so-called Consultative Group of Eighteen or CG18[149] – was established on a 'temporary' basis by the contracting parties to the GATT in order to deal with the major countries' desire for an issue-orientated consultative body', made up primarily of senior officials from capitals.[150] During its existence it could be said to have had something of a 'critical mass' character, given that the CG18 frequently represented a majority of the contracting parties, the overall trade weight of which was in excess of more than 90% of total share of world trade and thus of considerable influence to the multilateral trading system. However, the CG18 was used for thrashing out specific policy issues and building consensus around them but

146 Blackhurst, above n. 2, 299.

147 Blackhurst, *ibid*; Friedl Weiss, 'Globalization through WTO Integration: Neither Friend nor Foe' (2003) 30 *LIEI* 95-102 at 101.

148 Markus Krajewski, 'From *Green Room* to *Glass Room: Participation of Developing Countries and Internal Transparency in the WTO Decision Making Process'* (Berlin, TradeWatch, July 2000) 8-11.

149 The Consultative Group of Eighteen was established by Decision of the Council of 11 July 1975, GATT doc. L/4204, *BISD* 22S/15, later confirmed by means of a further Decision of 22 November 1979, GATT doc. L/4869, *BISD* 26S/289; *see* further *Note by the GATT Secretariat*, 9 June 1987, GATT doc. MTN.GNG/NG14/W/5.

150 Blackhurst, above n. 2, 302-303. The recently published *Sutherland Report*, above n. 7, 70-71, paras. 323-327, has suggested that a consultative body be established along similar lines to the CG-18; see also chapter II, section 3.3.

was not a decision-making forum. Despite becoming a permanent body in 1979, which effectively institutionalised this particular consultative body under the former GATT, the CG18 was eventually wound up in 1990.[151]

The green room process continued to operate throughout the GATT era and is still present in the WTO where it used less frequently and has undergone a change of name to 'small group meetings' due to the bad connotations which the term 'green room' conjures up for some Members.[152] It is also important to note the difference between Ministerial green rooms, such as those which gave rise to so much controversy at the First Ministerial Conference, held at Singapore in 1996 and the failed Third and Fifth Meetings of the Ministerial Conference, held at Seattle in 1999[153] and Cancun in 2003,[154] and ordinary green room meetings, held on WTO premises in Geneva. The former included informal meetings of restricted groups of Ministers while the latter are held at ambassadorial level in the WTO, at the initiative of the Director-General.[155] Currently, up to forty delegates can participate in such small group meetings although the average number is about twenty and the range of informal consultations has been extended to the regular WTO bodies in the form of committees and working parties at all levels of the organisation.

The small group meetings process has also been reinforced in recent years by the appearance of regional mini-ministerials and other regional meetings. Mini-ministerials are informal meetings held in advance of the biennial Ministerial Conference, sometimes on the fringes of a Ministerial meeting in another economic forum such as the OECD, in order to take stock of ongoing negotiations if an MTN is in progress and/or to discuss specific trade issues with a view to preparing participating Members for the forthcoming Ministerial Conference.

While the small group meeting, or former green room, process is seen by some Members, particularly developing countries, and many outsiders as secretive,

151 For details, see chapter II, section 3.4.

152 Sharma, above n. 32, 9.

153 *Summary Record of the Eighth Meeting* of the Ministerial Conference, Third Session, held at Seattle, 30 November – 3 December 1999, WT/MIN(99)/SR/8 (14 January 2000) (adjournment of the Session of the Ministerial Conference).

154 *Summary Record of the Ninth Meeting* of the Ministerial Conference, Fifth Session, held at Cancún, 10-14 September 2003, WT/ MIN(03)/SR/9 (closure of the Session of the Ministerial Conference) and adoption of the *Ministerial Statement* of the Ministerial Conference, Fifth Session, held at Cancún, 10-14 September 2003, WT/MIN(03)/20.

155 Blackhurst and Hartridge, above n. 130, 711-713

unrepresentative and lacking transparency,[156] particularly following the debacle of the Third Ministerial Meeting held in Seattle in 1999,[157] the membership does not seem in a hurry to change things. Despite periodic proposals to reform 'the hegemonic or parochial green room process',[158] for example by establishing a 'WTO executive committee' or 'WTO consultative board'[159] with a membership based on shares of world trade in order to better manage the WTO agenda, no progress has been made to date and is unlikely to as long as Members consider it in their interests to belong to the small group meeting process. This issue forms part of the discussion as to possible reform of the WTO's institutional structure,[160] including the decision-making and consultative processes, which are taken up in the overall conclusions to this book.

c) Chairpersons, facilitators and 'friends'

Although Members are responsible for decision-making in the various WTO bodies, the overriding importance of informal practices in the organisation also means that Chairpersons can play an important role in the consensus-building process at all levels.[161] The Chairpersons of WTO Bodies, from the General Council down to the smallest Committee are filled by delegates, drawn from the membership, on the basis of annual rotation with particular attention being paid to trying to achieve some sort of regional parity in appointments, although this is not the same thing as the equitable geographical distribution or EGD system which can be found in other, UN-based international institutions.

While the *Rules of Procedure for Meetings of WTO Bodies*[162] set out the formal functions of the Chairperson as to the conduct of meetings there are a number of practices surrounding the role of the Chair (and to some extent the Secretariat) in such bodies which can have a decisive influence on decision-

156 Former Indian Ambassador to the WTO, B. Lal Das, 'Why the WTO decision-making system of "consensus" works against the South', available at www.twnside.org.sg/title/bg13-ch.htm.

157 Georgiev, above n. 21, 40. Hartridge in Blackhurst and Hartridge, above n. 130, 711, does not see the Seattle Ministerial Conference as a turning point on this issue.

158 Weiss, above n. 5, 76.

159 Richard Blackhurst, above n. 2, 303-308 and also more recently Blackhurst and Hartridge, above n. 130, 708-710.

160 *See* the insightful comments by David Hartridge in Blackhurst and Hartridge, *ibid,* 715-716 and more recently, *The Sutherland Report*, above n. 7, 72, para. 333-335, especially at para. 335.

161 Sharma, above n. 32, 3.

162 *Rules of Procedure for Meetings of WTO Bodies*, above n. 12.

making. We have already noted that neither the Director-General nor the Secretariat enjoy any formal right of initiative in WTO decision-making (see section 2.1) but the very fact that this is not explicitly regulated has not deterred (former) Director-Generals[163] (and Deputy Director-Generals)[164] as well as Secretariat staff[165] and Chairpersons[166] acting under their own responsibility, from launching initiatives and tabling proposals for consideration by the broader membership.

It is also the Chairperson who usually decides whether certain issues will be discussed separately, whether personnel from the Secretariat should be included and who will intervene at critical moments when there is deadlock in a meeting of a Council or a Committee. Chairpersons can thus structure discussions in order to facilitate mutual understanding among Members or to find a compromise.[167] In short, as Georgiev states: '[I]n spite of the absence of formal substantive powers in the process of decision-making the chairpersons of WTO bodies and the Secretariat have considerable means to influence this process'.[168] Consideration of the particular significance and value of decisions taken by Members in various

163 *See* for example the role of former GATT Director-General, Arthur Dunkel in moving the stalled Uruguay Round negotiations forward when he produced the 'Dunkel Draft' or *Draft Final Act Embodying the Results of the Uruguay Round of Multilateral Trade Negotiations*, GATT Doc. MTN.TNC/W/FA (Dec. 20, 1991), which was subsequently tabled at the Brussels meeting in 1992 and eventually led to the successful conclusion of those negotiations based on this text.

164 *See* the role of former WTO Deputy Director-General, Miguel Rodriguez Mendoza on the *Proposal for Circulation and Derestriction of WTO Documents*, WT/GC/W/464 (7 December 2001) which he drafted following informal consultations with Members and which was subsequently presented to the General Council for adoption at its meeting of 18 and 19 July 2001, WT/GC/M/66 (10 August 2001), para. 95 *et seq*. *See* also *Proposal for Circulation and Derestriction of WTO Documents*, Revision, WT/GC/W/464, Rev. 1 (6 May 2002) adopted by the Members in the Meeting of the General Council on 13-14 May 2002, WT/GC/M/74 (1 July 2002), para. 16 *et seq*. Reported by Georgiev, above n. 21, 39.

165 *See* the increasing role of the Secretariat in drafting (and refining) chairman's texts that form the basis for negotiation during an MTN and in some negotiating *fora* under the built-in agenda items of certain Multilateral Trade Agreements, e.g. the *General Agreement on Services* or *GATS*; see further Xu and Weller, above n. 21, 264-267.

166 *See* the role of the Chairman of the Special Session of the DSB, Ambassador Péter Balas, who acting under his own responsibility, in April 2003 produced a draft text for reform of the *DSU*, known as the 'Chairman's Text'. It was reported to the Special Session of the Dispute Settlement Body in *Report of the Chairman to the Trade Negotiations Committee*, TN/DS/9, 6 June 2003, and included a revised version of the Chairman's Text issued on 28 May as Job(03)/91/Rev.1, appended to his report.

167 Georgiev, above n. 21, 39

168 Georgiev, *ibid.*

WTO bodies, based on 'Chairman's Statements' and 'Chairman's Texts', when seeking to amend treaty provisions and to develop secondary rules are considered in chapters IV and V.

In addition to the ordinary role of Chairpersons in decision-making, two new phenomena have appeared on the scene in the form of facilitators and 'friends', both of which have led to significant improvements in consensus-building among Members as part of the overall decision-making process. Facilitators were specifically used in seeking to overcome difficulties that Members had with a decision on the appointment of a new Director-General in 1999[169] and in getting developing country Members to agree to the inclusion of specific issues on the Doha Development Agenda at the Fourth Ministerial Meeting held in Doha in 2001.

'Friends of the Chair' in GATT/WTO practice have traditionally been 'delegates who are called upon by the Chair (who takes into account the need for a political balance among various interests) to assist in carrying out specific tasks'.[170] They were used extensively throughout the Uruguay Round MTN in various consultative procedures in order to bring closure on certain issues in draft texts that were taken up in negotiating groups, which reported to the Trade Negotiations Committee or TNC, and have been a regular feature of the WTO ever since, especially in further trade negotiations on the development of rules and disciplines.[171] The Friends of the Chair process can be important in helping to build consensus among a particular group of Members on a particular topic or in order to ensure that a reform process gets under way.

The process can also be instrumental in focusing Members' attention on specific draft texts that revise basic WTO rules and disciplines or introduce new ones. Some examples in practice include the work of the 'Friends of the Chair' group, which is redrafting special and differential provisions for submission to the Committee on Trade and Development,[172] the work of the 'Friends of Agriculture' and of the 'Friends of Antidumping negotiations', all of which are working on revisions to basic WTO Agreements, and 'Friends of Fish' in respect of proposed disciplines on the introduction of fishing subsides in the multilateral

169 Georgiev, *ibid*, 41 on the specific difficulties of reaching a consensus decision concerning the appointment of a new Director-General and where facilitators were used.

170 This is the official definition given by the European Communities on its web-site for external relations and is a common feature in other international *fora* where the EC is an actor; *see* http://biodiversity-chm.eea.eu.int/CHMIndexTerms/Glossary/F/friends_of_the_chair.

171 Blackhurst and Hartridge, above n. 130, 712.

172 'Friends of the Chair' looking to save WTO's S & D Review' (2003) 7, No. 21 *BRIDGES* 4.

trading system.[173] Such processes go a long way to explaining the attractiveness of informal practices whereby trade specialists with particular trading interests face each other across the table, exchanging drafts and negotiating until differences have been narrowed and the text has been cleared of brackets.[174]

4 Internal and external transparency in decision-making

The issue of greater transparency in WTO decision-making first reared its head at the Third Ministerial Meeting, held at Seattle in 1999[175] although the seeds of discontent were sown at the very First Ministerial Meeting, held in Singapore in 1996.[176] While a number of Members have expressed dissatisfaction with the way in which decision-making takes place in the WTO, with particular reference to the various informal practices,[177] it begs the larger question as to whether such dissatisfaction is shared by a broad enough constituency within the organisation to bring about change. It seems that the debate on greater internal and external transparency and effective participation of Members in decision-making processes has been mostly of a procedural nature but that the desire for reform of the decision-making process is less urgent.[178] Even so there are some issues that are worth highlighting.

On the matter of internal transparency, the process of decision making by consensus in the WTO is far from transparent[179] and this has a lot to do with the informal practices in which the Members engage. While popular among Members, such practices signal a key imperfection in this form of participation and one that does not speak well for the institutional effectiveness of WTO decision-making for a number of reasons.

First, most negotiations that precede the formal consensus decision-making process in a plenary body, such as the sessions of the Meetings of the Ministerial

173 All of these items form part of the *Doha Ministerial Declaration*, above n. 46, and the Doha Work Programme, which forms part of the *Declaration*, *see* specifically paras. 13 and 14 (agriculture) and para. 28 (fisheries subsidies) respectively.

174 Jacques J. Gorlin, *An Analysis of the Pharmaceutical-related Provisions of the WTO TRIPs (Intellectual Property) Agreement* (London: Intellectual Property Institute, 1999).

175 Garcia-Bercero, above n. 3, 103-115, Georgiev, above n. 21, 43-45.

176 *See* the various statements of delegates at the Singapore Ministerial Meeting of 1996 and the Seattle Ministerial Meeting of 1999, in Blackhurst, above n. 2, 295-299.

177 Some of the objections of developing country Members were addressed at the Fourth Session of the Ministerial Conference, held in Doha, 11-14 November 2001.

178 Georgiev, above n. 21, 45.

179 Sharma, above n. 32, 2.

Conference, or in the General Council, are conducted privately and no trace is left in the records. Second, informal meetings are usually by invitation only or operate through a process of self-selection, as was noted above when discussing the green room or small group meetings process. Third, the results of these informal processes, while known to their participants, may only be presented to the general membership at a fairly late stage of discussions, which gives rise to the perception for some Members of a *fait accompli*. Fourth, there may be undue reliance placed on the role and the discretion of the Chair at informal meetings. Fifth, concerns have been raised both by Members, particularly developing country delegates, and civil society organisations over the Heads of Delegations or HODs and the Friends of the Chair processes since these meetings are informal and no minutes or records taken, even though draft texts may be under discussion.

Within the WTO, Members deliberations on internal and external transparency have been ongoing for the past five years but with active participation of Members in 2000, under the guidance of a former Chairman of the General Council, Ambassador Kåre Bryn. To date Members have largely focused on the organisation of meetings and participation meetings and other consultative processes. Essentially Members have no desire for major institutional reform, but instead support the existing practice of consensus decision-making and continue to recognise that 'interactive open-ended consultation meetings play an important role in facilitating consensus decision-making'.[180]

On the more sensitive issue of informal consultative processes with participation restricted to certain individual Members or groups of Members, some delegates were of the view that they should be advised accordingly so that any Member with an interest in a specific matter under consideration could be given an opportunity to make its views known. Similarly, it was felt that assumptions should not be made about the representation of any Member in the group representing another Member not present and that the outcome of such consultations should be 'reported back to the full membership expeditiously for their consideration.'[181]

In late 2000, the European Communities produced a discussion paper, which summed up the situation,[182] since when not much progress has been made. The discussion paper records the fact that (i) Members do not foresee any changes which would 'alter the basic character of the Organisation and its decision-making

180 Minutes of the Meeting of the General Council of 17 and 19 July 2000, WT/GC/M/57 (14 September 2000), para. 134; Georgiev, above n. 21, 44.

181 *Ibid.*

182 *Improving the Functioning of the WTO System,* Discussion Paper of the European Communities to the WTO General Council, 2 October 2000, WT/GC/W/412 (6 October 2000),

process'; (ii) 'decisions should continue to be made by consensus, in accordance with Article IX of the WTO agreement' but (iii) there was 'a clear interest in seeking a number of improvements in WTO functioning, in order to achieve enhanced effectiveness, transparency and participation.' The paper then goes on to suggest proposals for measures in three main areas – improving decision-making, including the organisation and functioning of informal consultations, fostering the flow of information among Members and improving meetings of the Ministerial Conference and the General Council.[183]

On the matter of external transparency, the Members have largely confined themselves to what they perceive as the central issue in respect of decision-making, namely the faster derestriction of official WTO documents and an increase in the number and range of external contacts. Certain of these initiatives, such as symposia, workshops, conferences and so on, open the WTO up to a broader range of non-governmental participants, including select NGOs, business and industry organisations, parliamentarians and academics[184] although some of these initiative may be limited in practice if they are restricted to invitation-only events.

As a first step, the General Council adopted a decision in May 2002 on the circulation and derestriction of official WTO documents,[185] whereby all WTO documents that are not restricted are made available on the WTO web-site, once they have been translated into all three official languages of the organisation (English, French and Spanish) and all other restricted documents are subject to specific de-restriction procedures.[186] Another step was the decision in September 2005 by the Panels, hearing a complaint with respect to the continued suspension of obligations in the *EC – Hormones* dispute, and subsequent to a common request

183 Georgiev, above n. 21, 43.

184 *Ibid*, 42-43.

185 *Procedures for the Circulation and Derestriction of WTO Documents*, Decision of the General Council, 14 May 2002, WT/L/452 (16 May 2002) [hereinafter *Derestriction Procedures Decision*], paras. 1and 3.

186 Where a Member government specifically requests that a document produced by the Secretariat be restricted the period for de-restriction has been reduced from eight months to 6-8 weeks in accordance with the *Derestriction Procedures Decision, ibid*, para. 2(a). Under the new rules on de-restriction, it is also possible for a document produced by the Secretariat to be restricted by the issuing WTO body, whereupon it will be de-restricted 60 days after the date of circulation. WTO Members retain the right under the new procedures to restrict their own submitted documents, although they must renew their restriction requests monthly, following an initial period of 60 days or until its first consideration by the Members in the relevant WTO body; see *Derestriction Procedures Decision, ibid*, para. 2(b).

by the parties (Canada, European Communities and the United States),[187] to open up the first meeting of the Panels for public viewing, via a closed-circuit television broadcast at WTO headquarters in Geneva.

The issue of internal and external transparency properly belongs to the broader sphere of WTO governance and in particular accountability of the organisation. While an extremely interesting topic it is beyond the scope of this chapter to cover such governance issues. In the next section, we turn briefly to consider the form, legal bases and validity of WTO decisions.

5 Form, legal bases and validity of WTO decisions

WTO decision-making yields a range of decisions across a broad spectrum, along which the scope and bindingness of such decisions change as one moves along the continuum from left to right. To the left of the spectrum lie decisions that are legally-binding resolutions, such as the Final Act of a Ministerial Conference (including decisions leading to such a resolution that are sometimes characterised as preparatory acts), Ministerial Decisions taken at Ministerial Conferences and Decisions of the General Council, some of which may give rise to new treaty rights and obligations or to subsidiary rules. To the right of the spectrum lie decisions that are non-binding and these can vary from a decision of a fourth level subsidiary body, such as a committee or working party or working group, established under one of the Multilateral Trade Agreements, to a decision of second-level body such as the General Council, and even decisions that are merely hortatory in character, such as Ministerial Declarations and Understandings. In the middle lie a host of decisions, of a substantive and a procedural nature that may be classified as norm-creating or that may give rise to a process, which leads to normative action, while others are merely recommendatory in character. The results of decision-making in the WTO, to the extent that they have normative effect, are taken up in the following two chapters, IV and V.

One aspect of decision-making that is less well appreciated is the drafting of decisions and their timely submission for consideration. Either or both can have an influence on the outcome of the relevant decision and ultimately their validity. Not surprisingly confusion has arisen for Members with respect to the legal status

187 Communication from the Chairman of the Panels in *United States – Continued Suspension of Obligations in the EC – Hormones Dispute* (WT/DS320) and *Canada – Continued Suspension of Obligations in the EC – Hormones Dispute* (WT/DS321), 1 August 2005, WT/DS320/8, WT/DS321/8 (2 August 2005).

of decisions taken at sessions of certain WTO bodies, in particular the decisions adopted at Meetings of the Ministerial Conference, due to their format, language and drafting. Some decisions have the imprint of a Ministerial Declaration and hint at a political commitment while others are clearly a Ministerial Decision *pur sang* and are intended to be legally binding upon the Members.[188]

An example of this is the format, language and drafting of the text of the *Doha Ministerial Declaration*[189] and the *Declaration on the TRIPs Agreement and Public Health*[190] both of which differ significantly from that of the *Implementation Decision* taken at the Fourth Meeting of the Ministerial Conference, held in Doha in 2001. The two *Ministerial Declarations* are silent on the matter of the body competent to act on behalf of the organisation (although one might assume that this is the Ministerial Conference), thereby giving rise to the rebuttable presumption that it is the Members collectively rather than the Ministerial Conference that is acting on behalf of the organisation. The *Implementation Decision*[191] begins with the wording: 'The Ministerial Conference', thereby indicating that this is the body acting on behalf of the organisation.

A further problem has been the issuance of Chairman's statements where the Chair of a WTO body pronounces the details of a decision, which may be the result of painstaking consultations with a number of delegations but which has not been fully negotiated. The tendency for the membership to accept Chairman's statements as decisions, sometimes in the belief that in issuing the Statement the Chair was acting on his/her own responsibility and under the illusion that the membership had reached consensus on a particular matter, led to a rude awakening in *United States – Foreign Sales Corporation (US – FSC)* case.[192]

In *US – FSC* the Appellate Body distinguished between 'decisions' and 'Chairman's statements'. It determined that the Chairman's Statements were not legally

188 Steve Charnovitz, 'The Legal Status of the Doha Declarations' (2002) 5 *JIEL* 207-211 who questions the status and validity of the various decisions adopted by the Members.

189 *Doha Ministerial Declaration*, above n. 46.

190 *Declaration on the TRIPs Agreement and Public Health*, adopted on 14 November 2001 at the Ministerial Conference, Fourth Session, Doha, 9-14 November 2001, WT/MIN(02)DEC/2 (20 November 2001) [hereinafter *TRIPS and Public Health Declaration*].

191 *Implementation-Related Issues and Concerns*, Decision of 14 November 2001, WT/MIN(01)17 (20 November 2001) [hereinafter *Implementation Decision*].

192 *US – FSC*, Appellate Body Report, *United States – Tax Treatment for 'Foreign Sales Corporations'*, WT/DS108/AB/R, adopted on 20 March 2000, paras. 104-114; *see* further Pieter Jan Kuijper, 'Some institutional issues presently before the WTO', in Daniel L.M. Kennedy and James D. Southwick, *The Political Economy of International Trade Law: Essays in Honour of Robert E. Hudec* (Cambridge: Cambridge University Press, 2002) 81-110 at 107-108.

binding on Members but (and by implication) decisions were binding on Members.[193] Thus, should a Member to seek to rely on a Chairman's statement vis-à-vis another Member, as the basis for a particular course of action, it would only raise a rebuttable presumption that the Member in question was bound by that statement.

6 Conclusions

The process of decision-making in the WTO, as with all other international institutions, lies at the heart of its existence and permeates every aspect of its functioning. An analysis of the formal decision-making rules as laid down in Article IX *WTO Agreement* and procedural rules combined with the practice of decision-making in the WTO leads us to the following conclusions.

The first and most striking conclusion about the decision-making process is that while the WTO is equipped with an elaborate set of formal rules, as laid down in Article IX *WTO Agreement* (see fig. 2) only one rule operates in practice. The general rule on consensus contained in Article IX:1 *WTO Agreement*, which was applied in the former GATT, is the preferred means of adopting a decision in the organisation, with voting acquiring a residual character – a process which has been institutionalised in the WTO. The character of consensus decision-making in the WTO remains the same as in the former GATT, i.e. it is one of non-objection or passive consensus.

Second, the primacy of consensus decision-making is reflected both in the formal rules and the informal practices of the organisation. At the formal level this is evident from the number of provisions in the *WTO Agreement* and one or two of the annexed Multilateral Trade Agreements that mandate consensus, including the novel use of 'reverse consensus' for the adoption of panel and Appellate Body reports by the DSB. Informally, consensus is used throughout the organisation, by every institutional body and in every formal and informal meeting even where voting is ordinarily called for. The informal practice of consensus decision-making *in lieu* of voting has been formally recognised for decisions on waivers and accessions (WT/L/93) although no WTO Member is precluded from requesting a vote.

Third, the practice of consensus decision-making in the WTO favours majority interests in a less obtrusive way than weighted voting. It gives procedural significance to variations in economic power and status among larger trading partners

193 *US – FSC*, *ibid*, paras. 112-113.

in the WTO trading system (parity of interest) in the face of a numerically larger group of developing and LDC Members, with a very small or even insignificant share of world trade, the latter of which could dominate the process if a one-member one-vote or OMOV and/or an equitable geographical distribution or EGD system of voting were to be applied. (The only attempt to apply any form of EGD in the WTO in the interests of regional parity is in the appointments of chairs of the various Councils and committees, which take place annually). This third conclusion supports the view that consensus decision-making sustains the continuance of the major interests' norm, which we identified in Chapter II.

On the basis of this third conclusion, the prospects for the introduction of a system of weighted voting, or resort to a critical mass approach to decision-making, where Members agree to refrain from blocking consensus in the event that a critical number of them support the decision, do not appear to be realistic. The variation suggested in *The Sutherland Report*, whereby a Member considering blocking a measure, which otherwise has the very broad consent of the membership but can only do so provided certain conditions are met, including declaring the objection in writing and motivating it, is unlikely to find approval and might lead to polarisation of the membership.

Fourth, the use of consensus to reach a decision conveniently masks dissent, which has much to commend it in collective-action decision-making *fora* like the WTO. The popularity of consensus decision-making, despite its flaws, derives from the very process itself, which means that establishing consensus is a question of arriving at a point where no Member, large or small, actively opposes the decision to be adopted. This gives a Member a powerful veto over a decision which is otherwise not present in the case of voting.

Fifth, there are a myriad of informal practices that exist in WTO decision-making, which surround the actual process of arriving at consensus and further endorse the process. These include various consultative processes by means of informal sessions of Heads of Delegations or HODs, the use of small group or green room meetings, through caucuses and alliance building mechanisms organised along geographical lines or sectoral issues and the use of chairpersons, facilitators and 'friends' groups in order to push for Members' consensus on certain issues. Such informal practices play a vital role in building consensus and steering the decision-making process towards a successful conclusion.

Sixth, many of these informal practices have been criticised for the fact that they sustain a process of decision-making that lacks transparency and legitimacy. This has led to greater efforts on the part of the Members to make their internal and external aspects of WTO decision-making more transparent by means of better notification to the Members about informal consultation processes and externally by affording the public greater access to the results of the decision-making.

Seventh, there is growing awareness on the part of Members about the correct format, language and drafting of a decision in conformity with its substance as well as such matters as the relevant procedures for the adoption of the decision and whether a particular decision can be considering as binding upon the Members.

A final conclusion that can be drawn from our analysis is that the practice of WTO decision-making is rarely consistent with the formal rules on decision-making as laid down in its constituent instrument. Instead, informality reigns both in principle and practice. This development has its origins in the former GATT and is sustained both by the practice of consensus decision-making and the informal practices, which are largely of a consultative and consensus-building nature and which are designed to reach agreement among Members prior to the formal adoption of a decision.

Despite all its flaws, and its many detractors, the process of consensus decision-making as applied in the WTO is firmly in place and the practices surrounding it are unlikely to change. The effects of this on normative developments in the WTO will be taken up at various points in the following two chapters, IV and V, as part of the normative analysis of the organisation.

IV

PRINCIPAL RULE-MAKING

1 Introduction

The establishment of a formal organisational and institutional basis for the multilateral trading system signifies that the WTO has become the main forum for institutional developments in the field of international trade law. At the same time the *WTO Agreement* and the annexed Multilateral Trade Agreements provide a code of conduct for world trade in a larger normative framework than existed under the GATT and one which is noteworthy in a couple of respects.

First, there is a strong normative continuity between the former GATT and the current WTO, as evidenced by the results of the Uruguay Round, which build upon the normative structure of the GATT and the Tokyo Round Agreements, with revised and new agreements on sectoral issues and rules-based disciplines. This continuity is further endorsed by the GATT *acquis*,[1] which is the body of principles, rules and standards, as embodied in various legal instruments, decisions and customary practices that were adopted by the CONTRACTING PARTIES under the GATT 1947 and bodies established in the framework of the GATT 1947.[2] As the Appellate Body has stated in one of its earliest decisions:

1 The term *acquis* is coined from European Community law where it is understood as the patrimony or body of rules, principles, agreements, decisions, understandings, resolutions, positions, opinions, objectives and practices developed in the EC legal order; see A. Toth, *Oxford Encyclopaedia of European Community Law* (Oxford: Oxford University Press, 1990) Vol. I, 9. *Cf.* Gabrielle Marceau, 'Transition from GATT to WTO. A most pragmatic operation' (1995) 29 *JWT* 147-163 at 147, n. 1 thereof, who disputes the use of the term *acquis* as applied to the GATT in the wider European law sense of the word.

2 Article XVI:1 *WTO Agreement, The Results of the Uruguay Round of Multilateral Trade Negotiations: The Legal Texts* (Geneva: World Trade Organization, 1999) [hereinafter *The Legal Texts*], 17.

> Article XVI:1 of the *WTO Agreement* and paragraph 1(b)(iv) of the language of Annex 1A incorporating the *GATT 1994* into the *WTO Agreement* bring the legal history and experience under the GATT 1947 into the new realm of the WTO in a way that ensures continuity and consistency in a smooth transition from the GATT 1947 system.[3]

Second, the WTO's normative landscape has come to fulfil Wolfgang Friedman's notion of the 'horizontal' and 'vertical' expansion of international law.[4] The results of the Uruguay Round MTN are evidence of a horizontal expansion of international trade law not only through the increased number and variety of norms but also through a broadening of the scope and coverage of subject matter. Whereas the subject of the GATT 1947 was a multilateral regime for the reduction of tariffs and the development of a number of disciplines on trade in goods so as to protect the value of those tariff concessions, the Multilateral Trade Agreements go much further in adding new disciplines in the field of trade in goods, which include the gradual inclusion over time of trade sectors that were formally exempt from full GATT coverage (agriculture and textiles), in developing stricter disciplines on contingent protection measures (antidumping, subsidies and safeguards) and in introducing rules and disciplines where previously none existed (rules sanctioning the use of sanitary and phytosanitary measures, provided that they are administered on a non-discriminatory basis). In addition, for the first time in the history of the multilateral trading system the WTO adds rules on new subject matter (trade in services and trade-related intellectual property rights).[5]

There has also been a vertical expansion of international trade law because WTO rule-making now reaches more directly into the private conduct of natural

3 *Japan – Alcoholic Beverages II*, Appellate Body Report, *Japan – Taxes on Alcoholic Beverages,* WT/DS8/AB/R, WTDS10/AB/R, WT/DS11/AB/R, adopted 1 November 1996, p. 15. The Appellate Body has also pronounced on the concept of the GATT *acquis* in relation to the well-established practice of challenging domestic legislation under the GATT 1947, noting that 'this practice forms part of the GATT *acquis* which, under Article XVI:1 of the *WTO Agreement*, provides guidance to the WTO and, therefore, to panels and the Appellate Body', *see US – 1916 Act*, Appellate Body Report, *United States – Anti-Dumping Act of 1916*, WT/DS136/AB/R, WT/DS162/AB/R, adopted 26 September 2000, para. 61.

4 Wolfgang Friedman, *The Changing Structure of International Law* (New York: Columbia University Press, 1964) 5, 6 and 9.

5 Jonathan T. Fried, 'Governance in the Global Age: A Public International Law Perspective' in Porter, Roger B. and Sauvé, Pierre (eds.) *Seattle, the WTO, and the Future of the Multilateral Trading System* (Cambridge, MA: The Center for Business and Government, John F. Kennedy School of Government, Harvard University, 2000) 131-141, at 132.

and corporate entities, at national and regional levels.[6] The intrusion of international trade law into Members' domestic legal orders has highlighted the need for the creation or the reform of trade laws and practices in many domestic constituencies where international trade rules are exerting an influence on national policies far 'behind the border'.[7]

While the preceding chapters were largely dedicated to an institutional analysis of the WTO, including its institutionalised decision-making process which underpins and informs the normative process, this chapter and the next are dedicated to a normative analysis of the WTO and prospects for further normative developments in the organisation. The rules that will be examined are understood in the general sense in which they are used in the 1986 Vienna Convention on Law of Treaties between States and International Organizations or between International Organization as 'rules of the organisation', which means 'in particular, the constituent instruments, decisions and resolutions adopted in accordance with them, and established practice of the organization'.[8]

Primary treaty rules in WTO law are those rules that set out the rights and obligations of the Members as parties to a set of multilateral treaty instruments. These primary treaty rules seek to regulate the behaviour of States or international organisations by requiring them to do something (*prescriptive norms*) or not to do something (*prohibitive norms*). Secondary treaty rules[9] are rules, which have

6 *Ibid.*

7 Robert Z. Lawrence, Albert Bressand and Takatoshi Ito, *A Vision for the World Economy: Openness, Diversity and Cohesion* (Washington, D.C: The Brookings Institution, 1996).

8 Article 2:1(*j*) Vienna Convention on Law of Treaties between States and International Organizations or between International Organizations (adopted 21 March 1986, *not yet in force*) (1986) 25 *ILM* 543 [hereinafter VCLTIO] at 547, which may be considered as reflecting customary international law on this point. While not having the force of law, the VCLTIO would probably be accepted in evidence as determinative of general international law on matters of treaty law and practice involving states and international organisations before (international) courts and tribunals.

9 *See* K.C. Wellens, 'Diversity in Secondary Rules and the Unity of International Law: Some Reflections on Current Trends' (1994) XXV *NYBIL*, 3-37 at 7 reprinted in L.A.N.M. Baarnhoorn and K.C. Wellens, *Diversity in Secondary Rules and the Unity of International Law*, (The Hague: T.M.C. Asser Instituut/Martinus Nijhoff, 1995), who draws on the work of H.L.A. Hart, *The Concept of Law*, 2nd edition (Oxford: Clarendon Press, 1994), 78-79. Hart's concept of law consists of a union of primary and secondary rules wherein primary rules impose duties whereas secondary rules confer either public or private powers. Moreover, secondary rules comprise 'rules of recognition', 'rules of change' and 'rules of adjudication'. It should be borne in mind that Hart's analysis is based on the domestic legal order and therefore is not *ipso facto* transferable to the

their basis in and derive their authority from primary treaty rules and which operate in such a way as to revise the content or application of primary treaty rules because they have something to say about their modification and interpretation; on occasion the operation of secondary treaty rules may lead to the adoption of new primary treaty rules. This chapter applies this division between primary and secondary treaty rules in conducting a normative analysis of primary treaty rules in the WTO and assessing the application in the light of the 1969 Vienna Convention on the Law of Treaties.[10]

The remainder of the chapter proceeds as follows. Section 2 defines the issue of principal rule-making, with an examination of the normative framework in which primary treaty rules are developed, before discussing the development of primary treaty rules through the treaty-making process and the manner in which they are brought into force. In section 3, we turn to consider the other aspect of principal rule-making, which are the secondary treaty rules laid down in the *WTO Agreement* that revise or interpret primary treaty rules through amendment (and related practice), modification following (re-)negotiation of tariff concessions or services' commitments, the accession process, exercise of the waiver power and authoritative interpretation. Section 4 forms the concluding section to this chapter and provides the basis for an analysis of the role of subsidiary rule-making within the overall normative framework of the WTO – a matter that is dealt with separately in chapter V.

2 Principal rule-making: primary treaty rules

In the WTO context primary treaty rules[11] consist of the rights and obligations that bind States as Members of an international organisation and as parties to a set of multilateral treaty instruments. The term 'normative development' is understood to mean the creation, maintenance and revision of legally binding and non-

international legal order. For a critique of Hart's concept of primary and secondary rules in relation to international law, *see* Ian Brownlie, *The Rule of Law in International Affairs: International Law at the Fiftieth Anniversary of the United Nations* (The Hague: Martinus Nijhoff, 1998) 3-6.

10 Vienna Convention on the Law of Treaties (adopted 23 May 1969, *in force* 27 January 1980) (1969) 8 *ILM* 689 [hereinafter the VCLT].

11 For the purposes of describing the WTO's normative structure the general division of the WTO legal order into primary and secondary law draws on Wolfgang Benedek's analysis of the sources of law in the GATT legal order. While there are obvious differences between the two legal orders, the general division used by Benedek is followed

binding norms ('soft' law).[12] The concept 'norms' is understood to include principles, rules and standards. These three categories of norms, which underpin and inform the rights and obligations of the Members, as set out in the basis treaty rules, can be summarised as follows.

'Principles' form a normative category at the highest level of abstraction and constitute fundamental assumptions that underlie a particular legal regime, its rules and standards.[13] Or, as Sir Gerald Fitzmaurice has stated: '[B]y a principle, or general principle, as opposed to a rule, even a general rule, of law is meant chiefly something which is not itself a rule, but which underlies a rule, and explains or provides the reason for it.'[14] Examples of general principles that underpin key WTO rights and obligations include the principle of non-discrimination (and its antithesis, the principle of special and differential treatment), the principle of reciprocity and the principle of market access.[15]

'Rules' elaborate upon the rights and obligations that flow from general principles; they are more specific in content than general principles and indicate the behaviour that Members are obligated to follow at an operational level.[16]

in this chapter and the next in analysing the normative structure of the WTO legal order. However, it is not the intention here to seek to determine the sources of law in the WTO legal order as Benedek has done for the GATT legal order. *See* Wolfgang Benedek, *Die Rechtsordnung des GATT aus völkerrechtlicher Sicht* (Berlin: Springer-Verlag, 1990) 97-126.

12 Christine Chinkin, 'Normative Developments in the International Legal System' in Dinah Shelton (ed.), *Commitment and Compliance, the Role of Non-Binding Norms in the International Legal System* (Oxford: Oxford University Press, 2000) 21-42. For the particular application of soft law in international economic relations, *see* Ignaz Seidl-Hohenveldern, 'International Economic "Soft Law"' (1979) 163 *Receuil des Cours* 165-246.

13 Anthony Clark Arend, *Legal Rules and International Society* (New York, Oxford: Oxford University Press, 1999) 14.

14 G. Fitzmaurice, 'The general principles of international law considered from the standpoint of the rule of law' (1957) 92 *Receuil des Cours* 1-227, at 7. *Cf.* Michel Virally, 'Le rôle des "principes" dans le développement du droit international' in *Recueil d'études de doit international en hommage à Paul Guggenheim* (Genève: Faculté de droit de l'Université de Genève, Institut universitaire de hautes études internationales/Tribune, 1968) 531-544 at 534 who sees general principles as merely a concept or notion of the law. ('Les "principes" ne se présentent pas toujours sous la forme d'une proposition normative, mais parfois sous celle d'un concept'.)

15 For reference to some of these principles and others (principle of solidarity, the principle of accountability and the principle of fair trade) in the GATT context (*Systematik der Prinzipien des GATT*) and discussion thereof, *see* Benedek, above n. 11, 52-58.

16 Clark Arend, above n. 13, 15. *See* also Gennady M. Danilenko *Law-making in the international community* (Dordrecht: Nordhoff Publishers, 1993) 8.

For example, the introductory paragraph, or *chapeau* to Article II *GATT 1994*, which relates to the scheduling of tariff concessions, is a rule that reflects the principle of reciprocity by stating that '[E]ach [Member] shall accord to the commerce of the other …'[17]

'Standards' refer to the behaviour that one Member is expected to accord another[18] and therefore involve a judgement. They are usually articulated in terms of the grant of a right, or the imposition of an obligation as to the level or type of treatment that a Member can expect to receive or to have to give, thereby creating legitimate expectations. It is not unusual for a standard to be bound up with the rule which articulates it and this may have the unintended consequence of the standard being confused with the rule. For example, the GATT provision on most-favoured nation (MFN) treatment, which is contained in Article I:1 *GATT 1994*, is articulated as a rule when it is stated that 'each Member shall accord immediately and unconditionally (*rule*) … treatment no less favourable (*standard*)'.[19] In this case the rule indicates how the behaviour will be conducted while at the same time articulating the standard of treatment to be expected. A further feature of this particular provision is that while the rule and standard are explicitly stated the underlying principle of non-discrimination is implicit.

2.1 The normative framework and primary treaty rules

In terms of its normative character the WTO legal order is a body of principles, rules and standards, the antecedents of which are to be found in the GATT 1947 and the subsequent practice of the contracting parties (established practice under the GATT multilateral trade regime), supplemented by the results of the deliberate rule-making process which took place during the Uruguay Round. The latter is characterised by the process of negotiation and deliberation among the GATT contracting parties as part of a single negotiated undertaking,[20] by which all

17 Paragraph 1(a) of Article II *GATT 1994*, *The Legal Texts*, above n. 2, 488.

18 For a particularly good discussion of standards (Grundregeln) in the GATT context, *see* Benedek, above n. 11, 61-63.

19 The MFN standard, which is taken up in Article II *GATS* in relation to its application in the services' sector is different to its counterpart in Article I *GATT 1994*. Paragraph 2 of Article II *GATS* provides a potential exception to the rule set out in paragraph 1, such as to alter the scope of the rule by re-introducing 'conditional' MFN, provided conditions are met; *see* Article II *GATS*, *The Legal Texts*, above n. 2, 329.

20 For comments on a similar process of law-making through a process of negotiation in the law of the sea, which proceeded by means of consensus decision-making and used a composite negotiating text, which broke new grounds in terms of substance and

Members agreed to be bound as to the results of those negotiations. It eventually led to the adoption of the most comprehensive set of rules for the regulation of international trade in the history of the multilateral trading system.

However, there is a qualitative difference between normative developments in the GATT and in the WTO. The GATT 1947 was a multilateral agreement with treaty provisions aimed at the reciprocal reduction of tariffs and supplemented by 'general clauses' of obligation, which were designed to complement and protect any tariff-reduction measures. In turn, these general clauses were drawn from the specific chapter in the draft Charter for an International Trade Organization or ITO, which was devoted to rules on trade and which relied on bilateral treaty clauses for their inspiration.[21] Those general clauses contained 'precisely formulated legal rules, sometimes termed "contractual", which were to be directly applied without further elaboration'[22] and included the possibility of dealing with bilateral protests relating to the non-performance of specific treaty obligations. Whereas legalism prevails in bilateral treaties it is rare to find this in the field of multilateral treaties. Instead, norms are generally phrased as broad general principles or devoted to procedural matters. In this respect the treaty rules set out in the General Agreement are something of a rarity but can be explained on the basis of their provenance because they were intended to be in harmony with equivalent rules in the abortive ITO Charter.

GATT treaty provisions contained a mixture of obligations[23] that required the contracting parties to do something (*prescriptive norms*), for example to accord equal treatment to imported products as to products of national origin (Article III:4 GATT),[24] or not to do something (*prohibitive norms*), for example the

procedure, *see* R.Y. Jennings, QC, 'Law-Making and Package Deal' in *Mélanges offerts à Paul Reuter: Le droit international: unité et diversité* (Paris: Éditions A. Pedone, 1981), 347-355. *Cf.* Akiho Shibata, 'International Law-making Process in the United Nations: Comparative Analysis of UNCED and UNCLOS III' (1993-1994) 24 *CalWestInt'lLJ* 17-53, 45.

21 John. H. Jackson, *The World Trading System: Law and Policy of International Economic Relations* (Cambridge, MA: The MIT Press, 1997) [hereinafter *The World Trading System*] 38.

22 John. H. Jackson, *World Trade and the Law of GATT* (Charlottesville, VA: The Michie Company (The Bobbs-Merill Company, Inc.), 1969) § 1.4., 12-13., citing Harry Hawkins at the London meeting of the Preparatory Committee of the United Nations Conference on Trade and Employment, when speaking of the proposed ITO Charter.

23 *See* Joost Pauwelyn, *Conflict of Norms in Public International Law: How WTO Law Relates to Other Rules of International Law* (Cambridge: Cambridge University Press, 2003) 158-159 for his detailed overview and summary of the norms of international law.

24 Article III:1 *GATT 1994*, *The Legal Texts*, above n. 2, 490.

prohibition on the institution or maintenance of quantitative measures or other measures of similar effect on imports or exports (Article XI:1 GATT).[25] A prescriptive norm was occasionally interspersed with the grant of a right for contracting parties to do something (*permissive norms*), for example a contracting party may levy anti-dumping duties or countervail in order to offset or prevent the effects of dumping (Article VI GATT),[26] or the grant of a right not to do something *provided* certain circumstances are fulfilled (*exceptive norms*),[27] for example contracting parties may take emergency remedial action to deal with a sudden influx of imports that cause or threaten serious injury to domestic producers (Article XIX GATT).[28]

Even so, some of those same treaty provisions, while containing precise language, were phrased as broad general principles, for example the freedom of transit principle which is taken up in Article V GATT,[29] or were devoted to procedural matters and were relatively indeterminate, for example the provisions relating to the formation by contracting parties *inter se* of a customs union or free-trade area in Article XXIV GATT,[30] which called for a plan and schedule for the formation but were indeterminate on other matters such as coverage, for example the requirement of the elimination of duties and measures of equivalent effect on *substantially all trade*, or which provided no time-frame for the formation or completion of the customs union or free trade area.[31] In addition, some of the exceptive norms were aspirational in character (*programmatic norms*),[32] as

25 Article XI:1 *GATT 1994*, *The Legal Texts*, *ibid*, 500.

26 Article VI:2 *GATT 1994*, *The Legal Texts*, *ibid*, 494.

27 The Appellate Body has ruled on the distinction to be drawn between a permissive norm and an exceptive norm in *EC – Tariff Preferences*, Appellate Body Report, *European Communities – Conditions for the Granting of Tariff Preferences to Developing Countries*, WT/DS246/AB/R, adopted 20 April 2004, para. 88 (relationship between Article I:1 *GATT 1994* (MFN) and the Enabling Clause and the allocation of the burden of proof between complainant and respondent parties), relying on its earlier case-law *EC – Hormones*, Appellate Body Report, *EC – Measures Concerning Meat and Meat Products*, WT/DS26/AB/R, WT/DS/48/AB/R, adopted 13 February 1998, para. 104 (with respect to the *SPS Agreement*), *Brazil – Aircraft*, Appellate Body Report, *Brazil – Export Financing Programme for Aircraft*, WT/DS46/AB/R, adopted 20 August 1999, paras. 139-141 (*SCM Agreement*) and *EC – Sardines*, Appellate Body Report, *EC – Trade Description of Sardines*, WT/DS231/AB/R, adopted 23 October 2002, para. 275 (with respect to the *TBT Agreement*).

28 Article XIX *GATT 1994*, *The Legal Texts*, above n. 2, 518-519.

29 Article V *GATT 1994*, *The Legal Texts*, *ibid,* 492-493.

30 Article XXIV *GATT 1994*, *The Legal Texts*, *ibid*, 522-523.

31 *See* paragraphs 5 and 8 of Article XXIV *GATT 1994*, *ibid*, 523-524.

32 *See* Benedek, above n. 11, at 125 and 470.

for example was the case with the detailed principles and objectives in Article XXXVI GATT[33] pertaining to the grant of more favourable treatment to 'less-developed contracting parties', which endorsed the non-application of the principle of reciprocity (Article XXXVI:8 GATT).[34]

This had the overall effect that many GATT obligations were not always fully capable of implementation or they were laid open to varying interpretations by national authorities when it came to implementation in the domestic legal orders of the contracting parties. An example of this is the articulation of preferential treatment for developing countries under Article XXXVI GATT which could not take place until certain developed contracting parties had been granted a waiver from their MFN obligations under Article I:1 GATT and were able to introduce and maintain enabling legislation that was considered to be GATT-consistent, i.e. the waiver provided an exception to the application of the principles of non-discrimination and reciprocity.[35]

It will also be recalled that many of the contracting parties continued to apply the GATT on a provisional basis, by means of the Provisional Protocol of Application or PPA,[36] thereby reserving for themselves certain regulatory and policy competences in the matter of trade. This situation has been corrected since the *WTO Agreement* and the annexed Multilateral Trade Agreements are applied on a definitive basis.[37]

The legal framework for the conduct of world trade, as set out in the *WTO Agreement,* its annexes and the Schedules, substantially alters the normative landscape of the multilateral trading system by introducing a broader set of rules than previously existed under the GATT 1947. While maintaining the principles, rules and standards laid down in the GATT 1947, other legal instruments that entered into force under the GATT 1947 and various understandings, all of which

33 Article XXXVI *GATT 1994*, *The Legal Texts*, above n. 2, 533-534.

34 *See* paragraph 8 of Article XXXVI *GATT 1994*, *ibid,* 534.

35 Decision of the CONTRACTING PARTIES of 25 June 1971, relating to the establishment of 'generalized, non-reciprocal and non discriminatory preferences beneficial to the developing countries', *BISD* 18S/24, GATT Doc. L/3545, [*1971 Waiver Decision on the Generalized System of Preferences*] and Differential and More Favourable Treatment, Reciprocity and Fuller Participation of Developing Countries, Decision of the CONTRACTING PARTIES, 28 November 1979, L/4903, (1979) *BISD* 26S/203-205 [hereinafter the *Enabling Clause*].

36 *Protocol of Provisional Application of the General Agreement on Tariffs and Trade* (adopted 30 October 1947 *in force* 1 January 1948) 55 *UNTS* 308 [hereinafter *Protocol of Provisional Application*].

37 Jackson, *The World Trading* System, above n. 21, 48.

form part of *GATT 1994*,[38] the WTO absorbs nearly all of the disciplines on matters such as customs valuation, import licensing, anti-dumping, subsidies and countervail and technical standards, which were previously taken up in 'stand-alone' treaties concluded at the end of the Tokyo Round MTN.[39]

The results of the Uruguay Round add considerably to this body of rules with further agreements for the integration of agriculture and textiles and clothing into *GATT 1994*, the addition of disciplines to govern safeguards, trade and investment measures, rules of origin for non-preferential (or MFN) trade, pre-shipment inspection and the regulation of the use of sanitary and phytosanitary measures. Additionally, new sectoral agreements on trade in services (*GATS*) in Annex 1B and the regulation of trade and intellectual property rights (*TRIPs*) in Annex 1C are taken up as a result of those negotiations together with an annex on dispute settlement (*DSU*) in Annex 2 and another on trade policy review (*TPRM*) in Annex 3. All of the results of the Uruguay Round MTN form a 'single undertaking',[40] by which *all* Members are bound and this marks a major departure from the GATT trade regime, whereby only some of the contracting parties had committed themselves to the additional disciplines, taken up in the Tokyo Round Agreements.[41]

In normative terms, the results of the Uruguay Round of Multilateral Trade Negotiations or MTN have led to an increase in the number of permissive and

38 *See* paragraph 1-3 of the preliminary notes to Annex IA, being the General Agreement on Tariffs and Trade 1994 or *GATT 1994*, *The Legal Texts*, above n. 2, 21-23.

39 See the next section, 2.2 for details of how the results of negotiations in the Uruguay Round, including on the Tokyo Round codes, have been transformed into basic treaty rules.

40 During the Uruguay Round the term 'single undertaking' meant that countries could no longer pick and choose which parts of the agreement they would sign up to, as had occurred under the Tokyo Round (*see Declaration of Ministers*, approved at Tokyo on 14 September 1973, setting out rules and procedures for the 1973-1979 Tokyo Round of Multilateral Trade Negotiations (*Tokyo Ministerial Declaration*) *Basic Instruments and Selected Documents (BISD)* 20S/19 [hereinafter 'Tokyo Round MTN']). Instead, all agreements were to apply to all participating countries.
Currently, the term is understood to mean 'every item of the negotiation is part of a whole and indivisible package and cannot be agreed separately' "Nothing is agreed until everything is agreed"'; *see* WTO web-site at: www.wto.org. For comments on this approach, *see* Philip I. Levy, 'Do we need an undertaker for the Single Undertaking? Considering the angles of variable geometry', paper prepared for the CEPR/ECARES/World Bank Conference, Brussels, 14/15 July 2000 (revised 2004), available at www.yale.edu/ycias/globalization/levy_paper.pdf and for its abandonment, *see* Deepak Nayyar, 'The Existing System and the Missing Institutions' in Deepak Nayyar (ed.) *Governing Globalization* (Oxford: Oxford University Press, 2002) 356-384, at 366.

41 *See* 'GATT: a legal guide to the Tokyo Round' (1979) 13 *JWT Law* 436-447.

exceptive norms,[42] particularly in those multilateral trade agreements that elaborate new disciplines which defer to national rules and standards *provided* they do not lead to the imposition of domestic regulatory barriers. An example of a permissive norm is paragraph 1 of Article 2 of the *Agreement on the Application of Sanitary and Phytosanitary Measures* or *SPS* that builds on the language of the exception in Article XX (b) *GATT 1994*. It states: 'Members have the right to take sanitary and phytosanitary measures necessary for the protection of human, animal or plant life or health, *provided* that such measures are not inconsistent with the provisions of this Agreement'. Paragraph 3 of that same Article requires that '[M]embers shall ensure that their sanitary and phytosanitary measures do not arbitrarily or unjustifiably discriminate between Members ... or constitute a disguised restriction on international trade.'[43]

Similarly, as a result of the Uruguay Round negotiations there may be a need to take account of the fact that a Member's domestic law or policy does not permit a certain activity on grounds of public order or morality in which case an exception may apply as for example in paragraphs 2 and 3 of Article 27 of the *Agreement on Trade-Related Intellectual Property Rights* or *TRIPs*. This provision permits WTO Members to exclude from patentability certain inventions on the grounds of public order or morality (paragraph 2), or to prevent the patenting of certain

42 The usual type of exceptive GATT norm is a safeguard or an anti-surge measure, for example in the form of an emergency safeguard under Article XIX *GATT 1994*, which allows for the raising of a previously lowered tariff (contrary to Article II:1 *GATT 1994*), or the imposition of a quantitative restriction (contrary to Article XI:1 *GATT 1994*), and the use of a balance-of-payments safeguard on the basis of Article XII:1 *GATT 1994* (also Article XVIII:8 *GATT 1994* for developing countries), which allows for the temporary imposition of quantitative restrictions.
Similarly, there is a broader category of exemptive norms that are horizontal in character, e.g. the formation of a customs union or a free trade area on more preferential terms (Article XXIV *GATT 1994*/Article V *GATS*), the *Enabling Clause*, above n. 35, that allows developed country Members to extend more preferential treatment to developing and LDC Members in the matter of trade in goods (contrary to Article I:1 *GATT 1994*), the general exception that re-validates an otherwise *GATT 1994* or *GATS*-inconsistent measure (Article XX *GATT 1994*/Article XIV *GATS*) and the security exception (Article XXI *GATT 1994*/Article XIV*bis GATS*).
Besides introducing more exceptive norms, in addition to those which existed under the GATT 1947 (now *GATT 1994*), the contracting parties added disciplines to the exercise of some of them, e.g. the *Agreement on Safeguards* in order to discipline the use of Article XIX *GATT 1994*, the *Legal Texts*, above n. 2, 315-324.

43 *See* for example paragraph 1 of Article 2 of the *Agreement on the Application of Sanitary and Phytosanitary Measures* or *SPS Agreement*, *The Legal Texts*, *ibid*, 70.

diagnostic, therapeutic or surgical methods for treatment of humans or animals (paragraph 3(a)).

Even so, the exception is a limited one and does not apply to all subject matter, for example there is an exclusion in paragraph 3(b) of Article 27 *TRIPs* from patentability of 'plants and animals other than micro-organisms, and essentially biological processes for the production of plants or animals other than non-biological and microbiological processes', which is conditional upon Members establishing some form of plant variety protection within their jurisdictions by a system of patents or a *sui generis* system. This is a matter which is still the subject of ongoing negotiations among Members.[44] In this case, the exceptive norm is qualified by a prescriptive norm which sets out a positive obligation that is binding on Members.

The foregoing examples of permissive and exceptive norms in the *SPS* and *TRIPs Agreements* have a direct bearing on the national public order of individual Members and potentially also on their domestic value systems. Until recently it has generally been held that sovereign States enjoyed considerable freedom of action to determine their own domestic regulatory spheres and to act accordingly but this is changing. WTO norms, as set out in the Uruguay Round agreements, remind us that there has been a paradigm shift in the regulatory philosophy underlying the multilateral trading system.

Whereas the GATT legal system was principally based on a trade barriers regime, in which the contracting parties agreed to the progressive reduction of tariffs and the implementation of trade disciplines in order to protect those tariff concessions (a form of negative integration), the WTO legal system calls upon Members to legislate and enforce international principles, rules and standards in their domestic legal orders and this is having a profound impact on the domestic regulatory spheres of individual Members (a form of positive integration).[45] This paradigm shift in regulatory philosophy signals an associated move towards

44 Paragraphs 2 and 3 of Article 27 *Agreement on Trade-Related Intellectual Property Rights* or *TRIPs Agreement*, *The Legal Texts*, above n. 2, 379-380. For a summary of the process, *see Review of the Provisions of Article 27.3(b), Summary of issues raised and points made*, Note by the Secretariat, Council for Trade-related Intellectual Property Tights, IP/C/W/369 (8 August 2002) noting the Annex at 19-24.

45 *See* Veijo Heiskanen, 'The Regulatory Philosophy of International Trade Law' (2004) 38 *JWT* 1-36. In similar vein and characterizing the change in philosophy underlying rule-making from Geneva to Seattle as a forward shift into positive rule-making, *see* William A. Dymond and Michael M. Hart, 'Post-Modern Trade Policy: Reflections on the Challenges to Multilateral Trade Negotiations After Seattle' (2001) 34 *JWT* 21-38 and S.P. Shukla, 'From the GATT to the WTO and Beyond' in Nayyar, above n. 40, 267-272.

positive prescription, which is reinforced by the language in paragraph 3 of Article XVI *WTO Agreement* that sets out the duty of every Member government to 'ensure conformity of its laws, regulations and administrative procedures with its obligations as provided in the annexed Agreements' thereby establishing a positive obligation for Members to ensure that their domestic laws, regulations and procedures are WTO-compliant and mitigating against any over-reliance on exceptive behaviour.

2.2 The development of primary treaty rules through the treaty-making process

The primary means of creating rights and obligations, which are binding on the Members, is through the formal treaty-making process.[46] The *WTO Agreement* and annexed Multilateral Trade Agreements together with the Schedules of Tariff Concessions and Services Commitments represent the common agreement of the contracting parties with respect to the results of the Uruguay Round MTN[47] and comprise a set of legally binding provisions of a fundamental norm-creating character.[48] The results of the MTN process are bilateral in nature and have led to the conclusion of a set of reciprocal promises that while only binding on *one* Member 'also represent a common agreement among *all* Members'.[49] These trade

46 The relevant conventional international law that is applicable here is the VCLT, above n. 10. This is either because Members are parties to the VCLT, or in the event they are not, because a large number of its provisions apply on the basis that the VCLT is declaratory of certain customary international law rules on the matter.

47 The Uruguay Round MTN was launched at the Ministerial Meeting held in Punta del Este, Uruguay; see *Declaration of Punta del Este*, Ministerial Meeting, *BISD* 33S/19 [hereinafter *Uruguay Round Declaration*].

48 As a matter of treaty law and practice the *WTO Agreement* also constitutes the text of 'a treaty which is the constituent instrument of an international organization' adopted by States, in the sense of Article 5 VCLT, above n. 10; *see* Anthony Aust, *Modern Treaty Law and Practice* (Cambridge: Cambridge University Press, 2000) 9 and 54. Strictly speaking Article 4 VCLT also applies since the *WTO Agreement* was concluded after the entry into force of the VCLT.

49 See *US – Gambling*, Appellate Body Report, *US – Measures Affecting the Cross-Border Supply of Gambling and Betting Services*, DS/285/AB/R, adopted 20 April 2005, para. 159, in respect of Schedules of Services Commitments, relying on its decision in *EC – Computer Equipment*, Appellate Body Report, *European Communities – Customs Classification of Certain Computer Equipment,* WT/DS62/AB/R, WT/DS67/AB/R, WT/DS68/AB/R, adopted 22 June 1998, para. 109, where it stated: 'although each Member's Schedule represents the tariff commitments that bind *one* Member, Schedules also

obligations remain a collection of reciprocal or bilateral obligations,[50] which are synallagmatic in character,[51] but the primary treaty rules are 'mutually dependent on each other'[52] and thereby acquire an integral and intra-dependent character.[53] This phenomenon is typical of those multilateral treaties or sets of treaty obligations that are necessary for the maintenance of a regime or a system of reciprocal rights and obligations like the WTO (and the former GATT). In the remainder of this section, we briefly examine the way in which the results of the Uruguay Round MTN have been transformed into primary treaty rules through the application of the relevant provisions of general treaty law and rules of customary international law concerning the making and performance of treaties.[54]

The text of the *Final Act of the Uruguay Round (Final Act)*[55] was formally adopted at the final meeting of the Trade Negotiations Committee or TNC in

represent a common agreement among *all* Members' (emphasis in the original). Tariff Schedules and Schedules of Services Commitments are legally binding instruments and stand on an equal footing with other WTO rights and obligations.

50 *See* Joost Pauwelyn, 'A Typology of Multilateral Treaty Obligations: Are WTO Obligations Bilateral or Collective in Nature?' (2003) 14 *EJIL* 907-951at 928-941. According to Pauwelyn, WTO obligations, including the MFN norm, are bilateral even though part of a multilateral treaty and the system of rights and obligations thereby created *remains* as a collection (or bundling) of equivalent legal obligations of the reciprocal or bilateral type. He does, however, admit that some more recent regulatory types obligations, such as exist under the *GATS*, *SPS*, *TBT* or *TRIPs* Agreements may be collective in nature *'when it comes to rules on standing'*, which would allow parties to pursue a collective complaint '*in the general interest*', *ibid*, at 940.

51 Antonio Cassese, *International Law* (2nd edn rev Oxford: Oxford University Press, 2004), 14, points out that international rules in a multilateral treaty may address themselves to all States but often they 'confer rights or impose obligations *on pairs of States* only', which means that each State has a right or obligation in relation to one other State only and in this sense they are synallagmatic or reciprocal rights and obligations, as distinct from rights and obligations *erga omnes*.

52 Oscar Schachter, 'Entangled Treaty and Custom' in Y. Dinstein (ed.) *International Law at a time of complexity: essays in honour of Shabtai Rosenne* (Dordrecht: Nijhoff, 1989) 717-738, at 735.

53 Schachter, *ibid.*

54 Once again, the relevant conventional international law that is applicable here is the VCLT or those provisions of the VCLT that are declaratory of customary international law, above n. 46.

55 *Final Act Embodying the Results of the Uruguay Round of Multilateral Trade Negotiations*, LT/UR/A/1 (15 April 1994) [hereinafter *Final Act*], to which is attached the *Agreement Establishing the World Trade Organisation* (or *WTO Agreement*) (adopted 15 April 1994, *in force* 1 January 1995) LT/UR/A/2 and its Annexes) 1867 *UNTS* 3, (1994) 33 *ILM* 1125, with 'Introductory Note' by Amelia Porges, 1125-1132, reproduced in *The Legal Texts*, above n. 2, 2-3.

Brussels on 15 December 1993[56] and subsequently signed at the specially convened Meeting of participating Governments and the European Communities, on the occasion of the final session of the Trade Negotiations Committee at Ministerial level, held at Marrakesh from 12-15 April 1994. The *Final Act* itself is preceded by a '*Note*', which states that the text embodies 'all the results of the Uruguay Round of Multilateral Trade Negotiations' and that '[B]y signing this Final Act at the Marrakesh Ministerial Meeting, the participants will establish the texts set out in the Annexes, in accordance with international treaty practice', in addition to which reference is made to the process of establishing and authenticating the text of a treaty in accordance with Article 10 VCLT.

The *Final Act* is an important legal instrument, which explicitly recognises the fact that States have concluded a negotiating round[57] and have bound themselves by signature of the *Final Act* (a) to submit the *WTO Agreement* for approval by their competent authorities and (b) to adopt the Ministerial Declarations and Decisions in the *Final Act*[58] thereby bringing the WTO into existence,[59] i.e. it is both declaratory and constitutive. At the same time the *Final Act* deals with the pre-requisite conditions for acceptance of the *WTO Agreement* by States, which were not (yet) contracting parties to the GATT by requiring them to conclude negotiations for accession to the GATT and to become contracting parties before being able to accept the *WTO Agreement*.[60] Additionally, for those same States that had not become GATT contracting parties as of the date of the *Final Act* (i.e. by 15 April 1994) their Schedules would not be considered as 'definitive' until such time as they had been completed, whereupon they could accede to the GATT and subsequently the *WTO Agreement*.[61] Finally, signature of the *Final Act*

56 The text of the *Final Act*, as adopted, appears at (1994) 33 *ILM*, 11-12 with an 'Introductory Note' to the General Agreement on Tariffs and Trade: Multilateral Trade Negotiations Final Act Embodying the Results of the Uruguay Round of Trade Negotiations' [15 December 2003] by Amelia Porges at 1-8.

57 Paragraph 1 of the *Final Act*, above n. 55.

58 This is without prejudice to the *Understanding on Commitments in Financial Services*, *The Legal Texts*, above n. 2, 478-482, which although annexed to the *Final Act*, was not treated in the same manner as the other Ministerial Declarations and Decisions since it was negotiated as an optional package which a Member could if it wished reference in its schedule of market access commitments in services. Thus, the effect of the decision is plurilateral rather than multilateral in character since some but not all Members have agreed to it.

59 Paragraph 2 of the *Final Act*, above n. 55.

60 Paragraph 5 of the *Final Act*, *ibid.*

61 *Ibid.*

authenticates the texts attached thereto,[62] i.e. the *WTO Agreement*, its Annexes and the various Ministerial Decisions and Declarations.[63]

Alongside the *Final Act*, Ministers also adopted a Ministerial Declaration (the *Marrakesh Ministerial Declaration*)[64] in which they undertook to sign the *Final Act* and to adopt four associated Ministerial Decisions, one of which involved the process of transition from the GATT to the WTO.[65] However, it is generally understood that a State does not give its consent to be bound by the simple adoption or authentification of the text[66] of a treaty or even by signing the Final

62 Early GATT practice in the matter of recording the results of additional tariff negotiations confirms this; see for example, 'Documents to Embody the Results of the Torquay Negotiations', Report adopted by the CONTRACTING PARTIES on 15 December 1950, *BISD* II, 157-166 at 157, which explicitly states *inter alia*, at para. 3, that '[T]he Final Act serves to authenticate the texts of the three annexed instruments.'

63 Paragraph 6 of the *Final Act*, above n. 55.

64 *Marrakesh Declaration of 15 April 1994* (*Marrakesh Ministerial Declaration*), *The Legal Texts*, above n. 2, iii-v.

65 Sixth Recital, *Marrakesh Ministerial Declaration*, *ibid*. Ministers agreed to establish a Preparatory Committee in order to lay the ground for the entry into force of the WTO, whereupon they adopted the *Decision on the Establishment of the Preparatory Committee for the World Trade Organization*, LT/UR/D-6/4 (15 April 1994) (1994) 33 *ILM* 1270-2 [hereinafter the *PCWTO Decision*], reproduced in *The Legal Texts*, above n. 2, 473-475, which is largely procedural in character. It set up a transitional committee, determined its membership (all signatories of the *Final Act* and any contracting party eligible to become an original WTO Member) (paras. 2 and 5) its means of reaching decisions by consensus (para. 4), established its own terms of reference and, in accordance therewith, that the PCWTO would cease to exist upon the entry into force of the *WTO Agreement* (para. 8).

Two of Ministerial Decisions, which are not discussed here, were: the *Ministerial Decision on Organizational and Financial Consequences Flowing from Implementation of the Agreement Establishing the World Trade Organization*, LT/UR/D-6/3 (15 April 1994) (1994) 33 *ILM*, 1269-70, *The Legal Texts*, *ibid*, 472, which is purely operational in character, and the *Ministerial Decision on Trade and the Environment*, LT/UR/D-6/2 (15 April 1994) (1994) 33 *ILM*, 1267-69, *ibid*, 469-471, which establishes a new permanent body, the Committee on Trade and Environment, sets out its terms of reference and a list of topics for its consideration and review.

66 This includes such practices as the initialling of the text drawn up during negotiations or a signature *ad referendum*, i.e. signature given provisionally and subject to confirmation, the latter of which is common practice among WTO Members. This subsidiary point in international treaty making was taken up in Article 12:2 (a) and (b) VCLT, above n. 10.

While initialling or the placing of a signature *ad referendum* may establish the text *ne variateur*, i.e. recognise its authenticity that is not subject to change, and indicate the personal agreement of the person initialling or the signatory, this does not imply an element of consent on the part of that person's government; *see* further, Kaye Holloway,

Act of a conference,[67] which has been called for the purposes of concluding a set of negotiations and will eventually be transformed into an internationally binding legal instrument. Instead something more is required, namely that States (or international organisations) express their consent to be bound by means of 'signature, exchange of instruments constituting a treaty, ratification, acceptance, approval or accession or by another means if so agreed'.[68]

Thus, the Ministers undertook a commitment 'to ratify the WTO Agreement so that it [could] enter into force by 1 January 1995 or as early as possible thereafter', in pursuance of which they adopted the Ministerial *Decision on the Acceptance*[69] *of and Accession to the Agreement Establishing the World Trade*

Modern Trends in Treaty Law: Constitutional Law, Reservations and the Three Modes of Legislation (London: Stevens & Sons/Dobbs Ferry, NY: Oceana Publications, 1967) 35. Once confirmed, it constitutes full signature and will operate as one of the rules constituting a state's consent to be bound; *see* Report of the International Law Commission on the Work of the Second Part of its 17th Session (3-28 January 1966), UN Doc A/6309/Rev. 1 [hereinafter ILC Report 1966], Commentary to draft Article 1, paras. (4) and (5), at 305. *See* Aust, above n. 48, 77, who notes that as a matter of practice many States sign a treaty text *ad referendum* in order to indicate that the treaty in question must first be submitted for parliamentary approval before ratification can take place.

67 Aust, *ibid*, 75-76. Article 9 VCLT, above n. 10, (and repeated verbatim in Article 9 VCLTIO, above n. 8) governs the adoption of the text of a treaty at an international conference. Paragraph 1 of that provision deals with the consent of *all* States while paragraph 2 sets out a decision-making procedure for the adoption (2/3 majority vote), with the residual rule that States may apply a different rule for adoption if they so wish. However, adoption of the text is not the same as consent to be bound; *see* also Claus-Dieter Ehlermann and Lothar Ehring, 'Decision-making in the World Trade Organization: Is the Consensus Practice in the World Trade Organization Adequate for Making, Revising and Implementing Rules on International Trade?' (2005) 8 *JIEL* 51-75 at 56.

68 'Consent to be bound' is understood in the sense of Article 11 VCLT, above n. 10 (and repeated verbatim in Article 11 VCLTIO, above n. 8) and is considered to be declaratory of the customary international law rule on the matter, being evidence of a widespread and uniform practice of states over a considerable period of time; it thus binds even those States that are not parties to the VCLT.

69 According to the International Law Commission, upon the second reading of its draft articles on the law of treaties, the term 'acceptance' had not only become established treaty practice over the past twenty years (since 1945) but also had 'become established as a name given to two new procedures, one analogous to 'ratification' and the other to 'accession'. The result of this was that signature 'subject to acceptance' had become signature 'subject to ratification' while a treaty that was opened for acceptance without prior signature was akin to the process of accession; *see* ILC Report 1966, above n. 66, commentary to draft Article 11, paras. (10) and (11), at 309. This observation does not accord with GATT/WTO treaty law and practice where acceptance denotes a process

Organization (*Decision on Acceptance and Accession*).[70] This Ministerial Decision is important because paragraph 1 of Article XIV *WTO Agreement* makes it clear that only contracting parties to the GATT 1947, i.e. those States which have signed and ratified the GATT 1947 or one of the later Protocols to the GATT and have not withdrawn from the Agreement[71] together with the European Communities, are eligible to become 'original Members' of the WTO and can give their consent to be bound by means of acceptance.[72] The Ministerial *Decision on Acceptance and Accession* covers other situations of States and customs territories, which had participated in the GATT 1947 as *de facto* contracting parties, or were in the process of becoming contracting parties to the GATT 1947, one which would allow them to be considered as 'original members' of the WTO.[73] Such issues are also related to the potential coexistence of the GATT 1947 and the *WTO Agreement*

of consent to be bound, which in practice is signature, including signature *ad referendum*, followed by ratification and accession which is a completely separate process and is bound up with becoming a contracting party to the GATT/Member of the WTO.

70 *Decision on the Acceptance of and Accession to the Agreement Establishing the World Trade Organization*, LT/UR/D-6/1 (15 April 1994) (1994) 33 *ILM*, 1265-7 [hereinafter *Decision on Acceptance and Accession*], reproduced in *The Legal Texts*, above n. 2, 466-468.

71 On the basis of Article XXXI GATT 1947 four States did withdraw as contracting parties to the GATT in the 1950's. They were: Republic of China, effective 5 May 1950, 55 *UNTS* 196; Lebanon, effective 25 February 1951, 77 *UNTS* 367; Syria, effective 6 August 1951, 90 *UNTS* 324; and Liberia, effective 13 June 1953, 163 *UNTS* 375. *See Analytical Index: Guide to GATT Law and Practice* 6th edition (Geneva: GATT Secretariat 1994) [hereinafter *GATT Analytical Index*], 937. Each of these four States previously had no automatic right to rejoin the GATT or currently to become a WTO Member. Instead each of them has had to renegotiate their terms of accession. China acceded to the WTO in 2001 while the Lebanese Republic is in the process of negotiating its accession. Neither Liberia nor Syria rejoined the GATT although Syria has subsequently made a request for WTO accession, which has thus far not been granted by the Members.

72 The *WTO Agreement* expressly provides in paragraph 1 of Article XIV that it 'shall be open for acceptance, by signature', *The Legal Texts*, above n. 2, 16.

73 The *Decision on Acceptance and Accession* deals on the basis of paragraph 1(a) with: (1) certain least-developed GATT contracting parties that were given an additional year from 15 April 1994 to submit their schedules (third recital); (2) the position of *de facto* contracting parties to the GATT 1947 on the basis of Article XXVI:5(c) GATT 1947 (fourth recital); (3) any State or a separate customs territory, which became a contracting party to the GATT between 15 April 1994 and entry into force of the *WTO Agreement* on 1 January 1995 (fifth recital); and (4) on the basis of paragraph 5, with any other participant in the Uruguay Round in the process of becoming a contracting party to the GATT but not having done so by 15 April 1994, all of which would be considered as original Members rather than as acceding Members. Paragraphs 2(a) and (b) of the *Decision on Acceptance and Accession* deal with the situation whereby States or customs

and the participation of States in successive treaties that deal with the same subject matter[74] and form part of the our analysis of the manner in which the results of the Uruguay Round were brought into effect.

The contracting parties to the GATT met at the so-called 'Implementation Conference', which took place in Geneva on 8 December 1994, with a view to bringing the *WTO Agreement* into force on 1 January 1995.[75] The Implementation Conference adopted a series of decisions that were recommended by the Preparatory Committee for the World Trade Organization or PCWTO to allow for the smooth transition from the GATT 1947 to the WTO and to bring the results of the Uruguay Round into immediate effect as of that same date while taking into account ongoing obligations under the GATT 1947.[76] Those decisions and the manner in which they were adopted reflect the practice of States in applying the rules of Article 30 VCLT on the matter of successive treaties that deal with the same subject matter.[77]

The provision, which is considered by some commentators to be problematic,[78] contains a number of residual rules that codify customary international

territories were acceding to the *WTO* Agreement on the basis of Article XII *WTO Agreement* (fifth recital).

74 During the remainder of 1994, in the period leading up to the entry into force of the *WTO Agreement,* the United States put pressure on the other contracting parties to the GATT to examine the potential legal consequences that could arise from successive treaties on the same subject-matter, the legal consequences of withdrawal from a treaty for some parties *only* and the best way to deal with the parallel existence of the GATT 1947 and the *GATT 1994* with distinct membership. *See* further Marceau, above, n. 1,149-152. For an overview of the general law and practice pertaining to successor international institutions, *see* Hugo J. Hahn, 'Continuity in the Law of International Organisation' (1964) 13 *ÖZöR* 167-239.

75 The set of decisions adopted at the Implementation Conference as well as the process of orderly transition from the GATT 1947 to the WTO could serve as a useful case study for other international organisations should they decide at a future date to replace their founding treaties with a constitution and a revised institutional and normative framework. *See* Patrick M. More, 'The Decisions Bridging the GATT 1947 and the WTO Agreement' (1996) 90 *AJIL* 317-328, at 317.

76 Marceau, above n. 1, 154-161.

77 More, above n. 75, 318-324.

78 Ian Sinclair, *The Vienna Convention on the Law of Treaties* (2nd edn Manchester: Manchester University Press, 1984), 93-98 and Jan B. Mus, 'Conflicts between Treaties in International Law' (1998). 45 *NILR* 208-232. See in particular, E.W. Vierdag, 'The Time of the "Conclusion" of a Multilateral Treaty: Article 30 of the Vienna Convention on the Law of Treaties and Related Provisions' (1989) 59 *BYIL* 75-111, at 97, who maintains that 'there is in Article 30 VCLT no relevant legal connection between the abstract legal rules contained in "successive" treaties on the one hand, and the concrete

law on the matter.[79] For the purposes of the transition of the GATT to the WTO, paragraph 4 of Article 30 VCLT governing the situation where a later treaty is concluded between States that does not include all the parties to the earlier one, is of particular relevance since section (b) operates to ensure that a later treaty (*WTO Agreement*) cannot deprive a State which is not (yet) a party to it of its rights under the earlier treaty (GATT 1947). This is because 'as between a State Party to both treaties and a State Party to only one of the treaties, the treaty to which both State are parties governs their mutual rights and obligations'.[80]

The *Decision on Transitional Coexistence of the GATT 1947 and the WTO Agreement* (the *Transitional Coexistence Decision*)[81] gives effect to paragraph (b) of Article 30:4 VCLT by providing for a short period in which the GATT 1947 would govern the relationship between a WTO Member, which remained a GATT contracting party, and a GATT contracting party that was not a WTO Member, to the extent that the two treaties were compatible, in order to preserve the rights and obligations of the Parties.[82] First, those GATT contracting parties that had become WTO Members would not discriminate against any contracting party that had not yet become a Member nor would they maintain or adopt any measures inconsistent with the provisions of the *WTO Agreement* (and by definition its annexes). Second, disputes that had already arisen under Article XXIII GATT 1947 with respect to specific measures, and which were either already being

rights and obligations of States on the other hand'. Cf. Aust, above n. 48, 173, who claims that the topic of successive treaties on the same subject matter 'does not cause daily consternation in the legal departments of foreign ministries' even if it is gaining in importance due to the wealth and complexity of multilateral treaties.

79 Aust, *ibid*, 181-183; in the law of treaties residual (or 'residuary') rules are generally understood to be those rules (usually procedural) which come into play when the matter is insufficiently regulated in the treaty itself, *in casu* the secondary rules of the VCLT that do not prescribe conduct but leave this to States to elaborate upon.

80 Article 30:4(b) VCLT, above n. 10.

81 Decision of 8 December 1994 adopted by the Preparatory Committee for the WTO and the CONTRACTING PARTIES to GATT 1947 on the Transitional Co-existence of the GATT 1947 and the WTO Agreement, L/7583, *BISD* 41S/5 [*Transitional Coexistence Decision*]. *See* More, above n. 74, for a detailed discussion of the problems arising from successive treaties and the relevant co-existence decision, the necessity of which he questions in light of the experience gained from its application.

82 See More, above n. 75, 318-324, noting that the *Transitional Co-existence Decision* resolved the uncertain application of Article 30 VCLT, above n. 10, in some practical ways, in particular in assuring (i) the continued operation of the principle of non-discrimination, as determined by MFN treatment (ii) the avoidance of protectionism and (iii) the elimination of 'double jeopardy' in dispute settlement proceedings in the relationship of the GATT 1947 to the *WTO Agreement*.

pursued or were completed, would not be filed anew under Article 6 of the *Understanding on Rules and Procedures governing the Settlement of Disputes* or *DSU*. Third, the GATT 1947 would continue in existence for the duration of one year following the entry into force of the *World Trade Agreement.*[83]

A complementary *Decision on the Participation in Meetings of WTO Bodies by Certain Signatories of the Final Act Eligible to Become Original Members of the WTO* (the *Transitional Participation Decision*)[84] allowed those contracting parties to the GATT 1947 that were eligible to become original WTO Members, for a period of seven months from 1 January 1995, to be present and speak at all formal and informal meetings of WTO bodies, other than the Textiles Monitoring Body or TMB, and to have access to all documents, normally made available to Members at meetings of those bodies but without rights to decision-making in those bodies.[85]

The process of large-scale treaty-making following completion of a further MTN remains untested in the WTO because the negotiations that were launched

83 Similarly, two transitional decisions relating to Code Agreements negotiated under the Tokyo Round MTN, above n. 40, were adopted. One was the Decision of 8 December 1994 adopted by the Preparatory Committee for the WTO and the CONTRACTING PARTIES to GATT 1947 and transmitted to the Parties to the Agreement on Implementation of Article VI of the General Agreement on Tariffs and Trade (L/7584), *BISD* 41S/10 [hereinafter the *Transitional Anti-dumping Code Decision*]. The other was the Decision of 8 December 1994 adopted by the Preparatory Committee for the WTO and the CONTRACTING PARTIES to GATT 1947 and transmitted to the Signatories to the Agreement on Interpretation and Application of Articles VI, XVI and XXIII of the General Agreement on Tariffs and Trade (L/7586), *BISD* 41S/11 [hereinafter the *Transitional Subsidies and Countervailing Code Decision*].

84 Decision of 8 December 1994 adopted by the Preparatory Committee for the WTO and noted by the CONTRACTING PARTIES to GATT 1947 (L/7581), *BISD* 41S/15, relating to Participation in Meetings of WTO Bodies by Certain Signatories of the Final Act Eligible to Become Original Members of the WTO [hereinafter *Transitional Participation Decision*].

85 A further operational decision relates to the institutional transfer of property and assets belonging to the Interim Commission of the International Trade Organization or ICITO and the CONTRACTING PARTIES to the GATT 1947 to the WTO. The so-called *Transitional Arrangements on Transfers Decision*, Decision of 8 December 1994 was adopted by the Preparatory Committee for the WTO, the CONTRACTING PARTIES to GATT 1947 and the Executive Committee of ICITO, with attached an Annex embodying the Agreement on the Transfer of Assets, Liabilities, Records, Staff and Functions from the Interim Commission of the International Trade Organization and the GATT to the World Trade Organization (L/7580), *BISD* 41S/; see further chapter V, section 2.2(d) for the effects of this decision on the staff of the GATT (ICITO) Secretariat.

at the Fourth Meeting of the Ministerial Conference in 2001[86] (the Doha Development Round) have not yet been concluded. However, upon completion of the Doha Development Round MTN it can be expected that a further Meeting of Ministers will be specially convened in order to transform the results of that Round, including the amendments to existing treaty norms, into binding treaty provisions. This could either be done by means of multiple amendments in a single Protocol of amendments, which may not be desirable given that separate conditions may govern the acceptance and entry into force of different amendments,[87] or by means of the adoption of a series of amendments through individual Protocols,[88] as was agreed with respect to the results of the 1954-55 GATT Review Session.[89]

Amending Protocols should be distinguished from the Agreements that were concluded between some of the GATT contracting parties at the end of the Tokyo Round MTN,[90] the majority of which could be considered as the application of successive treaties on the same subject matter (Article 30 VCLT). However, the

86 WTO Ministerial Conference, Fourth Session, Doha, 9-14 November 2001, *Ministerial Declaration*, WT/MIN(01)/DEC/1, 20 November 2001 [hereinafter *Doha Ministerial Declaration*].

87 The possibility of drawing up a single Protocol of amendments was considered by the Legal and Drafting Committee under the GATT 1947 during the Ninth Session of the GATT Contracting Parties, held from 28 October 1954 through 18 March 1955 (the '1954-1955 Review Session'), which was charged with examining and restructuring the GATT in accordance with Article XXIX:4 GATT 1947.

88 'Report of the Legal and Drafting Committee on the Procedure for the Approval of Amendments to the General Agreement', W.9/173, p. 2, *GATT Analytical Index*, above n. 71, 930.

89 Of the various proposals for textual amendments to the GATT, only the *Protocol Amending the Preamble and Part II and III of the GATT*, GATT Doc. PROT/6 (adopted 10 March 1955, *in force* 10 July 1957) 278 *UNTS* 168 survived. In this connection, *see Continued Application of Schedules to the General Agreement on Tariffs and Trade*, Declaration of 10 March 1955, *BISD* 3S/79 (1955). Three other Protocols would have changed portions of GATT text, including Part I and Articles XXIX and XXX GATT 1947 (in this instance the Protocol was allowed to lapse), as well as providing for organisational amendments to the GATT. The 1955 Review Session led to the biggest textual change to GATT since the original text of 1947, followed in 1964 by the addition of Part IV to the GATT.

90 Tokyo Round MTN, above n. 40. The negotiations resulted in nine separate agreements or 'side codes': the *1979 Agreement on Implementation of Article VI*, the *Agreement on Interpretation and Application of Articles VI, XVI and XXIII*, the *Agreement on Implementation of Article VII*, the *Agreement on Import Licensing Procedures*, the *Agreement on Technical Barriers to Trade*, the *Agreement on Government Procurement*, the *Agreement on Trade in Civil Aircraft*, the *Arrangement Regarding Bovine Meat* and the *International Dairy Arrangement*.

Tokyo Round Agreements only bound those GATT contracting parties that had signed and ratified them, as GATT practice demonstrates,[91] and thus have more in common with *inter se* modifications in the sense of Article 41 VCLT. These 'stand-alone' treaties had their own separate signatory clauses, their own institutional measures, such as a committee of the signatories to a particular Agreement, and their own dispute settlement mechanisms.[92] Four of the Tokyo Round Agreements were still in force upon the entry into force of the WTO on 1 January 1995 and were included in Annex 4 to the *WTO Agreement*, as 'Plurilateral Trade Agreements'. Since then one has been re-negotiated,[93] two have been wound up[94] and the fourth remains in force without any changes.[95]

3 Principal rule-making and the application of secondary treaty rules

In the overall context of the treaty-making process, the inclusion of secondary treaty rules in a treaty such as the *WTO Agreement* allows for the revision of primary treaty rules. The majority of secondary treaty rules have their legal basis in and derive their authority from primary treaty rules but there may be other rules, which are based on decisions taken by the Members in one of the WTO bodies which have normative effect. These other rules should properly be characterised as forming part of the established practice of the organisation and may in turn

91 See 'Action by the CONTRACTING PARTIES on the Multilateral Trade Negotiations', L/4905, Decision of 28 November 1979, *BISD* 26S/201 (1980) which, in para. 3, states that '[T]he CONTRACTING PARTIES note that existing rights and benefits under the GATT of contracting parties not being parties to these Agreements, including those derived form Article I [MFN], are not affected by these Agreements.'

92 Jackson, *The World Trading System* above n. 21, 75-78, who also discusses the legal status of the Tokyo Round 'Side' Agreements.

93 *Agreement on Government Procurement* (adopted 12 April 1979, *in force* 1 January 1981) *BISD* 26S/33, 1235 *UNTS* 258, subsequently re-negotiated; *see Agreement on Government Procurement* or *AGP* (adopted 15 April 1994 , *in force* 1 January 1996) 1915 *UNTS* 103.

94 The *Arrangement Regarding Bovine Meat, BISD* 26S/84, 1186 *UNTS* 344 and *Termination of the International Bovine Meat Agreement*, Decision pursuant to Article VI:3, IMA/8 (30 September 1997) respectively the *International Dairy Arrangement*, *BISD* 26S/91, 1186 *UNTS* 54 and *Termination of the International Dairy Agreement*, Decision pursuant to Article VIII:3, IDA/8 (30 September 1997). Both treaty instruments had a termination date of 31 December 1997.

95 *Agreement on Trade in Civil Aircraft* (adopted 12 April 1979, *in force* 1 January 1980) *BISD* 26S/162, 1186 *UNTS* 170; *Agreement on Technical Barriers to Trade* (adopted 12 April 1979, *in force* 1 January 1980) *BISD* 26S/8, 1186 UNTS 276.

give rise to subsidiary rule-making by WTO bodies;[96] they are dealt with in the next chapter.

The secondary treaty rules, which are examined in the context of the WTO, include the amending law and practice of the WTO, the use of Protocols as supplementary agreements to the Schedules, the modification, rectification and certification of Schedules, rectification in the event of error, accession, the waiver power (both the general waiver and the use of 'mini-waivers') and the role of authoritative interpretation. Each of these secondary treaty rules is analysed separately on the basis of WTO treaty law and practice with reference to the provisions in the VCLT, which govern the observance, application and interpretation of treaties, i.e. performance generally (Part III VCLT), amendment and modification of treaties (Part IV VCLT), invalidity, termination and suspension of the operation of treaties (Part V VCLT) and the role of depositaries, notifications, corrections and registration (Part VII VCLT).

3.1 Amendment

In the past half century there has been a tremendous increase in multilateral treaty-making in the international legal order in terms of the number of treaties, the degree of complexity and technicality of the subject matter covered and the growth of quasi-legislative international treaty instruments, often doubling as the constitutional basis of an international organisation. One consequence of this increased engagement in multilateral treaty making is that it has become increasingly difficult to bring about even the most minor amendments to many of those treaties, including multilateral treaties that establish international organisations, otherwise known as 'constituent instruments',[97] and to achieve unanimity for the purposes of amendment. Consequently, it has become increasingly common for the constitutions of international organisations, and their related treaty instruments, to make it possible for States to adopt amendments by a majority of two-thirds of the votes cast at a conference or similar plenary session of the Members, called especially for that purpose.

96 See chapter V, section 2.

97 Aust, above n. 48, 215. Egon Schwelb, 'The Amending Procedure of Constitutions of International Organizations' (1954) 31 *BYIL*, 49-95, with particular reference to the amending provisions of the ILO, UNRAA, FAO, ICAO, UNESCO, WHO, ISO and WMO, as well as Articles 108 and 109 of the UN Charter; he also makes some reference to the Havana Charter for an ITO and to the GATT 1947.

Even so, there remains an inherent tension in modern treaty law and practice between the performance of a web of treaty obligations to which States have consented, often after lengthy and complex negotiations sometimes as the result of a package deal (1982 UN Convention on the Law of the Sea)[98] or a single undertaking (WTO), and the need to take account of the evolutionary character of international law in adapting to changing circumstances.[99] Given this situation States have devised elaborate means of amending treaty instruments 'to suit the particular needs of the organisation or treaty'.[100] While amending clauses may be rigidly drawn to prevent frequent recourse to them, thereby maintaining legal certainty and, in the case of a package deal or a single undertaking, preserving the integrity of the treaty instrument, in practice States frequently bypass formal amendment procedures in favour of exercising a range of flexibilities such as modifications *inter se* in the sense of Article 41 VCLT or interpreting treaty provisions in the sense of Article 31 VCLT.

The basic amending provisions in Articles 39 and 40 VCLT offer States the possibility of 'contracting out' in favour of more specific rules on amendment, as set out in the relevant multilateral treaty to which they are parties, and will govern the amendment(s) as between them. This is true in respect of the *WTO Agreement* which is fairly exhaustive as to the means for effectuating amendments to that particular instrument, as well as the rights and obligations of the Members in the annexed Multilateral Trade Agreements. Article 39 VCLT simply provides that a treaty may be amended by agreement of the parties but does not prescribe any rules for such amendment other than those set out in Part II of the Convention except in so far as the treaty itself may otherwise provide. Similarly, Article 40 VCLT on the amendment of multilateral treaties does not lay down any actual procedures for their amendment but simply notes the possibility of exercising the amending power in respect of a treaty, with deference to any procedures that a treaty itself might prescribe.

98 United Nations Convention on the Law of the Sea (adopted 10 December 1982, *in force* 16 November 1994) 1833 *UNTS* 3.

99 David Freestone and Alex Oude Elferink, 'Flexibility and Innovation in the Law of the Sea – Will the LOSC Amendment Procedures ever be used?' Paper for the Third Verzijl Symposium, Utrecht, The Netherlands, 3 December 2004, 1-46, at 5.

100 Aust, above n. 48, 216, citing Hans Blix and Jirina H. Emerson (ed.), *The Treaty Maker's Handbook* (Dobbs Ferry, N.Y: Oceana Publications, Inc./Stockholm: Almqvist & Wiksell, 1973) 225-239 for relevant examples of informal adoption procedures. For the problems that arise with the amending procedures in Articles 311-314 of the UN Convention on the Law of the Sea 1982 and the use of 'implementation agreements' to bring about amendments and modifications, *see* Freestone and Oude Elferink, *ibid*, *in extenso.*

Furthermore, the practice of States in the amendment of multilateral treaties, including constituent instruments like the *WTO Agreement*, have led to the evolution of rules and procedures for the adoption of amendments, which may also govern the entry into force of a particular amendment. Some or all of the following criteria are relevant in respect of the development of these rules and procedures:[101] (a) number of parties needed to support the amendment before it is put to all the parties, i.e. at the stage of the proposed amendment; (b) required majority for the amendment's adoption; (c) adoption of amendment by ratification, acceptance or otherwise; (d) number of parties needed to ratify or accept the amendment for it to come into force; (e) where ratification or acceptance is not required, whether the amendment can be adopted by tacit agreement (or by means of a 'quasi-legislative' or legislative activity of an institutional body in an international organisation); and (f) whether the amendment binds parties that have not accepted it, and if so on what conditions. The rules governing particular amendments to the WTO constitute combinations of the aforementioned criteria depending upon the provision to be amended.[102]

a) Amendment law of the WTO

Article X *WTO Agreement* sets out specific procedures for its amendment and also for the amendment of treaty provisions in the annexed Multilateral Trade Agreements. WTO treaty law in the matter of amendment adopts the basic rules contained in Article XXX GATT 1947,[103] despite some of the practical problems that have arisen in the past in amending the General Agreement.[104] Claus-Dieter

101 Adapted from the six points that Aust, *ibid*, lists and complemented with other features particular to the amendment procedures of international organisations in Schwelb, above n. 97, 55-60.

102 Blix and Emerson, above n. 100, 239 with reference to Article XXX GATT 1947.

103 The basic rule under Article XXX GATT 1947, *The Legal Texts*, above n. 2, 531, required unanimity for certain amendments to Part I (containing the MFN obligation and the schedules of tariff bindings) and provisions related to the Havana Charter in Article XXIX GATT 1947. In practice, the increasing difficulty which GATT contracting parties experienced with amending the General Agreement was one of the reasons for the development of the Tokyo Round 'side codes' and other special arrangements. *See* further John H. Jackson, *The World Trade Organization: Constitution and Jurisprudence* (London: The Royal Institute for International Affairs/Pinter, 1998) 44.

104 Jackson, *World Trade and the Law of* GATT, above n. 22, §3.6, 73-82, who reviews the practical problems of the Article XXX GATT 1947 unanimity requirement being applied to the modification and renegotiation of GATT Tariff Schedules, the issue of rectifications and certifications and the relationship of the amending power in Article XXX GATT 1947 to the waiver power in Article XXV:5 GATT 1947.

Ehlermann and Lothar Ehring consider Article X *WTO Agreement* to be stricter[105] than Article 40 VCLT with one exception but this is hardly surprising given the language of paragraph 1 of Article 40 VCLT which states: '[U]nless the treaty otherwise provides …', which is a *renvoi* to such specific rules on amendment as may exist in a particular multilateral treaty.

The most striking aspect of Article X *WTO Agreement* is its comprehensiveness with respect to the criteria that we have previously identified for the amendment of a multilateral treaty. It provides detailed rules governing such matters as the number of Members needed to support a proposed WTO treaty amendment (see (a) above) the required majority for the amendment's adoption (see (b) above) and the number of Members needed for ratification or acceptance for the amendment to come into force (see (c) and (d) above). The question whether the amendment can be adopted by tacit agreement (see (e) above) and whether the amendment binds Members that have not accepted it (see (f) above) depends upon the substance of the treaty provision and its legal character, in particular whether it *alters the rights and obligations of the Members.* We turn briefly to examine how these criteria have been taken up in the amendment law of the WTO in the remainder of this section before analysing the practice of WTO amendment in the next section.

As to the numbers of Members needed to propose or initiate a treaty amendment (criterion (a)), this differs depending upon the subject matter of the proposed amendment. In the case of a proposed amendment to the *WTO Agreement* or any of the Multilateral Trade Agreements in Annex 1, i.e. Annex IA: the Multilateral Agreements on Trade in Goods, Annex 1B: the *GATS* and Annex 1C: the *TRIPs*, any Member can initiate a proposal for amendment to the Ministerial Conference (or the General Council), on the basis of paragraph 1 of Article X *WTO Agreement.*[106] However, it is also possible for the membership to adopt a decision in one of the third level Councils, which oversees the respective Annex, proposing an amendment of the provisions in the corresponding Multilateral Trade Agreements.[107] Finally, any Member can initiate a proposal to amend either the *DSU* (Annex 2) or the *TPRM* (Annex 3) by submitting this to the Ministerial Conference, in accordance with paragraph 7 of Article X *WTO Agreement* without any provisions being made for the Members to initiate a proposal for amendment in the DSB or the TPRB, both of which operate as emanations of the General Council that does not of itself have right of initiative in amendment proposals.

105 Ehlermann and Ehring, above n. 67, 57.
106 Article X:1 *WTO Agreement, The Legal Texts*, above n. 2, 12, first sentence.
107 Article X:1 *WTO Agreement, ibid*, second sentence.

The remaining criteria for the amendment of WTO treaty rules, with respect to the required majority for the amendment's adoption at (b), the number of Members needed for ratification or acceptance for the amendment to come into force at (c) and (d), and whether the amendment binds Members that have not accepted it (f), vary according to the substance of the provision for which amendment is sought. First of all, the principle of unanimity has been retained in respect of certain fundamental principles relating to the decision making procedures (Article IX *WTO Agreement*) and any amendment to MFN (and the bindings) in the *GATT 1994*, or MFN in the *GATS* or the *TRIPs Agreement*[108] (Article X:2 *WTO Agreement*), all of which 'take effect only upon acceptance by *all* Members', which is the strictest form of amendment procedure both with respect to its adoption and its effects

The remaining amendment clauses contained in Article X *WTO Agreement* follow treaty law and practice in conferring upon a qualified majority of the Members, the power to adopt an amendment to the *WTO Agreement* and related annexes, potentially even against the wishes of the minority.[109] The only difference lies in whether the nature of a provision to be amended is such that it *would alter the rights and obligations of the Members*, in which case the amendment will only come into force after a certain percentage of the Members have accepted it (see criteria (c) and (d) above). In this respect, amendments to the *WTO Agreement* or one of the Multilateral Trade Agreements listed in Annex 1A: Trade in Goods (other than the MFN obligation of Article I:1 MFN for which the unanimity rule applies) or Annex 1C: *TRIPs* (other than Article 4 *TRIPs* for which the unanimity rule applies) *and* which are of a nature that *would alter the rights and obligations of the Members*, 'take effect for the Members that have accepted them upon acceptance by two-thirds of the Members and thereafter for each other Member upon acceptance by it' (criteria (c) and (d).[110] The same applies in respect of amendments to certain *GATS* provisions found in Parts I, II and III *GATS*[111] (other than the MFN obligation of Article II:1 *GATS* for which the unanimity rule applies).

In all of the foregoing cases the WTO's highest plenary body – the Ministerial Conference (or General Council acting in the interim) – can decide by a three-fourths majority of the Members that any Member which has not accepted such amendments within a period specified by the Ministerial Conference shall be free

108 Article X:2 *WTO Agreement*, *The legal Texts*, above n. 2, 13, contains a definitive or closed list of the provisions that require unanimity.

109 Schwelb, above n. 97, 51-52.

110 Article X:3 *WTO Agreement*, *The Legal Texts*, above n. 2, 13.

111 Article X:4 *WTO Agreement*, *ibid.*

to withdraw from the WTO or remain a Member with the consent of the Ministerial Conference, i.e. it can condition a Member's continuing membership of the organisation on its compliance with the acceptance of the amendment of a fundamental treaty provision (see criteria (d) combined with (f) above).[112]

The WTO process is somewhat different in respect of those provisions in the *WTO Agreement* or one of the Multilateral Trade Agreements listed in Annex 1A – Trade in Goods or Annex 1C – *TRIPs Agreement*[113] that *would not alter the rights and obligations of the Members*[114] or in respect of Parts IV, V and VI *GATS*[115] since these 'take effect for all Members upon acceptance by two thirds of the Members', i.e. the amendment binds even those Members that have not accepted it (criteria (c), (d) and (f)). Noteworthy too is the relative ease with which the *DSU*[116] can be amended by consensus and the *TPRM*[117] by approval of the Ministerial Conference and the fact that these amendments 'shall take effect for all Members upon approval by the Ministerial Conference' without the additional requirement of acceptance, as with is the case with all other WTO treaty provisions.

As to whether the amendment must be adopted by individual Members by means of ratification or acceptance and whether this must be express or implied, including the possibility of quasi-legislative or legislative activity by an institutional body, which allows for its tacit acceptance by the Members (see criteria (c) and (e) above), the *WTO Agreement* demonstrates an interesting departure from general international law in making a distinction between amendments to provisions in the *WTO Agreement* and the different Annexes. Paragraph 7 of Article X *WTO Agreement* expressly states that the adoption of amendments to the *WTO Agreement* and the Multilateral Trade Agreements in Annex 1 shall be by acceptance, with the deposit of an instrument of acceptance with the WTO Director-General and that this must occur within the period of acceptance specified by the Ministerial

112 This potential withdrawal or 'suspension' of rights flowing from Membership is identical to the consequences for GATT contracting parties set out in the residual clauses of the amending provision in Article XXX:2 GATT 1947, *The Legal Texts*, above n. 2, 531. The same process was foreseen in the abortive Havana Charter for an ITO; *see* Schwelb, above n. 97, 61.

113 Article X:4 *WTO Agreement, The Legal Texts*, above n. 2, 13.

114 In this respect, the WTO follows the Havana Charter for an International Trade Organization; *see* Schwelb, above n. 97, 56.

115 Final sentence in paragraph 4 of Article X *WTO Agreement, The Legal Texts*, above n. 2, 14.

116 Second sentence in paragraph 8 of Article X *WTO Agreement*, *ibid.*

117 Final sentence in paragraph 8 of Article X *WTO Agreement, ibid.*

Conference.[118] As Anthony Aust notes, the 'use of acceptance or approval was developed in order to enable some States to avoid constitutional requirements to obtain parliamentary authority to ratify, particularly when the parliamentary process was described as 'ratification', and no clear distinction was drawn by the parliament or the constitution between that process and ratification on the international plane'.[119]

The exceptions to this explicit treaty rule on acceptance are amendments to the *DSU* or the *TPRM* in Annexes 2 and 3, on the basis of paragraph 8 of Article X *WTO Agreement*, both of which only require approval by the Ministerial Conference for them to take effect for *all* Members, which means that acceptance is not required. The placement of those particular amending procedures in a separate provision immediately after the general rules on amendment sets those procedures apart and indicates that the drafters did not intend that individual Members should have to seek domestic parliamentary approval. As Aust points out, tacit procedures, such as those envisaged for *DSU* or *TPRM* amendments, are designed to avoid delays brought about by constitutional processes in some States, thereby enabling them to become effective more quickly than other substantive treaty amendments.[120]

However, he acknowledges that some domestic constitutions may require all treaty amendments, including (minor) changes, to be scrutinised by domestic parliaments. In the case of amendments to the DSU, it is likely that similar considerations would weigh heavily with some Member governments, which could see those Members departing from the letter of Article X:8 *WTO Agreement* in search of approval by their national assemblies. This is troublesome because it could bring the validity and effectiveness of *DSU* amendments into question, with some Members holding the view that they could not be bound by the amendments until they had received such approval. It could even lead to a situation where some Members would apply the DSU amendments and others would not – a situation that would be completely untenable especially where the amendments were of the type that involves the Members collectively, in the DSB.[121]

As a matter of treaty practice all amendments and changes to the *WTO Agreement* or one of the annexed Multilateral Trade Agreements, are published following

118 Article X:7 *WTO Agreement*, *ibid*.

119 Aust, above n. 48, 87. As the International Law Commission noted in the second reading of its draft articles on treaty law, in practice the term 'acceptance' is considered to be analogous to that of 'ratification', ILC Report 1966, above n. 66.

120 Aust, *ibid*, 218.

121 The proposed amendments to the DSU, which are designed to address the sequencing problem of Articles 21 and 22 DSU, are exactly of this type; see next section 3.1(b).

their adoption. Upon their entry into force all treaty instruments, including any modifications and rectifications thereto, and the texts of those instruments are deposited with the WTO Director General (Article XIV *WTO Agreement*)[122] and are registered with the UN Secretary General (Article XVI:6 *WTO Agreement*)[123] in both instances fulfilling the depository and registration requirements in Part VII of the VCLT.[124]

b) Practice of WTO amendment

The actual practice of amendment in accordance with the secondary treaty rules laid down in Article X *WTO Agreement* reveals two major problems. One is that since the WTO entered into force in 1995, there have been no major amendments to the *WTO Agreement* or other legal instruments that are taken up in the Annexes.[125] The other is that the amending provisions are just as difficult, if not more difficult to apply in the WTO than they were in the GATT. Not surprisingly, the practice thus far on amendments has been extremely limited and fraught with difficulties. This has led to stagnation in respect of two proposals for amendment and to one very pragmatic solution for dealing with the rigidity of these particular secondary treaty rules on another.

It is clear that at such time as the ongoing negotiations, launched at the Fourth Ministerial Meeting Conference held at Doha in November 2001, reach their conclusion, the results will most likely be taken up in a Final Act of the Doha Round, incorporating the amendments made to the legal instruments and adding any authoritative interpretations in the form of Understandings (as to interpretation), Decisions or Declarations, which the Members may adopt, along the lines of the Final Act of the Uruguay Round.[126] Alternatively, and more likely, the

122 Paragraph 3 of Article XIV makes a temporal distinction between the acceptance of the *WTO Agreement* and the annexed Multilateral Trade Agreements before and after their entry into force. In the former case, the depository is the Director-General to the CONTRACTING PARTIES to GATT 1947 while in the latter case it is the Director-General of the WTO.

123 Paragraph 6 of Article XVI *WTO Agreement* states that '[T]his Agreement shall be registered in accordance with the provisions of Article 102 of the Charter of the United Nations', i.e. with the Secretary General of the UN, and by implication any amendments thereto.

124 Articles 76-80 govern the designation and functions of the depository while paragraph 1 of Article 80 VCLT deals with the registration requirement.

125 *WTO Analytical Index: Guide to WTO Law and Practice* 1st edition (Geneva: WTO Secretariat/Bernan, 2003) [hereinafter *WTO Analytical Index*], 90.

126 *Final Act*, above n. 55.

results of the Doha Round MTN may be appended to a Protocol of Amendment, as was done previously with respect to certain amendments under the GATT 1947.[127]

Apart from the results of a negotiating round leading to possible amendment, there have only been two instances of practice where deliberate attempts have been made to amend provisions in two of the Multilateral Trade Agreements, annexed to the *WTO Agreement* and both say something about the status of WTO practice on amendment. The first relates to an in-built agenda item concerning *DSU* review, which is taken up in one of the Ministerial Decisions adopted at Marrakesh in 1994, and the second relates to a proposed amendment to Article 31 *TRIPs*, on the basis of a Decision of the General Council of August 2003.

At Marrakesh in April 1994, the Ministers adopted a *Decision on the Application and Review of the Understanding on Rules and Procedures Governing the Settlement of Disputes* (*DSU Review Decision*),[128] wherein they agreed 'to complete a full review of dispute settlement rules and procedures under the World Trade Organization within four years after the entry into force of the Agreement Establishing the World Trade Organization, and to take a decision on the occasion of its first meeting after the completion of the review, whether to continue, modify or terminate such dispute settlement rules and procedures', i.e. to take a decision before the end of 1999.[129] In launching the Doha Round of MTN, the original intention had been to keep the ongoing *DSU* Review outside the single undertaking because it was simply a continuation of the process of review that had still not

127 See for example the *Protocol Modifying Part I and Article XXIX of the GATT* (adopted 14 September 1948, *in force* 24 September 1952) 138 *UNTS* 334 and *Protocol Modifying Part II and Article XXVI of the GATT* (adopted 14 September 1948, *in force* 14 December 1948) 62 *UNTS* 80, both of which revised GATT 1947 in light of the Havana Conference; see further Jackson, *World Trade and the Law of GATT*, above n. 22, §3.4, 66-71, at 67.

128 *Decision on the Application and Review of the Understanding on Rules and Procedures Governing the Settlement of Disputes*, *The Legal Texts*, above n. 2, 465 [hereinafter *Ministerial Decision on DSU Review*].

129 While it is sometimes unclear as to whether there is a substantive difference between a treaty amendment and a treaty review (including a treaty revision process), *see* Freestone and Oude Elferink, above n. 99, at 2-3, in general international law it is settled practice that they amount to the same thing, *see* Ian Brownlie, *Principles of Public International Law*, (6th edn, Oxford: Oxford University Press, 2002), 630, fn. 122, and Aust, above n. 48, 220, who cites the ILC in finding no distinction between the processes of amendment and review. In the case of the WTO, the language of the actual *Decision on DSU Review*, *ibid*, speaks of the possibility of 'modifying' the rules and procedures in the DSU.

come to an end and it was not anticipated that DSU amendments would be exchanged for tariff concessions.

Unfortunately, due to the number of proposals for amendment and the discussion they subsequently generated, the deadline was extended in the *Doha Ministerial Declaration* such that Members would 'aim to agree improvements and clarifications [to the dispute settlement system] no later than May 2003.'[130] Ministers also stated that they would 'take steps to ensure that the results enter into force as soon as possible thereafter'.[131]

The point is that the decision to accept amendments to the *DSU* could be taken by consensus and could take effect for all Members upon approval by the Ministerial Conference, as foreseen in Article X:8 *WTO Agreement*, i.e. by tacit agreement conform criteria (e) above. Additionally, the *Doha Ministerial Declaration* specifically places 'the conduct, conclusion and entry into force', arising from the outcome of such negotiations on *DSU* improvements and clarifications, outside the single undertaking,[132] lending further support to the argument that what is required is a simple, more efficient means of bringing about amendments to this particular treaty instrument. However, the reality is somewhat different. While it may have been unintended, delayed completion of the DSU Review has meant that the whole review process has effectively become part of the Doha Round.

Notwithstanding the explicit language of Article X:8 *WTO Agreement* and the *Doha Ministerial Declaration*, Members have failed to meet the deadline of May 2003, and subsequent extension of that deadline, for completion of the review mandated in the 1994 *DSU Review Decision*, despite several extensions. The matter forms part of the work of the Special Session of the DSB, reporting to the TNC,[133] but the Members remain divided over exactly which provisions in the

130 *Doha Ministerial Declaration*, above n. 86, para. 30.

131 *Ibid.*

132 *Doha Ministerial Declaration*, *ibid*, para. 47, which states that '*[W]ith the exception of the improvements and clarifications of the Dispute Settlement Understanding*, the conduct, conclusion and entry into force of the outcome of the negotiations shall be treated as parts of a single undertaking' (emphasis added).

133 On the basis of paragraph 3 of the *Doha Work Programme*, Decision of the General Council of 31 July 2004, adopted at the Meeting of the General Council, 27 and 31 July 2004, WT/GC/W/535 (31 July 2004), [hereinafter *Doha Work Programme Decision*], at 4, in which 'The Council agrees to continue the negotiations launched at Doha beyond the timeframe set out in paragraph 45 of the Doha [Ministerial] Declaration, leading to the Sixth Session of the Ministerial Conference', it could be argued that the DSU review negotiations since they were not launched at Doha and they are not referred to in paragraph 45 but dealt with separately in paragraph 47 of the *Doha Ministerial Declaration*, above n. 86, do not enjoy the same grace period, i.e. up until the Sixth

DSU should be amended and how this should be achieved.[134]

While the *DSU* review process has encountered a number of difficulties from a procedural point of view the results of those negotiations could be adopted by the Members fairly quickly, using the aforementioned procedures, even before the end of the Doha Round.[135] Ironically, simple as those procedures might appear the fact that the decision approving such amendments can be taken by consensus provides the Members with an effective veto power, which at best could continue to delay the introduction of any amendments to the *DSU* amendments or at worst see them being held hostage to the winds of fortune, including the conclusion of the Doha Round negotiations.[136] Should the Ministerial Conference adopt a decision approving amendments to the DSU the question may arise as to whether individual Member governments could make reservations or interpretative declarations at the time of approval? If so, and there seems to be nothing in general treaty law and practice to the contrary, then such amendments, including any reservations and interpretative declarations, would take effect immediately for *all* Members. However, despite the fact that acceptance is not needed for *DSU* amendments and they could be adopted by tacit agreement, by means of a decision of the Ministerial Conference, it does not mean that this will occur in practice, as previously noted in section 2.1.

The proposed *TRIPs Agreement* amendment illustrates another aspect of WTO practice. An amendment to Article 31, operative paragraphs (f) and (h) of *TRIPs* has been under consideration by the General Council since it adopted a waiver decision on 30 August 2003, conform Article IX *WTO Agreement*, concerning the *Implementation of paragraph 6 of the Doha Declaration on the TRIPS Agreement and Public Health* (*Paragraph 6 Decision*), which gives effect to the

Ministerial Conference in Hong Kong, 15-18 December 2005, or in the alternative that the time-frame for their conclusion is indefinite!

134 The most comprehensive source documentation arising out of negotiations, and containing 42 proposals for clarification and amendment of the DSU, is the compilation of draft legal texts prepared by the Chairman of the Special Session of the DSB, Ambassador Péter Balas, on his own responsibility in April 2003 and known as the 'Chairman's Text'. It was reported to the Special Session of the Dispute Settlement Body in *Report of the Chairman to the Trade Negotiations Committee* (6 June 2003) TN/DS/9 [*Chairman's Report*] and includes a revised version of the Chairman's Text issued on 28 May (Job(03)/91/Rev. 1), which is appended to the *Chairman's Report*.

135 This happened in the case of the results of the Montreal Mid-Term Review in 1998, which were adopted before the end of the Uruguay Round on the basis of a Ministerial Decision; *see* General Agreement on Tariffs and Trade: Decisions Adopted at the Mid-Term Review of the Uruguay Round held at Montreal (1989) 28 ILM 1023.

136 See earlier comments in chapter III, at section 2.2 (b) on Mandated Consensus.

Ministerial *Declaration on the TRIPs Agreement and public health*, adopted at the Doha Ministerial Conference in 2001.[137] The *Paragraph 6 Decision* addresses the ongoing need for certain (mostly African) developing country and LDC Members faced with the HIV/Aids pandemic in their countries and without pharmaceutical manufacturing capacity, due either to lack of active ingredients or formulations or lack of technology, equipment, human resources or economic viability of domestic production,[138] to be able to import cheaper generic medicines produced under compulsory licence, and to do so without otherwise infringing pharmaceutical patents contrary to their international obligations, as set out in Article 31 *TRIPs*.[139]

The *Paragraph 6 Decision* temporarily waives an exporting Members' obligations under paragraph (f) of Article 31 *TRIPs* by allowing it to export pharmaceuticals produced under compulsory licence, contrary to the usual requirement that such licences be authorised 'predominantly' for supply of the domestic market, and waives an importing Member's obligations under paragraph (h) to ensure that adequate compensation is paid to the rights' holder.[140] It is intended that the waiver granted by the *Paragraph 6 Decision* will terminate on the date on which an amendment to the *TRIPs* Agreement takes effect. Work on the amendment was due to begin before the end of 2003 and be adopted within six months, with the Members explicitly agreeing that such an amendment would '*be based, where appropriate, on the Decision*' (emphasis added).[141] Not only has that deadline

137 *Implementation of Paragraph 6 of the Doha Declaration on the TRIPS Agreement and Public Health*, Decision of the General Council of 30 August 2003, WT/L/540 (1 September 2003) [hereinafter *Paragraph 6 Decision*], adopted pursuant to paragraphs 1, 3 and 4 of Article IX *WTO Agreement* and giving effect to the *Declaration on the TRIPs Agreement and public health*, adopted at the Fourth Meeting of the Ministerial Conference, Doha, 9-14 November 2001, WT/MIN(01)/DEC/2 (20 November 2001), paragraph 6.

138 Carlos M. Correa, *Implementation of the WTO General Council Decision on Paragraph 6 of the Doha Declaration on the TRIPs Agreement and Public Health*, Geneva, World Health Organization, 2004, doc. WHO/EDM/PAR/2004.4.

139 Article 31 *TRIPs*, *The Legal Texts*, above n. 2, 381-382, deals with the circumstances under which the (domestic) laws of a Member may allow for 'other use' (other than that under Article 30 *TRIPs*, which deals with the grant by Members of limited, specific exceptions to exclusive monopoly rights) without the authorization of the rights' holder and translates into a set of flexibilities and their potential application by Members.

140 The *Paragraph 6 Decision* has far-reaching consequences, in particular for exporting Members', many of which will need to make legislative amendments to their domestic intellectual property laws. So far Canada, Norway, France and the European Communities have draft implementing legislation in hand.

141 Paragraph 11 of the *Paragraph 6 Decision*, above n. 137.

been missed several times but also the transformation of the *Paragraph 6 Decision* (a general waiver decision) into a treaty amendment has been complicated by the fact that it was accompanied by a statement from the Chair of the General Council assuring Members that the *Decision* would not be misused.[142]

There are two points to note about the Chairman's Statement, which was worked out by the Chairman of the *TRIPs* Council with delegates from the US, Brazil, India, South Africa and Kenya, reflecting 'several key shared understandings of Members regarding to the Decision to be adopted',[143] and which smoothed the way for adoption by the Members of the *Paragraph 6 Decision* without changes. First, the Chairman's statement has an interpretative character with respect to certain substantive parts of the *Paragraph 6 Decision* but the language contained in the Chairman's statement differs sufficiently from that contained in the *Paragraph 6 Decision* as to call its interpretative value into question since this was arrived at on the basis of discussions with some but not all Members. For example the Chairman's statement states: 'all reasonable measures should be taken to prevent … diversion [of cheap drugs] in accordance with the relevant paragraphs of the Decision' and 'the provisions of paragraph 2(b)(ii) [products produced under licence should be clearly identified … through specific labelling or marking] apply … also to active ingredients produced and supplied under the system and to finished products produced using such active ingredients'[144] thereby adding language, which broadens the scope of that section of the *Paragraph 6 Decision*.

A further example is where the Chairman's statement notes that Members will seek to resolve any issues arising from use and implementation of the *Paragraph 6 Decision* 'expeditiously and amicably', by calling on 'the good offices of the Director-General or Chair of the *TRIPS* Council, with a view to finding a mutually acceptable solution'.[145] This additional language potentially mandates

142 A footnote to the *Paragraph 6 Decision*, *ibid*, notes that '[T]his Decision was adopted by the General Council in the light of a statement read out by the Chairman, which can be found in JOB(03)/177. This statement will be reproduced in the minutes of the General Council to be issued as WT/GC/M/82' [hereinafter Chairman's Statement]. *See* further the Minutes of the Meeting of the General Council of 25, 26 and 30 August 2003, WT/GC/M/82 (13 November 2003), para. 29 at pp. 6-7 and the 'Best Practices Guidelines', attached as Annex I to the Chairman's Statement, which Members and producers are encouraged to draw from and use, and to share information on their experiences in preventing diversion.

143 Chairman's Statement, *ibid*, preambular, introductory paragraph.

144 Chairman's Statement, *ibid*, second recital; *see* 'WTO Members Agree on TRIPs and Public Health Text' (2003) 6 *BRIDGES* 9.

145 Chairman's Statement, *ibid*, third recital, and *BRIDGES*, *ibid*.

a means of settling disputes arising under the *Paragraph 6 Decision* that is contrary to the letter and the spirit of paragraph 1 of Article 5 Article *DSU*, which makes it clear that alternative means of settling disputes such as good offices will be undertaken 'voluntarily' and provided the parties so agree.

Second, progress on moving the amendment process forward has been caught up in protracted discussions between developed and developing country Members over what should go into the amending text, including whether the Chairman's statement should be included as part of the amending text, either as a footnote, or within the body of the amendment. Members' views on the matter can be broken down into three separate groups. The first group largely supports the transformation *tel quel* of the *Paragraph 6 Decision* into a treaty amendment '*based, where appropriate, on the Decision*', with some modifications from a drafting point of view. In December 2004 the African Group of Members introduced the first substantive text of a proposal for amendment of Article 31 *TRIPs*[146] in a meeting of the TRIPs Council,[147] which it claimed was based on the *Paragraph 6 Decision* but for the purposes of amendment the text contained several modifications, including the elimination of a number of provisions in the *Decision* that were considered to be 'redundant in the context of an amendment or where their purpose would otherwise be served by existing provisions of the *TRIPs Agreement*, such as the provisions on compulsory licences read together with the provisions on enforcement'. At the TRIPs Council Meeting of 1-2 December 2004 the Kenyan delegate[148] stressed the need to clarify the fact that the Chairman's statement was not intended to be made part of the amendment.[149]

The second group of Members is more widely dispersed over developed and developing (exporting and importing) countries, including Canada,[150] Norway[151]

146 *Implementation of Paragraph 11 of the 30 August 2003 Decision*, Communication from Nigeria on behalf of the African Group to the TRIPs Council, IP/C/W/437 (10 December 2004), which was circulated ahead of the 1-2 December 2004 Meeting of the TRIPs Council at which it was discussed. See also *Implementation of Paragraph 11 of the 30 August 2003 Decision, Revision*, Communication from Nigeria on behalf of the African Group to the TRIPs Council, IP/C/W/437/Rev.1 (23 March 2005), which incorporates a textual amendment to the earlier proposal form the Delegation of Rwanda on behalf of the African Group.

147 Minutes of Meeting of the Council for Trade-Related Aspects of Intellectual Property Rights, held on 1-2 December 2004, IP/C/M/46 (11 January 2005) [hereinafter 'TRIPs Council Meeting, December 2004'].

148 *Ibid*, p. 24, paras. 119-120.

149 *Ibid*, para. 121.

150 *Ibid*, pp. 25-26, paras. 130-131, with reference to forthcoming legislation for implementation of the *Decision*, para. 147.

151 *Ibid*, p. 125, para. 129.

and the European Communities,[152] all three of which have already undertaken legislative initiatives in order to implement the *Paragraph 6 Decision* in their domestic legal orders[153] and the EC legal order.[154] Their views differ somewhat, for example the European Communities wants the amendment process to be a purely technical exercise, with a faithful transposition of the *Decision* into *TRIPs* language,[155] thereby excluding the Chairman's statement,[156] whereas Canada seeks its inclusion.[157]

The third group of Members includes the United States, which wants an amendment by way of a footnote that would include both the text of the *Decision* and the Chairman's statement because the latter is 'an essential part of the agreement of 30 August 2003'[158] and Switzerland, which supports an amendment 'by way of [a footnote] reference to incorporate the 5-page long text of the Decision into the TRIPs Agreement' and is also in favour of including the Chairman's statement as part of the implementation.[159]

The proposed solution by the United States is awkward and does not follow normal GATT/WTO treaty practice, where footnotes are used sparingly and

152 *Ibid*, p. 27, paras. 140 and 141 with reference to a proposal for a regulation on the matter, for details see below at n. 156.

153 For Canada, *see* Bill C-9, An Act to amend the Patent Act and the Food and Drugs Act (The Jean Chrétien Pledge to Africa), as passed by the House of Commons, May 4, 2004 (passed in the Senate without amendment on 13 May, and received Royal Assent on 14 May) [hereinafter 'Bill C-9'] *not yet in force.* Also Richard Elliott, 'Canada's New Patent Bill Provides a Basis for Improvement', Comment (May 2004) 5 *BRIDGES* 19-20. India, Korea and Switzerland are reportedly also working on putting enabling domestic legislation into place.

154 *See Proposal for a Regulation of the European Parliament and of the Council on compulsory licensing of patents relating to the manufacture of pharmaceutical products for export to countries with public health problems* (2004) COM 737.

155 Statement by the representative of the European Communities, *ibid*, para. 114. See the earlier statement by the European Communities, reiterating this point: *Implementation of the General Council Decision on Paragraph 6 of the Doha Declaration on the TRIPs Agreement and Public Health*, Communication from the European Communities to the TRIPs Council, IP/C/W/416 (21 November 2003), paras. 13-16, especially at para. 15.

156 This is borne out by the text of the proposed *Regulation* by the European Communities, above n. 154, which omits any mention of the Chairman's Statement.

157 Bill C-9, above n. 153, para. 21.02, including definitional clauses where the General Council Decision of August 30 2003 in respect of Article 31 *TRIPs* includes 'the interpretation of that decision in the General Council Chairperson's statement of that date'.

158 TRIPs Council Meeting, December 2004, above n. 147, p. 23, paras. 116-117, especially at 116.

159 *Ibid*, p. 25, paras. 124-125.

restricted 'to providing *information* to the reader'. Put differently, it is more usual for the text of the treaty to prevail and not the footnote. However, Switzerland's suggestion to 'reference' the *Decision* (with or without the Chairman's statement), as a new footnote to Article 31 *TRIPs* would be more consistent with GATT/WTO treaty practice where footnotes to substantive treaty provisions have often been included, sometimes containing references to a particular Decision of the GATT contracting parties, an interpretative statement or referencing another legal instrument or document. A further observation is that the legal effect of a footnote has been confirmed by the Appellate Body in *European Communities – Export Subsidies on Sugar*,[160] in construing the meaning of a footnote (to a Tariff Schedule) and in determining its conformity with a substantive WTO obligation.

Members opposed to the incorporation of the Chairman's statement into the amendment,[161] think that this action would unjustifiably upgrade its legal status, thereby giving it legal effect which it currently does not enjoy. Should the matter of the General Council's action be addressed in the context of dispute settlement much will turn on the circumstances surrounding the adoption of the *Paragraph 6 Decision*, including whether the Chairman's statement forms part of a single integrated package when taken with the *Decision*,[162] and could be construed as sufficiently representative of Members' understandings as to 'the way in which it would be interpreted and implemented' in practice.[163] The subsequent and diverging practice of individual Members in implementing the *Paragraph 6 Decision* into domestic law (Canada and Norway) and in the European Union could constitute an additional ground for interpretation not previously addressed.

Should agreement be reached on the final text and a decision is taken at the Ministerial Conference (or General Council) to adopt the amendment, then Article

160 *EC – Export Subsidies on Sugar*, Appellate Body Report, *European Communities – Export Subsidies on Sugar*, WT/DS265/AB/R, WT/DS266/AB/R and WT/DS283/AB/R, adopted 19 May 2005, paras. 169-200.

161 Argentina, Brazil, Hong Kong China, India, Jamaica, Kenya, Malaysia and the Philippines, according to (2005) 9 *BRIDGES* 7, reporting on the Meeting of the TRIPs Council of 30-31 March 2005 and the missed deadline of 31 March 2005 for agreement on the TRIPs amendment.

162 *See US – FSC*, Panel Report, *United States – Tax Treatment for 'Foreign Sales Corporations'*, WT/DS108/R, adopted 20 March 2000, as modified by the Appellate Body Report, WT/DS108/AB/R, paras. 7.73-7.85, especially at 7.84, confirmed by *US – FSC*, Appellate Body Report, *United States – Tax Treatment for 'Foreign Sales Corporations'*, WT/DS108/AB/R, adopted 20 March 2000, para. 49.

163 Remark by Canada, TRIPs Council Meeting, December 2004, above n. 147, p. 26, para. 130, further noting that at the time of the adoption of the Paragraph 6 Decision by the General Council 'no delegation had objected to it'.

31 *TRIPs* is the type of amendment that *would alter the rights and obligations of the Members* and would therefore require acceptance by two-thirds of the Members for it to take effect. This could only lead to further delays with respect to its entry into force although there is every reason to believe that the Members would continue to extend the waiver granted on the basis of the *Paragraph 6 Decision* until such time as the amendment came into force.

Given the difficulty in amending the *WTO Agreement* or any of the annexed Multilateral Trade Agreements there has been at least one occasion when the Members have resorted to a very pragmatic solution to the problem. Evidence of this is the decision of the General Council, upon the recommendation of the Committee on Budget, Finance and Administration or BFA Committee, to move to a system of biennial budgeting which could be read as a *de facto* amendment of Article VII:1 *WTO Agreement*.[164] The rationale behind this decision was the BFA Committee's desire 'to allow for better planning and strategic thinking for the organization' and 'to provide both Members and the Secretariat with greater predictability with regard to the financial requirements of the organization'.[165] The dilemma which with the Members were faced in switching from annual to biennial budgeting in the WTO centred on the amending provisions of paragraph 3 of Article X *WTO Agreement*, as is clear from the briefing paper which the BFA Committee requested the Legal Affairs Division to prepare, setting out the possible legal approaches that could be taken 'not simply as a means to get around the word "annual" in Article VII:1, but also to establish the new "biennial" practice on a sound legal basis'.[166]

Of the six options presented in that briefing paper – amendment to Article XVII *WTO Agreement*, authoritative interpretation (on the basis of Article IX:2 *WTO Agreement*), a decision of the Ministerial Conference (or General Council) under Article IX:2 *WTO Agreement*, which specifies the procedures to be followed by the Director-General, a collective waiver under Article IX:3 *WTO Agreement*, suspension of relevant parts of Article VII *WTO Agreement* in accordance with Article 57 VCLT and adaptation of the practice on budgeting – the membership decided to pursue the third option, i.e. adoption of a decision to this effect by the General Council. The solution chosen demonstrates some creativity in inter-

164 *See* Minutes of the Meeting of the General Council of 25, 26 and 30 August 2003, WT/GC/M/82 (13 November 2003) [hereinafter 'General Council Meeting August 2003'], p. 2, section 2, paras. 1-5.

165 General Council Meeting August 2003, *ibid*, para. 3.

166 *Biennial Budgeting in the WTO, Possible Legal Approaches*, briefing paper of the Legal Affairs Division to the Committee on Budget, Finance and Administration, WT/BFA/A/W/104 (16 July 2003).

preting a WTO provision, since the Director-General will henceforth be requested to present 'two estimated budgets covering a biennial period, with effect from the time of the estimates for 2004 and 2005',[167] which preserves the spirit of the annual budget estimate if not the letter of Article VII: 1 *WTO Agreement*. It also raises a question as to the validity of the decision, since it comes close to an authoritative interpretation,[168] on the basis of 2 of Article IX *WTO Agreement* and yet the manner of its adoption is not in conformity with the specific requirements of that provision nor does it take into account the prohibition against using the power of authoritative interpretation 'in a manner that would undermine the amendment provisions in Article X'.[169]

In summary, if we compare the amendment law of the WTO with the practice of WTO amendment there is a striking divergence in Article X *WTO Agreement* between the two. Also it is clear that the Members are all too aware of the difficulties of amending any WTO provision and in some instances, as with the move to biennial budgeting, have simply sought more practical solutions of a less formal nature even in the face of clear treaty language that warns against a *détournement de pouvoir*!

c) Protocols supplementing Schedules

The Members also continue in other ways to seek means of addressing the difficulty of 'modifying' primary treaty rules by supplementing them and this is the case with respect to the additional obligations concerning specific commitments in Members' Schedules, which arise out of a process of further negotiations.[170] The practice of supplementing obligations is not specifically regulated in the *WTO Agreement* but it is in line with the general rules of the VCLT, which allow parties to a treaty to 'contract out' in favour *either* of more specific rules contained in that treaty, i.e. the *WTO Agreement*, *or* where the matter is insufficiently regulated, to apply residual treaty rules. A presumption is then raised in favour of regulation of such matters through the established practice of the parties to the treaty. Some of the less formal procedures for supplementing WTO obligations are of this type

167 General Council Meeting August 2003, above n. 164, para. 4.

168 *See* below section 3.4.

169 Final sentence in Article IX:2 *WTO Agreement, The Legal Texts*, above n. 2, 11.

170 This process should be distinguished from that of renegotiating tariff concessions in accordance with Article XXVIII *GATT 1994* (or Article XXI *GATS*) which provide the possibility for an individual Member to modify or withdraw a tariff concession or service commitment, according to a simplified procedure: see Ehlermann and Ehring, above n. 67, 57-58, and which are discussed in section 3.1(d).

and arguably form part of the subsequent practice of the Members with respect to primary treaty obligations, which establish the agreement of some of the parties to 'modify' those treaty provisions.

The practice in question articulates the outcome of negotiations contained in a 'built-in agenda' item, usually involving the attainment of improved levels of liberalisation with respect to tariff reductions (goods sector) or the taking of specific commitments (services sector), which are open to participation by the entire membership but which are only ever concluded by a smaller group of Members (the 'participating Members'). The usual means for transforming the results of these forms of negotiations into binding treaty obligations is by the adoption of a Protocol,[171] to which are annexed the Schedules of Tariff Bindings (for goods) or the Schedules of Specific Commitments and Lists of Article II (MFN) Exemptions (for services) of the participating Members, each of which is made an integral part of the *GATT*[172] or *GATS*[173] respectively. The Protocol is then laid open for acceptance by those participating Member governments.[174]

During the first decade of the WTO's existence the results of further negotiations have been taken up in a limited number of additional protocols that have focused mainly on further liberalisation under the *GATS* in basic telecommunications and financial services and on improving liberalisation commitments in the

171 The use of the term 'Protocol' for such an instrument is not regulated in the *WTO Agreement* but follows the usual practice in general international law whereby the word may be used to designate a stand-alone treaty but is more readily applied to an amending or subsidiary treaty; *see* Aust, above n. 48, 333, noting also the generally unsystematic way in which treaties are designated or named.

172 According to the Appellate Body in *EC – Computer Equipment*, above n. 49, para. 84, Tariff Schedules are made an integral part of the *GATT 1994* by means of Article II:7 *GATT 1994* and the concessions provided for in that Schedule are part of the terms of the treaty, i.e. they constitute rights and obligations that bind the Members.

173 In *US – Gambling*, above n. 49, Panel Report, paras. 6.44 and 6.45, (confirmed by the Appellate Body, para. 160), the Panel stated, with reliance on the Appellate Body Report in *EC – Computer Equipment*, *ibid*, that 'schedules of specific commitments form an integral part of the *GATS*', at least for the purposes of interpretation. It means that schedules of services commitments under the *GATS* must be fully interpreted in the same way as tariff concessions under the *GATT 1994*.

174 *See Issues Concerning the Adoption of a Protocol to Conclude the Financial Services Negotiations*, Note by the Secretariat to the Committee on Trade in Financial Services, S/FIN/W/11 (1 May 1997) [hereinafter *Secretarial Note on Adoption of Protocols*] at 1-2, under the sub-heading '*The need for a protocol*' it is pointed out that 'where negotiations result in an agreed set of commitments [for services], a protocol is adopted as a legal instrument certifying the changes agreed', it is necessary to do this as a practical matter in order to bring the agreed changes into force simultaneously with the protocol.

movement of natural persons. At the end of the Uruguay Round too few specific commitments had been made in the two aforementioned services sectors,[175] or else horizontal commitments on MFN had been subjected to extensive exemptions, and Members had taken too few specific commitments with respect to certain categories of natural persons who supply services under mode 4 of the *GATS*.

Aside from Protocols that take up the results of further liberalisation in trade in services with respect to basic services commitments, no additional protocols have been adopted which reflect the results of new or revised rules under any of the Multilateral Trade Agreements. This is despite the fact that several of those Agreements contain explicit mandates for further rule-making, many of which form part of the so-called 'built-in agenda' left over from the Uruguay Round MTN.[176] While some of those mandates establish timetables for future work they do not include detailed procedures for the fulfilment of the mandate. Instead, this is a matter which is left to the collective action of the Members in the respective WTO body, i.e. Council, Committee, Working Party or Working Group to decide upon.

At the end of the Uruguay Round 73 countries had taken specific commitments on financial services in their initial schedules but it was realised that negotiations would need to continue in order improve upon market openings and initial commitments. Upon conclusion of the Uruguay Round, a technical legal device was added to the *General Agreement on Services* of *GATS* in the form of a specific annex, which was no more than a negotiating mandate and which was known as the *Second Annex on Financial Services*.[177] This allowed Members, notwithstanding the rules on re-negotiations, which ordinarily apply when a Member wishes to modify its schedules (Article XXI *GATS*), and contrary to the rule on the listing of MFN exemptions (Article II:2 *GATS*), to improve, modify, or withdraw all

175 Basic maritime services is another sector where broader liberalization is needed but thus far Members have been unwilling to proceed with further negotiations, due mostly to the intransigence of the United States. See for details of the history of stalled negotiations, Mary E. Footer and Carol George, 'The General Agreement on Trade in Services', in Patrick MacRory, Arthur Appleton and Michael Plummer (eds.) *The World Trade Organization: Legal, Economic and Political Analysis* (New York: Springer Science+ Business Media, Inc., 2005) 799-953, at 814 and 935-937.

176 There were well over thirty items in the original built-in agenda, immediately following the end of the Uruguay Round MTN. A number of them are now part of the Doha Development Round MTN and some of them have been updated. See for an overview of progress on rule-making under the *GATS* built-in agenda items, Mary E. Footer, 'The General Agreement on Trade in Services: Taking Stock and Moving Forward' (2002) 29, *LIEI* 7-25.

177 *Second Annex on Financial Services*, *The Legal Texts*, above n. 2, 358.

or part of the specific commitments contained in their Schedules of Specific Commitments over a 60 day period in the four months following entry into force of the *WTO Agreement*,[178] i.e. before 1 May 1995.

In fact negotiations became protracted and it was not until 21 July 1995 (two months after the elapsed time frame foreseen in the *Second Annex on Financial Services*[179] and pursuant to the *Decision on the Application of the Second Annex* by the Council for Trade in Services or CTS, which extended the negotiating deadline to 28 July 1995)[180] that participating Members finally completed negotiations on financial services. It resulted in twenty-nine Members[181] improving upon their original specific commitments and/or removing, suspending or reducing the scope of their MFN exemption[182] in financial services (banking, insurance and securities). An additional protocol, the so-called *Second Protocol to the General Agreement on Trade in Services* (*Second Protocol to the GATS*)[183] was

178 According to footnote 3 to the *Secretarial Note on Adoption of Protocols*, above n. 174, three Members exercised their rights under the *Second Annex on Financial Services*, *ibid*, and modified their Schedules and List of Article II (MFN) Exemptions in June 1995; *see* further, below in main text at section 3.1 (d) (Modification, rectification and certification of Schedules).

179 *Second Annex on Financial Services*, *ibid*, paragraph 2.

180 *Decision on the Application of the Second Annex on Financial* Services, adopted by the Council for Trade in Services, 30 June 1995, S/L/6 (4 July 1995), whereby: '[A] Member may notify changes to specific commitments on financial services inscribed in its Schedule and notify measures relating to financial services which are inconsistent with paragraph 1 of Article II of the *GATS* no later than 28 July 1995.'

181 The European Communities, or EC, counts as one Member on account of its single schedule.

182 An MFN exemption can be taken on the basis of Article II:2 *GATS* and the *Annex on Article II Exemptions*, *The Legal Texts*, above, n. 2, 352.

183 *Second Protocol to the General Agreement on Trade in Services* (adopted 6 October 1995, in *force* 1 September 1996) S/L/11 (24 July 1995) 35 *ILM* 203 [hereinafter *Second Protocol to the GATS*]. See the *Decision Adopting the Second Protocol to the General Agreement on Trade in Services*, 21 July 1995, S/L/13 (24 July 1995), adopted by the Committee on Trade in Financial Services or CTFS at its meeting on 21 July 1995, para. 4, which was taken on the basis of the *Decision on Institutional Arrangements for the General Agreement on Trade in Services*, adopted by the Council for Trade in Services, 1 March 1995, S/L/1 (4 April 1995). The latter *Decision* repeats verbatim the Ministerial *Decision on Institutional Arrangements for the General Agreements on Trade in Services*, LT/UR/D-5/3 (15 April 1994), *The Legal Texts*, above n. 2, 456, whereby the CTFS was established. The CTFS' mandate includes *inter alia* the following express powers that have been delegated to it by the CTS on the basis of that latter *Decision*: 'to formulate proposals or recommendations for consideration by the Council in connection with any matter relating to trade in the sector concerned' (paragraph 2(b)) and 'if there

drawn up and the results of the improved commitments attached thereto.[184] Colombia, Mauritius and the United States did not improve upon their initial commitments and all three subsequently took a broad MFN exemption to financial services, based on reciprocity; in particular, the absence of the United States was a cause for concern among the participating Members.

The participating Members were all too aware that the *Second Protocol to the GATS* might not enter into force 30 days after its acceptance, i.e. by 1 August 1996, due to the non-participation of the United States and so they adopted a contingent measure that would protect the results achieved while allowing them the right to reconsider their existing commitments, i.e. to continue negotiating if necessary.[185] Thus, the *Second Protocol to the GATS* provided for its entry into force 30 days following its acceptance by *all* Members concerned by 30 June 1996 but if this was not accomplished then, prior to 1 July 1996 the Members would decide on its entry into force. In this respect, WTO law and practice follow paragraph 1 of Article 24 VLCT,[186] which states that: '[A] treaty enters into force in such manner and upon such date as it may provide or as the negotiating States may agree.'

On 21 July 1995 the CTS,[187] acting on a set of recommendations of the Committee on Trade in Financial Services or CTFS at its meeting that same day,[188] adopted two decisions. One was the *Decision on Commitments in Financial Services*,[189] which notwithstanding the wording of Article XIX *GATS* and paragraphs 1 and 2 of Article II *GATS* together with the *Annex on Article II*

is an annex pertaining to the sector, to consider proposals for amendment of that sectoral annex, and to make appropriate recommendations to the Council' (paragraph 2(c)).

184 For the record, there is no 'First Protocol'. Originally, the name was reserved for some LDC commitments that were expected to take effect a few months after entry into force of the *WTO Agreement* and its annexed Multilateral Trade Agreements, including the *GATS*, i.e. after 1 January 1995, but eventually these delayed commitments were incorporated into the Schedules of Services Commitments, thereby making it unnecessary to adopt a separate protocol.

185 *Second Protocol to the GATS*, above n. 183, paragraph 3, read in conjunction with paragraph 2.

186 Article 24:1 VCLT, above n. 10.

187 Council for Trade in Services, Report of the Meeting held on 21 July 1995, Note by the Secretariat, S/C/M/5 (29 August 1995), para. 2.

188 Report of the Meeting of the CTFS, Afternoon, Note by the Secretariat, 21 July 1995, S/FIN/M/8 (26 July 1995).

189 *Decision on Commitments in Financial Services* adopted by the Council for Trade in Services, 21 July 1995, S/L/8 (24 July 1995). The *Second Protocol to the GATS* entered into force on 1 September 1996 and therefore this condition was not fulfilled.

Exemptions,[190] allowed a Member to modify or withdraw all or part of its commitments and to list MFN exemptions during a period of 60 days after 1 August 1996 should the *Second Protocol to the GATS* not enter into force. The other was the *Second Decision on Financial Services*,[191] which was an operative decision that would open the way for a Member, which had been involved in earlier negotiations on financial services, and notwithstanding Articles XIX and II *GATS*, to 'modify or withdraw all or part of the Specific Commitments on Financial Services inscribed in its Schedule' and to list MFN exemptions relating to financial services during a period of 60 days beginning on 1 November 1997.

The *Second Protocol to the GATS* entered into force on 6 September 1996,[192] thereby bringing the *Second Decision on Financial Services* into effect. Thus, this *Second Decision* allowed for further negotiations to take place whereby Members could improve upon the commitments in financial services they had already taken. These negotiations began in April 1997 and led to an improved package of market openings by the participating Members, including the United States, some eight months later. Eventually 56 schedules of commitments in financial services, representing 70 Members, were annexed to the *Fifth Protocol of the General Agreement on Trade in Services* (*Fifth Protocol to the GATS*).[193]

It remained open for acceptance by WTO Members until 29 January 1999 but once again the CTS, at its meeting of 12 December 1997, fearful that the *Fifth Protocol to the GATS* would not enter into force, adopted the *Decision of Decem-*

190 *Annex on Article II Exemptions*, *The Legal Texts*, above n. 2, 352.

191 *Second Decision on Financial Services* adopted by the CTS, 21 July 1995, S/L/9 (24 July 1995).

192 *Communication from Members which have accepted the Second Protocol to the GATS* to the Council for Trade in Services, 30 July 1996, S/L/25 (30 July 1996), whereby those Members that had accepted the *Second Protocol* before 1 July 1996 agreed that it would enter into force on 1 September 1996 and whereby that same group of Members requested the CTS to extend the period for acceptance of the *Second Protocol* until 30 November 1996, whereupon it would enter into force for those 'late' accepting Members 30 days thereafter. The CTS subsequently extended the deadline for acceptance of the *Second Protocol* to 30 November 1996, see *Decision on Acceptance of the Second and Third Protocols to the GATS*, adopted by the Council for Trade in Services on 30 July 1996, S/L/28 (30 July 1996).

193 *Fifth Protocol to the General Agreement on Trade in Services* (adopted 27 February 1998, *in force* 30 January 1999) S/L/45 (3 December 1997), 2065 *UNTS* 155 [hereinafter *Fifth Protocol to the GATS*]. *See* also the *Decision adopting the Fifth Protocol to the General Agreement on Trade in Services*, adopted by the CTFS at its meeting on 14 November 1997, S/L/44, (3 December 1997).

ber 1997 on Commitments in Financial Services[194] which had been proposed by the CFTS.[195] Again this contingency decision proved unnecessary as the *Fifth Protocol* entered into force on 5 February 1998.

Telecommunications services also form an integral part of the specific commitments that Members can take under the *GATS* on the basis of a specific *Annex on Telecommunications* or *Telecoms Annex.*[196] At the time of conclusion of the Uruguay Round very few commitments had been taken on basic telecommunications, including the all-important sector of basic voice telephony,[197] although there were a considerable number of initial commitments in the area of value-added, or enhanced, telecommunications services. Unlike financial services, in the case of telecommunications the Ministers adopted a Ministerial *Decision on Negotiations on Basic Telecommunications* (*Ministerial Decision on Basic Telecoms*)[198] at Marrakesh that was the starting point for Members to continue negotiating on basic telecommunications, in accordance with the *Annex on Negotiations on Basic Telecommunications* (*Basic Telecoms Annex*),[199] with the intention of further liberalising and opening up this sector.

The initial round of negotiations began with a group of 33 participating Members in May 1994 under the auspices of the Negotiating Group on Basic Telecommunications or NGBT, as provided for in the *Ministerial Decision on Basic Telecoms Decision*[200] and on the conditions set out in the *Basic Telecoms Annex*, which provided for a standstill on the application of MFN exemptions in basis telecommunications until the date of implementation of the results of further negotiations or, if they proved inconclusive, a final report of the NGBT to that effect no later than 30 April 1996. By that date a total of 53 Members were

194 *Decision of December 1997 on Commitments in Financial Services*, 12 December 1997, S/L/50 (12 December 1997).

195 Report of the Meeting of the CTFS, above n. 193.

196 *Annex on Telecommunications*, *The Legal Texts*, above n. 2, 359-363.

197 Paragraph 2(a) of the *Basic Telecoms Annex*, *The Legal Texts*, above n. 2, 359, contains an open-ended definition of telecommunications services as measures that "affect access to and use of public telecommunications transport networks and services". It therefore requires Members to ensure that service suppliers wishing to take advantage of scheduled commitments in this sector are accorded market access to and use of basic public telecommunications systems, both networks and services on a reasonable and non-discriminatory basis.

198 *Decision on Negotiations on Basic Telecommunications*, adopted by the Ministers at Marrakesh, 15 April 1994, [hereinafter *Ministerial Decision on Basic Telecoms Negotiations*], *The Legal Texts*, above n. 2, 461-462.

199 *Annex on Negotiations on Basic Telecommunications*, *The Legal Texts*, *ibid*, 364

200 *Ministerial Decision on Basic Telecoms Negotiations*, above n. 113, para. 3.

participating fully in the NGBT with 24 governments (some of them in the process of accession) enjoying observer status, with offers from 48 governments[201] although in this sector too it was realised that further negotiations were needed.

At this point WTO Director-General, Renato Ruggiero, personally intervened and suggested attaching the results achieved thus far to a Protocol but on the understanding that participants would re-examine their positions on market access and MFN treatment during a 30 day period in early 1997. This resulted in the *Fourth Protocol to the General Agreement on Trade in Services* (the *Fourth Protocol to the GATS*),[202] to which were annexed a total of 69 Schedules of commitments in basic telecommunications. The accompanying *Decision on Commitments in Basic Telecommunications*[203] of the CTS then confirmed the opportunity for participating Members, which had annexed a new Schedule of Commitments on basic telecommunications to the *Fourth Protocol to the GATS*, to continue negotiating on further supplementary commitments, or modifications, to those Schedules within a 30 day period from 15 January 1997 to 15 February 1997.

The rapid liberalisation of telecommunications also created concern about the regulatory environment post-market entry. During the negotiations some participating Members had suggested inscribing regulatory disciplines in the Schedules as additional commitments (in accordance with Article XXI *GATS*) in order to safeguard the value of market access commitments already undertaken. However, participating Members chose not to follow this route but instead agreed to a set of definitions and principles on the regulatory framework for basic telecommunications services, covering such matters as competition, interconnection guarantees, and transparency of licensing processes and the independence of regulatory authorities, to be set out in an optional *Reference Paper*. Members could choose to inscribe it in their Schedules of Specific Commitments but if the *Reference Paper* obligations were included as additional commitments then they were 'applicable only by Members that had included them in their schedules' and they applied 'only to basic telecommunications'.[204] By the end of February 1997, 63 of the 69

201 Of the forty-eight offers, there were actually thirty-four since the EC's schedule at the time counted for 15 Members in total.

202 *Fourth Protocol to the General Agreement on Trade in Services* (adopted 15 April 1997, *in force* 5 February 1998) S/L/20 (30 April 1996), 2061 *UNTS* 214.

203 *Decision on Basic Telecommunications*, adopted by the Council for Trade in Services on 30 April 1996, S/L/19 (30 April 1996).

204 *See Mexico – Telecoms*, Panel Report, *Mexico – Measures Affecting Telecommunications Services*, WT/DS204/R, adopted 1 June 2004, para. 7.33, where the Panel noted that

participating Members had submitted schedules that contained additional commitments on regulatory disciplines. The results of the negotiations were then attached to the (revised) *Fourth Protocol to the GATS*, which was opened for acceptance until 30 November 1997.[205]

The liberalisation of labour mobility with respect to service suppliers (known as the 'movement of natural persons supplying services' under mode 4 of the *GATS*)[206] is at the heart of the Third Protocol to the *GATS*.[207] Throughout the Uruguay Round negotiations developing countries maintained improved labour mobility of service suppliers as one of their key negotiating objectives but developed countries were opposed on the grounds that cross-border movement of personnel would require major changes in their visa and immigration policies. A compromise position was reached at the end of the Uruguay Round, with the inclusion of a separate annex to the *GATS*, known as the Annex on Movement of Natural Persons Supplying Services under the Agreement,[208] which primarily reflected the concerns of developed GATT Contracting Parties to allow only the cross-border movement of managerial, technical and supervisory staff.[209] Since developing countries Members were largely dissatisfied with the failure of developed country Members to generate improved offers in other areas of labour mobility of interest to them (primarily unskilled labour), a decision was taken to continue negotiations up to 28 July 1995[210] in order to achieve greater liberalisation under Mode 4.

As a result of the extended period for negotiations on movement of natural persons and completion of national schedules, the nature and extent of commit-

Mexico had inscribed the *Reference Paper* in its Schedule under 'Additional Commitments'.

205 The CTS extended the deadline for acceptance until 31 July 1998; *see* Decision on Acceptance of the Fourth Protocol to the General Agreement on Trade in Services, adopted by the CTS on 19 December 1997, S/L/51 (19 December 1997).

206 Footer and George, above n. 175, 908-909.

207 *Third Protocol to the General Agreement on Trade in Services* (adopted 6 October 1995, *in force* 27 July 1996) S/L/12 (24 July 1995), 2061 *UNTS* 193 [hereinafter *Third Protocol to the GATS*].

208 *Annex on Movement of Natural Persons Supplying Services under the Agreement*, *The Legal Texts*, above n. 2, 353.

209 In taking commitments with respect to Mode 4 (presence of natural persons), developed Members have usually interpreted this type of labour mobility as only applicable to managers and executives including intra-corporate transferees, corporate trainees and service sellers and/or individual service providers and specialists on specific services assignments.

210 *Decision on Movement of Natural Persons*, adopted by the CTS on 30 June 1995, S/C/W/4 (4 July 4 1995).

ments on liberalisation led to (1) improved commitments on the limitation of the number of natural persons entering the territory of a Member in order to supply services; (2) bound commitments specifying the nature and extent of liberalisation, e.g. entry and temporary stay of some categories of natural persons supplying services; (3) bound commitments specifying liberalisation of entry and temporary stay of certain categories of natural persons as service providers but subject to economic needs tests or quantitative ceilings; and (4) some horizontal commitments in relation to national laws that involve otherwise broad discretionary powers of immigration or labour ministries in some developed country Members. The aforementioned results were then inscribed in the 'additional commitments' column of the Schedules of participating Members, and attached to the Third Protocol to the *GATS*.[211]

The practice of the Members in transforming the results of these further liberalisation efforts in services commitments into legally binding treaty obligations has been criticised for the way in which Members have approached the process as a modification to the Schedules of Specific Commitments similar to the GATT practice on modification of Tariff Schedules,[212] and while there may be some support for this view based on GATT/WTO practice[213] the better view is that these Protocols are subsequent or supplemental agreements, which have their basis in the residual rules on amendment in treaty law and practice. The adoption of a Protocol to the *WTO Agreement*, or one of the annexed Multilateral Trade Agreements, as we have noted in the case of the *GATS*, appears on the face of it to have much in common with an ordinary amendment to a multilateral treaty in the sense of Article 40 VCLT.[214] However, since only some and not all of the Members participate in these supplementary Protocols to which the results

211 *Third Protocol to the GATS*, above n. 207. *See* also *Decision on Movement of Natural Persons Commitments*, adopted by the CTS on 21 July 1995, S/L/10 (24 July 1995) adopting the text of the *Third Protocol to the GATS*.

212 Pieter Jan Kuijper, 'Some institutional issues presently before the WTO', in Daniel L.M. Kennedy and James D. Southwick, *The Political Economy of International Trade Law: Essays in Honour of Robert E. Hudec* (Cambridge: Cambridge University Press, 2002) 81-110 at 90-94.

213 See for example the practice of the WTO with respect to modification, rectification and certification of Schedules, below at section (d).

214 Both Articles 39 and 40 VCLT, above n. 10, are facultative. They only prescribe rules to govern the act of amendment in so far as the treaty does not otherwise provide, i.e. they foresee the possibility of States 'contracting out' or prescribing their own rules to govern amendment, as in Article X *WTO Agreement*, which is one of the most detailed amending provisions of a multilateral treaty that doubles as the constituent instrument of an international organisation.

of additional negotiations are attached, they constitute a specialised forms of amendment,[215] such as the modification of primary treaty rules 'when some of the parties conclude an "inter-se agreement" altering the application of the treaty between themselves alone' pursuant to Article 41 VCLT or they result 'from the conclusion of a subsequent treaty'.[216]

As Ian Brownlie points out 'the Final Draft of the International Law Commission [1966] provided that "a treaty may be modified by subsequent practice in the application of the treaty establishing the agreement of the parties to modify its provisions".' He further notes that the relevant 'article was rejected at the Vienna Conference on the ground that such a rule would create instability', stating

215 This is clear from the wording of Article 41 VCLT, above n. 10, whereby the specialist rules on amendment are intended for the modification of multilateral treaties as between certain of the parties *only* and are aimed primarily at protecting third party rights and obligation of States not involved in the modification. Joel Trachtman is doubtful as to whether Article 41 VCLT, above n. 10, on *inter se* modifications is applicable in the WTO context because ordinarily they 'would be permitted only if they were not prohibited by the [WTO] treaty' and he is of the belief that they are prohibited; *see* Joel P. Trachtman, Book Review, (2004) 98 *AJIL* 855-861 (reviewing Joost Pauwelyn, *Conflict of Norms in Public International Law: How WTO Law Relates to Other Rules of International Law* Cambridge: Cambridge University Press, 2003) at 859.
In fact, the *WTO Agreement* and the annexed Multilateral Trade Agreements are silent on the matter of *inter se* modifications although it could be argued that certain paragraphs in Article X *WTO Agreement* (notably paragraphs 2 and 3) dismiss the possibility of such amendments if they were to *alter the rights and obligations of Members* while certain provisions like Article XXIV *GATT 1994* or Article V *GATS* may contain language that seeks to protect third party rights in the event of the formation of regional trade arrangements.
For an earlier discussion of Article 41 VCLT, above n. 10, in the WTO context, see Joost Pauwelyn, 'The Role of Public International Law in the WTO: How Far Can We Go?' (2001) 95 *AJIL* 535-578, at 548, who makes reference to the fact that *inter se* modifications include 'those further liberalizing trade as between some WTO Members only, for which the WTO Treaty has explicit rules'. While he does not indicate the type of liberalising measures he has in mind it is probable that these are limited to the formation of regional trade arrangements under Article XXIV *GATT 1994* or Article V *GATS*. In this latter regard, see also Thomas Cottier, 'The Legal Framework for Free Trade Areas & Customs Unions in WTO Law', Paper prepared for the Third Workshop jointly hosted by the State Secretariat for Economic Affairs (SECO) and the World Trade Institute (WTI) on *Multilateralism and Bilateralism after Cancún: Challenges and Opportunities of Regionalism*, Berne, 15 June 2004, 10-11. He deals with the phenomenon of regional arrangements according to the general treaty rules on the application of successive treaties on the same subject matter (Article 30 VCLT) and modifications *inter se* of multilateral treaties (Article 41 VCLT), above n. 10.

216 Brownlie, above n. 129, 601, cited in Freestone and Oude Elferink, above n. 99, 4.

that this is unsatisfactory *inter alia* because Article 39 VCLT provides for the amendment of a treaty *by agreement* without any formal expression of agreement [*sic*]. Moreover, he contends that consistent practice under the treaty 'may provide cogent evidence of *common* consent to a change' and that anyway this type of modification occurs in practice.[217] Aust, with reference to the residual character of the rules governing the amendment of multilateral treaties,[218] characterises this type of amendment as a supplementary treaty; he is also careful to distinguish between those treaties that *amend* and those that *supplement*.

The WTO practice of 'modifying' primary treaty rules by supplementing them is precisely the type of subsequent practice by parties to a multilateral treaty to which Brownlie and Aust are referring. More obviously this type of WTO practice follows GATT practice of the early 1950's where procedures for 'supplementary concessions' were established, thereby making it possible for any two or more GATT contracting parties to negotiate tariff concessions, which would be embodied in a protocol of supplementary concessions, and for those concessions to 'be regarded by the CONTRACTING PARTIES as a Schedule to the General Agreement.'[219] Similarly, the results of the negotiations among participating Members that lead to supplementary services' commitments are then annexed to a Protocol, which is laid open for acceptance by the respective Members in accordance with their constitutional procedures. Where the WTO differs from GATT is that the practice of modifying the treaty by means of subsequent or supplementary Protocols has its normative basis in a built-in agenda item contained in one of the Multilateral Trade Agreements or alternatively finds its basis in a decision of a WTO body.[220] Thus, not only does the VCLT allow parties to 'contract out' in favour of more specific rules but where the matter is insufficiently regulated, as is the case here with supplementary provisions, then residual treaty rules operate and a presumption is raised in favour of regulation through the established practice

217 Brownlie, *ibid.*

218 Aust, above n. 48, 220-221.

219 Jackson,, *The World Trading System*, above n. 21, 76, with details in fn. 12 of the *Procedures for Negotiations Between Two or More Contracting Parties*, Sales No. GATT/1952-3, *BISD* 1/116.

220 The *Agreement on the Expansion of Trade in Information Technology Products* was established pursuant the *Ministerial Declaration in Trade in Information Technology Products*, 13 December 1996 (WT/MIN(96)/16), adopted at the First Session of the Ministerial Conference, held at Singapore in 1996, and the provisions for the *Implementation of the Ministerial Declaration on Trade in Information Technology Products* (G/L/160), in order to carry out the provisions of paragraphs 3, 5, 6 and 7 of the Annex to the Declaration.

of the parties to the primary treaty instruments, i.e. the *WTO Agreement*, its Annexes and Schedules.

d) Modification, rectification and certification of schedules

The former General Agreement was extremely difficult to amend, in particular with respect to the obligations on MFN and the tariff bindings contained in Part I (Articles I and II of the GATT 1947 and the Schedules), due to the requirement that unanimity was needed for any amendment to Part I.[221] According to Jackson, some governments believed that the unanimity requirement applied to the Tariff Schedules on the grounds that paragraph 7 of Article II GATT 1947 clearly states that '[T]he Schedules annexed to this Agreement are hereby made an integral part of Part I' of the General Agreement,[222] while others were more pragmatic, particularly when it was realised that frequent changes would be needed to the Schedules. Thus, the need for a simpler means of amending the Schedules either as a result of tariff renegotiations on the basis of Article XXVIII GATT 1947, i.e. modifications, or due to errors in the original Schedules, i.e. rectifications, as opposed to substantive treaty amendments,[223] soon emerged in the practice of the contracting parties under the General Agreement.

As a result, there is a wealth of established practice in respect of certain amendments such as modifications to the Schedules, which are rendered necessary by the renegotiation of tariff concessions under Article XXVIII *GATT 1994* or specific commitments under Article XXI *GATS*,[224] combined with the process of 'certifications' and 'rectifications' to Schedules, including rectification in the event of error. These unregulated forms of 'amendment' form a continuum with previous practice under the GATT, where they were borne out of necessity due to the difficulty of amending the General Agreement, and are dealt with in this section.

In the early years of the GATT, modification and rectification of Schedules was carried out by means of a general protocol of 'Schedule' changes, i.e. a

221 Jackson, *World Trade and the Law of GATT*, above n. 22, § 3.6., 73.

222 Jackson, *The World Trading System*, above n. 21, especially fn. 1, and 75. The Appellate Body has confirmed that Tariff Schedules are an integral part of the GATT; *see EC – Computer Equipment*, above n. 49.

223 According to Jackson, *World Trade and the Law of GATT*, above n. 22, §3.6, 75, '[W]hen Schedule changes result from the application of various GATT "renegotiation" clauses, it can be argued that those clauses establish authority themselves for the changes in the Schedules.'

224 Ehlermann and Ehring, above n. 67, 57-58.

specific Protocol that would take up those 'modifications', 'rectifications', etc.[225] but some of them never came into force because they failed to achieve the necessary unanimity of the contracting parties that is required for changes to the Schedules in accordance with Article II GATT 1947 (Part I).[226] Instead, a practice developed of the most directly affected parties putting into effect the results of negotiations on tariff concessions, which were attached to the Protocols, even though those Protocols were not technically in force, and of the contracting parties treating them as if they were in effect.

Gradually this practice became more formalised as the result of a number of decisions of the CONTRACTING PARTIES in 1959 and 1968 whereby, in the case of modification or rectification of schedules, notification of the proposed modification had to be circulated and provided no objections were raised within a period (usually 30 days) the modification would take effect.[227] This was followed in 1980 by the formalisation of the procedure for the 'Certification' of modifications to the Tariff Schedules resulting from (a) action under Article II:6, Article XVIII, Article XXIV, Article XXVII and Article XXVIII GATT 1947 and (b) the recording of rectifications of a purely formal character.[228] The procedures were further adjusted by a Decision of the CONTRACTING PARTIES

225 *GATT Analytical Index*, above n. 71, 106.

226 Jackson, *World Trade and the Law of GATT*, above n. 22, §3.6, 76-77 with reference to fifteen Protocols of Rectification, or Rectification and Modification, of which five were technically not in force until 7 February 1969; see fn. 15 at 77, and table at §3.4, at 70.

227 *Procedures for Modification and Rectification of Schedules of Tariff Concessions* were adopted by the CONTRACTING PARTIES on 17 April 1959, *BISD* 8S/25, 19 November 1968, L/3131, *BISD* 16S/16, *GATT Analytical Index*, above n. 71, 106, 890 and 932.

228 *Procedures for Modification and Rectification of Schedules of Tariff Concessions*, Decision of the CONTRACTING PARTIES, 26 March 1980, L/4962, *BISD* 27S/25-26. Paragraph 1 of this decision states '[C]hanges in the authentic texts of Schedules annexed to the General Agreement which reflect modifications resulting from action under Article II, Article XVIII, Article XXIV, Article XXVII or Article XXVIII shall be certified by means of Certifications', *GATT Analytical Index*, *ibid*, 106. Jackson, *World Trade and the Law of GATT*, above n. 22, §3.6, 80, had earlier in 1969 noted the practice of the contracting parties in making a distinction between modifications and rectifications of a purely formal character. At another point, *ibid*, §10.6, 230, he remarks that whereas the process of renegotiation centres on the language of Article XXVIII GATT, which contains three authorisations for renegotiation. In the case of renegotiations pursuant to Article XXVII, Article XXIV:6 and Article XVIII:7 such authority is restricted to certain circumstances and is explicit. In the case of rectifications the authority is general and implied.

in 1983, with the introduction of the Harmonized System,[229] and another in 1991 with a simplified means for the recording of changes and rectifications in the Tariff Schedules.[230] Under the aforementioned procedures a draft Certification containing changes in the Schedule was communicated to all the contracting parties and, provided that no objection was raised by a contracting party within 90 days, the Director-General would proceed to notification and the Certification would take effect.[231]

In the case of Tariff Schedules, WTO practice still follows the procedures set out in the decisions, adopted under the former GATT in 1980, 1983 and 1991, as the 'legal basis' for rectifications and modifications although not always following those procedures in practice.[232] This is largely due to an unsuccessful attempt in 1997 by the Members in the General Council to try and consolidate those former GATT Decisions.[233]

The usual procedure for a Member seeking to make a change to its Tariff Schedule is to notify the Council for Trade in Goods or CTG, thereby bringing the matter to the attention of *all* the Members although in practice it has become

229 The change in GATT practice on certification is recorded in a Decision of the GATT Council on *GATT Concessions under the Harmonized Commodity Description and Coding System*, 12 July 1983, L/5470/Rev. 1, *BISD* 30S/17-21, *GATT Analytical Index*, *ibid*, 101-102. This 1983 Decision, which was applicable to those GATT contracting parties that adopted the Harmonized System, contained more detailed procedures than the 1980 Decision. It established the basic principle that bindings should remain unchanged and required specific documentation to be notified.

230 Decision of the GATT Council on *GATT Concessions under the Harmonized Commodity Description and Coding System, Procedures to Implement Changes in the Harmonized System*, 8 October 1991, Annex to L/6905, *BISD* 39S/300-301, *GATT Analytical Index*, *ibid*, 103.

231 The formalisation of GATT practice led to six certifications of Changes to Schedules between 1969 and 1987, whereafter changes to schedules were made and certified on an *ad hoc* basis as a result of the introduction of the loose-leaf system; see *GATT Analytical Index*, *ibid*, 112. However, there is further evidence that between 1980 and 1989, about 30 out of 62 schedules were submitted in loose-leaf format but very few of them were certified because of objections raised by other delegations; see *Rectifications and Modifications to Schedules of Tariff Concessions and their Certification*, Note by the Secretariat, to the Council for Trade in Goods, G/L/90 (6 October 1997) [hereinafter *1997 Secretariat Note on Rectifications and Modifications*], 6, Annex, para. 3.

232 *1997 Secretariat Note on Rectifications and Modifications*, *ibid*, Section I. Present Legal Basis for Rectifications and Modifications, 1-3, at paras. 3-10, noting also para. 11.

233 See for an attempt to arrive at consolidation of the 1980, 1983 and 1991 Decisions, the Meeting of Meeting of the Council for Trade in Goods, 6 October 1997 , G/C/M/23 (6 November 1997), 5, Section 2, Statement of the Chairman, pp. 5-8, para. 2.1-2.15. See also Anwarul Hoda, *Tariff Negotiations and Renegotiations under the GATT and*

more usual, for the Director-General in his capacity as depository, in accordance with paragraph 2 of Article 79 VCLT, acting through the Secretariat, to notify *all* Members by the means of circulation of documents under letter, known as the LET process.[234] In either event, Members still have a 90-day period in which to raise objections.[235] If none are received at the end of this period then the approval is taken to be definitive.[236] The Secretariat will proceed to certification of the modifications or rectifications, consisting of the formulation of a *procès-verbal*, listing the considerations for modification and stating the amendment, whereupon the Certification is deposited with the Director-General and, upon its entry into force, is registered with the UN Secretariat. Should a Member raise an objection the Secretariat does not proceed to certification but instead there is a *de facto* extension of the original 90-day period until the objection is lifted. Since no term is set for the removal of objections it means that a Member, which has not agreed to the proposed changes, can indefinitely block the entry into force of the Certification in exactly the same manner as under the former GATT.[237]

the WTO: Procedures and Practices (Cambridge: Cambridge University Press, 2001) 111-133, especially at 121-131.

234 See for example, the notification of a technical error in the text of Annex VII (Developing Country Members referred to in paragraph 2(a) of Article 27) of the *Agreement on Subsidies and Countervailing Measures*, curing the omission of Honduras from the original list of developing countries, which can benefit from the *de minimis* requirements for the maintenance of domestic subsidies for a limited on the grounds that Honduras became a GATT contracting party on 10 April 1994, on the eve of the opening of the text for acceptance at the Marrakesh Ministerial Meeting on 15 April 1994. A 30-day period was set by the Director-General for notification of objections, whereupon the Certification of the rectification would take place, WT/Let/366 (21 December 2000).

235 The period for raising objections in the case of the two plurilaterals – the Agreement on Trade in Civil Aircraft and the Agreement on Government Procurement – is 30 days under a simplified procedure inherent to each; see Hoda, above n. 233, 117, para. 16.

236 *See Dominican Republic – Import and Sale of Cigarettes,* Panel Report, *Dominican Republic – Measures Affecting the Importation and Internal Sale of Cigarettes*, WT/DS302/R, adopted on 19 May 2005, para. 7.34 with respect to the matter of non-objection in the certification of rectifications, *in casu* with respect to notification of the addition of 'other duties and charges, or 'ODC's' in accordance with paragraph 7 of the *Understanding on the Interpretation of Article II:1(b) of the General Agreement on Tariffs and Trade*, *The Legal Texts*, above n. 2, 23-24 at 24.

237 A 1985 Secretariat Note on *Loose-leaf Schedules Based on Harmonized System Nomenclature*, noted this problem: '[C]ertifications ... require the tacit approval of all contracting parties before being approved, by virtue of the (first) three-month period during which objections against proposed changes in Tariff Schedules can be raised. A contracting party with which agreement concerning the proposed changes has not been reached

Uncertified changes have no legal status.[238]

In the case of the Schedules of Specific Commitments, the CTS has taken a number of decisions on the basis of paragraph 5 of Article XXI *GATS* that have led to the adoption of slightly different procedures. Procedures for the Certification of modifications and rectifications of Schedules of Specific Commitments differ depending upon whether the modifications arise under Article XXI *GATS* or not. Following the end of the Uruguay Round, an *ad hoc* certification procedure was initially applied for the purpose of introducing changes or adding new commitments to Members' schedules, pending the adoption of a formal set of procedures under the provision that allows for the modification of schedules following re-negotiations (Article XXI *GATS*) and which was intended to be used whenever a Member wished to modify or withdraw a scheduled commitment.

This was followed in 1999 and 2000 with the adoption by the CTS of two separate sets of decisions that apply to modifications to Schedules of Specific Commitments, dependent on whether the matter referred to is a modification under Article XXI *GATS*[239] or entails 'new commitments, improvements to existing ones, or rectifications or changes of a purely technical character that do not alter the scope of the substance of the existing commitments', in which case the modifications and/or rectifications are governed by slightly different procedures that are the subject of a Certification procedure.[240]

can thus indefinitely block the entry into force of the certification', *GATT Analytical Index*, above n. 71, 115. The matter remains unchanged in the WTO.

238 A 1987 Secretariat Note on *Harmonized System Negotiations under Article* XXVIII, states that: 'Although the uncertified loose-leaf schedules represent important sources of information and bases for negotiations, they have *no* legal status (emphasis added). It follows that past protocols and other legal instruments continue to keep their legal status until the time of certification of the respective loose-leaf schedules or their entry into force by means of a Protocol'. See *GATT Analytical Index*, *ibid*.

239 At its meeting of 19-20 July 1999, S/C/M/38 (13 September 1999), the CTS adopted a draft Decision contained in document S/CSC/W/114, approving the draft procedures drawn up by the Committee on Specific Commitments or CSC, contained in document S/C/W/21; the text of the decision and the procedures were issued as *Decision on Procedures for the Implementation of Article XXI of the General Agreement on Trade in Services (GATS)*, S/L/79 (20 July 1999) and *Procedures for the Implementation of Article XXI of the General Agreement on Trade in Services (GATS) (Modification of Schedules*, S/L/80 (20 July 1999) [hereinafter *S/L/80 procedures*].

240 At its meeting of 14 April 2000, S/C/M/42 (9 May 2000) the CTS adopted a draft Decision contained in document S/CSC/W/26/Rev.1, approving the draft procedures drawn up by the CSC, contained in document S/C/W/133; the text of the decision and the procedures were issued as *Decision on Procedures for the Certification of Rectifications or Improvements to Schedules of Specific Commitments*, S/L/83 (18 April 2000)

In the case of modifications pursuant to Article XXI *GATS* a Member wishing to modify or withdraw a scheduled commitment must notify the Secretariat no later than three months before the intended date of implementation of such modification or withdrawal. The Secretariat then distributes the notification to all other Members in a secret document and includes the item on the next meeting of the CTS, thereby putting *all* Members on notice. This can lead to other Members seeking compensatory adjustment under paragraph 2 of Article XXI *GATS*, within 45 days of circulation of the notice of intent to modify, failing which the matter can be subject to arbitration between the Members.[241] The process is seen as an improvement to the overall system of modifications in the case of Schedules of Specific Commitments and one which still does not exist in the case of modifications to Tariff Schedules.

Modifications to the Schedules of Specific Commitments, resulting from action under Article XXI *GATS*, take effect by means of certification[242] but unlike those in respect of Tariff Schedules, enter into force after a 45-day circulation period, provided that no Member has raised an objection. Again unlike modifications to Tariff Schedules the objecting Member must as far as possible identify the specific elements of the modifications that have given rise to the objection.[243]

In the case of all other modifications to Schedules of Specific Commitments the procedures are simplified since they only involve certification and not renegotiations followed by certification, which lies at the heart of Article XXI *GATS* modifications. Thus, as soon as a Member has notified the Secretariat of proposed changes these are circulated to *all* Members that have 45 days to raise an objection, failing which the Secretariat advises all Members that the certification procedure has been concluded, and indicates the date of entry into force of the modifications.[244]

The process of objection to a certification follows that of Article XXI *GATS* certifications of modifications, save that the objecting Member(s) and the modifying Member must consult with each other as soon as possible and must try to resolve the matter within the 45-day period.[245] An important addition to the procedures is the rule that if the objections are not withdrawn by the end of that 45-day period then the certification procedures will cease to apply and the modify-

and *Procedures for the Certification of Rectifications or Improvements to Schedules of Specific Commitments*, S/L/84 (18 April 2000) [hereinafter *S/L/84 procedures*].

241 Article XXI:3 *GATS*, *The Legal Texts*, above n. 2, 345.

242 *S/L/80 procedures*, above n. 239, p. 3, para. 20.

243 *Ibid*, p. 4, para. 20.

244 *S/L/84 procedures*, above n. 240, p. 1, para. 1.

245 *Ibid*, para. 2.

ing Member can either withdraw its proposed modifications or initiate the procedures for Article XXI *GATS* modifications, i.e. start re-negotiations.[246] This avoids the inevitable situation of a Member indefinitely blocking the entry into force of the certification as frequently happens with Tariff Schedules.

e) Rectification in the event of error

There have been occasions where a Member government claims that it has made an error in concluding a multilateral treaty. Alternatively, it may claim that an error has been made post-conclusion during the so-called 'validation' process which reveals that an error in transforming the results of negotiations into the relevant treaty obligations. The situation of error in the treaty-making process as a ground for invalidity (Article 48 VCLT), should be distinguished from those situations whereby a Member seeks to invoke the invalidity of a treaty provision by claiming that its consent to be bound is in violation of its internal, domestic law (Article 46 VCLT)[247] or the authority of a representative to express a State's consent to be bound is subject to specific restrictions (Article 47 VCLT).

However, as Aust points out[248] while the matter of invalidity in the law of treaties cannot be taken lightly there is very little evidence of it in the practice of States. The actual grounds for invoking error in the sense of Article 48 VCLT are fairly narrowly construed – no doubt in order to avoid legal uncertainty. They require that the error relate to a fact or situation[249] which was assumed by the State to exist upon the conclusion of the treaty and formed an essential basis for its consent to be bound. There must be no contributory error on the part of the State by means of its own conduct or circumstances which would have put it on notice as to the possible error.[250]

246 *Ibid*, para. 4.

247 Here again Article 46 VCLT, above n. 10, should be distinguished from Article 27 VCLT, *ibid,* which provides that a party may not invoke provisions in its internal, domestic law as a justification for its failure to perform under the treaty.

248 Aust, above n. 48, 252-260.

249 It can be difficult sometimes to distinguish between law and fact, besides which a factual error can have legal consequences; see also Aust, *ibid*, 254, on this point.

250 The criteria set out in Article 48 VCLT, above n. 10, are taken from *The Case Concerning The Temple of Preah Vihear*, (*Cambodia* v *Thailand*) [1962] ICJ Rep 1962 6, at 26-27; see Aust, *ibid.*

There has been one instance in WTO practice, involving Hungary, where a Member has directly invoked Article 48 VCLT[251] on the grounds of error during the treaty-making process, with respect to an obligation involving Section II of Part IV of its Schedule LXXI. As a justification for the invocation Hungary cited the exceptional conditions brought about by the political and economic transition of the country and the fact that the error was essentially caused by circumstances external to the Hungarian Government.[252] A week later the representative of Hungary informed the Members of its invocation of Article 48 VCLT at a meeting of the General Council and expressed the readiness of his Government to hold consultations with any Members on the matter.[253] Three Members – Australia, Argentina and New Zealand – responded, with New Zealand expressing his delegation's surprise at Hungary's action.

The issue of error in treaty formation has also been addressed in the context of WTO dispute settlement in the case of *Korea – Measures Affecting Government Procurement (Korea – Government Procurement)*[254] when, in the course of considering a possible claim by the United States for nullification or impairment of benefits reasonably expected to accrue from negotiated concessions under the *Agreement Government Procurement* or *AGP*, the panel thought it better to enquire as to whether the United States was in error when it assumed that the Inchon International Airport or IIA in South Korea, was a 'covered entity' within the meaning of Article 1 *AGP*. In deciding the dispute, the panel applied Article 48 VCLT, even though the United States itself had not invoked the provision in the proceedings as a possible defence.

Instead the panel proceeded to consider whether the exclusionary clause in the second paragraph of Article 48 VCLT was applicable, thereby raising the defence for the United States and subsequently rebutting it when it found that the United States had not 'properly discharged' its duty of diligence in verifying the offers made by Korea. The panel concluded that the United States had not by its own conduct contributed to the error but that the circumstances surrounding the negotiations, the two and a half year delay involved between Korea's answer

251 *Invocation of Article 48 Vienna Convention on the Law of Treaties*, Communication from Hungary, WT/L/144 (3 May 1996) and *Invocation of Article 48 Vienna Convention on the Law of Treaties*, Communication from Hungary, corrigendum, WT/L/144/Corr.1 (21 May 1996).

252 *Ibid*, pp. 1-2.

253 Minutes of the Meeting of the General Council, 16 April 1996, WT/GC/M/11 (28 May 1996), p. 16, para. 7.

254 *Korea – Procurement*, Panel Report, *Korea – Measures Affecting Government Procurement*, WT/DS163/R, adopted 19 June 2000 paras. 7.120-7.126, especially at paras. 7.122-7.123.

to the question posed by the United States regarding coverage of airport construction and Korea's final offer, combined with the subsequent four month period, including time for verification and so on, were such as to put it on notice of a possible error.[255] This is a somewhat curious application of Article 48 VCLT because error is usually invoked by a State as a means of invalidating its consent to be bound,[256] as Hungary's invocation of the provision demonstrates, rather than as ground for the protection of legitimate expectations, which the panel thought was the issue in the case of *Korea – Government Procurement*.

3.2 Accession

Each time a country seeking WTO membership completes its negotiations on the terms of accession with existing Members the results of those negotiations, together with the rights and obligations of the new Member are attached to a Protocol, which is then opened for acceptance. The accession of a new Member is not usually thought of as an amendment but the *WTO Agreement* is modified in order to cover 'an additional subject of international law',[257] thereby changing the complex web of treaty relationships among *all* the Members on the basis of which they operate. The process of accession to the WTO consequently raises important legal issues concerning the rights and obligations of existing Members as well as the acceding Member. The following section reviews the substantive and procedural mechanism for countries wishing to accede to the WTO, focusing on the practice of the Members in creating and applying rules that regulate the accession process. It also raises some points regarding the consistency of the process with the rules of general international law.

Since the establishment of the WTO in 1995 the process of accession in accordance with Article XII *WTO Agreement* has become more complicated than the process of accession to the GATT 1947. This is due to the increased scope and coverage of the WTO arising from the results of the Uruguay Round and the exercise of a broader array of norms than under the GATT 1947. As a result there has been a need to ensure that the process is more structured and transparent[258] and this has led to qualitative changes of a procedural and substantive nature. The

255 *Korea – Government Procurement*, *ibid*, para. 7.125.

256 Aust, above n. 48, 254.

257 Ehlermann and Ehring, above n. 67, 57.

258 *Technical Note on the Accession Process*, Note by the Secretariat, Revision, WT/ACC/10/Rev. 2, 22 October 2004 [hereinafter *Technical Note on Accession, Revision 2004*], 1; on the need for greater internal and external transparency in the system *see inter alia*,

accession process is arguably the area of established practice of the organisation where the former GATT predominates. Accession to the WTO continues to resemble the accession of a contracting party to a multilateral treaty regime rather than the admission of a new Member to an international economic organisation.

The reason for this is a mixture of specific WTO rules and a long-standing practice, dating back to the former GATT that governs the ordinary procedure for accession. There are a limited number of positive rules on accession and the most relevant one is Article XII *WTO Agreement*, which is remarkable for its brevity.[259] It states:

> 1. Any State or separate customs territory possessing full autonomy in the conduct of its external commercial relations and of the other matters provided for in this Agreement and the Multilateral Trade Agreements may accede to this Agreement, on terms to be agreed between it and the WTO. Such accession shall apply to this Agreement and the Multilateral Trade Agreements annexed thereto.
> 2. Decisions on accession shall be taken by the Ministerial Conference. The Ministerial Conference shall approve the agreement on the terms of accession by a two-thirds majority of the Members of the WTO.
> 3. Accession to a Plurilateral Trade Agreement[260] shall be governed by the provisions of that Agreement.[261]

The language of paragraphs 1 and 2 of Article XII *WTO Agreement* follows almost *verbatim* the wording of Article XXXIII of the GATT 1947 on accession[262] and

Caroline Dommen, 'Raising Human Rights Concerns in the World Trade Organisation: Actors, Processes and Possible Strategies' (2002) 24 *HRQ* 1-50, at 29-32.

259 *Technical Note on Accession, Revision 2004*, *ibid*, 3.

260 Only two of the original four Plurilateral Trade Agreements – the (revised) Government Procurement Agreement and the Agreement on Trade in Civil Aircraft – are still in effect. For the other two Plurilateral Trade Agreements, *see Deletion of the International Dairy Agreement from Annex 4 of the WTO Agreement*, Decision of 10 December 1997, WT/L/251, 17 December 1997, and *Deletion of the International Bovine Meat Agreement from Annex 4 of the WTO Agreement*, Decision of 10 December 1997, WT/L/252, 17 December 1997.

261 Article XII, WTO Agreement, *The Legal Texts*, above n. 2, 15.

262 Article XXXIII *GATT 1994*, *The Legal Texts*, *ibid*, 532, reads as follows:
'Accession
A government not party to this Agreement, or a government acting on behalf of a separate customs territory possessing full autonomy in the conduct of its external commercial relations and of the other matters provided for in this Agreement, may accede to this Agreement, on its own behalf or on behalf of that territory, on terms to be agreed between such government and the CONTRACTING PARTIES. Decisions of the CON-

gives substance to the idea that WTO accession is still considered in terms of the accession of a new party to a multilateral treaty rather than the admission of a member to an international organisation, as was noted when analysing the organisational and institutional bases of the organisation.[263]

Moreover, as in the case of the former GATT, no guidance is given as to what should be understood by the wording 'on terms to be agreed' contained in the first paragraph of Article XII *WTO Agreement* nor is any specific procedure laid down for negotiating those terms. However, what might seem like a very obscure phrase is in fact highly significant. It is clear that the provision is copied from Article XXIII GATT 1947[264] and thus it should be read in light of GATT practice under that provision, the operation of which in the GATT era had both a formal and an informal character.

The phrase 'on terms to be agreed', and the practice surrounding it, is a direct reference to the fact that certain (standard) provisions have appeared in almost all GATT protocols of accession since the Annecy Protocol of 1949.[265] In the context of WTO accession, there are no guidelines as to what is meant by 'on terms to be agreed'[266] and thus considerable latitude is left for negotiations between the existing Members and the acceding country. The process of accession manifests itself in a set of substantive and procedural rules, which are wholly informal in character, arise out of the practice of the Members as former contracting parties to the GATT, and which can be interpreted by the Members as they see fit in order to govern the process of any country seeking accession to the WTO. The stipulation of specific rather than general conditions for each acceding country combined with *ad hoc* decision-making that is geared to each individual applicant, is considered a necessity in those international (economic) organisations 'where there is such strong interference with the domestic policies of the members that it is impossible to predetermine, in general terms, the demands which must be made on the applicant'.[267]

TRACTING PARTIES under this paragraph shall be taken by a two-thirds majority.'

263 *See* chapter I, section 3.3.

264 *See* text of Article XXIII GATT 1947, *The Legal Texts*, above n. 2.

265 The Annecy Protocol of Terms of Accession to the GATT (adopted 10 October 1949, *in force* 30 November 1949) 62 *UNTS* 122, *see* further *GATT Analytical Index*, above n. 71, 1021-1022 for further details and an illustration, drawn from the Decision and Protocol of Accession of Bolivia to the GATT.

266 Anna Lanoszka, 'The World Trade Organization Accession Process, Negotiating Participation in a Globalizing Economy' (2001) 35 *JWT* 575-602 at 589.

267 H. G. Schermers and N. M. Blokker, *International Institutional Law: Unity within diversity* (4th edn rev Boston, Leiden: Martinus Nijhoff Publishers, 2003) §97, 78, with reference to the accession provisions of the IMF (Article II, section 2), the European

The soft-law character of these informal, non-binding rules that make up the practice on GATT/WTO accession provides the Members with considerable flexibility in their negotiations with an acceding country. Some striking changes have taken place in WTO accession compared to the former GATT. Increasingly the accession process has the potential to influence economic policy and to foster institutional and regulatory reform within the country seeking accession. As Anna Lanoschka observes: 'by forcing higher regulatory standards, transparent policy-making, and by encouraging national treatment for the commercially present foreign suppliers of services, WTO legal rules can help build market-supporting mechanisms such as a professional judiciary to enforce contracts, secure property rights and ensure due process, administrative transparency in government agencies, and regulatory predictability to domestic policy making' – all of which are seen as beneficial outcomes.[268]

Not surprisingly the accession process has come in for criticism,[269] due to the increasing number and range of additional obligations that the Membership, as *demandeur* in the accession process, has required of certain developing countries and LDCs.[270] Even Lanoschka admits that there is a burden on acceding States 'to submit a *legislative plan of action* indicating implementation of the requested legislative changes and the introduction of the new commercial laws and regulations'.[271] The type of commitments that acceding States must currently make can be grouped into three basic sets. One is the set of commitments to observe all the rules included in the *WTO Agreement* and the annexed Multilateral Trade Agreements. A second set concerns commitments relating to the (non-)recourse to particular WTO provisions, such as transitional periods and developing country status (possibly with the application of special and differential treatment) under certain Multilateral Agreements. Finally, there are the commitments to abide by rules created in the commitment paragraphs that relate to extraneous economic

Union (Article 49) and the EFTA (Article 41), in addition to the WTO (Article XII) and the extensive literature on EU membership in fn. 109.

268 Lanoszka, above n. 266, 577.

269 Julia Ya Qin, '"WTO-Plus" Obligations and Their Implications for the World Trade Organization Legal System: An Appraisal of the China Accession Protocol' (2003) 37 *JWT* 483-522.

270 See the collection of papers arising from the meeting of the *Ad Hoc* Expert Group Meeting of the Secretary-General of UNCTAD: Issues and Problems Arising from the Integration of Countries into the Multilateral Trading System, Geneva, 9-10 April 2001, together with other collected papers of UNCTAD staff and experts, in *WTO Accessions and Development Policies*, UNCTAD/DIC/TNCD/11 (New York: United Nations, 2001), UN Sales No. E.02.II.D.19.

271 Lanoszka, above n. 266, 581.

policies and regulatory reform, for example privatization programmes, the dismantling of monopolies, price and profit controls, industrial policy and participation in the plurilateral agreements contained in Annex 4 (the *AGP* and the *Agreement on Civil Aircraft*).[272]

The substantive and procedural norms on WTO accession find their legal basis in the *WTO Agreement* together with a variety of instruments and practice arising from accession to the former GATT under the corresponding Article XXXIII GATT 1947.[273] The first of these norms is the GATT *acquis*, which is procedural in character because WTO practice on accession continues the practice followed by the CONTRACTING PARTIES to the GATT 1947 and guides the current Members when negotiating with acceding Members.

This is clear from the practice of the Secretariat, which following extensive consultations with interested Members, early in 1995 issued a *Technical Note on the Accession Process* (*Technical Note on Accessions*)[274] in order to assist the Members in 'the organisation and pursuit of accession negotiations' by individual Working Parties. It was understood that the *Technical Note on Accessions* would not be submitted to the Ministerial Conference (nor the General Council) nor to individual working parties for approval but instead would be accorded the status of a practical guide for use by delegations of Members and delegations of acceding governments without any formal endorsement of a general policy on accession negotiations. The *Technical Note on Accessions* is therefore considered to be a guide for WTO practice on accession but it does not bind the Members.

Thus, WTO accession follows a set of procedures, which date back to the establishment of the WTO but are modelled on those followed by the CONTRACTING PARTIES to GATT 1947. These GATT 1947 procedures include the *Complementary Procedures on Accession Negotiations* agreed by the Council of GATT 1947 in 1993[275] and the statement by the Chairman of the Council

272 See generally, Lanoszka, *ibid*, 584-585 and Jolita Butkeviciene, Michiko Hayashi, Victor Ognivtsev and Tokio Yamaoka, 'Terms of WTO Accession' in *WTO Accessions and Development Policies*, above n. 270, 230-264.

273 For practice on accession under Article XXXIII GATT 1947 *see GATT Analytical Index*, above n. 71, 943-952.

274 *Accession – Procedures for Negotiations under Article XII*, Note by the Secretariat, WT/ACC/1 of 24 March 1995 [hereinafter WT/ACC/1]. *See* also Gabrielle Marceau, 'Les procédures d'accession à l'Organisation mondiale de commerce (OMC)' (1997) *AcDI* 233-252, at 239 *et seq* and Antonio Parenti, 'Accession to the World Trade Organisation' (2000) 27 *LIEI* 141-157.

275 *Accession to the General Agreement – Complementary procedures to be followed in the organization and pursuit of negotiations*, with an Annex attached, being 'Outline Format for a Memorandum on the Foreign Trade Régime', Decision of the GATT

of GATT 1947 on the *Management of Accession Negotiations* in 1994,[276] which are described more fully hereunder since they give a clearer picture of the established practice of the GATT contracting parties/WTO Members in the matter of accession.

The *Complementary Procedures on Accession Negotiations* refer to the fact that following the receipt of 'a formal request for accession to the General Agreement and its approval by the Council or by the CONTRACTING PARTIES', the acceding government will be issued with details of the normal procedures for accession that are followed by working parties on accession. It will also be requested to submit a Memorandum on its Foreign Trade Regime. The practice is for participating Members in the Working Party on Accession to raise questions and for the discussion that takes place to be recorded in the report of the Working Party on Accession, which will eventually be attached to a draft Decision on Accession and the Protocol of Accession (see below).

Parallel to this, bilateral negotiations on tariffs and services commitments are held between the acceding government and individual Members participating in the Working Party on Accession, which will later be 'multilateralised' to *all* Members.[277] The results of those accession negotiations are then annexed in schedules of tariff concessions and schedules of specific commitments to the draft Protocol of Accession. Once accession negotiations have been concluded, the Report of the Working Party on Accession together with the draft Decision and Protocol of Accession are submitted to the Ministerial Conference (or the General Council acting in the interim) for adoption of the report and approval of the texts of the draft Decision and Protocol of Accession through the normal decision-making procedures relating to accessions. As with all Protocols, a Protocol of

Council, L/7317, (27 October 1993), *Basic Instruments and Selected Documents (BISD)* 40S/6-9 [hereinafter *Complementary Procedures on Accession*]; for details, *see GATT Analytical Index*, above n. 71, 1019.

276 Statement of the Chairman of the Council of GATT 1947 on the *Management of Accession Negotiations*, 10 November 1994, C/COM/4 (16 November 1994), *BISD* 41S, Vol. I/32-33 [hereinafter *Management of Accession Negotiations – Chairman's Note*], reported in *GATT Analytical Index, ibid*, 1020.

277 Marceau, above n. 274, 242. See further comments, *see* above section 2.1 with respect to the nature of WTO obligations, which are essentially bilateral and reciprocal, but as result of their multilateralisation also acquire an integral and intra-dependent character.

Accession enters into effect for the applicant Member[278] 30 days following acceptance[279] in accordance with paragraph 1 of Article XIV *WTO Agreement*.

By contrast, the Chairman's Note on the *Management of Accession Negotiations*, drawn up after consultations with delegations, is considered to be merely indicative in nature. Its aim is 'to rationalize the manner of work on accession negotiations when an unusually large number of requests for accession must be dealt with' and it should not be read as substituting for the established procedures on accession,[280] i.e. the procedures that are described in the *Technical Note on Accessions* and the *Complementary Procedures on Accession Negotiations*. The Chairman's Note includes such things as management of the process in order to 'ensure the wider acceptance and effective application of rules and disciplines under the GATT [WTO], thus contributing towards the reform processes in the applicant countries or territories …',[281] the fact that 'accession negotiations should be limited to issues related to GATT [WTO] rights and obligations including market access to the applicant country or territory',[282] the allowance of adequate lead time at all stages of accession from preparatory stages to finalisation of the examination process[283] and the involvement of the Secretariat with technical assistance to the acceding country[284] combined with active participation in the work of the GATT [WTO] by the acceding country through availing itself of training activities at the GATT [WTO], utilising its GATT [WTO] observer status, in particular by attending meetings of other accession working parties and of various committees.[285]

The second and third norms that govern accession are also procedural in character. One is paragraph 2 of Article XII *WTO Agreement*, stating that '[D]ecisions on accession shall be taken by the Ministerial Conference'. It might lead one to believe that a final decision on accession rests with the main plenary body in which Ministers will take the decision but this is misleading. As we noted

278 Details on the interpretation and application of the *Complementary Procedures on Accession*, above n. 175, can be found in the *GATT Analytical Index*, above n. 71, 1019.

279 The Protocol of Accession is usually signed *ad referendum*, i.e. subject to confirmation by the government of the person signing on behalf of the acceding Member, whereupon it will indicate its consent to be bound by ratification

280 Chapeau to the *Management of Accession Negotiations – Chairman's Note*, above n. 131, reproduced in the *GATT Analytical Index*, above n. 71, 1020.

281 *Management of Accession Negotiations – Chairman's Note*, *ibid*, point 1.

282 *Management of Accession Negotiations – Chairman's Note*, *ibid*, point 3.

283 *Management of Accession Negotiations – Chairman's Note*, *ibid*, points 5, 6 and 7.

284 *Management of Accession Negotiations – Chairman's Note*, *ibid*, point 8.

285 *Management of Accession Negotiations – Chairman's Note*, *ibid*, point 10.

previously,[286] the provision should always be read in conjunction with paragraph 2 of Article IV *WTO* Agreement, which makes it clear that the General Council, where governments are only represented at ambassadorial level, will usually take such a decision unless of course one of the two-yearly Meetings of the Ministerial Conference happens to be in session. Altogether twenty countries have acceded to the WTO over a ten year period since its establishment in 1995, based on a decision taken by the General Council[287] and to which a standard Protocol of Accession is attached.[288]

The other procedural norm that governs accession is the preference for consensus decision-making over voting, conform WTO practice. As noted in chapter III, while paragraph 2 of Article XII *WTO Agreement* states that 'the Ministerial Conference shall approve the agreement on the terms of accession by a two-thirds majority of the Members of the WTO', i.e. by a qualified majority vote, the practice has emerged of decisions on accession being taken by consensus. This practice has been recognised in the revised procedures for decision-making, which were adopted on the basis of a Chairman's Statement, where it was noted that the Members usually adopt decisions on waivers and accessions by consensus, i.e. by means of the so-called WT/L/93 practice, which operates *in lieu* of voting.[289]

Ecuador is the *only* country to have acceded to the WTO in accordance with Article XII:2 *WTO Agreement.* This was done because the meeting at which the matter was put to a vote was 'inquorate' and the aforementioned WT/L/93 practice, which proscribes consensus *in lieu* of voting, had not yet been put in place. Eventually recourse was made to a postal ballot[290] in order to comply with the

286 *See* chapter I, section 3.3.

287 The format for decisions taken by General Council in the matter of accessions was revised in January 2001; *see Technical Note on Accession, Revision 2004*, above n. 258, 39-40, with differences in drafting of the recitals to Accession Decisions in order to take account of the adoption of such decisions conform the WT/L/93 practice of consensus, *see* below, n. 289.

288 Annex 2 to the *Technical Note on Accession, Revision 2004*, above n. 258, 39-43.

289 The General Council adopted the decision on *Decision-making procedures under Article IX and XII of the WTO Agreement*, at its meeting of 15 November 1995, item 3, WT/GC/M/8 (13 December 1995), section V, pp. 7-8 and the relevant decision was issued in the 'L' or Legal Series, as a Statement by the Chairman, WT/L/93 (24 November 1995) [hereinafter *WT/L/93 Practice*]. *See* for further details, chapter III, section 2.2(c).

290 This was only done after consensus had been reached on the Report of the Working Party; see *Minutes of the Meeting of the General Council held on 31 July 1995*, WT/GC/M/6 (20 September 1995) and *Decision of the General Council of 16 August 1995*, WT/ACC/ECU/5 (22 August 1995). *See* also WT/ACC/ECU/6, which takes note of the General Council decision and informs Members that the Protocol of Accession (annexed

rules of procedure on the calling of meetings and decision-making in operation at the time.[291] The move to the use of consensus instead of voting on accessions (and waiver decisions) stems from some of the practical problems that exist with voting on matters that call for a qualified majority, where the decision must be taken according to the *number* of WTO Members present and voting while the use of consensus requires that a decision be taken on the basis of those present at the meeting.

On the issue of consensus, it should also be recalled that the General Council can use the ordinary consensus rule at any stage during the accession process including the handling of a request from a country wishing to accede to the WTO from the establishment of a Working Party on Accession up to the adoption of the Report of the Working Party on Accession, including the draft Decision and Protocol of Accession. The use of consensus to block the establishment of a Working Party can act as a very effective veto as happened on several, well-documented occasions in the case of Iran, which made 22 such requests from 1996 onwards but due to the opposition of the United States that request was only granted in May 2005.[292]

The fourth norm of relevance to the WTO accession process is substantive in nature and concerns the additional rule relating to the potential disapplication of the *WTO Agreement* and the annexed Multilateral Trade Agreements between an acceding country and the Members, pursuant to Article XIII *WTO Agreement (Non-Application of Multilateral Trade Agreements between Particular Members)*, which is sometimes called the 'exception of multilateralism' and is considered to be somewhat unusual in the law of international organisations.[293] The exceptional nature of this particular provision is evidenced in GATT/WTO law and

as *Protocol for the Accession of the Republic of Ecuador to the Agreement Establishing the World Trade Organization*) is open for acceptance in the Office of the Director of the Accessions Division, Room 2079. *See* further Lorand Bartels, 'The Separation of Powers in the WTO: How to Avoid Judicial Activism' (2004) 53 *ICLQ* 861-895 at 865 and Deborah Steger, *Peace Through Trade: Building the World Trade Organization* (London: Cameron May, 2004) 42.

291 *Rules of Procedure for Sessions of the Ministerial Conference and Meetings of the General Council*, adopted by the General Council on 31 January 1995, WT/L/28 (7 February 1995), Rule 16 in respect of a quorum and Rule

292 See Minutes of the Meeting of the General Council, held on 26 May 2005, WT/GC/M/95 (21 June 2005) 2, para. 1, following the United States' agreement two months earlier to drop its longstanding opposition in an effort to support attempts by the UK, France and Germany to persuade Iran to renounce its suspected attempts to develop nuclear weapons in return for a package of economic incentives, including WTO membership; see (1 June 2005) 19 *BRIDGES Weekly Trade News Digest*.

293 Schermers and Blokker, above n. 267, §43, 33.

practice by the fact that it can only be invoked if certain conditions are met in the same manner as under Article XXXV GATT 1947 (Non-application of the Agreement between Particular Contracting Parties).[294] Specifically, paragraph 1 of Article XIII *WTO Agreement* provides that '[T]his Agreement and the Multilateral Trade Agreements in Annexes 1 and 2 shall not apply as between any Member and any other Member if either of the Members, at the time either becomes a member, does not consent to such application.' In accordance with paragraph 3 of Article XIII *WTO Agreement* the disapplication provision can only be validly invoked by an existing Member as against an acceding one provided the existing non-consenting Member 'has so notified the Ministerial Conference' and has done this prior to 'the approval of the agreement on the terms of accession by the Ministerial Conference'.[295]

Thus far there have been eight invocations of Article XIII *WTO Agreement* by Members that have taken place, prior to the decision of the General Council whereby the Report of the Working Party is adopted and the Protocol of Accession is opened for acceptance. One has been by Turkey against Armenia,[296] another by El Salvador against China[297] and six by the United States against Romania,[298] Mongolia,[299] Kyrgyz Republic,[300] Georgia,[301] Moldova[302] and Ar-

294 For practice on invocation of Article XXXV GATT 1947 *see GATT Analytical Index*, above note 71, 1032-1033.

295 Marceau, above n. 274, 246. See also Wang, Lei, 'Non-Application Issues in the GATT and the WTO' (1994) 28 *JWT* 49-74.

296 *Accession of the Republic of Armenia – Invocation by the Republic of Turkey of Article XIII of the Marrakesh Agreement Establishing the World Trade Organization with respect to the Republic of Armenia*, 29 November 2002, WT/L/501 (3 December 2002).

297 *Ministerial Conference – Fourth Session – Doha, 9 – 13 November 2001 – Accession of China – Invocation by El Salvador of Article XIII of the Marrakesh Agreement Establishing the World Trade Organization with Respect to China*, 5 November 2001, WT/L/429 (7 November 2001)

298 *Marrakesh Agreement Establishing the World Trade Organization – Invocation of Article XIII, paragraph 1, by the United States*, WT/L/11 (27 January). The US informed the Director-General on 30 December 1994 but only formally invoked Article XIII:1 on 27 January 1995; *see WTO Analytical Index*, above n. 125, 97 at fn. 348.

299 *Accession of Mongolia – Invocation by the United States of Article XIII of the WTO Agreement,* 11 July 1996, WT/L/159 (17 July 1996),

300 *Accession of the Kyrgyz Republic – Invocation by the United States of Article XIII of the WTO Agreement*, 9 October 1998, WT/L/275 (10 October 1998).

301 *Accession of Georgia – Invocation by the United States of Article XIII of the Marrakesh Agreement Establishing the World Trade Organization with Respect to Georgia*, 30 September 1999, WT/L/318 (1 October 1999).

menia.[303] All but four of these invocations[304] have subsequently been revoked. Both Turkey's invocation against Armenia and El Salvador's invocation against China are still in force. The United States has subsequently revoked its invocations[305] with the exception of Armenia and Moldova.[306] By contrast, there are several examples in GATT practice of the application of Article XXXV GATT 1947, the most well-known of which was the mass invocation of the provision by some fifty contracting parties against Japan between the mid-1950's and 1970.[307]

A fifth and final procedural norm, which is of relevance to some acceding States, is the set of General Council Guidelines on the Accession of LDC's that seek to facilitate and accelerate the process of accession for least-developed countries by simplifying and streamlining the procedures.[308] Authority for their adoption is to be found in the *Doha Ministerial Declaration*.[309] These Guidelines have proven essential, given that currently fully one third of all acceding govern-

302 *Accession of the Republic of Moldova – Invocation by the United States of Article XIII of the Marrakesh Agreement Establishing the World Trade Organization with Respect to Moldova*, 2 May 2001, WT/L/395 (4 May 2001).

303 *Accession of the Republic of Armenia – Invocation by the United States of Article XIII of the Marrakesh Agreement Establishing the World Trade Organization with respect to the Republic of Armenia*, 9 December 2002, WT/L/505 (10 December 2002).

304 The United States invoked the non-application clause of Article XIII:3 with respect to Georgia, the Kyrgyz Republic, Moldova and Mongolia in accordance with the Jackson-Vanik Amendment to §402 of the 1974 United States Trade Act, which was introduced to allow the United States Government to deny unconditional MFN treatment to 'non-market economies', which deny or restrict the right of their citizens to emigrate; see Butkeviciene, Hayashi, Ognivtsev and Yamaoka, above n. 272, 254.

305 *See Marrakesh Agreement Establishing the World Trade Organization – Invocation of Article XIII.1 with respect to Romania – Withdrawal of Invocation by the United States*, WT/L/203 (20 February 1997), *Marrakesh Agreement Establishing the World Trade Organization – Withdrawal of Invocation of Article XIII by the United States with Respect to Mongolia*, 7 July 1999, WT/L/306 (8 July 1999), *Marrakesh Agreement Establishing the World Trade Organization – Withdrawal of Invocation of Article XIII by the United States with respect to the Kyrgyz Republic*, 18 September 2000, WT/L/363 (20 September 2000) and *Marrakesh Agreement Establishing the World Trade Organization – Withdrawal of Invocation of Article XIII by the United States with respect to Georgia*, 8 January 2001, WT/L/385 (10 January 2001).

306 *Technical Note on Accession, Revision 2004*, above n. 258, 29.

307 *GATT Analytical Index*, above n. 71, Table of Former Invocations of Article XXXV, which lists no less than fifty against Japan between September 1955 and February 1970, all of which were subsequently withdrawn.

308 *Accession of Least-Developed Countries*, Decision of the General Council, 10 December 2002, WT/L/508 20 January 2003).

309 *Doha Ministerial Declaration*, above n. 86, para. 42.

ments are LDCs and at the time of their adoption in 2002 not a single LDC had acceded to the WTO.[310]

The effect of this mix of substantive and mostly procedural norms governing the accession process on normative developments in the WTO is significant. In the absence of formal procedures for the admission of new Members, the *Technical Note on Accessions* and the *Complementary Procedures on Accession Negotiations* combined with the Chairman's Note on the *Management of Accession Negotiations*, both of which are non-binding instruments, substitute for any formal procedures.[311] Moreover, due to the nature of the *Complementary Procedures on Accession Negotiations* and the Chairman's Note on the *Management of Accession Negotiations*, which deal with the accession of contracting parties to the GATT 1947 and pre-date the entry into force of the WTO, GATT practice on accession is carried forward and forms part of the GATT *acquis* on accession. This established practice is further endorsed by preservation of the exception on multilateralism, which continues to permit the disapplication of substantive WTO rights and obligations between existing Members and certain acceding Members, in Article XIII *WTO Agreement* just as it did in the former GATT.

However, what none of these substantive and procedural norms regulate is the very heart of the accession process, i.e. the ever increasing number of terms and conditions that acceding Members are called upon to assume and have in some cases led to the accession on the basis of different sets of rights and obligations between acceding States and existing Members. As noted earlier,[312] this has potential consequences for the organisation but it also has consequences for normative developments within the WTO, since it extends the scope and application of some basic rights and obligations, besides adding new obligations in respect of some acceding Members.

3.3 Waivers

Some international organisations may waive or dispense with the obligations of their members in certain circumstances, including where a member has failed to

310 This has since been rectified with the accession of Cambodia and Nepal at the Fifth Session of the Ministerial Conference, held at Cancún in 2003. Even so, Cambodia has publicly gone on record at the Fifth Session of the Ministerial Conference, held at Cancún, 10-14 September 2003 in criticising the onerous accession process for LDCs.

311 The *Technical Note on Accession, Revision 2004*, above n. 258, simply adds to and endorses the procedures set out in the *Complementary Procedures on Accession Negotiations* and the Chairman's Note on the *Management of Accession Negotiations*.

312 *See* chapter I, section 3.3.

fulfil its obligations, for example where the payments on its annual contributions are in arrears.[313] However, the practice of international organisations demonstrates that this seldom occurs and the more usual procedure is for the members to waive the obligation of the delinquent member on grounds of special circumstances. Since a waiver of obligation is an exceptive norm, it should always be provided for expressly in the multilateral treaty or constituent instrument of the organisation, with details of the general and specific conditions that warrant it. Alongside the waiver in Article IX:3 *WTO Agreement* Henry Schermers and Niels Blokker cite examples of other international economic institutions, such as the IMF and the general conferences of some commodity councils, which contain provisions that may relieve their members of an obligation on account of exceptional or emergency circumstances.[314]

The exercise of secondary treaty rules like the waiver power can provide an organisation such as the WTO with the basis for rules that constitute an important supplement to the provisions of its constitution.[315] As Joseph Gold has remarked with respect to the IMF, 'the absence of an express authority to adopt procedures and criteria is not likely to prevent an organization from developing them, because the mere existence of a power to waive may suggest implied authority to regulate its exercise by general rules'. He goes on to caution that '[I]f ... the organization relies on implied authority to adopt general rules, it may encounter the question of the relationship of the power to the amendment.'[316] This problem has also been highlighted by Jackson[317] and Kenneth Dam[318] in the context of the

313 Schermers and Blokker, above n. 267, §1444, at 911 with cross-reference to §157 at 119.

314 *Ibid*, §1444 at 911, citing the example of Article VIII, sections (2) and (3) IMF whereby the Fund may authorize a waiver to the normal rule that IMF Members may not impose restrictions on payments of current international transactions or engage in discriminatory currency arrangements where exception or emergency circumstances prevail. Also some commodity agreements contain provisions whereby the general conference or a commodity council under the agreement may relieve a member of its obligations in exceptional circumstances, e.g. Article 47 of the Sixth International Cocoa Agreement, United Nations Cocoa Conference, 2000, Second Session, Geneva, 26 February – 2 March 2001, TD/COCOA.9/7 and Corr. 1, 13 March 2001, opened for signature 1 May 2001.

315 Joseph Gold, 'The "Dispensing" and "Suspending" Powers of International Organizations (1972) XIX *NILR* 169-200 at 178 when comparing the practice of the IMF to that of other international institutions, including the GATT 1947.

316 Gold, *ibid*, 178-179.

317 Jackson, *World Trade and the Law of GATT*, above n. 22, §5.6, 137-139 at 138.

318 Kenneth W. Dam, *The GATT: Law and International Economic Organization* (Chicago: University of Chicago Press, 1970) 352.

former GATT and the issue is still relevant in the WTO context where the ongoing debate relating to implementation of paragraph 6 of the *Doha Ministerial Declaration on the TRIPs Agreement and Public Health*, has at one point revolved around the choice of implementation, either by means of an authoritative interpretation under Article IX:2 *WTO Agreement* (see below at section 3.4), by means of a waiver under Article IX:3 *WTO Agreement*, by means of amendment of the *TRIPs Agreement* under Article X *WTO Agreement* or by means of a moratorium on dispute settlement.[319]

Where a primary treaty obligation is temporarily set aside or 'waived', as in the case of the WTO (or former GATT), it constitutes what Gold has termed the 'dispensing' powers of the organisation.[320] Schermers and Blokker have suggested that in the case of some international organisations like the WTO (or the former GATT) the operation of the waiver may affect not only the performance of an obligation by an individual Member but also effectively change the field of responsibility of the organisation thereby affecting *all* Members, i.e. the waiver may be granted by the Members to an individual Member, or group of individual Members, but the legal consequences arising from its grant affect the rights and obligations of *all* other Members *erga omnes partes*. Dam goes so far as to consider that when the application of a waiver does not involve a straightforward violation of a WTO obligation (nullification and impairment of benefits) it may 'rest on the unfamiliar principle of giving a remedy in the absence of a right'.[321] Arguably an example of this latter phenomenon is the so-called 'Kimberly Waiver' discussed in the following section.

a) General waiver power

The general waiver power, which the Members may exercise, stems from the former GATT multilateral trade regime where it existed in the form of a collective action decision taken by the CONTRACTING PARTIES on the basis of paragraph 5 of Article XXV GATT 1947.[322] In accordance with Article XXV:5 GATT 1947, a waiver decision could only be adopted by a super qualified majority

319 *Proposals on Paragraph 6 of the Doha Declaration on the TRIPS Agreement and Public Health: Thematic Compilation*, Note by the Secretariat, Revision, IP/C/W/363/Add.1 (23 July 2002) [hereinafter '*Secretariat Note: Thematic Compilation on Implementation of Paragraph 6 Decision*'].

320 Gold, above n. 315, 172-179.

321 Dam, above n. 318, 358, remarked upon by Gold, *ibid*, 175.

322 Article XXV:5 GATT 1947, *The Legal Texts*, above n. 2, 525-526; see also Jackson, *World Trade and the Law of GATT*, above n. 22, especially §§ 22.2 and 22.3, 537-552.

decision, consisting of a two-thirds majority of the votes cast in a meeting where more than half of the contracting parties had to be present and voting.

In the case of the WTO, the right of a Member to derogate from any WTO obligation must be expressly approved by the Ministerial Conference (or in the intervening period between sessions of the Ministerial Conference by the General Council) on the basis of paragraphs 3 and 4 of Article IX *WTO Agreement*. A waiver decision normally calls for a qualified majority vote, with three-quarters of the Members voting in favour.

However, as we already noted in respect of decisions on accession, in section 3.2, the General Council early on in the life of the new organisation resolved that future decisions on general waivers could be adopted by consensus instead of being put to a formal vote. On purely practical grounds consensus, as opposed to qualified majority voting, does not require that the number of Members present be counted when the decision is taken. Even so, this 'revised' decision-making procedure does not preclude a Member from requesting a vote on the matter.[323]

The actual conditions for the grant of a waiver are set out in Article IX *WTO Agreement*, where in accordance with paragraph 3 'exceptional circumstances' must prevail and a clear time frame must be established for termination of the waiver. On the basis of paragraph 4 of Article IX *WTO Agreement*, this major exception to WTO obligations can only be provided for the duration of one year, whereupon it is reviewable annually in order to establish whether the exceptional circumstances still apply and to allow the General Council to examine the conditions related to the grant of that waiver.

Based on the foregoing the general waiver is distinguishable from other so-called 'horizontal waivers' such as the general exception (Article XX *GATT 1994*[324] or Article XIV *GATS*[325]) or the security exception (Article XXI *GATT 1994* or Article *XIVbis GATS*), which may be invoked in order to justify an otherwise inconsistent WTO measure. These types of horizontal waiver provide limited exceptions from obligations under certain other provisions of the *GATT 1994* or the *GATS* but they only come into effect in the event of a dispute when

323 This a reference to the residual character of voting under the WT/L/93 practice in respect of waivers and accession, for which see above n. 289, and for further details on the practice of decision-making by consensus *in lieu* voting, chapter III, at section 2.2 (c).

324 *See* WTO Committee on Trade and Environment, *GATT/WTO Dispute Settlement Practice Relating to Article XX, Paragraphs (b), (d) and (g) of GATT: Note from the Secretariat – Revision*, WTO Doc WT/CTE/W/103 (8 March 2002) and more recently the references to additional case law of the Appellate Body on Article XX *GATT 1994* in *WTO Appellate Body Repertory of Reports and Awards, 1995-2004* (Cambridge: Cambridge University Press, 2005) [hereinafter *WTO Appellate Body Repertory*] 163-175.

325 *See* for an invocation of Article XIV *GATS*, *US – Gambling*, above n. 49, 293-366.

invocation of the exception by the respondent party gives rise to an affirmative defence, i.e. the party raising the exceptive measure bears the burden of proving that the challenged measure meets the requirements of the defence provision while the complaint must seek to rebut it.[326]

In the past the GATT contracting parties made extensive use of the waiver power and it was frequently abused; waivers were often of a general nature and were 'open-ended', i.e. no specific time-limits were set for their termination. In its new formula, the dispensing powers of the Members, to use Gold's term, are not so readily exercised. Currently, no Member has a right to derogate from one of the basic principles (including MFN), or a specific provision in the *WTO Agreement* or one of annexed the Multilateral Trade Agreements but instead must 'negotiate' the right to a waiver. Additionally, any such exception should be narrowly construed and hence the conditioning of the terms of the grant of the general waiver, which transforms it into a truly exceptive norm. Since a waiver is already granted by the membership, it will not normally be contestable in dispute settlement proceedings unless the Member that was granted the waiver has failed to comply with its conditions,[327] or its application leads to a non-violation complaint.

During the ten-year period since the establishment of the WTO around 150 waivers, or extensions thereof from the former GATT, have been adopted by the General Council under Article IX *WTO Agreement*.[328] One group of decisions concerns 'collective waivers' in relation to the extension of the time-limit for the purpose of enabling Members to implement recommended amendments to the Harmonized System or HS nomenclature in their Tariff Schedules.[329] A second group covers individual waivers granted to two or more Members for the formation

326 *US – Wool Shirts and Blouses*, Appellate Body Report, *United States – Measures Affecting Imports of Woven Wool Shirts and Blouses from India*, WT/DS33/AB/R, adopted 23 May 1997, p. 323 at 337.

327 *EC – Bananas III*, Appellate Body Report, *European Communities – Regime for the Importation, Sale and Distribution of Bananas*, WT/DS27/AB/R, adopted 25 September 1997, paras. 183-185, especially at para. 185.

328 A list of waivers granted between 1995 and 2003 in accordance with Article IX *WTO Agreement*, and extensions to waivers previously granted under Article XXV:5 GATT 1947 can be found in the *WTO Analytical Index*, above n. 125, 82-87.

329 *See* for example *Submission of HS96 Documentation*, Note by the Secretariat, Revision, G/MA/TAR/2/Rev.35 (22 March 2005), listing eleven so-called 'collective waivers', being *Decisions on the Introduction of HS changes into WTO Schedules of Tariff Concessions on 1 January 1996*, e.g. WT/L/124 + Corr.1, WT/L/173, WT/L/216, WT/L/243, WT/L/268, WT/L/281, WT/L/303, WT/L/338, WT/L/351, WT/L/379 and WT/L/400. Since 2001, the General Council has proceeded to issue individual waivers to requesting Members rather than collective waivers for the HS96 System.

of a regional trade arrangement,[330] or the extension of preferential treatment to a single territory[331] or a group of countries.[332] A third group of waivers deals with 'other forms', i.e. a category of miscellaneous waivers of a more general character, the most interesting of which is the *Waiver Concerning Kimberley Process Certification Scheme for Rough Diamonds* (*Kimberley Waiver*).[333]

Substantively, the *Kimberley Waiver* granted a waiver of obligation of the 'covered' Members from applying Article I:1 *GATT 1994* (MFN) and allowed for the imposition of an export or import ban in violation of Articles XI:1 and XIII *GATT 1994* (prohibition on quantitative restrictions), which came about as a result of a meeting at ministerial level in Interlaken, Switzerland on 5 November 2002, in order to stop the flow of conflict diamonds onto world markets while at the same time seeking to protect the legitimate diamond industry. The Kimberley process works through an international scheme of certification for rough diamond exports to, and imports from, participants, thereby breaking the link between the trade in rough diamonds and armed conflict groups such as exist in Angola, Liberia and Sierra Leone. It also takes into account relevant UN Security Council resolutions, adopted under Chapter VII UN[334] and the Kimberley Process Certification Scheme Participants' stated intent 'to contribute and support the implementation of the measures provided for in those resolutions', thereby incorporating UN Security Council practice by reference into WTO law. Some Members felt that there was no need for a waiver since the security exception in Article XXI *GATT 1994* ought to be sufficient to cover the situation and moreover, the *Kimberley waiver* does not place any restrictions on trade in conflict diamonds *between* Kimberley process participants.[335]

330 See for example *European Communities – The ACP-EC Partnership Agreement*, waiver decision adopted at the Fourth Session of the Ministerial Conference, Doha, 9-14 November 2001, WT/MIN(01)/15 (14 November2001), re-circulated as WT/L/436 (7 December 2001) valid until 31 December 2007.

331 *See* for example *United States – Former Trust Territory of the Pacific Islands*, waiver decision adopted by the General Council on 14 October 1996, WT/L/183 (18 October 1996) valid until 31 December 2006.

332 *See* for example *United States – Caribbean Basin Economic Recovery Act*, waiver decision adopted by the General Council on 15 November 1995, WT/L/104 (24 November 1995) valid until 31 December 2005.

333 *Waiver Concerning Kimberley Process Certification Scheme for Rough Diamonds* (*Kimberley Waiver*), decision adopted by the General Council on 15 May 2003, WTL/518 (27 May 2003) valid until 31 December 2006.

334 Special reference is made in the ninth recital to UN Security Council Resolution, S/RES/ 1459 (2003) supporting the Kimberley Process Certification Scheme.

335 Joost Pauwelyn, 'WTO Compassion or Superiority Complex?: What to make of the WTO Waiver for "Conflict Diamonds"' (2003) 24 *MJIL* 1177-1207.

Procedurally the waiver decision was adopted pursuant to paragraphs 3 and 4 of Article IX *WTO Agreement* and based on a set of 'Guiding Principles' adopted by the former GATT contracting parties in 1956[336] as well as the 1994 *Understanding in Respect of Waivers*,[337] both of which endorse the resort to dispute settlement should a Member feel that its benefits are being nullified or impaired as a result of the application of the waiver but interestingly the 1956 *Guidelines Principles* provide 'where appropriate, for arbitration' on the matter.[338] The inclusion of the 1956 *Guiding Principles* has to do with the fact that the *Kimberley waiver* is a major exception to the principle of non-discrimination as laid down in Article I:1 *GATT 1994* (MFN) and is only the second time in the history of GATT/WTO that it has been applied to Article XIII *GATT 1994* (Non-discriminatory Administration of Quantitative Restrictions).[339] The decision of the Appellate Body in *EC – Bananas III*[340] with respect to the Lomé waiver[341] makes it clear that the truly exceptional nature of waivers from the obligation of non-discrimination means that there must be an explicit reference in the waiver itself to that provision, or to the importance of the obligation contained therein.

A final point with respect to the *Kimberley Waiver* is that it was initially granted in favour of eleven Members listed in the Annex to the waiver – Australia, Brazil, Canada, Israel, Japan, Korea, Philippines, Sierra Leone, Thailand, United Arab Emirates and the United States. However, the decision offers other Members *prospectively* the opportunity to be covered provided that they notify the Council

336 *Article XXV – Guiding Principles to be Followed by the CONTRACTING PARTIES in Considering Applications for Waivers from Part I or Other Important Obligations of the Agreement*, Procedures adopted on 1 November 1956 by the Contracting Parties, *BISD* 5S/25 [hereinafter *1956 Guiding Principles*].

337 *Understanding in Respect of Waivers of Obligations under the General Agreements on Tariff and Trade 1994*, *The Legal Texts*, above n. 2, 34-35.

338 Paragraph *(d)* of the *1956 Guiding Principles*, above n. 336.

339 The reference is to the *Waiver Granted in Connection with the European Coal and Steel Community*, Decision of 10 November 1952, *BISD*, 1S/17, para. 3; see *WTO Analytical Index*, above n. 125, at 81, fn. 270.

340 *EC – Bananas III*, above n. 310, paras. 184-187.

341 Fourth ACP-EC Convention of Lomé, Extension of Waiver, Decision of 14 October 1996, WT/L/186 (18 October 1996), extended the waiver with respect to the Fourth ACP-EEC Convention of Lomé, granted by Decision of the CONTRACTING PARTIES of 9 December 1994, L/7604, until 29 February 2000; there was no explicit reference to a waiver in respect of Article XIII GATT 1947 (or *GATT 1994*).

for Trade in Goods accordingly,[342] which is something of a rarity in GATT/WTO waiver practice.

b) 'Mini' waivers

On occasion a Council or Committee with responsibility for overseeing a particular Multilateral Trade Agreement adopts a decision that has the effect of dispensing with a time limit for compliance with one or more obligations contained in that Agreement. The reference here is to a separate set of secondary treaty rules in certain Multilateral Trade Agreements that grant developing and/or least developing country Members, upon request, an exceptional waiver from their obligations under that Agreement for a certain period of time, including a transitional period, to be determined by the Committee or Council overseeing the relevant Agreement. These are what have been described as 'time-specified waivers'.[343] Some examples include paragraph 8 of Article 12 of the *Agreement on Technical Barriers to Trade* or *TBT,* whereby the Committee is 'enable to grant, upon request, specified, time-limited exception in whole or in part form obligations under this Agreement',[344] paragraph 4 of Article 27 of the *Agreement on Subsidies and Countervailing Measures* or *SCM* whereby a 'developing country deems it necessary to apply such subsidies beyond the eight-year period, it shall not later than one year before the expiry of this period enter into consultation with the Committee',[345] and paragraph 1 of Article 66 *TRIPs* whereby the 'TRIPs Council shall, upon duly motivated requested by a least-developed country Member, accord extensions' to the ten-year period for the date of application of the Agreement, as specified in paragraph 1 of Article 65, i.e. ten years from 1 January 1996.[346]

The practice with respect to some of these time-specified waivers reveals an emerging practice among the Members towards the extension of transitional periods for the implementation of a WTO obligation. However, these extensions have not

342 Paragraph 4 of the *Kimberley Waiver, ibid.* As of 31 December 2004 an additional eleven Members have subsequently notified the Council for Trade in Goods that they wish to be covered: Bulgaria, Croatia, Czech Republic, European Communities, Hungary, Mauritius, Romania, Separate Customs Territory of Taiwan, Penghu, Kinmen and Matsu, Slovenia, Switzerland and Venezuela; *see Annual Report 2004* (Geneva: World Trade Organization, 2005) 36, fn. a.

343 Kuijper, above n. 212, 97.

344 Article 12:8, *Agreement on Technical Barriers to Trade* or *TBT Agreement*, *The Legal Texts*, above n. 2, 138-162, at 154.

345 Article 27:4 *Agreement on Subsidies and Countervailing Measures* or *SCM Agreement*, *The Legal Texts*, *ibid*, 264-314, at 299.

346 Article 66:1 *TRIPs*, *The Legal Texts*, *ibid*, 399.

taken place on the basis of the general waiver power in paragraphs 2 to 4 of Article IX *WTO Agreement*, which sets out certain conditions for the grant of a waiver, or its extension, and therefore they amount to nothing less than the grant of mini-waivers. As might be anticipated, the practice has not been without its problems.

An example of such a mini-waiver is contained in paragraph 3 of Article 5 of the *Agreement on Trade-Related Investment Measures* or *TRIMs*. The provision explicitly states that: '[O]n request, the Council for Trade in Goods may extend the transitional period for the elimination of TRIMs notified under paragraph 1 for a developing country Member, including a least-developed country Member'.[347] On the basis of paragraph 2 of that same provision[348] developing country and least-developed country Members had already been granted longer periods of respectively five and seven years from entry into force of the WTO Agreement[349] in which to phase out and eliminate all previously notified trade-related investment measures. The notification period contained in paragraph 1 is important since it triggers the transitional period for the phasing out and elimination of these measures.[350]

The first Annual Report of the Director-General to the General Council in 1995 listed a total of 26 Members as having made a regular Article 5:1 *TRIMs* notification of the existence of trade-related measures, of which two were developed, five developing and seven LDC's.[351] A further point is that while most Members notified within the relevant time frame, a significant number of developing and LDC Members did not.[352]

347 Article 5:3 *Agreement on Trade-Related Investment Measures* or *TRIMs Agreement, The Legal Texts*, *ibid*, 163-167, 164.

348 Article 5:2 *TRIMs Agreement, The Legal Texts*, *ibid*, 163-164.

349 According to Article 5:1 *TRIMs*, *The Legal Texts*, ibid, the period of notification runs 90 days (3 calendar months) from the date of entry into force of the Marrakesh Agreement Establishing the World Trade Organization and its Annexes. Thus for the majority of WTO Members where the WTO Agreement entered into force on 1 January 1995, the notification period elapsed on 31 March 1995 while for others it is later.

350 The critical point is that Members must have notified existing TRIMs for the transitional period to take effect. Thus, failure to do so means that a Member cannot avail itself of the provisions in paragraphs 2 and 3 of Article 5 *TRIMs*, *The Legal Texts*, *ibid*, 163-164.

351 *World Trade Organization, Annual Report 1996*, Vol. 1 (Geneva: World Trade Organization, 1997) 109-110.

352 One was Brazil that actually introduced new trade restrictive investment measures into its automotive sector in 1996 and for which it unsuccessfully sought a 'waiver'. A second was India that in 1998 still maintained local content and trade balancing requirements, contrary to the measures contained in the 'Illustrative List' in the Annex to the *TRIMs*

However, what had not been anticipated was that between 1996 and 1999 a large number of developing countries Members would seek an extension for the phasing out and elimination of TRIMs-inconsistent measures in the CTG, including countries like Brazil and India that had not previously notified but wanted un-notified measures to enjoy the same benefits.[353] Just to complicate matters further one Member, the Philippines, which had previously notified under Article 5:1 *TRIMs*,[354] made a request to the CTG for an extension on the basis of Article 5:3 *TRIMs* but then entered into negotiations with the United States, leading to a bilateral agreement, whereby the United States granted the Philippines an extension or time-specified waiver on its TRIMs measures provided certain conditions were met. This was an extraordinary turn of events because it amounted to the grant of a mini-waiver by one Member whereas a waiver decision, whether adopted in the CTG pursuant to Article 5:3 *TRIMs* or in the General Council pursuant to Article IX *WTO Agreement*, is normally a collective action decision involving the membership.

Besides, as a matter of WTO law and practice the conclusion of a bilateral agreement between two Members can only be only condoned where the benefits are extended to all Members on an MFN basis.[355] Not surprisingly several Members condemned the practice, stating that decisions on time-limited waivers should be taken on a case-by-case basis by the CTG and that it was never the intention that individual Members should set their own conditions for the exercise of such a time-limited extension or mini-waiver.[356]

The matter did not rest there. Following the failure of the Third Meeting of the Ministerial Conference held in Seattle in 1999, several developing country

Agreement, The Legal Texts, above n. 2, 166-167. A third was Indonesia that became the target of dispute settlement proceedings in 1997, as a result of its 1996 National Car Programme whereby it maintained local content requirements in violation of Article 2 *TRIMs*; *see Indonesia – Autos*, Panel Report, *Indonesia – Certain Measures Affecting the Automobile Industry*, WT/DS54/R, WT/DS55/R, WT/DS59/R, WT/DS64/R, adopted 23 July 1998, paras. 6.1-6.27.

353 In fact only three developing countries had officially made such a request by the end of 1999 – they were the Philippines, Colombia and Mexico, for details see below, notes 354 and 357.

354 *Philippines – Request for Extension of the Transition Period under the Agreement on Trade-Related Investment Measures*, 4 October 1999, G/L/325 (5 October 1999) in respect of its domestic vehicle industry and local content for coconut based chemicals.

355 Jackson, *World Trade and the Law of* GATT, above n. 22, § 3.6, 76 and §10.4, 217, in respect of GATT practice on the matter.

356 Minutes of the Meeting of the Council for Trade in Goods or CTG, 24 January 2000, G/C/M/41 (29 February 2000), paras. 6-29, which was the first such meeting held after 31 December 1999. See the responses of the United States, the European Communities,

Members requested extensions, particularly in the period 18 – 28 December 1999.[357] The debate over a general extension continued right up until May 2000, when a decision was reached in the General Council concerning outstanding implementation issues[358] and included directing other WTO bodies 'to provide any appropriate inputs and to take any appropriate action' in pursuance of this decision.

At the same session the General Council adopted a decision on the implementation of the *TRIMs Agreement* (the *TRIMs Transition Decision*) wherein Members agreed to direct the CTG to give positive consideration to individual requests from developing countries, which had previously notified under Article 5:1 *TRIMs* for the extension of the transition period for implementation, in accordance with Article 5.3 *TRIMs*. With respect to those developing country Members that had *not* notified their TRIMs measures, or had not yet requested an extension, it was suggested in the same decision that informal consultations be pursued with these countries, as a matter of priority, under the aegis of the Chairman of the CTG, who should be invited to keep the General Council informed of the progress of those consultations.[359]

The whole episode with respect to the blanket disinvocation by developing and least-developing country Members of key operational provisions in the *TRIMs Agreement*, in favour of a time-limited exception for the phasing out and elimination of trade restrictive investment measures, bears a striking similarity to the mass

Canada and Japan to various request made by developing country Members for extensions.

357 *See* requests for extensions by the Philippines, above n. 354; by Colombia, *Request by Colombia under the Provisions of Article 5.3 of the Agreement on Trade-Related Investment Measures*, 29 November 1999, G/C/W/169 (1 December 1999) with respect to the problem of absorbing agricultural products due to rural poverty, illegal crop substitution and internal armed conflict; and by Mexico, *Request by Mexico under Article 5.3 of the Agreement on Trade-Related Investment Measures*, 20 December, G/C/W/171 (23 December 1999) in respective of its automotive sector.

358 Minutes of the Meeting of the General Council of 3 and 8 May 2000, WT/G/C/M/55 and the decision on 'TRIMs Transition Period Issues', which is taken up as Annex II to the Minutes of the Meeting (the '*TRIMs Transition Decision*').

359 *TRIMs Transition Decision*, *ibid*, fourth and sixth bullet points. The issues arising from the *TRIMS Transition Decision* fall within the broader framework of 'Implementation-Related Issues' that were dealt with by the General Council, beginning in the month of June 2000 and were eventually mostly resolved at the Fourth Meeting of the Ministerial Conference, held at Doha, 9-14 December 2001, *Implementation-Related Issues and Concerns*, adopted at the WTO Ministerial Conference, Fourth Session, Doha, 9-14 November 2001, *Ministerial Decision*, WT/MIN(01)/17, 20 November 2001[hereinafter '*Implementation-Related Issues and Concerns Decision*'].

disinvocation by a number of GATT contracting parties in the late 1950s[360] of time-specified waivers in favour of the continued application of quantitative restrictions, as a result of severe balance-of-payments problems on the basis of Article XII GATT 1947. These 'residual restrictions', as they were known in GATT-parlance, were a prominent feature of the post-war trading system that many GATT contracting parties had imposed in order to deal with severe balance of payments problems after the end of the Second World War and the intention was that the invoking countries would gradually remove them from the early 1950's onwards as economic conditions improved, i.e. 'disinvoke' those restrictions.[361] When it became clear that a number of GATT contracting parties, despite claiming disinvocation, still maintained a substantial number of quantitative restrictions, a 'hard core' waiver[362] was adopted by the CONTRACTING PARTIES in 1995 that called for stringent conditions for the justification of social hardship and required the petitioning contracting party government to commit itself to a plan for the removal of these residual restrictions within five years.[363]

The issue of TRIMs implementation eventually became absorbed into the more general discussion on implementation issues, which was taken up in the Doha Development Round MTN. Similarly, the 1950's hard core waiver was later abandoned as a result of improved economic performance combined with more stringent reporting procedures for residual restrictions that had been established under the hard core waiver. However, there are striking parallels between the practice under the GATT and under the WTO, where the core of the problems lies in a conflict between monetary policy and trade policy (the GATT hard core waiver) or between macro-economic industrial policy and trade policy (the TRIMs mini waivers).

However, where the parallels end is that the time-limited GATT waiver for balance-of-payments purposes eventually resolved itself, partly through the formation of the EEC in 1957, which was to prove a much bigger challenge to the fragile multilateral trading system. By contrast, the time-limited TRIMs extension

360 *See* Robert E. Hudec, *The GATT Legal System and World Trade Diplomacy* (2nd edn Salem, New Hampshire: Butterworths Legal Publishers, 1990) 265-285.

361 *Ibid*, 265-266.

362 The largest *demandeur* then, as now, was the United States although a number of other developed GATT contracting parties were also in support of tougher measures against extended balance-of-payment waivers.

363 Decision of the CONTRACTING PARTIES of 5 March 1955, *BISD* 3S/38. Termed a 'hard-core waiver' the Decision effectively allowed a number of contracting parties to the GATT to continue to maintain import restrictions for balance-of payments purposes. See also Hudec, above n. 360, 266.

have been shifted forward into a negotiating round,[364] where compliance issues can be bargained for in exchange for other concessions in areas such as improved market access in the agricultural and non-agricultural sectors, services, stricter disciplines on contingent protection measures (anti-dumping, subsidies and emergency safeguard measures) and special and differential treatment.

3.4 Authoritative interpretation

Another secondary treaty rule that can lead to modification of a primary treaty rule is the possibility that exists for Members, acting through the Ministerial Conference or the General Council, with exclusive authority, to adopt an authentic interpretation to the *WTO Agreement* or one of the annexed Multilateral Trade Agreements, on the basis of paragraph 2 of Article IX *WTO Agreement*. The Ministerial Conference and the General Council exercise this authority on the basis of a recommendation by the Council overseeing the functioning of the relevant agreement.[365] The means for adopting an authoritative interpretation is stated in paragraph 2 of Article IX *WTO Agreement* as being taken by a three-fourths majority of the Members[366] although in practice it is understood that the decision will only be taken by a qualified majority vote where consensus cannot be reached.[367] Finally, the last sentence of Article IX:2 *WTO Agreement* specifically states that this provision 'shall not be used in a manner that would undermine the amendment provisions in Article X',[368] i.e. such decisions if deemed an

364 This is an example of the more generally recognised phenomenon of 'forum shifting', i.e. the attempt by economic actors to shift a decision making process from one forum to another in order to derive a benefit from the forum that 'embeds the principles most valued by them' in resolving specific regulatory issues, for which *see* John Braithwaite and Peter Drahos, *Global Business Regulation* (Cambridge: Cambridge University Press, 2000) 28-29. Within a major international economic organisation like the WTO, this strategy is demonstrated by a number of Members in seeking to pursue the same agenda in more than one institutional setting within the organisation at large.

365 Second sentence, Article IX:2 *WTO Agreement, The Legal Texts*, above n. 2, 11.

366 Third sentence, Article IX:2 *WTO Agreement, ibid.*

367 *Secretariat Note: Thematic Compilation on Implementation of Paragraph 6 Decision*, above n. 319, p. 2, para. 8. *See* also *Biennial Budgeting in the WTO, Possible Legal Approaches*, paper prepared by the Legal Affairs Division at the request of the Committee on Budget, Finance and Administration, WT/BFA/W/104 (16 July 2003), p. 2, at (b) Authoritative interpretation, para. 7, last sentence [hereinafter *Biennial Budgeting Paper*].

368 Fourth sentence, Article IX:2 *WTO Agreement, The Legal Texts*, above n. 2, 11.

amendment would be open to possible challenge.[369] However, as Brownlie has observed, the concept of interpretation is legally distinct from that of modification or amendment but in practice that 'distinction is often rather fine'.[370]

Thus far Members have not resorted to the adoption of an authoritative interpretation on the basis of Article IX:2 *WTO Agreement* although the European Communities did make such a request in January 1999 to the General Council in respect of Articles 3.7, 21.5, 22.2, 22.6, 22.7 and 23 *DSU*.[371] The United States opposed the request on the grounds *inter alia* that the requested authoritative interpretation amounted to an amendment of substantive provisions of the *DSU*, contrary to the last sentence in Article IX:2 *WTO Agreement* and 'would needlessly damage the institutional fabric of this organization'.[372] Suggestions have been put forward for its use as an alternative to the amendment procedure and at least one decision could be conceived as of being an authoritative interpretation although the means for its adoption falls short of the requirements set out in the governing provision.

The adoption of an authoritative interpretation, pursuant to Article IX:2 *WTO Agreement* has been suggested for addressing possible legal approaches to a change from annual to biennial budgeting at the WTO,[373] on the grounds that it was a practical approach and possibly more 'legally acceptable' than other routes to amendment.[374] The resort to an authoritative interpretation was also proposed by Japan for a possible amendment of the DSU, following the European Com-

369 *Secretariat Note: Thematic Compilation on Implementation of Paragraph 6 Decision*, above n. 319, 2, para. 9.

370 Brownlie, above n. 129, 601.

371 *Request for an Authoritative Interpretation Pursuant to Article IX.2 of the Marrakesh Agreement Establishing the World Trade Organization*, Communication from the European Communities, 21 January 1999, WT/GC/W/133 (25 January 1999) and requested that a special meeting of the General Council be called to deal with the matter, Communication from the European Communities to the General Council, 4 February 1999, WT/GC/W/143 (5 February 1999), reported in *Secretariat Note: Thematic Compilation on Implementation of Paragraph 6 Decision*, 3, para. 10 at fn. 5.

372 *General Council – Procedures for Amendment and Interpretation of the Dispute Settlement Understanding – Response to European Communities' Request for an Authoritative Interpretation of the Dispute Settlement Understanding Pursuant to Article IX:2 of the WTO Agreement*, Communication from the United States, 4 February 1999, WT/GC/W/144 (5 February 1999).

373 *Biennial Budgeting Paper*, above n. 367, p. 2, at (b) Authoritative interpretation, paras. 7-9.

374 *Ibid*, para. 7.

munities' demarche in 1999[375] and has been considered for amending Article 31 *TRIPs* in order to take account of the *Paragraph 6 Decision*.[376]

Arguably there are precedents in WTO decision-making that could be characterised as authoritative interpretations in the sense of Article IX:2 *WTO Agreement*. One example is the decision on *Implementation-Related Issues and Concerns*, which was adopted at the Fourth Meeting of the Ministerial Conference, held at Doha, 9-14 November 2001[377] Each of the decisions taken in that Ministerial Decision could be characterised as 'mini' authoritative interpretations in the sense of Article IX:2 *WTO Agreement*, in which case the question arises as to whether they fulfilled the procedural rules set out in that provision for their adoption, in particular whether the Ministerial Conference (or General Council) exercised its authority on the basis of a recommendation from the Council overseeing the agreements in question (in this case from the CTG in respect of the *TRIMs Agreement*) and whether they could possibly have undermined the amending authority set out in Article X *WTO Agreement*.

The other is the General Council decision with respect to the issue of biennial budgeting, which as we have just noted was not adopted pursuant to Article IX:2 *WTO Agreement*.[378] Nevertheless, it is a decision which interprets Article VII:1 *WTO Agreement*, in a very similar fashion to the decision on *Implementation-Related Issues and Concerns*. In both these situations, it is unclear as to the legal nature and enforceability of the respective decisions. A possible solution might be construe both of them as a tacit revision of the terms of the treaty – the *WTO Agreement* in the case of biennial budgeting decision and the *TRIMs Agreement* in the case of *Implementation-Related Issues and Concerns* decision – which has taken effect through the subsequent practice or conduct of the parties in relation to that the treaty.[379] As Aust remarks: '[G]iven that the parties can agree later to modify the treaty, they can also subsequently agree on an authoritative

375 *See* Proposal by Japan, Minutes of the Meeting of the Special Session of the Dispute Settlement Body, 13-15 November 2002, TN/DS/M/6 (31 March 2003), p. 2, para. 3.

376 *See Secretariat Note: Thematic Compilation on Implementation of Paragraph 6 Decision*, above n. 319, pp. 2-3, paras. 7-10. See also the statement by Brazil in the Meeting of the Council for Trade-Related Aspects of Intellectual Property Rights, 17-19 September 2002, IP/C/M/37 (11 October 2002), 16, para. 60. *See* further, above section 3.1(b).

377 *Implementation-Related Issues and Concerns Decision*, above n. 359, paras. 1.2, 3.1, 3.4, 4.5, 5.2 and 12.2.

378 *Biennial Budgeting Paper*, above n. 367, p. 2, at (b) Authoritative interpretation, para. 9.

379 *See* Sir Gerald Fitzmaurice, 'The Law and Procedure of the International Court of Justice, 1951-1954: Treaty Interpretation and Other Treaty Points' (1957) 33 *BYIL* 211-252.

interpretation of its terms, and this can amount, in effect, to an amendment.'[380] Even so, there remains a very fine line between (authoritative) interpretation and amendment.

4 Conclusions

The *WTO Agreement* and the annexed Multilateral Trade Agreements provide a code of conduct for world trade in a larger normative framework than existed under the former GATT. The body of principles, rules and standards, which are taken up in the primary treaty instruments the *WTO Agreement*, the annexed Multilateral Trade Agreements and the Schedules of Tariffs and Schedules of Specific Commitments, represent the legal results of the negotiated rights and obligations of the GATT contracting parties, which have been extended to all original and acceding Members, upon the entry into force of the *WTO Agreement* in 1995.

Where the rights and obligations of WTO Members differ significantly from those of the contracting parties under the former GATT is that they are applied on a definitive basis rather than provisionally and they bind *all* Members, on the basis of the single undertaking in contrast to the fragmented system of the GATT 1947 and the Tokyo Round Agreements. Member governments are also under a positive obligation to ensure that their domestic laws, regulations and procedures are in conformity with their WTO obligations.

The type of primary treaty rules, which are taken up in the *WTO Agreement* and the annexed Multilateral Trade Agreements, reflect a broadening of the normative base of multilateral trading system compared to the GATT. This is linked to the underlying shift in regulatory philosophy from a process of negative integration under the GATT trade regime, whereby the contracting parties agreed to the progressive reduction of tariffs and the implementation of trade disciplines in order to protect those tariff concessions, to one of positive prescription in the WTO, which calls upon Members to legislate and enforce international principles, rules and standards in their domestic legal orders.

Whereas the GATT contracting parties were mostly concerned with tariff reductions and the pursuit of the complimentary goal of non-discriminatory international trade, which was reflected in the inclusion in the General Agreement of mostly prescriptive and prohibitive norms (with some exceptive norms), the WTO Multilateral Trade Agreements contain a large number of permissive and

380 Aust, above n. 48, 191; *see* also section 3.1(b) above.

exceptive norms, which reflect the obligations of Members to bring their laws, regulations and administrative procedures pertaining to domestic regulation into conformity with their international obligations but with the additional goal of harmonising standards in the certain fields such as health and food safety regulation, technical standards, the protection of intellectual property rights and domestic services' regulation.

These normative developments are linked to an increase in the number of primary treaty rules that have come about as the result of negotiations undertaken in the Uruguay Round MTN. Principal rule-making by means of the formal treaty-making process is still perceived as the primary means of giving effect to those results but the process itself has become strained due to the Members belief that they must adhere to the concept of the single undertaking in concluding the current Doha Development Round MTN before bringing those results into force.

While the single undertaking may preserve the integrity of the treaty instrument, in practice it leads to a concurrent practice of the Members bypassing formal, rigid amendment procedures. This practice manifests itself in the way in which the Members continue to apply the secondary treaty rules that revise or modify primary treaty rules, relying where necessary on GATT practice to inform their decisions concerning the application of those rules. An analysis of this practice leads to the following conclusions.

First, the amendment law of the WTO is honoured more in the breach of that law than in its observance. While Article X *WTO Agreement* contains a comprehensive set of treaty amending provisions, which conforms in terms of form and substance to the criteria that are generally accepted for the amendment of multilateral treaties, it is not used in practice. Instead, a practice has grown up, as occurred under the former GATT, of adopting other informal practices and procedures in order to achieve the effects of a formal treaty amendment.

Thus, the regulation of the proposed amendment to Article 31 *TRIPs* in order to take account of the urgent need for certain developing country Members to have access to essential medicines, in their fight against the HIV/Aids pandemic, is currently regulated by means of the waiver power under Article IX *WTO Agreement* until such time as a formal treaty amendment is adopted. In the case of the change to biennial budgeting in the WTO, this 'minor' amendment has for the time being been achieved by a decision of the General Council, which does not foreclose the possibility of a future treaty amendment on the matter. However, the manner in which this decision and some others have been adopted, for example the *Implementation-Related Issues and Concerns* decision, is questionable given that these are *de facto* authoritative interpretations, adopted by consensus in the main plenary body but without fulfilling the heavier procedural requirement of

Article IX:2 *WTO Agreement*, which requires a three-fourths majority vote of the Members.

Second, and linked to the first conclusion, the power of authoritative interpretation has never been used by the Members, despite having been invoked by the European Communities and Japan as a means of amending the *DSU*, a purpose for which it is not intended, and more belatedly as a suggestion for the organisation to move to biennial budgeting.

Third, the Members continue the GATT practice of 'modifying' primary treaty rules by supplementing them following negotiations in order to improve levels of liberalisation with respect to services commitments. These negotiations, which have their legal basis in a 'built-in agenda' item, are open to the entire membership but only some Members participate and only they are bound as to the results achieved, which are attached to a Protocol to the *GATS* and supplement the existing Schedules. This practice can be considered as the practice of concluding subsequent or supplement agreements by parties to a treaty and has its basis in the residual rules on amendment in treaty law and practice and not in the amending provisions of Article X *WTO Agreement.*

Fourth, a further practice that is not formally regulated in Article X *WTO Agreement* is the modification, rectification and certification of Schedules of Tariff Concessions or Services Schedules following re-negotiation by individual Members of tariff concessions, on the basis of Article XXVIII *GATT 1994*, or services commitments, on the basis of Article XXI *GATS*, the practice of which forms a continuum with former practice under the GATT except that there have been some minor adjustments in respect of the practice concerning the renegotiation of services' commitments that have come about as a result of the inclusion of the *GATS* at the end of the Uruguay Round.

Fifth, the WTO accession process can be read as a form of treaty amendment since it not only adds an additional Member to the organisation but also brings a new party into the multilateral treaty relationship. Article XIII *WTO Agreement* is based on Article XXIII GATT 1947 and so is the practice surrounding its application. As long as the provision on accession in the *WTO Agreement* contains no formal criteria for a State seeking accession to the WTO and/or the Members decide to draw up a definitive set of rules with respect to the terms on which a State must accede, the practice continues of the admittance of new Members being subject to a process of extended negotiations between the acceding country and individual Members. These negotiations are conducted within the framework of an elaborate set of non-binding instruments, which are largely procedural in character. Some Members continue to exercise the exception to multilateralism in the case of certain acceding States, invocation of which allows for the potential disapplication of WTO rights and obligations between an acceding country and the Member invoking the exception.

Sixth, the practice of granting a general waiver to an individual Member or group of Members, on the basis of Article IX *WTO Agreement*, is another means of temporarily setting aside, or dispensing, with the obligations with which Members must otherwise comply and is extensively used. The practice of the general waiver power stems from the former GATT trade regime but has been institutionalised in the WTO and formalised to the extent that it can now only be granted subject to certain exceptional conditions and for a limited period of time.

From the foregoing conclusions, it is possible to characterise the WTO as a far more dynamic organisation than its formal treaty structure might suggest. This is due to the fact that the Members are capable of resorting to a number of informal practices and procedures in the field of principal rule-making that belie the rigid character of its constituent treaty, particularly in the matter of amendment, and to adopt legally binding decisions with normative effect that lead to the creation of supplemental obligations or to the revision of primary treaty rules.

include the adoption of new treaties to which their Members may become parties.[8] It is also possible that a treaty management organisation may be actively involved in the development of certain standards and good practices through the adoption of soft-law instruments such as codes of conduct and guide-lines.[9] Seen in this light, the WTO cannot be said to function as a treaty-management organisation but, as we have already noted, is primarily a policy-making organisation and not one that exercises any real law-making function.

Instead the WTO exercises a 'legislative' power on the basis of paragraph 2 of Article III *WTO Agreement*, which emanates from and responds to the needs of the Members in implementing the results of negotiations among them.[10] The question that this chapter seeks to address is whether on the basis of that provision there exists an implied power for a WTO body, within the framework of the organisation, to engage in subsidiary rule-making and, if so, whether such subsidiary rule-making does take place, what forms it takes and how this activity contributes to normative developments in the WTO?

Second, any discussion of subsidiary rule-making invariably raises the question as to whether the members of an international organisation are bound by such a rule and, if so, under what circumstances? As a general matter, when discussing the provenance and existence of norms in international law, Prosper Weil has explained that 'the acts accomplished by subjects of international law are so diverse in character that it is no simple matter for a jurist to determine what may be called the normativity threshold, i.e. the line of transition between the non-legal and the legal, between what does not constitute a norm and what does'.[11] Put differently, it may not always be possible to establish a 'bright-line' between the legal and

8 Some international organisations such as the FAO and the UNESCO specifically mandate additional treaty-making, for example two specialised UN organisations, the Food and Agricultural Organization or FAO, (adopted 16 October 1945, *in force* 16 October 1945) as amended, in accordance with Article XIV FAO, and the United Nations Educational Scientific and Cultural Organization or UNESCO (adopted 16 November 1945, *in force* 4 November 1946) as amended, in accordance with Article 1.2(c) UNESCO.

9 Francis Maupain, 'International Labor Organization Recommendations and Similar Instruments' in Dinah Shelton (ed.) *Commitment and Compliance, the Role of Non-Binding Norms in the International Legal System* (Oxford: Oxford University Press, 2000) 372-393.

10 See chapter I, section 3.1.

11 Prosper Weil, 'Towards Relative Normativity in International Law' (1983) 77 *AJIL* 413-442 at 415.

the non-legal, the binding and the non-binding.[12] Subsidiary rule-making suffers from this normative imperfection.

While there is still a limited amount of subsidiary rules that are adopted by policy making organisations, or their subsidiary organs, and rules promulgated by treaty-making organisations in the form of technical regulations and recommendations, there are a greater number of non-binding or 'soft' law instruments,[13] which are adopted by international organisations in the form of guidelines, codes of conduct, understandings and other (interpretative) acts.[14] These soft law instruments are not necessarily binding on the Members at the time of their adoption but may crystallise or harden over time so that states, as Members of the organisation, acknowledge that they feel bound by the relevant guideline, code of conduct, understanding or similar interpretative act, as evidence of a practice that is general, uniform and consistently applied by other states Members of the organisation.[15] If the range and type of legal instruments that international organisations can espouse are placed on a continuum then we discover at one end norm-creating instruments, which have legally binding content and exert an obligatory pull, and a range of non-binding / non-law instruments or soft law instruments at the other end that do not,[16] or at least not to the same degree.[17] There are some further points to note in respect of soft law.

Whereas the development of soft law instruments and soft law processes is usually thought of as applying in such specialist fields as environmental law or human rights law it also prevails in the field of international economic regulation[18] and since the WTO follows this trend to some extent, where relevant it will be brought into the analysis. Soft law is sufficiently pliable, even when

12 *See* Christine Chinkin, 'Normative Developments in the International Legal System' in Shelton (ed.) *Commitment and Compliance,* above n. 9, 21-42.

13 Sommer, above n. 3, at 636.

14 Interpretative acts in the sense of paragraph 3 of Article 31 of the Vienna Convention on the Law of Treaties (adopted 23 May 1969, *in force* 27 January 1980) (1969) 8 *ILM* 689 [hereinafter the VCLT].

15 For a discussion of institutional acts, with or without normative effect, their bindingness and their lawfulness, see Sands and Klein, above n. 4, 279-297.

16 Christopher Joyner, 'The Legal Status and Effect of Antarctic Recommended Measures' in Shelton, above n. 9, 163-196 at 179.

17 Henry G. Schermers and Niels M. Blokker, *International Institutional Law: Unity within diversity* (4th edn Boston, Leiden: Martinus Nijhoff Publishers, 2003) §1320, 823, are of the view that the gap between binding and non-binding decisions may be narrowed, since some non-binding decisions have considerable practical effect.

18 *See* in particular the contributions by Beth Simmons and David Wirth in Shelton, above n. 9, at 244-263 and 330-344 respectively.

employed in a more formalised, institutional setting such as the WTO, to be susceptible to various permutations and is often used as a 'gap-filler' in complementing and adding to hard law in existing treaty provisions.

An example of soft law being used to fill a gap in the GATT/WTO context is the development of the 1979 'Enabling Clause',[19] which 'permits Members to provide "differential and more favourable treatment" to developing countries "in spite of" the MFN obligation of Article I:1'. The Enabling Clause is a decision of the GATT CONTRACTING PARTIES with normative effect that to all intents and purposes 'amends' the GATT.[20] In so doing, it incorporates by 'reference'[21] an earlier 1971 waiver decision of the GATT CONTRACTING PARTIES,[22] which provided the (temporary) legal basis for various industrialised countries to suspend the application of most-favoured nation (MFN) treatment in Article I:1 *GATT1994*[23] (previously GATT 1947) to developing and least-developed countries in favour of generalised, non-reciprocal and non-discriminatory (trade) preferences (known as the Generalized System of Preferences or GSP).[24]

The Enabling Clause references the 1971 GATT waiver, which gives expression to the notion that 'developed countries do not expect reciprocity for commitments made by them in trade negotiations …' by providing for the establishment of 'generalized, non-reciprocal and non-discriminatory preferences beneficial to developing countries', which is the legal basis for developed countries to grant preferential treatment to developing countries. The Enabling Clause

19 Differential and More Favourable Treatment, Reciprocity and Fuller Participation of Developing Countries, Decision of the CONTRACTING PARTIES, 28 November 1979, L/4903, (1979) *BISD* 26S/203-205 (1979) [hereinafter the *Enabling Clause*].

20 Schermers and Blokker have characterized the GATT/WTO waiver practice as effectively changing the field of responsibility of the organisation because all Members are affected; *see* section 3.6, introductory paragraphs.

21 *See* this chapter, section 3 hereunder, for an explanation of rule referencing when applied to the formation of new rules by means of this process.

22 Decision of the CONTRACTING PARTIES of 25 June 1971, relating to the establishment of 'generalized, non-reciprocal and non discriminatory preferences beneficial to the developing countries', GATT Doc. L/3545 (1971) *BISD* 18S/24, [*1971 Waiver Decision on the Generalized System of Preferences*].

23 Article I:1 GATT 1947 (now *GATT 1994*) in *The Results of the Uruguay Round of Multilateral Trade Negotiations: The Legal Texts* (Geneva: World Trade Organization, 1999) [hereinafter *The Legal Texts*] 486.

24 The exceptive norm in the general waiver fulfils the aspirational norm, set out in Article XXXVI:8 *GATT 1994* (previously GATT 1947), *The Legal Texts*, *ibid*, 534, which states that 'developed contracting parties do not expect reciprocity for commitments made by them in trade negotiations to reduce or removed tariffs and other barriers to trade of less-developed contracting parties'.

decision has been incorporated into the *GATT 1994*,[25] as part of the results of the Uruguay Round, whereupon it has been the subject of interpretation in a complaint brought by India against the EC's GSP in *EC – Tariff Preferences*[26] where the Appellate Body ruled that preference-giving countries could differentiate among GSP beneficiaries under certain conditions without this being considered discriminatory.[27]

Similarly, other soft law rules or standards may be upgraded to 'hard law' through their incorporation by reference into international treaty instruments whereupon they become binding on the parties to those instruments.[28] And finally, in an increasing number of instances non-binding norms or soft law may end up substituting for binding obligations on a whole range of issues due to the uncertainties and delay that exist in amending primary treaty rules in treaty-based international organisations like the WTO. This could eventually be the fate of the *Paragraph 6 Decision* of August 2003 on 'TRIPs and Access to Essential Medicines'.[29]

Third, traditionally it has been held that there is limited scope for subsidiary rule-making in most international organisations. As Krzysztof Skubiszewski has pointed out, while the number of decisions adopted by international organisations may be legion 'only a small fraction of them bear the characteristics of law-making'.[30] His view on decisions that have normative effect is derived from the definition of a law-making (or regulative) resolution as 'one which is binding on its addressees by virtue of the decision of the organization and which lays down general and abstractly formulated rules of conduct'. Likewise, he submits that

25 The Enabling Clause has been incorporated into the *GATT 1994* on the basis of paragraph 1(b)(iv) of the preliminary notes to Annex IA, being the General Agreement on Tariffs and Trade 1994 or *GATT 1994*, *The Legal Texts*, above n. 23, 21.

26 *EC – Tariff Preferences*, Appellate Body Report, *European Communities – Conditions for the Granting of Tariff Preferences to Developing Countries*, WT/DS246/AB/R, adopted 20 April 2004.

27 *EC – Tariff Preferences*, *ibid*, para. 108 (with respect to incorporation of the Enabling Clause in *GATT 1994*) and paras. 153-154 (with respect to the non-discriminatory application of a GSP regime).

28 Sommer, above n. 3, at 636 for the transition from soft law to hard law acts in the field of international environmental law and Sands and Klein, above n. 4, at 286-288, for recommendatory acts and practices that become binding upon on Members in the field of food safety standards at the *Codex Alimentarius Commission*.

29 See chapter IV, section 3.1(b).

30 Krzysztof Skubiszewski, 'Enactment of law by international organizations' (1965-1966) 41 *BYIL* 198-274, at 201. (His contribution is partly reproduced in Krzysztof Skubiszewski, 'Law-making by International Organizations' (1992) 19 (XIX) *Thesaurus Acroasium Thessaloniki* 357-384.)

'[T]he drafting, adoption, entry into force, validity, application, effects, modification, and termination of law-making resolutions of international organizations' are all 'regulated by the law, in particular the constituent instrument, of the organization which adopted the resolution in question', i.e. the organisation's internal law.[31] Accordingly, the bindingness of the law-making or regulative decision will depend upon the organisation's constitution although it may be supplemented by the practice of the organisation.[32]

Skubiszewski's characterisation of law-making resolutions, or decisions with normative effect, comes close to the definition on 'rules of the organisation' in the Vienna Convention on Law of Treaties between States and International Organizations or between International Organization, which is broad enough to encompass not only the organisation's 'constituent instruments' but also the 'decisions and resolutions adopted in accordance with [the organisation's constituent instrument], and established practice of the organization'.[33] The International Law Commission or ILC is currently considering the application of the term 'rules of the organisation' in the context of drafting a set of articles on the responsibility of international organisations but the task is proving to be a challenging one, particularly given the vast spectrum of international institutions, some of which have very few defining features in common.[34]

A final remark with respect to the term 'established practice'. In the case of international organisations the term is similar but *not* identical to the one which

31 *Ibid,* at 201. He also stresses that the law-making resolution is not a contractual instrument but the act of an international organisation, which is different from a treaty concluded either between the organisation and the Members or between the Members *inter se.*

32 Once again, Skubiszewski qualifies this statement by saying that only practice accepted as law by *all* the members of the organisation can provide the basis for the enactment of mandatory resolutions, i.e. resolutions that bind the Members, *ibid.*

33 Article 2:1(*j*) Vienna Convention on Law of Treaties between States and International Organizations or between International Organizations (adopted 21 March 1986, *not yet in force*) (1986) 25 *ILM* (1986), 543, at 547 [hereinafter VCLTIO]. *See* also chapter IV, section 1.

34 See for the work of the International Law Commission or ILC on this point, Report of the International Law Commission 56th Session (5 May – 6 June and 7 July – 8 August 2003), UN Doc. A/58/10) at 22 and Report of the International Law Commission 57th Session (4 May – 4 June and 5 July – 6 August 2004), UN Doc A/CN.4/553. For some of the problems to which this legislative drafting exercises gives rise for the European Union and the European Community in the context of international responsibility; *see* P.J. Kuijper and E. Paasivirta, 'Further Exploring International Responsibility: The European Community and the ILC's Project on Responsibility of International Organizations' (2004) 1 *IOLR* 111-138 at 113, 115-116 and 132-133.

is applied by States in the formation of customary international law rules.[35] While the established practice of international organisations shares with state practice the requirements that it should consist of a general practice, or *usus*, that is both extensive and virtually uniform,[36] in the case of international organisations the 'conviction that such practice reflects, or amounts to, law (*opinio iuris*) or is required by social, economic, or political exigencies (*opinio necessitatis*)'[37] may simply be 'an instance of procedure'.[38] As Zemanek explains '[I]f an organ departs from established practice, it does so with instant effect, and the only requirement for this deviating act to become new established practice is that it is consistently repeated'.[39] This comes close to the idea of *coutume sauvage* first expounded by René-Jean Dupuy[40] and pursued by Georges Abi-Saab[41] in the case of States where custom is not created by practice, or *usus*, coupled with *opinio iuris*, which they identify as *coutume sage*, but is generated by the obligatory force of the rule that States feel bound to accept as binding upon them following its declaration, coupled with the general and consistent application of that rule by States thereafter. It is submitted that the development of an established practice by the Members of an international organisation following a declaratory statement, evidencing their belief that they are bound by the act, is confirmation of this process of *coutume sauvage* at work in an international organisation.

In support of his argument, Zemanek gives the hypothetical example of a situation where the Security Council, in applying Article 27(3) UN, suddenly begins counting the abstention of a permanent member as a negative vote. He claims that if this practice were to be applied over and over again then 'the current established practice would be superseded by one more consistent with the wording of the provision'.[42] This instance of procedure or act of an institutional body, which may establish consistent practice over a period of some time, has already

35 Zemanek, above n. 1, 209-210.

36 *North Sea Continental Shelf Cases* [1969] *(Federal Republic of Germany v. Denmark and Federal Republic of Germany v. The Netherlands)* [1969] ICJ Rep. 3 [*North Sea Continental Shelf Cases*], para. 74.

37 Antonio Cassese, *International Law* (2nd edn Oxford : Oxford University Press, 2004) 119.

38 Zemanek, above n. 1, 210.

39 *Ibid.*

40 René-Jean Dupuy, 'Coutume sage et coutume sauvage' in *Mélanges offerts à Charles Rousseau: La communauté internationale* (Paris: Éditions A. Pedone, 1974) 75-86.

41 Georges Abi-Saab, 'Cours général de droit international public' (1987) 207 *Receuil des Cours* 9 at 173-178.

42 *Ibid.*

occurred in the WTO with respect to the further extension of the practice of consensus decision-making.

It will be recalled[43] that early on in the life of the organisation a statement by the Chairman of the WTO General Council records the Member's agreement that: 'On occasions when the General Council deals with matters related to requests for waivers or accessions to the WTO under Articles IX and XII of the *WTO Agreement* respectively, the General Council will seek a decision in accordance with Article IX: 1',[44] i.e. on the basis of consensus rather than by means of a vote (the WT/L/93 practice).[45] Thus, consensus has become the usual procedure for the adoption of a general waiver decision or a decision on accession.

It is submitted that the use of consensus *in lieu* of voting may simply be more practical because the use of qualified majority requires that a decision be taken according to the *number* of WTO Members present and voting while a decision by consensus is based on those present at the meeting. However, WT/L/93 could be cited as evidence of a belief by the Members that they are bound[46] by the practice of consensus decision-making with respect to these two types of decision, even in the face of qualified-majority voting as required by the *WTO Agreement*. The consistent and repeated application of consensus *in lieu* of voting over the past ten years, including the citation of the WT/L/93 statement itself, as the procedural basis for the adoption of a whole range of similar decisions on waivers and accessions, since the statement was issued, renders it part of the established practice of the organisation.

2 WTO bodies and subsidiary rule-making

Subsidiary rule-making that relies on decisions of international organisations with normative effect can be characterised in different ways, depending on a number of factors. These include such matters as whether the decision relies for its authority on an express or an implied power, whether the decision leads to the develop-

43 *See* further, chapter IV, section 2.2 (c).

44 The reference is to the statement of the Chairman of the General Council, upon this body's adoption of *Decision-making procedures under Article IX and XII of the WTO Agreement*, at its meeting of 15 November 1995, item 3, WT/GC/M/8 (13 December 1995), section V, pp. 7-8; the relevant decision was issued in the 'L' or Legal Series, as a Statement by the Chairman, WT/L/93 (24 November 1995).

45 See chapter III, section 2.2(c) for further details of this procedure.

46 The issue as to whether the Members consider themselves legally bound, or only politically committed, is often made clear in statements by individual Members upon the adoption of a particular decision.

ment of a new principle, rule or standard or has a more functional character, i.e. relates to the essential functioning of the organisation, whether the rule that emanates from the decision is addressed to States as members of the organisation,[47] or to individuals[48] and finally whether it is binding or non-binding on (some or all) Members. Taking these factors into consideration it is possible to arrive at a framework for analysing the subsidiary rule-making capacity of the WTO derived from an examination of the decisions adopted by the Members in various WTO bodies. Additionally, subsidiary rule-making may arise where a WTO treaty provision makes express reference to binding, or non-binding, rules or standards,[49] which have their provenance in another treaty outside the WTO legal order, or to principles, rules or standards, which have been developed by another formal or informal institution exogenous to the WTO and subsequently incorporated by reference into a primary treaty rule, i.e. 'rule referencing'.[50]

In some instances the basis for subsidiary rule-making is expressly laid down in the *WTO Agreement* or one of the Multilateral Trade Agreements. Where those instruments are silent as to the organisation's authority to enact subsidiary rules, the power to do so may be an implied power.[51] A WTO body may have delegated authority in subsidiary rule-making on the basis of a treaty provision.

In other instances, there are other types of subsidiary rule-making in the WTO, which are based on decisions that are internal in terms of their source, their

47 Schermers and Blokker, above n. 17, §1323, 824-827, also §1327 and §1328, 828-829, on the effects of Decisions addressed to governments.

48 As Schermers and Blokker, *ibid*, §1331, 830, 'the power to address Decisions to individuals is irrelevant' because most international organisations 'are concerned only with governments and have no competence to issue Decisions to individuals over whom they exert no governing power'.

49 'Standards' refer to the behaviour that one actor is expected to accord another. In inter-state relations standards are usually articulated in terms of the grant of a right, or the imposition of an obligation as to the level or type of treatment that one State can expect to receive from or to have to give to another State. With the development of standards as indicators of the behaviour by a range of non-State actors such as corporations or coalitions of trade unions or human rights NGO's concerning codes of practice or behaviour the notion of standards and standard-setting bodies has been expanded.

50 See below in this chapter, section 3.

51 Skubiszewski, above n. 30, 230 with reliance on the doctrine of implied powers of international organisations, as determined by various ICJ decisions with respect to the UN – *Reparation for Injuries Suffered in the Service of the United Nations* (*Advisory Opinion*) [1949] ICJ Rep174, at 179 [hereinafter *Reparation for Injuries*]; *Effects of Awards of Compensation Made by the United Nations Administrative Tribunal*, (Advisory Opinion) [1954] ICJ Rep 47 at 56-57 [hereinafter *Effects of Awards*]; and *Certain Expenses of the United Nations (Article 17, paragraph 2 of the Charter)* (*Advisory Opinion*) [1962] ICJ Rep 151 at 168 and 182 [hereinafter *Certain Expenses*]

substance and their normative effect but are essential for the functioning of the organisation, such as those rules which deal with the establishment of subsidiary WTO bodies and rules of procedure for meetings of WTO bodies (including inter-institutional arrangements between different bodies), the approval of the WTO budget and WTO staff regulations. However, some decisions adopted by WTO bodies may have normative effect on the external plane, as for example with certain operational decisions, which engage the organisation in activities of a broader, cooperative nature.[52]

Finally, decisions of adjudicative bodies such as the panels and the Appellate Body in the WTO dispute settlement system, while in first instance only containing recommendations and rulings addressed to the Members as parties in a dispute, may indicate a move towards judicial rule-making. Both the *ad hoc* panels and the Appellate Body have contributed significantly to the development of a body of procedural rules, including rules on evidence and proof, to govern complaints brought by Members in the dispute settlement system. In the context of deciding certain disputes, the panels and Appellate Body have also played a role in generating norms through the interpretation and application of principles, rules and standards in the *WTO Agreement* and the annexed Multilateral Trade Agreements, but mostly with respect to standard of review.

It is submitted that in most instances of subsidiary rule-making in the WTO, the addressees of the rules are the Members. There are however, a number of subsidiary rules, such as staff rules and regulations, that apply to personnel employed by the organisation and subsidiary rules on diplomatic privileges and immunities that operate in respect of certain categories of Secretariat staff and the Director-General.[53]

In the remainder of this chapter, the following clusters of subsidiary rule-making are analysed, beginning with forms of delegated rule-making based on express and implied powers in section 2.1, including a discussion, where appropriate, of the role that soft law may play in that particular process of subsidiary rule-making. This is followed in section 2.2 with a review of the other types of subsidiary rule-making that form part of the WTO's internal legal order. These concern the internal rules of WTO relating to the establishment of subsidiary bodies, rules of procedures and rules relating to its operational capacity, including financial and staffing matters. Section 2.3 highlights the contribution of adjudicative rule-making to the body of subsidiary rule-making in the WTO, primarily through procedural rules, and substantive rules that mostly relate to

52 See generally Schermers and Blokker, above n. 17, §§938-940, §§605-606 and §1208, 759-760.

53 Zemanek, above n. 1, 210-213.

standard of review. In section 3, we turn to a brief analysis of the phenomenon of rule referencing, whereby law may be created by reference, i.e. by turning non-binding or soft law rules and standards, which have their provenance in another treaty instrument or institutional norm, into rules that are binding on Members. In section 4 some conclusions are reached as to the effect of subsidiary rule-making on normative developments in the WTO.

2.1 Delegated rule-making

As noted previously[54] the results of the Uruguay Round led to an increase in the number of permissive and exceptive norms, particularly in those Multilateral Trade Agreements that elaborate new disciplines and defer to national rules and standards provided they do not lead to the imposition of domestic regulatory barriers. During the negotiations there were a series of domestic regulatory issues involving services and service suppliers, the use of sanitary and phytosanitary measures, technical standards and, to a lesser degree, intellectual property standards, that were considered by many GATT contracting parties to be so sensitive[55] that negotiating disciplines which could lead to harmonisation, mutual recognition and equivalence of different rules and standards of Members had to be put off to a future date. Some of the Multilateral Trade Agreements contain treaty provisions that delegate the authority to a Council or committee under a particular agreement to develop subsidiary rules for adoption by the Members.

In this section, two sets of different Multilateral Trade Agreements are examined to discover the extent to which subsidiary rule-making has been developed by the institutional bodies under those Agreements. The first example is the case of the *General Agreement on Trade in Services* or *GATS*,[56] with respect to domestic qualification requirements and procedures, technical standards and licensing requirements, and the exercise by a subsidiary body of the Council for Trade in Services or CTS of delegated rule-making on the basis of an express power. The second example is the *Agreement on Sanitary and Phytosanitary Measures* or *SPS Agreement*,[57] with respect to consumer health and safety require-

54 *See* further chapter IV, introductory remarks in section 1.

55 *See* for the matter of domestic regulation in the services sector, Geza Feketekuty, 'Trade in Services – Bringing Services into the Multilateral Trading System' in Jagdish Bhagwati and Hirsch, Mathias (eds.) *The Uruguay Round and Beyond: Essays in Honour of Arthur Dunkel* (Berlin: Springer Verlag, 1998) 79- 99 at 87.

56 *General Agreement on Trade in Services*, *The Legal* Texts, above n. 23, 325-364.

57 *Agreement on Sanitary and Phytosanitary Measures* or *SPS Agreement*, *The Legal Texts*, *ibid*, 69-84.

ments in the fields of sanitary and phytosanitary standards, where the SPS Committee has exercised delegated rule-making authority on the basis of an implied power.

We turn first to the issue of domestic regulation in the field of trade in services and paragraph 4 of Article VI *GATS*,[58] which contains an explicit mandate for the CTS to establish rules when it states:

> *Domestic Regulation*
>
> With a view to ensuring that measures relating to qualification requirements and procedures, technical standards and licensing requirements do not constitute unnecessary barriers to trade in services, the Council for Trade in Services shall, through appropriate bodies it may establish, develop any necessary disciplines. Such disciplines shall aim to ensure that such requirements are, inter alia:
>
> a) based on objective and transparent criteria, such as competence and the ability to supply the service;
> b) not more burdensome than necessary to ensure the quality of the service;
> c) in the case of licensing procedures, not in themselves a restriction on the supply of the service.[59]

Since government regulation is considered to be particularly pervasive[60] in the area of professional services,[61] where professional standards, including qualifications, licensing and certification procedures, are frequent barriers to entry for service suppliers in foreign service markets, the first step Members took in order

58 Article VI:4 *GATS*, *The Legal Texts*, *ibid*, 333.

59 The actual definitions of categories of measures covered in Article VI:4 *GATS* are contained in *The Relevance of the Disciplines of the Agreements on Technical Barriers to Trade (TBT) and on Import Licensing Procedures to Article VI.4 of the General Agreement on Trade in Services: Note by the Secretariat*, S/WPPS/W/9 (11 September 1996), para. 4. They are qualification requirements, qualification procedures, licensing requirements, licensing procedures and technical standards.

60 *See* Dale B. Honeck, 'Developing Regulatory Disciplines in Professional Services: the Role of the World Trade Organization' in Yair Aharoni and Lilach Nachum, *Globalization of Services Some implications for theory and practice* (London: Routledge, 2000) 52-72.

61 'Professional services', from the perspective of services' regulation, is one of the listed sub-categories under 'Business Services' in the Services Sectoral Classification List, MTN.GNS/W/120 (10 July 1991), which the GATT Contracting Parties used to negotiate specific commitments. It is broken down into ten further sub-sectors, as follows: a. Legal services; b. Accounting, auditing and bookkeeping services; c. Taxation services; d. Architectural services; e. Engineering services; f. Integrated engineering services; g. Urban planning and landscape architectural services; h. Medical and dental services; i. Veterinary services; j. Services provided by midwives, nurses, physiotherapists and para-medical personnel; and k. Other.

to implement Article VI:4 *GATS* was to adopt a Ministerial Decision at Marrakesh[62] recommending the adoption by the CTS of a *Decision on Professional Services*[63] and the establishment of a *Working Party on Professional Services* or *WPPS*[64] in order to examine and report on the work programme set out in Article VI:4 *GATS*.

The *Decision on Professional Services* proposed that the Working Party should, as a matter of priority, make recommendations for the elaboration of multilateral disciplines in the accountancy sector in order to ensure that: (a) domestic regulation is based on objective and transparent criteria and not more burdensome than necessary to ensure the quality of the service; (b) international standards are used in developing the disciplines; and (c) those disciplines facilitate the effective application of the GATS provisions for mutual recognition of (professional) qualifications. It also exhorted the Working Party 'to take account of the importance of the governmental and non-governmental bodies regulating professional services' in developing the disciplines.[65] This latter recommendation is an example of the contribution that epistemic communities,[66] i.e. groups of experts, scattered throughout multiple States in the international community but sharing a common core of values and beliefs, a specialised language, or practice, and a common policy enterprise, can make to rule-making within a formal, institutionalised setting. It was a common feature of the Uruguay Round MTN with respect to the negotiation of services disciplines[67] and therefore it is not unusual to see the practice continued in the field of subsidiary rule-making in the WTO.

Within a relatively short space of time the *WPPS* had succeeded in creating a set of voluntary *Guidelines for Mutual Recognition Agreements or Arrangements*

62 *Ministerial Decision on Professional Services*, *The Legal Texts*, above n. 23, 462-463.

63 *Decision on Professional Services*, 1 March 1995, S/L/3 (4 April 1995).

64 For an overview of WPPS activities, *see* the reports by the Working Party to the CTS, series S/WPPS/1-4, while detailed descriptions can be found in the Minutes of the Meetings of the Working Party, series S/WPPS/M/1-25.

65 *Decision on Professional Services*, above n. 63, para. 2, final sentence.

66 A useful definition of 'epistemic communities' is provided by Peter M. Haas, 'Introduction: epistemic communities and international policy coordination' (1992) 46 *International Organization* 1-35, at 3, as 'network[s] of professionals with recognised expertise and competence in a particular domain and an authoritative claim to policy-relevant knowledge within that domain or issue-area', and more particularly fns. 4 and 5, for use of the term and the characteristics that epistemic communities display.

67 William J. Drake and Kalypso Nicolaïdis 'Ideas, interests, and institutionalization: "trade in services" and the Uruguay Round' (1992) 46 *International Organization*, 37-100.

in the Accountancy Sector or *MRA Guidelines*,[68] which were adopted by the CTS in May 1997. The important point about the *MRA Guidelines* is that they consist of a series of recommendations to the Members on the form and coverage of mutual recognition agreements,[69] which could be applied not only to the accountancy sector but also, due to their general and more abstract nature, to other services sectors in order to deal with 'differences in education and examination standards, experience requirements, regulatory influence and various other matters, all of which make implementing recognition on a multilateral basis extremely difficult.'[70] While the inclusion of 'general and abstractly formulated rules of conduct' is generally seen as an essential feature of a law-making resolution that is binding on its addresses by virtue of a decision of the organisation[71] this was clearly not what the Members hand in mind when they adopted the *MRA Guidelines*. Instead, they wanted the *MRA Guidelines* to remain voluntary and to retain their recommendatory, non-binding character and this is clearly stated in the opening section.[72]

Meanwhile, work continued in the WPPS on developing a set of *Disciplines on Domestic Regulation in the Accountancy Sector* or *Accountancy Disciplines*,[73] one of the most important elements of which was the development of a mandatory 'necessity test' for all applicable regulatory measures, i.e. they should 'not be more trade-restrictive than necessary to fulfil a specified legitimate objective'. However, with the exception of the accountancy sector, no general necessity test on non-discriminatory domestic regulation has yet been developed.[74] The necessity test

68 *Guidelines for Mutual Recognition Agreements or Arrangements in the Accountancy Sector*, adopted by the Council for Trade in Services, S/L/38 (28 May 1997) [hereinafter *MRA Guidelines*].

69 According to the *MRA Guidelines*, *ibid*, 3-7, 'Section B: Form and Content of Agreement', there are a number of requirements that MRAs should meet. They should list the participants, set out the purpose and scope of the agreements, give details of the mutual recognition provisions, including eligibility requirements for recognition, and specify the conditions for the application of any additional supplementary requirements, provide mechanisms for implementation, deal with further licensing or related requirements and state the terms for their revision.

70 *MRA Guidelines*, *ibid*, at, 'Introduction'.

71 Skubiszewski, above n. 30, 201.

72 It is clearly stated in the opening paragraph of the *MRA Guidelines*, above n. 68, that '[T]hese guidelines are non-binding and are intended to be used by Members on a voluntary basis, and cannot modify the rights or obligations of the Members of the WTO.'

73 *Disciplines on Domestic Regulation in the Accountancy Sector*, adopted by the Council for Trade in Services, 14 December 1998, S/L/64 (17 December 1998).

74 Joost Pauwelyn, 'Rien ne Va Plus? Distinguishing Domestic Regulation from Market Access in GATT and GATS (2005) *WTR* 131-170 at 138.

requirement in the *Accountancy Disciplines* reflects the objective in the *GATS*,[75] and other Multilateral Trade Agreements,[76] of balancing the preservation of the freedom of Members to set and achieve regulatory objectives through measures of their own choice and the need to avoid regulatory protectionism, i.e. regulation that is *de iure* and *de facto* discriminatory and unduly trade restrictive.

The *Accountancy Disciplines* establish a number of requirements for Members to apply in the domestic regulatory sphere, which include matters such as the provision of a non-exhaustive list of legitimate objectives for their domestic regulation,[77] enhanced rules on transparency,[78] the application of less trade restrictive alternatives to residency requirements for foreign service suppliers,[79] 'reasonable' documentation,[80] mutual recognition of foreign licensing and qualifications on the basis of equivalency[81] and consideration of internationally recognised standards, prepared by 'relevant international organisations' that are open to *all* Members.[82]

However, when it came to giving legal form and potential entry into force of the *Accountancy Disciplines* there was a lack of consensus among the Members. Initially the Secretariat was asked by the WPPS to prepare an informal note, advising on the means of rendering this set of non-binding disciplines binding on Members.[83] Three options were proposed in the Secretariat's Informal Note:[84]

75 In the case of the *GATS* there are references to necessity in Article VI:4, paragraphs (a), (b) and (c) of Article XIV, paragraph 2(d) of Article XVI *GATS* and paragraph 5(e) of the *Annex on Telecommunications*, *The Legal Texts*, above n. 24, 333, 342 and 362 respectively.

76 Similar references to necessity exist in paragraphs (a), (b), (d) and (i) of Article XX *GATT 1994*, *The Legal Texts*, *ibid*, 519-520; Article 2.2 *SPS Agreement*, *The Legal Texts*, *ibid*, 70; and Articles 2.2 and 2.5 *Agreement on Technical Barriers to Trade* or *TBT Agreement*, *The Legal Texts*, *ibid*, 130 and 140.

77 *Accountancy Disciplines*, *ibid*, Section II, para. 2 where 'Legitimate objectives are, *inter alia*, the protection of consumers (which includes all users of accounting services and the public generally), the quality of the service, professional competence, and the integrity of the profession.'

78 *Accountancy Disciplines*, *ibid*, Section III, under 'Transparency', paras. 5 and 6.

79 *Accountancy Disciplines*, *ibid*, Section IV, under 'Licensing Requirements', para. 9.

80 *Accountancy Disciplines*, *ibid*, Section V, under 'Licensing Procedures', para. 15.

81 *Accountancy Disciplines*, *ibid* Section VI, under 'Qualification Requirements', para. 19.

82 *Accountancy Disciplines*, *ibid*, Section VIII, under 'Technical Standards', para. 26.

83 See *Working Party on Professional Services*, *Note on the Meeting held on 3 and 4 February 1998*, Note by the Secretariat, S/WPPS/M/15 (19 February 1998).

84 *Disciplines on Accountancy*, *Legal Form and Entry into Force*, *Informal Note by the Secretariat*, *Revision*, Job. No. 1144 (28 February 1998).

(a) an annex to the *GATS,* constituting an amendment to the *GATS,*[85] (b) a reference paper approach, similar to the one used in the supplemental commitments taken by Members in telecommunications services,[86] on the basis of which Members could schedule specific commitments under Article XVIII *GATS* (additional commitments); and (c) a decision by the CTS on the application of the disciplines on a provisional (voluntary) basis, pending the elaboration of further disciplines under Article VI:4 *GATS*.

The Members discussed the question of potential legal forms for the adoption of the accountancy disciplines in the WPPS, the outcome of which was a draft Decision of the CTS,[87] agreed to by the WPPS and recommended by the latter to the CTS for its adoption. Eventually the CTS adopted the *Decision on Disciplines Relating to the Accountancy Sector* or *Accountancy Disciplines Decision* in December 1998,[88] and then only on an *ad referendum* basis, i.e. approved provisionally and subject to confirmation (following consultation by individual Members with capitals), which is an indication of the lack of political will that exists in the membership in making progress on rule-making in the WTO outside a formal MTN round.[89] Currently, the *Accountancy Disciplines Decision* is being applied by Members that have scheduled specific commitments on accountancy on a voluntary basis.[90] The Decision also records the fact that Members will continue their work on domestic regulation, aimed at developing general disciplines for professional services while retaining the possibility of developing or revising sectoral disciplines, including accountancy (second

85 *See* chapter IV, section 3.1(a) and (b).

86 *See* chapter IV, section 3.1(c).

87 The draft CTS *Decision on Disciplines Relating to the Accountancy Sector*, (Job. No. 6481), was eventually adopted by the Members in the WPPS on an *ad referendum* basis, *see Working Party on Professional Services, Note on the Meeting held on 4 December 1998, Note by the Secretariat*, S/WPPS/M/24 (18 December 1998), 4, para. 20.

88 *Decision on Disciplines Relating to the Accountancy Sector*, adopted by the Council for Trade in Services, 14 December 1998, S/L/63 (December 15, 1998) [hereinafter *Accountancy Disciplines*].

89 This is a frequently recurring event in the services sector where so far the work on developing disciplines on emergency safeguard measures, subsidies and government procurement in the Working Party on GATS Rules or WPGR has all but ground to a halt; see Mary E. Footer and Carol George, 'The General Agreement on Trade in Services' in Patrick MacRory, Arthur Appleton and Michael Plummer (eds.) *The World Trade Organization: Legal, Economic and Political Analysis* ((New York: Springer Science+Business Media, Inc., 2005) 799-953, at 902-906.

90 *Accountancy Disciplines*, above n. 88, para. 1.

paragraph),[91] and that *all* Members, including those without *GATS* commitments in the accountancy sector, agree with immediate effect, and to the fullest extent consistent with their existing legislation, not to take new measures which would be in violation of the *Accountancy Disciplines Decision* (third paragraph).[92]

This latter element of the *Accountancy Disciplines Decision* is critical to determining the normative force of the underlying decision because while it is well established in international institutional law that a competent decision-making body may adopt decisions that are binding on its Members internally,[93] the real test of its legislative or rule-making competence comes in deciding whether it may adopt measures that are binding externally.[94] It is submitted that while the *Accountancy Disciplines* were intended to have externally binding effect this has not been achieved, except with respect to the 'standstill' provision of paragraph 3, by which *all* Members are bound, whether or not they have taken specific commitments in accounting services, and *ipso facto* the directly affected entities and sectors within their jurisdictions, i.e. national regulators and accountancy sectors. However, such standstill provisions have been taken previously in CTS decisions in relation to the adoption of the texts of Protocols to the GATS and they are generally understood by the Members to be of a political rather than a legally binding nature, which calls into question the legally binding effect, if any, of the *Accountancy Disciplines*

We turn next to the work of the Committee under the *SPS Agreement* with respect to delegated rule-making, pursuant to implementing requirements on equivalency in the Agreement, which is of a different order and rests on an implied power. The wording of Article 4 SPS reads as follows:

91 *Accountancy Disciplines*, *ibid*, para. 2. Since 1999 work has continued on the development of horizontally applicable disciplines on domestic regulation in the Working Party on Domestic Regulation or WPDR, which was established by the *Decision on Domestic Regulation* adopted by the Council for Trade in Services on 26 April 1000, S/L/70 (28 April 1999), and is the successor body to the WPPS. The WPDR has focused on the elaboration of a necessity test, which introduces the principle of proportionality, enhanced transparency, and the related issues of equivalency (of qualifications) and international standards. *See Article VI:4 of the GATS: Disciplines on Domestic Regulation Applicable to All Services, Note by the Secretariat*, S/C/W/96, 1 March 1999 for further details.

92 *Accountancy Disciplines*, *ibid*, para. 3.

93 Schermers and Blokker, above n. 17, § 1327, 828-829.

94 Jochen Abr. Frowein, 'The Internal and External Effects of Resolutions by International Organisations' (1989) 49 *ZaöRV* 778-790 at 778.

Equivalence

1. Members shall accept the sanitary or phytosanitary measures of other Members as equivalent, even if these measures differ from their own or from those used by other Members trading in the same product, if the exporting Member objectively demonstrates to the importing Member that its measures achieve the importing Member's appropriate level of sanitary or phytosanitary protection. For this purpose, reasonable access shall be given, upon request, to the importing Member for inspection, testing and other relevant procedures.
2. Members shall, upon request, enter into consultations with the aim of achieving bilateral and multilateral agreements on recognition of the equivalence of specified sanitary or phytosanitary measures.[95]

In 2000 and 2001 the SPS Committee began work on examining the concerns of developing country Members on how to deal with problems that they confront from importing Members when seeking recognition of equivalence of their SPS measures for the protection of human, animal or plant life or health (including food safety and environmental measures). The Committee's examination involved one of the international standard-setting bodies designated under the *SPS Agreement*,[96] the *Codex Alimentarius Commission*,[97] which was already in the early stages of its work programme on the matter of equivalence agreements for food safety control, inspection and certification systems and on the judgment of equivalence. In order to generate discussion, and as part of the information gathering processes surrounding the equivalence debate, the SPS Committee held a number of informal meetings with observer organisations (and governments).[98]

The work programme eventually led to the adoption by the SPS Committee of the *Decision on the Implementation of Article 4 of the Agreement on the*

95 Article 4 *SPS Agreement*, *The Legal Texts*, above n. 23, 72.

96 The three designated standard-setting bodies in accordance with Annex A, section 3 to the *SPS Agreement*, *The Legal Texts*, *ibid*, 79, are: (1) the FAO/WHO *Codex Alimentarius Commission*, established in 1963 by FAO and WHO, which is responsible for developing food standards, guidelines and related texts such as codes of practice under the Joint FAO/WHO Food Standards Programme; (2) the International Office of Epizootics or OIE for animal health and zoonoses; and (3) the Secretariat of the International Plant Protection Convention or IPPC, which sets international standards, guidelines and recommendations for plant health within the framework of the IPPC.

97 For details, *see Equivalence: Consideration of Article 4 of the SPS Agreement, Summary of the Discussions of the SPS Committee*, Report by the Chairman, G/L/423 (29 November 2000) 1-2, paras. 4 and 11-12.

98 *See* further *Committee on Sanitary and Phytosanitary Measures – Equivalence: Consideration of Article 4 of the SPS Agreement – Summary of Informal Discussions on Equivalence, Second Report by the Chairman*, G/L/445 (21 March 2001).

Application of Sanitary and Phytosanitary Measures (*SPS Equivalency Decision*).[99] The key elements of the *SPS Equivalency Decision* are acceptance of the concept of equivalence in respect of specific SPS measures, or measures related to a certain product, or on a systems-wide basis,[100] and support for the view that: (1) the importing Member shall explain the objective and rationale of the SPS measure and clearly identify the risks that the measure is intended to address; (2) the importing Member shall indicate the 'appropriate level of protection' which its SPS measure seeks to achieve,[101] taking into account the *Guidelines to Further the Practical Implementation of Article 5.5*, adopted by the SPS Committee in 2000,[102] and (3) the exporting Member shall provide appropriate science-based and technical information to support its objective and demonstrate that its measure achieves the appropriate level of protection identified by the importing Member.[103]

Unlike the *Accountancy Disciplines* adopted by the CTS, upon a recommendation of the WPPS, for which the legal basis and authority is explicitly laid down in Article VI: 6 *GATS*, the *SPS Equivalency Decision* (and its later revision in 2004) was adopted by the SPS Committee, on the basis of paragraph 1 of Article 12 *SPS Agreement*, which is silent as to the Committee's authority to exercise

99 *Decision on the Implementation of Article 4 of the Agreement on the Application of Sanitary and Phytosanitary Measures*, adopted by the Committee on Sanitary and Phytosanitary Measures, G/SPS/19 (26 October 2001)], which was subsequently revised, in accordance with paragraph 13 of the original *SPS Equivalency Decision*, by means of the *Decision on the Implementation of Article 4 of the Agreement on the Application of Sanitary and Phytosanitary Measures, Revision including clarifications adopted by the Committee*, Revision, G/SPS/19/Rev.1 (2 April 2004) [hereinafter collectively referred to as the *SPS Equivalency Decision*]. The revised *SPS Equivalency Decision* of 2004 clarifies a number of paragraphs in the 2001 *Decision*, including the more recent work of the *Codex Alimentarius* and the OIE on the recognition of equivalence.

100 *SPS Equivalency Decision*, *ibid*, para. 1.

101 *SPS Equivalency Decision*, *ibid*, para. 2.

102 *See Guidelines to Further the Practical Implementation of Article 5.5*, adopted by the Committee on Sanitary and Phytosanitary Measures at its meeting of 21-22 June 2000, G/SPS/15 (18 July 2000). The *Guidelines*, which consist of a set of soft law recommendations and procedures, which deal in a descriptive and explanatory manner with the application of risk analysis, in terms of risk assessment and risk management, were adopted on an *ad referendum* basis, giving Members the opportunity to consult with capitals before 14 July 2000 whereafter if no objections had been raised the *Guidelines* would be considered adopted, fn. 1 ((there were no objections).

103 *SPS Equivalency Decision*, para. 4, which also states that 'this information may include, *inter alia*, reference to relevant international standards, or to relevant risk assessments undertaken by the importing Member of by another Member'.

Opinion on the *Effects of Awards of Compensation Made by the United Nations Administrative Tribunal (Effects of Awards)*, when it decided that the UN General Assembly in establishing the Administrative Tribunal had not delegated the performance of its own functions but had exercised a general power, which it had under the Charter to regulate staff relations.[113]

The rules on the establishment and functioning of WTO subsidiary bodies are spread throughout the *WTO Agreement* and the annexed Multilateral Trade Agreements and are based on a mixture of delegated and attributed powers. The Ministerial Conference exercises a specific power to establish subsidiary bodies, which is attributed to it on the basis of paragraph 7 of Article IV *WTO Agreement*. It has established the Committee on Trade and Development, the Committee on Balance-of-Payments Restrictions and the Committee on Budget, Finance and Administration together with the rules governing their mandates on the basis of Article IV:7 *WTO Agreement* and has proceeded to establish other subsidiary bodies at its first and subsequent meetings.[114]

In the case of the General Council there is no express authority in the *WTO Agreement* for it to establish and regulate subsidiary bodies. However, it exercises the functions of the Ministerial Conference in the intervals between meetings of this principal body and derives its authorisation to act from an implied power since Article IV:7 *WTO Agreement* makes it clear that it can 'establish such additional Committees with such functions as it may deem appropriate'. As noted previously, the Market Access Committee was established by means of a decision of the General Council,[115] on the basis of Article IV:7 *WTO Agreement* after the Council for Trade in Goods or CTG failed to act.[116] It also established the Committee on Trade and Environment or CTE[117] and the Committee on Regional Trade

113 *Effects of Awards*, above n. 49, 47-63, at 61. *See* Zemanek, above n. 1, 204-209, who critically assesses, in light of this Advisory Opinion, the establishment of the UN Tribunal for the former Yugoslavia by the Security Council, pursuant to UNSC Res 808 (3 May 1993) UN Doc S/25704 of 3 May 1993 and the *Addendum* (19 May 1993) UN Doc S/25704/Add., and UNSC Res 827 of 25 May 1993 (1993) 32 *ILM* 1159.

114 *See* chapter I, section 3.2(a).

115 *WTO Committee on Market Access, Decision of the General Council on 31 January 1995*, WT/L/47 (17 February 1995), adopted at the first Meeting of the General Council on 31 January 1995, WT/GC/M/1 (28 February 1995), para. 7(2); Decision WT/L/47 also contains the Terms of Reference for the Committee on Market Access.

116 See chapter I, section 3.2(c).

117 The Committee on Trade and Environment or CTE, was also established at the first meeting of the General Council, held on 31 January 1995, *ibid*, pursuant to the Ministerial Decision on Trade and Environment adopted by Ministers at the Meeting of the Trade Negotiations Committee in Marrakesh on 14 April 1994 (the *Marrakesh Ministerial Decision on Trade and Environment*), *The Legal Texts*, above n. 23, 469-471.

Arrangements or CRTA[118] on the basis of Article IV, paragraphs 2 and 7 *WTO Agreement*. Moreover, it is the General Council rather than the Ministerial Conference that establishes working parties on accession, on the basis of delegated powers, in accordance with *Accession – Procedures for Negotiations under Article XII*, which forms part of the GATT *acquis* on accession[119] and for a limited time, i.e. the duration of the accession process.

For the third level specialised Councils, i.e. the CTG, the CTS and the TRIPs Council, the rules governing their power to establish subsidiary bodies are explicitly stated in paragraph 6 of Article IV *WTO Agreement*. So far the CTG has exercised this power on a limited number of occasions with the establishment of the Working Group on State Trading Enterprises,[120] pursuant to paragraph 5 of the *Understanding on the Interpretation of Article XVII of the GATT 1994*,[121] the Working Group on Notification Obligations and Procedures, established pursuant to Part III of the *Marrakesh Ministerial Decision on Notification Procedures*;[122] and some ten working parties on various regional trade arrangements. The Council for Trade in Services has established the Committee on Trade in Financial Services or CTFS,[123] the Committee on Specific Commitments or CSC,[124] the Working Party on Professional Services

118 The Committee on Regional Trade Arrangements or CRTA was established by a Decision of the General Council of 6 February 1996, at its meeting of even date, WT/GC/M/10 (6 March 1996), para. 11.

119 *See* for further details chapter IV, section 3.2.

120 Meeting of the Council for Trade in Goods, 20 February 1995, G/C/M/1 (27 March 1995), para. 5(A), *WTO Analytical Index: Guide to WTO Law and Practice* 1st edition (Geneva: WTO Secretariat/Bernan, 2003), [hereinafter *WTO Analytical Index*], 53-54.

121 *Understanding on the Interpretation of Article XVII of the GATT 1994*, *The Legal Texts*, above n. 23, 25-26.

122 *Marrakesh Ministerial Decision on Notification Procedures*, *The Legal Texts*, *ibid*, 444-445. The Ministerial Decision was later endorsed by General Council (rather than the CTG) in its *Decision on Notification Procedures*, adopted at the first Meeting of the General Council, 31 January 1995, above n. 113, para. 9.

123 The power of the CTS to establish the Committee on Trade in Financial Services (CTFS) was explicitly granted in one of the Ministerial Decisions taken at the end of the Uruguay Round; see *Marrakesh Decision on Institutional Arrangements for the General Agreement on Trade in Services*, *The Legal Texts, ibid,* 456, para. 3. The Ministerial Decision was later endorsed by the Council for Trade in Services in its *Decision on Institutional Arrangements for the General Agreement on Trade in Services*, 1 March 1995, S/L/1 (4 April 1995).

124 The Committee on Specific Commitments, or CSC, was established by the Council for Trade in Services in 1995; see *Decision Establishing the Committee on Specific Commitments*, adopted by the Council for Trade in Services on 22 November 1995, S/L/16 (24 November 1995).

or WPPS[125] (in 1999 it was transformed into the Working Party
Regulation or WPDR),[126] and the Working Party on GATS Rules

In a few instances, fourth level bodies, i.e. Committees unde… Multilateral Trade Agreements have established subsidiary bodies and regulated their operation, on the basis of either express or implied powers. An example is the establishment by the Committee on Subsidies and Countervailing Measures of a Working Party on Subsidy Notifications,[128] established pursuant to Article 24.2 SCM,[129] on the basis of an expressed power contained in paragraph 2 of the Article 24 of the *Agreement on Subsidies and Countervailing Measures* or *SCM Agreement*.[130]

b) Rules of procedure of WTO bodies

An important set of subsidiary rules in the life of an international organisation is the body of procedural rules that regulate the right of Members to attend meetings and participate in its decision-making process.[131] Normally the rules of procedure that govern meetings of the institutional bodies will include the rules for the calling of meetings, the agenda, credentials, officers and deputation, conduct

125 The Working Party on Professional Services or WPPS, was established pursuant to the Uruguay Round *Ministerial Decision on Professional Services,* and the *Decision on Professional Services*, adopted by the Council for Trade in Services, 1 March 1995, S/L/3 (4 April 1995).

126 The Working Party on Domestic Regulation or WPDR, is the successor to the WPPS, and was established by *Decision on Domestic Regulation* adopted by the Council for Trade in Services on 26 April 1999, S/L/70 (28 April 1999).

127 The Working Party on GATS Rules or WPGR, was established at the second meeting of the CTS in order to carry out the negotiating mandates contained in the *GATS* on emergency safeguard measures, government procurement in services and subsidies, *see* Council for Trade in Services, Report of the Meeting held on 30 March 1995, Note by the Secretariat, S/C/M/2 (28 April 1995), paras. 23-25.

128 The Working Party on Subsidy Notifications is charged with reviewing the annual updates of Members' subsidy notifications in accordance with Article 8.3 *Agreement on Subsidies and Countervailing Duties* or *SCM Agreement, The Legal Texts,* above n. 23, 276.

129 The Working Party on Subsidy Notifications was established at a special meeting of the Committee on Subsidies and Countervailing Duties (SCM Committee) of 22 February 1995, G/SCM/1 (4 April 1995).

130 Article 24.2 *SCM*, *The Legal Texts,* above n. 23, 296, states: 'The Committee may set up subsidiary bodies as appropriate'.

131 Zemanek, above n. 1, 210-211.

of business, including the means of establishing whether the meeting is quorate, the form of decision-making, language(s) of the meeting and so forth.[132]

It has become established practice – on the basis of an implied or even inherent power[133] – for an international organisation, and by analogy any of its principal or subsidiary bodies (including any judicial or quasi-judicial bodies), to establish its own rules of procedures.[134] Where the organisation's constituent instrument requires that there be rules of procedure, it is on the understanding that those rules should be adhered to by Members, i.e. they are bound by them as long as they have not been expressly amended. Put differently, there exists a presumption against the implicit amendment of rules of procedure in the established practice of international organisations.[135]

The WTO has chosen to apply a fairly standard set of rules of procedure to all of its bodies, with the exception of two of its judicial and quasi-judicial bodies – the Appellate Body and the panels.[136] The rules of procedures governing meetings of the Ministerial Conference and the General Council,[137] which were adopted upon establishment of the organisation with revisions, serve as a template for almost every body in the organisation and are drawn from the rules of pro-

132 Such specific rules relating to the calling and conduct of meetings but more particularly the means of deliberation and decision-making, have been referred to by Philip Jessup as 'parliamentary diplomacy'; *see* his case study of the UN in the application and legal effect of rules of procedures, in Philip C. Jessup, 'Parliamentary Diplomacy: An Examination of the Legal Quality of the Rules of Procedures of Organs of the United Nations' (1956) 89 *Receuil des Cours* 181-320 at 203

133 Schermers and Blokker, above n. 17, §1201, 754.

134 Skubiszewski, above n. 30, 226-227; Zemanek, above n. 1, 211; see also Ronnie Sabel, *Procedure at International Conferences: A study of the rules of procedure of conferences and assemblies of international inter-governmental organizations* (Cambridge: Cambridge University Press, 1997).

135 Schermers and Blokker, above n. 17, §1205, 757-758.

136 Since the Dispute Settlement Body or DSB is an emanation of the General Council, *see*, chapter I, section 3.2(b), it follows the rules of procedure of that body, with a few minor changes.

137 *Rules of Procedure for the Ministerial Conference and the General Council*, WT/L/28 (7 February 1995), adopted at the Meeting of the General Council, held on 31 January 1995, WT/GC/M/1 (28 February 1995), at 5, para. 4.I.(a), as amended by the General Council on 3 April 1995 with regard to Chapter V – Officers, and on 18 July 1996 with regard to Annex 3. The extant version contains the *Rules of Procedure of the Ministerial Conference and General Council,* WT/L/161 (25 July 1996) [hereinafter *Ministerial Conference and General Council Rules of Procedure*]. They have been reproduced together with the Rules of Procedure adopted by the other WTO councils and committees in *OMC/WTO Rules of Procedure for Meetings of WTO Bodies* (Geneva: WTO Secretariat, July 1997).

cedure that governed meetings of the CONTRACTING PARTIE Council and various committees under the former GATT.[138] The the foregoing are the judicial and quasi-judicial bodies, with the exc DSB, which is an emanation of the General Council and therefore op ... under a slightly modified version of the *Rules of Procedure* governing meetings of that body.[139]

The *Understanding on Rules and Procedures Governing the Settlement of Disputes* or *DSU*,[140] sets out the rules and procedures that 'shall apply to disputes brought pursuant to the consultation and dispute settlement provisions of the agreements listed in Appendix 1 to ... [the *DSU*]'[141] and referred to as the 'covered agreements'.[142] They constitute the primary treaty rules for the settlement of disputes between Members. However, it is submitted that there also exists a body of subsidiary rules made up of various working procedures (and practices) for complaints brought before panels, the Appellate Body and other adjudicating bodies in the WTO.[143] The question that arises within the institutional context of the WTO is to what extent, if any, are the panels and the Appellate Body able to exercise a margin of discretion in adopting additional rules and procedures. Put differently, are there any limitations on the exercise of the inherent powers

138 Rules of Procedure for Sessions of the CONTRACTING PARTIES, the most recent of which consisted of a consolidated text which appeared at (1964) *BISD* 12S/10-16, *see* further *Analytical Index: Guide to GATT Law and Practice* 6th edition (Geneva: GATT Secretariat 1994) [hereinafter *GATT Analytical Index*], 1094 and fn. 14.

139 The *Rules of Procedure for the Dispute Settlement Body*, were adopted at the Meeting of the Dispute Settlement Body, held on 10 February and 25 April 1996 and incorporate by reference the *Ministerial Conference and General Council Rules of Procedure*, above n. 137 and issued as WT/DSB/9 (16 January 1997).

140 *Understanding on Rules and Procedures Governing the Settlement of Disputes* or *DSU*, *The Legal Texts,* above n. 23, 404-433.

141 Appendix 1 to the *DSU*, 'Agreements Covered by the Understanding', *The Legal Texts, ibid*, 429-430 gives a definitive list of those 'covered agreements'. Appendix 2 to the *DSU*, contains a list of 'Special or Additional Rules and Procedures Contained in the Covered Agreements', *ibid*, 430.

142 Paragraph 1 of Article 1 *DSU, The Legal Texts, ibid,* first full sentence. The second sentence of that same provision makes it clear that the rules and procedures in the *DSU* also apply to any disputes brought by Members concerning their rights and obligations under the *WTO* Agreement and the *DSU* itself or in combination with the covered agreements.

143 P. Monnier, 'Working Procedures before Panels, the Appellate Body and other Adjudicating Bodies of the WTO' (2002) 1 *Law and Practice of International Courts and Tribunals* 481-538.

of a (quasi-)judicial body to establish and to amend its own rules of procedures, including working procedures?

While Article 12 *DSU*[144] contains the basic provisions governing panel procedures, paragraph 1 thereof directs panels to follow the Working Procedures in Appendix 3 to the *DSU*.[145] Also relevant is paragraph 2 of Article 13 *DSU* that directs panels to apply 'the rules and procedures set forth in Appendix 4[146] of the DSU in situations in which expert review groups have been established'.[147] These Working Procedures for panels and expert review groups advising panels have remained unchanged since their adoption as Appendixes 3 and 4 to the *DSU* but the practice with respect to their application has changed over time.

It is recognised that panels have 'a wide margin of discretion to deal, always in accordance with due process, with specific situations that may arise in a particular case and that are not explicitly regulated'.[148] In other words, there is an established practice of panels developing their own working procedures on an *ad hoc* basis in order to govern individual disputes,[149] which gives rise to an interesting example of subsidiary rule-making by an (*ad hoc*) institutional body within the WTO's internal legal order. The rule-making activity usually consists of the panel expanding on the rules and procedures contained in Appendix 3 (and sometimes Appendix 4 if expert reviews are involved) in order to cover additional procedural rules governing the written submissions, oral hearings, composition of delegations, issues of evidence, requests for preliminary hearings (including on jurisdiction), format of documentation and service of documents, as can be seen from the Working Procedures for the Panel in the *US – Gambling* dispute.[150] Even so, there are limits to the exercise of this discretion, as the Appellate Body recalled in *India – Patent Protection for Pharmaceutical and Agri-*

144 Article 12.1 *DSU*, *The Legal Texts,* above n. 23, 414.

145 Appendix 3 to the *DSU*, *The Legal Texts*, *ibid*, 431-432, contained a fairly detailed but non-exhaustive list of procedures for panels to follow, combined with a 'proposed timetable for panel work'. Paragraph 11 of Appendix 3 specifically foresees the possibility of '[A]ny additional procedures specific to the panel'.

146 Appendix 4 to the *DSU*, *The Legal Texts*, *ibid*, 4, 433, contains further rules governing the participation in expert review groups, their duties and scope of work, as well as a confidentiality of information clause (paragraph 5).

147 *EC – Hormones*, Appellate Body Report, *European Communities – Measures Concerning Meat and Meat Products*, WT/DS26/AB/R, 26/DS/48/AB/R, adopted 13 February 1998, para. 148.

148 *EC – Hormones*, *ibid*, fn. 138 to para. 152. *See* also Monnier, above, n. 143, at 484-485.

149 A recent innovation is that, following the settlement of a dispute, panels have begun to make their working procedures public.

150 See for example the Working Procedures for the Panel, attached as Annex A to *US – Gambling,* Panel Report, *United States – Measures Affecting the Cross-Border Supply*

cultural Chemical Products (*India – Patents (US)*)[151] where it ma
panels, in determining their own procedures, should not disregard or
explicit provisions of the DSU, including in particular Article 7
governs the jurisdiction of a panel, which is established by that panel's terms of reference.

An unusual aspect of the panel's Working Procedures is that they are amenable to review by the Appellate Body during the ordinary course of proceedings. This is in contrast to other international courts and tribunals, which act autonomously in the determination of their rules of procedure and conduct, an activity that is usually considered to flow from the inherent power of a judicial body to determine the scope and limits of its jurisdiction and to regulate it accordingly. In the case of standing judicial bodies such as the International Court of Justice it is common for a Rules Committee to establish and amend its rules of procedure and to issue practice directions from time to time.[153]

In the case of *ad hoc* judicial and quasi-judicial bodies it is the particular judicial body itself which determines its own rules and procedures, except where the procedure is conducted in an institutional setting or resort is made to an existing set of rules and procedures, as is common in the field of international arbitration. Some examples of Appellate Body review of the working procedures for panels as set out in Appendix 3 to the *DSU*, combined with subsequent panel practice, reveal a number of factors. One is the view that panels would be better served if they 'had detailed, standard working procedures that allowed *inter alia* for preliminary rulings'[154] and another is that there should be a working pro-

of Gambling and Betting Services, WT/DS DS/285/R, adopted 20 April 2005 as modified by the Appellate Body Report, AB/DS285/AB/R, Page A-1and B-2.

151 *India – Patents (US)*, Appellate Body Report, *India – Patent Protection for Pharmaceutical and Agricultural Chemical Products*, WT/DS50/AB/R, adopted 16 January 1998, para. 92.

152 Article 7 *DSU* 'Terms of Reference of Panels', *The Legal Texts,* above n. 23, 410-411.

153 For example, the International Court of Justice has a Rules Committee that meets regularly in order to update its rules, pursuant to Article 30 of the Statute of the International Court of Justice; *see International Court of Justice, Rules of Court* (1978), adopted on 14 April 1978 and entered into force on 1 July 1978, with the most recent amendment concerning written pleadings coming into force on 14 April 2005, available at: http://www.icj-cij.org.

154 *EC – Bananas III*, Appellate Body Report, *European Communities – Regime for the Importation, Sale and Distribution of Bananas*, WT/DS27/AB/R, adopted 25 September 1997, paras. 143-144.

cedure for 'appropriate factual discovery at an early stage in panel proceedings'.[155]

It is clear that the Appellate Body does not enjoy the same margin of discretion as the panels do in the adoption of working procedures[156] in order to deal with a specific situation as became clear in the case of *European Communities – Measures Affecting Asbestos and Asbestos Containing Products* (*EC – Asbestos*).[157] In order to manage the anticipated flood of *amicus curiae* (or friends of the court) briefs the Appellate Body adopted an additional procedure in order to manage the *amicus curiae*, which was subsequently circulated to Members and posted on the WTO web-site.[158] What happened next was unusual in terms of judicial propriety and called into question the judicial independence of the Appellate Body.

Following an extraordinary meeting of the General Council,[159] at which the membership expressed its dissatisfaction with the Appellate Body's adoption of an additional working procedure since this can only be done *in consultation* with the Chairman of the DSB and the Director General,[160] the Appellate Body rejected all of the applications for leave to file an *amicus* brief and continued to do so, discarding any that had been received.[161] As noted earlier,[162] it is clear

155 *India – Patents (US)*, above n. 151, para. 95.

156 The Appellate Body is empowered under Article 17:9 *DSU*, *The Legal Texts*, above n. 23, 418, to draw up its own working procedures but it must do so '*in consultation* with the Chairman of the DSB and the Director-General'. Following its fifth revision, the current *Working Procedures for Appellate Review* (4 January 2005), are a consolidated, revised version which reflect amendments to Rules 1, 18(5), 20, 21, 23, 27 and Annex I, as well as the addition of a new Rule 23*bis* and a new Annex III, as discussed in documents WT/AB/WP/W/8 and WT/AB/WP/W/9. The new rules of procedures or working procedures are applicable to appeals initiated after 1 January 2005.

157 *EC – Asbestos*, Appellate Body Report, *European Communities – Measures Affecting Asbestos and Asbestos Containing Products*, WT/DS135/AB/R, adopted 5 April 2001.

158 *Additional Procedure Adopted under Rule 16(1) of the Working Procedures for Appellate Review*, WT/DS135/9 (8 November 2000) [hereinafter *Additional Procedure*]. The *Additional Procedure* was communicated to the parties and third parties in *EC – Asbestos* on 7 November 2000. The following day, the Chairman of the Appellate Body, Florentino Feliciano, informed the Chairman of the DSB in writing of the *Additional Procedure* adopted and the procedure was circulated to WTO Members.

159 *Minutes of the Meeting of the General Council*, 22 November 2000, WT/GC/M/60 (23 January 2001), para. 12.

160 Article 17:9 DSU, *The Legal Texts,* above n. 23, 418. Following the *amicus curiae* debacle the DSB adopted *Additional Procedures for Consultation between the Chairperson of the DSB and WTO Members in Relation to the Working Procedures for Appellate Review*, at its meeting of 19 December 2002, WT/DSB/31 (20 December 2002).

161 *EC – Asbestos*, above n. 157, paras. 53 and 55-57.

that the Appellate Body does not enjoy the same inherent powers as c national judicial bodies[163] in determining its own rules of procedure or working procedures and where it has sought to exercise such competence specific limits have been place upon it by the DSB, which is a political body and thus calls its judicial independence into question.[164]

Finally, as part of its subsidiary rule-making in the area of internal rules relating to dispute settlement, the DSB established *Rules of Conduct for the DSU*[165] at its meeting in December 1996. The *Rules of Conduct* are ethical rules that apply to each person serving on a panel, on the standing Appellate Body,[166] as an arbitrator or as an expert participating in the dispute settlement mechanism[167] as well as to the now defunct Textiles Monitoring Body or TMB.[168] The R*ules of Conduct* also govern such matters as self-disclosure requirements with respect to the independence and impartiality of persons involved in the DSU mechanism, confidentiality requirements, procedures on subsequent disclosure and material violation, and issues relating to receipt of evidence where Secretariat staff may be involved (to be dealt with in conjunction with WTO staff regulations).

162 *See* for a broader discussion, chapter I, section 3.2(b).

163 On this aspect, *see* Friedl Weiss, 'Inherent Powers of National and International Courts' in Federico Ortino and Ernst-Ulrich Petersmann (eds.) *The WTO Dispute Settlement System 1995-2003* (The Hague: Kluwer Law International, 2004) 177-190.

164 Steve Charnovitz, 'Judicial Independence in the World Trade Organization' in Laurence Boisson de Chazournes, Cesare Romano and Ruth Mackenzie, *International Organizations and International Dispute Settlement* (Ardsley NY: Transnational Publishers, Inc., 2002) 212-240.

165 *Rules of Conduct for the Understanding on Rules and Procedures Governing the Settlement of Dispute*, adopted by gavel at the meeting of the Dispute Settlement Body on 3 December 1996 (WT/DSB/M/27, item 1); the document embodying the rules can be found at the WT/DSB/RC/1 (11 December 1996) [hereinafter *Rules of Conduct for the DSU*].

166 The Appellate Body had already adopted these *Rules of Conduct for the DSU*, upon its establishment in 1995 on a provisional basis. Following their adoption by the DSB they were directly incorporated and became part of the *Working Procedures for Appellate Body Review*, above n. 156. *See* further Gabrielle Marceau, 'Rules on Ethics for the New World Trade Organization Dispute Settlement Mechanism' (1998) 32 *JWT* 57-97.

167 *Rules of Conduct for the DSU,* above n. 165, para. 1, *IV. Scope.*

168 The Textiles Monitoring Board or TMB no longer exists after the demise of *Agreement on Textiles and Clothing* or *ATC*, *The Legal Texts,* above n. 23, 85-137, and its integration into the GATT.

c) Operational rules: WTO budget, finance and administration

There are certain rules in the WTO's internal legal order that are essential to the functioning of the organisation, more particularly pertaining to its budget, finance and administration. Such matters as the size of the budget of an international organisation and the means of assessing Members' contributions are fundamental to any international organisation.[169] The budget is considered to be 'a legal act by which the income and expenditure of an international organization is estimated. It authorizes the organization to incur certain expenditure and it constitutes the legal basis for the payment of contributions'.[170] The consequences of this are that the budget, which directly concerns the rights and duties of the Members, as a result of their contributions towards expenses, is usually adopted by the organisation's plenary body by means of simple or qualified majority vote. In the case of the WTO, its constituent instrument, on the basis of paragraph 3 of Article VII *WTO Agreement*,[171] calls for the 'annual budget estimate' to be adopted by the General Council by means of a super-qualified majority vote consisting of 'a two-thirds majority comprising more than half the membership' although in practice this decision has only ever been adopted by consensus.[172]

Most of the WTO's income for its annual operating budget comes from the contributions of the Members, which are established according to a complex formula based on their share of international trade (imports and exports) in relation to the overall international trade of *all* Members and other factors,[173] in addition

169 Sands and Klein, above n. 4, 565.

170 Schermers and Blokker, above n. 17, §1091, 691, citing J. David Singer, *Financing International Organizations: The UN Budget Process* (The Hague: Nijhoff Publishers, 1961) 54-55, who distinguishes four functions of the budget of an international organisation: (1) basis for decision-making organs to expand; (2) operational plan according to which the secretariat will execute its responsibilities; (3) allows the secretariat to estimate operating costs; and (4) serves as a yardstick by which the auditing agency may compare expenditure with appropriation.

171 Article VII:3 *WTO Agreement, The Legal Texts,* above n. 23, 10.

172 *See* chapter III, section 2.3(b). *See* also William J. Davey, 'Institutional Framework' in McRory, Appleton and Plummer, *The World Trade Organization,* above n. 89, 51-87 at 66 and 82.

173 At its Meeting of 15 November 1995, WT/GC/M/8 (13 December 1995), the General Council approved the recommendation of the Joint WTO/GATT Committee on Budget, Finance and Administration concerning a new methodology for the calculation of the assessment of Members' contributions to the WTO budget, with each Contracting Party/ Member's share in the annual operating budget of the GATT/WTO being established on the basis of that country's (or separate customs territory's) international trade (imports plus exports) in relation to the total international trade of all GATT Contracting Parties/

to which certain miscellaneous income is earned from rental fees and sales of WTO publications. Increasingly, and more particularly, since the launch of the Doha Development Round MTN in November 2001, the WTO has been managing a number of trust funds, to which Members contribute on an individual and voluntary basis. The purpose of these trust funds is primarily to support special activities for technical cooperation and training that are designed to assist developed and LDC Member countries participation in the multilateral trading system.[174]

WTO law and practice in the matter of budget finance and administration follows that of its predecessor the GATT. The process of transition from GATT to WTO was facilitated by the *Organizational and Financial Consequences Decision*[175] adopted by Ministers at Marrakesh, which led to the preparation of recommendations and decisions on organisational changes, resource requirements and staff conditions of service brought about by the creation of the WTO. The Committee on Budget, Finance and Administration or BFA Committee existed as a joint GATT/WTO Committee[176] for a transitional period of one year, i.e. 1995, whereupon the current BFA Committee succeeded its predecessor under the GATT.[177] Subsequently, the General Council, on the basis of paragraph 3 of Article VII *WTO Agreement*[178] adopted a set of internal rules in the form of *Financial Regulations of the World Trade Organization* and *Financial Rules*

WTO Members and other factors (WT/BFA/6, L/7633). A later modification, recommended by the BFA Committee (WT/BFA/44), was approved by the General Council at it Meeting of 17 December 1999, WT/GC/M/52 (3 January 2000) to reflect a minimum contribution of those Members whose share in the total international trade of all WTO Members was less than 0.015 per cent..

174 For details concerning the WTO's budget and current budgetary levels, *see* the organisation's web-site at *www.wto.org/english/thewto_e/secre_e/budget05_e.htm.*

175 *Decision on Organizational and Financial Consequences Flowing from Implementation of the Agreement Establishing the World Trade Organization*, LT/UR/D-6/3 (15 April 1994), 33 *ILM* (1994) 1269-70 [hereinafter *Organizational and Financial Consequences Decision*], reproduced in *The Legal Texts*, above n. 23, 472.

176 For the terms of reference of the Joint GATT/WTO Committee on Budget, Finance and Administration, see GATT doc. L/5964/Rev.9 of 20 March 1995 and WT/L/44 of 23 February 1995.

177 This moment of institutional succession was recorded in the Minutes of the Meeting of the Committee on Budget, Finance and Administration or BFA Committee, held on 29 January 1996, WT/BFA/20 (21 February 1996) by means of a notification of the terms of reference and composition of the 'new' WTO Committee and recorded in a single handover of the chairmanship of the Committee.

178 Article VII:3 *WTO Agreement*, *The Legal Texts,* above n. 23, 10.

of the World Trade Organization,[179] which govern the preparation of budget estimates, adoption of the budget, collection and use of funds, the surplus account, the working capital fund, custody and investment of fund, internal control and external audit. In August 2003, following the specific recommendations of the BFA Committee, the General Council[180] adopted a Decision whereby 'the Director-General would be requested to present to the Committee BFA two estimated budgets covering a biennial period' and it simultaneously approved revised a set of *Financial Regulations*[181] in respect of the matter.

d) WTO staff rules and regulations

As in other international organisations,[182] the WTO has a number of subsidiary rules and regulations that apply to its staff and personnel and form part of the internal law of the organisation. Generally speaking these rules and regulations can be broken down into three topic areas, concerning: (1) appointment of staff and terms of employment; (2) legal position of the staff, including protection at law; and (3) the independent character of staff employed by the WTO, including where relevant the grant of privileges and immunities to certain categories of personnel.

One of the Ministerial Decisions adopted at Marrakesh was the Decision on *Organizational and Financial Consequences Flowing from Implementation of the Agreement Establishing the WTO*,[183] which mandated the Preparatory Committee for the PCWTO or PCWTO to 'consider organizational changes, resource requirements and staff conditions of service proposed in connection with the establishment

179 *Financial Regulations of the World Trade Organization*, WT/L/156 (5 August 1996) and *Financial Rules of the World Trade* Organization, WT/L/157 (5 August 1995), adopted by the General Council at its Meeting of 15 November 1995, WT/GC/M/8 (13 December 1995), 15, under E, pursuant to a recommendation of Joint WTO/GATT Committee on Budget, Finance and Administration (WT/BFA/13, L/7649).

180 Minutes of the Meeting of the General Council held on 25, 26 and 30 August 2003, WT/GC/M/82 (13 November 2003), para. 2 at 1-2, adopting the proposal of the BFA Committee, WT/BFA/W/105/Rev.1, with annexed thereto *Financial Regulations of the World Trade Organization*, WT/L/156/Rev.1 (21 November 2003) with amendments to Regulations 5 and 6.

181 See chapter IV section 3.1(b) for a discussion of the process that was used to do this, which is nothing less than a 'backdoor' amendment of the *WTO Agreement*.

182 Schermers and Blokker, above n. 17, §516-§545, 359-386.

183 *Decision on Organizational and Financial Consequences Flowing from Implementation of the Agreement Establishing the World Trade Organization*, LT/UR/D-6/3 (15 April 1994), (1994) 33 *ILM* 1269-70 [hereinafter *Organizational and Financial Consequences Decision*] reproduced in *The Legal Texts,* above n. 23, 472.

of the WTO ... and take decisions, to the extent necessary, on the adjustments required'. At various meetings held between October 1995 and April 1998 the General Council adopted a series of Decisions,[184] which regulated the terms of service applicable to WTO staff and personnel during a transitional period from the establishment of the WTO on 1 January 1995 and April 1998 and which involved the transfer of the former ICITO (GATT) Secretariat staff to the WTO.[185] The WTO Secretariat finally came into existence in October 1998 on the basis of paragraph 3 of Article VI *WTO Agreement*,[186] and henceforth the members of staff of the WTO Secretariat are appointed on the basis of the *Staff Regulations*[187] which govern the conditions of service and the personnel practices of the Secretariat and set out the rights, duties and obligations of staff members.

It is intended that the *Staff Regulations* should serve as a set of guiding principles for the Director-General in the staffing and administration of the Secret-

184 *Conditions of Service Applicable to the Staff of the WTO Secretariat*, WT/L/91, Decision adopted by the General Council, at its Meeting of 30 October 1995, WT/GC/M/7 (11 December 1995), section 1 and *Conditions of Service Applicable to the Staff of the WTO Secretariat*, WT/L/197, Decision adopted by the General Council, at its Meeting of 7, 8 and 13 November 1996, WT/GC/M/16 (18 November 1996), section 6; *Working Group on Conditions of Service Applicable to the Staff of the WTO Secretariat*, WT/L/205, Decision concerning its establishment, adopted by the General Council at its Meeting of 7 February 1997, WT/GC/M/18 (19 March 1997), section 3; *Conditions of Service Applicable to the Staff of the WTO Secretariat*, Decision adopted by the WTO General Council and ICITO Executive Committee on 1 July 1997, WT/L/223, adopted by the General Council at its Meeting of 30 June-1 July 1997, WT/GC/M/20 (10 July 1997), section 1; and *Conditions of Service Applicable to the Staff of the WTO Secretariat*, Decision adopted by the WTO General Council and ICITO Executive Committee on 24 April 1998, WT/L/269, adopted by the General Council at its Meeting of 24 April 1998, WT/GC/M/28 (8 May 1998), section 1. (The fourth recital to the Joint Decision of 24 April 1998 makes reference to the fact that 'the WTO is a *sui generis* organization established outside the United Nations system'.)

185 Until 1998, the WTO Secretariat had not been officially appointed in accordance with paragraph 3 of Article VI *WTO Agreement* but continued to operate on the basis of an exchange of letters between the Executive Secretary (later the title was changed to Director-General) of the GATT and the Secretary-General of the United Nations that went back to August 1952.

186 It followed the adoption of a joint decision of the WTO General Council and ICITO Executive Committee on *Conditions of Service Applicable to the Staff of the WTO Secretariat*, 16 October 1998, WT/L/282, (21 October 1998).

187 The *Staff Regulations*, *Pension Plan Regulations*, *Staff Rules*, *Administrative Rules of the Pension Plan* and *Compensation Philosophy* are all taken up as Annex 2 to Decision WT/L/282, *ibid.*

ariat. A further set of *Staff Rules*[188] provide the means for implementing the provisions of the Staff Regulations. The Director-General has the authority to issue *Staff Administrative Memoranda* in elaboration of the *Staff Rules*.[189] The *Staff Regulations*, *Staff Rules* and *Staff Administrative Memoranda* apply to all staff members of the Secretariat holding contracts of twelve months' duration or more, i.e. there is a separation made on the basis of permanent and temporary appointments.[190] For the latter type of appointment, it is the Director-General who establishes separate conditions of service based on the *Staff Regulations, Staff Rules* and *Staff Administrative Memoranda.*

An important aspect of this body of internal rules is that they also regulate the independence of the Secretariat staff as international civil servants. A fundamental aspect to the proper functioning of an international organisation[191] is that the principles of independence, impartiality and loyalty to the organisation are upheld.[192] The international character of the responsibilities of the Director-General and of the staff of the Secretariat is expressly stated in paragraph 4 of Article VI *WTO Agreement*,[193] and endorsed in Regulation 1.4 of the *Staff Regulations*, on the basis of which '... staff members shall neither seek nor accept any instruction relating to the performance of their duties from any government or other entity or person external to the WTO, and shall at all times respect the exclusively international character of their positions and maintain their independence.'[194] Regulation 1.4 also references to the 'Standards of Conduct in the World Trade Organization' required of WTO staff members.[195]

188 For the *Staff Rules* see Annex 2, *ibid.*

189 The Director-General is authorized to do this on the basis of Regulation 2.4 of the *Staff Regulations*, above n. 187.

190 Schermers and Blokker, above n. 17, §518-§523, 359-366.

191 See ILO Administrative Tribunal (ILOAT) Judgement No. 2232 of 16 July 2003 in the *Bustani* case, involving General José Bustani, the former Director-General of the Organization for the Prohibition of Chemical Weapons or OPCW at *http://www/ilo.org/public/English/tribunal*, where the independence of civil servants is considered to be an essential guarantee for the proper functioning of the organisation; for a critical account of this decision, *see* Jan Klabbers, 'The *Bustani* case before the ILOAT: constitutionalism in disguise'(2004) 53 *ICLQ* 455-463.

192 Schermers and Blokker, above n. 17, §524, 366.

193 Article VI:4 *WTO Agreement*, *The Legal Texts,* above n. 23, 9-10.

194 *Staff Regulations*, above n. 187, Regulation 1.4.

195 *Staff Regulations*, *ibid*, second sentence of Regulation 1.4, which refers to Annex B 'Standards of Conduct in the World Trade Organization', which according to a footnote are adapted in part from the ICSAB Report on Standards of Conduct in the International Civil Service 1954.

Another feature of the conditions of service of the Secretariat staff in the *Staff Regulations* is that provision is made for their protection at law, including where staff members have problems or grievances or wish to appeal an administrative decision, including disciplinary measures. In both cases, the *Staff Rules*¸ which give effect to the *Staff Regulations*, contain a set of rules governing a complaints procedure. In the case of problems and grievance, recourse can be made to an impartial mediator or mediators in order to try and resolve the matter.[196] Where a staff member wishes to appeal an administrative decision the process is different. A preliminary request for review has to be made to the Director-General,[197] whereupon the possibility for appeal to the Joint Appeals Board or JAB exists.[198] In the event of a disciplinary measure the process is slightly different, since the staff member in question will have recourse to an appeal directly to the Administrative Tribunal of the International Labour Organization or ILOAT.[199]

As noted previously, the Ministerial Conference (or the General Council acting in the interim) has the power, on the basis of paragraphs 2 and 3 of Article VI *WTO Agreement*, to appoint the Director General and to adopt regulations setting out the powers, duties, conditions of service and terms pertaining to the office of the Director-General and to adopt regulations governing the duties and conditions of service of the Secretariat. Matters have not always proceeded so smoothly in the appointment of Directors-General. Following bitter divisions between the Members over the appointment of a Director-General to succeed Renato Ruggiero in 1999, which eventually led to an unprecedented term sharing arrangement, a comprehensive set of rules and procedures for future appointments of WTO Director-Generals,[200] was adopted by a decision of the General Council at the end of 2002.

The set of rules and procedures is concerned with the smooth conduct of the appointment process, which is led by the Chair of the General Council, who is assisted by two facilitators (the Chair of the DSB and the Chair of the TPRB). The rules and procedures include such details as length of time for the process, nominations, qualifications of candidate, the consultations phase in order 'to identify candidate around whom consensus can be built',[201] term of office,

196 *Staff Rules*, above n. 187, Rule 114.1.

197 *Staff Rules*, *ibid,* Rule 114.3(a).

198 *Staff Rules*, *ibid*, Rule 114.5(b); Rule 114.2 governs the composition and 'jurisdiction' of the Joint Appeals Board or JAB.

199 *Staff Rules, ibid*, Rule 114.3(b).

200 *Procedures for the appointment of Directors-General*, adopted by the General Council, 10 December 2002, WT/L/509 (20 January 2003); *see* also chapter I, section 3.2 at (f).

201 *Ibid*, para. 17.

remuneration and contract of employment of the future Director-General. The aforementioned rules and procedures for the appointment of WTO Director-Generals is an example of the exercise of subsidiary rule-making by the General Council on the basis of a specific power in Article VI:2 *WTO Agreement.*

It is also usual practice in international institutional law and practice to recognise that the staff (including temporary staff) and delegates of missions attached to an international organisation enjoy certain privileges and immunities in connection with their function on the basis of conventions, headquarters agreements and other instruments laying down privileges and immunities of the staff of international organisations. In the case of the WTO, the Director-General, members of staff of the Secretariat and delegates from permanent missions to the WTO enjoy certain functional immunities which are based on the privileges and immunities of the WTO in accordance with paragraph 4 of Article VIII *WTO Agreement.*[202] This has the consequence that such persons do not fall completely within the legal order of the host state (in this case Switzerland), or any other State while carrying out their functions for the organisation. The extent to which these aforementioned categories of persons will also enjoy diplomatic privileges and immunities varies in accordance with the terms of their appointment and whether they carry the rank of diplomat.

e) Rules giving effect to assigned functions in the *WTO Agreement*

Another body of subsidiary rule-making concerns those rules of the organisation that are necessary to its functioning on the external plane and have been assigned to it, or one of its institutional bodies, on the basis of its constituent instrument. Separate provisions of the *WTO Agreement* govern functions that call for decisions to be taken by various WTO bodies, which can lead to the elaboration of subsidiary rules regulating such matters as the relationship between the WTO and other intergovernmental organisations (and non-governmental organisations).

An example of such subsidiary rule-making are the rules which have been developed by the General Council in order to define the ongoing relationship between the WTO and the UN on the basis of Paragraph 1 of Article V *WTO Agreement* and which govern 'appropriate arrangements for effective cooperation with other intergovernmental organizations that have responsibilities related to

202 These privileges and immunities are similar to those privileges and immunities set out in the Convention on the Privileges and Immunities of the United Nations (adopted by the UN General Assembly on 13 February 1946, *entry into force*, 17 September 1946) 1 *UNTS* 15; *see* also chapter I, section 3 introductory remarks.

those of the WTO',[203] since the WTO is not a specialised agency of the UN nor does it have any formal links with the UN.[204] In April 1995, the General Council approved revised arrangements for effective cooperation in the relationship between the WTO and the UN[205] on the basis of a Report of the PCWTO,[206] which led to an exchange of letters between WTO Director-General, Renato Ruggiero and UN Secretary General, Boutros Boutros-Ghali in September 1995.[207] Among other things, it was agreed that the WTO-UN relationship would be the same as the GATT-UN one,[208] there would be arrangements for the reciprocal exchange of information, the WTO would participate in the UN Administrative Committee on Coordination or ACC (now the UN Chief Executives' Board or CEB)[209] and its subsidiary bodies, and there would be continued cooperation between WTO and UN secretariats on statistics and administrative matters.

The latter two points are particularly important to the organisation. While the WTO is not a specialised agency of the UN, nor does it maintain any formal links

203 Article V:1 *WTO Agreement*, *The Legal Texts,* above n. 23, 9.

204 This is unlike its predecessor the GATT, which historically hadmaintained formal links with the UN based on the fact that Article 86:1 of the draft Charter for the International Trade Organisation or ITO (1948), UN Doc E/Conf.2/78; ICITO/1/4 (April 1948) (the so-called 'Havana Charter') would have brought the ITO into a relationship with the UN through a specialised agency agreement with the Economic and Social Council (ECOSOC) under Article 63 UN.

205 Minutes of the Meeting of the General Council, held on 3 April 1995, WT/GC/M/3 (20 April 1995), para. 13, 5-6.

206 *Report of the Preparatory Committee for the WTO*, 31 January 1995, in particular para. 54, thereof, which 'saw no grounds for formal institutional links between the WTO and the United Nations, although the need for the establishment of cooperative ties between the two organizations was underscored' in Minutes of the Meeting of the General Council, 31 January 1995, *ibid*, para. 13.

207 *Communication from the Director-General to the General Council, Arrangements for the Effective Cooperation with other Intergovernmental Organizations, Relations between the WTO and the United Nations*, 15 November 1995, WT/GC/W/10 (3 November 1995).

208 The arrangements and practices, which previously existed between the UN and the GATT are described in UN GA Doc. of 9 March 1976 (A/AC.179/5).

209 The UN Administrative Committee on Coordination or ACC is currently known as the United Nations System Chief Executives' Board or CEB for Coordination, which acts as a forum for the executive heads of 25 organisations, including the WTO, in order to further co-ordination and cooperation on a range of substantive and management issues facing the UN system. It is chaired by the UN Secretary-General and meets twice a year. Participation by the WTO in the CEB includes participation in the High Level Committee on Management or HLCM, which has been re-shaped out of several subsidiary bodies, including the former UN Consultative Committee on Administrative Questions or CCAQ.

with that organisation, it relies heavily on the UN statistical services in providing the Members and their trading partners with accurate information and is essential for several key operational divisions of the Secretariat, including the Trade Policy Reviews Division, which services the Trade Policy Review Body or TPRB, the Economic Research and Statistics Division and the Trade and Finance Division.

There is also a duty incumbent on the WTO to register the *WTO Agreement* and any amendments thereto, including modifications to schedules brought about by supplemental Protocols, and modifications to Schedules following renegotiations of Tariffs Concessions or Services Commitments,[210] in accordance with Article 102 UN on the basis of paragraph 6 of Article XVI *WTO Agreement*. This task is fulfilled by the Director-General, on the basis of paragraphs 3 and 4 of Article XIV *WTO Agreement*, who acts as depository, from which flow a number of administrative and legal consequences. It should be recalled that the role of the depositories, the issue of notifications, rectifications and registrations are designated in Part VII VCLT.[211] In practice, a member of WTO staff, acting as registrar, assists the Director-General on a full-time basis in fulfilling the function of depository of the *WTO Agreement* and the annexed Multilateral Trade Agreements, including the Tariff Schedule and Schedules of Services Commitments.

2.3 Adjudicative rule-making

A further area where subsidiary rules-making may take place is by means of the development of principles, rules and standards through the adjudicative process of an international organisation although this will vary from one organisation to

210 *See* Chapter IV, sections 3.1(c) and (d).

211 Article 77 VCLT lists the functions of the depository (a) custody of the original text of the treaty; (b) preparation of certified copies of the original texts of the treaty and transmission to the parties, i.e. Members, and 'to States entitled to become parties to the treaty'; (c) receipt of any signature and receipt and custody of any instruments of ratification, acceptance or accession and all notifications and communications relating thereto; (d) examination of such signature, or any instrument, notification or communication relating to the treaty in order to ensure that it is in due and proper form; (e) informing parties, i.e. Members, and States of acts, notifications and communications relating to the treaty; (f) informing States entitled to become parties to the treaty when the number of signatures, instruments of ratification, approval or accession required for entry into force of the treaty, or modifications thereto have been received or deposited; and (g) registration of the treaty with the UN Secretariat in accordance with Article 102 UN, upon its entry into force. *See* further Anthony Aust, *Modern Treaty Law and Practice* (Cambridge: Cambridge University Press, 2000) 268-269.

another dependent upon the scope and exercise of the functions by its judicial organ(s).[212] Even so, in the case of the WTO the judicial function of the panels and Appellate Body is limited entirely to the settlement of state-to-state disputes, i.e. only the Members have standing to bring complaints before the dispute settlement bodies relating to 'whether one WTO Member's actions violate WTO law or impair trade benefits'[213] under the 'covered agreements', and there is no provision for third parties, including individuals or international organisations, whether governmental or non-governmental, to bring claims.[214] No Member (or its representatives) or WTO staff member has a right of action against an administrative act of the WTO or one of its subsidiary organs, including the Director-General (or by implication the Secretariat) in the WTO dispute settlement system.[215]

Irrespective of the limited scope of the judicial function in the WTO the possibility still exists for the Appellate Body and to a lesser extent, the panels, to develop subsidiary rules during the ordinary course of settling disputes between Members on the basis of paragraph 2 of Article 3 *DSU*. This development has been viewed with criticism in some quarters and labelled as an act of judicial activism because it flies in the face of the wording in that provision, which counsels: '[R]ecommendations and rulings …cannot add to or diminish the rights or obligations provided in the covered agreements'.[216] Nevertheless, it is submitted that the creation of subsidiary rules by judicial bodies such as the Appellate

212 See Cesare P.R. Romano, 'International Organizations and the International Judicial Process: An Overview' in Boisson de Chazournes, Romano and Mackenzie, above n. 164, 3-36, at 3.

213 Charnovitz, in Boisson de Chazournes, Romano and Mackenzie, *ibid,* 164, 223.

214 Article 3.2 *DSU*, *The Legal Texts,* above n. 23, 405. See *US – Shrimp*, Appellate Body Report, *United States – Import Prohibition of Certain Shrimp and Shrimp Products*, WT/DS58/AB/R, adopted 6 November 1998, para. 89.

215 In the UN system there are specialist tribunals, for example the United Nations Administrative Tribunal or UNAT, which was established by GA Res. 351A (IV) of 24 November 1949, as subsequently amended. It is competent to hear and pass judgement upon applications alleging non-observance of contracts of employment of staff members of the United Nations Secretariat or their terms of appointment and applications alleging non-observance of the regulations and rules of the United Nations Joint Staff Pension Fund.
Similarly, the Statute of the International Labour Organization Administrative Tribunal or ILOAT (successor of the League of Nations Tribunal), which was also established in 1946, hears complaints from serving and former officials of the International Labour Organization or ILO. It is also competent to hear complaints against more than 40 other international organizations that recognise its jurisdiction including the WTO for staff complaints on appeal from the Joint Appeals Board or JAB, above n. 198.

216 Article 3.2 *DSU*, *The Legal Texts,* above n. 23, 405, third and final sentence.

Body (and to a lesser extent quasi-judicial bodies like the panels), is an inevitable outcome of a vibrant judicial dispute settlement and a necessary one in order to ensure that these bodies are engaged in the proper exercise of their judicial function.

Judicial rule-making in the sense that it is employed here is limited to identifying those principles, rules and standards that have been developed in GATT/WTO dispute settlement, which are either (a) procedural in character and necessary to ensure due process and the efficient and timely settlement of disputes or settlement process, or (b) which are predominantly interpretative in character adding light and shade to substantive WTO rights and obligations that are found in primary treaty rules. Each of these types of judicial rule-making is briefly reviewed in order to assess the extent to which the Appellate Body and panels have been able to build on existing principles, rules and standards, found in the Multilateral Trade Agreements in settling disputes.

a) Procedural rules, including evidence and proof

The jurisprudence of the Appellate Body has been critical to the development of a body of subsidiary procedural rules, particularly those on evidence and proof, where in the absence of a set of written rules or practice directions, it has had to develop its own. During the course of hearing an appeal, it could be expected that the Appellate Body will consider issues of procedural law that the panel has applied or omitted to apply in reaching its recommendations. However, as the Appellate Body itself has cautioned, in the interests of due process, procedural rules 'are designed to promote, not the development of litigation techniques, but simply the fair, prompt and effective resolution of trade disputes'.[217]

Thus far the Appellate Body has ruled on a number of procedural issues, thereby adding to the body of procedural rules. These rulings address various aspects of due process, such as the opportunity of parties (and third parties) to respond to claims[218] and evidence submitted[219] (both are aspects of the *audi*

217 *US – FSC*, Appellate Body Report, *United States – Tax Treatment for "Foreign Sales Corporations"*, WT/DS108/AB/R, adopted 20 March 2000, para. 166.

218 *India – Patents (US)*, above n. 149, para. 94 and *Australia – Salmon*, Appellate Body Report, *Australia – Measures Affecting Importation of Salmon*, WT/DS18/AB/R, adopted 20 August 1999, para. 278.

219 *Australia – Salmon*, *ibid*, para. 272.

et alteram partem rule), to raise timely objections,[220] 'enhanced' third party rights[221] and the issue of *amicus curiae*, or friends of the court, briefs by non-WTO Members[222] and Members,[223] as well as the adoption of an additional procedure.[224] It has also ruled on procedural issues pertaining to its own jurisdiction and the proper exercise of its judicial function including the application of the principle of *jura novit curia*,[225] potential *non-liquet*,[226] i.e. the situation where there is a gap in the law,[227] the notion of judicial economy, which dictates

220 *Mexico – Corn Syrup (Article 21.5 – US)*, Appellate Body Report, *Mexico – Anti-Dumping Investigation of High Fructose Corn Syrup (HFCS) from the United States – Recourse to Article 21.5 of the DSU by the United States*, WT/DS132/AB/RW, adopted 21 November 2001, para. 50.

221 *US – FSC (Article 21.5 – EC)*, Appellate Body Report, *United States –Tax Treatment for "Foreign Sales Corporations" – Recourse to Article 21.5 of the DSU by the European Communities*, WT/DS108/AB/RW, adopted 29 January 2002, para. 243 and *US – 1916 Act*, Appellate Body Report, *United States – Anti-Dumping Act of 1916*, WT/DS136/AB/R, WT/DS162/AB/R, adopted 26 September 2000, para. 150.

222 *US – Shrimp*, above n. 214, para. 89-110, and *US – Lead and Bismuth II*, Appellate Body Report, *United States – Imposition of Countervailing Duties on Certain Hot-Rolled Lead and Bismuth Carbon Steel Products Originating in the United Kingdom*, WT/DS138/AB/R, adopted 7 June 2000 , para. 39-42.

223 *EC – Sardines*, Appellate Body Report, *European Communities – Trade Descriptions of Sardines*, WT/DS231/AB/R, adopted 23 October 2002, concerning the *amicus curiae* brief submitted by WTO Member, Morocco, paras. 161-170.

224 *EC – Asbestos*, above n. 157, paras. 51-56.

225 *EC – Tariff Preferences*, Appellate Body Report, above n. 26, para. 105, with reliance on the application of the principle of *jura novit curia* by the International Court of Justice in *Case Concerning Military and Paramilitary Activities in and against Nicaragua (Nicaragua* v. *United States of America)* [1986] ICJ Rep 14, para. 29, *Fisheries Jurisdiction Case (United Kingdom of Great Britain and Northern Ireland* v. *Iceland)* [1974] ICJ Rep 9, para. 17.
The panel also recalled the principle of *jura novit curia* in *EC – Export Subsidies on Sugar*, Panel Report, *European Communities – Export Subsidies on Sugar*, WT/DS265/R, WT/DS266/R and WT/DS283/R, adopted 19 May 2005 as modified by the Appellate Body Report, WT/DS265/AB/R, para. 7.121, fn. 437.

226 In *US – Hot-Rolled Steel*, Appellate Body Report, *United States – Anti-Dumping Measures on Certain Hot-Rolled Steel Products from Japan*, WT/DS184/AB/R, adopted 23 August 2001, paras. 125-126; *see* Charnovitz in Boisson de Chazournes, Romano and MacKenzie, above n. 164, 233 and fn. 96, where he states: the Appellate Body 'detected a lacuna in Article 19.4 of the Anti-dumping Agreement, but stated that the appeal did not raise the issue of how the lacuna might be overcome'.

227 *See* further Daniel Bodansky, 'Non Liquet and the Incompleteness of International Law' in Laurence Boisson de Chazournes and Philippe Sands (eds.) *International Law, The International Court of Justice and Nuclear Weapons* (Cambridge: Cambridge University Press, 1999) 153-170, cited in Charnovitz, *ibid*; for a more exhaustive analysis of the

that a (quasi-)judicial body is not required to examine *all* legal claims raised by the complainant[228] since the aim of the dispute settlement system is to settle disputes not to 'make law' by clarifying existing WTO provisions outside the scope of the dispute,[229] and completion of the legal analysis where the factual findings of the panel and the undisputed facts in the panel record provide an insufficient basis for the Appellate Body's own analysis.[230]

On the subject of evidence and proof, the necessity of developing subsidiary rules is vital given that the matter is scarcely regulated in the *DSU*. The Appellate Body has thus far ruled on matters of evidence pertaining to the submission of evidence (no time limits in Article 11 *DSU*)[231] (acceptance, rejection and weighing of evidence)[232] (exercise of due diligence)[233] expert opinion (any individual, body or source)[234] and scientific evidence.[235] With respect to issues of proof, it has ruled on burden of proof, including allocation[236] and reversal of the burden

existence of *non liquet* and a doctrinal discussion of its treatment by international courts and tribunals, *see* Gerald Fitzmaurice, 'The Problem of Non Liquet: Prolegomena to a Restatement' in *Mélanges offerts à Charles Rousseau: La communauté internationale*, above n. 40, 90-112.

228 *US – Wool Shirts and Blouses*, Appellate Body Report, *United States – Measures Affecting Imports of Woven Wool Shirts and Blouses from India*, WT/DS33/AB/R, adopted 23 May 1997, para 323.

229 *US – Wools and Blouses*, *ibid*, and *Australia – Salmon*, above n. 219, para 223.

230 *EC – Asbestos*, above n. 157, paras. 78-79. *See* also the more extensive resort to the practice of completing the legal analysis on other occasions in *WTO Appellate Body Repertory of Reports and Awards, 1995-2004* (Cambridge: Cambridge University Press, 2005) [hereinafter *WTO Appellate Body Repertory*], 122-128.

231 *Argentina – Textiles and Apparel*, Appellate Body Report, *Argentina – Measures Affecting Imports of Footwear, Textiles, Apparel and Other Items*, WT/DS56/AB/R, adopted 22 April 1998, para. 79.

232 *US – Shrimp*, above n. 214, para. 104.

233 *US – Cotton Yarn*, Appellate Body Report, *United States – Transitional Safeguard Measure on Combed Cotton Yarn from Pakistan*, WT/DS192/AB/R, adopted 5 November 2001, paras. 77-78.

234 *US – Shrimp,* above n. 214, para. 104 and *Argentina – Textiles and Apparel*, above n. 232, para. 82 and 84.

235 *Japan – Apples*, Appellate Body Report, *Japan – Measures Affecting the Importation of Apples*, WT/DS245/AB/R, adopted 10 December 2003, para. 179.

236 *US – Wool Shirts and Blouses*, above n. 229, para 323, *EC – Hormones*, above n. 147, para. 98 and *EC – Sardines*, above n. 223, para. 275 and *Canada – Dairy (Article 2.5 – New Zealand and US II)*, Appellate Body Report, *Canada – Measures Affecting the Importation of Milk and the Exportation of Dairy Products – Second Recourse to Article 21.5 of the DSU by New Zealand and the United States*), WT/DS103/AB/RW2, WT/DS113/AB/RW2, adopted 17 January 2003, para. 66.

of proof,[237] presumption,[238] including a prima facie case[239] and affirmative defences.[240]

b) Substantive rules, mostly standard of review

The situation with respect to the development of any subsidiary rules of a substantive nature by the adjudicative bodies under the DSU is extremely limited. Paragraph 2 of Article 3 *DSU* makes it clear that the adjudicative function, i.e. the function of applying the law, is different from law-making, when it states that 'recommendations and rulings of the DSB cannot add to or diminish the rights and obligations of Members under the covered agreements'.[241] While the task of the panels and Appellate Body is largely restricted to clarifying and giving meaning to existing WTO provisions in accordance with the customary rules of interpretation of public international law,[242] the wording of Article 3.2 *DSU* should not be read as an obstacle to those bodies making a contribution to the rule-making process by means of subsidiary rules and in fact they do this during the ordinary course of adjudication, interpretation and clarification. In this section, we examine two means by which the recommendations and rulings of the panels and the Appellate Body can influence normative developments at the WTO in the context of subsidiary rule-making, either by clarifying and applying principles, rules and standards in basic WTO provisions or by establishing new rules or standards during the articulation of those provisions.

A number of general principles of public international law have been applied in the context of interpreting WTO rights and obligations. These have covered the application of the principle of proportionality with reference to the public international law rules on state responsibility in the case of countermeasures (safeguard actions),[243] the application of the principle of good faith (in curing

237 *Canada – Dairy (Article 2.5 – New Zealand and US II)*, *ibid*, paras. 71 and 98.

238 *US – Wool Shirts and Blouses*, above n. 228, p. 323 at 335.

239 *Canada – Aircraft*, Appellate Body Report, *Canada – Measures Affecting Importation of Civilian Aircraft*, WT/DS70/AB/R, adopted 20 August 1999, para. 192 and *Japan – Apples*, above n. 235, paras. 159-160.

240 *US – Wool Shirts and Blouses*, above n. 228, p. 323 at 337.

241 Final sentence, Article 3.2 *DSU*, *The Legal Texts,* above n. 23, 405.

242 Second full sentence, Article 3:2 *DSU*, *ibid.*

243 *US – Cotton Yarn*, above n. 234, paras. 119-120 and *US – Line Pipe*, Appellate Body Report, *United States – Definitive Safeguard Measures on Imports of Circular Welded Carbon Quality Line Pipe from Korea*, WT/DS202/AB/R, adopted 8 March 2002, para. 257 and 259.

an *abus de droit* or abuse of rights)[244] (in the resolution of disputes)[245] (as required by the principle of *pacta sunt servanda*)[246] and the application of the precautionary principle.[247] In seeking to clarify WTO provisions 'in accordance with customary rules of interpretation of public international law, as required in paragraph 2 of Article 3 *DSU*,[248] the Appellate Body has applied the principle of effectiveness (*ut res magis valeat quam pereat*)[249] as '[O]ne of the corollaries of the 'general rule of interpretation in the *Vienna Convention*' in order to 'give meaning and effect to all the terms of the treaty'[250] and 'to give effect to a legally operative meaning' (*effet utile*).[251]

It has also ruled on the application of the principle *in dubio mitius* (deference to State sovereignty in the matter of treaty interpretation) as a supplementary means of interpretation, which is 'widely recognised in international law'.[252] In the view of the Appellate Body, the principle of *in dubio mitius* is to be applied where 'the meaning of a term is ambiguous' in which case 'the meaning is to be preferred which is less onerous to the party assuming an obligation, or which interferes less with the territorial and personal supremacy of a party, or involves less general restrictions upon the parties'.[253] In other words, where there are two possible interpretations of a treaty provision, the interpreter should adopt the one that least constrains the sovereignty of the parties to the treaty.

Finally, the Appellate Body has applied the doctrine of legitimate expectations in the matter of treaty interpretation. In *India – Patents (US)*[254] it said that 'the

244 *US – Shrimp*, above n. 214, para. 158.

245 *US – FSC*, above n. 217, para. 166.

246 *EC – Sardines*, above n. 223, para. 278 and *US – Offset Act (Byrd Amendment)*, Appellate Body Report, *United States – Continued Dumping and Subsidy Offset Act of 2000*, WT/DS217/AB/R, WT/DS234/AB/R, adopted 27 January 2003, with reliance to the principle of *pacta sunt servanda* articulated in Article 26 VCLT, above n. 14.

247 *EC – Hormones*, above n. 147, paras. 123-124.

248 Article 3.2 *DSU, The Legal Texts,* above n. 23, 405.

249 *Japan – Alcoholic Beverages II*, Appellate Body Report, *Japan – Taxes on Alcoholic Beverages,* WT/DS8/AB/R, WT/DS10/AB/R, WT/DS11/AB/R/, adopted 1 November 1996, p. 97 at 106.

250 *US – Gasoline,* Appellate Body Report, *United States – Standards for Reformulated Gasoline and Conventional Gasoline*, WT/DS2/AB/R, adopted 20 May 1996, p. 3 at 21.

251 *Canada – Dairy*, Appellate Body Report, *Canada – Measures Affecting the Importation of Milk and the Exportation of Dairy Products*, WT/DS103/AB/R, WT/DS113/AB/R, Corr. 1, adopted 27 October 1999, para. 133.

252 *EC – Hormones*, above n. 147, para. 165 with reference to the principle in fn. 154.

253 *EC – Hormones, ibid.*

254 *India – Patents (US)*, above n. 151.

legitimate expectations of parties to a treaty [were] reflected in the language of the treaty itself'.[255] This was reinforced in *EC – Computer Equipment*[256] where the Appellate Body made it clear that the purpose of treaty interpretation as set out in Article 31 VCLT was 'to ascertain the *common* intention of the parties'. In its view, such '*common* intentions cannot be ascertained on the basis of the subjective and unilaterally determined "expectations" of *one* of the parties to a treaty.'[257]

The extent to which the Appellate Body has generated other subsidiary rules that articulate or give effect to basic WTO rules of a more substantive type has mostly been limited to the development of standards of judicial review where national authorities have enacted trade remedies in the form of anti-dumping, countervailing or safeguard measures and the dispute settlement system effectively acts as a review process for those actions under the respective Multilateral Trade Agreements.[258] This situation has changed over the course of the past decade as an increasing number of complaints brought by Members in the dispute settlement system address violations of WTO rules that encourage Members to adopt positive integrationist measures in order to bring their domestic regulatory systems into line with their international obligations.

This development has led panels and the Appellate Body to establish the structure for a more principled case law in the matter of standard of judicial review which seeks to balance conditions of market access and the application of the principle of non-discrimination with other societal values, enshrined in Members' domestic policies. In the remainder of this section, we turn first to consider some examples of this aforementioned occurrence. This is followed by some observations concerning subsidiary rule-making in the context of jurisprudential development and its relationship to subsidiary rule-making in other WTO bodies.

There are a growing number of complaints brought by WTO Members involving challenges to measures by national regulatory authorities (other than trade remedies such as anti-dumping, countervail and safeguards). The trend highlights

255 *India – Patents*, *ibid*, para. 45.

256 EC – *Computer Equipment*, Appellate Body Report, *European Communities – Customs Classification of Certain Computer Equipment,* WT/DS62/AB/R, WT/DS67/AB/R, WT/DS68/AB/R, adopted 22 June 1998, para. 84

257 *EC – Computer*, *ibid.*

258 The emergence of a consistent jurisprudence in applying standards of review to rules-based disciplines such as anti-dumping, subsidies and safeguards has been well-established; see *Appellate Body Repertory*, above n. 230, 421-434 and Holger Spamann, 'Standard of Review for World Trade Organization Panels in Trade Remedy Cases: A Critical Analysis' (2004) 38 *JWT* 509-555 and Matthias Oesch, 'Standards of Review in WTO Dispute Settlement' (2003) 6 *JIEL* 635-659.

the underlying regulatory philosophy that underpins the multilateral trading system[259] and which is characterised by an increase in the number of permissive and exceptive norms. This has in turn led to the elaboration of new disciplines which defer to national rules and standards *provided* they do not lead to the imposition of domestic regulatory barriers (sanitary and phytosanitary measures, technical barriers, intellectual property rights and licensing, qualification requirements and procedures and so on in the field of services).

Under the *GATT 1994* it is sufficient for a complainant to allege that a regulatory measure of a contracting party 'nullifies or impairs' benefits that would otherwise accrue to it under the GATT. The complainant bears the burden of proof and of establishing a prima facie case, whereupon the burden of proof shifts to the defendant to show that the measures is justified under an exceptive provision, the best known of which is the general exception of Article XX *GATT 1994*. Having done this, Article XX sets up a strict standard of judicial review which requires that the party raising this affirmative defence must be able to demonstrate that its regulatory measure is not arbitrary, unjustifiably discriminatory or a disguised restriction on trade.

The defendant may also be required to demonstrate that the measure was 'necessary' under certain headings of paragraphs (a) (b) or (j) of Article XX *GATT 1994* which, in accordance with established case law under that provision, 'involves in every case a process of weighing and balancing a series of factors' including the contribution of the compliance measures to enforcement of the law and the importance of common interests and values,[260] i.e. the necessity test is introduced in order to demonstrate that no less trade-restrictive alternative measure was available. This adds an additional element to an otherwise strict standard of review in respect of Article XX *GATT 1994*.[261] A further test that has been introduced into Article XX *GATT 1994* case law is the test to determine that the measure in question was rationally related to its purpose, and is primarily related to a defence brought under paragraph (g) of Article XX.[262]

The application of standard of judicial review in the foregoing example relates to a measure under an agreement, the primary aim of which is the norm of non-

259 *See* chapter II, section 3, introductory remarks and chapter IV, section 2.1.

260 *Korea – Various Measures on Beef*, Appellate Body Report, *Korea – Measures Affecting Imports of Fresh, Chilled and Frozen Beef*, WT/DS161/AB/R, WT/DS169/AB/R, adopted 10 January 2001, para. 164.

261 *See* for a similar application of the necessity test in the case of the exception in Article XIV GATS, *US – Gambling*, above n. 150, paras. 304-325 and especially its finding at para. 326.

262 *US – Shrimp*, above n. 214, para. 141.

discrimination, as we noted with the respect to the former trade barriers regime, but is it applicable to a measure adopted under an agreement, the primary aim of which is harmonisation, such as the *SPS*, *TBT* or *TRIPs Agreements*? Put differently should a more deferential standard be applied in these types of cases because the underlying aim of the agreement is of a different nature?

In the first case of its kind under the *SPS Agreement* where there was no issue of discrimination, the Appellate Body in *EC – Hormones*, which involved the European Communities' ban on imports of hormone-treated meat and meat products, upheld the inconsistency of the EC measure with Article 5.1 *SPS* because it was not supported by a sufficiently specific risk assessment. However, the Appellate Body added a further test to the standard of judicial review under this provision by requiring that there should be a rational relationship between an SPS measure and a risk assessment,[263] i.e. a rational relationship between the means and the ends (the so-called 'rational basis test').[264]

Essentially, the application of this test, if satisfied should preclude the need to pursue an enquiry into whether the measure was also necessary in the sense that there was no alternative less-trade restrictive measure available (the test under Article *XX 1994* case law), authority for which can be found in *EC – Sardines* case.[265] The application of the rational basis test, which began with *EC – Hormones,* has been endorsed in later case-law relating both to *SPS*[266] and non-harmonising agreement measures. In the context of an Agreement like *SPS* it is considered as offering a margin of discretion to governments in the protection of their national regulatory autonomy. The stricter test of necessity, which is found in Article XX *GATT 1994* and Article XIV *GATS* case law,[267] with its emphasis on the application of the principle of proportionality in weighing and balancing the otherwise GATT-infringing measure with other common interests and societal values, does not offer the same margin of discretion. Thus, in conclusion the Appellate Body has through clarification and application of the law, contributed

263 *EC – Hormones*, above n. 147, para. 193.

264 Viejo Heiskanen, 'The Regulatory Philosophy of International Trade Law' (2004) 38 *JWT* 1-36 at 33.

265 The Appellate Body was called upon by the European Communities to consider the rational relationship between an international standard and a technical regulation in respect of a measure that was 'based' on an international standard in *EC – Sardines*, above n. 223, para. 248.

266 See for example, *Japan – Apples*, above n. 235, para. 77.

267 See for example, *Korea – Beef*, above n. 260, para. 164 and *US – Gambling*, above n. 150, para. 326.

in at least one area to the development of a standard of judicial review, which is of a substantive and not merely a procedural nature.[268]

3 Rule referencing

A different type of subsidiary rule-making altogether is the phenomenon of 'rule referencing' or the creation of rules on the basis of provisions in an international treaty instrument, which reference by means of 'incorporation' other binding or non-binding rules or standards which exist in another treaty instrument, or have been developed by a formal or informal institution or body. While rule referencing is more commonly found in the field of private international law with respect to foreign rules incorporated by reference into domestic legal systems, in the field of public international law the phenomenon of 'incorporating legal rules with a different origin' into treaty regimes is not new, as demonstrated by the 1982 UN Convention on the Law of the Sea.[269] In this latter convention references appear in a number of provisions to 'generally accepted international rules and standards',[270] for example with respect to the protection and preservation of the marine environment in the case of pollution from vessels(Article 211)[271] or to the duties of the flag state to ensure compliance with 'applicable international rules and standards' (Article 217).[272]

In the case of the WTO several of the Multilateral Trade Agreements reference binding and non-binding rules or standards, which have their origin in another treaty or which have been developed by an institutional or conventional body outside the organisation, as a basis for the adoption of international standards, guidelines and recommendations. The use of rule referencing in a policy-making organisation like the WTO raises a number of questions. First, do such rules of reference have the effect of incorporating into WTO law rules and standards in other treaties, or developed by other bodies that have a law-making function and by what process does this occur? Second, are rules of reference capable of creating

268 Spamann, above n. 258, 635-659, noting conclusions at 547 and 554-555.

269 United Nations Convention on the Law of the Sea (adopted 10 December 1982, *in force* 16 November 1994) 1833 *UNTS* 3 [hereinafter UNCLOS].

270 W. van Reenen, 'Rules of Reference in the New Convention on the Law of the Sea, in particular in connection with the pollution of the sea by oil from tankers' (1982) 12 *NYIL* 3-44.

271 Paragraph 2 of Article 211 UNCLOS, above n. 265. *See* also the 'conflicts rule' in Article 237 UNCLOS which deals with obligations under other conventions on the protection and preservation of the marine environment.

272 Paragraph 1 of Article 217 UNCLOS *ibid.*

law by reference, i.e. turning non-binding 'soft law' into rules that are binding on the Members? Put more simply, what is the effect of rule-referencing where this occurs in certain Multilateral Trade Agreements and does the process of incorporation of a rule or standard by reference have the effect of turning a non-binding WTO norm into a binding one?

Examples of rule-referencing in WTO law and practice include efforts under Article 3.1 *SPS Agreement* to harmonise sanitary and phytosanitary measures as widely as possible, using as their basis[273] international standards, guidelines and recommendations in accordance with the definitions contained in section 3 of Annex A to the *SPS Agreement*. In the case of food safety this means standards, guidelines and recommendation, as developed by the FAO/WHO *Codex Alimentarius Commission*[274] (paragraph (a)), while for animal health and zoonoses, it means those standards, guidelines and recommendations as developed under the auspices of the International Office of Epizootics or IOE[275] (paragraph (b)) and for plant health the definition extends to international standards, guidelines and recommendations developed under the auspices of the Secretariat of the International Plant Protection Convention[276] or IPPC (and cooperating regional organisations within the framework of the IPPC) (paragraph (c)). For matters under

273 In *EC – Sardines*, above n. 223, para. 243, the Appellate Body stated, with reliance on its ruling in *EC – Hormones*, above n. 147, that the proper meaning to be attributed to 'an international standard [in Article 2.4 *TBT*]... "as the basis for" a technical regulation [is] when it is used as the principal constituent or fundamental principle for the purpose of enacting the technical regulation'.

274 Created in 1963 as a joint initiative of two specialised UN agencies, the FAO and the WHO, the *Codex Alimentarius Commission* develops food standards, guidelines and related texts, such as codes of practice under the Joint FAO/WHO Food Standards Programme; for further information *see http://www.codexalimentarius.net/* and Alexandrowicz, above n. 5, 75-82. For a comprehensive analysis of the ongoing process of standard-setting and rule-making by *inter alia* the FAO/WHO *Codex Alimentarius* Commission (CAC) in the field of food safety see *Ad Hoc* Group on Food Safety, *Overview and Compendium of International Organisations with Food Safety Activities*, OECD, 27-28 May 2000, SG/ADHOC/FS(2000)4/FINAL and for a briefing, Steve Suppan, *Consumers International's Decision-Making in the Global Market. Codex Briefing Paper* (August 2004) available at: *www.tradeobservatory.org/library.cfm?RefID=36988*.

275 The *International Office of Epizootics* (*Office international des epizooties*), now more commonly known as the *World Organisation for Animal Health*, was established by the International Agreement for the Creation of an Office International des Epizooties in Paris (adopted 25 January 1924, *in force* for various parties from 1924 onwards) 57 *LNTS* 135.

276 International Plant Protection Convention (adopted by FAO Conference, 6th Session, 6 December 1951, subsequently amended in 1979, *in* force 4 April 1991, later amend-

the *SPS Agreement* that are not covered by any of the aforementioned bodies, rule-referencing may also occur in the case where 'appropriate standards, guidelines and recommendations are promulgated by 'relevant international organizations open for membership to all Members, as identified by the [SPS] Committee' (paragraph (d)).[277]

However, it should be noted that in *EC – Hormones*, the Appellate Body has specifically stated that Article 3.1 *SPS Agreement* should not be read 'as requiring Members to harmonize their SPS measures *by conforming those measures with international standards*, guidelines and recommendations' because to do so would be 'to vest such international standards, guidelines and recommendations (which are by the terms of the Codex *recommendatory* in form and nature) with obligatory force and effect'.[278] In other words, their incorporation by reference cannot 'transform those standards, guidelines and recommendations into binding *norms*'.[279]

In answer to the first question, it would suggest that the process of incorporation by reference to a rule, standard or guideline laid down in another treaty, or developed by another international body can play a role in the harmonising process, which is their aim in the *SPS Agreement*. In answer to the second question, it is clear that the process of rule-referencing does not have the effect of turning non-binding soft law into law that is binding on the Members.

The issue of rule-referencing with respect to non-binding norms in contexts other than harmonising or standardisation measures has been addressed in WTO dispute settlement cases with respect to unfair trade in the matter of export subsidies. In cases arising from the Brazil/Canada aircraft dispute the Panels and Appellate Body have made reference to the non-binding OECD Export Credits Arrangement[280] in order to establish the boundaries of a WTO obligation with respect to the prohibition on export subsidies and a permissible defence under

ment of November 1997 *in force* 2 October 2005). The 1997 text is available at: http://www.ippc.int.

277 Article 3.2 *SPS Agreement* and paragraph 3 of Annex A, *The Legal Texts*, above n. 24, 71 and 79 respectively.

278 *EC – Hormones*, above n. 147, para. 165.

279 *EC – Hormones*, *ibid.*

280 The OECD Arrangement on Officially Supported Export Credits, 2005, is available at: www.oecd.org. The OECD Export Credits Arrangement is a 'Gentleman's Agreement' that is open to participants which represent an OECD Member Government. It sets out the most generous export credit terms and conditions that may be supported by its participants. The OECD also provides details of the monthly updates of Commercial Interest Reference Rates or CIRR, which represents the relevant government bond rate plus one hundred base points.

Item (k) of the Illustrative List of Export Subsidies, annexed to the *SCM Agreement*.[281]

In *Brazil – Aircraft*[282] the Appellate Body concluded that the indirect reference to the OECD Export Credits Arrangement in the second paragraph of Item (k), upon which Brazil was relying for the financing of its aircraft export trade (PROEX), was sufficient to bring this non-binding instrument into the dispute as an example of what might constitute a 'material advantage'. It went on to determine that 'the second paragraph of item (k) [was] a useful context for interpreting the "material advantage" clause in the text of the first paragraph'. More significantly, the Appellate Body considered the OECD Export Credits Arrangement 'as one example of an international undertaking providing a specific market benchmark by which to assess whether payments by governments, coming within the provisions of item (k), are "used to secure a material advantage in the field of export credit terms"'. On this view it proceeded to determine that the 'appropriate comparison' to be made was between the effective interest rate in a PROEX transaction with the relevant Commercial Interest Reference Rate or CIRR[283] (in accordance with the OECD Export Credits Arrangement),[284] thereby explicitly referencing the rules governing interest rates in this soft law instrument.

When confronted with the issue of the 'matching' of derogations under the OECD Export Credits Agreement, as a means of disciplining export credits in

281 Item (k) of the Illustrative List of Export Subsidies, being Annex A to the SCM Agreement, *The Legal Texts*, above n. 23, 304-307 at 306. The first paragraph of Item (k) of the Illustrative List identifies the grant by governments (or government-controlled entities) of export credits at rates below market rates as an example of an export subsidy *in so far as they are used to secure a material advantage in the field of export credit terms*'. The second paragraph of Item (k) provides a 'safe haven' by indicating that if the export credit is granted by a Member participating in an international undertaking (or a successor undertaking) on official export credits (and this is a reference to the OECD Export Credits Arrangement) *or* if a Member applies the interest rate provisions of that undertaking, i.e. the CIRR rates, above n. 280, then such export credits are not an export subsidy.

282 *Brazil – Aircraft*, Appellate Body Report, *Brazil – Export Financing Programme for Aircraft*, WT/DS46/AB/R, adopted 20 August 1999, para. 180.

283 *Brazil – Aircraft*, *ibid*, para. 182.

284 This approach was confirmed at the appeal stage of an Article 21.5 compliance proceeding, brought by Canada in *Brazil – Aircraft (Article 21.5 – Canada)*, Appellate Body Report, *Brazil – Export Financing Programme for Aircraft, Recourse by Canada to Article 21.5 of the DSU*, WT/DS46/AB/RW, adopted 4 August 2000, para. 67.

the field of aircraft subsidies, the Panel in *Canada–Aircraft Credits and Guarantees*[285] was careful to distinguish between the OECD Export Credits Arrangement and the *SCM Agreement*.

> Unlike the *OECD Arrangement*, the SCM Agreement is not an "informal" "gentleman's agreement". The SCM Agreement therefore does not need to allow recourse to the matching of derogations in order to instil discipline. The SCM Agreement is a binding instrument, and is therefore enforceable through the WTO dispute settlement mechanism.[286]

This statement clearly marks the boundary between applicable soft law and binding WTO obligations under the 'covered agreements'. It also cautions against the notion that the process of incorporation by reference of rules, standards and guidelines developed and maintained by another international body can turn non-binding law into law that is binding on WTO Members.

4 Conclusions

The subject of subsidiary rule-making, its diversity and complexity within the overall normative framework of the WTO is only just beginning to be understood. A few further preliminary conclusions are in order.

285 *Canada –Aircraft Credits and Guarantees*, Panel Report, *Canada – Export Credits and Loan Guarantees for Regional Aircraft*, WT/DS222/R, adopted, 19 February 2002, para. 7.180 (findings).

286 *Canada – Aircraft Credits and Guarantees, ibid*, relying on *Canada – Aircraft (Article 21.5)*, Panel Report, *Canada – Measures Affecting the Export of Civilian Aircraft – Recourse by Brazil to Article 21.5 of the DSU*, WT/DS70/RW, adopted 4 August 2000, paras. 5.125, 5.132 and 5.134 and *Brazil – Aircraft – Second Article 21.5* (*Brazil – Export Financing Programme for Aircraft – Second Recourse by Canada to Article 21.5 of the DSU*, Panel Report, WT/DS46/RW/2, adopted 23 August 2001, paras. 5.114-5.115 and 5.117.
The matching provisions in the OECD Export Credit Arrangement were also introduced by the Panel in *Korea – Commercial Vessels*, Panel Report, *Korea – Measures Affecting Trade in Commercial Vessels*, WT/DS273/R, adopted 11 April 2005, when responding to the charge by the European Communities that Korea could not claim reliance on the 'matching' provisions, which would allow the Korean Export-Import Bank or KEXIM to finance at below cost, although ultimately the Panel did not rule on the issue of matching, at paras. 7.105 and 7.106, with reliance on *Canada –Aircraft Credits and Guarantees*, above n. 285, para. 7.180.

From the limited amount of delegated rule-making, that has thus far taken place at the WTO, we can conclude that this is moving at different speeds depending on the subject matter and coverage of Members' existing domestic regulation and the extent to which an individual Member's regulatory measures in the fields of environmental and consumer protection, health and safety standards, technical standards and intellectual property protection are coming under challenge at the WTO. Such delegated rule-making as exists has been exercised by the body (or subsidiary body) established under the relevant Agreement, on the basis of an express or an implied power.

A large portion of subsidiary rule-making is related to the internal legal order of the organisation and the WTO is no exception. These rules are established by the Members in WTO bodies and they pertain to the WTO' s internal function, as for example with respect to rules for the establishment of WTO subsidiary bodies, rules of procedure for those bodies, the WTO *Financial Rules* and *Final Regulations* and the WTO *Staff Rules*, *Staff Rules* and *Staff Administrative Memoranda*.

Some subsidiary rules while internal in origin have external effect in order to comply with obligations that the organisation owes to other actors in the international community. This could be on the basis of the recognition of privileges and immunities of the WTO to its staff and, where relevant, diplomatic privileges and immunities. Separately, certain internal rules and procedures are necessary in order that the WTO may fulfil its international obligations with respect to other intergovernmental organisations, including the UN, in particular with respect to the depository function of the Director-General.

There is also some limited scope for subsidiary rule-making by adjudicative bodies in the WTO dispute settlement in the matter of the development of procedural rules, particularly as a response to the need to fill the gap left by the lack of adequate procedural rules in the *DSU* and the absence of rules on evidence and proof. A more interesting development is the creation by the Appellate Body (and to a lesser extent the panels) of new rules and standards during the ordinary course of dispute settlement, particularly with the development of a more principled jurisprudence in balancing the normative interaction between WTO rules and domestic regulation with the development of a standard of judicial review.

When it comes to rule-referencing the matter is somewhat different. The incorporation of rules and (international) standards by reference to another treaty or their formulation and adoption in a formal or informal institutional body, like the *Codex Alimentarius Commission* or the *ISO*, may potentially have the effect of normatively transforming what were non-binding of soft law norms into norms that are binding on Members by virtue of the referencing process in the basic WTO treaty rule. However, as we have seen from the rulings of the Appellate Body in *EC – Hormones* and in the *Brazil – Aircraft/Canada – Aircraft* cases the process of rule referencing does not necessarily turn non-binding norms or soft law into rules that are legally binding on the Members.

In summary, it can be stated that while some subsidiary rule-making does take place in the WTO it is insufficiently developed. It is also somewhat contradictory as to its legal force and effects, as for example is the case with delegated rule-making. Consequently, it is also premature at this stage to be able to draw any real conclusions as to the effects that subsidiary rule-making may have on normative developments in the WTO.

CONCLUSIONS

Since the WTO came into existence in 1995 it has established itself as the preeminent international institution for the reciprocal reduction of tariffs and the opening up of domestic markets to foreign services and service suppliers, the removal of non-tariff and other regulatory barriers and the administration and enforcement of a common set of trading rules designed to enhance peace, prosperity and economic welfare in the international community. At the same time its constituent instrument establishes an international organisation for the governance of world trade although, as we noted at the outset of this study, the WTO has become better known for its role as an enforcer of trade rules than as an international organisation. The purpose of this study, as set out in the introductory chapter of this book, has been to conduct an analysis of the institutional and normative bases of the WTO in the hope of reaching a better understanding of its governance structure and functioning, without which only a partial and incomplete assessment can be made of the institutional and normative challenges the organisation faces.

The concluding remarks presented here bring the findings and conclusions in the preceding chapters together in addressing the twin propositions set out in the introductory chapter with respect to institutional and normative developments in the WTO. First, the WTO is incapable of fulfilling a proper institutional role and becoming a pillar for global economic governance as long as its individual Members continue to shape the organisation to their own ends through a variety of informal arrangements and established practices. Second, the rigidity of the WTO's amending provisions coupled with its institutional decision-making processes results in an ineffective exercise of the organisation's rule-making capacity.

Indeed, there is a disparity between the formality of the treaty rules, which arise from the treaty-making process and embody the rights and obligations of the Members coupled with the near impossibility of amending them, and the amount of informal practices and procedures that individual Members continue to pursue in the decision-making and rule-making processes. The prospects for future institutional and normative developments are therefore considered in the light of these two propositions coupled with the peculiar dynamics of the organisation to which the juxtaposition of formal and informal practices and procedures in the WTO give rise.

1 Institutional Developments

The WTO has been created as a specialist functional organisation under international law. The organisation is considered by its Members to be *sui generis* in character, which is a view that stems from its establishment in 1995 when it was decided by the contracting parties to the GATT that the new organisation should be neither a specialised UN agency nor form part of the UN system. It is reinforced by the notion that the WTO itself perpetuates of being a 'member-driven' organisation.[1] This is a concept that is examined by the Consultative Board in *The Sutherland Report*,[2] which is of the view that the WTO needs a convincing and persistent voice, but the *Report* does not consider the issue on its own merits which would mean questioning the status of the WTO as an international organisation with a will of its own, independent of that of its Members. In terms of institutional developments, the combination of this notion of a *sui generis* organisation coupled with the WTO's identity as a 'member-driven' organisation, sets it apart from other international organisations and may over time contribute to the WTO's sense of self-imposed isolation.[3]

The organisation itself is a complex, over-burdened hierarchy of institutional bodies which operates at four different levels (three when the Ministerial Conference is not in session) consisting of over 70 institutional bodies. Within this institutional hierarchy, almost all WTO bodies are open to *all* Members, with just a few bodies of limited composition, such as the Appellate Body. Formally speaking *all* Members can be represented in the remainder of the WTO bodies, which are not of limited composition, and *all* matters are decided upon by the membership as a whole, either by ministers (who meet at least once every two

1 *See* the WTO web-site, at www.wto.org where it is stated: The WTO is 'member-driven', with decisions taken by consensus among all member governments.'

2 *The Future of the WTO – Addressing institutional challenges in the new millennium*, Report of the Director-General's Consultative Board (Geneva: World Trade Organization, 2004) [hereinafter *The Sutherland Report*] 76-77, paras. 359-364.

3 In similar vein, *see* Joost Pauwelyn, 'The Sutherland Report: A Missed Opportunity for Genuine Debate on Trade, Globalization and Reforming the WTO' (2005) 8 *JIEL* 329-346 at 334.

years in the Ministerial Conference) or by their ambassadors or delegates (who meet in the intervening sessions of the Ministerial Conference throughout the year in Geneva). In practice, it is more common for meetings of the second and third level bodies, i.e. General Council and specialised Councils to be well represented, and for those Members most interested in a particular trade matter to be in attendance at meetings of other bodies; some developing country and LDC Member representatives are unable to attend all or even some of the Geneva-based meetings, due to the lack of government representation in Geneva.

While the scope of the organisation is expressly laid down in the *WTO Agreement* in terms of its mandate, which is divided into five main functions, the organisation has arguably expanded the scope of its constituent treaty when Member governments conferred a sixth function on the organisation, in adopting the Doha Ministerial Declaration in November 2001. Henceforth, the WTO also fulfils the function of providing technical assistance and capacity building to developing country Members. In institutional terms, this new function could prove problematic if the WTO were to overreach itself in its fulfilment such that it might become a development agency – a move that is strongly resisted by the majority of the membership.

This particular institutional development raises a number of issues. First, the additional function makes more demands on the WTO in terms of its coordination role with other institutions and agencies in the field of development in the international community and calls for greater policy coherence not only in terms of global economic policy-making (a function which the WTO exercises with the IMF and the World Bank on the basis of Article III:5 *WTO Agreement*) but also in the field of development policy. Second, there is a danger of the WTO's scope and mandate creeping into the functions of other institutions and agencies, especially the World Bank and UNDP. The situation is not unthinkable given a similar development, which has occurred in the past in the international economy. The IMF has stood accused of 'mission creep' in fulfilling its functions with respect to international cooperation and crisis management through various extended loan facilities and the establishment of economic development goals, which potentially encroach on the functions of the World Bank and other agencies.

The primary function of the WTO is to act as an (ongoing) forum for negotiations among its Members and to exercise executive, legislative and (quasi-) adjudicative powers through its constituent bodies in order to implement and administer the results of those negotiations. All three functions are overwhelmingly political in character, given the fact that it is Member governments which are represented in those bodies exercising such powers.

The majority of institutional bodies in the WTO are involved in the implementation and administration, or oversight, of existing Multilateral Trade Agreements, through the Councils and Committees structure, which since they are all bodies of the whole give rise to potential mass management of the organisation's activities by and for the Members. Unlike some other international economic organisations such as the World Bank and the IMF, the WTO does not have an executive body of limited membership, which is functionally separate from a plenary body that could retain a 'legislative oversight' function.

The *Sutherland Report*[4] does recommend an executive body for the WTO but takes a different approach. It merely recommends a 'senior level consultative body', along the lines of the Consultative Group of Eighteen (CG18) in the GATT, without any executive or negotiating powers and as 'an alternative approach' to senior government policy makers from capitals being in Geneva more often. There is an underlying assumption on the part of the Consultative Board that in making this recommendation what worked for the GATT will work for the WTO but times have changed. While there is both formal and informal continuity between the GATT and the WTO trade regimes in institutional and normative terms, the idea of 'institutionalising' the major interests norm in this manner while seemingly informal in character, is likely to be fraught with debate as to which Members should be invited to such a forum. Put differently, it might raise the issue of whether invitations to attend this forum or indeed any other consultative process, as for example with small group or limited access meetings (formally 'green room' meetings), should have a 'critical mass' character in order to link them to consensus-building efforts, which surround the consensus decision-making process, or should be based on some other criteria, such as equitable geographical distribution or EGD representation,[5] as exist in other international institutions.

The Director-General, elected by the Members, heads the organisation and is assisted by a Secretariat, which fulfils a support role for the membership in this Member-driven' organisation. Although there is now a legal basis for the Director-General and the Secretariat in the *WTO Agreement* their powers and duties are not specifically regulated nor do they enjoy a right of initiative in making proposals to the membership for legislative or executive action. There are further consequences for institutional developments in the WTO that are related to the foregoing since the Director-General is not considered by the Members as fulfilling a leadership role nor can the Secretariat, despite the wealth of knowledge and expertise that resides in its professional staff, make any formal contribution to policy-making or policy-co-ordination in the organisation. Nevertheless, as was noted in Chapter III, while neither the Director-General nor the staff of the Secret-

4 *The Sutherland Report*, above n. 2, 70, paras. 323-327.
5 *The Sutherland Report*, *ibid*, 72, para. 335.

ariat enjoy any formal right of initiative in WTO decision-making they do from time to time act informally in launching initiatives and tabling proposals for the membership to consider, as well as advising Members on trade matters. It is also not uncommon for the Director-General to be party to informal consultations among Members (sometimes together with the Chair of the General Council or one of the specialised Councils) and to play a role in steering the discussions that take place.

The Sutherland Report[6] recommends enhancing the role of the Director-General, beginning with the adoption by the Ministerial Conference of regulations setting out the powers, duties, conditions and terms of office of the Director-General, which could include, as the *Report* suggests, specific provision for the Director-General to chair the General Council meetings, and which could establish that person's duties with respect to management of the Secretariat. In terms of institutional developments, this would not only clarify the position of the Director-General, as head of the organisation, internally vis-à-vis the Members and externally vis-à-vis the international community but also institutionalise the role of the WTO Director General – a move that would be entirely in keeping with its institutional character and that of other international organisations in the international community.

The legislative or rule-making function, the exercise of which forms part of the normative analysis of the WTO and normative developments within the organisation, is exercised by the membership collectively primarily through the MTN process and is implicit in the WTO's function as a forum for negotiations and as a framework for implementation of those negotiations. The exercise of legislative power, initiated by the Members and responding to the need to elaborate further treaty rules between the MTN rounds, is implicit in the *WTO Agreement*, while express provision is made in some Multilateral Trade Agreements for negotiating rights and obligations pertaining to certain subject-matter, on the basis of 'built-in agenda' items left over from the Uruguay Round MTN, and on which Members need to continue negotiating. The only constitutional limits that are placed on the exercise of this legislative competence in the WTO is by the Members themselves in the context of a Ministerial Meeting where they may determine on the basis of 'explicit' consensus not to proceed with a negotiating mandate, as happened with respect to three of the four Singapore Issues at the Cancún Ministerial Meeting in September 2003.

The (quasi-)adjudicative function is exercised by the Dispute Settlement Body or DSB, together with the panels and the Appellate Body, which are in turn

6 *The Sutherland Report*, *ibid*, 73-76, paras. 342-356, especially at 73-74, paras. 342-347.

responsible to the DSB. In a rare instance of a WTO body being granted a specific rather than a general executive function, the DSB is charged with administering the dispute settlement system on the basis of Article 2.1 *DSU*. Additionally, it is tasked on the basis of the *DSU*, with the surveillance and monitoring of Members' compliance with recommendations and rulings of panels and the Appellate Body and can order the suspension of concessions as retaliation in the event of non-compliance. The adjudicative function proper, i.e. clarification and interpretation of WTO rules, falls to *ad hoc* panels and the Appellate Body, the mandate, composition and functioning of which is set out in the *DSU*. Neither of these adjudicative bodies enjoy inherent powers that are normally found with respect to an arbitral or judicial body in international law, i.e. the inherent power to determine their own jurisdiction and to establish their own rules and procedures as necessary for the proper exercise of their judicial functions.

The institutional bodies under the *DSU* are only open to States and the European Communities as Members of the WTO. No non-Member (including an acceding country) or individual has standing to bring a complaint, nor to take part in the proceedings as is clear from the first constitutional crisis to arise in the WTO involving the procedure, which was instigated by the Appellate Body in *EC – Asbestos* in order to receive *amicus curiae* briefs, and which was challenged by the Members in an extraordinary meeting of the General Council. Moreover, the fact that other institutional bodies involved in rule implementation may undertake a review of a Members' actions, following the receipt of a complaint by another Member, for example with respect to the continued maintenance of balance-of-payments restrictions, does not exclude the possibility of a Member seeking the establishment of a panel to hear the same complaint – a situation that has already led to a challenge concerning a breach of the principle of institutional balance in the WTO.

From an institutional standpoint, it is clear that while the WTO may not be *sui generis* in character, its adjudicative function, with its curious mix of quasi-judicial and judicial functions is somewhat unusual in the law of international institutions. Its importance in developing principles, rules and standards in WTO law is already of inestimable value and has established it as a successful example of institutionalised dispute settlement within an international organisation.

An understanding of the practice of the members with respect to institutional developments is critical before any suggestions for institutional reform can be pursued. From reading the WTO as an international regime we can conclude that the WTO is a dynamic organisation that draws on the practices and procedures of the former GATT trade regime and sustains the underlying norms of that regime.

In institutional terms the WTO marks the institutionalisation of a number of *ad hoc* arrangements that existed under the former GATT. This includes the norm of multilateralism, which is articulated through the practice of collective decision-making in the WTO whereby potentially every institutional body is a body of the whole and has actually been reinforced and made more coherent through its institutionalisation in the WTO, beginning with the Members' continued adherence to meetings of Ministers in its highest decision-making body, the Ministerial Conference and the regular meetings of second, third and fourth level bodies. The general rule on consensus decision-making, which has been institutionalised in Article IX:1 *WTO Agreement*, and forms part of the GATT *acquis*, is applied collectively by the Members in every institutional body for every type of decision, even when not required, thereby further completing the formalisation of the norm of multilateralism.

By contrast, the major interests' norm, which was present in the GATT trade regime, has manifested itself in a renewed commitment to the club-model of decision-making, i.e. the means of facilitating cooperation among a smaller group of Members, usually focused on achieving consensus on single issues. This has occurred by means of a myriad of informal practices that sustain the use of the club model even in the face of its critics, especially such consultative procedures as the small room or green room meetings, which are seen as lacking transparency and legitimacy but mostly by those that are excluded from the process. Many more of these consultative procedures have sprung up since the WTO came into existence in the form of chairpersons, facilitators[7] and 'friends', all of which can bring considerable influence to bear on the process of decision-making since they are considered vital to the process of building consensus around a particular issue, ahead of the adoption of a formal decision in one of the institutional bodies.

However, while the club model works well for trade negotiations, it is proving less effective in dealing with the complexity of normative and procedural issues that arise from the WTO's burgeoning agenda, especially with respect to the increasing number of 'linkage' issues, such as trade and environment, trade and intellectual property protection, trade and health and safety. As we noted in chapter III, the use of consensus decision-making sustains the continuance of the major interests' norm because it favours majority interests in a less obtrusive way than weighted voting by giving procedural significance to parity of interest among the individual Members rather than having to take equality of voting power of Members into account.

7 *The Sutherland Report*, *ibid*, 72, para. 331, indirectly recognises the role of facilitators in order bring about consensus on negotiating single issue items on the agenda at a Ministerial Conference.

The practice and procedure of consensus decision-making in the WTO is essentially one of non-objection but by its very nature the veto aspect of the consensus rule, as applied in WTO decision-making, means that it can be used to obstruct the adoption of decisions and lead to a paralysis of action.[8] One proposal has been to introduce a critical mass approach into consensus decision-making, whereby Members agree to refrain from blocking consensus in the event that a critical number of them support the decision. *The Sutherland Report* comes up with a variation on this whereby a Member which is considering a blocking measure which otherwise has the broad support of the membership should have to declare in writing, with reasons included, that the matter is of national interest.[9]

Another suggestion that is often heard is to 'reintroduce' voting, or more specifically the threat of voting, where consensus cannot be reached, especially for those decisions where provision is made in the *WTO Agreement* for simple majority voting but more particularly for those certain decisions where qualified majority voting is called for, as with decisions on accessions and waivers. The proposal overlooks an important aspect of the consensus rule and that is that it has become institutionalised in the WTO and is part of the culture of the organisation, to the extent that there are Members prepared to defend its continued use, even if they are openly critical of the process. It is considered by many Members to be against the informal rules of the club to push for voting and this brings us to the next conclusion.

Another drawback is the source of the threat itself. In the case of the IMF and the World Bank weighted voting (or the threat of voting) favours those developed countries that are the largest contributors and can easily outvote the developing countries. The situation is reversed in the WTO where the developing countries can easily outvote the rest simply on the basis of the equality of voting power and so adherence to the consensus principle is very much in the interests of certain key developed country Members.

However, all of these proposals have their merits in terms of improvements to the consensus decision-making process, which could reflect positively on the governance of the organisation. While there may be doubts as to viability of any of them as a means of resolving the 'veto' problem of the consensus principle, the Members should at least consider them even if at the end of the day, consensus decision-making, for all its evils, remains exactly the way it is.

These institutional developments would suggest that the WTO does not sufficiently fulfil the role of an international organisation, with a will of its own

8 Gary Clyde Hufbauer, 'Inconsistency between Diagnosis and Treatment' (2005) 8 *JWT* 291-297, at 295.

9 *The Sutherland Report*, above n. 2, 63-65, paras. 280-290.

and identity separate from that of its Members. Moreover, the self-styled 'Member-driven' character of the organisation demonstrates that Members are continuing to shape the organisation to their own ends and will probably do so into the foreseeable future. While *The Sutherland Report* has highlighted a number of institutional challenges that the WTO faces, it was commissioned by the Director-General, on his own initiative, and not the Members but this should not detract form its significance in providing a valuable source of recommendations for the Members to take note of and to consider implementing in practice.

2 Normative Developments

The WTO also owes much of its dynamic normative character to the previous GATT trade regime and an analysis of the prevailing norms under that latter regime leads to the following conclusions. The number and range of normative developments that have taken place as a result of the Uruguay Round MTN are significant. There has been a vast increase in primary treaty rules that are taken up in the *WTO Agreement*, the annexed Multilateral Trade Agreements and the Schedules that collectively represent the rights and obligations of the Members, as negotiated during the Uruguay Round.

The scope and coverage of basic WTO treaty rules has increased in respect of the sheer amount of treaty-making that has taken place but also in respect of the types of norms that have been created. Whereas the GATT trade regime was characterised by a process of negative integration which focused on the progressive reduction of tariffs and the complimentary goal of non-discriminatory international trade, the WTO represents a move to a system of positive integration whereby Members must undertake to legislate and enforce measures relating to technical standards, health and safety standards and intellectual property rights, the goal being to harmonise such standards among Members. A further feature of those particular Multilateral Agreements such as the *SPS Agreement,* the *TBT Agreement* and the *TRIPs Agreement*, which embody positive prescription rules, is that they are institutionally embedded in a broader network of norms and institutions since those Agreements incorporate by reference, secondary rules and standards laid down in other treaty instruments or developed by other institutional bodies, outside of the WTO. This may see the Members being faced with a greater number of regulatory issues, as a result of the interface of trade with rules and standards emanating from international rule-making and standard-setting bodies extraneous to the WTO, and which may be a sign of the further encroachment of international rule-making on policy areas that have traditionally been considered to form part of the *domain reservé* of Members.

As far as most Members are concerned the MTN process is still the main forum for negotiating new rights and obligations, which is reinforced by the notion left over from the Uruguay Round of the 'single undertaking', whereby *all* the Members are bound by *all* of the Agreements. The concept of the single undertaking appears to have entered the collective psyche of the organisation and is stymieing efforts to the organisation in a new direction, including the possibility of adopting new plurilateral trade agreements to which some but not all Members are parties, for regulation of trade linkage issues such as trade and investment or trade and competition, as the failure of the Fifth Meeting of the Ministerial Conference in Cancún demonstrates.

The *WTO Agreement* and its annexed Multilateral Trade Agreements appear as difficult to amend as the former GATT. The overall conclusion that arises from an analysis of the practice of amendment of WTO rules reveals that Article X *WTO Agreement*, while it contains a number of provisions designed to revise or modify existing WTO provisions, all of which meet the criteria that are generally accepted for the amendment of multilateral treaties on the basis of the *VCLT*, the practice of the Members deviates considerably. The problem with Article X is related to the ordinary process of decision-making at work in the WTO, which is dominated by consensus, whereas nearly all the amending clauses in Article X call for voting majorities with respect to the adoption of the decision on amendment and for certain majorities to apply for the acceptance, i.e. consent to be bound, and entry into force of a particular amendment. Seen in this light Members have resorted to other means to effect modifications and revisions that are less onerous but perhaps less satisfactory. Some of those means include modifications to existing obligations through the temporary suspension of the operation such as the general waiver decision, on the basis of Article IX:3 and 4 *WTO Agreement*, or the adoption of decisions of an interpretative character ('authoritative' interpretation by means of an ordinary decision), which amounts to a *de facto* amendment of an WTO obligation without using the amendment clauses of Article X *WTO Agreement*.

Other conclusions that are derived from the analysis reveal that the power of authoritative interpretation has never been used by the Members, despite being proposed on more than one occasion but instead members have reverted to adopting decisions by consensus that 'interpret' WTO obligations. The reasons for failure to adopt an authoritative interpretation arise from the fact that a qualified majority vote is called for on the basis of Article IX:2 *WTO Agreement* and the warning against using this as a disguised means of amendment, the latter calls for the ordinary voting majorities and majorities for acceptance and entry into force that are not present in an authoritative interpretation decision.

Members also continue to apply certain practices for revision or modification of primary treaty obligations that are not regulated in Article X *WTO Agreement* and have their origin in GATT practice. One is the modification of primary treaty rules by supplementing them, following the conclusion of negotiations in order to improve levels of liberalisation in the case of services commitments under the *GATS*, as was done by the contracting parties under the GATT 1947 with respect to supplemental tariff concessions. Another is the continued practice of modification, rectification and certification of Schedules of Tariff Concessions and Services Schedules following re-negotiation by individual Members of tariff concessions on the basis of Article XXVIII *GATT 1994*, or services commitments on the basis of Article XXI *GATS*.

A further practice is the process of accession to the WTO, as a new Member of the organisation, which from a normative point of view brings in an additional party to the underlying multilateral treaty. Article XII:2 *WTO Agreement* contains no formal criteria for a State seeking accession to the WTO but instead the whole process of accession is one of extended negotiations between the acceding country and individual Members. These negotiations are conducted within the framework of an elaborate set of non-binding or 'soft' law instruments, which are largely procedural in character and of a non-binding character, but which provide the Members with considerable flexibility concerning the terms and conditions that can be set for the accession of new countries to the WTO.

These normative developments suggest that while the entry into force of the WTO has led to the establishment of a code of conduct for world trade, as a result of the Uruguay Round MTN, and a more sophisticated normative framework for the Members to operate in, it does not necessarily bring with it a stricter adherence to formal treaty-making processes, in particular the application of the existing rules on revision and modification of primary treaty rules as set out in Article X *WTO Agreement*. Instead, the Members have devised a number of practical means of by-passing the existing rules in favour of informal procedures and practices.

As long as there is no major reform of the decision-making process, and even if there were and consensus were to be introduced as the formal means of adopting decisions on amendment, instead of voting as required for many of the Article X amendment clauses, the possibility still exists for a Member to block the process by vetoing the proposed amendment, as we have observed with efforts in the *DSU* review process, where the consensus principle can be applied to amend the *DSU*, but Members have still not managed to agree on which amendments should be taken forward.

While there would appear to be some scope for the development of subsidiary rule-making by institutional bodies on the based of the conferral of delegated powers, either explicitly or implicitly, this has been very limited so far and Members have been cautious about endorsing a process that could lead to legally binding rules. As is the case with many other international organisations,[10] there is no inherent legislative authority for WTO bodies to create rules that are directly binding on States, not even as Members of the organisation and the WTO is no exception. Even so, where subsidiary rule-making does take place, it is driven by the consensus process that is used in the various institutional bodies and which can effectively be used to block the adoption of a decision that might have normative effect, i.e. be binding on the Members

These normative developments suggest that future prospects for further rule-making, including the results of the Doha Development Round at such time as they may be concluded, are limited. In particular our analysis demonstrates that the rigidity of the WTO's secondary treaty rules on amendment coupled with the institutional decision-making processes are such as to render the revision and amendment of primary treaty rules difficult or impossible to achieve for the foreseeable future and therefore the Members will continue to follow established practice under the prevailing treaty, which is dominated by informality and consensus decision-making, in order to regulate the matter. In this respect the *WTO Agreement* and its annexed Multilateral Treaties can be considered as a 'living' treaty, which can 'generate "secondary" [subsidiary] or "delegated" soft law, that is statements and practice that develop around a treaty to supplement or correct the text',[11] in a manner which is no different from some other framework treaties, as Christine Chinkin has demonstrated in her appraisal of the diversity of soft law forms and their application in the international legal order.

10 Paul Szasz, 'General Law-making Processes' in Christopher C. Joyner, *The United Nations and International Law* (Cambridge: American Society of International Law/ Cambridge University Press, 1997) 27-64 at 58.

11 Christine Chinkin, 'Normative Developments in the International Legal System' in Dinah Shelton (ed.) *Commitment and Compliance, the Role of Non-Binding Norms in the International Legal System* (Oxford: Oxford University Press, 2000) 21-42.

BIBLIOGRAPHY

1 Books and Monographs

1.1 International Law and International Relations: General Works

Alexandrowicz, Charles H., *The Law-Making Functions of the Specialised Agencies of the United Nations* (Sydney: Angus & Robertson in association with the Australian Institute of International Affairs, 1973)

Amerasinghe, C.F., *Principles of the institutional law of international organizations*, (Cambridge: Cambridge University Press, 1995)

Arend, Anthony C., *Legal Rules and International Society* (New York, Oxford: Oxford University Press, 1999)

Aust, Anthony, *Modern Treaty Law and Practice* (Cambridge: Cambridge University Press, 2000)

Bekker, Peter H.F., *The Legal Position of Intergovernmental Organizations: A Functional Necessity Analysis of Their Legal Status and Immunities* (Dordrecht/Boston/London: Martinus Nijhoff Publishers, 1994)

Birnie, Patricia and Alan Boyle, *International Law & the Environment*, 2nd edition (Oxford: Oxford University Press, 2002)

Blix, Hans and Emerson, Jirina H. (ed.), *The Treaty Maker's Handbook* (Dobbs Ferry, N.Y: Oceana Publications, Inc./Stockholm: Almqvist & Wiksell, 1973)

Blokker, Niels M. and Schermers, Henry G. (eds.), *Proliferation of International Organizations: Legal Issues* (The Hague, Kluwer Publishing, 2001)

Brownlie, Ian, *Principles of Public International Law* 6th edition (Oxford University Press, 2002)

Brownlie, Ian, *The Rule of Law in International Affairs: International Law at the Fiftieth Anniversary of the United Nations* (The Hague: Martinus Nijhoff, 1998)

Buergenthal, Thomas, *Law-Making in the International Civil Aviation Organization* (Syracuse, NY: Syracuse University Press, 1969)

Cassese, Antonio, *International Law* 2nd revised edition (Oxford: Oxford University Press, 2004)

Chayes, Abram and Antonia Handler Chayes, *The New Sovereignty: Compliance with International Agreements* (Cambridge, MA: Harvard University Press, 1995)

Coicaud, Jean-Marc and Heiskanen, Veijo (eds.), *The legitimacy of international organizations* (Tokyo: The United Nations University Press, 2001)

Cox, Robert W. and Jacobsen, Harold K., *The Anatomy of Influence – Decision Making in International Organization* (New Haven: Yale University Press, 1973)

Crawford, Richard M.A., *Regime Theory in the Post-Cold War World* (Aldershot: Dartmouth Publishing Co. Ltd, 1996)

Danilenko, Gennady M., *Law-making in the international community* (Dordrecht: Nijhoff, 1993)

Economides, Constantin P., *Le pouvoir des décisions de organisations internationales européenes* (Leiden: Sythoff, 1964)

Eeckhout, Piet, *The External Relations of the European Union* (Oxford: Oxford University Press, 2004)

Fawcett, James, *Law and Power in International Relations* (London: Faber and Faber, 1982)

Friedmann, Wolfgang, *The Changing Structure of International Law* (New York: Columbia University Press, 1964)

Hart, H.L.A., *The Concept of Law* 2nd edition (Oxford: Clarendon Law Series, 1994)

Holloway, Kaye, *Modern Trends in Treaty Law: Constitutional Law, Reservations and the Three Modes of Legislation* (London: Stevens & Sons/Dobbs Ferry, NY: Oceana Publications, 1967)

Jenks, C. Wilfred, *The proper law of international organisations* (London: Stevens/ Dobbs Ferry, NY: Oceana, 1962)

Keohane, Robert O. and Nye, Joseph S., *Power and Interdependence: World Politics in Transition* (Boston: Little Brown, 1977)

Klabbers, Jan, *An Introduction to International Institutional Law* (Cambridge: Cambridge University Press, 2002)

Krasner, Stephen D. (ed.), *International Regimes* (Ithaca: Cornell University Press, 1983)

Sabel, Robbie, *Procedure at International Conferences: A study of the rules of procedure of conferences and assemblies of international inter-governmental organizations* (Cambridge: Cambridge University Press, 1997)

Sands, Philippe and Klein, Pierre, *Bowett's Law of International Institutions* (London: Sweet & Maxwell, 2001)

Sarooshi, Danesh, *The United Nations and the Development of Collective Security* (Oxford: Oxford University Press, 1999)

Schachter, Oscar, *International Law in Theory and Practice* (The Hague: Martinus Nijhoff, 1991)

Schermers, Henry G. & Blokker, Niels M., *International Institutional Law: Unity within diversity*, 4th revised edition (Boston, Leiden: Martinus Nijhoff Publishers: 2003)

Schwarzenberger, Georg, *A Manual of International Law* 5th edition (London: Stevens & Sons Ltd., 1967)

Simma, Bruno (ed.), *The Charter of the United Nations: A Commentary* 2nd edition (Oxford: Oxford University Press, 2002)

Simon, Herbert A., *The Science of the Artificial* 3rd edition (Cambridge, MA., MIT Press, 1996)

Sinclair, Ian, *The Vienna Convention on the Law of Treaties* 2nd edition (Manchester: Manchester University Press, 1984)

Singer, J. David, *Financing International Organizations: The UN Budget Process* (The Hague: Nijhoff Publishers, 1961)

Szasz, Paul C. and Brown Weiss, Edith, *Selected essays on understanding international institutions and the legislative process* (Ardsley NY: Transnational Publishers, 2001)

Toth, A., *Oxford Encyclopedia of European Community Law*, Vol. I – Institutional Law (Oxford: Oxford University Press, 1990)

Triggs, Gillian D., *The Antarctic Treaty regime: law, environment and resources* (Cambridge: Cambridge University Press, 1989)

Young, Oran R., *International Governance: Protecting the Environment in a Stateless Society* (Ithaca NY: Cornell University Press, 1994)

1.2 International Economic Law, GATT/WTO and International Trade Law: General Works, including Reference Works

Analytical Index: Guide to GATT Law and Practice, GATT/LEG/2, 6th edition (Geneva, GATT Secretariat, 1994)

OMC/WTO Rules of Procedure for Meetings of WTO Bodies (Geneva: WTO Secretariat, July 1997)

WTO Analytical Index: Guide to WTO Law and Practice (Geneva: WTO Secretariat/Bernan, 2003)

WTO Appellate Body Repertory of Reports and Awards, 1995-2004 (Cambridge: Cambridge University Press, 2005)

Benedek, Wolfgang, *Die Rechtsordnung des GATT aus völkerrechtlicher Sicht* (Berlin: Springer-Verlag, 1990)

Bossche, Van den, Peter, *The Law and Policy of the World Trade Organization: Text, Cases and Materials* (Cambridge: Cambridge University Press, 2005)

Braithwaite, John and Drahos, Peter, *Global Business Regulation* (Cambridge: Cambridge University Press, 2000)

Cornes, Richard and Saddler, Todd, *The Theory of Externalities, Public Goods and Club Goods* 2nd edition (Cambridge: Cambridge University Press, 1996)

Curzon, Gerard, *Multilateral Commercial Diplomacy: The General Agreement on Tariffs and Trade and its Impact on National Commercial Policy and Techniques* (London: Michael Joseph, 1965)

Dam, Kenneth W., *The GATT: Law and International Economic Organization* (Chicago: University of Chicago Press, 1970)

Gardner, Richard N., *Sterling-Dollar Diplomacy in Current Perspective* (New York: Columbia University Press, 1980)

Goode, Walter, *Dictionary of Trade Policy Terms* 4th edition (Cambridge: Cambridge University Press, 2003)

Gorlin, Jacques J., *An Analysis of the Pharmaceutical-related Provisions of the WTO TRIPs (Intellectual Property) Agreement* (London: Intellectual Property Institute, 1999)

Hoda, Anwarul, *Tariff Negotiations and Renegotiations under the GATT and the WTO: Procedures and Practices* (Cambridge: Cambridge University Press, 2001),

Hoekman, Bernard M. and Kostecki, Michel M., *The Political Economy of the World Trading System* 2nd edition (Oxford: Oxford University Press, 2001)

Hossain, Kamal, *Legal Aspects of the New International Economic Order* (London: Pinter Publishers, 1980)

Hudec, Robert E, *Essays on the Nature of International Trade Law* (London: Cameron May, 1999)

Hudec, Robert E., *The GATT Legal System and World Trade Diplomacy* 2nd edition (Salem, NH: Butterworths Legal Publishers, 1990)

Jackson, John H., *World Trade and the Law of GATT* (Charlottesville, VA: The Mitchie Company [The Bobbs-Merrill Company, Inc.] 1969)

Jackson, John H., *The World Trading System: Law and Policy of International Economic Relations* 2nd edition (Cambridge, MA.: The MIT Press, 1997)

Jackson, John H., *The World Trade Organization: Constitution and Jurisprudence* (London: The Royal Institute for International Affairs/Pinter Publishers, 1998)

Kostecki, Michel M., *East-West Trade and the GATT System* (London: Macmillan Press for the Trade Policy Research Centre, 1979)

Lawrence, Robert Z., Bressand, Albert and Ito, Takatoshi, *A Vision for the World Economy: Openness, Diversity and Cohesion* (Washington DC: The Brookings Institution, 1996)

Long, Olivier, *Law and its Limitations in the GATT Multilateral Trading System* (London: Graham & Trotman/Martinus Nijhoff, 1987)

Lowenfeld, Andreas, *International Economic Law* (Oxford: Oxford University Press, 2002)

Meerhaeghe, Van, M.A.G., *International Economic Institutions*, 5th revised edition (Dordrecht: Kluwer Academic Publishers, 1987)

Pauwelyn, Joost, *Conflict of Norms in Public International Law: How WTO Law Relates to Other Rules of International Law* (Cambridge: Cambridge University Press, 2003)

Qureshi, Asif H. *The World Trade Organisation: Implementing International Trade Norms* (Manchester: Manchester University Press, 1996)

Shihata, Ibrahim F.I., *The World Bank in a changing world: selected essays* (The Hague: Nijhoff, 1991)

Steger, Debra, *Peace through Trade: Building the World Trade Organization* (London: Cameron May, 2004)

Verloren van Themaat, Pieter, *The Changing Structure of International Economic Law: a contribution of legal history, of comparative law and of general legal theory to the debate on a new international economic order* (The Hague: T.M.C. Asser Institute/Martinus Nijhoff, 1981)

Wilcox, Clair, *A Charter for World Trade* (New York: The Macmillan Co., 1949)

Xu, Yi-chong and Weller, Patrick, *The Governance of World Trade: International Civil Servants and the GATT/WTO* (Cheltenham: Edward Elgar, 2004)

2 Journal Articles

Abeyratne, R.I.R., 'Law Making and Decision Making Powers of the ICAO Council – a Critical Analysis' (1992) 41 *Zeitschrift fuer Luft- und Weltraumrecht*, 387-394

Alvarez, José E., 'The WTO as Linkage Machine' (2002) 96 *American Journal of International Law*, 146-158

Anderson, David H., 'Law-Making Process in the UN System' (1998) *Max Planck Yearbook of United Nations Law,* 23-50

Barnett, Michael N. and Finnemore, Martha, 'The Politics, Power and Pathologies of International Organizations' (1999) 53 *International Organization*, 699-732

Bartels, Lorand, 'The Separation of Powers in the WTO: How to Avoid Judicial Activism' (2004) 53 *International and Comparative Law Quarterly*, 861-895

Blackhurst, Richard and Hartridge, David, 'Improving the Capacity of WTO Institutions to Fulfil their Mandate' (2004) 7 *Journal of International Economic Law*, 705-716

Blay, S.K.N., 'New trends in the protection of the Antarctic environment: the 1991 Madrid Protocol' (1992) 86 *American Journal of International Law*, 377-399

Bogdandy, von, Armin, 'Law and Politics in the WTO – Strategies to Cope with a Deficient Relationship' (2001) 5 *Max Planck Yearbook of United Nations Law*, 609-674

Brölmann, Catherine, 'A Flat Earth? International Organizations in the System of International Law' (2001) 70 *Nordic Journal of International Law*, 319-340

Bronckers, Marco C.E.J., 'More Power to the WTO?' (2001) 4 *Journal of International Economic Law*, 41-65

Brunnée, Jutta, 'COPing with Consent: Law-Making Under Multilateral Environmental Agreements' (2002) 15 *Leiden Journal of International Law*, 1-52

Buzan, Barry, 'Negotiating by Consensus: Developments in Technique at the United Nations Conference on the Law of the Sea' (1981) 75 *American Journal of International Law*, 324-348

Cassese, Antonio, 'Consensus and Some of its Pitfalls' (1975) 58 *Revista di diritto internazionale*, 754-761

Charney, Jonathan, 'United States interests in a Convention on the Law of the Sea: the case for continued efforts' (1978-79) 11 *Vanderbilt Journal of Transnational Law*, 39-75

Charnovitz, Steve, 'The Legal Status of the Doha Declarations' (2002) 5 *Journal of International Economic Law*, 207-211

Charpentier, J., 'La procédure de non-objection (À propos d'une crise constitutionelle de l'ONU)' (1966) 70 *Revue Générale de Droit International Public*, 862-877

Churchill, Robin R. and Ulfstein, Geir, 'Autonomous Institutional Arrangements in Multilateral Environmental Agreements: A Little-Noticed Phenomenon in International Law' (2009) 94 *American Journal of International Law*, 623 –659

Cottier, Thomas and Takenoshita, Satoko, 'The Balance of Power in WTO Decision-Making: Towards Weighted Voting in Legislative Response' (2003) 59 *Aussenwirtschaft*, 171-214

Decker, Claudia and Mildner, Stormy, 'Wo ware der Wille in Cancún: der Fehlschlag der WTO-Ministerkonferenz' (2003) 58 *Internationale Politik*, 57-60

Dommen, Caroline, 'Raising Human Rights Concerns in the World Trade Organisation: Actors, Processes and Possible Strategies' (2002) *Human Rights Quarterly,* 1-50

Donnelly, Jack, 'International human rights: a regime analysis' (1986) 40 *International Organization*, 599-642

Drake, William J. and Nicolaïdis, Kalypso, 'Ideas, interests, and institutionalization: "trade in services" and the Uruguay Round' (1992) 46 *International Organization*, 37-100

Dymond, William A. and Hart, Michael M., 'Post-Modern Trade Policy: Reflections on the Challenges to Multilateral Trade Negotiations after Seattle' (2000) 34 *Journal of World Trade*, 21-38

Ehlermann, Claus-Dieter and Ehring, Lothar, 'Decision-making in the World Trade Organization: Is the Consensus Practice of the World Trade Organization Adequate for Making, Revising and Implementing Rules on International Trade?' (2005) 8 *Journal of International Economic Law*, 51-75

Elliott, Richard, 'Canada's New Patent Bill Provides a Basis for Improvement', Comment (2004) 5 *BRIDGES*, 19-20

Ellis, Mark E., 'The New International Economic Order and General Assembly resolutions: the debate over General Assembly resolutions revisited' (1985) 15 *California Western International Law Journal*, 647-670

Evenett, Simon, 'Systemic Research Questions Raised by the Failure of the WTO Ministerial Meeting in Cancún' (2004) 31 *Legal Issues of Economic Integration*, 1-6

Fawcett, J.E.S., 'The Place of Law in an International Organisation' (1960) 36 *British Yearbook of International Law*, 321-342

Fitzmaurice, Sir Gerald, 'The Law and Procedure of the International Court of Justice, 1951-1954: Treaty Interpretation and Other Treaty Points' (1957) 33 *British Yearbook of International Law*, 211-252

Footer, Mary E., 'The Role of Consensus in GATT/WTO Decision-making' (1996-97) 17 *Northwestern Journal of International Law and Business Studies*, 653-680

Footer, Mary E., 'The General Agreement on Trade in Services: Taking Stock and Moving Forward' (2002) 29 *Legal Issues of Economic Integration*, 7-25

Frowein, Jochen Abr., 'The Internal and External Effects of Resolutions by International Organisations' (1989) 49 *Zeitschrift für ausländisches öfffentliches Recht und Völkerrecht*, 778-790

Garcia, Frank J., 'The Universal Declaration at 50 and the Challenge of the Global Markets: Trading Away the Human Rights Principle' (1999) 25 *Brooklyn Journal of International Law* (1999), 51-97

García Bercero, Ignacio, 'Functioning of the WTO System: Elements for Possible Institutional Reform' (2000) 6 *International Trade Law and Regulation*, 103-115

Gautier, Philippe, 'The Reparation for Injuries Case Revisited: The Personality of the European Union' (2000) 4 *Max Planck Yearbook of United Nations Law*, 331-361

Gold, Joseph, 'The "Dispensing" and "Suspending" Powers of International Organizations (1972) XIX *Netherlands International Law Review*, 169-200

Haas, Ernst. B., 'Why Collaborate? Issue-Linkage and International Regimes' (1980) 32 *World Politics*, 357-405

Haas, Peter M., 'Introduction: epistemic communities and international policy coordination' (1992) 46 *International Organization*, 1-35

Hahn, Hugo J., 'Continuity in the Law of International Organisation' (1964) 13 *Österreichische Zeitschrift für öffentliches Recht*, 167-239

Haight, G.W., 'The New International Economic Order and the Charter of Rights and Duties of States' (1975) 9 *The international lawyer*, 591-604

Heiskanen, Veijo, 'The Regulatory Philosophy of International Trade Law' (2004) 38 *Journal of World Trade*, 1-36

Hufbauer, Gary Clyde, 'Inconsistency between Diagnosis and Treatment' (2005) 8 *Journal of International Economic Law,* 291-297

Ismail, Faizel, 'A Development Perspective on the WTO July 2004 General Council Decision' (2005) 8 *Journal of International Economic Law*, 377-404

Jackson, John. H., 'The WTO "Constitution" and Proposed Reforms: Seven "Mantras" Revisited' (2001) 4 *Journal of International Economic Law*, 67-78

Jenks, C.W., 'Some structural dilemmas of world organization', (1973) 3 *Georgia Journal of International and Comparative Law*, 1-17

Klabbers, Jan, 'The *Bustani* case before the ILOAT: constitutionalism in disguise' (2004) 53 *International & Comparative Law Quarterly*, 455-463

Krasner, Stephen D., 'Structural Causes and Regime Consequences: Regimes and Intervening Variables' (1982) 36 *International Organization*, 185-205

Kratochwil, Friedrich V. and Ruggie, John Gerard, 'International organization: a state of the art on the art of the state' (1986) 40 *International Organization*, 753-775

Kuijper, P.J. and E. Paasivirta, 'Further Exploring International Responsibility: The European Community and the ILC's Project on Responsibility of International Organizations' (2004) 1 *International Organizations Law Review*, 111-138

Kunz, Josef L., 'The Danube Regime and the Belgrade Conference' (1949) 43 *American Journal of International Law*, 104-113

Lanoszka, Anna, 'The World Trade Organization Accession Process, Negotiating Participation in a Globalizing Economy' (2001) 35 *Journal of World Trade*, 575-602

MacLean, Robert M., 'The Lessons of Seattle and the Need for WTO Institutional Reform' (2000) 6 *International Trade Law and Regulation*, 1-5

Marceau, Gabrielle, 'Transition from GATT to WTO: A most pragmatic operation' (1995) 29 *Journal of World Trade*, 147-163

Marceau, Gabrielle, 'Les procédures d'accession à l'Organisation mondiale de commerce (OMC)' (1997) *Annuaire canadien de Droit International*, 233-252

Marceau, Gabrielle, 'Rules on Ethics for the New World Trade Organization Dispute Settlement Mechanism' (1998) 32 *Journal of World Trade*, 57-97

McWhinney, E., 'The international law-making process and the new international economic order' (1976) 14 *Canadian Yearbook of International Law*, 57-72

Monnier, P., 'Working Procedures before Panels, the Appellate Body and other Adjudicating Bodies of the WTO' (2002) 1 *Law and Practice of International Courts and Tribunals*, 481-538

More, Patrick M., 'The Decisions Bridging the GATT 1947 and the WTO Agreement' (1996) 90 *American Journal of International Law*, 317-328

Mus, Jan B., 'Conflicts between Treaties in International Law' (1998) 45 *Netherlands International Law Review*, 208-232

Norton Moore, John, 'The Regime of Straits and the Third United Nations Conference on the Law of the Sea' (1980) 74 *American Journal of International Law*, 77-121

Oesch, Matthias, *Standards of Review in WTO Dispute Settlement* (2003) 6 *Journal of International Economic Law*, 635-659

Parenti, Antonio, 'Accession to the World Trade Organisation' (2000) 27 *Legal Issues of Economic Integration*, 141-157

Pauwelyn, Joost, 'Rien ne Va Plus? Distinguishing Domestic Regulation from Market Access in GATT and GATS' (2005) 4 *World Trade Review*, 131-170

Pauwelyn, Joost, 'The Sutherland Report: A Missed Opportunity for Genuine Debate on Trade, Globalization and Reforming the WTO' (2005) 8 *Journal of International Economic Law*, 329-346

Pauwelyn, Joost, 'A Typology of Multilateral Treaty Obligations: Are WTO Obligations Bilateral or Collective in Nature?' (2003) 14 *European Journal of International Law*, 907-951

Pauwelyn, Joost, 'WTO Compassion or Superiority Complex?: What to make of the WTO Waiver for "Conflict Diamonds"' (2003) 24 *Michigan Journal of International Law*, 1177-1207

Pauwelyn, Joost, 'The Role of Public International Law in the WTO: How Far Can We Go?' (2001) 95 *American Journal of International Law*, 535-578

Pauwelyn, Joost, 'Enforcement and Countermeasures in the WTO: rules are rules – towards a more collective approach' (2000) 94 *American Journal of International Law*, 335-347

Pellet, Alain, 'The Normative Dilemma: Will and Consent in International Law-making' (1992) 12 *Australian Yearbook of International Law*, 22-53

Petersmann, Ernst-Ulrich, 'The Transformation of the World Trading System through the 1994 Agreement Establishing the World Trade Organization' for 'Symposium: The World Trade Organization and the European Union' (1995) 6 *European Journal of International Law*, 161-221

Qin, Julia Ya, '"WTO-Plus" Obligations and Their Implications for the World Trade Organization Legal System: An Appraisal of the China Accession Protocol' (2003) 37 *Journal of World Trade*, 483-522

Raustiala, Kal, 'Rethinking the Sovereignty Debate in International Economic Law' (2003) 6 *Journal of International Economic Law*, 841-878

Reenen, W., van, 'Rules of Reference in the New Convention on the Law of the Sea, in particular in connection with the pollution of the sea by oil from tankers' (1982) XIII *Netherlands Yearbook of International Law*, 3-44

Rhodes, Sylvia A., 'The Article 21.5/22 Problem: Clarification Through Bilateral Agreements?' (2000) 3 *Journal of International Economic Law*, 553-558

Rigo Sureda, Andrés, 'Informality and Effectiveness in the Operation of the International Bank for Reconstruction and Development' (2003) 6 *Journal of International Economic Law*, 572-576

Schwelb, Egon, 'The Amending Procedure of Constitutions of International Organizations' (1954) 31 *British Yearbook of International Law*, 49-95

Scott, Karen, 'Institutional Developments within the Antarctic Treaty System' (2003) 52 *International & Comparative Law Quarterly*, 473-487

Seyersted, Finn, 'Objective International Personality of Intergovernmental Organizations' (1964) 34 *Nordisk Tidsskrift for international Ret*, 1-112

Shibata, Akiho, 'International law-making process in the United Nations: comparative analysis of UNCED and UNCLOS III' (1993-1994) 24 *California Western International Law Journal*, 17-53

Skubiszweski, Krzysztof, 'The Elaboration of General Multilateral Conventions and of Non-Contractual Instruments having a Normative Function or Objective, Resolutions of the General Assembly of the United Nations', 'Provisional Report' (1965) 61 *Annuaire de l'Institut de Droit International*, 154-158

Sommer, Julia, 'Environmental law-making by international organisations' (1996) 56 *Zeitschrift fuer auslaendisches oeffentliches Recht und Voelkerrecht*, 628-667

Spamann, Holger, 'Standard of Review for World Trade Organization Panels in Trade Remedy Cases: A Critical Analysis' (2004) 38 *Journal of World Trade*, 509-555

Szasz, Paul, 'Improving the International Legislative Process' (1979) 9 *Georgia Journal of International and Comparative Law*, 519

Trachtman, Joel P., Book Review (2004) 98 *American Journal of International Law*, 855-861 (reviewing Joost Pauwelyn, *Conflict of Norms in Public International Law: How WTO Law Relates to Other Rules of International Law*, Cambridge: Cambridge University Press, 2003)

Trachtman, Joel P. 'The International Economic Law Revolution' (1996) 17 *University of Pennsylvania Journal of International Economic Law*, 33-61

Vierdag, E.W., 'The Time of the "Conclusion" of a Multilateral Treaty: Article 30 of the Vienna Convention on the Law of Treaties and Related Provisions' (1989) 59 *British Yearbook of International Law*, 75-111

Vignes, Claude-Henri, 'Towards the Harmonisation of Health Legislation: The Role of the World Health Organization' (1995) 46 *International Digest of Health Legislation*, 422-427

Wang, Lei, 'Non-Application Issues in the GATT and the WTO' (1994) 28 *Journal of World Trade*, 49-74

Weil, Prosper, 'Towards Relative Normativity in International Law?' (1983) 77 *American Journal of International Law*, 413-442

Weiler, J.H.H., 'The Rule of Lawyers and the Ethos of Diplomats: Reflections on the Internal and External Legitimacy of WTO Dispute Settlement' (2001) 35 *Journal of World Trade*, 191-207

Weiss, Friedl, 'Globalization through WTO Integration: Neither Friend nor Foe' (2003) 30 *Legal Issues of Economic Integration*, 95-102

Wilkinson, Rorden, 'The WTO in Crisis: Exploring the Dimensions of Institutional Inertia' (2001) 33 *Journal of World Trade*, 397-419

Wolfe, Robert, 'Regulatory transparency, developing countries and the WTO' (2003) 2 *World Trade Review*, 157-182

Zamora, Stephen, 'Voting in International Economic Organizations' (1980) 74 *American Journal of International Law*, 566-608

3 Contributions to Collected Works

Abi-Saab, Georges, *Cours général de droit international* (1987) 207 *Receuil des Cours*, 9

Akande, Dapo, 'International Organizations' in Evans, Malcolm (ed.), *International Law* (Oxford: Oxford University Press, 2003), 269-297

Bayne, Nicholas 'International economic organizations – More policy making, less autonomy' in Reinalda, Bob and Verbeek, Bertjan, *Autonomous Policy Making by International Organizations* (London: Routledge, 1998), 195-210

Benedek, Wolfgang, 'Die Konstitutionalisierung der Welthandelsordnung: Kompetenzen und Rechtsordnung der WTO' in *Entschädigung nach bewaffneten Konflikten. Die Konstitutionalisierung der Welthandelsordnung* (Heidelberg: C.F. Müller Verlag, 2003), 283-330

Blackhurst, Richard and Hartridge, David, 'Improving the Capacity of WTO Institutions to Fulfil their Mandate' in Ernst-Ulrich Petersmann (ed.), *Reforming the World Trading System: legitimacy, efficiency and democratic governance* (Oxford: Oxford University Press, 2005), 455-467

Blackhurst, Richard, 'Reforming WTO decision-making: Lessons from Singapore and Seattle' in Deutsch, Klaus Günter and Speyer, Bernhard (eds.), *The World Trade Organization Millennium Round: Freer Trade in the Twenty-first Century* (London: Routledge, 2001), 295-310

Bodansky, Daniel, 'Non Liquet and the Incompleteness of International Law' in Boisson de Chazournes, Laurence and Sands, Philippe (eds.), *International Law, The International Court of Justice and Nuclear Weapons* (Cambridge: Cambridge University Press, 1999), 153-170

Butkeviciene, Jolita, Hayashi, Michiko, Ognivtsev, Victor and Yamaoka, Tokio, 'Terms of WTO Accession' in *WTO Accessions and Development Policies, WTO Accessions and Development Policies*, UNCTAD/DIC/TNCD/11 (New York: United Nations, 2001), UN Sales No. E.02.II.D.19, 230-264

Charnovitz, Steve, 'Judicial Independence in the World Trade Organization' in Boisson de Chazournes, Laurence, Romano, Cesare, and Mackenzie, Ruth, *International Organizations and International Dispute Settlement* (Ardsley NY: Transnational Publishers, Inc., 2002), 212-240

Chinkin, Christine, 'Normative Developments in the International Legal System' in Shelton, Dinah (ed.), *Commitment and Compliance, the Role of Non-Binding Norms in the International Legal System* (Oxford: Oxford University Press, 2000), 21-42

Curtin, Deirdre and Dekker, Ige F., 'The EU as a "Layered" International Organization: Institutional Unity in Disguise' in Craig, Paul and de Burca, Gráinne (eds.), *The Evolution of EU Law* (Oxford: Oxford University Press, 1999), 83-136

Davey, William J., 'Institutional Framework' in Patrick MacRory, Arthur Appleton and Michael Plummer (eds.) *The World Trade Organization: Legal, Economic and Political Analysis* (New York: Springer Science+Business Media, Inc., 2005), 51-87

Dupuy, René-Jean, 'Coutume sage et coutume sauvage' in *Mélanges offerts à Charles Rousseau: La communauté internationale* (Paris: Éditions A. Pedone, 1974), 75-86

Fektekuty, Geza 'Trade in Services – Bringing Services into the Multilateral Trading System' in Bhagwati, Jagdish and Hirsh, Mathias (eds.), *The Uruguay Round and Beyond: Essays in Honour of Arthur Dunkel* (Berlin: Springer Verlag, 1998), 79- 99

Finalyson, Jock A. and Zacher, Mark W., 'The GATT and the regulation of trade barriers: regime dynamics and functions' in Krasner, Stephen D. (ed.), *International Regimes* (Ithaca: Cornell University Press, 1983), 273-314

Fitzmaurice, Gerald, 'The problem of non liquet: prolegomena to a restatement' in *Mélanges offerts à Charles Rousseau: La communauté internationale* (Paris : Éditions A. Pedone, 1974), 90-112

Fitzmaurice, Sir Gerald, 'The general principles of international law considered from the standpoint of the rule of law' (1957) 92 *Recueil des Cours*, 1

Footer, Mary E. and George, Carol, 'The General Agreement on Trade in Services' in MacRory, Patrick, Appleton, Arthur and Plummer, Michael (eds.) *The World Trade Organization: Legal, Economic and Political Analysis* (New York: Springer Science+Business Media, Inc., 2005), 799-953

Fried, Jonathan T., 'Governance in the Global Age: A Public International Law Perspective' in Porter, Roger B. and Sauvé, Pierre (eds.), *Seattle, the WTO, and the Future of the Multilateral Trading System* (Cambridge, MA: The Center for Business and Government, John F. Kennedy School of Government, Harvard University, 2000), 131-141

Georgiev, Dencho, 'The Decision-making Process in the World Trade Organization', in Borght, Kim, van der (ed.), with Remache, Eric and Wiener, Jarred (ass. eds.), *Essays on the Future of the WTO: Finding a New Balance* (London: Cameron & May, 2003), 25-46

Honeck, Dale B., 'Developing Regulatory Disciplines in Professional Services: the Role of the World Trade Organization' in Aharoni, Yair and Nachum, Lilach (eds.), *Globalization of Services Some implications for theory and practice* (London: Routledge, 2000), 52-72

Howse, Robert L., 'Adjudicative Legitimacy and Treaty Interpretation in International Trade Law: The Early Years of WTO Jurisprudence' in Weiler, Joseph H.H., *The EU, the WTO and the NAFTA: Towards a Common Law of International Trade* (Oxford: Oxford University Press, 2000) 35-69

Hurrell, Andrew, 'International Society and the Study of Regimes: A Reflective Approach' in Rittberger, Volker (ed.), *Regime Theory and International Relations* (Oxford: Clarendon Press, 1993), 49-72

Jenks, C. Wilfred, 'Unanimity, the Veto, Weighted Voting, Special and Simple Majorities and Consensus as Modes of Decision in International Organization' in Jennings, R.Y. (ed.), *Cambridge Essays in International Law: Essays in*

Honour of Lord McNair (London: Stevens & Sons/Dobbs Ferry, New York: Oceana Publications, Inc., 1965) 48-63

Jennings, Robert Y. 'Law-making and Package Deal' in *Mélanges offerts à Paul Reuter: Le droit international: unité et diversité* (Paris: Éditions A. Pedone, 1981), 347-355

Jessup, Philip 'Parliamentary Diplomacy. An Examination of the Legal Quality of the Rules of Procedure of the United Nations' (1956) 89 *Recueil des Cours*, 181-320

Joyner, Christopher, 'The Legal Status and Effect of Antarctic Recommended Measures' in Shelton, Dinah (ed.), *Commitment and Compliance: The Role of Non-binding Norms in the International Legal System* (Oxford: Oxford University Press, 2000), 163-196

Junne, G.C.A. 'International Organizations in a period of globalization: New (problems of) Legitimacy' in Coicaud, Jean-Marc and Heiskanen, Veijo (eds.), *The legitimacy of international organizations* (Tokyo: The United Nations University Press, 2001), 189-220

Keohane, Robert O., 'Neoliberal Institutionalism: A Perspective on World Politics' in Keohane, Robert O., *International Institutions and State Power: Essays in International Relations Theory* (Boulder, Col: Westview Press, 1989), 1-20

Keohane, Robert O. and Nye, Joseph S., 'The Club Model of Multilateral Co-operation and Problems of Democratic Legitimacy' in Porter, Roger B., et al. (eds.) *Efficiency, Equity, and Legitimacy: The Multilateral Trading System at the Millennium* (Washington, DC: Brookings Institution Press, 2001), 264-294

Klein, E., 'International Régimes' vol. 2 *Encyclopaedia of Public International Law*, revised edition (Amsterdam: North Holland, 1995), 203-207

Kuijper, Peter Jan, 'Some institutional issues presently before the WTO' in Kennedy, Daniel L.M. and Southwick, James D., *The Political Economy of International Trade Law: Essays in Honour of Robert E. Hudec* (Cambridge: Cambridge University Press, 2002), 81-110

Lang, Winfried, 'Regimes and Organizations in the Labyrinth of International Institutions' in Ginther, Konrad, Hafner, Gerhard, Lang, Winfried, Neuhold, Hanspeter, Sucharipa-Behrmann a.o., *Völkerrecht zwischen normativem Anspruch und politischer Realität, Feschrift für Karl Zemanek zum 65. Geburtstag* (Berlin: Duncker & Humblot, 1994), 275-289

Lauterpacht, E., 'The Development of the Law of International Organizations by the Decisions of International Tribunals' (1976) 152 *Receuil des Cours*, 377

Lauterpacht, E., 'The Legal Effect of Illegal Acts of International Organisations' in *Cambridge Essays in International Law*: *Essays in honour of Lord McNair* (London: Stevens & Sons/ Dobbs Ferry, New York: Oceana Publications, Inc., 1965), 88-121

Marks, Susan, 'Democracy and international governance' in Coicaud, Jean-Marc and Heiskanen, Veijo (eds.), *The legitimacy of international organizations* (Tokyo: The United Nations University Press, 2001), 47-68

Martenczuk, Berend, 'Decisions of Bodies established by International Agreements and the Community Legal Order' in Kronenberger, Vincent (ed.), *The European Union and the International Legal Order: Discord or Harmony?* (The Hague: T.M.C. Asser Press, 2001)

Maupain, Francis, 'International Labor Organization Recommendations and Similar Instruments' in Shelton, Dinah (ed.), *Commitment and Compliance, the Role of Non-Binding Norms in the International Legal System* (Oxford: Oxford University Press, 2000), 372-393

McRae, Donald M., 'The Contribution of International Trade Law to the Development of International Law' (1996) 261 *Recueil des Cours*, 99

Müller, Harald, 'The Internationalization of Principles, Norms and Rules by Governments: The Case of Security Regimes', in Rittberger, Volker (ed.), *Regime Theory and International Relations* (Oxford: Clarendon Press, 1993), 361-388

Nayyar, Deepak, 'The Existing System and the Missing Institutions' in Nayyar, Deepak (ed.), *Governing Globalization* (Oxford: Oxford University Press, 2002), 356-384

Ostry, Sylvia, 'World Trade Organization: Institutional Design for Better Governance' in Porter, Robert B., Sauvé, Pierre, Subramanian, Arvind and Beviglia Zampetti, Amerigo (eds.) *Efficiency, Equity, and Legitimacy: The Multilateral Trading System at the Millennium* (Washington, D.C: Brookings Institution Press, 2001), 361-380

Redgwell, Catherine, 'Multilateral Environmental Treaty-Making' in Gowland-Debbas, Vera, (ed.), *Multilateral Treaty Making: The Current Status of Challenges and Reforms Needed in the International Legislative Process* (London: Kluwer Law International, 2000), 89-107

Roht-Arriaza, Naomi, 'Soft Law' in a "Hybrid" Organization: The International Organization for Standardization' in Shelton, Diana (ed.) *Commitment and Compliance. The Role of Non-Binding Norms in the International Legal System* (Oxford: Oxford University Press, 2000), 263-281

Roessler, Frieder 'The institutional balance between judicial and political organs of the WTO' in Bronckers, Marco C.E.J. and Quick, Reinhard (eds.), *New directions in international economic law: essays in honor of John H. Jackson* (The Hague: Kluwer International Ltd., 2000), 325-346

Romano, Cesare P.R., 'International Organizations and the International Judicial Process: An Overview' in in Boisson de Chazournes, Laurence, Romano, Cesare and Mackenzie, Ruth, *International Organizations and International Dispute Settlement* (Ardsley NY: Transnational Publishers, Inc., 2002), 3-36

Schachter, Oscar, 'Entangled Treaty and Custom' in Dinstein, Y. (ed.), *International Law at a time of complexity: essays in honour of Shabtai Rosenne* (Dordrecht: Nijhoff, 1989), 717-738

Schott, Jeffrey J., 'The WTO after Seattle' in Schott, Jeffrey J. (ed.), *The WTO after Seattle* (Washington, DC: Institute for International Economics, July 2000), 3-41

Seidl-Hohenveldern, Ignaz, 'International Economic "Soft Law"' (1979) 163 *Recueil des Cours*, 165

Shukla, S.P., 'From the GATT to the WTO and Beyond' in Nayyar, Deepak (ed.), *Governing Globalization* (Oxford: Oxford University Press, 2002), 254-283

Strange, S., '*Cave! Hic dragones*: A Critique of Regime Analysis' in Krasner, Stephen D. (ed.), *International Regimes*, (Ithaca: Cornell University Press, 1983), 337-354

Strange, Susan 'Why do international organizations never die?' in Reinalda, Bob and Verbeek, Bertjan *Autonomous Policy Making by International Organizations* (London: Routledge, 1998), 213-220

Szasz, Paul 'General law-making processes' in Joyner, Christopher C. (ed.), *The United Nations and International Law* (Cambridge: American Society of International Law and Cambridge University Press, 1997), 27-64

Trotman, LeRoy, 'The WTO: the institutional contradictions' in Moore, Mike (ed.), *Doha and Beyond: The Future of the Multilateral Trading System* (Cambridge: Cambridge University Press, 2004), 19-25

Virally, Michel, 'Le rôle des "principes" dans le développement du droit international' in *Recueil d'études de doit international en hommage à Paul Guggenheim* (Geneva: Faculté de droit de l'Université de Genève, Institut universitaire de hautes études internationales/ Tribune, 1968), 531-544

Weiss, Friedl, 'WTO decision-making: is it reformable?' in Kennedy, Daniel M. and Southwick, James D. (eds.), *The Political Economy of International Trade Law: Essays in Honor of Robert E. Hudec*' (Cambridge: Cambridge University Press, 2002), 68-80

Weiss, Friedl, 'From Havana to Marrakesh: Treaty Making for Trade' in Klabbers, Jan and Lefeber, René (eds.), *Essays on the Law of Treaties: A collection of Essays in Honour of Bert Vierdag* (The Hague, Boston, London: Martinus Nijhoff Publishers, 1998), 155-170

Weiss, Friedl, 'The WTO Dispute Settlement System and the Economic Order of WTO Member States', in Dijck, Pitou, van and Faber, Gerrit (eds.), *Challenges to the New World Trade Organization* (The Hague: Kluwer Law International, 1996), 77-91

Weiss, Friedl, 'Inherent Powers of National and International Courts' in Ortino, Federico and Petersmann, Ernst-Ulrich (eds.), *The WTO Dispute Settlement System 1995-2003* (The Hague: Kluwer Law International, 2004), 177-190

Wellens, K.C. 'Diversity in Secondary Rules and the Unity of International Law: Some Reflections on Current Trends' in Baarnhoorn, L.A.N.M. and Wellens, K.C., *Diversity in Secondary Rules and the Unity of International Law*, (The Hague: T.MC. Asser Instituut/Martinus Nijhoff, 1995), 3-37

Wickmerasinghe, Chanaka, 'Immunities enjoyed by Officials of States and International Organizations', in Evans, Malcolm (ed.), *International Law* (Oxford: Oxford University Press, 2003), 387-413

Young, Oran R., 'International Regimes: Problems of Concept Formation' in Krasner, Stephen D. (ed.), *International Regimes* (Ithaca and London: Cornell University Press, 1983), 332-357

Zamora, Stephen, 'Economic Relations and Development' in Schachter, Oscar and Joyner, Christopher C., (eds.), *The United Nations legal order* (Cambridge: American Society of International Law and Cambridge University Press, 1997), 503-576

Zemanek, Karl, 'The Legal Foundations of the International System', *General Course on Public International Law* (1997) 266 *Recueil des Cours*, 9

Zemanek, Karl, 'Majority Rule and Consensus Technique in Law-Making Diplomacy' in McDonald, R.St.J. and Johnston, D.M. (eds.), *The Structure and Process of International Law* (Dordrecht, Boston: Martinus Nijhoff, 1983), 857-887

4 Other Publications including Reports and Papers

Bièvre, Dirk, de, 'Judicialisation and Positive Integration in the WTO', paper prepared for 5th Pan-European International Relations Conference organised by the Standing Group on International Relations (SGIR) of the European Consortium for Political Research (ECPR), Netherlands Congress Centre, Den Haag, 9-11 September 2004

Committee on the Accountability of International Organisations, International Law Association (ILA), New Delhi Conference (2002), *Third Report, Consolidated, Revised and Enlarged Version of Recommended Rules and Practices ("RRP-s")*

Cottier, Thomas, 'The Legal Framework for Free Trade Areas & Customs Unions in WTO Law', Paper prepared for the Third Workshop jointly hosted by the State Secretariat for Economic Affairs (SECO) and the World Trade Institute (WTI) on Multilateralism and Bilateralism after Cancún: Challenges and Opportunities of Regionalism, Berne, 15 June 2004

Cottier, Thomas, 'WTO Dispute Settlement and Multilateral Trade Negotiations: Is There a Need for Inter-Round Negotiations?', paper prepared for the World Trade Forum 2002, *Dispute Settlement and Decision Making in the Multilateral Trading System: Current Operation and Options for Reform*

Freestone, David and Oude Elferink, Alex, 'Flexibility and Innovation in the Law of the Sea – Will the LOSC Amendment Procedures ever be used?' Paper for the Third Verzijl Symposium, Utrecht, The Netherlands, 3 December 2004, 1-46

GATT, Trends in International Trade, A Report by a Panel of Experts, (Geneva: GATT Secretariat, [*The Haberler Report*] 1958)

Gehring, Thomas, *Integrating integration theory: neofunctionalism and international regimes*, EUI Working Papers no. 95/39 (San Domenico: European University Institute, 1995)

Krajewski, Markus, 'From *Green Room* to *Glass Room*': Participation of Developing Countries and Internal Transparency in the WTO Decision Making Process' (Berlin, TradeWatch, July 2000)

Moravscik, Andrew, 'Why the European Union Strengthens the State: Domestic Politics and International Cooperation', Center for European Studies, Harvard University, Working Paper Series #52 (1994)

Narlikar, Amrita, 'WTO Decision-making and Developing Countries', Working Paper, no. 11, Trade-Related Agenda, Development and Equity' (T.R.A.D.E.) (Geneva: South Centre, November 2001)

Report of the Director-General's Consultative Board, *The Future of the WTO – Addressing institutional challenges in the new millennium*, (Geneva: World Trade Organization, 2004) [*The Sutherland Report*]

Report of G-7 Finance Ministers and Central Bank Governors, *Strengthening the International Financial System and the Multilateral Development Banks*, 7 July 2001, Rome, Italy

Sharma, Shefali, 'The Decision-making Process and the Single Undertaking', Institute for Agriculture and Trade Policy, paper for Panel on 'Investment in the WTO? Myth and Realities' WTO Symposium, 17 June 2003

Schott, Jeffrey J. and Watal, Jayashree, *Decision-making in the WTO*, International Economics Policy Brief No. 00-2, Institute for International Economics, Washington, DC, March, 2000

Schott, Jeffrey J., 'The WTO after Cancún', paper prepared for the Conference on Sustainable Development in the WTO: Trade, Investment and Environment after Cancún', Royal Institute for International Affairs, 23 February 2004

Sharma, Shefali, 'The Decision-making Process and the Single Undertaking', Institute for Agriculture and Trade Policy, Symposium paper, 17 June 2003

Slater, Terry, *Strategic Organizational Review: Structure and Staffing Resources of the World Trade Organization Secretariat* (Geneva: World Trade Organization, 2001)

Stoler, Andrew L., 'The Current State of the WTO', paper for a *Workshop on the EU, the US and the WTO,* Stanford University, 28 February – 1 March 2003

Suppan, Steve, Consumers International's Decision-Making in the Global Market. Codex Briefing Paper (August 2004) available at: *www.tradeobservatory.org/library.cfm?RefID=36988.*

INDEX

Abi-Saab, Georges, 278
abus de droit, 316
access to justice
- *amicus curiae*, 52-53, 300-301, 313, 332
- appellate review, *see* Appellate Body

accession, 241-252
- criticism of process, 244-245
- decisions, 74, 148, 152, 154, 160, 241-242, 248, 255, 279
- GATT, 195, 197-198, 241
- membership, 71-74, 337
- norms, 245-252
  · procedural, 245-249, 251-252
  · substantive, 249-250
- protocols, 63, 152, 246-250
- working parties, 36, 63

accountancy services
- disciplines, 67, 284-288, 290-291
- mutual recognition, 284-285

ACP Group, *see* African, Caribbean and Pacific Group
ACP-EC Partnership Agreement, 48, 145, 257 fn
ad hoc committees, 62, 67
ad hoc working groups, 63
adjudication
- affirmative defences, 256, 315, 318
- burden of proof
  · allocation, 188, 314
  · reversal, 314-315, 318
- DSU, *see* Dispute Settlement Understanding
- due process, 298, 312
  · *amicus curiae*, *see* access to justice
  · *audi et alteram partem* rule, 312-313
  · third party rights, 101, 313
  · timely objections, 313
- evidence, 314
  · presumption of, 315
  · *prima facie*, 315, 318
- interpretation, 77, 90, 332
  · aid to, 23, 32
  · *effet utile*, 36
  · *in dubio mitius*, 316
- judicial economy, 313
- *juris novit curia*, 226
- *non liquet*, 226

Administrative Committee on Coordination (ACC), *see* Chief Executives' Board for Coordination (CEB)
Administrative Tribunal of the International Labour Organization (ILOAT), 307, 311 fn
African Caribbean and Pacific (ACP) Group, 166
African Development Bank, 158 fn
African Group, 113, 166-167, 217
agriculture, 182, 190
- agreement (AoA), 24, 65
- committee, 65 fn, 119, 164

alliances, *see* decision-making practices
amendment
- decision-making, 146, 152-155, 204, 207-209, 212, 214-215, 220, 336-338
- *de facto*, 97, 220, 336
- GATT, 94, 233
- law, 8, 203-211, 221, 268
- modification, 184, 231-232, 337, *see also* modification, rectification and certification
- practice, 8, 205-206, 211-221, 268
- presumption against, 296
- residual rules, 230, 232
- supplementary treaties, 204, 232

anti-dumping practices, 15 fn, 67, 99 fn, 188, 190, 264
- *Ad hoc* Working Group on Implementation, 67
- agreement (ADP), 67-68, 313 fn
- Anti-Dumping Code, *see* Tokyo Round MTN
- Anti-Dumping Practices Committee, 67
- circumvention, *see* Informal Group on Anti-Circumvention
- committee, 9, 64 fn, 67
- implementation, *see Ad hoc* Working Group on Implementation
- Informal Group on Anti-Circumvention, 67

Appellate Body, 29-31, 38, 77, 281, 331-332
- additional procedure, 52, 300-301, 313
- powers, 53, 301
- Rules of Conduct, 301
- Rules of Procedure, 296
- special procedure, *see* additional procedure
- working procedures, 52-53, 297, 300

Asian Development Bank, 158 fn
Association of South East Asian Nations (ASEAN), 165
Aust, Anthony, 210, 232, 239, 266
authoritative interpretation, 46-47, 54, 96, 152, 155, 184, 204, 211, 220-221, 254, 264-267, 269, 336
- decision-making, 54, 96, 155, 184, 204, 220-221, 254, 264-265, 269, 336
- *de facto*, 268

authoritative treaty norm, 93-95
autonomous institutional arrangements, 11, 18, 45, 74-75, 115

balance-of-payments, 30-31, 263, 332
- committee (BOP Committee), 30, 53, 62, 119, 121, 293
- GATT *and*, 120
- exceptions for developing countries, 94, 97, 104, 119
- residual restrictions (GATT), 263
- Understanding on Balance-of-Payments, 104, 120

Berne Convention, 98 fn
bilateral agreements, *see* dispute settlement
Blackhurst, Richard, 167
Blokker, Niels, 253-254
Brownlie, Ian, 231-232, 265
Bogdandy, von, Armin, 28-29
Bossche, Van den, Peter, 33, 146
budget
- annual, 53, 155-156, 221, 302-304
- biennial, move to, 96, 109, 220-221, 265-266, 268-269, 304
- committee (BFA Committee), 62, 96, 156, 220, 303-304

burden of proof, *see* adjudication
Bryn, Kåre, 174

Cairns Group, 166
Caucuses, *see* decision-making practices
Chairman
- notes, 160
- statements, 160, 172
- texts, 172, 177-178

Chinkin, Christine, 338
Churchill, Robin, 18

Chief Executives' Board for Coordination (CEB), 309
Civil aircraft
- Agreement on Trade in Civil Aircraft, 25 fn, 37, 49 fn, 95-96, 202-203 fn, 245
club model, 110-114, 125, 333-334
code of conduct
- international trade, GATT, 13
- world trade, WTO, 106, 181, 267, 337
Codex Alimentarius, 89
- Commission, 98 fn, 289, 321, 325
coherence
- macro-economic policy, 32, 35, 102-103, 329
- development policy, 105
collective action
- GATT, 16
- WTO, 75, 223
- decisions, 96, 162, 179, 254, 261
common institutional framework, *see* WTO Agreement
consensus, *see* decision-making procedures
consent to be bound, 153-156, 196-198, 239, 241, 336
Consultative Board on the Future of the Multilateral Trading System, 40, 123, 130, 328, 330
Consultative Group of 18 (CG18), 41, 76, 122-123, 168, 330
CONTRACTING PARTIES (GATT), 117, 120-122, 181, 234, 245-246, 254, 263, 275, 297
- acting jointly, 17 fn, 44-45, 90, 108
- meaning of, 108 fn
Convention on Biological Diversity (CBD), 149 fn
Cottier, Thomas, 161
Council for Trade in Goods (CTG), 37, 133, 235, 258-262, 293
- powers, 53-57, 66
Council for Trade in Services (CTS), 53, 224-226, 228-230, 237-238, 282-285, 287-288, 290, 294
- powers, 57-61
countervailing duties, *see* Agreement on Subsidies and Countervailing Duties (SCM)
Cox, Robert, 26
critical mass, *see* decision-making practices
Curtin, Deirdre, 16

Dam, Kenneth, 253-254
decision-making practices
- alliances, 165-166, 179
- caucuses, 164-165, 179
- chairperson, role of, 160, 170-171
- critical mass, 161-162, 168, 179, 330, 334
- equality of voting power, 151, 157-161
- 'green room' meetings, 113-114, 131, 164, 167-170, 174, 179
- informal practices, 130-131, 157, 163-164, 170, 173, 178-180
- parity of interest, 151, 157-161
- regime, 83-85, 87, 94, 100, 106, 124
- small room meetings, *see* 'green room' meetings
decision-making procedures
- accessions, 74, 148, 152, 154, 160, 241-242, 248, 255, 279
- amendment, 146, 152-155, 204, 207-209, 212, 214-215, 220, 336-338
- annual budget, 53, 155-156, 220-221, 281, 292, 301, 304
- authoritative interpretations, 54, 96, 155, 184, 204, 220-221, 254, 264-265, 269, 336
- consensus
  · explicit, 44 fn, 141-142, 331
  · *in lieu* of voting, 148-149, 155, 178, 248, 255 fn, 279
  · mandated, 142-147

· primary rule, 137-142
· qualified, 148-149
· reform, 132, 161-162
· reverse, 29 fn, 143, 178
- consultative, 131, 172, 333
- decisions
· status of, 176-178
- improvements, 5, 172, 334
- 'kick-up' rule, 36, 56, 66
- reform, 132, 161-162, 170, 173, 337
- rules of procedure
· meetings, 36, 132, 151, 170, 249, 281, 292, 295-296
- voting, 149-151
· qualified majority, 151-156
· simple majority, 150-151
· super-qualified majority, 155
· weighted, 150-151, 157-159, 161-163, 178-179, 333-334
- transparency
· external transparency, 175
· internal transparency, 173-175
- unanimity, 156
- waivers, 148-149, 154, 178, 248, 252, 255, 279, 334
- WT/L/93, 74 fn, 148, 155, 178, 248, 279
Dekker, Ige, 16
détournement de pouvoir, 155, 221
developing countries
- accession, terms of, 244-245
- balance-of-payments exceptions, 94, 97, 104, 119, 191 fn
- club model, 112-113
- Enabling Clause, 104, 125, 191 fn, 275-276
- 'green room' meetings, 113, 167-169
- labour mobility, 229-230
- major interests' norm, 114
- 'mini' waivers, 259, 261-262
- preferential treatment, 188-189, 275-276
- representation, 54, 64, 174, 329
- *and* Singapore Issues, 141-142, 331
- special and differential treatment, 104-105, 125, 245
- technical assistance, 33, 71, 76, 104-105, 125, 134, 247, 321
- time-limited exceptions, *see* 'mini waivers'
- TRIPs waiver, 215-216, 268
- TRIMs waiver, *see* 'mini waivers'
development
- committee, on trade and (COMTD), 62
- norm, 90, 104, 107, 120, 125
- policy, 35, 105, 329
Director-General, 68-70
- Appointment of, 46-47, 132, 172, 306-308
- powers, 70, 75
- right of initiative, 69, 75, 133-134, 171
dispute settlement, *see also* adjudication
arbitration, 238, 258
bilateral settlement, 144
binding arbitration, reasonable period of time, 50-51
sequencing problem, 144
systemic issue, 101
Dispute Settlement Body (DSB), 29, 35, 77
- adoption of reports, automatic, 100, 143
- Chair(man), 300, 307
- decision-making
· consensus, use of, 142, 144
· reverse consensus, 29 fn, 143, 178
- monitoring, *see* powers, surveillance
- political body, 29-30, 49 fn, 51, 76-77
- powers
· express, 50-51
· implied, exercise of, 50
· specific, 49-50, 332
· surveillance, 101, 125
- quasi-adjudicative, 49, 76, 297, 331
- Rules of Procedure, 296-297

Dispute Settlement Understanding (DSU), 29, 96, 101, 121, 201, 297
- reform, 121, 167, 171 fn
- review of, 147 fn, 212-213
- Rules of Conduct, 50, 301

Doha Development Round MTN, 2, 5, 119 fn, 125, 166, 202, 263, 268, 303, 338
- agenda, 125, 121, 176 fn
- DSU negotiations, *see* Dispute Settlement Understanding (DSU), review of
- work programme, 33, 96 fn, 104, 164

domestic regulation
- *see* GATS

Donnelly, Jack, 90, 92, 100
due process, *see* adjudication
Dunkel, Arthur, 171 fn
Dupuy, René-Jean, 278

ECOSOC, *see* United Nations Economic and Social Council
effet utile, *see* adjudication
Ehlermann, Claus-Dieter, 206-207
Ehring, Lothar, 206-207
emergency safeguard measures, *see* GATS
Enabling Clause, *see* Developing Countries
environment, 12, 23, 320
- committee (CTE), 62, 196 fn, 293
- trade and, 46, 333

equitable geographical distribution (EGD), 157 fn, 160, 170, 179, 330
equivalence, *see* sanitary and phytosanitary measures
European Bank for Reconstruction and Development (EBRD), 72 fn
European Communities
- authoritative interpretation request, 265
- Member, 71-72, 165 fn, 195, 224 fn, 332
- representation, 136 fn, 150 fn
- waivers
  · ACP-EC Partnership Agreement, 48, 145, 257 fn
  · Kimberley, 259 fn
  · Transitional Banana Tariff Quota, 48, 145
  · TRIPs, Paragraph 6 Decision, 218

European Court of Justice (ECJ)
European Union (EU), *see* European Communities
exceptive norms, 188, 191-193, 253, 256, 267, 275 fn, 282, 318

Facilitators, 172
FAO, *see* Food and Agriculture Organization
Final Act
- GATT, 15 fn
- Havana Conference, 14 fn, 16
- Uruguay Round, 93, 194-196, 201, 211

financial services, 161 fn, 222-227
- committee, (CTFS), 58, 224 fn, 225, 294

Finlayson, Jock, 90, 92, 104, 119-120, 124
Fitzmaurice, Gerald, 185
Food and Agriculture Organization (FAO), 204 fn, 273, fn
forum organisation, 26, 78, 80
Friedmann, Wolfgang, 182
'friends', 131, 170-173, 179, 333
- of the Chair, 172, 174

Functioning of the GATT System (FOGS), 2, 102-103

GATS, 24, 57-60, 66-67, 71, 104, 153-154, 156, 186, 190, 207-208, 223-231, 233, 237-239, 255, 269, 282-289, 294-295, 319, 337
- *and* accession, 246
- 'built-in' agenda, 27 fn, 66, 100, 126, 171 fn, 222-223, 232, 269, 331
- modification, 233, 237-238

- specific commitments
  · committee (CSC), 58, 294
  · schedules, 4, 59, 71, 237, 267, 287-288
- supplementary protocols, 221-231

GATT *acquis*, 3 fn, 88, 133 fn, 137, 162, 181, 245, 252, 294, 333

GATT 1947
- accession, 241-243, 245-246, 249-253, 269
- amendment, difficulty of, 233-234
- Annecy Protocol, 159 fn, 243
- *de facto*
  · contracting parties, 159, 198
  · international organisation, 17, 108
- Director-General, 69
  · Executive Secretary, formerly, 116-117 fn
- Enabling Clause, *see* developing countries
- dispute settlement, 143, 200, 203, 214 fn, 312
- GSP waiver (1971), 275
- history, 16-18
- International Trade Organization (ITO), 16, 116, 156
- Part IV, 17 fn, 94, 104, 121, 125
- Protocol of Provisional Application (PPA), 15-16 fn, 99, 189 fn
- residual restrictions, *see* balance-of-payments
- Review Session (1954-1955), 17 fn, 94, 202
- trade (barriers) regime, 90, 92, 160
- treaty regime
  · multilateral, 23, 182, 187
  · semi-institutionalised, 2, 7, 17, 74, 79
- waiver power, 254, 256, 259

General Agreement on Trade in Services, *see* GATS

General Agreement on Tariffs and Trade 1947, *see* GATT 1947

General Council, 35, 48-53
- Chair(man, person), 69 fn, 70, 75, 154, 164, 170-171, 216, 307, 331
- DSB, *see* Dispute Settlement Body
- executive function, 29, 48
- internal rules
  · financial regulations, 303-304
  · staff rules and regulation, 304-305
- non-governmental organisations, 33 fn
- powers
  · attributed, 49-50
  · delegated, 62, 294
  · executive, 48-49
  · implied, 50-51
  · specific, 49-53
  · waiver, 47
- representation, 48, 329
- Rules of Procedure, 36-37, 42, 53, 132-133, 151, 249, 296
- TNC, *see* Trade Negotiations Committee
- TPRB, *see* Trade Policy Review Body

Generalized System of Preferences (GSP), 275-276

Georgiev, Dencho, 143, 171

Gold, Joseph, 253-254, 256

government procurement
- agreement (AGP), 25fn, 37, 95, 202 fn, 240-241
- transparency, 27 fn, 44-45 fn, 63, 112, 141, *see also* Singapore Issues

'green room' meetings, *see* decision-making practices

Group of 21 (Group of 20), 114, 166

Group of LDC Members (LDC Group), 113, 166

Group of Latin American and Caribbean Members, 166

'hard core' waiver, *see* waivers

Heads of Delegation (HODs), 122, 179
- meetings of, 163-164, 167

High Level Committee on Management (UN), 309 fn
Harmonized Commodity Description and Coding System (HS System), 235-237, 256
- tariff schedules, 256, *see also* Tariff Schedules
'horizontal' committees, 36, 53, 62-63
human rights, 7, 12, 80, 274
- normative character, 91
- regime theory, 86, 90-92, 100-101
ICITO, *see* International Commission for the International Trade Organization
ILA, *see* International Law Association
ILC, *see* International Law Commission
ILO, *see* International Labour Organization
IMF, *see* International Monetary Fund
implementation
- Implementation Conference (1994), 199
- Implementation-Related Issues, *see* Ministerial Conference, Decisions
- norms, 100-103, 124, 189
- Paragraph 6 Decision, *see* TRIPs
in dubio mitius, *see* adjudication, interpretation
informal practices, 7, 8, 110-111, 118, 126, 268, 270, 327-328, 333
- *see also* decision-making practices *and* institutional, practices
information technology products, trade in
- agreement, 38, 232 fn
- committee, participants on the expansion, 45fn
institutional
- balance, principle of, 26, 30-31, 77, 101, 332
- design, 89, 115
- practices, 4, 16, 116
  · informal, 68
- reform, 2, 5, 121, 123, 130, 170, 177, 332
  · GATT, 17 fn, 118
  · WTO, 5, 123, 174, 332
intellectual property rights, 60, 89, 97, 102, 153, 215 fn, 282, 318, 325, 335
- trade-related aspects of, 111, 182, 190, 333
  · agreement (TRIPs), 60-61, 96, 102, 156, 214-218, 254, 335
  · Paragraph 6 Decision, 96 fn, 214, 216-220, 254
  · *and* public health, 177, 214-218, 254
Inter-American Development Bank (IADB), 158 fn
Interim Commission for the International Trade Organization (ICITO), 14 fn, 116, 201 fn
- arrangements with UN, 116
- secretariat (GATT), 116-117, 201 fn, 305
International Bank for Reconstruction and Development (IDRB), *see* World Bank
International Bovine Meat Agreement (IMA), 95, 147, 203 fn, 242 fn
International Civil Aviation Organization (ICAO), 99, 109, 204 fn, 272 fn
International Court of Justice (ICJ)
- standing judicial body, 29
International Dairy Agreement (IDA), 95, 147, 203 fn, 242 fn
international institution, 2, 110, 129, 133, 327
- theory, 89
International Labour Organization (ILO), 153 fn, 204 fn
- Administrative Tribunal, 307, 311 fn
International Law Commission (ILC), 42, 85 fn, 231, 277
International Monetary Fund (IMF), 2, 13, 28, 40-41, 68, 76, 81, 110, 123, 253
- executive body, 41
- relationship with WTO, 32, 35, 329-330
- weighted voting, 149-150, 157-158, 162, 340

International Plant Protection Convention (IPPC), 289 fn, 321
international regime, 79-80, 332
- concept and application, 75-76
international standards, 91-92, 97-98, 126, 272 fn, 284, 288-290, 319 fn, 320-322, 325
- International Standards Organization (ISO), 89, 204 fn, 325
International Telegraphic Union (ITU), 83 fn
International Trade Centre (ITC), 32 fn
International Trade Organization (ITO), 7, 12, 17, 25, 75, 108, 116-117, 187, 209 fn
- Charter (Havana), 14-16, 94 fn, 153 fn, 156, 187, 204 fn
- normative structure, 13, 187
interpretation, 77, 90, 184, 204, 211, 219, 281, 315-317, 332
- aid to, 23
  · Ministerial Declaration, 34
  · Preamble to WTO Agreement, 22-23
- authoritative, 8, 54, 96-97, 155, 204, 220-221, 254, 264-267, 336
- effectiveness principle, 316
- treaty rules, 274, 312, 316
investment measures, trade-related, 90, 190, 263
- agreement (TRIMs), 133, 260-262, 266
IPPC, *see* International Plant Protection Convention
ITU, *see* International Telegraphic Union

Jackson, John, 117, 121, 157, 233
Jacobson, Harold, 26
jewel in the crown, 1
Joint Appeals Board, 307

Keohane, Robert, 110, 113-114
Klabbers, Jan, 41
Krasner, Stephen, 83
Kuijper, Pieter Jan, 43, 50, 53, 57, 59, 61

Lanoschka, Anna, 244
LDC Group, *see* Group of LDC Members

major interests norm, 90, 107-108, 110-112, 114, 125, 131, 157, 160-161, 179, 330, 333
market access, 46, 73, 90-91, 106, 185, 228, 247, 264, 317
- committee, 36, 56, 64, 293
- norm, 106
Marrakesh Agreement Establishing the World Trade Organization, *see* WTO Agreement
McRae, Donald, 71, 73
MEA, *see* multilateral environmental agreement
member-driven organisation, 28, 40, 75-76, 328, 330
- criticism of, 40
membership, 71-74
- accession, 241-252
- original, 71-73, 189, 201
mini-ministerials, 169
Ministerial Conference
- Decisions, 33-35, 44, 74, 176-177
  · ACP-EC Partnership Agreement, *see* waivers
  · Basic Telecommunications, 227
  · DSU Review, 96, 147, 212
  · Implementation-Related Issues, 48, 104, 145, 177, 262, 266, 268
  · Notification Procedures, 56, 294
  · Paragraph 6 Decision (TRIPs), *see* waivers
  · Professional Services, 284, 295
  · Trade and Environment, 62 fn, 196 fn, 293
  · Transitional Banana Tariff Quota, *see* waivers
  · Work Programme (Doha Round), 33, 164

· WTO Acceptance and Accession, 73 fn, 197-198
- Declarations, 27, 34, 177
 · coherence, macro-economic policy, 32
 · Doha, 28, 33, 43, 76, 103, 105, 141, 177, 202, 213, 251, 329
 · Geneva, 43
 · Marrakesh, 196
 · Singapore, 27, 43, 45, 113, 141, 162 fn
 · Trade in Technology Products, 38, 220 fn
 · TRIPs and Public Health, 177, 214-215, 254
- functions, 27, 54
- Meetings, 35, 45-46
 · fifth (Cancún), 2, 44 fn, 63, 114, 141-142, 164, 166, 169, 252, 331
 · first (Singapore), 27, 38, 43, 44 fn, 45, 48 fn, 63, 113, 141-142, 169, 173
 · fourth (Doha), 28 fn, 33, 43, 46, 48, 61 fn, 63, 72 fn, 96, 105, 107 fn, 141, 145, 172, 177, 202, 211-212, 214-215, 263, 266, 303, 329, 338
 · second (Geneva), 43, 48 fn
 · sixth (Hong Kong), 213-214 fn
 · third (Seattle), 2, 48 fn, 113, 129, 169-170, 173, 262
- powers, 43-48, 49, 54-55, 62
- Rules of Procedure, 36-37, 42, 132-133, 151, 249, 296

Ministerial Decisions and Declarations, *see* Ministerial Conference
'mini' waivers, *see* waivers
Montreal Ministerial Mid-Term Review Conference, 31, 143 fn, 214 fn
multilateral environmental agreements (MEAs)
- permanent secretariats, 68-69, 117-118

Multifibre Arrangement, 112 fn, *see* textiles and clothing
most favoured nation treatment, 99 fn, 186, 275
multilateralism
- exception to, 249-252, 269
- norm, 90, 107-111, 124

multilateral trade negotiations (MTN), 96, 113, 169, 193-194, 331
- Doha Round, *see* Doha Development Round MTN
- Tokyo Round, *see* Tokyo Round MTN
- treaty-making, as a result of, 201, 336
- Uruguay Round, *see* Uruguay Round MTN

Multilateral Trade Agreements, 3-4, 23-25, 36, 43, 47, 54-55, 62, 64-65, 71, 76-77, 93, 96, 98, 102, 104, 107, 124-126, 133, 153, 155, 176, 178, 181-182, 191, 193, 205-210, 212, 220, 223, 230, 232, 242, 244, 249-250, 256, 264, 267, 280-282, 286, 293, 295, 310, 317, 320-321, 331, 335-336
mutual recognition, 98, 106, 127, 282
- agreements, 284-286
- professional qualifications (GATS), 284

negative integration, 89, 98, 126-127, 192, 267, 335
Negotiating Group on Trade Facilitation, 63, 142
non-discrimination
- norm, 106, 127
- principle, 90, 185-186, 258, 317

non liquet, see adjudication
Nordic Group, 165
norms
- accession, 245-252
 · procedural, 245-249, 251-252
 · substantive, 249-250
- creation of, 7, 100, 335

- development, 90, 104, 107, 120, 125
- enforcement of, 100
- exceptive, 188, 191-193, 253, 256, 267, 275 fn, 282, 318
- implementation, 100-102
- indeterminacy of, 188, 273-274
- maintenance of, 7, 12
- market access, 106
- non-binding ('soft' law), 184-185, 276, 322, 325-326
- non-discrimination, 106, 127
- permissive, 188, 190-192, 267, 282, 318
- prescriptive, 183, 187-188, 192, 267
- procedural, 11, 24, 90-91, 108, 124, 126, 245, 252
- programmatic, 105, 188
- prohibitive, 183, 187, 267
- promotional, 100, 103-104
- reciprocity in trade concessions, 106
- *and* regime theory, 83-85, 87, 89, 90-92
- revision of, 7
- safeguard, 90, 97, 107, 119-120
- special and differential, 104, 105 fn, 107, 120
- substantive, 88, 90-91, 106, 124-125, 245, 252
- trade liberalisation, 90, 99, 106
- treaty-based, 91, 98, 100, 202
- transparency, 103-104, 107

Nye, Joseph, 110, 113-114

Organization for Economic Cooperation and Development (OECD), 110, 169
- Export Credits Arrangement, 322-324

Office International des Epizooties or International Office of Epizootics (OIE), 289-290 fn, 321

one member one vote (OMOV), 157, 160, 179

Organization for the Prohibition of Chemical Weapons (OPCW), 306 fn

pacta sunt servanda, 316

Panitchpakdi, Supachai, 40, 123

Paris Convention, 60 fn, 98 fn

PCWTO, *see* Preparatory Committee for the World Trade Organization

Permanent Group of Experts, *see* subsidies and countervailing measures

permissive norms, 188, 190-192, 267, 282, 318

plurilateral (trade) agreements, 25, 36-37, 49 fn, 95-96, 119, 147, 203, 242, 245, 336
- bodies, 36

positive prescription, 89, 98, 126-127, 193, 267, 335

Preparatory Committee for the World Trade Organization (PCWTO), 196 fn, 199, 304, 309

prescriptive norms, 183, 187-188, 192, 267

principles, 16, 83-85, 87, 89, 91-92, 126, 182, 185, 187-189, 190, 256, 267, 271, 280-281, 310, 312, 315, 332
- definition, 185
- effectiveness, *see* interpretation
- institutional balance, 26, 30-31, 77, 101, 332
- market access, 90, 185
- non-discrimination, 90, 185-186, 258, 317
- *pacta sunt servanda*, 316
- reciprocity, 90, 185-186, 189, 225
- special and differential treatment, 90, 185
- transparency, 103

privileges and immunities, 21-22, 281, 304, 308, 325, *see also* United Nations

procedural norms, 11, 24, 90-91, 108, 124, 126, 245, 252

programmatic norms, 105, 188

prohibitive norms, 183, 187, 267

promotional norms, 100, 103-104

Protocol of Provisional Application (PPA), *see* GATT 1947

Quad Group of Countries, 168

Raustiala, Kal, 111
reciprocal trade concessions
rectification of treaty, in event of error, 239-241, *see also* treaty rules, secondary
reform
- decision-making, 5, 132, 161-162, 170, 172, 337
- Dispute Settlement Understanding (DSU), 121, 167, 171 fn
- governance, 5
- institutional, 2, 5, 121, 123, 130, 170, 177, 332
- non-agricultural market access, 166
- organisational (GATT), 17fn, 118
- regulatory, 244-245
- trade laws, 183
- WTO, 6-7
regime
- concept in international relations, 80-82
- theory, 12, 84, 87-89, 106, 124, 130-131
  · application, 6-7, 79-80, 87, 124
  · definition, 82-84
  · development of, 7, 12
  · *and* legal scholarship, 80-87
  · *and* WTO, 88, 93-106
regional trade
- committee (CRTA), 62
regulation, presumption in favour of, 221, 232
regulatory philosophy, 89, 127, 192, 267, 318
residual restrictions, *see* balance-of-payments
rule-referencing, 8, 98, 280, 282, 320-324, 325-326
rule-making, 2, 4-5, 7-8, 28-29, 77, 125-127, 135, 161, 167
- delegated, 4, 8, 67 fn, 102, 224 fn, 280-281, 282-291, 325-326
- presumption against implicit amendment, 296
- principal, 6, 126, 132, 181, 181-270
- subsidiary, 6-9, 42, 51, 96, 102, 132, 184, 204, 271-326, 337
rules
- definition, 185-186
rules of origin, 190
- agreement, 24 fn
- committee, 65 fn, 66

safeguards, 107, 125, 182, 190, 317
- agreement, 107
- committee, 25-26 fn, 64 fn
- norm, 90, 97, 107, 119-120
sanitary and phytosanitary measures, 112 fn, 182, 190-191, 282-283, 318, 321
- agreement (SPS), 98, 191, 282-283, 321
- committee, 25 fn, 64, 65fn
- equivalency, 282-283, 290
Schachter, Oscar, 12, 86
Schermers, Henry, 253-254
Schott, Jeffrey, 40, 166
SCM Agreement, *see* Agreement on Subsidies and Countervailing Measures
Secretariat, 5, 68-71
- duties and conditions, 46-47
- GATT, 117, 123
- lack of powers, 69, 75, 78, 118
- reform of, 5-6, 71, 75, 331
- right of initiative, 69, 75, 134, 170-171
- role as depository, 236-238
- Rules of Conduct, 50, 301
- staffing of, 47, 116
Sectoral Cotton Initiative, 164, 167
semi-institutionalised, *see also* treaty regime
- treaty bodies, 91
separation of powers, 26, 29-30, 76-77
services commitments
- Schedules, 4, 71, 194

· modifications, 237-238
Singapore Issues, 141-142, 331
single undertaking, 93, 95, 186, 190, 205, 212-213, 267-268, 336
Skubiszewski, Krzysztof, 276-277
'soft' law, 7, 87-88, 110-111, 185, 244, 273-276, 282, 290 fn, 321-325, 337-338
- delegated, 338
special and differential treatment, *see also* developing countries
- norm, 104, 105 fn, 107, 120
- principle, 90, 185
specialist councils, 53-55
specific commitments, *see* GATS
Staff Rules and Regulations, *see* Secretariat
standards, 6-7, 66, 84, 87, 89, 91, 98, 103, 126, 181, 185, 189, 267, 271, 273, 276, 280-282, 310, 312, 315, 320, 332, 335
- definition, 186
- international, 92, 97-98, 126, 192, 267, 284, 320-322, 324-325
- judicial review, 315-317, 325
- national, 92, 97-99, 191, 282, 318
subsidies and countervailing measures, 4, 38, 94, 99, 103, 114, 125, 164, 182, 190, 259, 264, 322, 324
- agreement (SCM), 38, 103, 259, 323-324
- committee, 64-65 fn
- *and* Export Credits Arrangements (OECD), 324
- illustrative list, 323
- notifications, 103
- Permanent Group of Experts (PGE), 38, 66
- time-limited exceptions, 259
- Working Party on Subsidy Notifications, 65, 295
substantive norms, 88, 90-91, 106, 124-125, 245, 252
Sutherland, Peter, 47 fn, 123
Sutherland Report, 5, 70-71, 75-76, 130, 161, 179, 328, 330-331, 334-335
synallagmatic obligations, 194

Takenoshita, Satoko, 161
tariffs
- progressive reduction, 23, 73, 89, 94 fn, 110 fn, 182, 192, 267, 335
- Schedules, 4, 15, 71, 194
· GATT 1994, integral part of, 222 fn, 233 fn
· modification, rectification and certification, 204, 233-239, 269
· GATT 1947, 59 fn, 230, 233-234
· WTO, 235, 238
· rectification in the event of error, 59, 239-241
- reciprocal reduction, 2, 13 fn, 187, 327
technical assistance, 33, 76, 104-105, 125, 134, 247, 329
- training-related (TRTA), 71
technical barriers to trade, 89, 112 fn, 190, 268, 282-283, 325, 335
- agreement (TBT), 103, 259, 318
- committee, 65 fn
technical standards, *see* technical barriers to trade
textiles, 182, 190
- agreement (ATC), 37
· status, 37, 107 fn, 301 fn
- monitoring body (TMB), 36-37, 201, 301
Tokyo Round MTN, 4, 24-25 fn, 75, 94, 99-100, 119, 125, 153 fn, 162, 181, 190, 201 fn, 202-203, 267
trade facilitation, 141-142
- negotiations, *see* Negotiating Group on Trade Facilitation
trade liberalisation norm, 90, 99, 106-107
Trade Negotiations Committee (TNC), 9, 36, 46, 172, 194, 213
trade policy review, 102 fn
- body (TPRB), 35, 49, 101, 310
- mechanism (TPRM), 31, 190

transparency
- norm, 103-104, 107
- principle, 103
treaty regime
- semi-institutionalised, 2, 7, 17, 74, 79
treaty rules
- primary, 7-8, 58, 77, 93, 96, 102-103, 125, 184-186, 193, 297, 312, 337-338
  · definition of, 183
  · transformation of results of MTN, 194-201
- secondary, 8, 93 fn, 96, 184, 203-204, 211, 253, 259, 268, 271, 338
  · accession, 241-252
  · amendment law, 8, 203-211, 221, 268
  · amendment practice, 8, 205-206, 211-221, 268
  · authoritative interpretation, 46-47, 54, 96, 152, 155, 184, 204, 211, 220-221, 254, 264-267, 269, 336
  · definition of, 183-184
  · modification, 94 fn, 162, 184, 204, 230-232, 277, 337
  · rectification and certification of Schedules, 59, 204, 233-239, 269
  · rectification, in event of error, 239-241
  · revision leading to supplementing Schedules, 221-222, 231-232
  · waiver, 254-260, *see also* waivers
TRIPs Council, 36, 53-54, 64, 102, 125, 259, 294
- Chairman's Statement, 216
- powers, 60-61

Ulfstein, Geir, 18
UN, *see* United Nations
UNAT, *see* United Nations Administrative Tribunal
UNCLOS, *see* United Nations Conference on the Law of the Sea
UNCTAD, *see* United Nations Conference on Trade and Development
Understanding on Rules and Procedures Governing the Settlement of Disputes, *see* Dispute Settlement Understanding
UNDP, *see* United Nations Development Programme
UNESCO, *see* United Nations Educational, Scientific and Cultural Organization
United Nations
- Convention on Privileges and Immunities of, 22 fn, 308
- Convention on Privileges and Immunities of Specialized Agencies of, 116
- and GATT, 308-309
- General Assembly, 81-82, 293
- relations with WTO, 211, 308-309, 328
- Secretariat, 236, 309
- Secretary General, 116, 134 fn, 211, 309, 325
- Security Council, 257
United Nations Administrative Tribunal (UNAT), 311 fn
United Nations Conference on the Law of the Sea (UNCLOS), 205, 320
United Nations Conference on Trade and Development (UNCTAD), 17 fn, 140 fn
United Nations Conference on Trade and Employment, 14
  · Preparatory Committee, 14-15, 99 fn
United Nations Development Programme (UNDP), 32 fn, 35 fn, 329
United Nations Economic and Social Council (ECOSOC), 14, 204 fn
United Nations Educational, Scientific and Cultural Organization (UNESCO), 134 fn
Universal Postal Union (UPU), 150 fn
UPU, *see* Universal Postal Union
Uruguay Round MTN, 2, 4, 17, 31-32, 46, 93, 95, 100, 103-106, 115, 120-121,

124, 126, 166, 172, 223, 227, 229, 237, 284, 331, 336
- results of, 106, 181-182, 190-195, 199, 241, 268-269, 276, 282, 335, 337

ut res magis valeat quam pereat, *see* interpretation, effectiveness principle

Vienna Convention on Diplomatic Relations (VCDR), 86 fn
Vienna Convention on the Law of Treaties (VCLT), 184, 204, 316
Vienna Convention on the Law of Treaties between States and International Organizations or between International Organizations (VCLTIO), 41-42, 183, 277

waivers, 254-260
- ACP-EC Partnership Agreement, 48, 145, 257 fn
- 'collective', 256
- decisions, 148-149, 154, 178, 248, 252, 255, 279, 334
- exceptive character, 253, 256, 275 fn
- GATT, 275
- general, obligation, 47, 96, 107, 145, 152, 184, 189, 204, 249, 253, 268, 270, 275, 279, 336
- 'hard-core', 263-264
- horizontal, 255
- Kimberley, 254, 257-258
- 'mini' waivers, 61, 66, 259-261
- Paragraph 6 Decision (TRIPs), 96 fn, 214, 216-220, 254
- transitional, 145-146
- Transitional Banana Tariff Quota, 48, 145

Weil, Prosper, 273
WIPO, *see* World Intellectual Property Organization
WMO, *see* World Meteorological Organization
Working Group on the Interaction between Trade and Competition, 63
Working Group on Notification Obligations and Procedures, 55
Working Group on the Relationship between Trade and Investment, 63
Working Group on State Trading Enterprises, 55
Working Group on Trade, Debt and Finance, 63
Working Group on Trade and Transfer of Technology, 63
Working Group on Transparency in Government Procurement, 63
Working Party on Domestic Regulation (WPDR), 59, 66-67, 295
Working Party on GATS Rules (WPGR), 59, 66, 295
Working Party on Professional Services (WPPS), 58 fn, 284-288, 290 295 fn
Working Party on Subsidy Notifications, *see* subsidies and countervailing measures
World Bank, 13, 32, 40, 68, 76, 81, 103, 110, 150, 157-158, 160, 329-330, 334
- relationship with WTO, 32, 35, 329

World Health Organization (WHO), 204 fn, 272 fn
- Advisory Opinion (ICJ), 19
- FAO/WHO Codex Alimentarius, *see* Codex Alimentarius

World Intellectual Property Organization (WIPO), 32 fn, 109
World Meteorological Organization (WMO), 204 fn
World Trade Organization
- functions, 6-7, 12-13, 21, 22-35, 75-77, 105, 329, 332
- legal personality, 20-21, 80
- objectives, 6-7, 12, 22-35, 76
- organisation
  - forum, 26, 78, 80

· international, 2-3, 5-7, 12, 19-21, 72, 74-75, 77, 79, 115, 327-328, 332, 334
· specialist, 77, 328
- powers, 20-21, 22-35, 103, 329, 332
· adjudicative, 5-6,, 29-30, 34, 76-77, 315, 329, 332
· executive, 5-6, 26, 28-29, 38, 40, 76-77, 329-330, 332
· 'legislative', 5-6, 26-30, 76-77, 273, 288
- reform of, 130, 170
- scope, 2-3, 23, 29, 76, 126, 329
- structure
· governance, 2, 5, 74, 77, 327
· hierarchical, 35, 49
· institutional, 3, 12, 23, 25, 41, 43, 62, 68, 75-76, 170
· normative, 126, 181, 189-193
- *sui generis* character, 28, 291, 305 fn, 328, 332

WTO, *see* World Trade Organization
WTO Agreement
- Annexes to, 24-26, 50, 77, 79-88, 157, 189, 195-196, 200, 208-211, 233, 250
- code of conduct, 181, 267
- common institutional framework, 18, 24, 75
- constitutional contract, 3
- normative template, 4
- Preamble, 18, 22, 34

Zacker, Mark, 90, 92, 104, 119-120, 124
Zemanek, Karl, 271, 298

LEGAL ASPECTS OF INTERNATIONAL ORGANIZATION

1. S. Rosenne: *Procedure in the International Court.* A Commentary on the 1978 Rules of the International Court of Justice. 1983 ISBN 90-247-3045-7
2. T.O. Elias: *The International Court of Justice and Some Contemporary Problems.* Essays on International Law. 1983 ISBN 90-247-2791-X
3. I. Hussain: *Dissenting and Separate Opinions at the World Court.* 1984 ISBN 90-247-2920-3
4. J.B. Elkind: *Non-Appearance before the International Court of Justice.* Functional and Comparative Analysis. 1984 ISBN 90-247-2921-1
5. E. Osieke: *Constitutional Law and Practice in the International Labour Organisation.* 1985 ISBN 90-247-2985-8
6. O. Long: *Law and Its Limitations in the GATT Multilateral Trade System.* 1985 ISBN 90-247-3189-5; Pb: 0-86010-959-3
7. E. McWhinney: *The International Court of Justice and the Western Tradition of International Law.* The Paul Martin Lectures in International Relations and Law. 1987 ISBN 90-247-3524-6
8. R. Sonnenfeld: *Resolutions of the United Nations Security Council.* 1988 ISBN-90-247-3567-X
9. T.D. Gill: *Litigation Strategy at the International Court.* A Case Study of the Nicaragua versus United States Dispute. 1989 ISBN 0-7923-0332-6
10. S. Rosenne: *The World Court.* What It is and how It works. 4th revised ed. Prepared with the assistance of T.D. Gill. 1989 *For the 5th revised ed., see below Volume 16*
11. V. Gowlland-Debbas: *Collective Responses to Illegal Acts in International Law.* United Nations Action in the Question of Southern Rhodesia. 1990 ISBN 0-7923-0811-5
12. Y. Beigbeder: *The Role and Status of International Humanitarian Volunteers and Organizations.* The Right and Duty to Humanitarian Assistance. 1991 ISBN 0-7923-1190-6
13. A.B. Avanessian: *The Iran-United States Claims Tribunal in Action.* 1993 (also published in *International Arbitration Law Library*) ISBN 1-85333-902-4
14. R. Szafarz: *The Compulsory Jurisdiction of the International Court of Justice.* 1993 ISBN 0-7923-1989-3
15. Y.Z. Blum: *Eroding the United Nations Charter.* 1993 ISBN 0-7923-2069-7
16. S. Rosenne: *The World Court.* What It is and how It works. 5th revised ed. 1994 ISBN 0-7923-2861-2
17. P.H.F. Bekker: *The Legal Position of Intergovernmental Organizations.* AFunctional Necessity Analysis of Their Legal Status and Immunities. 1994 ISBN 0-7923-2904-X
18. S.A. Voitovich: *International Economic Organizations in the International Legal Process.* 1994 ISBN 0-7923-2766-7
19. S.A. Alexandrov: *Reservations in Unilateral Declarations Accepting the Compulsory Jurisdiction of the International Court of Justice.* 1995 ISBN 0-7923-3145-1
20. M. Hirsch: *The Responsibility of International Organizations Toward Third Parties.* Some Basic Principles. 1995 ISBN 0-7923-3286-5
21. A.S. Muller: *International Organizations and their Host States.* Aspects of their Legal Relationship. 1995 ISBN 90-411-0080-6
22. T. Kanninen: *Leadership and Reform.* The Secretary-General and the UN Financial Crisis of the late 1980s. 1995 ISBN 90-411-0102-0

23. C. Tomuschat (Ed.): *The United Nations at Age Fifty.* A Legal Perspective. 1995 ISBN 90-411-0145-4
24. R. Frid: *The Relations Between the EC and International Organizations.* Legal Theory and Practice. 1995 ISBN 90-411-0155-1
25. M.M. Martin Martinez: *National Sovereignty and International Organizations.* 1996 ISBN 90-411-0200-0
26. M. Pomerance: *The United States and the World Court as a 'Supreme Court of the Nations': Dreams, Illusions and Disillusion.* 1996 ISBN 90-411-0204-3
27. E. Denters: *Law and Policy of IMF Conditionality.* 1996 ISBN 90-411-0211-6
28. P. van Dijck and G. Faber (Eds.): *Challenges to the New World Trade Organization.* 1996 ISBN 90-411-0236-1
29. C. Peck and R.S. Lee (Eds.): *Increasing the Effectiveness of the International Court of Justice.* Proceedings of the ICJ/UNITAR Colloquium to Celebrate the 50th Anniversary of the Court. 1997 ISBN 90-411-0306-6
30. B. Conforti: *The Law and Practice of the United Nations.* 1996 ISBN 90-411-0233-7
31. N.L. Wallace-Bruce: *The Settlement of International Disputes.* The Contribution of Australia and New Zealand. 1998 ISBN 90-411-0567-0
32. B. Fassbender: *UN Security Council Reform and the Right of Veto.* A Constitutional Perspective. 1998 ISBN 90-411-0592-1
33. R.A. Wessel: *The European Union's Foreign and Security Policy.* A Legal Institutional Perspective. 1999 ISBN 90-411-1265-0
34. A.D. Efraim: *Sovereign (In)equality in International Organizations.* 2000 ISBN 90-411-1310-X
35. P. van Dijck and G. Faber (eds.) *The External Economic Dimension of the European Union.* 2000 ISBN 90-411-1383-5
36. B. Conforti: *The Law and Practice of the United Nations.* Second Revised Edition. 2000 ISBN 90-411-1414-9
37. N.M. Blokker and H.G. Schermers (eds.): *Proliferation of International Organizations.* Legal Issues. 2001 ISBN 90-411-1535-8
38. K.G. Bühler: *State Succession and Membership in International Organizations.* Legal Theories *versus* Political Pragmatism. 2001 ISBN 90-411-1553-6
39. E. Riesenhuber: *The International Monetary Fund under Constraint.* Legitimacy of its Crisis Management. 2001 ISBN 90-411-1577-3
40. Mohammed Sameh M. Amr: *Role of the International Court of Justice as the Principal Judicial Organ of the United Nations.* 2003 ISBN 90-411-2026-2
41. Terry Gill (ed.): *Rosenne's The World Court.* What It Is and How It Works. 6th revised edition. 2003 ISBN 90-04-13633-9
42. B. Conforti: *The Law and Practice of the United Nations.* Third Revised Edition. 2005 ISBN 90-04-14308-4
43. Hector Olásolo: *The Triggering Procedure of the International Criminal Court.* 2005 ISBN 90-04-14615-6
44. Niels Blokker and Nico Schrijver (eds.): *The Security Council and the Use of Force.* 2005 ISBN 90-04-14642-3
45. Ralph Zacklin, *The Amendment of the Constitutive Instruments of the United Nations and Specialized Agencies.* 2005 ISBN 90-04-14800-0
46. Mary E. Footer, *An Institutional and Normative Analysis of the World Trade Organization.* 2006 ISBN 90-04-14961-9

MARTINUS NIJHOFF PUBLISHERS – LEIDEN / BOSTON